Volume 3

The Political Economy of Japan
is a three-volume work under the
general editorship of Yasusuke Murakami
and Hugh T. Patrick.

Volume 1 is *The Domestic Transformation*,
edited by Kozo Yamamura and Yasukichi Yasuba.
Volume 2 is *The Changing International
Context*, edited by Takashi Inoguchi and
Daniel I. Okimoto.

Edited by Shumpei Kumon and Henry Rosovsky

The Political Economy of Japan

Volume 3

Cultural and Social Dynamics

Stanford University Press, Stanford, California

Stanford University Press
Stanford, California
© 1992 by the Board of Trustees of the
Leland Stanford Junior University
Printed in the United States of America
Original printing 1992
Last figure below indicates year of this printing:
01   00   99   98   97   96   95   94   93   92

CIP data appear at the end of the book

Original printing published with the
assistance of the Japan Foundation

Japanese language rights assigned to
the National Institute for Research Advancement
37F Shinjuku Mitsui Building, 2-1-1 Nishi-Shinjuku,
Shinjuku-ku, Tokyo, Japan

The Japan Political Economy Research Committee
acknowledges with deep appreciation the support
provided by the two core funding institutions for the project,
the National Institute for Research Advancement, Tokyo,
and the East-West Center, Honolulu.

Contents

Part III: Trends

Tables

Rohlen: Learning

Lebra: Gender and Culture

Figures

Kumon: Japan as a Network Society

Aoki: Decentralization-Centralization

Imai: Japan's Corporate Networks

Lifson: Managerial Integration in America

Cole: Cultural and Social Bases of Japanese Innovation

Contributors

Masahiko Aoki, Henri and Tomoye Takahashi Professor, Department of Economics, Stanford University

Robert E. Cole, Professor of Business Administration and Sociology, University of California, Berkeley

John O. Haley, Professor, School of Law, University of Washington

Ken-ichi Imai, Senior Fellow, Institute for International Studies, Stanford University, and Director of Research, Stanford Japan Center

Ryushi Iwata, Professor, International University of Japan

Shumpei Kumon, Professor, International University of Japan

Takie Sugiyama Lebra, Professor of Anthropology, University of Hawaii

Thomas B. Lifson, Management Consultant, Berkeley, California

Yasusuke Murakami, Professor, International University of Japan, and Director, Center for Global Communications

Hugh T. Patrick, R. D. Calkins Professor of International Business and Director, Center on Japanese Economy and Business, Columbia University

Thomas P. Rohlen, Professor of Education and Senior Fellow, Institute for International Studies, Stanford University

Henry Rosovsky, Lewis P. and Linda L. Geyser University Professor, Harvard University

Haruo Shimada, Professor, Economics Department, Keio University

Robert J. Smith, Goldwin Smith Professor, Cornell University

Preface by the General Editors

The genesis of the three volumes that make up *The Political Economy of Japan* lies in the profound transformation of both Japan and the global political-economic system since World War II. Japan's sustained surge of rapid economic growth has brought it to the forefront of nations. The implications continue to be far-reaching and deep—within Japan in terms of societal and cultural as well as economic and political change, and internationally in terms of the mutual accommodation between the global system and Japan at a time of Japanese resurgence on the one hand and a decline in the capacity of the United States to serve as world leader on the other.

A new era is emerging—for Japan and the world as a whole. Since the early 1970s, Japan's political economy, and the international system as well, have undergone a sea change. In historical perspective—by economic criteria at least, such as living standards, levels of technology, and growth rates—the changes were so great that by 1980 the postwar era could be said to have come to an end. Japan is now in a transition to a new era, the major features of which can only be sensed imperfectly. Yet even with its economic transformation Japan is a remarkably stable democracy and society, seemingly without major political, economic, or social problems. Nor are there ideological or social schisms so pervasive or profound as to threaten that stability. Embedded in Japanese culture are great historical continuities that endure and yet are unusually susceptible to pragmatic adaptation as conditions change. These characteristics are well reflected in the ongoing evolution of economic, political, and social institutions.

The major purpose of these volumes is to evaluate the political economy of Japan as it approaches the 1990s. Explaining where Japan is today requires some explanation of how it arrived at that point; our intention, however, is not a history of the evolution of Japan's postwar political economy. The papers in these volumes are in principle future-oriented—they raise questions about where Japan is going as it approaches the twenty-first century and offer insights, albeit speculative, about future tendencies, prospects, and problems. The analysis of Japan's political economy is important in its own right. In addition, it will help us better understand the present and future of all industrial democracies; they face similar problems, and their futures will be inextricably linked.

Japan's economic performance and behavior over the long run, and particularly in transition periods, cannot be explained by standard economic variables alone. Nor can Japanese political performance and behavior be explained solely by political variables. The rules of the game, matters of policy, and the institutional environment are determined by the state—bureaucrats and politicians. Hence the political economy approach of these volumes. Yet even that is too narrow. A broader interdisciplinary, analytical approach is needed to take into account social and cultural variables, some of them changing significantly, others important for their very stability. In the short run it may be possible to isolate and analyze certain phenomena on the assumption that nothing else changes, but in the longer run one must take into account an intricate web of complex interactions between economic, political, social, and cultural forces and structures. However, social science has yet to develop generally accepted, comprehensive analytical frameworks that are operational. Each of the participants in this project found that even a political economy approach required substantial stretching beyond standard disciplinary boundaries.

What major changes marked the end of the postwar era? From a Japanese perspective, Japan in the 1970s had finally "caught up with the West." From a Western perspective, Japan had become a major affluent, industrial, high-technology power, the world's second largest market economy, and indeed the major challenger to U.S. industrial and technological supremacy. By 1970 Japan's domestic economic policies and performance had such an impact on the United States and Western Europe by way of trade that it could no longer be dismissed as a "small-country economy." Rather, U.S. and European government and business decision makers felt increasingly compelled to respond to Japanese competitive pressure; and Japan in turn could no longer take the world political-economic environment as a given. By the late 1970s, some Japanese large firms were at the technological frontiers in virtually every civilian goods industry and in the commercial application of basic scientific research, though not in basic science itself. By the mid-1980s, Japan had become the world's largest net exporter of capital in the now highly developed system of international financial markets.

Japan's economic prowess stands in sharp contrast to its modest military strength. Since World War II, Japan has persisted in a very low military posture of only limited self-defense capabilities. It has become an economic superpower, commensurate with the United States and Western Europe, while abjuring military power. Japan has depended for military security on its alliance with the United States, also by far its most important economic partner. This comprehensive alliance has been crucial for Japan; it has also become increasingly important for the United States.

The international political and economic environment has changed dramatically in the past fifteen years or so. Détente came to an end; the Soviet Union rose to nuclear parity with the United States. The hegemonic power—military and economic—of the United States declined but by no means disappeared. The Bretton Woods system of fixed exchange rates collapsed, to be replaced by a system of flexible exchange rates that has developed problems of its own. The two oil shocks of the 1970s contributed greatly to world inflation, a slowing of world growth, high interest rates, subsequent disinflation, an intractable Third World debt problem, and emergent protectionism in the United States and Western Europe. The international trading and monetary systems have come under immense strain. The sharp decline in world oil prices, interest rates, and the overvalued dollar in the mid-1980s continue the uncertain process of international adjustment and transition.

Japan has been as much affected by these international shocks and systemic changes as any other major nation. For these as well as internal reasons, Japan's formerly super-fast economic growth rate slowed sharply after 1973. Japan has nonetheless achieved more rapid economic growth than other industrial nations and has performed better in such areas as employment, price stability, productivity improvement, and structural adjustment. It has also fared better in terms of political and social stability. Even so, the sharp appreciation of the yen in the mid-1980s must have a substantial impact on domestic economic structure and performance, with implications for the rest of the world as well.

The question of where the present period of transition is leading pervades the papers in these volumes. Within Japan, we can anticipate an aging population; still further urbanization; and increased homogenization as mass media reduce regional and other variations, coupled, however, with the increased individuality of an affluent new middle class that forms Japan's great majority. Yet Japan's economy and institutions may well manifest greater decentralization, reflecting new opportunities as well as heterogeneity within a homogeneous society. Japan may well become the new, information-based society par excellence as a new technological era comes to dominate the turn of the new century.

Undoubtedly economic, political, and social institutions will continue to evolve in response to changing needs and pressures. Basic values and behavioral patterns, however, change more slowly. Indeed, they are a major source of domestic stability; yet they are also a source of international misunderstanding, confusion, and even conflict. Nonetheless, values, and the behavior they shape, are not static. Will the transition be predominantly technological and economic? To what extent will the new era embody even more profound societal and cultural changes? Or will basic values and preferred behavior patterns provide the stability to make the transition easier to deal with?

The international system—economic, political, military—also appears to be in transition, with its future characteristics unclear. The U.S-USSR confrontation continues to dominate the global military arena. The rise of Japan to major international economic prominence has generated pressures from the United States and Western Europe for Japan to play a far greater role in maintaining and strengthening the open international economic system, to prevent a systemic retreat into protectionism. The foreign desire for Japanese leadership has been matched so far by Japanese caution. Will a new era of reduced U.S.-USSR military tension emerge? Will Japan's economic role be stabilizing or destabilizing? Will protectionism become more significant, and if so, will it be sectoral rather than geographic? We do not pretend to answer these or a host of other questions comprehensively, but at least they are addressed.

The editors of each volume of *The Political Economy of Japan* expand upon the general themes raised here in their introductions to the volumes, setting the themes in their particular context. Volume 1, subtitled *The Domestic Transformation*, takes essentially a domestic approach, while recognizing the impact of the rest of the world on Japan and Japan's interaction with it. Volume 2, *The Changing International Context*, correspondingly takes an international approach, while examining the global effects of Japan's domestic political economy. Volume 3, *Cultural and Social Dynamics*, presents a quite different but equally essential perspective. Culture is the medium in which economic and political behavior rests; it embodies underlying norms, values, and tastes. Society and its institutions are essential features of any political economy. The linkages between Japan's political economy, society, and culture are clearly important. They are also extraordinarily difficult to analyze. In Volume 3, a wider range of social scientists analyze certain of these linkages. Whereas Volumes 1 and 2 aim to be definitive, Volume 3 is overtly exploratory. Its aim is to open new avenues of research for our understanding of Japan.

The basic themes and issues addressed in the volumes are broad and comprehensive. Every nation, like every individual, has its unique features. But far more important are the similarities, and the subtle degree and specific nature of the differences. In principle, these studies are explicitly comparative, interdisciplinary, and future-oriented. These are difficult goals to achieve, as anyone conversant with the current state of social science theory and methodology knows full well. In practice, most of the comparisons are between Japan and the major market-oriented industrial democracies of the West, particularly the United States. In many respects they are the most appropriate comparison group. Financial and human resource constraints precluded an even more ambitious approach. The Japanese economy, polity, society, culture, and people are not nearly so monolithic, centralized, homogeneous, or vertically structured as they have on occasion been stereotypically portrayed in the West. Nor are they as unique as some Japanese would maintain. On the other hand, the United States stands at the opposite pole among the industrial nations in terms of heterogeneity and decentralization. A comparison between Japan and the United States, the world's largest market economies, is therefore of crucial importance in our search for insights into Japan's political economy.

The contributors to these volumes confronted a complex mixture of evolutionary change, discontinuous change, and enduring continuities in their analyses of Japan's current state and future possibilities. They bravely responded by delving beyond their normal, comfortable disciplinary limits. We believe that, thanks to their efforts, these volumes will contribute substantially to establishing both the substance and the approach of future social science research on Japan. Although these studies push forward the frontiers of our knowledge, we still have much to do.

In recognition that no one scholar could adequately address the array of topics and issues incorporated in these volumes, in 1982 the binational Japan Political Economy Research Committee was formed, with Yasusuke Murakami and Hugh Patrick as co-chairmen, in order to plan and carry out this comprehensive project. The committee, together with other scholars, held numerous planning workshops to prepare six substantive conferences between 1984 and 1987, two for each volume.

The committee members were: Takashi Inoguchi (Political Science, University of Tokyo), Kazuo Koike (Economics, University of Kyoto), Ryutaro Komiya (Economics, University of Tokyo), Shumpei Kumon (Social Systems Analysis, University of Tokyo), Yasusuke Murakami (Economics, University of Tokyo), Yukio Noguchi (Economics, Hitotsubashi University), Daniel I. Okimoto (Political Science, Stanford University), Hugh T. Patrick (Economics, Columbia University), Kenneth B. Pyle (History, University of Washington), Thomas P. Rohlen (Anthropology, Stanford University), Henry Rosovsky (Economics, Harvard University),

Seizaburo Sato (Political Science, University of Tokyo), Gary Saxonhouse (Economics, University of Michigan), Akio Watanabe (International Relations, University of Tokyo), Kozo Yamamura (Economics, University of Washington), and Yasukichi Yasuba (Economics, Osaka University). The committee benefited greatly from the participation of many other scholars in the planning, particularly Marius Jansen (History, Princeton University), Barbara Ruch (Japanese Literature and Culture, Columbia University), and Robert Smith (Anthropology, Cornell University).

The project and its scope were made possible by the visionary funding commitments made early in the planning stage by the National Institute for Research Advancement (NIRA) in Tokyo and the East-West Center in Honolulu. Their early enthusiasm and financial underwriting were crucial. Additional funding for various key components of the intellectual package was received from the Mellon Foundation, the Japan–United States Educational Commission, the United States–Japan Friendship Commission, and the Japan Foundation.

Our great debt, as co-chairmen of the committee, is to the scholars who have written, rewritten and rewritten again the papers appearing in these volumes. This was no ordinary project and certainly no ordinary series of conferences. Each author made a deep intellectual commitment, reflected in immense amounts of time and energy devoted to planning and meeting as well as research and writing. We thank especially the editors of each of the three volumes for their dedication, leadership, and sheer hard work. By far the greatest financial source of support for this project, as with much social scientific research, was the cost of the scholars' time, borne by their universities; all too often we take for granted the universities' central role in making such research efforts possible.

The project had a rather loose, semiautonomous administrative structure, which worked—from beginning to final publication—because of the behind-the-scenes efforts of many persons, all of whom we deeply thank. We mention only three stalwarts by name: Mikio Kato, Executive Director of the International House in Tokyo, who administered the NIRA grant and the three conferences and many planning sessions held in Tokyo; Charles Morrison, Research Fellow at the East-West Center, who oversaw the East-West Center's role as conference host and funder; and Grant Barnes, Director of Stanford University Press, who personally shepherded these manuscripts through the publication process.

Yasusuke Murakami
Hugh T. Patrick

Postscript

As this the final volume is published, the three-volume work *The Political Economy of Japan* and the multidisciplinary, multinational research effort on which it is based are brought to completion. We are profoundly thankful to all those who have collaborated with us on this project.

Two of the central themes of these volumes have been the complex combination of continuity and change within Japan's domestic political economy, and the perception that both Japan and the international political, economic, and security systems of which it is part are in transition to a new era. Events both in Japan and internationally since the first publication of the foregoing Preface in Volume 1 in 1987 have reaffirmed the importance not only of these themes, but of their treatment in these volumes; the descriptions and analyses of patterns and trends have well stood the test of recent times.

To be sure, there have been some major surprises. This was less so in Japan—though the rapidity and extent of Japanese business investment abroad, particularly in the United States and Western Europe, were not anticipated by many specialists, nor were the full political economy implications of the Tokyo stock market crash of 1990. The real surprises have been the ending of the cold war and of the confrontation between the United States and the Soviet Union, the collapse of communism in Eastern Europe (though not in China, North Korea, or Indochina), and the dissolution of the Soviet Union into independent states. Nonetheless, although it is clear that we are indeed approaching a new era—a new world order—its political, economic, and security contours remain shadowy.

What is clear is that Japan will play an increasingly important global and regional role. The Gulf War of 1991 not only tested Japanese leadership and found it wanting, it accelerated the debate within Japan over the country's proper global role. While many people in other countries are hoping that Japan will exercise more leadership, there are also those who have expressed fears of such a prospect. The reluctance of the polity and people of Japan to exercise, much less initiate, far-reaching new policies is only gradually diminishing, particularly beyond the economic domain. And within Japan, while the process of internationalization proceeds, it does so gradually and in tandem with an enhanced pride in domestic performance and continuing preoccupation—as is true of all the great powers—with major domestic concerns.

Yasusuke Murakami
Hugh T. Patrick

The Political Economy of Japan

Volume 3

Introduction

This is the final volume of the series entitled *The Political Economy of Japan*. Volume 1 dealt with *The Domestic Transformation*. Volume 2 focused on *The Changing International Context*. And now we introduce Volume 3, *Cultural and Social Dynamics*.

The series has a number of distinctive characteristics which perhaps emerge most clearly if we contrast it with its spiritual ancestor, *Asia's New Giant*, edited by Hugh Patrick and Henry Rosovsky (1976).[1] Both are collections of essays by different authors, intended to give mainly non-Japanese readers a broad, balanced picture of the post–World War II Japanese economy. But the differences are far more important than the similarities. First of all, *New Giant* was planned and assembled well before the growing dominance of the Japanese economy was widely recognized. Only a few insiders followed events in East Asia at that time, and the principal purpose of *New Giant* was to educate relatively ignorant readers. Today, the degree of sophistication and the desire for knowledge about Japan are higher than ever before; consequently, *The Political Economy of Japan* has been able to go well beyond the confines of an introductory survey. Second, *New Giant* was written nearly entirely by American economists, who—with the assistance of younger Japanese scholars—undertook the interpretation of Japan to foreign audiences. By contrast, the majority of the authors of the present volumes are Japanese, explaining their own country. Third, we have progressed from economics—only one chapter in *New Giant* was written by a non-economist[2]—to the currently very popular concept of political economy. Only Volume 1 of the new series is solidly dominated by economists. The other volumes bear a much more interdisciplinary stamp.

The movement from economics to political economy is significant; it certainly means more than simply the desire to include political factors in understanding Japan's current position and future prospects. The recent revival of political economy[3] was a direct result of increasing dissatisfaction with the perceived narrowness and lack of realism that characterized much of traditional economics, with its almost exclusive emphasis on markets and simultaneous deemphasizing of history and institutions. The revived political economy approach intends to reintroduce the missing ingredients: primarily government, but other social forces as well.

The need to move beyond economics should, perhaps, have been especially strongly felt by students of Japanese society. It was fairly clear that modern Japanese economic history could not adequately be analyzed without reference to public policy and institutions. As Japanese economic success was becoming more evident, it also became increasingly obvious that many assumptions of liberal and orthodox economics yielded—in Japan—counterintuitive results. After all, here was a country in which, to cite but a few examples, oligopolies were strong, labor mobility low, government interference high, and yet the efficiency of the economy in terms of output, productivity growth, and competitive power could not be doubted.

For all these reasons, the general editors of *The Political Economy of Japan* chose a much broader canvas than *New Giant*, not only featuring the traditional elements of the domestic economy, but adding the international context and, most daringly, the "cultural and social dynamics" associated with economic growth in Japan.

The particular difficulties suggested by the topic of Volume 3 were eloquently anticipated many years ago by the well-known American sociologist Nathan Glazer:

However imprecise and uncertain economists take their analyses and interpretations to be, they are based on the most rigorous of the social sciences, one which manipulates well-defined concepts, to which numbers can generally be attached and which can be grouped into well developed and frequently tested generalizations. However loose the realm of political science may be considered to be, it deals with one set of institutions, the political, which can be specifically delimited. There is no difficulty in perceiving the significance of the political system for the functioning of the economy, though disagreement may exist about which manipulates which, and how. But around both the economic complex and its particular political environment there is discernible another environment that is the concern of the sociologist, the anthropologist, and the social psychologist. It is a murky environment indeed, and despite the importance that men attribute to it, has not been ordered—and apparently cannot be ordered—in any simple manner. Or, rather, it has been ordered in so many ways by so many different scholars that little guidance akin to science seems available. And yet this further realm—let it be called "the social and cultural factors in Japanese economic growth"—cannot be ignored.[4]

What can we add to this "murky environment that cannot be ignored"? Neither the contributors to Volume 3 nor the authors of this Introduction can claim to have constructed a general theory concerning the ties between sociocultural dynamics and economic growth. What we offer and claim is much more modest: we hope to have produced a complement to and enrichment of the preceding volumes by analyzing certain neglected features of Japan's economic performance, such as some aspects of culture, the role of the legal system, political power, the system of learning, and, most of all, the characteristic behavior of Japanese firms (the so-called J Firm), with special emphasis on types of networks. Well over half the essays in Volume 3 deal with the J Firm and networking, and one of our authors (Kumon) attempts the difficult task of providing an overall framework for this important topic.

It seems to us that recent changes in attitudes outside of Japan—especially in the West—have made the subjects treated in this volume particularly relevant. Views and evaluations of Japan have shown great historical variation, and we have frequently had occasion to observe that many characteristics of Japanese society that were condemned as "bad" or "feudal" in the early postwar period are today considered worthy of study and conceivably even of emulation. Among the many possible examples would be the Japanese system of management, especially those aspects of it dealing with labor relations.

Looking back to the beginnings of modern economic growth in Japan during the Meiji era, we can in fact suggest three sets of attitudes that lasted for very uneven periods. From the 1880s, when modern economic growth began, until the early 1970s—effectively for a century—Japan was seen by Westerners as an economically backward country, gradually catching up with the leading-edge economies of Europe and North America. That is also how the Japanese saw themselves: indigenous characteristics gradually came to be viewed by both sides as deformations that would be eliminated by the inevitable forces of convergence.

Beginning in the early 1970s, many Japanese economic practices became widely admired and, to some degree, emulated in the West; in the words of the old proverb, "Imitation is the sincerest form of flattery." This was, of course, the decade in which Japan "caught up" with the United States; when a number of major industries in Japan became undisputed world leaders in quantity of production and level of technology. In the mid 1980s, Japan became the world's leading creditor nation, while many observers noted the end of American political and economic hegemony. Primarily in the United States, there now arose self-conscious efforts to adopt Japanese ways of doing things: management by consultation, quality circles, fewer job categories, longer-term employment, and so on. For the first time, increasing numbers of non-Japanese managers were willing to entertain the possibility that idiosyncratic Japanese economic practices—perhaps rooted in culture and civilization—could, to a significant degree, account for a national economic performance unparalleled in modern history.

The idea that convergence between East and West—conceived of as Asians adopting Euro-American ways—is either desirable or inevitable has lost much of its plausibility on both sides of the Pacific, and Rodney Clark's startling observation is undoubtedly correct: "The organization of Japanese and Western industry was probably more similar in 1910 than in 1970."[5] The Japanese gradually developed their own methods of managing modern economic growth, and they proved to be at least as good as those of their teachers.

Sometime in the 1980s, coexisting with the new feelings of admiration and emulation, there was born what is now known as the "Japan Problem." Both conceptions sprang from the same root system: one branch, benign and outward-looking; the other, resentful, frustrated, and sometimes malignant. It is not easy to define the Japan Problem with any degree of rigor because it is largely a matter of feeling. In 1982, Michel Jobert, France's minister of foreign trade, is reported to have said: "How much nicer a world this would be if there were no Russians or Japanese!"[6] We can certainly understand his feelings about the Russians (back then), but why the Japanese? Precisely because those now sometimes admired, imitated, and deeply rooted non–Euro-American practices had created, in the opinion of some critics, a world in which Japan could and did take unfair advantage of many countries. Its trade was said to be adversarial; its actions caused the international economy to malfunction, leading to chronic international disequilibria. Japan could never, it was alleged, be an open free-market economy. And thus, the central question created by the Japan Problem came to be whether the systemic differences between Japan and other modern industrial nations were so deep, profound, intransigent, and unchanging (on both sides), resulting in an incompatibility so great, that either a new international economic system would have to be developed or special rules would have to be devised for dealing with Japan.[7]

Many reputable authorities have taken positions on either side of these questions.[8] The Japan Problem is not at all a specific theme of Volume 3. However, it should be clear that an understanding of the issues posed by raising "The Problem" requires an intellectual excursion beyond the more conventional categories of the first two volumes. That is one of our purposes.

In this series, the political economy of Japan has been analyzed at three different levels. Although some overlap does exist, we can say that Volumes 1 and 2 focused, first of all, on functional traits. One major category of these can be described as measures of performance: economic growth, productivity, international competitiveness, and similar matters. Another category fits the policy rubric and would include such issues as protection versus free trade, foreign policy, the welfare state, and so on. Both performance and policy variables share the characteristic of relatively rapid changeability. For example, the era of Japan's double-digit GNP growth lasted for just about two decades; in less than a single decade, Japan moved from high to low tariffs, and from being a debtor to being a creditor nation—all very major changes.

Both earlier volumes also dealt extensively with structural traits of Japan's political economy. These are usually best described as specific institutions: big business, *keiretsu* (groups of corporations), dominant political parties, pressure groups, and so on. Structural changes may, in general, be slower than changes in the values of the types of functions considered here, but the point is that they do change within the life span of a typical observer. Defeat in World War II and the subsequent spurt of economic growth left almost no Japanese institution unaffected.

Volume 3 adds another dimension to the study of Japan's political economy: the introduction of some deeper, very slowly changing traits, more abstract and general traits or propensities, frequently described by such terms as *group-orientedness, diligence, vertical hierarchies,* and so forth. The emphasis now turns more on world outlook and especially values. Thus, for example, Masahiko Aoki's study of the J Firm pays considerable attention to "Japanese-style" information-processing; Haruo Shimada concentrates on the value system underlying labor-management relations—with, we might add, considerable criticism of the current state of affairs; and Ken-ichi Imai builds a whole concept of industrial organization on the basis of corporate networks.

The adjective *deeper* is vague, but its use does help to stress the important point that the traits associated with the description of any "political economy" vary in the degree to which they are embedded in society. Those embedded most deeply form part of Japanese culture (*bunka*). Those that are, by their very nature, more changeable, have been labeled aspects of civilization (*bummei*) by some Japanese scholars. None of the authors of Volume 3 use this distinction, first introduced by Tadao Umesao, Shuntaro Ito, Shumpei Kumon, and Esyun Hamaguchi.[9] But it will nevertheless be helpful for readers to keep the distinction in mind, despite the fact that in considering any real society, a sharp classification of traits is very difficult. The movement from culture to civilization is a continuum. We would, however, stress two points. First, all the volumes in this series discuss aspects of Japanese culture and civilization, but this final volume devotes proportionately far greater attention to culture: to those characteristics of society that change only very slowly. Second, the concept of degrees of changeability may be useful in considering possible policy alternatives. From the point of view of the previously mentioned Japan Problem, it would be more fruitful to press for changes in less deeply rooted characteristics—for example, an excessive export orientation—while taking values associated with culture as more or less constant. In fact, it is useful to think of Japan—in common with many other countries—as possessing a very slowly changing culture that has produced forms of social organization manifestly capable of rapid alterations. Appropriate examples would be the Meiji Restoration and post–World War II democracy.

Our subtitle is *Cultural and Social Dynamics*. The notion of social dynamics should not create difficulties or ambiguities: readers will be familiar with the scope of the social sciences. Cultural dynamics may require more elaboration, especially because the contributors to Volume 3 do not adhere to a single, consistent definition of culture.

The most general definition is given by Robert J. Smith in the first chapter: "[Culture is] the array of formal and informal rules that guides the members of a society in their selection of appropriate behavior and provides the framework for the construction of ideology. It is the context in which all economic and political behavior must make sense. While not determinative of behavior, it does establish the range of choices for action." Thus, according to Smith, culture is neither ideology nor behavior. It is a framework: "members of a society behave in accordance with shared understandings acquired by virtue of shared experience. Culture, then, can be viewed as a learned and shared information pool."

Smith's conception is close to the formulation adopted much earlier by Ruth Benedict, who treated culture as "assumptions about the conduct of life" and "the eyes through which one looks."[10] A related definition is given by Edward and Mildred Hall, and it stresses more explicitly the transmission of information, a topic of special relevance for this volume:

Each culture has a hidden code of behavior that can rarely be understood without a code breaker.

Members of a common culture not only share information, they share methods of coding, storing, and retrieving that information. Some 80 to 90 percent of the significant features of a culture are reflected in its nonverbal messages. These are usually taken for granted and transmitted unconsciously.

Culture can be likened to an enormous, subtle, extraordinarily complex computer. It programs the actions and responses of every person, and these programs must be mastered by anyone wishing to make the system work.[11]

Although we are quite comfortable with these definitions as background to the chapters in this volume, it may be helpful to provide a few elaborations. We—the editors—think of culture as the design principles or fundamental patterns that act as organizers of more derivative social characteristics, such as a particular world outlook, set of policies, or forms of organization. Culture provides the design principles; the product of these principles we have called civilization. Culture, by definition, changes more slowly than other social characteristics and much of it is transmitted unconsciously and nonverbally from generation to generation. The fundamental patterns or design principles associated with culture can—at least in theory—be divided into four main classes:

1. Those used for recognition and evaluation
2. Those employed in decision making
3. Those determining the framework for action and interaction
4. Those providing the principles for formation of social systems (organizations) of all types

Every chapter in Volume 3 fits into one or more of these classes and examines the relationship between a class or classes and the economy.

One of the common assignments for all editors and authors in this series on the political economy of Japan is speculation about the future. In a sense, it is a most appropriate task for us because sociocultural dynamics change very slowly—certainly more slowly than the economic and political factors whose analysis forms the core of Volumes 1 and 2. The safest and easiest forecast would simply say that "things" will remain more or less the same in the foreseeable future. But we do believe that a little more can be said concerning the future against the background of the essays contained in Volume 3.

In considering the current state of Japanese-American relations, it sometimes seems to us as if one is caught between two wholly unsatisfactory extremes: so-called "Japan bashers" and followers of *Nihonjin-ron*.[12] Both argue that Japan is "different" for cultural reasons: *Nihonjinron* advocates say that these differences simply have to be accepted, and bashers urge special rules. Unfortunately, few partisans have bothered to make clear what specific reasons account for these mysterious differences. Furthermore, it must also be obvious that culture is only one factor affecting action and performance: the environment, policies, and history should all be part of any explanation. And, as we have already noted, there are no generally accepted integrated theories.

This situation, we hope, increases the value of Volume 3. None of the essays in it relies for explanations solely on culture; all take for granted the concurrent validity of economic and political interpretations. The essays all employ a broader approach, which highlights the subtlety required in using cultural explanations. The authors focus on factors of varying depth or changeability in society. For example, Robert Smith, Yasusuke Murakami, Ryushi Iwata, and Robert Cole deal with what—

no doubt—will be least changeable: social exchange, corporate values, interpersonal relations. Haruo Shimada, on the other hand, examines areas where alterations are likely to happen more quickly, such as in the role of unions and the distribution of political power.

These essays are not merely useful because of their broader approach to a complicated topic; they are particularly appropriate for consideration of future relations between advanced industrial countries. The postwar competition and conflict between capitalism and socialism has ended; capitalism is the winner. But this does not mean the end of competition between systems. In the future we shall surely witness competition between alternative views of the world, institutions, and policies. Different forms of capitalism—the products of various national cultures or, to use the Japanese conception, "civilizations"—may well describe future forms of struggle. If the competition between varieties of capitalism turns into cultural conflict between nations, we shall have gained little. Indeed, these conflicts could be worse than the cold war. But we see an important ray of hope in the future: a renewed, powerful, and rather different wave of convergence.

At the beginning of this Introduction, we mentioned the astute observation of Rodney Clark to the effect that Japanese and Western industry were more similar in 1910 than in 1970. We predict with a high degree of confidence that Japanese and Western economic structures will become more similar by 2030—and, most likely, much earlier. The move toward convergence has already started, and it will not be stopped.

When the industrial revolution moved from the West to East Asia—specifically to Japan—the task of receiving countries was to adopt Western institutions and techniques in the most efficient manner. That meant reformulations more suitable for local conditions, and ultimately this created the truth behind Clark's observation. It is a tribute to the Japanese genius for improved adaptation. While this historical process was occurring—and it took nearly a century—two attitudes were prominent in the West. The first may be labeled "enlighten Japan": help a backward country to become more like us, to reach the "higher" level of Western culture and civilization. The second attitude gradually gained adherents as Japan became more powerful: "contain Japan," because it is not becoming more like us and is taking unfair advantage of the differences in our cultures.

However, what had been a one-way street for over a century has become a heavily traveled two-way street: technical and organizational progress moves from country to country, and from East to West as easily as from West to East. In the advanced countries outside Japan, the current attitude increasingly stresses mutual learning and reorganization on the basis of that learning, while attempting to formulate rules for global competition and cooperation. We may hope that this attitude will lead to renewed convergence: toward a more universal economic civilization.

These are hopeful signs, indicating the possibilities of more harmony in the future. We think that Volume 3 can make a contribution toward that end by describing some elements that need to be better understood if convergence is to occur.

Part I

Broad Frameworks

Robert J. Smith

The Cultural Context of the
Japanese Political Economy

Among the many ways of thinking about the concept of culture,[1] one of the most common is to see it as the array of formal and informal rules that guides the members of a society in their selection of appropriate behavior and provides the framework for the construction of ideology. It is the context in which all economic and political behavior must make sense. While not determinative of behavior, it does establish the range of choices for action. Another way of putting it is that members of a society behave in accordance with shared understandings acquired by virtue of shared experience. Culture, then, can be viewed as a learned and shared information pool.[2] It is not static, for new information is constantly added to the pool, other information is allowed to fall away, received information takes on new relevance, and the development of new understandings leads to changes in behavior.

However routinely economists ignore or assume it away, the concept of culture enters economic analysis fundamentally through the two basic constructs of the utility function and the production function. These I take to be economists' basic formulations of what individuals and the organizations to which they belong want, and how they go about acquiring it through the process of production.[3] Tastes, preferences, attitudes toward risk-taking and risk-avoidance, trade-offs in allocating time to work and to leisure, balancing present and future consumption, and the like are all shaped by cultural considerations.[4] So, too, are the processes of production.[5] Let me provide one deceptively simple illustration of these points.

Food preferences fundamentally affect the economy of any society and deeply ramify in policy formation. Climatic conditions, availability of water, the nature of soils, and a host of similar considerations may enter into any explanation of why a people grow wheat, millet, or rice, but not why they choose not to grow an equally viable alternative crop or why one crop displaces another. Early in their history, the Japanese shifted from other grains to the cultivation of rice with such single-mindedness that they eventually developed strains that can be grown as far north as inhospitable Hokkaido. Much more recently there has been a dramatic shift from the consumption of rice to wheat products, owing in part to changes in government policy, of course, as well as to economic pressures. The persistence of tastes and preferences among the older generations and the development of new ones among younger Japanese have resulted in marked intergenerational differences in rice and wheat consumption. At the same time, the consumption of beef and pork has risen sharply with the continued waning of the authority that once promoted the observance of Buddhist food taboos in the face of the new doctrines of the promoters of "modernity" and the dicta of the nutritionists.[6]

A shorthand way of putting all this is that culture has a great deal to do with the political economy. That being the case, we must have a clearer understanding of the concept, which is notoriously difficult to define.

The Concept of Culture

Just because a thing is hard to describe does not mean that it is any less real than a thing easily described, or that it is any less important. Although we understand matters like stellar evolution and DNA better than we do religion, personality, mental illness, and magic,[7] we have little difficulty talking about religion and magic, personality and mental illness. Where we encounter problems is when we seek agreement on the best definition of those terms. So it is with culture.

Were disagreement over the proper definition of the concept of culture sufficient grounds for dismissing it, then sociology would be deprived of the idea of social class and the concept of the stereotype, psychology would have to make do without the notions of intelligence and cognition, and political science without the concepts of power and authority. The lack of consensus does require, however, that we be as clear as possible about what we mean by the term *culture*. I take it to be concerned with motivation, rationalization, choice, decision making, and the exercise of options, insofar as it sets the broad limits within which action is conceivable and performance undertaken. It has everything to do with definitions of propriety, appropriateness, acceptability, and the right and wrong of things. Beliefs, meanings, understandings, values, prescriptions, and proscriptions all lie within the cultural realm, as do definitions of social goals and what constitutes the common good. Culture is not "tradition," as we shall see, although aspects of tradition inevitably figure in the configuration of culture and ideology of any society in a given period of its history. Culture is neither static nor something out there waiting to be discovered; it is a construct to be inferred from behavior and its products.

There is no aspect of the political economy in which culture is not implicated, for it is the context in which all decisions are made. The challenge faced by the contributors to this volume is to show precisely how, in the case of Japan, culture and the political economy are interrelated. I use the word *concepts* deliberately, for it is easily forgotten that "politics" and "economy" are no less constructs than are "society" and "culture." Because politics and economy are constructs of a particular kind, however, the elements that comprise them can readily be expressed as variables. We are quite accustomed to discussing the effect of economic variables on demographic trends. It is commonly observed that one or another political variable affects the way social welfare policy is framed. Even social variables, often labeled *institutional*, are routinely introduced into discussions of political economy. History is accorded respectful attention as shaper or modifier of the present.

The use of the concept of culture in these kinds of discussions is more limited, perhaps because it seems to lack their apparent clarity and specificity, whereas history and institutions are usually invoked as if they have a concreteness, a reality. To do so betrays a profound misunderstanding of the nature of all three terms, however, for all are constructs in precisely the same sense—they are simply ways of trying to render coherent a welter of events, records, perceptions, and assumptions.[8]

It is tempting here to plunge into the vortex and take up the issue of epistemology. What is an explanation? How do we decide when we really know something? What constitutes acceptable authority for a statement? How do we choose to end an investigation, confident of our findings? I shall not do so, but what follows reflects my concern with all these questions and the answers to them.

Culture as Legacy

One of the most common themes in the study of social and cultural change in Japan has been the attempt to assess the degree of continuity and discontinuity between the premodern (Tokugawa) era and the present as it is reflected in institutions, practice, and values. Andrew Gordon has contributed to this literature a remarkably detailed study of a century of development of labor relations in Japanese heavy industry up to 1955. He writes:

Some of the earliest works on labor relations in Japan used the simple and misleading notion of the carry-over of feudal values to explain subsequent institutional development. To deny the explanatory power of this notion is by no means to deny all connection between the Tokugawa past and the modern factory. Preindustrial practices or values did not determine the course of subsequent development, but a legacy from the past did influence managers and workers as they defined the labor relationship. This legacy embraced patterns of behavior and organization, as well as attitudes, but it drew only in part on a value system of the feudal era stressing obedience, loyalty, hard work, and paternalistic "beautiful customs."[9]

Commenting on one of the most arresting features of the labor union movement in Japan, he adds: "The tendency of Japanese workers to organize their unions in factory or workshop units is a . . . basic trait of the labor relationship with roots in the past. With no tradition of effective guild networks as a model [they] organized by workshop and factory with hardly a second thought."[10] From these and many other passages, it is clear that Gordon sees some continuities between the past and Japan's modern present. They are not only historical and institutional, but cultural as well. More important, the aspects of Japanese society he deals with are presented as the product of a perpetually changing amalgam of all three—partly cultural, partly historical, partly institutional.

Ronald Dore long ago made the same point.[11] How, he asks, did the Japanese get their contemporary institutions? Did they create them de novo to conform to their cultural predispositions? Did they choose them from various contexts and eclectically synthesize those that conformed to their cultural purposes? Did they carry forward from the past some institutions that existed in embryo and make use of them in the present? "In Japan's case," he asserts, "the answer is . . . a bit of all three."[12]

Dan Henderson reaches the same conclusion in his discussion of the three distinctive forms of conciliation that characterize contemporary Japanese legal practice.[13] One, *jidan*, is straight out of Tokugawa village practice. The second, *chōtei*, was devised piecemeal in Japan between the world wars. The third, *wakai*, is a direct borrowing from German practice.

In this connection, Gordon makes an invaluable point about the development of labor relations in Japanese industry that applies to a wide range of contexts in Japan:

Factory workers and corporate managers first appeared on the stage of Japanese history in the middle of the nineteenth century. For the following century they both confronted each other and compromised; in so doing they worked out the terms of their participation in factory life. Ironically enough, the social relations of production most resembled those of the West at the outset. Several times since then, Japan's workers and managers have substantially reshaped the Japanese labor relationship, producing by the 1950s, a social form notably different from the West.[14]

Dare we say that, over time, the Japanese labor relationship has become increasingly Japanese? The claim is not a tautology, for although the model was Western, the outcome is not. This is not to say merely that there is a congruence between Japanese institutions and Japanese values. How could there not be? If a thing works in Japan, of course it has something to do with Japanese values, and by definition it must conform to Japanese principles of organization. It would be truly remarkable if we could identify any institutional arrangement in Japan that failed to do so. It is the great merit of Gordon's analysis that he details the process by which the terms of agreement, of congruence, were negotiated over time by the three principal parties—government, labor, and management. The planning that results in the "fit" between institutions and values is an issue I return to below.

Recognizing the essential fluidity of the amalgam referred to above, Gordon reminds us that cultural values are not shared by all members of the society, and they change over time. They are given variant interpretations and manipulated differently by different groups. This suggests that an identical cultural value may be used by different groups in society to achieve divergent aims, and indeed such was the case. Management attempted to avoid improving working conditions by appealing to Japan's "beautiful customs," while labor based its demands for higher pay and a greater degree of participation in the enterprise on precisely the same grounds.[15] That there was conflict on several levels in the development of labor relationships is undeniable; that it occurred within a shared system of meanings is equally apparent.

Culture as Principle and Pattern

If culture is important, then all manner of institutions in the society ought to reflect that fact. Do the principles of organization found in the institutions described by Gordon appear elsewhere as well? He has argued that the workshop and the factory were the natural bases for union organization in Japan in light of the Tokugawa past. Now, it is widely reported that in Japan associations and organizations of all kinds tend to be localized and territorially based. Whether or not this tendency has its origins in the character of the Japanese village, as is often claimed, does not much matter. Tadashi Fukutake does make that argument in contrasting the case of Japan with those of China and India where, he points out, sociorelational bases for group formation are typically found.[16] Even common-interest groups appear to be linked closely with territorial units,[17] and in a comparison of citizens' movements in Western Europe, Australia, and Japan, T. R. Rochon finds that activists in Japan are far more likely than their counterparts elsewhere to be rooted in their communities and to rely on existing local community-level organizations for their base.[18]

Analogously, C. Scott Littleton reports that the techniques of contemporary Japanese business management and decision making are quite similar to those employed in the planning and organization of the local festival in a Tokyo neighborhood he studied.[19] Consensus is sought; potentially conflicting interests are balanced through appeals to harmony; interlocking hierarchies are involved in the process, and their formal leadership is responsive to pressures from below.

From another Tokyo neighborhood, Theodore Bestor offers a broader consideration of the role of "traditionalism" in the formation of contemporary Japanese social groupings:

> In the . . . process of socially constructing its identity, institutions and residents of Miyamoto-cho define the neighborhood by referring to particular aspects of its history and its customary practices, selecting out certain events or activities with which to press their case. Although many of the events or institutions to which they refer are recent in occurrence or origin, this does not diminish their utility or significance as emblems of neighborhood tradition and distinctiveness.
>   . . . Although idioms of traditionalism and elements of traditional social patterns are invoked in the symbolic creation and maintenance of the neighborhood as a community, this should not blind analysts from examining them for what they are—consciously and unconsciously manipulated metaphors—rather than for what they are not—evidence of historical continuity or cultural stagnation of the individuals and social groups involved.[20]

Similar accounts of the creation of community in contemporary Japan abound.[21] In all of them, the rhetoric used by organizers of movements and programs extols the models and patterns of the past as the essential building blocks of the new towns and neighborhoods of the future. It is yet another example of the well-attested tendency of the Japanese to clothe new concepts in traditional garb.[22] The creators of community in Eyal Ben-Ari's combined new housing estate and old village, the new housing estate in Stephen Nussbaum's Hatoyama New Town, and Jennifer Robertson's peripheral Kodaira do not base their appeals and programs on claims to be building anything new and unprecedented, but argue rather that they are restoring, retaining, or recapturing valuable features of a specifically Japanese past in order to guarantee the perpetuation of a specifically Japanese future. It matters not at all whether theirs is an accurate version of history and past institutions, nor is it important that the appeal is to traditionalism rather than to tradition construed as culture.

The recurrence of such patterns may be taken as evidence of the importance of cultural factors in the structuring and restructuring of social institutions in any society. But there are other ways in which members of a society behave in accordance with shared understandings acquired by virtue of shared experience—a hallmark of virtually all definitions of culture. Ben-Ari provides a useful discussion of the hotly debated issue of "groupism" in Japanese society, contending that in his newly formed community, the structuring of the athletic meet, or field day (*undōkai*), exhibits all the features of any such social aggregate— permanent or ad hoc—in Japan. Consumption of alcohol, recreational activities, and ceremonies are used to facilitate the creation of solidarity and a climate fostering close interaction among the participants. He suggests that a profitable redefinition of *groupism* must take into account the fact that Japanese acquire "a basic orientation to groups that is the outcome of membership in and links with a great number of concrete groups." Through the process of socialization, most middle-class Japanese acquire a learned capacity to move from and relate to a succession of groups throughout their lifetimes. "This is related to the complex process of socialization (direct, anticipatory and vicarious), and to an individual's procession . . . through . . . play and neighborhood gangs, kindergarten and various school classes, school and sports teams, student clubs, coteries of friends, task and work groups, and so on." Through a process of meta-learning, then, individuals acquire the capacity to move from one frame to another: "That is, they learn to relate to the constant 'idea' or 'construct' of a group although they may move successively or concurrently through many concrete or actual groups."[23]

Put another way, when faced with a task, or upon adopting a goal, the cultural preference (and the common practice) in Japan is to form a group, which in terms of sentiment and structure will conform to type. That does not mean that Japanese culture is unique in this respect or that it is unchanging. It does strongly suggest, however, that at any moment in history, the character of institutions in any society will of necessity represent in some degree a combination of past usages and present dispositions. Cultural factors do play a part in the structuring of institutions, therefore, and have a great deal to do with how the members of a society interpret their history.

How Culture Changes

As we have seen, in its most extreme formal definition, culture may be conceived to be a kind of "information economy,"[24] in which information is received, stored, retrieved, utilized, transmitted, created, or lost. It is stored in the minds of the members of the society and in its artifacts. Roy D'Andrade has elaborated on the notion of culture as a shared and learned information pool:

It is not just physical objects which are products of culture. . . . Behavior environments, consisting of complex messages and signals, rights and duties, and roles and institutions, are a culturally constituted reality which is a product of our socially transmitted information pool . . . the cultural pool contains the information which defines what the object is, tells us how to construct the object, and prescribes how the object is to be used. Without culture, we could not have or use such things.[25]

It may be objected that in this view anything that comes into the head of any member of Japanese society has the potential for becoming part of Japanese culture. However unpalatable the notion, that is exactly what it means. Christmas trees, undeniably artifacts thoroughly embedded in American culture and emblematic of what is perhaps its most important festival, are no less so because they happen to have originated elsewhere. Such a construction of the concept of culture permits us to blink but not flinch when the suggestion is advanced that Beethoven's Ninth Symphony has become an integral element in the cultural inventory of the Japanese New Year's celebrations, as is in fact the case. Nor should we be surprised at the following account of a high-tech consequence of that unexpected development:

Today's CD [compact disk] machine is the result of a technological race among electronics firms to develop a laser-based music system. It was won in 1987 by two companies working together, Sony of Japan and Philips of the Netherlands. Philips originally designed a 60-minute disk [a not-unpredictable culturally based decision], but Sony convinced its ally that the current 75-minute version would be better. Recalls Sony Chairman Akio Morita: "The reason was so that we could put Beethoven's Ninth Symphony on one record. The Ninth has a special significance in Japan because we traditionally play it over and over at year end."[26]

Thus, the information pool recently has expanded to incorporate a new item, now defined as an aspect of tradition. Today the number of Japanese who can render the melodies of Beethoven's Ninth surely exceeds that of those who can deliver an acceptable version of "Takasago," a classical song once thought appropriate to all felicitous occasions.[27]

Culture as Explanation

In this section I take up three cases in which cultural considerations seem to me to play a demonstrably important role. The first may be called a "pure" Japanese case, presented here precisely because it is so unusual, for I wish to make the point that such rare instances of the cultural effect are nonetheless instructive. The second, like the first, is highly specific to Japanese culture, but less pure analytically. The third is not peculiarly Japanese at all, but rather deals with a domain that has a marked cultural component in all societies. They are, respectively, the effect of a coincidence of zodiacal signs on the crude birthrate and its ramifications, the connection between political and economic policies

TABLE 1

Birthrates in Two Hinoe-uma *(fire/yang/horse) Years*
Compared with Surrounding Years

	Birthrate per 1,000	Increase (decrease)	% increase (decrease) over preceding year
1905	30.6	0.0	0.0
1906	29.0	(1.6)	(5.2)
1907	33.2	4.2	14.5
1965	18.6	0.9	5.1
1966	13.7	(4.9)	(26.3)
1967	19.4	5.7	41.6

and the involvement of a pariah group in the beef-processing and leather-goods industries, and the system of medical care.

The "Pure" Case: Hinoe-uma

Twice in the twentieth century Japan's crude birth rate has responded to a purely cultural factor.[28] Understanding why it has done so requires a bit of background. In addition to the Gregorian calendar, the older lunar one, and an even more ancient solar system of reckoning, time is measured in Japan in terms of the sexagenary cycle (*eto*), a 60-year sequence of combinations of the 12 animal signs of the zodiac, the 5 elements, and yin and yang. There are several ways in which this system may have some bearing on the life of an individual, most of which are part and parcel of the lore of fortune-tellers today. That divining sticks and other traditional devices are giving way to the computer in no way alters the basic assumptions about the *eto*. The underlying notion is that the individual is obliged to cope with forces determined by circumstances entirely beyond human control. The only recourse, therefore, is to maximize the positive elements available and minimize the negative forces to which one may be exposed.

The one dramatic and very telling instance of a relationship between the individual's life-course and the turning of the sexagenary cycle is my pure case. It has to do with the beliefs relating to women (there is no comparable year for men) born in the year in which the twelve stems and ten branches combine to produce what it called *hinoe-uma*, the year of fire/yang/horse. Such women, thought to be virtually unmarriageable, are said to be extremely strong-willed and even liable to destroy a man unlucky or unwise enough to take one as wife. There have been two such coincidences of signs in this century, in 1906 and 1966. In both years the crude birth rate registered remarkable shifts, as did the abortion rate in the latter (See Tables 1 and 2).

TABLE 2
Comparative Abortion Rates for the Years
1965, 1966 (Hinoe-uma [fire/yang/horse]), and 1967

	Live births	Abortions	Total pregnancies	Abortion rate per 1,000 pregnancies	
				Observed	Expected
1965	1,823,697	161,617	1,985,314	33.8	33.0
1966	1,360,974	148,248	1,509,222	43.1	30.6
1967	1,935,647	149,389	2,085,036	28.0	28.8

In 1906 the crude birth rate dropped 5.2 per cent from the 1905 figure, and it jumped 14.5 per cent in 1907. This is dramatic evidence that some credence was given the notion that it would be preferable not to have a daughter born in *hinoe-uma*. The corresponding figures for 1965–67 are extraordinary. In 1966 the crude birth rate dropped an astonishing 26.3 per cent from the rate of 1965, and it rose a heavily compensatory 41.6 per cent in 1967. No similar short-term swings of comparable magnitude are to be found anywhere else in Japan's modern population statistics. The effects of the 1966 *hinoe-uma* were dramatic, for the class that entered first grade in 1972 was and remained by far the smallest in the system right through graduation from high school in 1984. Nationally there were 10,000 fewer first-grade homerooms in 1972 and far less severe competition for places in colleges and universities in 1984. Other economic consequences were a drop in the commercial wedding-hall business early in 1966, heavy pressure on obstetrical facilities in 1967, and a boom in the infants' clothing manufacturing and retail enterprises in 1967, following the slump in 1966. As Table 2 shows, abortion clinics reported a sharp rise in business from mid 1965 to mid 1966.

The case is instructive in several ways. Among other things, it demonstrates quite clearly that acceptance of culturally defined beliefs is not universal, or, alternatively, that they may or may not serve as guides to action—after all, quite a lot of children were born in *hinoe-uma*. There is no problem here, for it has been a very long time since any anthropologist has argued that all members of a society share equally in all aspects of its culture. It is of more than passing interest to students of social change in Japan, however, that the effect of *hinoe-uma* seems to have been far more marked in 1966 than in 1906 (I say "seems" because the sources of data are not strictly comparable). The major implication surely is that it is naive to assume that economic development necessarily obliterates all such aspects of "traditional culture." Indeed, so taken for granted is the cultural construction of the meaning of this year of the cycle that in its 1985 New Year's Day edition, the *Asahi Shinbun* reported without comment that in 1984 the number of live births in Japan had dropped below 1.5 million "for the first time, with the exception of the two *hinoe-uma*," in the modern period. It may be objected that this pure case comes along only once in sixty years and even then seems not to affect even the majority of Japanese married couples. There is no doubt that the curve of birthrate trends can be smoothed to eliminate the unusual stutter in the trendline, but I reject the assumption that statistical frequency is the best guide we have to the importance of a phenomenon. The point is not only that cultural factors can have an effect in the demographic domain, but that in this case they alone account for a situation that otherwise would remain inexplicable.[29]

Beef, Leather Goods, and Their Invisible Processors

It is perfectly possible to analyze the Japanese government's policies toward beef and leather imports primarily in economic terms. It is even possible to discuss the politics behind the economic policies as though they reflected just another case of a special-interest group exercising its political clout to secure protection or other favorable treatment.[30] Neither approach requires a thoroughgoing treatment of the very special cultural, historical, and institutional factors that have contributed to the formation of present policies, however.

This is not the place to go into the intricacies of the situation of Japan's *burakumin*, often characterized as untouchables, outcasts, or pariahs. Suffice it to say that they represent a social category of persons viewed by significant elements of the population as ritually polluting and are subject to the most extreme forms of discrimination (major firms will not knowingly hire them). Direct contact with them is still regarded with abhorrence by many. Rising militancy on their part has led the government to set in place extensive "uplift" programs designed to improve their standards of living, educational opportunities, and competitiveness in the labor market.[31]

Most *burakumin* are not engaged in the traditionally polluting occupations (they are for the most part farmers and factory workers), but significant numbers are directly involved in leather-goods manufacture and the processing and sale of beef. Protection of these interests has been disproportionate to their voting power, although to be sure other interest groups have benefited enormously from the willingness of the government to stand firm, especially on beef import controls. To the extent that this protectionist policy is successful, it represents an indirect transfer of payments to members of the *burakumin* community. The last manufacturing industry to enjoy outright import quotas was leather shoes.

The difficulty of obtaining hard information on this aspect of the formation of government policy makes it impossible to estimate its importance in the overall scheme of things. The matter is rarely mentioned, and then only in passing.[32] Some Japanese publishing houses routinely accede to demands that references to the *burakumin* be deleted from books, and translations from the English often omit such passages as a matter of course.[33] The reasons behind the silence and the protectionist stance are not difficult to guess, however.[34] The *burakumin* have developed a formidable technique of confrontation and denunciation that is tacitly approved by the authorities. Frank Upham offers the following assessment:

The effectiveness of denunciation in economic issues in Osaka is paralleled on a small scale on the national level in terms of leather and beef import restrictions. Even though restraints on both items have been highly visible irritants in the U.S.–Japan relationship, Japan has strongly resisted liberalization. One reason is the concentration of *burakumin* in these sectors, particularly in leather working and beef butchering and wholesaling, and the B(uraku) L(iberation) L(eague)'s strong opposition to any liberalization. To ensure the continuation of current policies, key officials in MITI and other ministries are regularly visited by BLL representatives.[35]

Such visits may also be occasioned by particular grivances, as in the BLL's reaction to the publication of two articles by Austrian economists that identify the *burakumin* as a source of trade friction with the EEC. Deeming both libelous, the BLL was particularly upset that one of the articles was actually published in a JETRO (Japan External Trade Organization) magazine. Meetings with representatives of MITI, the Ministry of Foreign Affairs, and JETRO produced no concrete result, apparently, leaving the BLL fearful that the government might have the "intention to allow the Burakumin to be used as scapegoats in this trade battle."[36] However that may be, it is clear that with respect to leather goods and beef-marketing policies, the efficiency of the market is a secondary consideration at best. Nevertheless, the power of such cultural factors to determine a government's course of action is not absolute. Finally, in the summer of 1988, Japan's policymakers did liberalize beef imports in response to intense pressure by the United States and the government of Australia. Even so, it was a grudging concession to lower tariff rates from 70 to 50 per cent over a three-year period, though quotas were indeed substantially increased and will be eliminated by 1991—a major change.

The Medical-Care Delivery System

How a modern society deals with the domain of medicine is profoundly shaped by all manner of forces—government policy, financial considerations, the general state of health of the population, and systems of diagnosis and treatment. In Japan, medical pluralism has been encouraged by the authorities,[37] with a result that will seem exotic only to those foreign observers who are unaware of the extent to which their own medical-care systems are an amalgam of traditions, assumptions, and preconceptions. Medical systems are shaped by accepted definitions of wellness and illness, concepts of what is treatable and what the best treatment is, aims of rehabilitation, assignment of responsibility for caretaking of the ill and infirm, and a host of other culturally defined concerns and beliefs.[38] All these may change over time, but the cultural is never far removed from the political economy of medical care.[39]

The current medical scene in Japan is characterized by a thorough blending of several systems by means of which health is defined and appropriate treatment of illness prescribed. Indeed, the practice of modern biomedicine is interwoven with the practice of what may be called holistic ("Chinese") medicine. The Meiji government promoted the establishment of Western biomedical science, to be sure, but it made no move to stamp out the indigenous system, itself a blend of Japanese and continental practices. Although the authorities did institute controls over medical practice, they also fostered the integration of the two systems into one that has flourished to the present day. One bit of evidence for the effectiveness of that integration is that the recent boom in the use of herbal medicines can be traced in part to their promotion by Japan's great pharmaceutical houses.[40] In contemporary Japan, the benefits of medical pluralism do not derive from marginal survivals holding out against the inroads of a powerful alien system; the two are perceived as complementary.

As in all societies, definitions of health, illness, and therapy are crucially shaped by beliefs concerning the body, concepts of the self and personal identity, and the individual's relationship to society. Popular medical knowledge and belief are everywhere deeply embedded in the formal definitions of proper health maintenance, the symptomology of illness and its effective treatment, and the role of medication in the curing process, but perhaps to a greater degree in Japan than in other industrial societies. The contributors to a recent volume edited by Edward Norbeck and Margaret Lock all attempt to show how what may seem to be purely technical medical decisions, such as length of hospital stay, degree of intrusiveness of treatment, and definitions of the numerous new syndromes "discovered" by the media, are infused with social and cultural understandings. "At the level of institutionalization there are indeed clear demarcations between folk, traditional literate, and biomedical systems of medicine, but using a cultural and structural . . . analysis, it is possible to demonstrate . . . that there are certain concepts and values, such as those based upon ideas of purity and impurity . . . that surface in a wide range of religions and medical settings, including modern hospitals."[41]

It goes without saying that cultural considerations are not the only important ones. For example, how should we account for the finding that the average length of hospital stays in Japan is 38.3 days as opposed to 8 in the United States? The sharp contrast can be explained in part by a difference in types of hospitals in the two societies; in Japan no distinction is drawn between acute and chronic care facilities, as is the case in the United States. There also are important differences in the structure of health insurance plans, and the Japanese permit lengthier hospitalization. And there are notions about the importance of bed rest and nurturant care of the patient.[42] So length of hospital stay is determined by considerations having little to do with the nature of the illness. It is a function of economic and political decisions (which are themselves partly cultural), as well as of definitions of proper treatment, images of the body, and the like. Such definitions can change (remember that culture is not static), as has happened in the United States, where surgery that formerly required up to two weeks in a hospital is now assigned to the category "same-day." That dramatic change has a lot to do with the economics of medical care; it also requires a major revision of notions about what the body can take and how it is best restored to normal functioning.

In the Japanese case, it would be foolish to ignore the effects of the political clout of the Japan Medical Association,[43] or the impact of the national health insurance plan on, say, the frequency with which elderly patients visit their physicians. Relative cost of treatment is also a factor of importance, but not the determining one, for the boom in the use of herbal medicines has occurred despite their higher cost, except perhaps in cases of chronic illness. Furthermore, the fees of the herbalists (as opposed to those of physicians) are not reimbursable under terms of the national health insurance plan, yet their clientele continues to grow.

This complex issue deserves far more extended treatment than I can offer here. Suffice it to say that the system of medical care of any society represents the outcome of a series of decisions about what can and should be done to preserve health and treat illness. Indeed, Article 25 of the Constitution of Japan requires the state to assume responsibility for promoting and extending social welfare and public health.[44] The state has assumed that responsibility only in recent years. What is deemed possible reveals much about political and economic constraints; what is said to be desirable reflects the kinds of cultural predispositions discussed above. It is always the task of the maker and implementer of policy to square the two.

Culture and Ideology

The nature of the relationship between culture and ideology, widely debated in recent years, deserves serious consideration in any discussion of Japan. Clifford Geertz has warned us that

the view that social action is fundamentally an unending struggle for power leads to an unduly Machiavellian view of ideology as a form of higher cunning and, consequently, to a neglect of its broader, less dramatic social functions. The battlefield image of society as a clash of interests thinly disguised as a clash of principles turns attention away from the role that ideologies play in defining (or obscuring) social categories, stabilizing (or upsetting) social expectations, maintaining (or undermining) social consensus, relieving (or exacerbating) social tensions.[45]

Ideological statements in Japan commonly include appeals to cultural themes and historical precedent. If we take Geertz's advice and use the word *ideology* in as neutral a sense as possible, then we are no longer required to dismiss the cultural content of ideology as mere window dressing, empty rhetorical devices designed to conceal the true (read "reprehensible") motives of the miscreants who formulated the ideology and refuse to own up to what they really are trying to accomplish. That cultural themes are invoked in such contexts is not evidence of manipulative, ill-intentioned, corrupt, or vapid motives; nor is their introduction necessarily fraudulent or specious. Indeed, as Robert Heilbroner has observed, ideology may very well express what the dominant class sincerely believes to be the best answer to the questions it faces.[46]

Whatever one's position on this matter, however, it is clearly unwise to ignore the cultural rhetoric that infuses statements of policy. It is at the very least an important datum that the cultural contextualization of ideology is thought to be necessary and is so widely employed. It is the rare modern society in which those in authority fail to make use of ideological appeals; it must be even less common to find appeals that are devoid of culturally specific components. Such is surely the case in Japan, as Ronald Dore and Thomas Rohlen have pointed out, where intensive efforts are made to create firm-specific ideologies.[47] Carol Gluck sets the issue in a larger framework: "Although no society is innocent of collective notions about itself, some countries have made more of ideology than others. From the time Japan began its deliberate pursuit of 'civilization' in the mid-nineteenth century, ideology appears as a conscious enterprise, a perpetual civic concern, an affair, indeed, of state."[48]

Does the ideological framework within which political economic policy is constructed really make any difference? Of course it does, for ideology aims to render social reality unproblematic by giving meaning to the institutions of society and clarifying the place of the individual in them:

Since different people construe their world differently, there is always a multiplicity of ideological formations within a society. The question then arises, which—or whose—set of values and meanings becomes dominant and by what means. Gramsci's conception of hegemony recognizes that when a social group is successful in persuading others of the validity of its own world view, force does not greatly exceed consent. The consent, moreover, so permeates the society that to many it seems commonsensical, natural, and at times invisible. On the other hand, the means by which this permeation occurs are visible indeed. They include the disseminating institutions, both public and private, which though unconnected in their activities—schools and newspapers, for example—help to construct a shared ideological universe.[49]

The construction of any shared ideological universe must rely on the utilization of elements of the culture of a society. An example of the relationship between the two in the Japanese case is offered by Winston Davis:

While there is evidence of a work ethic among the working classes [at an earlier period in Japanese history], this ethic achieved national significance only after it was rationalized and propagated as a part of civil theology, the business ideology, and in the new national image making of Japan Theory. Whether or not there is such a thing as a "central value system," there clearly is a *resonance* here between the work ethic of the common people and the work ideology of the cultured and industrial elites. That resonance is not natural or accidental: it was planned.[50]

I have argued elsewhere that the Japanese have proved extremely adept at manipulating the past for present purposes.[51] Successful use of this strategy depends largely on the extent to which appeals for change resonate (to use Davis's apt word) with basic principles and sentiments on which the entire social system rests. A national work ethic could not have been invented out of whole cloth and sold to the people. Outright falsification of the past will fail, but an adroit combination and reordering of some of its elements that remain faithful to existing predispositions will be of great benefit to those who wish to persuade the people of the legitimacy of their goals and secure their cooperation in the attainment of them. The successful ideologue capitalizes on those elements of culture that can be used to further his ends. The Japanese government and the business elite have an enviable record in the successful conflation of culture and ideology. What they have produced is not a population sunk in "false consciousness"[52] but one whose behavior suggests strongly that they subscribe wholeheartedly to the virtues the system seeks to promote.

What of the Future?

I am not in the habit of making predictions, perhaps because I have so often been disappointed by those who do. Like the demographers of

Allen Otten's account,[53] predictors must make do with information gleaned from the record of the past and observations made in the present, on the basis of which they perforce extrapolate. It is for this reason that the well-advised seer opens with "Barring unforeseen developments . . ." or "Granting continued stability in the . . ." or, most egregiously, "All things being equal. . . ." I do not know what Japan will be like in the next century, nor does anyone else. There could well be a massive disruption of its oil supply. The anticipated Second Kanto Great Earthquake might devastate its capital city. Who knows? Certainly Japan's current problems are complex and difficult of solution, but in thinking about the ability of the Japanese to meet the challenge, I was reminded of another time of crisis and another forecast: "While Japan is presently beset by a host of difficult and complex economic problems, one cannot be pessimistic about 85 million intelligent, ingenious, and industrious people. In both the immediate and somewhat more distant future, clear lines of action are open to them and doubtless others less readily discernible at present will in due course suggest themselves to a people whose ability to adjust to changing world conditions has little parallel in history."[54] Thus Jerome Cohen, concluding his review of the economy at the moment that Japan regained its sovereignty. His account is grim, the economic prospects he sees are dim, and the picture is one of unrelieved gloom. The passage made an impression on me when I first read it, for here was an economist who pinned his hopes for Japan's postwar recovery on its people. Intelligence, ingenuity, industriousness, and the ability to adjust to changing conditions were the characteristics that seemed likely to see the Japanese through, despite all the negative signs in the economic picture.

Social commentators in Japan are much given to observing that momentous changes are in train, changes so far-reaching in their import that Japanese society "as we know it" is being transformed irrevocably. Some applaud its impending disappearance; others lament its passing. The young are denounced as feckless or heedless on the one hand and declared tragically stunted and diminished by the demands of the educational treadmill on the other. Trust based on long-established interpersonal relationships is said by many to be fast becoming a thing of the past; others welcome the dawn of a new era of openness and universalism in human relations. About equal numbers of these commentators point with despair to the erosion of the work ethic or note with approval the disappearance of the workaholic unable to make use of leisure time. The list of perceived threats and promises is endless, the concern genuine. The fear seems to be that the social fabric has become so badly frayed that it may be rent apart by the demands of those who seek the fulfillment of self-interest rather than service to the common good.

To the distant observer like myself, the furor seems disproportionate to the urgency of the problem or the likelihood of systemic change. That perception is no doubt related to my conviction that American society has been more fundamentally transformed since World War II than Japanese society. In the foregoing pages I have touched on several aspects of Japan's society and culture that seem to be likely to prove as perdurable in the future as they have in the past. Let me summarize them briefly. It seems to me that the perception that change is inevitable (or, as a Japanese student of mine put it, that stability is the exception and change the rule) is a great strength. Experience has taught the Japanese that lesson with a vengeance, leading to the understanding that the task for the future is to continue to manage change. One way to achieve that end is to clothe new concepts in traditional garb, a technique that has served the Japanese authorities very well in the past. I can see no reason why it should prove ineffective in future.

A key characteristic of Japanese social organization is the emphasis on territoriality and the sense of community. Again, the social commentators frequently note the erosion of that very sense, but as earlier delimited communities (e.g., *mura* [villages]) have been displaced/replaced by new ones (such as *kaisha* [companies]) for significant numbers of Japanese, it seems to me entirely likely that other devices will be identified or developed to take the place of those now being eroded. Among some of these are the programs devoted to community-building (*mura-tsukuri*), community-awakening (*mura-okoshi*), and the manufacture of a quite new "consciousness of native place," *furusato* being the key word, whose promotion has been met with a widely underestimated degree of success. Those who belittle the effort fail to understand its very deep resonances with the concern to find contemporary ways of defining what it means to be Japanese.[55] An important aspect of all these programs just mentioned is the skill with which groups are organized, the hierarchy of achievement exploited to reach their goals, and the interweaving of culture and ideology managed.

In short, while it is obvious that Japanese society and culture, like all others in the world, are in a state of flux, I cannot see that they are on their way to becoming something unrecognizable. Jerome Cohen's 85 million are now half again as many in number, but I share his view that those attributes that carried them through and beyond the decades of the 1940s and 1950s will see them through the current need to respond to new challenges. In that effort, the importance of the role of the government cannot be overestimated, as Prime Minister Takeshita (see note 55) has observed. I close with one of my favorite observations about Japan, confident that it was accurate when it was made, clearly holds true today, and is entirely likely to be the case at least a generation hence. Upon his return from Nagasaki to Batavia in 1813, Dr. D. Ainslee wrote to the Secretary of the Government of Java: "In Japan the Government pervades and animates every fibre of the frame of society, it identifies itself with its Subjects, and every Individual of its numerous population moves by its impulse."[56]

In many, perhaps most respects, Japan is just like all other contemporary industrial nations. There are those who argue, however, that because of the very peculiar characteristics of this particular nation, the future it faces is uniquely challenging and likely to prove ultimately transformative in fundamental ways. Perhaps so, but it appears to be the lot of every generation to interpret its time as somehow qualitatively different from all others. The old are given to seeing the future as a loss of the past; the young have only the dimmest perception of what that past was like. Nevertheless, the future is theirs to shape, and the system they devise surely will seem to them thoroughly Japanese.

John O. Haley

Consensual Governance:
A Study of Law, Culture, and the
Political Economy of Postwar Japan

To many, law seems to have little bearing on either the configuration or the performance of Japan's postwar economy. A postwar dearth of lawyers, litigation, and—at least as process—law is repeatedly said to distinguish Japan from its Western peers. Law as a means of governmental control and mechanism of governance in postwar Japan seems extraordinarily weak. Conciliation and administrative guidance, not law and order, become the watchwords. Legal rules from constitution to contract appear to yield to compromise and pliant manipulation, while formal processes atrophy.

As nearly all observers also agree, the bureaucrats play a special part in governance in Japan.[1] Simply put, theirs is a widely accepted managerial role that entitles and, in some instances, requires them to intervene and participate in all spheres of social, political, and economic activity. Here, too, legal controls seem extraordinarily weak. As a result, government involvement in the economy seems unlimited in scope and administrative discretion without bounds. Establishment laws (*setchi hō*) for governmental organizations become in effect a means of territorial division, allocating managerial jurisdiction over discrete segments of the entire terrain. Government offices thus constitute the fora for a broad range of economic decisions left to the marketplace in most market economies.

Authority Without Power

Paradoxically, despite the scope of such pervasive managerial authority, government officials in Japan rarely exercise or even possess some legal powers that are taken for granted in either command or intensively regulated economies. Absent too are the extensive formal procedures for administrative decision making of other industrial democracies, as well as the coercive restraints of other bureaucratic regimes. In Japan governmental policies are not carefully articulated in either legislative enactments or legally binding administrative pronouncements. Nor does the bureaucracy exercise the array of formal coercive legal powers, the mere threat of which usually assures compliance, common in other industrial states. Although decisions are made within governmental institutions with the active participation of bureaucratic officials, few can be accurately described as bureaucratic decisions in the sense that officials decide or direct policy elsewhere. As Richard Samuels comments:

Although the Japanese state pervades the market, it does not lead, guide, or supervise private interests. There is little evidence that state actors have ever been able to resist political pressures in the absence of alliances with parts of the private sector. In three hundred years of coal markets and a century of oil and electric power, where have state actors systematically denied access to particular groups in the policy process? Where have they ignored the demands of labor or small business with impunity? Where have state initiatives been adopted without evisceration and without guarantees? Transformations of energy markets have always preceded state intervention, and state intervention has always conformed to and reconfirmed evolving energy markets. Again we ask . . . not why the Japanese state is so pervasive in the economy but why the pervasive state is so congenial to private firms.[2]

Language fails in fact to convey the nature and process of governance in Japan. No commonly accepted paradigm of how policy is made and enforced seems to fit. Neither "regulation" nor "market" seems apt. Why? The answer, I argue, lies in what might be called an enthymeme of authority, an unstated premise in nearly all legal and political orders, except Japan, that with authority there is also power. The authority of the state to command thus necessarily implies the coercive power of the state to implement and enforce its commands. Divorce power from authority, as in Japan, however, and the capacity of the state to direct and control, not just to intervene and participate, becomes a function of its ability to persuade, bargain, or cajole in order to induce consent. "The Japanese bureaucracy does not dominate, it negotiates," Samuels notes.[3]

In such contexts, governmental decisions cannot be unilateral. Indeed, to describe them as governmental decisions at all is in many instances simply to locate the situs of the action but not the actor. This is because with only authority to make policy and without the power to enforce it, those who govern must have the consent of those whose cooperation or compliance is necessary for it to be implemented successfully. Consequently, by necessity those affected have a significant voice in the process of forming policy and an even greater opportunity to participate in the enforcement process. The separation of power from authority thus denies the state the capacity to choose to permit participation. It is forced upon it.

This process of rule—perhaps most aptly labeled consensual governance—is not therefore itself the result of intentional political choice.
Rather, it is, I believe, the product of Japan's unique institutional history
and cultural environment. The unstated premise of authority without
power is an inextricable feature of the Japanese legal order. In both the
West and the sinofied legal traditions of East Asia, law defines the state's
authority and its powers and thus becomes the dominant instrument of
social control by the state. Consensual governance thus implies a very
different paradigm of the nature of law and its function, one that varies
considerably from those of both Japan's East Asian neighbors and its
Western partners. One cannot, then, begin to understand Japan's postwar political economy without at least an intuitive appreciation of these
contrasts.

Law as Culture

This endeavor is made more formidable, however, by the threshold
difficulties of definition. What do we mean by authority, power, culture,
and, above all, law?

My aim in this essay is to explain the peculiar separation of power
from authority in Japan, and its reliance upon consensual mechanisms
of social ordering for the effective implementation of public policy. In so
doing, I offer an interpretative analysis of the role of law in shaping
Japan's postwar political economy. Stated as succinctly as possible, the
central argument is that the peculiar configuration of Japan's legal order
has long contributed to chronic dependence upon consent for effective
governance.

At least for the purposes of this analysis, *authority* is used to mean an
accepted entitlement to command and to receive respect and compliance. With authority inevitably comes influence, but not necessarily
power in the sense of a capacity to force or coerce others to do what they
would not otherwise do. *Power* is therefore used here to mean more than
merely a capacity to influence or persuade, to manage or control the
environment in ways that give rational actors incentives to become
willing to act in the desired fashion. It involves the ability of those who
hold and exercise it to coerce compliance with prescribed standards or
rules of behavior. Power is thus more than persuasion and influence,
although in many contexts it may be difficult to delineate where influence
ends and power begins. For instance, an official's orders may at face
value seem to reflect both authority and power, but if on closer scrutiny
one finds that the order can be disobeyed with impunity, and that
compliance is best explained by a tacit understanding or explicit decision
by those subject to the command that they choose without being com-

pelled to obey, the commander may be said to have authority without power.

By *culture*, I mean quite simply the identifiable values, habits, and expectations shared generally, if not unanimously, by a people, here the Japanese. Not all the components of a culture need be indigenous, as illustrated by the contributions of both Buddhism and neo-Confucian thought to Japanese culture. Nor are structural or institutional arrangements irrelevant. Political organization and other institutional features of a society both shape and are shaped by prevailing values, habits of thinking, behavior, and expectations. Cultures thus evolve and change in a historical process of institutional change.

Defining what is meant by *law* is an even more elusive task. Law is, after all, itself a self-defining cultural artifact. Simply put, a legal order is no less a "belief system" than an institutionalized religious order. Constitutions and codes are its sacred texts; legal theory and terminology, its doctrines and creeds; definitions of the nature of law, its theology. Individual legal systems independently define what is meant by law and which roles or standards share law's attributes. The concept of law thus encompasses the shared habits, expectations, and values—in other words, the legal culture—of a given legal system. Take, for example, the simplest rules governing individual conduct in society, requiring payment of debts or proscribing violence. Legal systems define these rules as law differently. Although one finds functional equivalents across cultures and legal systems, whether such rules are "legal" and share any common attributes as law depends upon what H. L. A. Hart has described as the "secondary" rules of recognition of a particular legal order: the rules or standards that determine the recognition or acknowledgment of law.[4] Discrete legal systems thus internally define which rules and standards are to be accorded the status of law by delineating the legitimate institutional processes for making and enforcing legal rules. In the United States, for example, the regulations of public institutions, such as the rules governing access to buildings at a public university, are by definition binding, justiciable legal rules. To be effective they must comply with prescribed procedural requirements. Yet identical rules established by private universities are not recognized as legal rules and do not share their attributes. In short, there are rules and rules in any complex legal order. Some are legal; others are not, despite functional and even substantive equivalence.

For purposes of this essay, it is therefore important for the reader to keep in mind that the words *law* and *legal* as used in the context of the Japanese political system refer to those norms and sanctions or processes for making or enforcing law that, in Hart's terminology, satisfy "secondary" rules of Japanese law prescribing recognition of what rules or norms constitute legal rules. The point is important because of the tendency, detailed below as one of the principal "premises" of the American reformers of Japan (as well, I might add, of most postwar observers), to assume that functional distinctions can be made between law and moral, market, or other extralegal rules of social conduct, and that law is the primary, if not the exclusive, legitimate instrument for ordering political, economic, and social life. The consequence of this error is to neglect the operation of social rules and mechanisms of enforcement, as though they do not matter or bear little if any relationship to the law. For example, an agreement among producers to limit production can be as effective and legitimate an instrument of policy to deal with problems of overcapacity as direct government regulation. Once this is understood, the need for analysis of differences in outcome between a pro-cartel policy versus direct regulation becomes apparent.

The reader should thus understand that here at least notions such as legal orders versus moral or social orders, legal controls versus moral or social controls, are not differentiated in functional terms, except, perhaps, by attributes that attach within the particular context of the Japanese political system at a particular moment in time.

Legal Cultures in Conflict: The Occupation Reforms

The domination in Japan until the mid nineteenth century of a concept of law derived from the imperial Chinese bureaucratic tradition was critically important to the Japanese legal culture, first in that it defined law narrowly in terms of state-made and bureaucratically enforced penal and administrative regulations, a definition that excluded the vast majority of the rules and standards that actually governed the lives of most Japanese. This preexisting concept of law also explains the tension that resulted when Japan introduced continental European notions of law following the Meiji Restoration.

By subjecting more areas of private life and relationships to governmental control through law, Western legal orders were more inclusive. Yet, paradoxically, by denying legitimacy to competing sources of social control, they were concomitantly more exclusive. This is illustrated by the tendency in Western societies to regard various forms of private coercion and self-help, such as refusals to deal, to be illegitimate unless authorized by law. The state thereby defines what forms of social sanctions, even for private transactions, are acceptable. Within the contours of either the traditional or the modern Japanese legal order, customary rules could be articulated and recognized as legal rules by adjudicating authorities—and thus become generally binding and enforceable—or be disregarded and denied even particularistic formal enforceability. Nevertheless, beyond the law's domain, such rules or standards could continue to have whatever effect is permitted by extralegal systems of prescription and enforcement. Thus, in the case of pollution, a customary rule regarding compensation for unforeseen consequences of economic conduct may be overridden by a requirement of negligence in a civil code (see Civil Code of Japan, art. 709) and yet still be subject to undisputed extralegal enforcement by public condemnation and possibly political action.

The consequence, of course, was an allocation of power. Those who controlled effective extralegal sanctions controlled the viability of whatever rules and norms were enforced, and thereby the political, social, or economic order they produced. The interrelationships, conflicts, and tensions between Japan's legal order and competing systems of social control thus had profound consequences for Japan's political and economic environment. None was greater, however, than the influence of the Occupation reforms on the political economy of postwar Japan, which paradoxically highlight and obscure the pattern of consensual governance in Japan.

The American occupiers of Japan imposed an extensive agenda of legal reforms, ranging from a new constitution to an equally enduring array of regulatory statutes. The extension of legal controls under the Occupation was pervasive, and their endurance throughout the postwar era to regulate both political and economic activity has been equally remarkable. The story of the impact of Occupation policy is one not only rich in irony and paradox but also telling of the interrelationships of law and culture. Premised in large measure on implicit assumptions concerning the role and efficacy of law derived from an alien, American experience, the Occupation reformers created an institutional framework that shaped the political and economic order of postwar Japan. In the course of the confrontation of dissimilar premises, Occupation legislation was necessarily adapted, transformed, or ignored, but not without influencing Japanese attitudes and assumptions about law and its role.

The Occupation reforms are equally important, however, for the perspective they provide on the more fundamental issues of governance and law in postwar Japanese society. The fact that most of Japan's basic regulatory statutes in force today date from the Occupation is itself revealing. At the very least, some explanation is required of why these statutes, many of which represented emergency controls, have endured. Consequently, the conflict of premises regarding the nature of authority and role of law that the Occupation reforms reflect is central to any analysis of the political and economic environment of postwar Japan.

For Japan's postwar economy, the consequences of the reforms and their transformation were profound. Despite reform and new legal controls, the resulting configuration of Japan's legal order further contributed to dependence upon societal consensus for the effective implementation of public policy. In turn, however, such dependence enabled Japan to restore and then maintain a market-driven economy notwithstanding the appearance of substantial governmental intervention. It also necessitated emphasis not only on extralegal means of societal control but on mechanisms for building or preserving consensus. One consequence was for legal institutions intended to assure the primacy of law and legal control, such as the judiciary, to function instead as important new sources for influencing consensus. Instead of being a system of binding, coercive rules of command forcing conformity, law in postwar Japan served less directly as a source of legitimized norms that were ultimately left to the discretion of constituent communities, including the family and the firm, to enforce by means of extralegal social sanctions.

The Occupation reforms were overwhelmingly legalistic. Not only did they take the form of statutory initiatives and of revisions of existing codes and statutes, they also reflected a complex and often subtle set of tacit premises about the role and efficacy of law as a vehicle to effect social and political change. As exemplified by the new constitution, pervasive economic legislation, and revision of nearly all of Japan's basic codes, the Occupation authorities relied on law as the primary instrument of social and political change. In so doing, they sought to realize their vision of a new political regime for postwar Japan. To say that they attempted to legislate a new democratic political and economic order is far more than an idle quip.

The Occupation's program rested on a set of implicit beliefs with respect to the instrumental function of law in society. Although seldom, if ever, fully articulated, these assumptions included a naive faith in the efficacy of law, not only in creating new political and social institutions, but also in controlling or channeling their function and impact. The new constitution and other legal reforms, it was apparently believed, could provide the institutional environment most likely to produce a liberal democratic political order. New economic legislation, ranging from land and tax reform to the "democratization" of Japanese company law, novel capital-market regulation, and stringent antitrust controls were similarly intended to produce an economic order regulated American-style. Equally fundamental was the peculiarly American emphasis on the ideological primacy of legal rules and standards as a means of political and social ordering—what Judith Shklar has described in part as "legalism."[5] Law was tacitly accepted as the principal, if not exclusive, means of organizing political and economic life. The Occupation authorities thus relied upon legal rules and standards as if no other instrument or means of controlling or regulating political or economic behavior existed. For the most part, they simply ignored market forces and other forms of extra-legal ordering as alternatives or, more to the point, competing systems of social control.

In addition to a parenthetical tendency to view prewar Japan as an Asian variant of German fascism, the Occupation reformers generally accepted the U.S. New Deal as the ideal of progressive, but pragmatic, governance in an industrial democracy. They envisioned the state playing an active role in channeling economic activity by means of selective intervention and regulatory controls, yet constrained by legal controls over its law-making and law-enforcing powers. Rejected were the extremes of both a command economy and laissez-faire capitalism. Because legitimate state intervention was assumed to take the form of legal rules embodied in legislation or administrative regulations, legislative supremacy and judicial review were considered to be crucial elements of the political order to assure the accountability of state officials to the citizenry in general.

The failure of the reformers to question the most obvious of these assumptions is not surprising. As shared premises about the role of law and proper governance, they were simply taken for granted. Consequently, legal and political models derived from the American experience tended to be imposed without evaluation of alternative patterns and practices from either continental Europe or even English-based parliamentary systems, much less the Japanese cultural experience.

The cluster of assumptions and values underlying much of the Occupation's legal program were in many instances characteristic of U.S. legal culture. They were the shared beliefs of a particular group of Americans at a specific moment in time. The vision of the function of law as an instrument of social change shared by the Occupation authorities was not, however, uniquely American. Such attitudes reflected assumptions derived from Western legal culture in general. Among the most fundamental were peculiarly Western views on the nexus between law and morals. Such questions as the morality of civil disobedience—whether breaking the law is morally or ethically wrong—and the conflict between natural law and positivist legal theories, not to mention exaltation of the "rule of law," all manifest the assumption that such a nexus exists. Indeed, our word *justice* embodies this fusion of morality and law. The Chinese equivalent *zheng yi* (in Japanese *seigi*), although commonly translated as "justice" or "righteousness," has no law-related nuance. What was "good and fair" was conceptually distinctive in the Chinese tradition from what was lawful or unlawful.

Detailed analysis of the interrelationships of law and morals in the Western legal tradition is well beyond the scope of this paper. Suffice it to say, however, that law in the Western tradition has never been completely divorced from its religious foundations. From Hammurabi's Code and Judaic law through early Greek and Roman law, the deistic origins of the earliest legal rules were explicitly acknowledged. As the notion of the secular state governing society by means of legal rules divorced from any supernatural or metaphysical command evolved, the idea of "justice" persisted in a universally applicable set of "higher" legal norms controlling alike those who governed and those being governed, albeit freed from their religious moorings. A principal concern of modern Western jurisprudence thus centers on the tension between recognition of binding legal norms apart from legislative, judicial, or other institutional law-making processes[6] and positivist views of legal rules as restricted to those articulated by the formal law-making institutions within a given political system.

Equally symptomatic of the identification of law and morals in Western legal culture are contemporary efforts to redefine both concepts in ways that deny any conflict. Judith Shklar, for example, argues that "law . . . is social, objective, and coercive" whereas "morals are individual, subjective, and voluntary."[7] The result of such definitions, however, is less to resolve the tension than to wish away social systems ordered by coercive moral controls that function apart from law and the legal order (as internally defined), as in imperial China, and theocratic systems, as in Saudi Arabia, within which no differentiation is made between the two.

This equation of moral values with legal rules pervades attitudes toward law in all Western societies, but in few does it appear as pervasive an influence as in the United States. What is lawful is deemed moral; what is unlawful, immoral. And no behavior considered immoral by the majority can long remain insulated from legal proscription. Such attitudes not only give law added legitimacy and force in regulating social behavior, they also reinforce reliance on the formal law-making and law-enforcing institutions of the state in ordering society. Nonetheless, it was as presumptive during the Occupation as it is today to believe that law has similar legitimacy and force across legal cultures, or that all societies share or ought to share a similar willingness to rely on governmental direction.

Concomitant with this subsumption by law of all forms of social control is a shared assumption of the legitimacy of the monopoly of the state over the means of coercion. Once accepted, at least in liberal democratic political orders, this premise then necessitates in theory and fact the assertion of effective mechanisms for legal controls over the state and its organs. Unless state law-making and law-enforcing institutions and officials themselves can be effectively coerced by law into complying with prescribed legal rules, the absence of alternative forms of controls leads inexorably to some form of state absolutism. Out of the need to prevent such absolutism arises the uniquely Western emphasis on the "rule of law." In other words, some effective means of law enforcement against the state becomes critical. Indeed, the paradox of liberal legal orders is the claim to absolutist powers of legal coercion by some organs of the state, especially the judiciary, in order to coerce other organs into compliance with the law.

Although the "legal subculture" of the Occupation—shared, I hasten to add, by most contemporary Western legal writings—led to a paramount concern with law-making processes and their regulation by law at the expense of interest in effective law enforcement, the ideal of the "rule of law" itself presupposes both facets. Not only are government policies to be expressed in legal rules as legislated or articulated by formal law-making institutions, such as parliaments and courts, but also the processes of law-making, such as adjudication, legislative action, or administrative regulation, are similarly to be governed by procedures established by law. The Occupation authorities (like most contemporary observers) paid scant attention to the issue of enforcement, however, except in terms of legal controls over criminal prosecution and "voluntary" administrative action. How were legal rules to be enforced? Who was to enforce them? And what difference did it make?

For many Americans, especially members of the legal profession, the answers may seem self-evident. The courts are the ultimate enforcers. The independent judiciary constitutes the institutional prerequisite for the "rule of law." As a separate organ of the state independent of both the legislative and executive branches, the courts alone function formally to enforce against other institutions and offices of government the legal rules they impose upon themselves or are subject to under a constitution. Absent the judiciary, however, legal rules may still be enforceable, but through the political rather than the formal process. Yet, as David Danelski notes, the establishment of a judiciary with express authority for judicial review was included almost as an afterthought in the early Occupation drafts of Japan's postwar constitution.[8] Little if any concern was directed to its powers and capacity to enforce its judgments adequately.

The organization of the judiciary, its powers, and procedures were left to the Courts and Law Division of the Government Section of the Supreme Commander for the Allied Powers (SCAP) to work out. The division was headed by Alfred C. Oppler, a German emigré to the United States who had served as an administrative law judge in the Weimar Republic. Its staff included Thomas C. Blakemore, one of the few American lawyers in SCAP with any training in both Japanese language and law. Despite their unique qualifications, apparently neither they nor anyone else appreciated how radical a departure from Japanese and continental European practice an American-style judiciary represented.

Paradigms of Governance: The Legacy of Japan's Legal Tradition

The Japanese, too, adhere to a particular set of assumptions about law and other means of social control. Some are common to the East Asian legal tradition generally—thus shared with China, Korea, and parts of Southeast Asia—others are as uniquely Japanese as many of the Occupation's premises were American. Whatever their origin, however, several central and especially relevant premises within the Japanese legal culture can be identified.

First, law had rarely, if ever, been the predominant means of social control. By the mid nineteenth century, a complex variety of informal social relationships evolved to order the lives of the vast majority of the Japanese population. The *mura* (village) provided the paradigm of the Japanese community. Often distantly and, at least from the late sixteenth century, indirectly regulated by the governing authorities, the people of the *mura* were in effect left to develop the means of consensual, extralegal self-governance.

The relocation of occupying warriors to newly established castle towns (*jōkamachi*) at the end of the sixteenth century resulted in a nationwide pattern of semi-autonomous villages, governed indirectly through the accountability of village headmen to often distant samurai officials. This system of indirect governance for the vast majority of Japanese, which endured for two and a half centuries, precluded effective central or regional bureaucratic control as in China and Korea, or direct coercive control on the European pattern, in which local feudal warriors evolved into manorial lords and, ultimately, landowner-aristocrats.[9] In other words, absent the quasi-officials and *yamen* "runners" connecting the regional bureaucracy to local communities as in China, the local presence of *sori* clerks and *yangban* aristocrats as in Korea, or the development of manorial rule as in Europe, the Japanese *mura* effectively preserved community autonomy, insofar as the village could avoid official intervention by maintaining at least an appearance of tranquility and law-abidingness.[10]

Outward submission to authority did not necessarily entail a diminution of community or individual freedom from control, however, or result in compliance with legal rules. Rather, the system reflected a trade-off between submission and autonomy, in that outward deference to authority ensured greater freedom from regulatory control by governing officials. Among other effects, it thereby diminished the efficacy of formal legal controls, while strengthening the need for and use of informal, extralegal rules of conduct and sanctions to assure their compliance. To preserve its autonomy and avoid direct intervention by *bakufu* or *han* officials, the *mura* had to develop consensual community controls to contain conflict and maintain order and stability.

Moreover, unlike China, Japan lacked a substitute for legal ordering in the form of a universally applicable set of moral or ethical standards for social and political control. As William Alford persuasively argues, the moral belief system of Chinese Confucianist thought embodied a cosmology that, whether effective or not, in theory at least subjected ruler and ruled alike to a set of definable standards of conduct, operating apart from the legal order to regulate all of society, including those who governed:

> The ancient Chinese state was not free to exercise unrestrained power . . . even in the presumed absence of specialized legal bodies within which disputes could be adjudicated with the help of specialized legal personnel applying specialized legal rules. Positions of power, believed the Chinese, were to be occupied by individuals of high virtue, whose particularly well-developed sense of morality and whose commitment to continue to improve their moral being would regulate their discharge of official authority. . . . Thus, although the ruler was vested with considerable formal legal authority to discharge his duty to lead the people, and although the populace typically deferred to his presumed greater wisdom and moral insight, if the ruler exercised his power in violation of these ethical bounds, he could no longer be called a ruler.[11]

Like Western legal theory in the nineteenth century, much of this moral belief system was introduced into Japan. It was a significant alien influence imposed from above, not evolved from within. Claims to enduring, hereditary imperial and shogunal authority prevented assimilation of the Chinese concept of the mandate from Heaven. Japan therefore lacked the sort of pervasive and universally applicable moral standards that functioned in Chinese society as an alternative to law and in Western societies as a syncretic element of the legal order (although, as Ronald Dore notes, the legitimacy of authority and power rests in Japan at least in part on benevolent and fair behavior).[12] Custom and social convention, only partially informed by either Confucianist or other "moral" principles or law, served as the principal source of social standards for most Japanese communities. What, then, was the dominant source of legitimacy in Japan? In a word, tradition. Legitimacy in Japan derived above all else from history as a shared present perception of the past and of custom.

Equally important, the lack of an effective means of formal regulatory enforcement by the governing authorities within the *mura* meant that the means of coercion, including both the sanctions used and the manner in which they were applied, were necessarily also informal and equally dependent upon convention or custom. As a result, unless an offense was perceived as likely to invite outside authorities to intervene, and thus to interfere in the *mura*'s autonomous governance, even rules imposed from above, whether by Confucianist tenets or by law, could effectively be ignored unless internalized by the community as custom or convention. Thus, by paying their rice tax when due, repairing roads and bridges as official regulations prescribed, and otherwise maintaining outward, visible conformity and community peace and harmony, the *mura* could generally expect to remain free of any direct, obtrusive governmental supervision or control. Furthermore, by controlling the means and process of enforcement, the community thereby controlled the efficacy of any legal or moral rules imposed upon it. Yet to maintain order—a prerequisite for the preservation of autonomy—the *mura* also had to ensure that its informal mechanisms for enforcement were effective. With such incentives, the Japanese developed an extraordinarily effective system of social controls.

Inexorably, Japanese villages evolved an elaborate system of consensual ordering among equals in legal status—what might well be labeled "government by contract." In a formal, legal sense, members of the community were equal in legal status within a system in which formal inherited status distinctions determined the most basic differentiations of applicable legal rules and standards. "Nothing," Dan Henderson notes, "had a more constitutional impact on Tokugawa law than the rigid, hereditary hierarchy of statuses established to classify the entire Tokugawa populace."[13] Such equality in legal status effectively inhibited the development of a fixed hierarchy of authority enabling upward social mobility, and contributed significantly to consensual means of governance. Although significant inequalities in wealth and power existed, the people of the *mura* lived within an ideological framework in which they were equals, and could thus aspire to higher economic and social status. This factor, I believe, further reinforced reliance on consensual means of governance.

Japan was consequently largely governed by contract, with ostracism, fines, and other conventional village sanctions (including sanctioned violence) being the principal means of coercion. Analyzing Tokugawa village documents, Henderson observes:

Considering how agreements were used in the village three points stand out: (1) they were pervasively used in all aspects of life; (2) many types of agreements were standardized as to form and meticulously executed so that they could be enforced; and (3) most significantly they were signed or sealed by village officials, relatives, and neighbors as custodians, recorders, guarantors and witnesses so that many formal "private" agreements had a public aspect and were indeed instruments of such village-wide consequence that I have suggested that they were in fact methods of consensual governance, performing something like constitutive, legislative, or judicial functions. Given the tight interdependence and immobility of most villagers, one suspects that social pressure was enough to enforce the consensual arrangements embodied in the usual multi-party village agreements.[14]

The *mura* was, however, only one of two paradigms of governance in the Japanese tradition. The other was the castle town, or *jōkamachi*. Whereas the *mura* was undergoverned, at least by law, the *jōkamachi*, established as a means of facilitating control over samurai retainers, was one of the most intensively regulated communities in the world. Although pockets of *mura*-like autonomy may have existed, here law governed in the form of regulatory, public law as understood in the imperial Chinese bureaucratic tradition, with status and power relationships rigorously controlled.

Hardly compatible within either the paradigm of governance by contract of the *mura* or the regulatory legal order of the *jōkamachi* was a third element of Japan's legal tradition—a sophisticated system of adjudication and judicial governance. Paralleling Western European experience, the political rulers of feudal Japan had early discovered in adjudication an efficient and effective means for establishing legitimacy and maintaining order. By the fourteenth century, judicial institutions had become the predominant vehicle for both the recognition of legal rules and their enforcement.[15] Judicial governance did not, however, fit comfortably within the framework of either the consensual or contract culture of the *mura* or the sinofied regulatory system of the *jōkamachi*. Nevertheless, litigation and judicial institutions remained. Albeit constrained by procedures for conciliation and other barriers, judicial law enforcement continued to hold a significant situs in Tokugawa governance as the number of commercial and intravillage suits increased with the expansion of commercial activity and economic growth.[16]

The complexity and institutional ambivalence in Japan's legal tradition helps to explain the nature of Japan's early accommodation of Western law and the significance of the Occupation reforms. That Japan had so little difficulty in adapting first continental European legal institutions and later American law models deserves special emphasis. Japan, in fact, readily absorbed new Western legal institutions, codes, statutes, and procedures with remarkable ease. No one argues, for instance, that European company law was ill suited to Japan's cultural environment. Nor did it take Japanese entrepreneurs long to recognize and pursue the advantages of organizing themselves into limited-liability partnerships or joint-stock companies. Moreover, as John Henry Wigmore noted in the 1890s in a noteworthy series of essays in the *Japan Weekly Mail*, even in the first Civil Code of 1890, which was subsequently scrapped in favor of the still-existing Civil Code of 1896 and 1898, few institutions of modern European law were without some analogue or parallel in customary Japanese practice, if not in the more formalized rules of Tokugawa law.[17]

Law in Japan, as in the West, also appears to have provided an important source of legitimacy. Although, as noted above, in Japan, as in China, legal rules did not represent moral commands, and moral rules were not necessarily embodied in legal commands, codified law does seem to have had a special legitimizing effect, especially when it could be argued to reflect tradition, quite apart from its instrumental use. As exemplified by the proliferation of legal codes promulgated by various daimyo in the sixteenth century[18] and Tokugawa edicts, particularly in the Buke shohatto (statute for warriors), in Yoshiro Hiramatsu's phrase, "a moralistic charter,"[19] law had acquired a hortatory quality. Among the best modern examples, however, are the attempts by the Meiji reformers to define in law the role of the emperor and to allocate legal authority within the family, justified by tradition.

The Meiji constitution recognized the emperor as combining in his person "the rights of sovereignty" (art. 4). From this it followed that he exercised "the legislative power with the consent of the Imperial Diet" (art. 5); issued all "ordinances necessary for the carrying out of the laws or for the maintenance of public peace and order" (art. 9); determined the organization of the administrative bureaucracy and the appointment, remuneration, and dismissal of all civil and military offices (art. 10); and functioned as supreme commander of the army and navy (art. 12). Explicating these provisions, surely with the model of the Kaiser in mind, the German jurist Hermann Roesler noted that they negated any thought that the "Supreme Sovereign" might reign but not rule, that executive or "ministerial" powers might be exercised independently of the emperor. Japanese ministers of state, he wrote, "perform their function subject to the supreme decision of the Emperor and are responsible to him."[20] Roesler was wrong, of course. As any serious student of Japanese governance knows, the emperor did indeed reign but not rule. The emperor personally neither determined nor directed policy. Hence, accountability to the emperor rather than another branch of government, whether phrased as an exercise of authority "in the name of the Emperor" as in the case of the judiciary (art. 57) or in terms of "direct access," as in the case of the military's high command in the 1930s, in effect meant autonomy and independence from control by other offices of government.

The Meiji constitution did not, then, mean what it said, at least to Western lawyers like Roesler. The drafters of the Meiji constitution could not have stated that the emperor had none of the powers of a ruling monarch without diminishing the authority they sought to invest in him.

The language used was purposely employed as a legitimizing device. Its function as law was didactic and ideological, not instrumental. The separation of authority and power could not be described in legal terms. It had to remain an implicit conventional understanding.

Closely related is the example of the civil code postponement controversy in 1892 and the revised family-law provisions eventually enacted and put into effect in 1898. To summarize the background to the dispute, in 1890 the 30-year effort to legislate a modern civil code with the French legal scholar Gustav Boissonade as the principal foreign adviser culminated in the enactment of a code based on French models but painstakingly drafted, as noted previously, to conform to preexisting customary practice. Before the code became effective, however, it was attacked by a group of influential scholars and publicists led by Yatsuka Hozumi and the "English School," representing the Tokyo Imperial University Law Faculty. A variety of concerns—not the least of which was a mounting sense that Japan had absorbed too much too quickly from the West to the detriment of valued traditions—fueled the dispute. It centered, however, on the family-law provisions of the 1890 code.

Drawing on a mélange of Shinto and Confucian themes, Hozumi and others construed the emperor and the state in familial terms. What unites the Japanese as a nation, Hozumi had earlier written, is "the authority of ancestors" and that authority "does not lie in a promise among equals" (in other words, the "social contract") but rather, "In the house [*ie*], the head of the house, representing the authority of the ancestors, exercises the patrimonial power over the family; in the nation, the emperor, representing the authority of the Sun Goddess [as mythological founder of Japan], exercises the sovereign power over the nation. Patrimonial power and sovereign power: both are powers whereby the emperor-father protects the children beloved of the ancestors."[21]

Construing the state and the role of the emperor in this manner, Hozumi and others predictably reacted with aghast fury against the family-law provisions of the new code. Article 449, for example, read: "Parental authority shall be exercised by the father. In the event of the decease of the father or of his inability to exercise parental authority, it shall be exercised by the mother." The critics attacked the provision for diluting the authority of the father, because, as Richard Rabinowitz explains, "paternal authority became merely a particular instance of the more general category of parental authority rather than standing as the supreme authority."[22]

From a functional or instrumental premise, such criticisms fail to persuade. Parental authority is not an empty abstraction. Even in a patrimonial regime, in the absence of the father, it follows logically that such authority must be exercised by the mother. However, Hozumi and the other critics did not evaluate provisions such as Article 449 from an instrumental perspective; they were concerned with paternal authority as an ideological principle. In their view, the code's provisions on authority within the family as a social unit had to conform to the recognition of sovereign authority in the person of "emperor-father." As in the case of the Meiji constitution, they were less concerned with the allocation of functional legal powers within real Japanese families than with an abstract ideal of paternal authority as the counterpart to imperial authority. Law thus had a legitimizing purpose that bore little, if any, relation to its functional use as a means of coercive ordering. It is therefore unlikely that critics of the 1890 code were at all dismayed by— indeed, they may have welcomed—later judicial decisions excoriating heads of households for arbitrary actions and denying them the power to exercise what otherwise appeared to be absolute rights granted them under the revised code.[23]

Needless to say, however, Tokugawa Japan did not replicate the legal orders of Western Europe. Tokugawa definitions of law and the legal process were bound within the East Asian tradition. Official, sinofied notions of which rules or norms were "legal" did not encompass village agreements or judicial law-making, however similar they may have been in effect or function. Alien to that tradition was the idea of legal rules subjected to private control over their application and enforcement through lawsuits—the essence of what I have called private law orders.[24] Conceptually, law meant the regulatory commands of those who ruled. There was no concept of law as a means of private, autonomous ordering. This is evidenced by one of the initial Japanese impressions of the French civil code, which was "truly unparalleled and without precedent," Joun Kurimoto, designated as ambassador to France in 1867, recorded in a pamphlet published upon his return. "I think that nothing short of the genius of Confucius could even have imagined it. Almost every government order issued by Napoleon [III], the present emperor, is rooted in this code."[25]

Any distinction between private and public law, between coercive state regulatory rules and legal norms enforced in an adjudicatory process subject to the initiative and control of interested parties as defined by the allocation of "rights" and "duties" was lost on Kurimoto. Rather he, like, I believe, most Japanese at that time and many today, thought of law in sinofied terms as rules and regulations issued by those who governed and subject to their discretionary enforcement.

Whatever misconception Kurimoto may have had about the nature of Western civil law and processes for its enforcement, he correctly perceived the expansiveness of the Western conception of law as the primary means of social ordering. Kurimoto's wonderment at the pervasiveness of regulation by legal rules and the domination of legal controls over all aspects of social life is telling of the absence of similar legal controls in Japan. Indeed, it was this expansion of the law's domain, combined with the reliance on litigation for enforcement, that proved to be more difficult than any substantive rules of Western law for Japan to absorb.

However divided those in power from the 1890s through the 1930s may have been over the acceptability of particular substantive provisions in Japan's new codes and statutes, they could agree that their private enforcement through litigation should be curtailed as disruptive. The debates over family law, rural and urban tenancy law, and labor codes in the 1920s ended with a standoff as to substantive reforms, but agreement as to the desirability of introducing formal conciliation (*chōtei*) as a substitute for litigation.[26] Both sides to these disputes were thus willing to permit the resolution of individual cases through conciliation and compromise, thereby avoiding the application of legislated rules as the primary standards for the social order in favor of the imposition of customary standards or a mutually agreed compromise.

The reception of nineteenth-century Western law in Japan did, of course, introduce new legal rules and institutions, although, as noted, few were totally inconsistent with preexisting patterns of behavior. And whatever the conceptual or ideological inconsistencies between traditional paradigms and their enforcement through private lawsuits, those benefited by them readily applied and fought to preserve them. Litigation rates in prewar Japan are startlingly high relative to the postwar experience. On average nearly twice as many cases were filed per capita each year in district courts between 1890 and 1935 than in any year since 1945.[27] The enactment of conciliation statutes in the 1920s and 1930s thus produced, not less litigation, but instead a substantial increase in the total number of disputes handled in some formal process.[28]

In the end, the nineteenth-century liberal constitutional orders of Western Europe, with their emphasis on private law ordering and laissez-faire restrictions on direct governmental direction, provided Japan's Meiji reformers with few legal or political models on which to build a more effective authoritarian state. The institutions and prevailing ideologies of nineteenth-century Europe could only buttress the preexisting paradox of an apparently authoritarian state with limited direct control over its subject citizenry (or even, as the events of the 1930s reveal, over agencies of the state with autonomous authority, such as the military). The modern Japanese state continued to depend to a remarkable degree on social controls and consensus in order to assure an essential degree of effective rule. This need to buttress consent and thus the legitimacy of governance in modern Japan explains, at least in part, the emphasis by political leaders on unifying national symbols of governance, from the imperial institution and "state Shinto," to definitions of national identity in terms of harmony and Japan's "virtuous ways and beautiful customs." The importance of appeals to cultural values as a means of securing the legitimacy of new patterns of bureaucratic rule and to assure order should not be minimized. They reflected an intuitive understanding of the limits of legal controls and the need to direct and manipulate Japan's complex system of social controls.

In turn, neither the ideology of harmony and order nor the prevalence of continued social controls should obscure the reality of conflict and change. "Yet the most cursory survey of the record," Robert J. Smith reminds us, "reveals a domestic political world far from harmonious, rendered pluralistic, contentious, and often perilous by the very granting of the [Meiji] constitution."[29] We need not turn back to the remote past for examples of how private violence has been used as an effective instrument for power and reordering. Directed violence has accompanied most, if not all, of contemporary Japanese political and social movements.[30] The fact that most Japanese still "go about their business"[31] despite such threats to the social order is owing less to expectations and reliance on law and the state for order than to the resilience of the Japanese social fabric and private ordering.

By the eve of the Pacific War, Japan had successfully transformed the Meiji legal order. The laws and legal institutions of modern Japan remained thoroughly Western, but the process of law enforcement had been fundamentally altered. The rules and theory of a nineteenth-century Western private law order remained formally intact, but without adequate means of enforcement to make them generally viable.

Neither, however, should the role of the state in directing the economy in Japan be overemphasized. It was not until the 1930s that Japan began to experiment with the types of regulatory economic controls that had become familiar in the United States and Western Europe two decades earlier. As noted below, even Japan's wartime controls permitted a degree of industry autonomy that was unthinkable in the United States. It was not, therefore, until the Occupation that the Japanese felt the impact of a totally authoritarian regime, with law as the primary instrument of control. Unlike the nineteenth-century European legal models, the regulatory regime of the U.S. New Deal included an arsenal of instruments for effective state control. What nineteenth-century European law lacked, twentieth-century American law offered in full measure.

The Occupation Reforms and Their Impact

There is general agreement as to both the basic features of the political and legal reforms of the Occupation and their impact on the postwar political economy. Stated briefly, the new constitution and implementing statutes established a parliamentary system with executive accountability through the political process and ruling political parties. The constitution also envisioned an American-style judiciary that, in exercising the power of judicial review, would assure legislative and administrative conformity to both constitutional and statutory requirements. Additionally, the Occupation produced an extensive array of regulatory statutes, some designed to achieve long-term reform goals and others to cure immediate economic ills. The list includes land-reform measures, dissolution of the *zaibatsu,* stringent antitrust legislation, labor law, and capital-market and tax reforms, as well as control of foreign investment and foreign trade.

The irony of the Allied Occupation as an attempt to impose democratic institutions by authoritarian means is equally well known. In Chalmers Johnson's words:

> Ironically, it was during the Occupation that the fondest dreams of the wartime "control bureaucrats" (*tōsei kanryō*) were finally realized. With the militarists gone, the zaibatsu facing dissolution, and SCAP's . . . decision to try to get the economy back on its feet, the bureaucracy finally found itself working for a *tennō* [MacArthur] who really possessed the attributes of "absolutism" (*zettai-shugi*).[32]

The institutional legacy of the Occupation, indeed, deserves careful reevaluation from a contemporary perspective. Above all the Occupation accomplished two goals: it restored Japan and ensured extraordinary stability of political rule for three decades. The price paid was in giving up any immediate realization of its democratic goals.

First, the Occupation decision to rule indirectly through the existing bureaucracy, a decision that precluded both any massive purge of civilian officials who had supported or participated in Japan's war effort and direct allied military rule, as in Germany, secured for at least a generation the political influence of Japan's bureaucratic elite. In addition, the Occupation introduced a series of economic controls, many of which were designed as short-term expedients to deal with emergency conditions. These regulatory statutes, along with a variety of long-term regulatory reforms, provided Japan's postwar economic bureaucracies with the most elaborate and extensive governmental controls they had ever possessed. Although they were theoretically subject to a variety of constraints in formal enforcement, the Occupation entrusted to the principal economic ministries a broad range of instruments that could and would be used for indirect, extralegal control.

For Japan's postwar economy, the Foreign Exchange and Foreign Trade Control Law (initially drafted by Jan V. Mladek of the International Monetary Fund at SCAP's invitation) proved to be the most critical of all the Occupation regulatory statutes. It provided the Ministry of Finance and the newly created Ministry of International Trade and Industry (MITI) with control over foreign-exchange allocations and access to foreign markets for imports and exports. For an economy dependent upon imports of raw materials and export markets, and thus on foreign exchange, this single statute and the regulations issued for its enforcement supplied these two ministries with sufficient indirect and extralegal levers to direct the domestic economy for over a decade. No Diet before or since could have legislated so sweeping a set of economic controls.

Initially restrained more by bureaucratic rivalries than by democratic pressures, the economic ministries, some recreated like MITI out of prewar ministries as the Occupation ended, retained the emergency controls that they could effectively use, while endeavoring to dismantle other Occupation reforms that threatened to reduce or restrict their powers. Their influence within Japan's conservative political parties, which they had helped to create, assured them of at least partial success. Once the Occupation ended and Japan regained full sovereignty, various American-inspired independent regulatory agencies, ranging from the Securities and Exchange Commission to the Labor Relations Board, were quickly consolidated within the appropriate ministries and thus made submissive to ministerial command. The few that remained, such as the Fair Trade Commission (FTC), were soon staffed with ex-bureaucrats from approved ministries or affiliated agencies. In rapid succession, Occupation legislation prohibiting the use of zaibatsu names was repealed; the Trade Association Law was substantially revised; and an effort was mounted to amend, if not exorcise completely, the general antitrust statute, as well as the new constitution. Left intact as an instrument for discretionary economic controls, however, were the emergency statutes establishing controls over foreign exchange and foreign trade and investment. Yet, even in the heyday of bureaucratic control, the representative political institutions fostered by SCAP's constitutional and political reforms prevented elimination of all the statutory or institutional restraints on bureaucratic power. Albeit weakened, the FTC, for example, remained, as did the constitution itself.

In the longer run, the institutional reforms represented by the postwar constitution did begin to work. Without the autonomous rule-making power enjoyed under the Meiji constitution, the economic bureaucracies were now dependent on legislative delegations of authority and subject to legislative and, in theory at least, judicial controls over their discretionary powers. Their ability to dominate economic policy thus depended upon either effective influence over the legislative process or resort to extralegal means of control.

Direct bureaucratic influence in the legislature is too often overstated. Except for the election of 1949, in which 37 former government officials, including 25 Yoshida recruits, entered the Diet, and 1952, in which 48 former officials, some depurgees, including Nobusuke Kishi, were elected, ex-bureaucrats did not make any significant gains in the Diet in any postwar election.[33] Rarely has the number of newly elected former bureaucrats exceeded a dozen.[34] In fact, there is no evidence that Japan's bureaucracies have any greater influence over the content of legislation introduced by the cabinet than those in other industrial democracies.[35] The consequence has been a demonstrable need for the bureaucracy generally to work closely with Diet members, often compromising significant policy goals, and increasingly to rely on extralegal, consensual means of governance.

Other SCAP reforms more directly limited the legal powers of the economic bureaucracies. The principal device for formal enforcement of administrative policies—the Administrative Enforcement Law—was repealed and the administrative police were abolished without any thought of providing an alternative means for formally enforcing regulatory statutes. SCAP officials paid little if any heed to the need for legal enforcement powers. They apparently assumed the universality of the American model of judicial enforcement of administrative orders and failed to take into account the fact that judicial enforcement ultimately rests on the contempt power of the courts. Without the coercive sanction of contempt of court, judicial decrees add nothing to administrative orders. Although it could have been argued that contempt is an inherent judicial power that the postwar constitution vested in "whole" in the judiciary, Japanese judges trained in a tradition of European law would have had to be radically reeducated even to consider the availability of so significant an addition to their customary authority. Whatever the cause or possible cure, however, the Occupation reforms in effect left the Japanese government nearly devoid of effective formal means of administrative law enforcement, except through the criminal process, especially ill suited in Japan for prompt enforcement or the prosecution of socially or politically sensitive cases.[36]

Moreover, even at the height of bureaucratic influence, during the period between 1953 and 1958, the elite economic ministries were not in full political control. Bureaucratic rivalries and the increasing influence of business on the conservative parties—merged in 1955 to create the ruling Liberal Democratic Party (LDP)—together with the promotional thrust of Japanese economic policy limited the ability of these ministries to override others in the Japanese establishment.[37]

As many American scholars have recently begun to recognize,[38] both the making and implementing of economic policy in Japan have involved complex interrelationships within each firm and industry, as well as among bureaucrats and politicians at each level of government. Each of these scholars finds a notable lack of power, but not necessarily of authority, in the bureaucracies of the central government. Samuels provides the most insightful observations:

Reciprocal consent is not uniquely Japanese. In Western Europe similar negotiations over the nature and extent of state intervention have resulted in a market presence for the state—often with considerable support from industry and labor. In Japan the state has been diverted away from market competition entirely. What makes Japan different is the routinization of economic policy which the durability of elites and their constituencies makes possible. Japan is not merely a vat of competing interests; neither is Japan a European government in an American business environment. Rather, the institutionalized routine of negotiation, reciprocal consent, is the tie that binds.[39]

During the 1950s, the Japanese economic ministries could perhaps rely upon their authority to allocate capital, foreign exchange, and access to raw materials and foreign markets as inducements to win compliance with informal commands, and thus have a reasonable expectation that informal policy enforcement (administrative guidance) would work. However, as Japan's economy recovered, such bureaucratic leverage diminished; the ostensible success of Japan's economic ministries in rearranging the postwar economy itself eroded bureaucratic power. Economic expansion and the resulting prosperity of industrial enterprises reduced their dependency for capital, for foreign-exchange allocations, or even for export and import licenses. Moreover, the larger the firm, the more difficult it was for government officials credibly to threaten to deny it access to the capital, raw materials, or export markets necessary for its survival. Too many others—employees, suppliers, creditors—would be affected, and it would be unthinkable for government officials to be responsible for any significant injury to these interests. The smaller the firm, the more effectively it could evade legal or extralegal restrictions imposed. So long as the amounts involved were small, foreign exchange, raw materials, and access to foreign markets could often be obtained illegally or indirectly.

Given the fundamental weakness in direct, formal enforcement of economic policies, as well as this diminishing bureaucratic control over resources, rule by consensus became an increasing imperative. It must be stressed that few direct or formal controls are needed when government officials promote rather than regulate, as was the case with Japan's postwar economic policies. In such contexts, cooperation and consultation are intrinsic to the policies being implemented. Although administrative actions adverse to some industries and some firms are inevitable even in these circumstances, such conflicts can be contained by agreement over general ends and means. Nevertheless, the behavior of Japanese firms has evidenced full appreciation of the costs of dependency and benefits of autonomy. As illustrated by Idemitsu and Toyota, Japa-

nese firms place high value on independence and freedom from government or private outside control. Formation of *keiretsu* (corporate groups)
and other examples of dependency relationships among business enterprises can be argued to result from an overriding need for security,
which has often masked the more basic drive for autonomy.[40]

Symptomatic of the Japanese government's reliance on consensual
governance is the role of trade associations and cartels as fora for
negotiating policy and its implementation. The pattern is not a postwar
phenomenon. It began in the 1930s and had become entrenched by the
end of the war. Contrary to conventional wisdom, Japan was not extensively cartelized until the late 1930s. Although the first trade associations
were formed in the 1880s, primarily in the textile industry, and attempts
were made to form voluntary cartels to stabilize prices at various times
between the first Sino-Japanese War (1894–95) and World War I, most
involved small-scale exporters and were short-lived and rarely effective.[41] Even as late as 1935, despite the 1931 Major Industries Control
Law, William Lockwood estimates, there were only 35 compulsory cartels, 4 voluntary cartels, and 80 trade associations, mostly for exporters.[42]
The numbers grew, however, with the imposition of wartime controls.
For both zaibatsu managers and the civil bureaucracies, indirect and
informal controls via collective industry organizations provided mutually
acceptable mechanisms for negotiating wartime allocations of resources
and procurement. Their use permitted a greater degree of autonomy for
both business vis-à-vis the government and the economic bureaucracies
vis-à-vis the military.[43]

It can be argued to the contrary, of course, that trade associations,
cartels, and even compulsory control organizations could have functioned as a less formal conduit for government direction rather than as
an autonomy-preserving alternative to direct regulatory controls. Because formal regulation costs more for all concerned than informal,
cooperative arrangements, the argument runs, it is in the interest of both
sides, regulator and regulated alike, to rely on informal mechanisms for
implementing policy. Consequently, informality is not necessarily equated
with negotiated policymaking or greater autonomy for those subject to
government direction. Japan's wartime experience, however, refutes
such claims. Reliance on indirect, informal controls resulted not in
effective implementation of government policies but rather in a degree
or disorganization and inefficiency that by all accounts caused serious
injury to the war effort. The military's dismay over such failures led
finally to the creation of the Munitions Ministry under the Tojo cabinet
as an attempt to establish a system of more direct control.[44]

Trade associations and cartel arrangements in the postwar period
should, I believe, be similarly explained. Reflecting the limits of legal

ordering by either government regulation or private contract, they have provided a structure within which consensual ordering could take place. As a consequence, Japanese public policy, no less than private contractual arrangements, has tended to reflect a process of continuous adaptation to changing market and other external demands. The informality and flexibility of Japanese governance, like the prevalence of private collusive—or, in less pejorative terms, cooperative—arrangements, are not therefore themselves the product of conscious government choice or planned policy, but are rather "cultural" phenomena produced by historical patterns and institutional arrangements that diminish the coercive powers of the state.

To the extent, then, that negotiated or consensual policymaking and enforcement have prevailed in postwar Japan, our attention should focus on consensus and consensus-inducing factors rather than the formal elements of the policymaking process. However, as Chalmers Johnson again reminds us, in Japan, consensus is "a process that changes its meaning, content and typical procedures over time. Indeed there is often little difference between the means used to achieve consensus in Japan and jawboning, lobbying, pork barreling, influence peddling, and other ordinary, dubious, or corrupt practices used in Western governments and legislatures for producing agreement without confrontation."[45] There is a difference, but the contrast lies in its use by the bureaucracy in Japan, not just in the process of forming policy but also in the process of implementing policy.

More to the point, reliance on consensus and informal means of enforcing economic policy did not contract as national consensus on economic growth, as well as effective extralegal means of inducement and coercion, diminished. Instead, the economic ministries began to rely even more on informal enforcement as the costs of economic success to both consumers and the environment became increasingly apparent and bureaucratic control of resources eroded in the 1960s and 1970s.[46] They had no alternative. They were forced to involve affected parties increasingly in both forming and implementing policy. Government officials thus were rarely policymakers, at least in the sense in which that term is used in the West. Rather, they functioned at times as policy initiators, but most often as policy coordinators or mediators. Nearly always they had to persuade rather than command.

The task of the economic bureaucracies in this context became increasingly difficult. The greater the number of participants in the process of building consensus, the more difficult the burden of persuasion. Increasingly, government officials had to provide benefits, to grant exceptions, to compromise policies, to become mediators rather than managers. And the number of participants grew.

Effective protectionist legal barriers prevented foreign competition, and the expansion of the Japanese economy and the domestic market thus invited new domestic entrants. Except for banking and other financial services, which were regulated under prewar statutes that effectively precluded entry unless expressly permitted by the Ministry of Finance, the economic ministries were unable, despite considerable efforts, to prevent new domestic firms from entering the market in almost every major industry: integrated steel, automobiles, electronics, pharmaceuticals, even retailing. In addition, as political and legal challenges to economic policies by local authorities and citizens' consumer and environmental groups increased, the economic ministries were forced to accommodate a very different assortment of players. They could cope only by radical shifts in policy and approaches.[47]

The political arrangements of the immediate postwar period were also subject to gradual, but steady, change. The constitutional and electoral reforms created a structure in which a politician with strong local support could withstand pressure to acquiesce to bureaucratic initiatives and an exceptionally astute politician would inevitably grasp that ostensible deference to bureaucratic wishes might fetch a price measured by access to the inner circles of power. Once admitted, however, the tables could easily turn, for power within, such as control over a major economic ministry, could be used to strengthen a local political base even further, thereby gaining even greater autonomy from bureaucratic control. Inevitably, therefore, the Japanese postwar political system had to produce a Kakuei Tanaka, who successfully challenged bureaucratic domination of the political process. Tanaka's rise to power as a politician manipulating the bureaucratic process, instead of being manipulated by it, thus ended an era in Japan's postwar political economy—political stability by means of bureaucratic influence—and ushered in at least a transitional period, out of which some new form of stable, predictable rule has yet to emerge.

In summary, all observers of postwar Japan have been struck by the pervasive strength of extralegal forms of social and market control. From administrative guidance to trade association cartels, informal, consensual methods of regulation and coercion have seemed to constitute the predominant mechanism of social and economic ordering. Japanese society is thus popularly characterized by Japanese and non-Japanese alike as remarkably free from effective legal regulation, whether in the form of constitutional or statutory constraints on bureaucratic action or of civil code rules for private behavior. Law and lawyers have played a minor part in the postwar political economy.

For some, the lack of legal controls is considered to be a reflection of either traditional attitudes or "deep culture." [48] Others have recently begun to develop more sophisticated explanations in terms of bureaucratic power. Frank Upham, for example, argues that the bureaucracy, aided by the other two elements of the conventional triumvirate, conservative LDP and business leaders, has been able to prevent litigation and "the threat that it poses to the pervasive informality on which the government relies in setting and implementing its own policies."[49] Michael Young similarly suggests that those who govern Japan purposefully created a third pattern of government intervention in the economy, one that falls between direction and control of the economy and total nonintervention.[50] Neither, however, is willing to credit the bureaucracy's lack of effective legal controls, and the resulting strength of extralegal forms of social and economic ordering, to either Japan's peculiar historical experience or the impact of Occupation reforms. Nevertheless, unless one is willing to accept the proposition that the Japanese bureaucracy in the postwar period was powerful enough to get what it wanted, yet deliberately refrained from exerting its full influence, such alternative explanations are persuasive.

Consensus, Culture, and the Role of Law in Postwar Japan

Few could accurately have predicted the significance of the Occupation legal reforms. Instead of producing a new legitimacy for majoritarian, representative government or a more democratized New Deal version of the administrative state—in either case with the authority coupled with power to shape Japan's postwar social and economic order through law—the Occupation reforms resulted in a regime chronically dependent upon consensus for effective governance. Unable to manipulate the legislative process, Japanese bureaucracies resorted to cooperative policymaking and administrative guidance, thereby strengthening preexisting patterns of consensual governance. In turn their dependency on consent necessitated an extraordinary need to nurture mechanisms for building consensus and, in effect, redefined who governed in terms of those whose assent was necessary for the effective implementation of policy.

This redefinition has permitted most Japanese a remarkable degree of autonomy from governmental control. In many instances, the government has simply been unable to act. In others, action has required painstaking efforts to achieve a consensus of at least those whose cooperation has been necessary. For Japan's bureaucracy, the consequence has been to assure the effectiveness of otherwise competitive markets, despite interfirm cooperation and ostensible government intrusion. Political and legal restraints have prevented the translation of bureaucratic authority into effective power and thus ensured that market forces would be more determinative in shaping or directing government policy than government policy in regulating or controlling market forces.

What is unusual about Japan's postwar governance, however, is less dependency on consensus itself than the extent of that dependency and its legitimacy. Some level of societal consensus as to the legitimacy of the norms that legal rules reflect, as well as the institutional processes for making and enforcing them, is necessary in all legal orders, even the most repressive. Moreover, even regimes born of terror or fear may ultimately acquire legitimacy from habit and custom. In this sense, institutional or structural patterns become cultural phenomena by definition. Thus Japan's dependency on consensus can be argued to have acquired from habit and expectation a particular and self-reinforcing legitimacy. In this context, formal law-making and law-enforcing processes, whether legislative, bureaucratic, or judicial, function primarily as consensus-building processes.

In Japan, the legitimacy of governance by consensus allows—perhaps even requires—focus on the adequacy of processes for creating consensus. For example, a bill passed by a bare majority in either a European parliament or the Japanese Diet becomes law, but because that law can be more effectively implemented without consensus in a European state than in Japan, majoritarian rule is more apt to be considered legitimate there than in Japan. By the same token, less attention need be paid in a European state than in Japan to the role of legislative deliberations about the means of developing public consent to legislation. In Japan a government must focus on the efficacy of the process of establishing consent. Denial of support by opposition parties is thus more effective politically in Japan than in Europe as an expression of refusal of consensus to a particular legislative action and the failure of the party in power to achieve the requisite assent.

As a consequence, the equation of participation in legislative, party, or ministerial councils with political power in Japan is as misleading as the appearance of bureaucratic control. Access to the media and the courts has also assured influence over consensus and thus effective political participation. Postwar economic policies designed to limit new entry, promote concentration, or otherwise foster economies of scale also had political justification in making consensus-building more manageable. In the end, however, because the efficacy of legal rules has depended upon the assent of those they are designed to regulate, political power has been increasingly diffused. The particular configuration of the postwar legal order in Japan has also in effect preserved a remarkable degree of autonomy for the lesser communities or modern "villages" of Japanese society, especially the firm. As governmental controls have not fully penetrated into Japanese economic, political, and social life, overt deference to state officials has masked the reality of nonconformity. Consequently, societal order has been maintained in Japan more by a complex network of interpersonal and informal obligations and sanctions than by those imposed by law. As a result, the predominant controlling norms of Japanese society have depended directly upon consensus and the structure of authority within particular groups as well as upon the raw exercise of power—both physical and economic.

In this context, Japan has enjoyed a special type of pluralism, difficult perhaps to discern by those who define pluralism in terms of ethnic, religious, and ideological diversity, or of individual rather than group autonomy. Japanese pluralism is less a product of self-selection into voluntary associations than a consequence of cohesion born out of need for security and order. Cohesion has meant that the values and norms shared within the firm, an industry, and other constituent communities of Japan carry more force and impact in determining the conduct of their members. Similarly, however, social recognition that legal rules do reflect consensus gives them a special impact and influence. As in the past, however, law continues to possess considerable legitimacy and didactic influence.

That the recognition of certain norms as legal rules, particularly in the context of constitutional adjudication, has had direct bearing on political consensus is illustrated by the seemingly endless series of lawsuits brought throughout the postwar period challenging the validity of Japan's Self-Defense Forces under Article 9 of the postwar constitution. In the 1982 Nagamura case, for example, as expected, the Supreme Court denied the justiciability of the issue.[51] This was surely anticipated by the plaintiffs in their refusal to consent to a special appeal to the court, which would have bypassed a time-consuming appeal to the high court. The legal outcome being relatively certain, these suits cannot be understood in terms of the plaintiffs' expectations of a favorable judgment. Rather, they reflect an appreciation of the courts' political role in affecting public attitudes toward the legitimacy of the Self-Defense Forces. By continuing to challenge the Self-Defense Forces' constitutionality under Article 9, opponents are at least able to retard public opinion from crystallizing in accepting their legitimacy.

Similarly, the highly publicized pollution cases in the 1970s helped create the political consensus necessary to achieve enactment of stringent pollution controls and victim-compensation schemes.[52] What mattered most was the protracted process of litigation, not the eventual judgments, as the media-dramatized trials assured national and international exposure of disfigured children and fearfully labeled diseases caused by mercury and cadmium poisoning.

The political responses to the recent malapportionment decisions, in which the Supreme Court reiterated its prior judgment that the House of Representatives was unconstitutionally constituted as a result of imbalanced electoral representation, also amply demonstrate the powerlessness of the courts to effect change directly through their judgments, but also their indirect impact on the political process.[53]

Law in postwar Japan thus presents a paradox. It serves as a means for legitimating norms while it remains relatively ineffective as an instrument of coercive control. Substantive legal norms thus operate as principles—*tatemae*—that both shape and reflect consensus. Without effective formal enforcement, they can only partially bind or command. They do not fully control or determine conduct, but they do influence and restrain. Law as *tatemae* also promotes autonomy as outward compliance and the effectiveness of social controls lessen the need to develop stronger means of coercive law enforcement.

On the one hand, in a society in which consensus within both society at large and its constituent communities is critical to preserving order, formal legal rules have special significance in their capacity to establish basic standards of conduct. As *tatemae*, legal norms may not command obedience, but they do demand respect and induce some level of outward conformity. As reflections of consensus, they establish parameters of acceptable, legitimate behavior that subject those who violate them to the risk of the penalty of social condemnation. On the other hand, their weakness as an instrument of control also promotes the development of cohesive constituent communities within society by reinforcing the need for attendant social controls to provide security and preserve social order.

The imposition of American-style legal institutions in postwar Japan also had a profound influence on the perceptions of the Japanese of their own legal tradition and on their attitudes toward law and governance. As Japanese and Americans became increasingly aware of differences in the premises underlying the role of law and the legal process, both sides began to write about differences in "rights consciousness," litigiousness, and dispute resolution.[54] Although comparison with the United States is rarely explicit, the Japanese legal tradition has generally been defined almost exclusively in terms of perceived contrasts with the United States, which has tended to be viewed as representative of all "Western" legal cultures. Ignored are not only salient differences between Japan and other countries in East Asia but also the complexity of Japan's actual historical experience.[55] The claim to "tradition" is less important for its accuracy, however, than for its use and effect. The Japanese legal tradition as redefined has legitimated a new—but not novel—set of values and expectations. Whereas in the 1920s and 1930s, substitutes for private lawsuits were considered by Japan's elite as a means of preserving traditional Japanese values,[56] in the postwar period, a dearth of litigation was viewed as a reflection of traditional values that were subject to change as Japan "progressed" toward modernity. Thus, as in the legitimization of consensus by habit, the redefinition of tradition to explain postwar reality contributed to a subtle change in Japanese culture and again to the legitimization of existing institutional arrangements, in which law and formal law enforcement serve to reinforce consensual patterns of governance.

Finally, and perhaps most important, the paradox of law in Japan helps to explain the ultimate paradox of modern Japan as a society of both continuity and change and its solution to the challenge to the liberal state of preserving an ordered, but free, society.

Yasusuke Murakami and Thomas P. Rohlen

Social-Exchange Aspects of the Japanese Political Economy: Culture, Efficiency, and Change

The character of the postwar Japanese political economy remains an enigma to many. The persistent key question is: "How different is Japan?" Experts seeking to model the Japanese political economy for comparative purposes rarely arrive at the same conclusions. While much of the debate centers around the pivotal question of the government's role in fostering growth, managing change, and coping with external economic forces, a series of fundamental theoretical issues are also involved. Is Japan's political economy essentially a system determined by market forces, as most economists would argue? Or do other, "nonmarket," forces (organizational strengths, industrial policies, and culture being three common themes) significantly determine outcomes? If nonmarket factors are central, should Japan be regarded as a special case? A special case of what? Even those who assert that the economists' focus on efficient markets is too simplistic disagree on where the emphasis belongs. Is the most pertinent nonmarket factor industrial policy, or bureaucratic power, or interlocking corporate groups, or union-management alliances, or business-government networks, or historical insularity or a communal ethic or some combination?

Indeed, one might wonder what is new here, since questions of market-system purity animate theoretical discussions about every capitalist political economy. Or, to put it differently, the neoclassical economic paradigm has its friends and enemies everywhere. Even the various disciplinary predispositions within social science in favor of one or another interpretation of Japan's distinctive qualities seem largely predictable (e.g., political scientists emphasizing the government, or anthropologists dwelling on culture). One wonders at times whether the "enigma" is largely the result of academic prejudices and blinders.

Nevertheless, with a shift in focus away from the far easier comparisons between capitalist and socialist economies, the case of Japan stands

out as especially important. It cannot be denied that culturally, historically, and institutionally, Japan is notably different from the West. But
these differences are neither as systematic nor as explicit as contrasts
between capitalism and socialism. Nor are they concentrated in public
institutions alone. To compare Japan with Western capitalist systems is
to focus on more than ideology, planning, and command structures. It
requires an understanding of the basic transactional patterns fundamental to the whole. Building an appropriate model of the Japanese political
economy is thus a formidable interdisciplinary task.

In this essay we analyze certain problematic elements of the overall
political economy using the perspective of exchange theory, an approach
that we find especially suitable to the task of integrating market and
institutional factors at an intermediate level where major players interface with one another. The elements we consider are relationships
between (1) government and industry, (2) companies and unions, and
(3) firms and their subcontractors. We are interested in the common
underlying patterns characteristic of all three, since we view such com-
monalities (or isomorphisms) as illustrative of Japan's distinctiveness.

We begin by noting that theories of political economy have long
contrasted organizational and market features as if only these two options existed.[1] If neoclassical economic theory virtually ignores all but
market mechanisms, the approach popularly labeled "Japan, Inc." con-
ceives of Japan as closely knit and hierarchically ordered, with the
government controlling the economy in a top-down fashion through
regulation and other mechanisms.[2] Certainly both perspectives have a
relevance to elements of the overall political economy, especially if we
acknowledge that their relative weight has been changing throughout
the postwar period. But neither alone provides an adequate picture. Nor
does a combination of market and organizational considerations adequately account for many central phenomena.

A closer examination of politico-economic phenomena in postwar
Japan reveals certain paradoxes that defy theories that dwell exclusively
on markets or hierarchical organizations. Despite the absence, inactivity,
or weakness of formal hierarchical authority, for example, distinctive
levels of coordination are achieved in many industries and between
unions and management. Furthermore, there are many cases in which
simple market rationality cannot explain voluntary actions on the part
of companies and unions. Not only must regulative and competitive
phenomena be seen as intermingled to achieve a more satisfactory level
of analysis, but the recognition of a third category of social activity,
located between the conventional dualistic notions of competition and
regulation, appears necessary if a range of such paradoxes is to be
explained.

Our model accepts the argument that the formal institutional structure of the postwar Japanese political economy is as pluralistic and competitive as those in other advanced industrial countries, but, at the same time, it stresses the importance of inclusive, informal networks as a considerable source of coordination, information flow, and patterned choices that interact with market mechanisms and lend power to regulative efforts. The underlying, typical character of certain types of networks is what we propose to explain using an exchange-theory framework.

It appears that the informal structure of transactions in Japan is receiving greater attention as scholars seek to approximate empirical reality more closely.[3] Other chapters in this volume on networks and cooperative bargaining illustrate this tendency. While there is much variation of interpretation, a common thread running through this recent research is the importance of embedded relationships to such things as decision making, business alliances, and processes of economic adjustment.

To define the relational foundation of economic "networks" more rigorously takes us into the realm of basic cultural and social patterns. This in turn highlights the contrasts between economic theorizing and the assumptions of other social sciences. Throughout this analysis, we walk a tightrope of sorts by contending that the patterns of relationship we describe are products of *both* existing cultural patterns and fortuitous postwar economic circumstances. We do not believe in cultural or economic determinism. But we do see each era of political economic development as the result of a confluence of continuous and discontinuous qualities. Many arguments about national character (*nihonjinron*) tend to paint Japanese society with a single sweeping brush, and thus exaggerate both its homogeneity and its historical stability, but we find that many of the often-cited "cultural" characteristics have actually come into prominence in the sphere of economic activity only in the postwar period and, moreover, can be shown to be partially contingent on certain conditions specific to that era. Furthermore, these conditions appear to be changing. In other words, we see the underlying relational character of the political economy as contingent on both cultural models and political economic conditions.

Paradoxical Characteristics

Let us look more closely at the examples we have chosen to analyze: government-business, management-union, and subcontracting relationships. Each has been treated as distinctively Japanese, and each appears problematic, given Western practice and theoretical expectations. First, the labor-management relationship in large firms involves much more than is stipulated in the legal employment contract, which in Japan is typically a very simple document implying a permanent relationship in which disagreements will be worked out amicably. It thus covers a long period (so-called "lifetime" employment), and, because it states the formation of a general relationship, the contract leaves open all other issues. For example, there are unstated expectations that wage increases and promotions will be largely seniority-based and that consultations on working conditions will be frequent. Thus, what is implicit and customary includes the recognition and acceptance of consultative patterns of authority and compliance, joint commitments to certain common interests, and other matters as they arise. The relationship is thus broadly and richly conceived, if not explicitly detailed. Much is left to "mutual consultation." Compared to Western labor contracts that rest on efforts to specify all details exhaustively, and thus provide prior solutions to as many problems as possible, the Japanese example is more diffuse. Rather than frequently working out new contracts or renewals, the Japanese approach hinges on the interactive working out of problems within the framework of a permanent relationship. The question is, how does the Japanese approach avoid being misused? Labor is not protected from exploitation, and management is not provided with the option of terminating employees as a form of discipline. Put differently, what keeps the ideal of a mutuality of interests alive and prevents free riding? How is effective cooperation preserved?

In the case of industrial policy, the legal foundation for Japanese government action is not well developed, and actual efforts at control are necessarily largely informal and rich in maneuver, give-and-take, and negotiation. No regulatory statute, for example, gives the government the power to force its intentions on private firms. Thus, even when some Japanese firms (e.g., Sumitomo Metals or Honda) have disregarded directives from the Ministry of International Trade and Industry (MITI), they could not be subjected to legal sanctions. The question then becomes one of discovering the mechanisms of enforcement or the reasons for compliance involved. There is no question that business has followed industrial policy initiatives, but what has made this so effective?

Turning to small-scale subcontractors, we find that their relations with their "parent" firms have been far more stable over time and far more closely cooperative than ordinary firm-to-firm relations in the West. A parent firm's linkage with its subcontractors includes not only the purchase of parts and services but also unwritten commitments to financial intermediation, as well as mutual technological consultation, joint planning, and even personnel exchange. This extensive involvement has not meant, however, that subcontractors are "vertically integrated" into their parent firms. The much larger customer has relatively more power, to be sure, but it, too, is heavily dependent on its stable of allied subcontractors. The overlap of interests is potentially very large because of the inclination to extensive integration of activities like joint development and investment. The relation is more a long-term hierarchically ordered association, then, based again largely on implicit understandings, involving diverse kinds of transactions other than simple buying and selling of products. How competitive and cooperative aspects of these relationships are ordered and developed over time presents a serious dilemma to our conventional modes of analysis, because subcontracting evidences both market and organizational qualities. We think explaining the mix of cooperation and autonomy involved requires a different approach, one based on exchange theory.

The postwar political economy is rich in similar examples of extensive relational development among quasi-independent economic actors. To summarize briefly, all three examples just cited illustrate a particular type of transaction, one occurring in a framework that is (1) long-term, (2) largely informal, (3) multifaceted, (4) based on mutual interests that are general and negotiable, (5) somewhat hierarchical and semi-autonomous, and (6) self-defining by nature. Within this kind of framework, many important forms of economic settlement occur in Japan. Litigation or other external sources of forceful settlement are rare.

Crucial to our approach is the fact that even when no contract exists or the contract is very vague, settlements are accomplished if the relationship is part of a framework of implicit common understanding. There are, of course, numerous examples of such exchanges in the zone between the economic and noneconomic spheres of every society. Matters involving services, information, honor, status, power, and emotion, for example, are typically adjusted on the basis of informal settlement. If we then contrast these to a "simple, purely economic" contract that is (1) formal, (2) single-faceted, and (3) short-term in orientation, we are in a position to examine the "geographical" distribution of each type in any particular society. Along with most others, we assume that it is the tendency in modern, industrial societies for the application of "simple, pure economic contracts" to expand into economic spaces where before more personalized, long-term dealings had dominated. Personalized relationships, we assume, give way to impersonal ones in the history of modern industrial development.[4]

The reasons for this have to do with mobility, complexity, and information in modern societies. The longer the duration of a contract, for example, the more likely are unpredictable disturbances that alter the costs and benefits expected. In a modern social environment, where we cannot know very much about most of the people we are dealing with, preference grows for shorter timespans and explicit agreements that are narrow in focus. The less information is available about the other party, in other words, the more limited is the element of trust. It is almost axiomatic that modern societies involve increasingly larger proportions of transactions involving very little information about the other party. Thus formal contracts help reduce the number of surprises. For reasons like these, the growth of "spot-market" and "arm's-length" activities in every economy is undeniable. But some key relationships do not necessarily fit these conditions very well. If they are recurrent, long-term, and amenable to cooperative solutions that are not zero-sum in nature, it may prove useful to organize them on different principles. The documentation of a contract implies that all issues can be specified in legal terms as a single package, and in cases where this is unlikely, an explicit, formal approach can mean inflexibility and conflict. We are referring to a kind of gray area within any modern society where precisely how transactions are settled is open to considerable variation. As a rule, this gray area is the hardest to analyze theoretically, and it is often relegated to a peripheral place in the thinking of economists or mistakenly reduced to either a market or an organizational set of assumptions.

That this gray area is large in Japan is now increasingly being recognized. The importance of institutionalized relationships based on longer-term, multifaceted informal settlements in Japan has not escaped notice, yet so far their overall conceptual analysis remains primarily descriptive. A theoretical analysis that strengthens the foundation of comparative work is needed.

Exchange Theory

The notion of exchange is fundamental to nearly all social science, but the variety of forms of exchange is still open to considerable theoretical debate. For our purposes, the distinctions we have been making between "simple, purely economic" transactions and the qualities we have listed as characteristic of the relationships occupying gray areas in the Japanese political economy are of central importance. For comparative purposes, can we understand the conditions that enhance the efficiency of relational transacting? Can we specify the prior cultural assumptions upon which efficient relational transactions are developed? The theory of social exchange has been developed by many well-known scholars, including Marcel Mauss, Georg Simmel, George Homans, Peter Blau, and Claude Lévi-Strauss. "Social exchange . . . refers to voluntary actions of individuals that are motivated by the returns they are expected to bring and typically do in fact bring from others," Blau writes.[5] But he also observes:

Social exchange differs in many important ways from strictly economic exchange. The basic and most crucial distinction is that social exchange entails *unspecified* obligations. The prototype of an economic transaction rests on a formal contract that stipulates the exact quantities to be exchanged. . . . Social exchange, in contrast, involves the principle that one person does another a favor, and while there is a general expectation of some future return, its exact nature is definitely *not* stipulated in advance.[6]

Evidently, what Blau here calls "social exchange" is exchange in its widest sense, yet not all possible types of human interaction fall under Blau's definition. For example, any action forced by physical violence cannot constitute an exchange, since it is not voluntary. Similarly, actions arising from internalized belief (religion, philosophy, value judgment, or whatever) or devotion to a charismatic leader cannot be an exchange, because no return is expected. Furthermore, an action mainly oriented toward nature cannot be an exchange, since it is not a human interaction.

More crucial is Blau's distinction between *social exchange*—exchange with unspecified obligations, and *economic exchange*—exchange with specified obligations. Still, some ambiguity remains, because the meaning of *specified* and *unspecified* is not sufficiently clear. To gain greater clarity, let us note that Blau points out the evident fact that exchange generally serves two kinds of goals. The first is the material benefit or utility gained from the objects exchanged. Blau labels this *extrinsic utility*. The second goal is the value or gratification one feels in the act of exchange itself— that is, a beneficial or desired effect arising from the mutual association and trust engendered or assured through the process of exchange. Blau calls this *intrinsic utility*. Most acts of exchange serve both goals albeit in differing proportions, so we must be cautious here. Commonsense usage would have us conclude that in general the term *economic exchange* would denote those exchanges that aim mainly at "extrinsic" utilities, whereas *social exchange* would denote those mainly concerned with "intrinsic" benefits. For most acts of exchange, social or economic, to be possible, however, the participants must share a considerable amount of agreement about both the environment they share and the relationship they have jointly built. Although the two parties' cognitive maps are certainly not identical, the actions each takes must make sense to the other and carry roughly the same order of value. Of course, simply not bumping into one another on the sidewalk can be said to be an exchange of civility and therefore a successful kind of social exchange, but in this essay we are focusing on much more complex forms of involvement and much more complex shared understandings regarding material objects, means to multifaceted goals, institutional participants, uncertain time horizons, and the like. As a useful rule of thumb, it is helpful to acknowledge that economic exchanges centering exclusively on material goods (like money and commodities) may rest on relatively simple systems of cognitive agreement. Currency traders, for example, need speak only a few words of a common language and have access to a common data pool and communications equipment in order to do business. By contrast, social exchanges (involving many kinds of nonmaterial values) are much more complex phenomena.

We, of course, take this kind of complexity for granted in everyday relations—that is, until we encounter other social circumstances where our understandings fail to work. The "culture shock" experienced by outsiders to a particular framework of social exchange (e.g., Japanese gift giving or the rules and manners of the Mafia) serves to highlight the rich fabric of unconscious assumptions upon which social exchanges typically depend.[7] Meaning and value, in other words, are fundamental to social exchange. Furthermore, what confirms and maintains this set of common understandings is successful social exchange itself. Embedded in what might be called the "living social world" context is a system of meaning and value that cannot readily be simplified or abstracted without destroying its character. In other words, what makes sense in a specific social context does not easily survive reduction to universal constructions of rationality.

We know people often prefer to interact with specific other parties, even if the material rewards are less than maximal. Family, friends, classmates, and neighbors all represent intrinsic worth to specific "others." Similarly, people prefer to feel trust, friendship, and affection toward others they deal with. The circle of such others is necessarily limited, because it takes time to generate and maintain these feelings. We also give priority to intrinsic value when we prefer a particular style of conducting relationships. Candor, warmth, politeness, sensitivity, indirection, patience, and other qualities are also elements of mutual understanding shaping social exchange. Because all such systems of preferences rest on humanly generated systems of shared meanings (i.e., they are cultural in nature), they are never universal or absolutely fixed in time or space.

Economists tend to define the concept of utility only at the level of objects, taking as given the meaning or value of the objects exchanged. The value of the relationship itself is typically ignored and the impersonality of the transaction is assumed. As is well known, the economist's convention is that the value of objects (i.e., extrinsic utility) can be separated from other matters having to do with nonmaterial goals and preferences. That is, ignoring the complexity of underlying relationships greatly facilitates many kinds of theorizing. Perfect markets are, by definition, depersonalized. Trust, friendship, courtesy, memory, and the like are of no account. Under actual circumstances (putting aside the economist's convention), of course, preferences for objects are intermingled with preferences for persons and relationships.

Lest we forget just what a leap of faith the economist's convention really is, recall the fact that the very acceptance and credibility of money rests on a shared *a priori* system of evaluation particular to each society. Even money cannot be explained simply in terms of extrinsic utility. The point is that even narrow economic exchanges, in Blau's terminology, rest on a degree of cooperative maintenance of shared assumptions. What Blau calls social exchange, by comparison, involves much more developed levels of mutual understanding and cooperation. On this basis, trust and other values are generated. It helps, at this point, to assume a spectrum of possibilities that runs between the polar ideals of pure "economic" and pure "social" exchange. Moving from the former to the latter involves an increase in the social component of the relationship, meaning that the various qualities we have defined as characterizing social exchange increase. The fact that the social aspects of exchange are cultivated and can be increased fits the view that we are in the final analysis dealing with matters of degree. Nevertheless, contrasting the two types of exchange highlights the pertinent differences involved.

Underlying exchange relationships are each participant's attachments to the interaction itself and to the people involved in it. These attachments constitute both a source of values and (because they can be increased) a goal of the relationship. Trust is not absolute, for example; it is developed, and each successful interaction leads to a deepening of this quality. Thus each participant can contribute to the realization of what we might call a common image, just as in families a common image of "our" family develops. In the typical relationship, of course, *conscious* give-and-take centers on physical objects (money, goods, the purchase of time, etc.), yet *taken for granted* is a world of shared assumptions (part of the image) that are also relevant and susceptible to change.

This point is crucial to our concern with the greater complexity of social exchanges, especially as they are generated and maintained in longer time frames. Some general observations are in order:

1. Exchange relationships that last typically develop more and more complexity on the intrinsic level. They assume a style; things like trust increase; and the parties find increased intrinsic value. Parties become more attached to a relationship over time if it works to satisfy nonmaterial as well as material needs.

2. As a relationship develops in its capacity to satisfy such intrinsic needs, it can survive the transformation of many material details. If two parties trust each other and like working together, for example, they are likely to do so even if the prices or goods involved change. Trust and liking make for greater mutual flexibility.

3. The more developed the relationship in terms of trust, liking, and so forth, the less the regular need for detailed specification of extrinsic

details. In simple terms, vagueness is more acceptable when people trust one another. Friends have less need for lawyers is another way of putting it.

4. The greater the intrinsic value developed, the greater the tolerance for long-term agreements. Proven capacities for cooperation, for example, make for longer time horizons because there is a higher sense of security and a higher value placed on the relationship itself.

While these propositions are commonsensical enough when we get past the abstract terminology and consider concrete examples, their implications for our study of the Japanese political economy are still far from clear.

Economic Exchange

In modern society, the conventional understanding that underlies "economic" exchange is that the *only* variables are the values of objects. The dominant form of economic exchange is, of course, monetary. Yet even money itself is not an exchangeable object in the original sense. Obviously, money is but a symbol representing a predetermined institution that consists of (1) the identification and quantification of an arbitrary commodity, (2) its authorization by some political power, and (3) the regularization of the bidding process to ensure a steady price for the commodity.

Even economic exchange needs a minimal level of mutual trust to support it. Barter, for example, carries the possibility of fraud, which can be obviated only by some means of establishing mutual reliability. In monetary exchanges, the minimal degree of mutual trust required is embodied in a predetermined institutional framework, which we generalize as the "market"—that is, a system of laws and customs (such as a commercial code, the authorization of money, the official identification and measures of commodities, means of documentation, and other commercial practices). Such trust-generating institutions are typically the historical outcome of accumulated experience from previous less-evolved forms of exchange. In this sense, any market implicitly retains the basic fabric of past experiences throughout an evolutionary process. However seemingly impersonal, that is to say, all conventional market transactions are embedded in considerable intrinsic value of an institutional kind, which is only apparent in cases of their breach (as, for example, in the case of hyperinflation, when trust in money breaks down). All in all, however, while individual acts of economic exchange presuppose institutionalized reliability (and confirm it to a degree), they are not expected to enlarge it. In other words, economic exchange is a system that neutralizes or depersonalizes transactions. This is because the common values and understandings among participants become fixed and mechanical. There is no expectation that transactions will lead eventually to a deepening of the social aspects of the relationships.

Social Exchange

Social exchange, on the other hand, gives primacy to specifications made primarily in terms of the participants. We are especially inclined to base our evaluations more on people (e.g., on their reliability and capacity) than on strictly material considerations when it comes to matters marked by ambiguities and uncertainties. When markets are not precise, or our information about them is sketchy, we prefer to rely on our judgments of the people we are dealing with. Take, for instance, relations of the so-called "principal-agent" type (e.g., doctor-patient, lawyer-client, teacher-student, etc.), in which our judgments of the person providing the service typically determine choice. Why? Because we cannot measure the service precisely enough to treat it like a commodity and because quality varies greatly according to the person providing the service. Ambiguities also arise when we are unable to anticipate and specify exactly all aspects of a transaction (say in the case of choosing a contractor to remodel one's house), and in such cases of uncertainty, we typically rely on our judgment of people. We emphasize the intrinsic aspects of the relationship, in other words, hoping that our preference will provide cooperative solutions to unforeseen problems.

As social exchange pivots around persons, one of its aims is to strengthen human ties via the process of exchange itself. Gift giving, for example, typically carries this meaning. It is not primarily the goods given and received that are important, but the symbolization of goodwill that is central. The essential point is that because social exchange can deepen in character, it is something to cultivate and develop. Doing so generates value. It creates opportunities.

Among neighbors, friends, and family, social exchange operates as a kind of insurance policy, providing a reservoir of goodwill (future assistance), even if this is not a primary goal. In general, cultivating social-exchange relationships provides networks of such goodwill on a reciprocal basis and thus works to reduce risk, as well as to increase unspecified opportunities.

Social exchange, on the face of it, however, appears to be casual and even inappropriate to the rationalized world outside the intimate realms of family, friends, and neighborhood. As already noted, it is not anchored in formal, explicit agreements, and this seeming lack of specificity (diffuseness) makes it appear casual, less calculated, and less straightforward. Because, by definition, social exchange is focused on both objects and relationships, it is inherently complex in terms of the mix of values and goals involved. Since it deals with a social milieu that is impossible to reduce to an explicit exchange of objects, the language of social exchange typically relies on the specification of general under-standings (e.g., "We are allies" or "We can work out the details as we go along") that join together many issues in a manner that preserves flexibility. All this depends, obviously, on the degree of trust involved. The greater the trust, presumably the greater the role for those qualities of exchange we have defined as "social."

It is helpful to note that building trust takes time; that a "track record" is one usual measure of trust; that trust is enhanced by actions that occur over and above the strict observance of rules and contracts; and that building trust implies an investment in the time dimension of relation-ships. Trust implies relative permanence, certainly by comparison to "economic" types of exchange. This extended time dimension, in turn, creates a more complex field for settlements, in which there is greater tolerance of temporary imbalances and fuzzier equivalences. The trust-ing assumption is that "in time" such imbalances will be redressed.[8] Trust is rarely perfectly confirmed in practice, and for this reason, social-exchange relations, especially in the political economy, where competi-tion and suspicion are inherent, require very high maintenance. Parties to social exchanges continue to discuss and clarify and adjust the rela-tionship throughout its existence. It is defined and redefined by the process itself. Of necessity, the right to renegotiation is assumed.

We might also observe that social-exchange relationships come in many structural forms. Patron-client relations, friendships, marriage, and so forth all fall into this category and together illustrate that there is no inherent requirement that social exchange follow a particular hierar-chical, egalitarian, or complementary mode. This is noteworthy, because it illustrates the possibility that within any particular example of social exchange, variability and transformation in this regard are possible. Neither a hierarchical nor a symmetrical form is necessitated.

Although Blau does not mention it, another crucial aspect of social exchange is that the parties to it are both specified and limited in number. Personalized transactions inherently imply the importance of precisely who the "other" is. A preference system, then, is almost by definition an inherent attribute of social exchange. Equally logical is the fact that the nature of social-exchange relationships implies a limitation on the numbers of participants. If there were no limits on the number of specified participants, there would be no focus on quality and no capacity to cultivate specific ties. Just as one can have only so many "good" friends, and a club can only have a limited number of members if it seeks to establish meaningful standards or relationships, so social ex-change implies exclusiveness of one form or another. The fewer the "others," the greater the guarantees of "quality" in terms of the measures we have been discussing (e.g., trustworthiness and common values). Similarly, the fewer the numbers, the better the communication and coordination, the greater the stability over time, and the more focused the resources for maintenance.[9] Virtually by definition, social exchange means limiting the numbers of participants.

In the political economy at large, this characteristic often proves to be unattractive to modern sensibilities based on impersonal ideals of justice. Similarly, the long-term and "fuzzy" commitments involved in social exchange appear to carry great potential for inefficiencies that derive from "entrenched interests." Typically, in the American political economy the labels for dealings of the social exchange type are pejorative: "special favor," "privileged access," "log rolling," "pork-barreling," "patronage," "cliques," the "spoils system," "insider deals," "collusion," and a host of similar terms illustrate the degree of disapproval of social-exchange relationships in the public and semi-public domains of contemporary society. They also illustrate, incidentally, just how widespread and inherent social exchange is in these domains. All pejorative judgments depend on a contrast with some ideal. In this instance, the contrast, of course, is with a set of ideals that distinguish economic exchange—namely, impersonal and rational means of contracting, "arm's-length" dealing, full public disclosure of information, short time horizons, and "equal" access for all potential participants. Yet despite its lack of fit with the reigning public ideology, social exchange prospers in areas of all industrial societies, apparently because it succeeds where formalized impersonal institutions are absent or where they function poorly for one reason or another.

Relevant here is that the efficiencies of dealings of the social exchange type are difficult to calculate precisely in advance. We have to assume that it is confidence in the relationship itself (a kind of practical faith) that motivates mutual commitments. This confidence is focused on the other's general qualities and potential, but may also be a result of ill-considered habit. Thus, social-exchange relationships have greater potential for either positive synergy and/or entropy when compared to economic exchange. When effective, the upside of social exchange is rich with potential for long-term growth, stemming from superior levels of coordination, but when misused, social exchange easily becomes stale and inflexible, its isolation from competition causing it gradually to fulfill all of its detractors' expectations.

Some of the reasons the impersonal institutions of economic exchange may work poorly should also be noted. As already noted, in times of uncertainty, risk-sharing is not a characteristic of economic exchange, whereas social exchange assumes a degree of uncertainty to be normal. The means for quality control in economic exchange are limited largely to termination of the relationship. It is not our purpose here to enumerate an exhaustive list of pros and cons, but we should note a few congenital problems with transactions of the economic-exchange type. For example, (1) decision-making processes can become very bureaucratic and costly when trust is absent and applicant numbers are unlimited, (2) long-term results and consequences are ignored, (3) there is less flexibility within each formally fixed contract period, and (4) dispute resolution can be problematic if the contract has failed to anticipate the problem. It is conventionally assumed by economists, however, that such costs (many difficult to demonstrate) do not outweigh the gained efficiencies deriving from depersonalized institutions of the kind we have been labeling economic exchange. The attractions of the market remain axiomatic, or nearly so for many economists.

The fact remains, however, that while money, commodities, and other things can be dealt with by economic exchange quite efficiently, some forms of economic and political transactions are difficult to reduce to depersonalized, institutional processes.[10] It is precisely in such areas of the political economy where we find considerable variation. Relations in Japan between the government and business, between management and labor, and between suppliers and assembly "parent" firms exemplify such areas.

We are arguing that many so-called "unique" Japanese phenomena can effectively be interpreted as occupying this area of the economy and explained in terms of a theory of social exchange. The historical question of which came first, economic or social exchange, and the evaluative question of which is more normal for what areas of the economy require more space to discuss than we can allot here, but it is useful to note again the conventional assumptions that the world has moved, and is moving, from social to economic exchange, and that the entire political economy is inherently (and even rightly) destined to be governed by economic exchange in the future. We disagree when it comes to the gray area of interface between major economic actors. Social exchange, we think, can expand at the expense of economic exchange, and vice versa, within certain domains. Which direction this dynamic has taken in postwar Japan is ultimately an empirical question, but we shall make our opinion clear in the next section.

Finally, cultural patterns and attitudes do indeed shape the practices of social exchange and color public judgments of it as well, but the cultural variation possible does not contradict the theoretical framework we are proposing for social exchange. There are important differences between Japan and the West, but they are best contrasted and understood within a common framework. This is rather different from saying that Japan is unique for cultural reasons.

Social Exchange and the Political Economy

We are now ready to examine our main hypothesis, namely, that (a) the mode of social exchange has diffused more significantly into the economic sphere in postwar Japanese society than in most other industrial societies, and (b) this has occurred because of both cultural legacies and favorable economic circumstances. A key term here is *economic sphere*, since, almost by definition, the mode of social exchange is assumed to be pervasive outside the economic sphere in any society. Let us define the economic sphere as those activities involving money. In other words, the economy in this sense includes not only the market system itself, but also the interface area between the market and nonmarket spheres. In fact, this is a very traditional definition of the economy.

How to demarcate the three areas—the market system proper, the interface area, and the noneconomic sphere—is always a focus of dispute between economic liberalism and other philosophies of political economy. Economic liberals argue that ideally the market proper should be expanded as much as possible, which, by implication, means the interface area ought to be minimized. Yet, patently, even in the most liberal of societies, the interface area does not and will never disappear. All societies depend on market-government linkages, exemplified in such conventional matters as tax collection and the governmental supply of public goods and services. Market-government linkage cannot be reduced to a system of monetary exchange. Furthermore, governmental intervention in the market system is a constant reality everywhere in the industrial world, and its extent depends fundamentally on the prevailing ideology and special circumstances that shape the degree of trust between government and private actors (compare, for example, wartime and peacetime economies). Even among neoliberals, opinion differs as to the proper extent of governmental interference in such matters as central bank activities and antimonopoly regulation.

The interface area also includes certain linkages between private relationships and market activities. The provision of services through direct personal contact is one very broad area of interface, typified by professional services (medical care, legal service, etc.), information services (education, consultants, etc.), entertainment, and so forth. To some degree, even the administrative services provided by modern bureaucracies have an element of personalization. These service actvities obviously involve much more than pure economic exchange. What is notable is that the actual value (and quality) of the benefits from these "exchanges" is difficult to specify precisely in advance because the quality often hinges crucially on factors such as personal character, mutual trust, and communication between the supplier and recipient (such as between lawyer

and client). Put differently, lawyers are not like tons of wheat or television sets, in that (1) they are not standardized, (2) quality is discovered
through personal knowledge, and (3) differences arise from the content
of the relationship itself. Nor are ordinary labor services in factories or
offices immune from problems of poor pre-specifiability of quality and
the intrusion of human and relational factors, particularly if long-term
performance is at issue. Dealings with people are different in many ways
from those centering on inanimate objects, especially given the variability relationships bring. When it comes to human services, a closer look
reveals persistent evidence of potential for "market failure." Most industrial societies have a tendency to deal with these problems within the
ideological framework of a market system by recourse to additional
regulation, such as accreditation (for doctors, lawyers, teachers, hospitals, schools, etc.), fee setting, labor standards, and so forth. In this
general area of the economy, one full of uncertainties, it is quite natural
that social exchanges become very important for what often only they
can ensure—namely, consistent quality over time. This suggests that the
diffusion of social exchange into certain areas of the economy can provide
better solutions to certain problems inherent to the area of interface.[11]

In more accurate terms, for areas of interface in the political economy,
neither pure social nor pure economic exchange should be taken as the
universal prior condition. This carries an important corollary: we cannot
assume that human nature inherently prefers one or the other mode.
This is a matter of importance, given the long-running debate over
whether Western individualism is to be taken as universal and, therefore,
whether Japanese "psychology" (dependency, human nexus-centered,
or whatever) is to be treated as exceptional. The crucial point is that
areas of interface in the economy are inherently areas of some mix
between social and economic exchange, with each mode providing value
and efficiency in a distinctively different manner.

The rate of change in industrial society must be recognized as setting
limits on the role of social exchange. New technologies appear one after
the other, industrial structure shifts, people change jobs, and so on,
producing what Lévi-Strauss terms a "hot" society (in contrast to what
he labels a "cold" society, in which human relations are largely static, as
in preliterate, preindustrial situations).[12] The popular belief is that, in a
"hot" social context, the stability of cognitive and evaluative agreements
is very difficult to maintain. It would follow that the framework of
specification supportive of social exchange would be particularly unstable or weak in areas attached to the modern economic sphere, the "hottest"
part of a "hot" society. One corollary of this notion would be that modes
of exchange will become polarized in modern industrial society between
economic and private activites, with each belonging to very separate

contexts. Industrialization typically means that legal institutions, markets, and money gain influence, and the mode of economic exchange thus expands. As deplored by many, human life in modern industrial society is prone to commercialization and depersonalization, to rational and legal forms of bureaucratic power, and to the dominance of short-term contractual interactions. Human ties are thus limited to a very narrow range of persons and contexts, characterized as spheres of private human emotion. It is assumed that any interaction outside such a sphere is likely to take the form of an economic exchange, subject to utility calculus. In this way, a polarization of exchange modes is thought to arise, with both polar types moving toward their ideal or pure form. The possibilities of an intermediate or mixed mode of exchange are not regarded as very great or theoretically very interesting. This is the current conventional view regarding exchange in modern society.

Indeed, social exchange does tend to be unstable in the economic sphere, at least when compared to preindustrial societies. However, the view that social exchange is inherently unsustainable in that sphere is patently not correct. To accept this point, it is necessary that we see social exchange as providing certain societal long-term efficiencies in realms of human uncertainty and that we see any particular mode or mixture of modes of exchange as resting on a set of shared understandings and evaluations that are both cultural in nature and created in time (rather than being culturally inherent or socially permanent).

The Game-Theoretic Viewpoint

The theory of social exchange by itself, however, is not comprehensive enough to explain larger developments in time and space. In fact, Blau himself conceded several years after his seminal work that "exchange theory is most directly concerned with face-to-face relations, and thus it must be complemented by other theoretical principles that focus on complex structures with institutionalized values."[13] If we approach the more complex issues of organizations, market structures, and the role of politics, we need to consider a broad field of multilateral interactions and their dynamic outcomes, acknowledging that they rest on a basic structure of human interaction in which exchange possibilities are unevenly distributed among possible participants. Here we have recourse to the viewpoint of the theory of games.

A theory of games delineates how players decide their moves when faced with complex interactive situations. The theory seeks to visualize all possible outcomes of a given range of interactions, using the tool of a payoff matrix, which portrays the general contours of the circumstances facing the players—not only the interactive pattern among them but also, to some extent at least, the potential of the general circumstances surrounding them.[14] As a concrete example, if the participants are nations, the payoff matrix shows an interactive pattern of nations in terms of each nation's alternative economic policy choices, and it will inform us of the potentiality of the world economy as a whole as well as provide a list of strategies to be adopted in international bargaining. Here we assume that it can also be used to illustrate the circumstances surrounding an industry, an organization, and other extensive circumstances.

In fact, a game-theory-like approach to the dynamics of industrial society has been attempted by a number of analysts.[15] Various phases of industrial society can be represented by the diverse possibilities of the payoff matrix, but for our present purposes it suffices that a viable system of social exchange may be interpreted as a stable "cooperative game" where the payoffs are the net rewards of social exchange. In other words, the obvious benefits of exchange may be represented as lying in those types of payoff matrices in which cooperative strategies result in very high returns, compared to noncooperative strategies.

In any cooperative game of repeated plays, all players must have perfect information about the payoff matrix as a whole—that is, they must know not only their own payoffs but also those of all other players. This is a very stringent requirement. Theoretically, whether this is an absolute necessity or not remains, in a way, an open question.[16] Practically, however, it is more important to note that each payoff matrix already implies a specification of the framework of players as well as strategies. Since there is almost always the possibility of a disturbance by potential players or strategies outside such a framework, it follows that the stability of a cooperative game necessitates some prior categorical restriction on participants and their actions. Specifically, distinguishing insiders from outsiders is crucially important. Thus, any cooperative game presupposes a fundamental consensus (represented as a particular payoff matrix) that includes not only the payoffs themselves but also a restriction of participants and strategies.

However, even in the case where all players are well aware of the potential benefits of cooperation, there is almost always room for strategic moves by some coalition of players that will make the solution unstable. As shown in the literature of game theory, the stability of cooperative solutions is hard to guarantee. Game theorists have been trying to formulate diverse bargaining processes to achieve stable results and various conceptual frameworks supporting stable cooperative solutions, yet despite many technical sophistications, the point remains that in the final analysis, some rule or norm must be superimposed on simple individual rationality. In order to realize cooperation, a basic consensus is needed, and this should be both cognitive and evaluative in the sense that the participants share (and indicate) some norm of cooperative intent. This implies that the stability of cooperative outcomes rests on relationships as well as rational calculation, that a system or culture supporting cooperation is essential.

Two Conditions for Social Exchange in the Contemporary Context

A game-theoretic formulation thus suggests that, in order to effect a stable pattern of social exchange, two conditions are necessary: a cognitive consensus and an evaluative consensus. Having in mind the current theme—that is, the role of social exchange in the economic sphere of industrial society—these two conditions may be summed up as follows:

1. A favorable environment for economic cooperation exists when the economic sphere provides a set of conditions favoring the creation by a group of participants of a cognitive consensus that predicts high profitability from cooperation and little resistance to this mode or consensus from outside the group.

2. The cultural background is favorable when there exists a relational and organizational tradition capable of and inclined to the formation of an evaluative consensus for cooperation among participants not related by ascriptive human ties (such as family, kinship, or locality).

In game-theoretic terms, the first condition promises visibly higher payoffs for a cooperative strategy. For example, in a village ravaged by a flood or a nation devastated by war—cases where natural or political disaster has removed past assets and vested interests—the fact that the benefits of cooperation (e.g., reconstruction of infrastructure) are very large is perhaps obvious to every inhabitant.

Another, more economic example of this condition is that of an industry facing a highly predictable prospect of future declining average cost. In this type of situation (where a strategy set is not convex), market competition (i.e., a noncooperative strategy) will be unstable and will result in cutthroat price competition and an investment race. The more predictable the prospect of average cost declines is, the more severe and unstable the competition is likely to be. The standard answer for this situation according to the economic theory of competition is the emergence of a giant monopoly. Since this outcome is obviously very costly to all other suppliers, as well as to all purchasers of the monopolized product, the potential benefit of avoiding total competition leading to monopoly seems sufficiently obvious. In other words, such very favorable conditions encourage a cognitive consensus that seeks both to limit competition and to restrain monopoly formation.

Another quite different example would be that of an industry facing a predictable prospect of stagnation, in which technological possibilities and demand potential have already been exploited. In such a case, managerial efforts must concentrate on strategic price-setting competition. This, too, is a very unstable state in a game-theoretic sense, one that approximates a zero-sum game, in which theoretically there is no room for cooperative action. Yet, as is well known, under these conditions cartels and other collusive practices are likely to arise if firms in the same industry are permitted to cooperate. Only if consumers demonstrate serious resistance, as in forcing the passage of an antimonopoly law, is it difficult for such a system of collusion to arise and prevail.

Turning to our second, "cultural" condition, we must ask how the evaluative consensus comes about. Generally speaking, it will not be based on a norm of individual rationality (which cannot specify, among other things, a range of participants), but must come from some existing model of cooperative social exchange—that is, from prior experiences of cooperative attempts. Yet because industrial society constantly transforms itself, past experience can easily become irrelevant. There is no fixed cultural form that is invariably reliable for such consensus. Yet if the same type of relationship has again and again proven its viability and survived the vicissitudes of change, then the pattern latent in it becomes a cultural legacy that can serve as the basis of a new evaluative consensus. Such legacies provide a readily available basis for new cooperative solutions, and they have existed in relative abundance in the economic sphere of Japanese society from the beginning of industrialization, even if in many spheres they were not immediately applied or seen by all parties as relevant or even desirable. That is, while all societies presumably have legacies of cooperative effort, in most industrial societies (including many aspects of prewar Japan), the application of traditional modes of social interaction to "modern" economic activities is not supported ideologically. In Japan, however, as industrialization progressed, preindustrial forms of cooperative social exchange were gradually revived in the economic sphere as effective means of solving problems arising from the instability of market outcomes.

The Japanese collectivistic orientation as a traditional legacy has been widely recognized.[17] That this legacy has been flexible enough in its conceptual nature to be readily extended into spheres of economic activity has also been noted.[18] Shumpei Kumon, Seizaburo Sato, and Yasusuke Murakami, in particular, have identified the historical origin of an achievement-oriented group pattern in the organizational tradition of the samurai household (ie) and village (mura) in the Tokugawa period.[19] The focus on traditional social relations has had a parallel in the concern with the continuity of traditional values and ethos into the modern period. Obviously, to a degree, the separate topics are mutually reinforcing. But debate continues as to how deterministic these legacies have been in shaping modern Japan, since there is little evidence of steady linear continuity to the present and many contemporary circumstances can be pointed to as counter to the argument of cultural determination.

In this regard, our position is that the diffusion and relative stability of social exchange in the economic sphere in postwar Japan have depended on a combination of unusual economic circumstances and a particular cultural tradition, a combination of conditions that is historically *sui generis*. The argument is that a workable system of social exchange in a modern economy patently requires a cultural foundation and yet is also contingent on an economic environment that makes social-exchange solutions viable. No cultural tradition alone can perpetuate the workability of social exchange in the economic sphere. Nor can a favorable environment alone, without an appropriate cultural legacy, produce such a result.

What we are asserting can have two variants, for example, depending on whether one emphasizes the cultural tradition or the economic environment. Many scholars, Japanese as well as non-Japanese, tend to see great persistence in the Japanese cultural tradition, and they thus predict the future continuation of a distinctive or "unique" character to the Japanese political economy (i.e., the persistence of social-exchange patterns in the economic sphere). Those inclined to discount the cultural tradition, on the other hand, would see such patterns of cooperation as contingent on economic conditions, and therefore readily susceptible to change. To predict the obstinacy of a cultural tradition in general is one thing, but to predict it for key areas of a political economy is another. At issue are two distinct questions: how contingent is the pattern on economic conditions, and how readily do embedded cultural norms change? By answering the first question, we can differentiate two schools of argument, one stressing the cultural continuity of certain kinds of social-exchange relationships (often in a social nexus) and one focusing on the economic contingencies that contributed to the rational logic of cooperation. Our inclination in this essay belongs ultimately more to the contingency school, in the sense that we predict significant future change owing to new economic conditions.

More fundamentally, we are arguing that many so-called "unique" Japanese phenomena can be effectively interpreted without recourse to either strictly economic or cultural determinism if we adopt exchange theory as a basic framework. Embedded social patterns and attitudes can indeed shape the practices of social exchange and color public judgments of its appropriateness to interface relations as well, but such cultural variation does not contradict the basic underlying realities of exchange we have been exploring. We repeat, there are important differences between Japan and the West, but they are best contrasted and understood within a common framework—which is, again, different from saying that Japan is unique for reasons of culture alone.

Three Cases of Social Exchange

Labor Relations

The elements distinguishing large Japanese firms in the postwar period include the following organizational features: (1) "lifetime employment" (or long tenure of employment); (2) seniority-based wage and promotion systems; (3) elaborate welfare, bonus, and other benefit systems; (4) company-based labor unions; (5) considerable inter-job mobility within a firm; (6) small-group activities (e.g., QC circles) at the shop-floor level; (7) intensive training and socialization by companies; and (8) attention to developing a corporate culture and managerial philosophy.[20] Since features (5), (6), and (7) are closely interrelated—that is, inter-job mobility requires intensive training, which is conducted mainly as small-group activities—they will be combined together in our discussions as one feature.

The essence of the system spelled out above is a particular type of labor agreement between employer and employee. There will be no objection to viewing these features as "Japanese management," or at least as its core characteristics. It is rather obvious that this employment relationship is a type of social exchange, since it is long-term, multi-issue, and based on an informal agreement.

There is another aspect of the Japanese management system worth noting initially. A central feature common to large-scale Japanese firms may be the principle of consensual rule and the frequent practice of "bottom-up initiative." In other words, it seems to be an implicit rule of Japanese decision making, compared to its Western counterpart, that lower-ranking managers (or even workers in some cases) should actively participate in suggesting, drafting, and formulating major managerial policies, and that their unanimous support of a final decision is proper and desirable, if not essential. This decision-making mode itself includes an element of social exchange (between higher-ranking and lower-ranking personnel). Although this, too, is an important aspect of the Japanese firm, we will not delve into it here, since an examination of the labor agreement is sufficient to substantiate the main theme of this essay.

The contract each employer and employee sign in large-scale Japanese firms is indeed a legal document, but this "contract" is very brief and general, and lacks specific details of rights and duties. It merely symbolizes the substance of an implicit and inclusive agreement between the two sides. The implicit agreement promises, first of all, that employment will typically continue up to some not-fully-specified retirement age—so called "lifetime employment." Another aspect of the agreement is that the employee can count on wages and status increasing according to length of service (*nenko joretsu*). Under this arrangement, then, a certain level of security is assured, but the details of wages, actual tasks, and career paths remain unspecified. This leaves considerable room for mixed systems that also emphasize merit-based achievement. Less specification means that jobs and skills are more adaptable to technological progress over the worker's long tenure. Job shifts linked with intrafirm training (intrafirm mobility) are thus another essential aspect of the implicit agreement. Such mobility helps to reconcile the inflexibilities of lifetime and seniority-based promotion with the pursuit of worker efficiency.

Job shifts may be viewed differently by workers in different industrial systems. Craft-union practice in Britain, for example, holds that workers usually prefer their old jobs to new, unfamiliar ones. On the other hand, Japanese workers appear willing to accept a job shift if it means a chance to learn new technologies and keep abreast with overall progress. This attitude coincides well with management's eagerness to pursue technological progress and to provide necessary training for workers. Postwar Japanese workers not only accepted job shifts but actually expected them as a benefit.[21]

Moreover, each employee in a typical large-scale Japanese firm reasonably expects various benefits from the firm, such as bonuses, housing, medical care, and facilities for leisure activities. Even the warmth of human relations in small groups in the office or on the shop floor is an expected benefit. What are counted as "fringe benefits" (or even managerial cooptation) in other countries constitute an essential part of Japanese corporate culture.

In exchange, management (or the employer) also benefits from this implicit agreement. First, the labor union tends to be committed to the company rather than to the nationwide or industrywide labor organization. Company-based unionism arose as a result as well as a cause of the long-term employment guarantee and the system of extensive benefits. These guarantees and benefits constitute a complex multi-issue relationship that varies from firm to firm. Such a relationship can only be negotiated between each individual firm and its union, since such matters as profits, size, history, and business fortunes make each company's circumstances different. A company-based union contributes greatly to the lessening of labor conflict and reduces labor costs in the sense that costly inflexibility and conflict are avoided in the context of the long-term implicit agreement between management and union. Japanese company-based unions also join in industrywide and then nationwide organizations (e.g., Sōhyō or Dōmei) that play symbolic roles in the national political scene. But these have no substantial influence on each company-based union's decisions on such key matters as wage negotiations, personnel policies, and working conditions.

Naturally, the employer benefits from the flexibility of interjob mobility. Firms can reshuffle their personnel in response to changing technologies without replacing employees or causing serious labor unrest. The result has been a remarkable technological adaptiveness. As this implies, Japanese firms can effectively harvest a rich yield from their "human investment" in their employees. This positive result from management/labor cooperation has been substantially shared between the two parties through such mechanisms as frequent consultations and extensive information sharing (including information on the firm's business and profit situation).

Thus, the Japanese employer-employee relationship is a system of social exchange similar to a cooperative game strategy.[22] Of course, the relationship originated from a typical economic exchange between wage and labor service in factory work in the early industrial period, yet, over time, and especially after World War II, the social-exchange aspects and benefits accruing to both sides from cooperation were greatly enlarged. Job and income security, dignity, and a supportive work environment benefited labor, while cooperative unionism, motivated and skilled workers, and responsiveness to technological change were the benefits for management.

It is to be noted that this social exchange is not the mere outcome of rational give-and-take between two opposing interests. Rather, the benefits to the two sides are inextricably interwoven, forming a single organizational whole. Furthermore, the weaving of these interests occurred over decades, and they were quite patently influenced initially by traditional legacies.[23] Indeed, the system shows a remarkable resemblance to certain premodern Japanese organizations, particularly the merchant household (ie). There is little doubt that a tradition of "ie-type functional collectivism" played a significant role in providing an underlying cognitive and evaluative consensus (e.g., "corporate familism" and the slogan "Every effort for the company's growth!").[24] Most notable from our perspective is that merchant household organizations (such as Mitsui and Sumitomo) offered rough models for nearly all the distinctive elements of the large Japanese firm (e.g., long-term employment, seniority rule and pay, management philosophy, and extensive training). It may even be said that the firm as a formal modern entity offered opportunities for the revival of premodern organizational traditions that were barely discernible in the early stages of Japanese industrialization.

Contemporary Japanese firms are not, however, mere replicas of some premodern organization. As in any industrial society, the firm in Japan is an achievement-oriented organization that in principle seeks to maximize profit. The traditional organizational pattern had to be modified to vitalize the modern firm effectively. As far as factory workers are concerned, the Japanese management system started experimentally in the 1920s, was maintained and strengthened through the experience of the war, and finally assumed its present form after much trial and error in the decade following 1945. The end of this transitional decade was symbolized by the Nissan labor dispute in 1953 and the emergence of a new leadership in the national Sōhyō labor organization in 1954.[25] Against a background of rapid economic growth, expectations on both sides were thereafter generally satisfied, and the system became more and more stable. As a result of this evolutionary pattern, one combining traditional patterns of social exchange with advancing modern technology under favorable circumstances, the Japanese management system assumed its present form. It is neither totally continuous nor discontinuous with the past, has never been static, and is still evolving.

What postwar conditions favored lifetime employment and gave it a strong economic rationale? Or, under what economic conditions could a system of promotion based on seniority be reconciled with a market-oriented theory of the firm? One key to answering these questions lies in the relationship between social exchange and investment activity. It may be said quite generally that social exchange is an "investment" in the sense that to both sides, it is essentially a long-term debtor-creditor relationship. In Blau's words, "the establishment of exchange relations involves making investments that constitute commitments to the other party."

Contemporary examples of investment activity are almost always embedded in organized relations among people. In creating a firm, for example, an entrepreneur-manager usually has to get help from at least two key sources—that is, investors and workers. Investors must have confidence in the entrepreneur. In this sense, even financial transactions are partnerships that require some broader agreement and deeper mutual trust than in the ordinary selling and buying of commodities.[26]

Turning to investments in human capital, we need to step back and consider a longer historical perspective on the evolution of internal and external labor markets. For the sake of simplicity, let us divide industrial history into two long stages: laissez-faire capitalism (roughly until the 1870s) and, after that, organized capitalism. In the latter, interfirm and intrafirm organization became increasingly complex and central to all economic activities. The watershed technologically was the introduction of electricity to production. Before the age of electricity, machines in factories were powered by steam or hydraulic power, and for many reasons, operating them required much individual skill. As David Landes points out, skilled masters therefore played an important role as subcontractors within the factory proper, maintaining their craftsmanship and controlling their own apprentices.[27] In contrast, electric machines were far more flexible, and they ushered in vast new production processes and revolutionized the organization of factory labor. Skills became much easier for average workers to learn because machines were more manageable. At the same time, to adjust to more flexible use of machines, even within a single factory, workers were required to obtain a broader range of skills and knowledge.

Accordingly, human investment by the firm gained great potential as a contributor to overall efficiency. Parenthetically, this kind of skill requirement may have been one of the reasons why elementary education expanded so rapidly in this period. Nevertheless, economies of scale and the development of mass-production facilities during the first half of the twentieth century led to a dominant managerial logic that ignored the potential gains from worker participation in the development of firm-specific efficiencies. F. W. Taylor's "scientific management," for example, essentially viewed manual employees as analogous to machine parts. The underlying assumption was that managerial people had enough capacity to grasp all technological problems in the firm and/or that average workers were lacking in general skills and knowledge. Taylor himself had in mind a situation in which workers were by and large illiterate.[28] But particularly in the later half of the twentieth century, production technology became increasingly firm-specific and thus largely embodied in the employees of the firm. Human investment, in this sense, is almost a sine qua non for the contemporary industrial economy. Taylorism and its descendants in the West viewed investments in human-capital formation as separate from the firm, whereas in Japan the trend has been to see such investments as essential to the long-term growth and efficiency of the firm. Firm-specific technology and human-capital formation by the firm were thus linked in a positive manner.

This took the form, again over time, of a particular kind of relationship, in which social-exchange aspects became more and more important. The uncertainty of returns and the evaluation of equitable distribution were dealt with in a social-exchange mode. The postwar Japanese management system is, in this sense, a major departure from Taylorism and from the assumptions of capitalism in the late nineteenth and early twentieth centuries. We should acknowledge here that this fortuitous development did not occur primarily as the result of economic wisdom, but in a rather ad hoc way, with union pressures and financial constraints playing a significant role. The point is that the conditions existed to confirm the potentiality of this approach to the problem.

This now widely emulated "Japanese" approach is not necessarily a universal solution, however. First, wartime devastation provided a favorable environment for economic cooperation among the Japanese people at large. Second, "organized capitalism" entered a stage of mature global expansion. Progress in technology, the expansion of the market for mass consumer durables, and consequently the smooth expansion of major industries (and thus particular firms) became more predictable than ever, establishing a common optimism. Third, in the case of the Japanese economy, borrowing technology was easy, and overseas markets—particularly the U.S. market—were open, thanks to the stability of the IMF–GATT regime. Finally, a pro-growth conservative government held power throughout the period, although this must be viewed as an outcome as well as a cause of economic growth. In short, major Japanese industries enjoyed economies of scale and decreasing average costs, a situation that offered unprecedented opportunity and incentives for each firm to expand, and that was very favorable to the expansion of social exchange in the area of labor-management relations. Obviously, the viability of lifetime employment and of the seniority-based advancement system (both notably long-term) depends heavily on the predictable growth of the company. The extensive application of the Japanese management system must be seen as a response to the nature of this era's overall economic environment and not simply as a product of cultural continuity.

Since the oil crisis of 1973–75 and the end of the fixed-exchange-rate regime, however, most of the above fortuitous conditions have disappeared or waned considerably. Major industries such as steel, automobiles, oil, petrochemicals, and even electronics have lost momentum, both in terms of technological opportunities and because the level of predictable demand growth has declined. Company expansion in these industries has visibly decelerated. Most large-scale Japanese corporations clearly faced a difficult time of transition. Although the ethos of management-labor cooperation has not been lost, there is considerable indication that there is much erosion in the actual arrangements involved in most firms. The core of workers for whom the social-exchange arrangement is pertinent is declining, for example, and while employers seek to lessen their exposure to "permanent employment's" fixed costs, new generations of workers are arriving on the scene with attitudes uninformed by the insecurities and optimism of the postwar era. To them, the vaunted Japanese management system is a tradition that is outgrowing its usefulness.

The postwar period in Japan, it might be argued, was equivalent to the situation following a natural disaster in the face of which all members of a community pull together in unusually close cooperation. Victory in the war had much the opposite effect in the United States and the United Kingdom, and only lately as the result of increased competition from Japan has the trend been toward more cooperation in those countries.

In the longer run, however, this new tradition seems likely to conflict with the economic imperatives of the coming era as far as Japan is concerned. Japan faces a new set of conditions, characterized by technological breakthroughs (rather than incremental learning) and by greater volatility and diversity of demand. Firm-level strategies are to pursue economies of *scope* instead of economies of *scale*. In recent years, many large Japanese firms have been attempting to enter new industries, such as new materials, biological engineering, leisure services, and real estate, by starting offshoot subsidiary companies. Such diversification seems to aim at maintaining the overall scale of corporate activity, thereby helping keep management's implicit employment guarantee to its workers. Interestingly, labor unions seem to comply with these new approaches by management, in spite of the fact that they include wage freezes and occasionally even layoffs or the discharge of some workers. In a word, unions in hard times remain company-based and preoccupied with the social-exchange arrangement that centers on stable employment. By sharing the same primary aim of defending "their company," management and union are keeping the postwar tradition alive, and the value of social exchange is thus much in evidence still.[29]

There are, however, limits to such efforts. Sooner or later, Japanese management will have to be restructured. The extent of the restructuring will vary with each firm's capacity for technological innovation and, for Japan as a whole, with the rate at which the world market grows. We expect that efficiency considerations will cause large-scale Japanese firms to withdraw, one by one, from some of the key practices identified with Japanese management. The first to go may be the rule of seniority-based promotion, which will gradually decline in relation to considerations of merit. This change will then begin to undermine the lifetime employment commitment to the unions. Some traditions of Japanese management, such as bottom-up consensus, are, however, likely to survive, and, certainly, all parties will adhere, as long as they can, to the notion that the company is eternal. This dilemma of efficiency versus social exchange—of increasing disharmony between the economic environment and the postwar legacy of social exchange and its associated values—is one of the key issues Japanese society is now facing.

Government-Business Relations

Early in this essay we noted that Japanese industrial policy cannot be explained simply by recourse to a model of regulatory organization built on legal authority. The question before us now is how to explain the broad compliance of business with government's so-called "administrative guidance." We argue here that the government-business relationship is more adequately explained by a theory of implicit give-and-take operating in a long-term framework in which both government and private firms get what they want—that is, a social-exchange framework. Again, neither market nor organizational model seems fully appropriate.

The major characteristics of Japanese industrial policy are most clearly evidenced in the relationship of a government bureau and a particular industry's trade association. They are:

1. *Informal membership specification.* In each leading industry in postwar Japan, all leading firms (except foreign ones) and the government branch with jurisdiction over the industry (usually a bureau section in a ministry) are constantly in close, informal mutual contact, primarily through the intermediation of a trade association. As a result, each trade association operates under strong bureaucratic influence and vice versa. This was partly an outcome of the wartime experience when affiliation in government-sponsored trade associations was compulsory for each firm. The postwar trade association similarly serves, in our terms, to specify the participants in an exchange relationship.

But at present this relationship is informal, having no legal ground for compulsory affiliation. Firms are not formally forced to join. Furthermore, legally established penalties to strengthen industrial policies are in force only in the exceptional cases of protection for seriously declining industries such as textiles, cement, and aluminum.

It is true that the ministry with jurisdiction over an industry can utilize a range of policy instruments (such as financing, tax concessions, subsidies, government contracts, and R & D grants) to support its goals, but these instruments are all promotional, rather than prohibitive, in character. We must note, in this regard, however, the strong legal authority for regulation of imports and foreign investment in Japan until the mid 1970s. This control over external economic forces was indeed a powerful form of authority, but it contrasts quite remarkably with the very different approach taken domestically. At the time, these externally oriented regulatory powers were of major significance in the protection of many industries, but they did not involve ministry direction of private-sector decision making. In other words, an individual firm was legally free to act against the policy intentions of the ministry of jurisdiction, if it was determined to do so. It is easy to point out specific examples of noncompliance. Kawasaki Steel and Sumitomo Metal, for example, built big steel mills contrary to MITI's policy of investment coordination in the steel industry. Car manufacturers, particularly Honda, resisted a merger plan recommended by MITI. Although these cases were exceptional, they show that policy guidance was not a matter of absolute legal authority. To fill out the picture, in this regard, failure to comply with MITI's "guidance" has often provoked some form of indirect reprisal in a totally separable context, often at a later date. Even without legal authority, in other words, MITI has had the capacity to enforce its initiatives indirectly. For this, and in order to seek favor for their industry, Japanese firms in the key industries have generally complied with the government's directives, particularly during the period of rapid growth. Control has been informal in nature and phrased in terms of long-term mutual benefit for industries as a whole.

2. *Cognitive consensus.* In spite of scattered examples of noncompliance, firms in all leading industries generally followed the government's guidance. A kind of patron-client relationship was formed, characterized by social exchange. The original basis of this relationship was apparently a growing belief, shared by all participants (government and firms alike), that "their industry" was facing a rare opportunity for sustained development—borrowable technology, ample high-quality labor, expanding demand (domestic and worldwide), and a capacity to control foreign invasion of domestic markets. This opportunity implied that each firm would be able to enjoy expanding economies of scale. In other words, all faced a situation in which the expected average cost would decrease in the future. Under such conditions, if firms compete freely, they will expand their production capacity as quickly as possible and thereby lower the product price as much as possible. According to standard economics, this will eventually lead to the emergence of a single giant monopoly and the destruction of all other firms in the industry. This is the kind of instability the Japanese most feared during the period of rapid growth. The label commonly applied to this form of instability was "excessive competition." Recognition of the merits and dangers of such an environment was shared by the government and by private firms. This was the cognitive consensus that constituted the basis of the informal trade association mentioned above. One may question the extent to which the danger of "excessive competition" was real, or at least the explosiveness of the instability. We cannot doubt, however, that such shared cognition was a cornerstone of the social-exchange relationship between the association (or each firm in it) and the government. The resultant cooperation would bring exceptionally smooth economic development.

3. *Long-term, multi-issue basis.* A shared cognitive consensus is not enough, however, to guarantee cooperative behavior. The participants, particularly the government, exploited and elaborated a set of strategies to strengthen the ethos of cooperation. Promotional policies were long-term, eclectic, and numerous. That is, the government made full use of the long-term, multi-issue nature of Japanese industrial policy in an approach consistent with the nature of social exchange as presented in this essay. First, short-run promotional policy measures cannot work well to prohibit a firm's "undesirable" behavior. However, if firms are convinced that a policy will continue for a long time, they are likely to accept government guidance, since whether they accept it or not will make a major difference to their long-run benefit. In the long run, promotional measures can be almost tantamount to prohibitive regulations, provided the government maintains the same attitude. Second, because the Japanese bureaucracy is vertically segmented, one government branch virtually monopolizes jurisdiction over each industry (controlling, for example, the issuance of various licenses and so forth). This gives it considerable coercive influence through its capacity to delay or refuse permission for new operations. Often exercised quite arbitrarily and without the balance of viable legal recourse (examples include import licenses and licenses in matters relating to factory operations, such as water use), this power is a threat to the private sector. Ministry jurisdiction over seemingly unrelated matters is potentially applicable to promotional policies and matters of administrative guidance that amount to effective pressure supporting bureau influence. Long-term, multi-issue interactions thus constitute the de facto basis for the effectiveness of administrative guidance as a general pattern.

4. *Intragroup impartiality.* Another important feature of this system is that the members of an industrial association are treated impartially by the relevant government agency. This intragroup impartiality is necessary because favoritism gives rise to internal dissension and the formation of opposition to coalition rule within a group. In practice, impartiality has meant that the government typically offers a policy proposal in the form of a fixed formula that acknowledges and preserves the market-share status quo among member firms. MITI, for example, usually suggests the rule of "proportional share," according to which it assigns shares of increased production capacity to each firm in proportion to the firm's existing share in the market. In the petrochemical industry, MITI has even adopted a rule of equal shares. In these and other instances, a major concern of Japanese bureaucrats has obviously been to avoid all appearances of favoritism. Impartiality is an essential moral requisite of any modern bureaucracy, but in the case of postwar

Japan, it is an acute functional requisite for the effectiveness of the group management aspect of industrial policy. This clublike logic and the high moral standards of most ministries—the mission psychology of career bureaucrats—both help explain why the postwar Japanese bureaucracy has been relatively free of corruption, which in turn has been an important source of trust in the overall arrangement.

The group structure thus established—a trade association composed of equals under one guiding/mediating agent (its ministry)—resembles in form the Tokugawa ideal of the village under a local official. The merchant guild (*kabu nakama*) of that period was also very similar in organizational pattern. The social structure we are describing is a mixture of hierarchical and egalitarian principles. Many firms form a club and the government is the supervising referee, so to speak. If Japanese firms, in their greater reliance on a seniority-based hierarchy, resemble premodern (extended) households (*ie* or *dozoku*), so trade associations find a precedent in the more egalitarian nature of preindustrial villages and merchant guilds.

5. *Entry control.* All of the abovementioned characteristics (informal membership specification; cognitive consensus; long-term, multi-issue nature; intragroup impartiality) presuppose that the group is clearly specified and entry to it limited. Of course, entry and exit are legally free in nearly all Japanese industries (except public utilities and basic-resource industries such as oil), yet as far as informal trade associations are concerned, free entry and exit are controlled. Ease of entry would presumably destabilize the cognitive consensus and undermine the long-term, multi-issue basis of industrial policy and the informal agreement already reached among existing members. Recognizing the importance of limiting membership for the purposes of establishing consensus, the ministries have explored every means to restrict entry or at least to screen entrants into such major industries as steel, automobiles, synthetic fibers, petrochemicals, and various financial activities. It is not an overstatement to say that a main theme in the history of each of these industries is the story of tense conflicts and negotiations between the ministry and new applicants for entry. In most industries, aggressive newcomers overrode the barriers set up by the ministries after much effort and time, and during the period of rapid growth, the number of firms within each industry increased considerably. The fact remains, however, that in Japan's case, barriers to entering an industry have existed, not because of economic logic, but because of the system of administrative guidance. Notable also is the fact that foreign firms were not legally permitted to operate in Japan until the early 1970s and were thus excluded from access through trade associations to close relations with government. These various efforts aimed at stabilizing the categor-

ical specification of participants are best understood in the context of the social-exchange pattern we have been discussing.

As in the case of Japanese union-management relations, all of these practices have depended on a "favorable environment of economic cooperation," which implies, among other things, the danger of market instability, or "excessive competition." In a way, the restrictive measures attempted by government—entry control, recession cartels, investment coordination, and so on—aimed at avoiding this implicit danger. We cannot say that Japanese firms meticulously followed ministry guidance, and, as noted, ministries had little direct power to impose their will on most industries. Yet administrative guidance exerted substantial influence on the behavior of Japanese firms. MITI, the Ministry of Finance, and other ministries did in the long run succeed in preventing excessive competition from seriously disturbing the performance of the whole economy. The typical outcome in the leading Japanese industries before the first oil crisis in 1973 was intense competition among a limited, yet relatively large number of firms (typically 5–10), simultaneously expanding rapidly at roughly the same pace. As far as the total impact on economic growth is concerned, the most crucial contribution of Japanese industrial policy, we would argue, has actually been the prevention of excessive competition. The direct promotion of industrial growth, however important in its own right, was a secondary result, one that would have emerged anyway because of the unprecedented favorable circumstances of the postwar period.

These circumstances have obviously changed since the first oil crisis in late 1973. Rates of technological progress and expansion of demand have both leveled off, and the situation of declining average cost has largely disappeared in many key manufacturing industries. These prime movers of rapid growth are now only relevant in a few industries. It follows logically that the original reasons for Japanese industrial policy have receded significantly, as has the size of the threat posed by foreign competition. The danger of "excessive competition" has now disappeared. Administrative guidance is no longer legitimated (in the eyes of the industry and government) by the environment, except in a minority of new "high technologies," such as semiconductors, that possess the same characteristics of declining average cost (although the aspect of technology borrowing is largely gone).

Even the environment for "high-tech" industries is different today. Consumption demand has not been large enough to justify constant high investment rates, and many high-tech industries suffer ups and downs. Even the computer industry has failed to achieve the rate of growth that consumer durables did during the 1960s. In many ways, the current situation appears comparable to that prevailing at the end of the nineteenth century, when new technologies appeared, but mass demand for new consumer products had not yet developed. The likelihood that the postwar boom will be repeated in high-tech industries is not very great.

Under these conditions, there is little industrial policy can do except to promote technological innovation. The increasing weight of the Japanese economy in the world market has created a new set of difficult tasks for the ministries, centering on market liberalization. The context is now global rather than domestic. Liberalization may well undermine the very social-exchange foundation of traditional Japanese industrial policy. More specifically, the entry of foreign firms into Japan will radically affect the country's informal trade associations. Their exclusive, clublike arrangements will be upset, and new rules and means of regulation will be required. Some foreign firms may want to play by the existing rules and develop their own social-exchange relationships with ministries (whether as part of or separate from trade associations), but it is doubtful whether the shared understandings achieved will suffice to sustain very high levels of mutual reliance.

The globalization of the Japanese economy has had other effects that also weaken the role of government. Industrial policy proved of little help in coping with the appreciation of the yen. Japanese companies had to reduce their costs drastically on their own. Moreover, the largest Japanese firms are themselves expanding internationally and diversifying the scope of their activities far beyond the boundaries of their original industries. The trade association is thus gradually losing its centrality and meaning. In this context of change, the postwar relational framework of Japanese industrial policy is being significantly weakened. Conditions now discourage relationships of the social-exchange type, and over time the ministry–trade association linkages will erode. To the degree that they continue to exist, they will be useful as a form of defensive symbiosis protecting stagnant industries (particularly from foreign competition) and/or as a vehicle for implementing coordinated responses to overseas protectionism (the poorly executed agreement on semiconductors is one recent example). In either case, Japanese industrial policy will primarily serve stagnant industries (Japanese and foreign) and the organizational interests of the ministries themselves. Ironically, overseas protectionism now becomes the final source of legitimacy for the ministries, allowing them to intervene in specific private industries in the administrative-guidance mode in the name of maintaining international stability.

The ministries will also continue to play a role in sponsoring technology. The much-publicized cooperative research projects (such as the fifth-generation computer project) organized by MITI are leading examples. Technological innovation in postwar Japan has, however, been almost entirely by private firms using their own money, and this will continue. The willing cooperation of firms in joint development is shifting to an alliance structure that depends very little on MITI and cuts across the lines of the trade associations. Economic ministries such as MITI are inherently limited in what they can do to sponsor innovation (a situation quite different from their effective promotion of technology imports) and the framework of the trade association is poorly adapted to exploitation of most new technologies. For these reasons, government-sponsored cooperation is largely restricted to the research stage.

To summarize, relationships between the government and business of the social-exchange type are in steady decline and will erode more rapidly than those in the labor-relations arena. Only severe international or domestic crises of an economic kind might revitalize the framework that we have been discussing.

Small-scale Firms and Subcontracting

Small-scale firms account for a larger portion of national economic activity in Japan than in any other industrial country. Explaining the viability of this vast sector of the Japanese economy requires that we first recognize three very different types of small business: farming, retailing, and industrial subcontracting. The three have much in common, of course, but from the perspective of exchange theory the differences are more apparent. Small-scale activities in the agricultural and retail sectors have long enjoyed important protection, subsidies, and tax breaks from the ruling Liberal Democratic Party in exchange for voting support. The scale of the political element in these areas of the economy has been huge. This is clearly a type of social exchange operating on a mass basis. Particularly, at the local level (between individual politicians and agricultural and commercial associations), it assumes all of the interpersonal richness of social exchange as we have been defining it. Entertainment, personal favors, and many other such activities consume a politician's time as he seeks to maintain numerous sets of relationships with groups that will provide votes, money, and other support based on a common perception of interests. This kind of framework tends to be long-term, multifaceted, and based in support-group structures, in clear distinction from the ideal of individual voting based on issues. That it is very much person-centered helps explain the extensive intergenerational continuity in political dynasties in certain localities.

But small-scale industrial subcontracting is not political in nature, and its viability is owing to heightened levels of efficient cooperation between small and large firms. Earlier explanations of the prevalence of the industrial subcontractor system in Japan have argued that subcontractors are essentially exploited by large firms, and that the subcontractors, in turn, exploit their workers. Subcontractors have been viewed as buffers in poor economic times, too weak to resist pressures on prices and unable to protest being squeezed in downturns. Workers in small-scale manufacturing have similarly been seen as poorly paid buffers with no employment security. This explanation contains considerable truth for the early postwar phase of rapid economic growth. As for more recent periods, however, the exploitation model loses credibility. The secret of the viability of subcontractors today is their noneconomic or extracontractual relationships with their parent firms. And this relationship, albeit asymmetrical, is not necessarily one of domination by the large firm. A mutual interdependence model, which fits the social-exchange framework very nicely, is much more appropriate.

Large corporations try to maintain their levels of employment according to the implicit rule of lifetime employment, whereas subcontractors (with small cores of permanent employees and no unions) can more easily adjust their employment levels to meet the demands of cost reduction from the parent firms. In financing, however, parent firms often mediate and endorse credits that subcontractors could not have raised alone. Moreover, parent firms and subcontractors have learned to cooperate closely in developing and improving the components or parts the subcontractors supply to the parent firm. In other words, subcontractors and parent firms share the burden of risk in three key areas—employment, financing, and the development of new technology—in different proportions. This is clearly an exchange of unspecifiables, or a social exchange by our definition. Although contracts are regularly reviewed, and are renewed if satisfactory, most subcontractors enjoy long-standing ties with their customers. Large manufacturers, for their part, organize subcontractor associations and try in other ways to reduce the numbers of participants with which they deal directly. Finally, as the relationship deepens, more and more issues or ways of cooperating are typically found.[30]

Nor are subcontractors necessarily worse off than large corporations in terms of business results. Statistically, the average profit among small-scale manufacturers has always been higher than that of large-scale manufacturers. And these figures probably understate the real status of small-scale firms. From the latter half of the period of rapid growth onward, smaller firms were much more leniently treated in tax terms, because the conservative government was fearful of being politically abandoned by owners and workers of the small firms, voters essential to the Liberal Democratic Party's electoral majority. The effective profit rates of smaller firms are almost certainly higher than their reported earnings. It is also true, however, that both the variance of profitability and the bankruptcy rates have been much higher among small-scale manufacturers than among large firms.

From the viewpoint of the owners of a small enterprise, furthermore, independence is an important value and motivation that goes beyond simple profit calculations. In fact, most workers in small-scale Japanese firms dream of starting their own businesses to capitalize on their accumulated technological know-how. In order to realize this dream, a would-be owner often asks for help from his employer and tries to utilize various human connections he has built up in the course of his experience as a worker. The employer may have mixed feelings about this, but very often he helps his former employee gain independence. This can be interpreted as a way of compensating the employee for his service to the employer. The relationship thus continues, with the former employer retaining some influence over the new enterprise. His social prestige and influence are enhanced and he has gained a subcontractor, while the new entrepreneur begins with a reliable customer base and some insurance against risk in the form of a patron. This practice has a long historical tradition, called *noren wake* (the splitting or sharing of a firm's goodwill), going back to the Tokugawa period. Generated in this manner, the mode of social exchange is found everywhere in the world of small manufacturing. Small firms can survive only in the nexus of human relations, and even when some become large firms, they tend to retain the core of that business culture. As Hugh Patrick and Thomas Rohlen have emphasized, the most important capital to small-scale firms is human relationships.[31]

We must ask, however, how long this pattern will continue in the Japanese economy. The elaborate subcontractor system is likely to be weakened, not, as some would argue, with the large swallowing the small, but with the small gaining greater autonomy. For one thing, financing has become increasingly easy for small-scale firms owing to an oversupply of capital in the past decade. Also, the balance of technological strength is shifting, with subcontractors strengthening their capacities for independent innovation. Some of the more successful small-scale firms are thus gaining greater overall independence, diversifying their customer base, exporting directly overseas, developing their own technologies, and, in short, shifting out of a dependent subcontractor status. In the manufacturing sector, small firms as a whole seem to be doing as well as large corporations. Notable here is the fact that the latter are bound by the implicit employment rule they committed themselves to in the period of postwar growth, whereas for small firms (free of unions) no such binding arrangement with employees exists.

Turning to the agricultural sector, we should note first that its prosperity hinges on whether the government continues its agricultural
protectionism in the face of increasing external pressure and the gradually rising discontent of Japanese consumers with high prices for farm
products. The "political" exchange relationship between politicians and
voters in rural areas will play a key role in determining the outcome. In
all likelihood, Japan's minuscule farms will have to be drastically restructured, not simply because politicians will shift their policy focus
toward nonfarming constituencies, but also because members of the
younger generation are unwilling to take over their parents' farms.

The future of small firms in the distribution and service sectors depends most heavily on tax reform. Under current tax practice, these
firms, including small shopkeepers, are enjoying something close to
virtual tax exemption. In April 1989, a new tax reform was put into
effect, but it carefully gave considerable leeway to small shopkeepers
and firms. Great political turmoil was the result. The opposition parties
gained in popularity by attacking the measure, and the Liberal Democratic Party suffered a severe setback in the House of Councilors in the
June 1989 elections. No one can forecast the rate at which the LDP will
change its orientation away from small farmers and businesses, but
clearly there is not only international pressure to do so but much domestic pressure as well. Foreign governments have successfully complained about governmental limits on large-scale retailing, and the price
support subsidies for Japan's rice farmers have been substantially lowered. Finally, the growing labor shortage and wage increases ahead in
the 1990s will put small businesses at a serious disadvantage compared
to the more efficient larger firms.

Proportionally, small-scale businesses are likely to decline and the role
of social exchange is thus also likely to recede gradually in the future.
Although new types of small service businesses will certainly appear, it
is difficult to imagine what conditions might arise that would encourage
enough new small-scale entrepreneurship to counterbalance the negative forces we have been discussing. Lastly, the social ties between small
shops and their customers will also gradually weaken as urban neighborhoods become more impersonal. In sum, Japan may remain a country
of small firms when compared to most other industrial countries because
of its strong tradition of social exchange in face-to-face economic relationships, yet this feature will be less conspicuous in the future.

Summary: The Implications of the Three Cases

The above three examples far from exhaust the possibilities for illustrating the importance of social-exchange relationships in the postwar

Japanese political economy. An analysis of the relationship between the ruling party and the bureaucracy would certainly reveal close parallels with what we have been discussing, since the LDP and elite bureaucrats engage in much informal dealing based on social exchange. The corporate groupings known as *keiretsu* also fit our social-exchange framework, although economists have substantiated that they did not play a leading role in Japan's rapid growth. For the purposes of this essay, however, the three cases we have considered in some detail should be sufficient to illustrate the nature and possibilities of cooperation in a social-exchange mode, as well as to show the limits of such relationships when conditions are not favorable.

Particularly notable at this point is the fact that from the perspective of outsiders (domestic and international), all of the relationships we have listed as fitting the social-exchange mode are problematic, because they are exclusive in nature. They do not operate according to the ideals of market transactions. Economic exchange is an open system, whereas social exchange is a closed one. International outsiders have made this point frequently and with growing intensity, and their position hardly needs further elucidation. What, however, about Japanese "outsiders" in Japan? There is little evidence of much public complaint in the postwar period from "outside" groups like consumers, and outside political parties and religious groups appear to have organized their own exclusive collectives. The evidence points to a near-universal orientation toward building exclusive ties of one's own as the best avenue to security in the face of discrimination. "If you can't beat them, copy them" is the psychology that has prevailed with virtually all firms, large and small, actively striving to develop as many ties of the social-exchange type with banks, customers, and the government as possible. Failure to do so has almost inevitably meant that in difficult times the firm has had no loyal friends willing to share its risks. International markets have also served a particular function in this regard, allowing some firms that are relative outsiders (Sony and Honda come to mind) to expand despite the difficulties they have faced in the domestic market. The exclusiveness arising from social-exchange building has not been limited to elite groups or to only large actors for this reason, but extends to all levels of the political economy and even to relations among protest groups themselves. We have been arguing that this tightly knit world of relational transacting is changing, and yet it is also important to point out that it is certain to change slowly, for it is indeed a central underlying feature of the Japanese political economy. The difficulty in acknowledging this so far has been both a theoretical problem of definitions and neoclassical assumptions and a problem of discerning the informal patterns that operate in interface areas.

Contrary to neoclassical economic expectations, furthermore, relationships of the social-exchange type can, under certain circumstances be quite efficient, as in the case of subcontracting in Japanese manufacturing. Our point is not that they are inherently efficient—Japanese agriculture and retailing certainly show that they are not—but that they can be efficient in certain circumstances. Even under positive economic conditions, the actual construction of effective relations of the social-exchange type is far from automatic. In this regard, the extensive historical foundation (social and cultural tendencies to this mode of dealing) in Japan cannot be ignored for comparative purposes.

We have argued that a fundamental distinguishing characteristic of the postwar Japanese economy has been the centrality of such cooperative relationships to certain economic activities. A particular cultural legacy and the favorable postwar socioeconomic environment were both necessary for this mode of social exchange to penetrate so significantly into the economic sphere of society. This argument is one that challenges existing theories reliant on only one or the other of these factors to explain the Japanese case. Since we see the special qualities of the Japanese management system, Japanese industrial policy, and the vitality of small-scale suppliers as the products of a fortuitous combination of economic and cultural conditions, our predictions about the future must also take both into account. Specifically, despite the continuation of many aspects of cultural tradition in Japanese society in general (however varied and dynamic), we see considerable change in the economic sphere, specifically, a decline of the social-exchange mode as the economic environment enters a new, more volatile phase. The ethos of social exchange will remain common to many aspects of personal relations and will thus be potentially available to the economic sphere, but its utility will, as a rule, decline.

Culture may shape the social response to economic circumstances, but the opposite is also true. The crucial question may actually be: How will the new economic environment reshape Japanese culture? Let us note here that the essence of the patterns of human relations in postwar Japan that we have described does not lie in any singular organizational form or its attributes. Nor did those patterns simply replicate traditional forms such as the *ie* (household), *mura* (village), and *noren wake* (merchant household subdivision). Postwar economic interactions in Japan are better understood as the adaptive result of a process of fitting a generalized traditional mode of social exchange to various relational situations in the modern economic sphere. The cooperation thus made possible became the answer to various problems of economic organization and development in the postwar Japanese context. Compared to the prewar period, Japanese postwar organizational culture might be characterized by a preference for (or tendency toward) informal and semi-autonomous social relations as opposed to formal, hierarchical ones. For example, prewar conglomerates were more hierarchical than the large corporations or informal trade associations of postwar Japan. Within the postwar Japanese corporation, furthermore, workers have been much less stratified and the distinction between white collar and blue collar has been blurred. Given the homogenizing effects of high mass consumption on the Japanese public, this trend of decreasing formality and weakening hierarchy will continue. One might say that the egalitarian *mura* pattern is superseding the more hierarchical *ie* one. As one symbolic example, the authoritarian/paternalistic father image has decisively weakened in various postwar Japanese groups, including the family itself. This trend is part of what Yasusuke Murakami once called "new middle mass phenomena."[32] Indeed, Japanese organizational culture seems to show signs of continual evolution in this direction.

This does not mean, however, that the Japanese are heading for Western-style individualism. The current Japanese situation is more paradoxical, or at least contrary to the typical sociopsychological assumptions about the dynamic of industrial society offered, for example, by Abraham Maslow.[33] There used to be an argument that the Japanese, particularly the younger generation, would release themselves from a sociocentric condition (defined by group and cooperative ties) and become more self-assertive, or, in Maslow's terms, more prone to "self-actualization," once Japanese society achieved material affluence. Contrary to this forecast, the newly achieved affluence tends to make the Japanese more, rather than less, interested in the elaboration of the human nexus, at least in the private sphere. Examples are numerous. The custom of gift exchange is growing beyond the old rules in terms of both its range and expense (specification of persons and objects). Wedding parties are becoming more and more a family-to-family matter and increasingly lavish and conspicuous. *Fashionable* and *trendy* were the catchwords of the youth consumption culture of the 1980s. In consumptive activities, a new mode of enriched and conspicuous social exchange seems to be appearing. During the period of rapid economic growth, social exchange was an instrument to upgrade long-term economic efficiency in workplaces, firms, business associations, industries, and so forth. Now, with material affluence, the Japanese orientation toward the human nexus seems to be focusing more and more on private, psychological, and consumptive domains. Thus, it appears that personal- or private-sphere social exchange is gradually eclipsing in importance those patterns we have been discussing for the economic sphere. At least individual attention is being drawn in such a direction.

Clearly, the mode of social exchange is pertinent to the current pattern of technological innovation, since innovation can now no longer be a one-man project, but must be a team effort among many. This point is an important exception to our general interpretation that the role of social exchange is weakening in the Japanese economy. Some have also argued that the coming of an "information society" will encourage—and be encouraged by—the patterns of human-nexus orientations. (See the essays by Shumpei Kumon and Ken-ichi Imai in this volume.) This second argument suggests that "twenty-first-century capitalism" tends to be less individualistic, in the sense that "information networks" bring people into a broader pattern of interdependence and linkage. Such conjectures may include considerable truth, but information networks also allow for new forms of autonomy and thus (at least) expressive individualism.

But no society changes overnight. In this volatile new era, the manufacturing systems of large Japanese firms are still crucial to the issue of how the postwar organizational tradition will be adapted to frontier technologies and research efforts. At least for some time, Japanese manufacturing corporations will remain dominant in the political economy. Japan's affluence and status as an economic "superpower" depend heavily upon their performance, and high-tech R & D will rely mostly on the diversification efforts of these giants in the absence of new entrants. Technological and informational innovation must still arise from a matrix of existing culture, mundane commitments, and institutional relations that reflect past efficiency and, concommitantly, present inertia.

In the international sphere, the same big corporations will also be the main actors representing the Japanese economy. They will not only export in vast amounts, but also control a huge volume of overseas investment. They are in many respects multinational corporations and must become more so. The liberalization of Japanese domestic markets also depends crucially on their behavior, since how they procure components and protect their powerful domestic sales networks will determine much of the future "openness" of the economy. They are likely to abandon some of their well-developed networks with other Japanese firms, particularly their subcontractors, in exchange for foreign partnerships and foreign sources of components, technologies, and overseas distribution. Thus, they will have to reexamine the basic structure and culture of their organizations if they are to survive their own multinationalization. They will also have to adapt flexibly to other types of business cultures represented in their overseas factories or joint ventures. As with all multinationals, Japanese business culture will have to become naturalized in each society where Japanese investment goes.

This will force Japanese multinationals to internationalize at home (e.g., place non-Japanese top executives among their managing directors).

Large-scale Japanese corporations have been a model of postwar socioeconomic success. Their organizations have come to symbolize the late-twentieth-century cooperative mode of production. Employment in a large firm has been the ideal for the average Japanese. But these giants have come to a major crossroads. Will they adapt their organizational culture to the new tasks of innovation, multinationalization, and liberalization? Or will they become devoted primarily to various forms of security out of concern for the existing system of social relations? The close symbiosis of patrons and clients is at issue. The various government ministries especially are facing a hard choice: Should they become effective catalysts for international adaptation or remain guardians of domestic vested interests? The primary issue is obvious: Can the Japanese mode of social exchange, with its tendencies to greater relational exclusiveness and security, adapt once again to new environmental challenges requiring that existing relationships be revitalized, transformed, and, in some cases, destroyed? This is not a choice that can be avoided. Nor is it one for which easy answers exist. Adaptation within the Japanese cultural context, but away from the social-exchange patterns of the postwar era, should be expected of those firms and ministries that will lead the nation in the coming decades.

Even if the response to these challenges turns out to be largely conservative, the Japanese postwar experience will stand out as a major accomplishment in the history of capitalism. The complete dominance of economic exchange appears to most people to be undesirable. It presupposes a process of "homogenized quantification" that eliminates many basic human values deriving from social interaction, and it drains society of any but material satisfactions. An ideal economy is not exclusively a market economy. To the degree that social exchange can complement economic exchange, it is a general benefit. The rub is its incompatibility with an international liberal trading order. Social exchange should be seen, not as an anachronistic (or traditional) mode, but as one of the keys to a future society that is both efficient and satisfying. It is also clear that this complementarity will have to take a less restrictive form in the future if the liberal world order is to be maintained.

Part II

The J Firm and Networking

Shumpei Kumon

Japan as a Network Society

The period of particularly high growth in the Japanese economy ended in the early 1970s. However, Japan has since weathered the two oil shocks of the 1970s and the "high-yen shock" of the late 1980s, and today its economy plays an increasingly important role in the global economy. Moreover, similar economic success stories are evident in Japan's Asian neighbors, the newly industrializing economies (NIEs).

At times, the success of Japan and the Asian NIEs has been attributed not only to their politico-economic systems but also to their cultural uniqueness. This has led to the view that, to deal effectively with Japan and the NIEs, these nations' trading partners must make changes in their foreign policy, as well as in the international economic order, and even to arguments for reevaluating their own culture itself and changing or abandoning at least part of it.[1] Some argue, however, that the quality that has brought prosperity to Japan and the NIEs is not unique to Asia but, rather, has a universal character that can be nurtured in other regions: nations should seriously study the success of this region, particularly that of Japan, and learn from it.[2]

Before any meaningful attempt can be made to reach conclusions in this debate, however, the following points require clarification:

1. What is the nature of the Japanese politico-economic system? How is it similar to or different from systems in the industrial nations of the West or in the Asian NIEs?

2. What are the causes (geographical, international, historical, cultural, or policy-related) of the special features of the Japanese system? How will this situation change in the future? If it becomes necessary to change course, how can that be done?

3. If the Japanese politico-economic system is in fact significantly different from those in the advanced Western nations, what sort of international order would be satisfactory to both Japan and the West?

Will internal changes be necessary to achieve such an international order, and, if so, what sort of changes?

4. What models or methods of analysis in social science will be most effective in grappling with these problems?

As readers of this series know, JPERC research tries to elucidate exactly such questions as these. From the viewpoint of social science, we are particularly concerned here with issues 1 and 4 above. The arguments of Karel van Wolferen and Stephen Krasner reveal the perception that neither the hierarchical organizations model nor the market model, both standard tools in social science, exactly fit the Japanese case; that is, neither the rules governing markets nor behavioral norms inferred from hierarchical organizations produce the desired results when applied to Japan.[3]

No general theoretical model can be expected to exactly fit an actual society. Even theories and models formulated with Western societies in mind may very well be inadequate for those societies once they or their constituent entities start to undergo change (as, for example, in the spread of the "alternative organizations" or "networking" movements in the United States in recent years).[4] It would be even more ridiculous to expect a Western model to fit the Japanese "muddle."[5]

Of course, when one particular theoretical model yields poor results in comparing different societies, it is the task of researchers to construct models that will explain those societies. The "network model" I present later in this chapter is precisely one such attempt. However, at the same time, researchers must construct a model at a higher order of abstraction and with a greater degree of universality by which the individual models can in turn be compared. Otherwise the comparison of models, much less the comparison of societies, will be meaningless.[6]

The Network Approach

Conspicuous in Japanese studies in recent years is a trend toward searching out new concepts and theoretical models in place of those in standard use in the social sciences. One in particular has been the concept of the network. Examples abound even among works by contributors to this volume.

Several years ago Daniel Okimoto coined the phrase *network state* to characterize the relationship between the public and private sectors in Japan.[7] This approach differs from market-oriented models in its emphasis on the mutual interdependence of government and private industry. And in its portrayal of an exchange of information among equals, rather than a more hierarchical relationship in which the government hands down orders to private industry, Okimoto's approach also differs from the "developmental state" model of Chalmers Johnson. Okimoto argues that "the state's role in Japan is to conduct by bringing out the best in others, not forcing musicians in the orchestra to play state compositions. Indeed, if one uses musical metaphors, the most appropriate may not be that of an orchestra conductor but that of a lead piano in a jazz ensemble; all instruments in the ensemble adapt, improvise, blend, harmonize with each other (instead of being directed by a single conductor)."[8]

In his essay in this volume, Ken-ichi Imai proposes using the generic term *corporate networks* to characterize the industrial organizations and connections between business firms in modern Japan. Thus, in Japan, the prewar *zaibatsu* system, an early form of the corporate network, was transformed in the postwar period into the system of business groups (as in the Mitsubishi group). This system is still evolving, leading to what Imai suggests calling a "network [in his narrowest sense] industrial organization," characterized by loose, nonhierarchical ties between relatively small business units based on the sharing of information.

Thomas Lifson's essay analyzes what he terms the *administrative network* in Japanese firms, namely, "a set of relationships existing among managers that enables them to contract with one another for the sharing of information, influence, or other resources without invoking formal organizational procedures." Administrative networks, he argues, serve as an informal but highly significant information-channeling process within (and between) large Japanese firms and are "most useful in situations with a high degree of change and uncertainty, and a high level of complexity and interdependence, where speed is important." Lifson believes that such networks are founded on reciprocity, a universal norm in human culture, but that they are particularly large-scale and prevalent in Japan and play a major role in Japanese-style management.

In the three examples cited above, the term *network* is used to characterize different levels and aspects of Japanese society: government-business relations, relations among business firms, and relations among departments or individuals within a firm. But to what extent is it possible to formulate a common definition of a "network" that will encompass all these, and to build a general theory based upon that? And in what way is a network different from either a hierarchical organization or a market?

As will be seen below, the concept of networks (hereafter referred to as the network approach) has been in use for some time in social science in the West, employed for the most part in the analysis of Western societies. However, it is only relatively recently that the network approach has been applied to analysis of Japanese society. Careful examination of its relevance to Japanese studies is therefore essential. Okimoto and Lifson have asserted that networks are particularly useful for analyzing the Japanese society of today, and Imai argues that they can be used to predict future changes in Japanese society. If such claims are valid, we are faced with the question of why that should be the case. In particular, what definition of *network* and what theoretical models would be most fruitful? And exactly what new knowledge will they afford us?

In this essay I have sought answers to these questions. Although I have not been able to answer them fully and completely, I hope that readers will nevertheless find some value in my efforts in this regard.

A Network as a Physico-Mathematical Concept

As a scientific term, *network* is given a rigorous physico-mathematical definition.[9]

Avoiding mathematical rigor, suppose there is a set of entities (say, cities), each connected by a certain relation (say, by highways) to others. If one can further define a set of variables with their domains in such a relation (and in some cases also in the entities), say, quantity of traffic between cities and population of cities, then one obtains a network in a physico-mathematical sense. An electrical circuit is a typical example of such a network, while a group of people connected through channels of communication is another example.

Obviously, such a physico-mathematical definition of a network is very broad and can be applied to an extremely wide range of empirical objects. In this sense, not only genuinely physical systems but almost all social systems—be they markets, organizations, or the more complex systems these comprise—can be regarded as networks. Such an approach could doubtless be adopted immediately and widely in social scientific analysis, not an insignificant point. However, it will clearly be insufficient for defining and analyzing a social system that is neither a market nor an organization.

How then should the concept of networks be dealt with in the social sciences?

The Network in Social Science

The network approach, in combination with social-exchange theory or role theory, has been widely applied in the social sciences—in sociology, anthropology, social psychology, human geography, and political science. Those applications range from large-scale social systems composed of multiple organizations to informal interpersonal connections within organizations.[10]

Generally speaking, the network concept spread in anthropology and sociology as the focus of research shifted from internal relations in relatively small-scale social systems, such as families and communities, to the relations tying these small-scale systems to their environment or to similar systems and, further, to the larger-scale, complex (less structured) societies that encompass such relations. I think such changes in viewpoint are quite relevant. The problem, however, is that such social relations are generally called "networks," which in turn have been defined as the "totality of all the units connected by a certain type of relationship."[11] This is almost identical to what I have called a physico-mathematical definition of a network and is obviously too broad a definition to be useful, because almost all social relations, including market, organization, family, and community, can belong to networks according to this definition. However, it seems to me that what those sociologists and anthropologists have really been interested in studying are different types of social relations, as well as different social systems, either those of small groups (families or communities) or formal organizations. At the same time, these different social relations must not be those found in marketplaces—in other words, they are not those that economists have specialized in analyzing. If so, there must be a better, more specific way of characterizing such relations and the social systems composed of them.

A somewhat different approach has been taken by another group of scholars. They concentrate on the analysis of communication networks, consisting of "interconnected individuals who are linked by patterned flows of information," and regard communication, very aptly, not as "a linear, one-way act," but as "a convergent process . . . in which the participants create and share information with one another in order to reach a mutual understanding."[12] Thus they virtually treat a communication network as a social system, with "communication links," not "individuals," as the units of analysis, though they do not distinguish it from different types of social systems.

At any rate, with these new developments in the social sciences in mind, it is not difficult to understand why this network approach began to attract the attention of Japan scholars. If, as some argue, the traditional theories of organizations and markets have shown themselves to be inadequate for the analysis of Japanese society, we shall have to look for other theories that better fit Japanese reality. And if the "network" approach provides a promising new approach in social science, it may be useful for Japan studies, too.

In what follows, I want, first, to present a new, narrower definition of a network as a social system different from an organization or a market, and, second, to study Japanese society from the new viewpoint of networks. Because terms such as *value*, *power*, and *organization* carry different meanings in the social and physical sciences, I think it should be permissible to adopt the same convention with respect to *network* as a term used in both areas of science. I would like here to formulate a social-science definition of a network, which must inevitably be placed within a "context." With a general conceptual and theoretical framework of social systems, one can characterize a network in contrast to other generic types of social systems. Let me therefore first present, as simply as possible, my framework for social systems in general.

Actors and Social Systems

A "society" is an entity composed of the totality of the interactions among its constituent elements—that is, among individuals and groups. In contrast, a "social system" is, in my thinking, a conceptual model for analysis of the empirical entity "society." The specific point of view I want to adopt here regards a society as a system having "actors" as its main elements. By the term *actors*, I refer to a conceptual model constructed by focusing on certain traits of individuals and groups as components of society. Those traits are specific qualities those individuals and groups possess beyond the mere fact of being physical entities or living creatures. That is, they refer to the fact that individuals and groups have the capability to engage in subjectively purposeful behavior comprising the following four aspects: (1) they think and communicate by operating ideas and concepts, both verbally and nonverbally; (2) they mentally perceive and evaluate the world—namely, themselves and the surrounding environment; (3) they plan to and actually use various physical means to act upon the world for the purpose of attaining certain goals they have chosen; and (4) they enjoy (or accept) what they have achieved (or failed to achieve) in the world (see Figure 1). Thus an *actor* is an entity that *acts*—namely, seeks goals subjectively.[13] But the state of the goals involved is determined not solely by the actor's own acts but as a joint outcome of those acts and other actions originating in the *environment*, both social (other actors) and natural (non-actors).

An act involves the choice and use of means on the basis of consciously purposeful mental activities (information-processing), as well as performing the consequent physical actions—namely, use of means. In particular, *economic acts* are those whose direct goal is the acquisition and management of the means themselves. Economic acts, as will be discussed later, constitute one of the three main types of acts; the other two types are cultural and political acts.

Even while submitting to many environmental constraints, an actor still retains considerable freedom to act, or at least feels this to be the case. In the end, of course, the actor must make choices and accept the

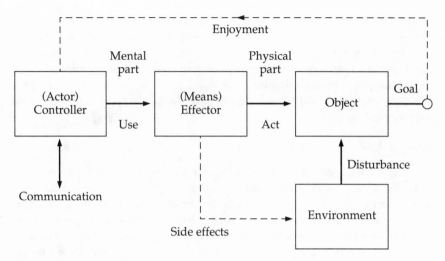

Fig. 1. The actor and his acts.

consequences. At the same time, however, there is no necessity for an actor always to act in complete isolation and independence from other actors. One can fully imagine actors voluntarily sharing information and jointly evaluating and deciding on an act—and carrying it out together as well, either jointly or separately, but in a coordinated fashion. Or perhaps certain actors might even give up a measure of their freedom to act and follow the lead or orders of other actors in particular matters. At any rate, the fact that actors can decide from moment to moment which particular acts to perform would indicate that criteria for such decisions must exist within individual actors or groups of actors. In this context, the "worldview" or "sense of values" of an actor can be regarded as constituting such a set of criteria for decision making.[14]

If we use the term *culture* to describe those traits distinguishing an actor (or group of actors) from other actors, then culture includes:

1. Traits of the actor's knowledge as defined above (conceptual framework and images)

2. Traits involving the acts of the actor (such as the decisions he or she makes, the means used, and the goals set)

3. Traits of the ways he or she establishes (or reestablishes) and maintains status as an actor

For present purposes, however, it will be more useful to define culture more narrowly so that it is made up only of the basic principles or criteria of choice that lie behind the emergence of the three abovementioned kinds of traits;[15] that is, it encompasses the factors, the most fundamental knowledge in other words, that unconsciously influence an actor's conscious mental and physical activities. Actors' worldviews and values are precisely culture in this sense. Consequently, when used hereafter, *culture* is meant in this narrower sense—as the worldviews/values of an actor (or group of actors), which can be divided into principles for interpretation/evaluation, decision making, carrying out acts, and (re)organizing oneself.[16]

Mutual Acts

Next let us consider mutual relations among actors by way of their acts. Imagine a world in which there are multiple actors whose acts exert some sort of effect, physical and/or informational, upon the goal states of other actors; in other words, actors help or hinder each other not only in their mental activities but also in the achievement of their respective goals. Let us then use the term *mutual act* for an act performed by an actor in conscious awareness of its external effect on other actors. Mutual acts for the direct purpose of controlling the acts of other actors (to prompt, cut off, maintain, or stop their acts) can be called *political acts*, and *communication* is a series of mutual acts performed for the purpose of mutually sharing knowledge among actors through exchanges of information, particularly symbols. Communication by which actors seek to share, develop, and maintain a common "culture" among themselves can be called *cultural acts*.[17]

We can also classify mutual acts according to whether their intended effect is to improve or worsen the degree to which other actors enjoy their goals (hereafter called *states of others*). Thus, an act intended to improve the states of others can be called *cooperation*; an act intended to worsen the states of others can be called *attack*.

Political acts effected through communication can be divided into *demands* and *negotiations*. Demands by one actor are specifications of what acts or states other actors should or should not perform or seek or not seek to achieve. If an actor accepts a demand without question, then the demander can be said to have *influence* over the demandee.

Negotiations are demands with conditions. They can be divided into three ideal types: (1) *threat*, or conveying the intention of attack if a demand is not met; (2) *exchange*, or conveying the intention of cooperation if a demand is met; and (3) *consensus*, or mutual understanding, on the basis of identification between the actors that following the course of acts mutually agreed upon will lead to improvement in the state of each actor.[18]

Other political acts do not involve direct demands or proposals. The political act of forcing others, ignoring their actorship, to behave so as to satisfy the actor is *coercion*. *Inducement*, on the other hand, consists of

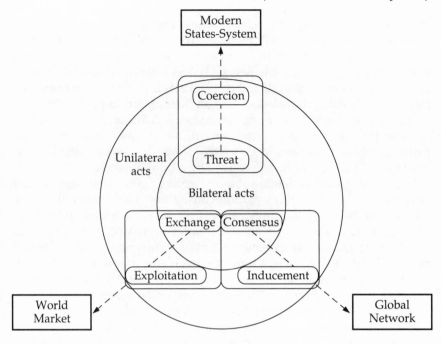

Fig. 2. Types of mutual acts and social systems.

providing certain environmental conditions for others, admitting their actorship, in the expectation that these will eventually lead them to choose a desired act. *Exploitation* refers to gaining temporary freedom for one's act by catching others off guard.

Of these six types of political acts, coercion has some affinity with threat, as does exploitation with exchange, and inducement with consensus. That is, attack, an indispensable condition for threat, is akin to coercion. Participants in an exchange tend to doubt the effectiveness of cooperation promised by others. In other words, they are frequently, and justly, afraid of being cheated and exploited by their exchange partners. Similarly, if one cannot fully trust others, it is not easy to distinguish a process of joint consensus formation from inducement by one or another of the parties (as, for example, informing others that a certain stock should soon increase in value in the hope of inducing them to buy that stock). Thus political acts can conveniently be grouped into three pairs: threat/coercion, exchange/exploitation, and consensus/inducement (see Figure 2).

A social system may be defined as a whole composed of a number of actors sharing the same culture and interconnected subjectively and/or objectively through constant, patterned, and regular mutual acts.

The meaning of the terms *actor, culture,* and *mutual acts* should now be clear. No explanation will be necessary for the term *constant* either. *Patterned* refers to the fact that most of an actor's individual acts are not unique but are patterned into several types. (Our classification above of acts into economic, political, and cultural acts is just one such example.) *Regular* implies that the effect of acts on their objects is predictable with a fair degree of accuracy. *Interconnected subjectively* implies that actors, the constituent parts of a social system, are themselves aware of the existence of such a whole, while *interconnected objectively* implies that the existence of such a whole is perceived by a third observer.

In a social system as defined above, members' acts will be constrained by various social as well as natural constraints. They "share the same culture" in the sense that they possess similar worldviews and values. Both as a basis for and as an outcome of "constant, patterned, and regular mutual acts," an extensive set of patterned rights and duties will be established there, constituting the main framework for social constraints. Let me, then, use the term *social order* to refer to the set of social constraints placed on mutual acts in a given social system.

It is possible to classify social systems into several types according to various criteria. For example, we can use as one such criterion the above groupings of political acts into three basic pairs. That is to say, depending on what particular group of political acts occupies the dominant position in the system, we have: (1) the threat/coercion-oriented type, (2) the exchange/exploitation-oriented type, and (3) the consensus/inducement-oriented type.

There are, of course, other ways of classifying social systems. One way is by looking at whether or not a given social system can itself be regarded as an actor. If a social system can also be regarded as an actor, it will be called a *complex actor* (or an *organization*) and, if not, a *societal system*. In this sense, a complex actor can be viewed as a supra-actor made up of other (sometimes themselves complex) sub-actors.[19]

Based on this conceptual differentiation of actors, we can introduce a partial ordering of the constituent actors of a social system according to whether they are sub-actors, supra-actors, or neither vis-à-vis one another. Let us call the top-ranking actor(s) in such a partial ordering the *state(s)*, and a social system having more than one state a *states-system*. A states-system is, by definition, a social system of the non-actor type.[20]

Complex Social Systems: Three Basic Types

Social systems made up of social systems (whether they are complex actors or non-actors) can be called *complex social systems*. In particular, let us pay attention to those complex societal systems of the non-actor type in which both the systems themselves and their constituent complex actors are organized according to the same orientation with respect to the dominant mutual acts. We can then consider complex social systems centered on (1) threat/coercion, (2) exchange/exploitation, or (3) consensus/inducement.[21] With this classificatory scheme in mind, let us take a reinterpretative look at the evolution of modern society in the West.

The first constituent organizations of a societal system to emerge in the modern West were based on the concept of all-inclusive rights of actorship (in other words, state sovereignty). They were complex actors freely employing political acts of the threat/coercion type: so-called *modern sovereign states*.[22] These modern sovereign states were the constituent organizations of the large-scale societal system that we can refer to as the *modern states-system*, in which "international law," such as the "law of war and peace," recognized as legitimate the sovereignty of each state and political acts of the threat/coercion-oriented type based on that sovereignty, while at the same time partially constraining them. That is to say, modern sovereign states and the modern states-system took, on the whole, the form of a complex social system of the threat/coercion-oriented type. In this type of societal system, the constituent organizations tended to make the guiding principle of their acts the acquisition of territory (colonies) and subjects as a means of maintaining comprehensive self-sufficiency and the autonomy of the state as an independent actor.

Thus, in the early modern era, modern sovereign states worked, often deliberately and artificially, to acquire new territory and colonies. At the same time, when they joined the states-system—that is, international society—they agreed to the possibility that their territory and colonies might be transferred to other states through war or diplomacy. That is to say, becoming a member of the states-system implied that they in fact gave up, though partially, their inviolability and indivisibility as sovereign states.

In contrast to this, *modern industrial firms*, which emerged out of the industrial revolution, are constituent organizations that treat property rights as inviolable and widely employ acts of the exchange/exploitation-oriented type. They emphasize this type not only in their mutual acts with other firms but also within themselves—that is, among their members. The *modern world market* is a societal system primarily composed of modern industrial firms.[23] This large-scale social system, while recognizing the social legitimacy of property ownership and rights to use, as well as the exchanges that take place on those grounds, has at the same time produced various rules of exchange, so that exercise of those rights is partially restricted. In this type of societal system, the constituent organizations tend to make it a guiding principle to own and use the means that help them to be effectively engaged in acts of the exchange/exploitation-oriented type.

Thus, modern industrial firms often deliberately and artificially produce such means as artifacts. And when they participate in the world market, they transform these artifacts into *commodities*. That is to say, entering the market implies agreeing to hand over to other actors, under certain conditions (say, that the price they set will be paid as compensation), their rights to own or to use those artifacts.

I suggest that, accompanied by both technological innovations (the so-called information revolution) and a change in people's consciousness (the emergence of a new form of self-consciousness that goes beyond individualism) that are ongoing today, still another type of societal system and its constituent organizations have been emerging. They make predominant use of consensus/inducement-oriented acts, based on information rights. I would like to use the terms *modern network organizations* to refer to this new type of constituent organization and *global network* for a large-scale societal system composed of them. In a global network, social legitimacy is granted to consensus/inducement-oriented acts, to information rights, and to the consequent obtaining and transmission of information/knowledge.[24] At the same time, various rules will be imposed on communication, such that the exercise of those information rights is partially restricted. In this type of societal system, the constituent organizations tend to make the guiding principle of their acts the creation and sharing of means (in this case, information and knowledge) that help them effectively engage in consensus/inducement-oriented acts.

Thus, modern network organizations often deliberately and artificially produce such means in the form of symbol information. And when they participate in the global network, they will convert this symbol information into *sharables*. That is, entering the global network implies agreeing to let other actors share information/knowledge under certain conditions (say, that the priority right concerning the shared piece of information/knowledge is guaranteed by its recipients).[25]

In today's world, we see both the states-system/modern sovereign states and the world market/modern industrial firms as real entities. But what about the global network/network organizations? In the United States many people have noticed, since the mid 1960s, the emergence of so-called "alternative" (nonhierarchical and democratic) organizations or networks, or of "Another America."[26] In more recent years, particularly as computer communication has spread all over the world, there has been a mushrooming of various sorts of network organizations, connected both internally and externally by computer communication channels. They are gradually forming what I have called the global network.[27]

A Network as a Social System

Let us generalize the previous discussion so that we may obtain a general definition of a network as a social system. I posit that a network as a generic social system is one in which, no matter whether it is a complex actor or a societal system, the major type of mutual acts is consensus/inducement-oriented. Networks are organized under the premise that information rights are legitimately established in some form or other and at the same time partially restricted within themselves. The main reasons for individual actors to join a network are to share useful information/knowledge with other members, to achieve better mutual understanding, and to develop a firm base for mutual trust that may eventually lead to collaboration to achieve actors' individual as well as collective goals.[28]

Networks in general can, then, be divided into two subcategories: (1) those that are simultaneously organizations, and (2) those that are not organizations—namely, those that are societal systems. Let us call the former *network organizations* and the latter *societal networks*. Thus, modern network organizations and the global network mentioned above are respectively concrete examples of network organizations and societal networks. Needless to say, however, they are not the only concrete examples of what I call networks here. For example, there used to be and still are many traditional network organizations and societal networks, though for the most part, say, in American business, or for that matter, all over the world, they remain informal.[29] As we shall see later, Japanese society can be characterized as a society in which such networks are ubiquitous, not only informally but also in a formally institutionalized form. But before we proceed to a discussion of networks in Japan, one theoretical point has to be clarified.

Here I am not contrasting a network directly to a market or to an organization, as a third major form of social system. To do so, I am afraid, is misleading in the sense that it leads to an interpretation of a network being neither an organization nor a market or being some mixture of both, making the network concept rather ambiguous.

To avoid such ambiguity, I have here introduced an alternative, two-dimensional classification of social systems, the first dimension being a dichotomy of organizations versus non-organizations (societal systems), and the second dimension being a trichotomy of threat/coercion-oriented, exchange/exploitation-oriented, and consensus/inducement-oriented systems. I adopt *network* as the generic name for consensus/

inducement-oriented social systems in general, which can therefore contain both organizations (namely, "network organizations") and non-organizations (namely, "societal networks") at the same time. In this classificatory scheme, *organization* (a complex actor, in other words) is the generic name for one category of social system in the first dimension, while *market* (particularly the modern world market) signifies a subcategory of societal (non-organization type) exchange/exploitation-oriented systems *and* systems of the consensus/inducement type. In this sense, it is not relevant, first of all, directly to compare an organization and a market as if they belonged to the same level of the categorical hierarchy of social systems.[30]

The Structure of Japanese Society

What do we find if we look at today's Japanese society, particularly its industrialized sector, from the social-systemic point of view developed in the previous section? The picture that emerges is that of a complex social system with a three-stratum structure of constituent social systems and individual actors:

1. A suprastratum composed of multiple layers of numerous networks, societal networks as well as network organizations, most of which are either formally or semi-formally institutionalized

2. A middle stratum composed of a number of what have been called *ie*-type organizations, the key social units of Japan since the medieval period

3. A substratum composed of people who share "contextualist" culture

Thus, depending on which stratum one focuses on, Japan can be characterized as either a network society, an *ie* society, or a contextualistic society. Let me explain more fully the meaning of each of the three strata, beginning with the last.

Japanese as Contextualists (Aidagara-shugi-sha)

Contrary to stereotype, most Japanese have a sense of individual psychological self; thus they are capable of behaving as actors, at least to a certain extent. But this "self" is strongly conditioned by a "contextualist" culture and frequently firmly "embedded" in group-oriented social relations, particularly *ie*-type organizations. This is not only objectively observed but is also subjectively recognized by most Japanese. It is in this sense that they can be characterized as "contextualists," not as mere "contextuals." I cannot here fully spell out all the components of the contextualist culture. Let me simply mention a few of its basic traits that I think to be congruent with social systems of the network type.[31]

In the first place, the Japanese tend to have a strong desire to identify themselves with others (other people or a supralevel social system), most probably based on the prototype of the mother-child relationship. Thus, on the one hand, they want, at least as much as their peers, to *amaeru*—namely, to be passively loved and identified/integrated with, and then to be allowed to depend on certain others they like, just as children do with their mothers. But, on the other hand, they also want to *sewa o yaku*—namely, to love actively and assimilate others and then to take care of them as nondiscriminately and equally as possible, just as a mother does her children.[32] Taken in part, this relationship is asymmetric, if not necessarily hierarchical. But, as a whole, it comprises a multilateral relationship of mutual dependence and caretaking in which one plays the role of a dependent on someone at one time, and the role of a caretaker for someone else at another time. This desire to identify with others and the sense of identity thus achieved, if satisfied to a sufficient degree, will form firm ground for effective communication and "networking" among them.[33]

Second, Japanese, like Mediterraneans, are "high context" communicators in E. T. Hall's sense. That is to say, a premise of their communication process is the preaccumulation of a large amount of commonly shared knowledge and information concerning the topic of communication and those with whom they communicate. This implies that a relatively small amount of new information is required for effective communication and networking.[34]

In addition, I should mention two more cultural traits: (1) most Japanese are "accommodators" to the environment in the sense that, when they perceive some disequilibrium in their relation with the environment and want to cope with it, they tend to change themselves rather than controlling or changing the environment;[35] and (2) in doing so, they tend to adopt a "soft" style in Sherry Turkle's sense, or "situational logic" in Ruth Benedict's sense.[36]

Ie-*type Organizations*

Together with two other colleagues, I have argued that the single most important type of actor in Japan since the medieval period has been a complex actor called the *ie*-type organization.[37] As an organization with a functionally differentiated hierarchical system of roles, and in the sense that it regarded, particularly before industrialization, threat/coercion as its most important political act for survival and development, the *ie* resembles the modern sovereign state. At the same time, the *ie* resembles an "individual" in Western individualistic society in that it shares certain individualistic values such as independence, autonomy, and self-sufficiency. In fact, *ie*-type organizations could be said to be more individualistic than Western individuals because they have often succeeded in practically rejecting formation of supralevel organizations other than those of a network type. That occurred especially conspicuously in the period after World War II, when they evolved into organizations engaging in industrial activities (grafting onto themselves some part of industrial civilization of Western origin).[38]

There was a period, however, when *ie*-type organizations were engaged mainly in wars against one another in a societal system similar to the modern states-system (the Warring States period from the late fifteenth century through the sixteenth century), and there have also been periods in which they coalesced, partly voluntarily and partly through coercion, into a supralevel, state-organized (in a homomorphic way) single giant *ie* (the Kamakura state formed in the late thirteenth century and the Tokugawa state established at the beginning of the seventeenth century) through a process we have termed "emulative expansion." From such a viewpoint, one may interpret the process of social evolution after the Meiji Restoration (1867) as an abortive attempt by the founders of the Restoration to disintegrate the constituent *ie*-type organizations (the *han* of daimyo) in order to form a huge, single, highly centralized *ie* with the emperor at its apex, as a partial replica of the modern sovereign state.

At the same, however, the new state also stimulated the development of highly independent, decentralized *ie*-type organizations at the level beneath the *han*. Not only the former warrior class, but also farmers, artisans, and merchants were allowed to organize their own *ie*, either separately or in coalescence. They were also encouraged to graft onto them the Western institutions of modern industry, governmental administration, and constitutional politics, which were gradually syncretized with the traditional form of *ie*-type organization, thus producing, among other things, so-called Japanese management. They then conspired, sometimes voluntarily and semi-formally, sometimes encouraged and/ or authorized by governmental bureaus, to form various kinds of network-type supra-organizations or societal systems, thus practically undermining the highly centralized system of rule of the modern sovereign state and replacing it with a conglomerate of networks.

Japan as a Network Society

No one will deny that Japanese society, viewed as a whole, is organized into a "state" (a complex actor with no supra-actor). However, Japan is more like a network organization, or even a societal network, than a modern sovereign state. Hence Daniel Okimoto's characterization of Japan as a "societal state" (see note 8). Many question Japan's status as a full-fledged sovereign state because it has maintained an asymmetrical, passively dependent type of alliance with the United States to assure its security. Externally, it has, by its constitution, renounced war as a means of solving international conflicts. Internally, it rarely uses legal coercion, let alone violence, as a form of regulatory command in its process of rule. At the same time, as John Haley explains in his essay in this volume, "the idea of legal rules being subject to private control over their application and enforcement" is alien not only to the Japanese government but also to the people themselves. Nevertheless, social integration and order are somehow maintained, not by the rule of law, argues Chie Nakane, but by a kind of dynamic regulatory relation operating among individuals and groups, comparable, in her image, to a starfish.[39]

At the same time, this "network state" overlaps with a nationwide societal network called Nihon, in which the mass media play the leading role in the process of consensus formation and inducement. In this sense, it would be appropriate to call Japan's mass media the most influential complex actors (of the network-organization type, or maybe even non-actors, in the sense of societal networks). I shall further discuss this aspect later.

This huge "network state" cum "societal network" is "vertically" divided, at its suprastratum, into a number of "worlds" (*kai*), such as the political, business, bureaucratic, educational, sports, and arts worlds, each of which is further divided into various subworlds. Thus, for example, the arts world is subdivided into the subworlds of movies, music, painting, and so on. These "worlds" are typical examples of societal networks, both in terms of the dominant type of mutual political act and of the motives of individuals (contextuals, to be more exact) in joining those networks. Moreover, these "worlds" or "subworlds" can be viewed as being composed of various kinds of network organizations. Some of those organizations consist solely of members (usually *ie*-type organizations) belonging to one and the same (sub)world. It also happens frequently that a network organization itself is composed of sub-level network organizations. Thus, for example, manufacturers of synthetic fibers form a network organization called the Association of Synthetic Fiber Manufacturers, which is a member of the Federation of Textile Industries, which, in turn, is a member of the Japan Federation of Economic Organizations (Keidanren), all of which are formally institutionalized corporations.[40]

Individual firms are also often members of a semi-formally organized transindustrial network organization called a "firm group" or "(horizontal) *keiretsu*," usually with a bank or trading company as the leader or the main "caretaker." thus, for example, Mitsubishi Rayon is a member of the Mitsubishi Group, and Toray is part of the Mitsui Group. Another example of a business network organization is the so-called vertical *keiretsu* composed of a big firm and its subsidiaries and/or subcontractors.

There also are a series of "transworld" network organizations, formally or semi-formally institutionalized, that connect individual industrial "worlds" to organizations belonging to other "worlds": political, mass media, academic, consumers' unions, and so on, mediated by concerned governmental offices. Their most representative form is that of legally established "councils" (*shingikai*) both on national and local levels. A council usually has a large number of subcouncils, sectional meetings, and small committees, each specializing in one particular area or problem. There are also less formal (not established by law) and thus "private" counseling groups or study groups for ministers, chiefs of bureaus, and so on, again with numerous subcommittees. The members of such organizations consist of former officials of concerned ministries; representatives of relevant industrial associations, labor unions, or consumer groups; and other learned or respected figures (scholars, journalists, etc.). The concerned government department acts as secretariat. These groups are typical network organizations in that they meet regularly, their members and the secretariat bringing in information to be shared by all. They use this information to obtain a common perception of present conditions surrounding them both at home and abroad, as well as to forecast future trends and to reach an overall consensus on how the public and private sectors in question should respond to environmental conditions, especially to their changes through enacting a new law, adopting a new policy, agreeing to engage in a certain type of act, and so on. The final conclusion of such joint discussion is usually confirmed in the form of a document (often called the "vision" for a certain industry). It is primarily the secretariat's role to provide basic information, conduct the backstage negotiations called *nemawashi*, and hammer out the draft of final conclusions, though the intervention of members at formal sessions and the testimony of outside persons at hearings are also important. Above all, statements (or silence) by full-fledged members of a council at its general meetings often convey symbolic implications about the success or failure in consensus formation.

However, the decisions of *shingikai* are not legally binding. Nor do their recommendations necessarily produce a new law or policy. In principle, whether or not to respect and act on those conclusions is entirely the prerogative of the individual members to determine. In more cases than not, however, members choose of their own "free will" to act in accordance with the decisions of the *shingikai*.[41]

Integration and Order in a Network Society

How, then, are a sufficient social integration and order maintained in a society composed of numerous overlapping networks? Let us first consider some of the traits of consensus/inducement processes in Japanese networks in general.

One conspicuous trait is that the consensus/inducement process tends to be based mainly on perceptions and evaluations that are commonly shared, or are thought to be commonly shared, throughout the network. In other words, individual and intentional attempts to persuade or manipulate other members do not play an important role in Japanese networks. Rather, all members make their best attempts to sense and accept, quite spontaneously, the perceptions, evaluations, and sentiments (in short, the *kūki*, or group sentiment) of the network as a whole,[42] and each seeks to agree with decisions and acts that naturally result from this *kūki* more ardently and actively than other members so as to occupy a higher position than others.[43]

Another conspicuous trait of networks in Japan is a tendency for consensus/inducement to be based on strong sentiments (likes and dislikes) about people, things, and circumstances, generated under the influence of value orientations rather than on the basis of precise factual recognition or reasoning. It is crucial that networks, particularly the nationwide societal network, Nihon, possess means of communication that allow efficient sharing of information and knowledge. During the modernization of Japan, the mass media played an indispensable role in the formation and maintenance of Nihon, paying particular attention to providing information about people's evaluation and sentiments (or morals in the broad sense). In other words, the strongest cohesive force for the societal network of Nihon has been the sharing of common feelings of joy, anger, sorrow, and pleasure.

Exemplifying this trait is a shared fantasy of Japanese: on New Year's Eve all the Nihonjin (that is, members of the societal network, Nihon) are envisaged as gathering with their families in front of their television sets or radios to listen to the annual popular song contest on the national broadcasting system, NHK, to laugh and cry simultaneously with all the others, experiencing a collective catharsis. Then, after watching other New Year celebrants in various parts of the archipelago, and even the planet, as the watch-night bell rings, they see off the old year and greet the new, all going at once to pay their first visit of the year to a nearby shrine or temple, without quite following the command or suggestion of anyone else.[44]

Another example is the way news is handled in Japan. For instance, the Japanese mass media tend to treat overseas news largely from the perspective of whether any Nihonjin are involved, or of how it will affect Nihon. In general, their emphasis is on the effect of the news in evoking specific common value judgments or sentiments, rather than on examining how factually true the news is or on analyzing its background (why and how a certain event occurred).[45]

The sharing of information and knowledge—about recognition and evaluation of facts, the setting of goals, and action to achieve those goals—is the prime concern of networks in general and network organizations in particular. As already pointed out, the largest societal network in Japan today (one that may largely exist only in people's minds) is Nihon, with the Nihonjin as its members. Conversely, we may redefine the Nihonjin as those individuals and groups who are recognized by the majority of the people living on the Japanese archipelago as the subjects and the objects of information-sharing in it.

It is often pointed out that the Japanese do not convey much information about themselves, especially information of the self-assertive kind. That is no doubt correct for communication outside their networks, and, in this sense, networks tend to be informationally closed to their environment.[46] Within Japanese networks, however, there is a vigorous process of gathering and sharing information, even though this may be mainly to promote each member's "synchronization and competition" with others.[47] Particularly conspicuous is the tendency to share information enthusiastically by discussing (or gossiping about) (1) the homogeneous traits shared by members (in other words, the shared "uniqueness" of members vis-à-vis outsiders),[48] and (2) the relative status and performance of other members in the network that differentiate individual members vis-à-vis their fellow members. The Japanese are also known for actively acquiring information from outside concerning matters they themselves are particularly interested in. We can include in this category evaluative information on the Japanese from outsiders.

The Political Traits of Japan's Network Organizations

So far, we have examined the traits of Japan's networks in general. What, then, about the traits of Japan's network organizations? To the extent that it is an organization (a complex actor), a network organization has to organize both its mental and its physical activities as a single collectivity. In particular, it must have ways to reach collective decisions. That is to say, it needs some arrangement to control itself, a political system that institutionalizes the structure of political acts in a complex actor, especially those of sub-actors vis-à-vis the complex actor itself. The sub-actors, either cooperatively or competitively, are involved in political acts to influence the decisions and acts of the complex actor as a whole. Like the economic system or the cultural system, the political system is, in this sense, one of the subsystems of the complex actor.

Generally speaking, one can conceive of various types of political systems. The distinction between a democratic system and an autocratic system is just one example. I shall introduce three dimensions to classify political systems here.

1. *The range of sub-actors who are allowed to participate in or influence the complex actor's decision making.* If only one sub-actor controls the complex actor's decision making, I shall call it an *autocratic system.* If most sub-actors can participate more or less equally, I shall call it a *democratic system,* though it goes without saying that there can be varying degrees of democratization. (Let us call those sub-actors who are allowed to participate in the process of collective decision making *qualified sub-actors.*)

2. *The way decisions are reached in systems having some degree of democracy.* If a decision cannot be made because of the opposition of just one of the qualified sub-actors, I shall call such a system a *unit-veto system.* If an effective decision can be made when a certain proportion—say, more than half, two-thirds, or three-fourths—of qualified sub-actors agree, I shall call such a system a *majority-rule system.*[49]

3. *The type and range of decisions a complex actor can make.* I shall call a political system in which, as a matter of principle, there is no particular limit on the type and range of decisions a *system of unlimited decision.* A political system that has restrictions on the type and range of decisions imposed by supra-actors or by cultural, religious, or ideological principles can be called a *system of limited decision.*

In terms of the three dimensions given above, Japan's network organizations tend, as an ideal at least, to aim at a fully democratic, unit-veto political system of unlimited decision. Let me cite just a few examples.

To most Japanese, especially after World War II, *democracy* has always meant, first of all, the right to become a qualified sub-actor with unit-veto power in an organization. Ryokichi Minobe, a progressive scholar and for many years the very popular governor of Tokyo, received public applause for often quoting the so-called "philosophy about a bridge" from the work of the French West Indian revolutionary Frantz Fanon to the effect that if anyone in a community opposes building a bridge, it should not be built, even if it would be useful to most other people.

In this sense, political power in Japan is above all the power of local autonomy, or the power to say "no" to others' intervention. Taichi Sakaiya, a well-known literary critic and a former MITI officer, observes:

If adjustment and reform of the parts of something is seen as more important than its overall reform or introduction of rapid progress in ideas, then inside an organization the opinions of those in charge of the parts will be valued more than those of the leaders of the whole organization. In other words, there is no need for strong leaders, since progress can be made through the piecemeal work of individuals. As a result there are no strong leaders worthy of being called dictators to be found in Japan. Instead there are tens of millions of power-holders. Thus, it is established practice that even division heads or chief clerks have veto power: "If one stakes one's job on absolute opposition, one can get things stopped."[50]

If there is unanimous consensus in a perfectly democratic system, can the complex actor then make decisions unlimitedly? Within the Japanese tradition, the answer seems to be, "Yes, of course." As was made abundantly clear during the Lockheed scandal in 1976, Japanese organizations, whether they are networks or *ie*-type organizations, tend to ignore, if not pressed to comply with them by the *kūki*, the laws and morality established in the name of supra-actors (the state, especially) or transcendental entities (such as God) that restrict the organizations' freedom of decision and action. There is a deep-rooted belief that as long as a unanimous and spontaneous decision is reached in a "democratic" organization, the organization should be allowed to do whatever it wants. Also, there is a tendency to distinguish between ethics that apply to acts within one's own organization and those that apply to the outside world.[51]

A political system like this may appear to be one that unjustly restricts the rights of the majority to control the collective decision-making process. That is to say, it may seem to be a system that places unfair importance on the rights of the minority. This is certainly why those in a position to govern or those who belong to the majority often lament the "lack of freedom" in Japanese society. Nevertheless, it does not at all mean that those in the minority fully enjoy their rights and freedom in any positive way. In such a system, almost everyone tends to end up complaining about the system's "tightness."

There is no guarantee, therefore, that a minority will always have veto power. In particular, if a minority is alienated from the collective decision-making process, its opinions and wishes, and sometimes even its very existence, are likely to be ignored or suppressed. That "unlimited" decision-making capability, which in fact is only the capability of qualified sub-actors who can achieve a consensus among themselves, can become quite dangerous if it manifests itself in dealings with an unqualified minority.

On the other hand, it is also obvious that, if complete unanimity is always required, a complex actor can lose its effective decision-making capability, resulting in functional paralysis. This danger increases with the actor's size. Therefore, even though each sub-actor seriously believes that unit-veto power should be guaranteed as a matter of principle (at least to himself), if he also agrees that the complex actor should not be completely paralyzed or disintegrated, then he will have to admit that unrestrained allowance of the unit veto must somehow be curbed. One ideological solution for this, I think, is the introduction of *wa* (harmony) as a countervailing principle to the unit veto, demanding that "egoistic" conduct by sub-actors be restrained for the good of the organization as a whole. One important role of a "caretaker" or a "mediator" in Japan's political system is to propagate and interpret this second principle in concrete terms, so as effectively to persuade the minority (in some cases the majority) to yield.[52]

The Paramarket for Goods and Services

In this attempt to characterize Japanese society, I have so far paid attention largely to *political acts*. However, there are at least two more basic types of mutual acts in a social system: *economic acts* and *cultural acts*. In today's Japan, a highly industrialized society, business firms, organizations specializing in economic acts, are the single most important group of actors. Therefore, we should take into account the additional point of view of the economic subsystem, the subsystem that deals with the appropriation and distribution of goods (means for acts) and services (acts done for you by others).

In this regard, Karl Polanyi's classification of different types of economic systems is highly suggestive. According to one summary of his views on this, "Polanyi has identified three general types of the social organization of economic activities under the heading forms of integration. These are: 'reciprocity, redistribution, and exchange.'" *Redistribution* "is derived from the actual physical movement of goods into a central place from which they are redistributed." However, "the 'centricity' of the redistributive pattern refers to the fact that the power to determine rights and obligations is located at an identifiable center, from which these are distributed through a matrix of formal rules and authority which order the movement of things between persons."[53] Thus, in our terms, redistribution is a subsystem within a complex actor (organization) which has its government (identifiable center).

If we turn now to *exchange*, "its characteristic motive is rational self interest. Its characteristic institution is the market, which is not to say that all markets fit the pattern. The self regulating or 'price-making' market of the modern West is the prototype of the exchange system."[54]

The central feature of *reciprocity*, Polanyi's third type of economic system, "is that the sanctions, the validation, for goods and person movements into and out of the economy, and the productive uses of the material stuff of the substantive economic process are to be found in some part of the societal structure, like the kinship system, which has a function and a rationale that is not necessarily independent of, but goes beyond that of its role in ordering the relations between persons in the economic process."[55] Reciprocity is thus similar to exchange insofar as it, too, is a subsystem embedded within a larger social system that determines economic relations. However, in the case of reciprocity, such determinations are not explicitly made by a clearly defined governmental function within a complex actor, but are, rather, made in accordance with "the behavioral norms of the particular social structure which rules in the given case."[56]

Polanyi wanted to emphasize, by way of such a theoretical construction, that economic decisions are not always made in a "self-regulating" way through the capitalist market mechanism developed in modern Western society. In other words, one can think of many other arrangements in which economic relations are embedded in other types of social systems.

I shall now attempt to incorporate Polanyi's conceptual framework into my own. Earlier I outlined three different types of complex social systems that emerged in the modern Western world: sovereign states/ states-system, industrial firms/world market, and network organizations/global network. We can view these as concrete examples of "the particular social structure which rules in a given case." Of these three, however, special attention should be given to the third pair and its rules for the distribution of goods and services.

I also defined *exchange* as a form of negotiation in which one party conveys its intention to cooperate if its request is met. Let me introduce here another kind of mutual act that is similar but not quite identical to exchange: cooperation that is given one-sidedly, multilaterally, and repeatedly, in return for support in the past or in anticipation of support in the future. Let us call this type of cooperation *reciprocation*. (In the present context, *multilateral* means that it is not necessary for the recipient of the cooperation and the provider of support to be one and the same other actor.) Reciprocation in this sense, however, can better be regarded not as a form of exchange but rather as a form of inducement (if it is made in anticipation of support from its recipient in the future), or an outcome of inducement (if it is made as repayment for past support). In other words, we can regard reciprocation as one important variant of mutual acts of the consensus/inducement type that can be widely used as economic acts in social systems of the network type to complement mutual acts for consensus-building.

In contrast to reciprocation, exchange (as defined above) is bilateral and either takes place at the same time (or same period of time) or at a time clearly agreed upon; it involves mutual acts that do not necessarily have to be repeated. Consequently, if we consider an economic (sub)system of the non-actor type that relies on reciprocation, rather than exchange, with respect to the social distribution of goods and services, we shall need some other term than *market* to conceptualize it most appropriately. In doing so, we should also regard such economic (sub)systems based on mutual acts of the consensus/inducement type as a kind of network. Let us call such economic systems *paramarkets*[57] and use the terms *para-commodities* for the goods and services supplied in a paramarket, in order to distinguish them from ordinary commodities (that is, the goods and services exchanged in markets).[58]

By taking out the paramarket as a subcategory of the network that specializes in economic acts, we can make the political nature of, so to speak, the "genuine" network even more evident: its fundamental raison d'être is in sharing information, achieving mutual understanding, and arriving at a consensus among its members through mutual acts of the consensus/inducement-oriented type. In particular, there is little reason for the network organization to distinguish itself from its political sub-system, because it is a political system par excellence.

Within social relations based on reciprocation, the notion of credit and debit (*kashi-kari*) is given important significance: *credit* refers to an actor's state of having not yet been repaid for his cooperation, while *debit* refers to his not yet having repaid support received from others. Of course, it is not always a simple matter to devise objective standards (that is, standards with which the majority of system members will agree) to measure exact amounts of credit and debit. Indeed, a large degree of subjectivity is inevitable in evaluating credit-debit relations.

In paramarkets, as in markets, the goods and services provided can include information goods and information services. But it is no exag-geration to say that paramarkets are better suited to the circulation of information goods than markets are, since, as is well known, such information goods can easily be copied by buyers, as well as by sellers. The rapid development of copying and telecommunications technology in recent years has made copying even easier. Once the possibility of resale (re-exchange) of copies is taken into consideration, it becomes extremely difficult to fix a price for information goods that can satisfy both parties in a bilateral transaction at one point in time. However, in a paramarket, the credit-debit relations of seller A and buyer B will not necessarily be damaged even if copies of a given piece of information are circulated to other parties. If buyer B finds out that seller A has sold the same information to buyer C, then B can simply reduce the amount of his debit toward A. Similarly, if B resells its copy to D, then B's debit toward A and A's credit toward B will increase. In fact, one of the key features of the paramarket is that it is not necessary to determine uniquely and ultimately the amount of credit-debit that the parties involved in reciprocation respectively have. Paramarkets have a large degree of flexibility in that such values can vary according to the parties involved and that they can change over the course of time as circumstances change.

Needless to say, commands and reports circulated within a hierarchical organization in accordance with the rules and procedures the organization itself has set, while information, do not constitute information goods subject to exchange in a market, or to reciprocation in a paramarket. There is thus no need to make payment for receiving commands, reports, or any other incidental materials (for example, expense allowances from above or goods produced in the factory). Neither does the receiver thereby incur a debit or credit. The same principle applies to information circulated within a network organization or a societal network. Since networks are social systems formed for the explicit purpose of sharing information, information shared within them according to the stipulated rules is not regarded as exchange or reciprocation in a market or paramarket. Such information also differs in nature from commands and reports.[59]

How does this theoretical analysis apply to today's Japan? I have been arguing that both network organizations and societal networks are widespread. Equally noteworthy is the widespread and complementary existence of reciprocation in the guise of market exchange among business firms or among firms and households, as well as the existence of the paramarket as the site of such reciprocation. In other words, a significantly large proportion of what seem to be market exchanges of goods and services in Japanese society is, I posit, actually characterized by a large element of reciprocation. It would probably be closest to the mark to regard such paramarkets as subsystems of networks in the sense in which I have defined them.

The Future of Network Society: Its Strengths and Weaknesses

There are at least two advantages to adopting a network point of view in the analysis of Japanese society. First, it provides a theoretical approach with universal applicability: there is, for example, nothing "uniquely Japanese" in the conceptual framework given in previous sections of this article. This makes comparison of Japanese and other societies more meaningful. In contrast, authors such as van Wolferen and Fallows have adopted what may be called a negative approach: they emphasize how contemporary Japan differs from the West, on the grounds that Japan *is not* quite a modern sovereign state in the Western mold, or that the Japanese market *is not* quite a classically free market. But then what *is* Japan? I believe we can take a more positive approach, in regarding

Japanese society as a whole, say, as a network/*ie*/contextualist society onto which institutions that originated in Western civilization—the modern sovereign state, industrial firms, and markets—have been grafted, giving rise to a gradual process of syncretism and, possibly, to a new evolution.

In fact, what I have described here as traits of Japan's social systems, especially networks, can be universal in the sense that similar social systems or similar traits do exist or are emerging in other societies, too. For instance, two recent personal experiences are revealing: in a U.S.–Japan joint seminar of business people on contemporary corporations, the American participants almost unanimously reminded Japanese colleagues of the fact that what the Japanese pointed out as characteristics of "Japanese management" were widely shared by American business corporations at least until the early 1960s;[60] then Henry Rosovsky referred me to an article by a sociologist on "collectivist organizations" that emerged in the United States in the 1970s as an alternative to bureaucratic organizations. I was dumbfounded to find that most of what the author identified as the main traits of this type of organization are the very traits of Japanese organizations![61]

Moreover, rapid progress in the technology of computer-aided telecommunication is making it possible for everyone to become a provider of information—as a "sharable"—for others, thus making the formation and maintenance of networks (network organizations as well as societal networks) much more effective and "democratic." This corresponds to the emergence of a new communication form, group communication, in contrast to personal and mass communication,[62] which suggests that networks as social system may come to play more significant roles all over the world, acquiring a new positive meaning and social legitimacy. It also suggests that the social systemic principles underlying Japanese society can not only be better understood in a positive sense but also accepted and even emulated. After all, in this "noncontemporary" and "heterogeneous" world, where there are many different world outlooks and value systems, let alone "gods," the peaceful coexistence and cooperation of human beings may require systems of better universal applicability. It is not so difficult to imagine this role being filled by Japanese-style consensus-making, based more on shared emotion than on allegedly cool, rational reasoning, as well as by Japanese management of network organizations, based more on collective goals, decentralized mutual acts, and spontaneous coordination than on a bureaucratic and hierarchical system of commands and reports or on sheer force and threat. That is to say, the Japanese way of running a society may, if well understood and widely adopted, contribute significantly to coping with today's global problems, societal as well as environmental, thus bringing about a more peaceful and prosperous future with better mutual understanding.[63]

However, this does not mean at all that the existing Japanese society is perfect. On the contrary, I believe there remain a number of negative aspects or limits that hinder Japan and the Japanese in their attempts to be more acceptable and responsible members of the global community.

First of all, networks in Japan tend to be closed and selfish in the sense that they select "homogeneous" members who share their basic world outlook and values and that their goals are often defined narrowly in terms only of their members' welfare. As Joyce Rothschild-Whitt points out, this may be a common trait of what she calls "collectivist organizations."[64] At any rate, to some extent, this is an inevitable cost for social systems relying mainly on consensus/inducement-oriented mutual acts. That is, information-sharing and consensus formation in networks can only take place effectively when based on long-standing and stable relations of mutual trust. And, conversely, when a network functions effectively, mutual trust among its members will be reinforced. Consequently, in networks, success tends to lead to complacency in and closedness of the system, with members becoming more introverted. Of course, they will show some interest in the outside world insofar as it continues to be the source of some useful information, or other goods and services, but they will have little genuine interest in, or sympathy for, the outside world as such.[65]

Similarly, paramarkets—that is, economic systems that constitute societal networks—cannot be free from the same limit. As we have seen, reciprocation in a paramarket is a form of cooperation that takes place one-sidedly, multilaterally, and repeatedly, in return for past support or in anticipation of future support. Therefore, it is only natural that the range of actors who can participate in such continuing relations will be considerably narrower than in the case of the market, which is characterized by temporary, bilateral relations. One can enter a market just once and promptly exit from it, if one so desires, but this is not easy in a paramarket. Moreover, the depth of such reciprocal relations can differ for each pair of participants in a paramarket. Generally speaking, new actors who want to join a paramarket will first have to go through a probation period, so to speak, during which they gradually build up their credibility through a series of reciprocation processes with other members until they are finally accepted as full-fledged members of that paramarket. In other words, members of a paramarket do not necessarily have equal credibility or the same depth of reciprocity with all other members.[66] On the other hand, those actors in a paramarket who are assured of a stable supply of the goods and services they need, under more or less satisfactory conditions, will have no strong incentive to invite new members into it. In this sense, the more successful a given paramarket is, the more self-sufficient and complacent, and hence closed, its members will tend to be. They will be more interested in expanding their reciprocal relations or building their credibility among themselves and will be largely indifferent to the interests of outsiders.

How can we expect this limit of networks to be overcome? In my opinion, it is neither realistic nor desirable for the Japanese to sacrifice and discard all the coziness and amenity provided by networks for the sake of unconditional openness to outsiders and complete equality among themselves. Rather, they should make more serious attempts to invite more newcomers into their networks, be more tolerant of internal heterogeneity, and listen more modestly and open-mindedly to criticism and demands from outside, while trying to understand more self-consciously and explain more clearly the essential characteristics of networks, their strengths as well as their weaknesses.

A second negative aspect of Japan's networks is the overemphasis on emotion and value judgments, rather than on facts and reason, in their process of communication. All too often, this is accompanied by a kind of situation-dependent choice of act. To many outside observers, such behavior seems to lack principles or to be a double standard and hence "irrational" and "unfair." Moreover, if it is further combined with the belief that organizations are as a matter of principle free to make any decision they like and to act accordingly as long as there is an internal consensus, no wonder the Japanese look like a group of formidably untrustable and opportunistic people. Here again, however, I do not think it necessary or desirable totally to deny the useful role that shared emotion can play in achieving group consensus rapidly. Likewise, situation-dependent choice can very well be a higher-order form of rationality and ethics as long as it embodies a firm core of cognitive and moral principles. Also, it is not a bad thing to assure individual actors of as much freedom in their acts as possible. The problem is that the Japanese seem to have gone too much to one extreme. This is particularly true of postwar Japan, when strict control over one's emotions came to be seen as "unnatural" or "inhuman," and it was thought that the only way for a small, war-beaten nation like Japan to survive was to be as shrewdly and cunningly adaptive as possible to the external conditions of international society. It is time to regain balance by coming back to a more middle-of-the-road position.

A third weakness is the tendency for the Japanese to put too much emphasis on consensus/inducement as a means of accomplishing mutual acts, ignoring other means, especially threat/coercion. It is true that, in recent years, the legitimacy of sovereign states competing to expand their territories and colonies through threat and coercion, to say nothing of pursuing world hegemony, has been largely abrogated throughout the world. It is also true that domestic use of threat/coercion as the means of rule has lost popularity. To that extent, Japan was correct in renouncing force as a means of resolving international disputes in its postwar constitution. It is also prudent that Japanese governments, central and local, have been most reluctant to adopt force as a means of suppressing opposition. Nevertheless, it is obvious that world peace has not arrived and that there still are groups and individuals who do not hesitate to use arms to achieve their own goals. Thus the need remains for individual states or some form of supra-state organization to maintain and use armed force to assure constabulary security both domestically and internationally. Nevertheless, if Japan, out of an excessive fear, say, of a resurgence of prewar militarism, should fail to contribute adequately, not only financially but also physically, to the maintenance of international security, it will not escape the criticism of other nations.

Moreover, one cannot wholly ignore the possibility of armed political groups fighting against one another to control a larger political entity such as a state in a revolutionary or civil-war situation, such as that which Japan experienced some 120 years ago. Even though it is disgusting for people to kill one another for some cause, whether it be political, ideological, or religious, it would be too optimistic categorically to assume away the possibility and necessity of the use of some forms of threat/coercion.

In fact, the Japanese-style political system of network organizations described above has at least two inherent drawbacks—in other words, two types of systemic errors. Type 1 is for the system as a whole to be impotent in terms of reaching an effective decision as a result of one or more of its sub-actors not rescinding its unit-veto power, in spite of the existence of the complementary principle of *wa* (harmony). Type 2 is for the system unanimously to reach a decision that is wrong. A typical example of the latter was Japan's decision to declare war against the Allied nations, while an example of the former was Japan's failure to reach the decision to end the war, a deadlock only the emperor was able to break and thus save Japan.

The Japanese themselves seem to have been aware of the possibility of errors of type 1 but it is doubtful they have been ever aware of the possibility of errors of type 2.[67]

One practical device widely accepted in Japanese network organizations is to graft rule by majority decision onto a unit-veto system, but in reality this supplementary system of decision making is seldom used. It is simply a means of intimidating the minority into compromising with the majority's position: "Well, if you are such blockheads, we can always vote, you know? Why don't you save face by avoiding that?" But then the minority can retort: "Of course you can call for voting. But that will leave an antagonistic feeling [*shikori o nokosu*] among us, you know. What will happen then when you people are in the minority?"

Another more "systemic" device is to superimpose on the consensus-oriented, excessively "democratic" political system an autocratic system of rule by elements heterogeneous to the rest of it. This is, I want to argue, the role the emperor system was expected to play, at least partially, in the Meiji state. In spite of the official ideology that it was a single huge "family-state," in reality its political system was a network organization composed of various politically influential groups, such as the Diet, the military, the Privy Council, and ministries. This implies that there was a real possibility of those holders of unit-veto powers failing to reach a consensus, paralyzing the decision-making function of the state. It was on such occasions that the throne as the transcendental institution was invited to intervene and make the final decision on behalf of those groups. At the same time, however, the emperor was also expected to play the part of the affectionate great mother who takes care of the people as her beloved children. This latter role was, in reality, entrusted to functionally divided governmental bureaus.[68]

In the postwar state of Japan, this peculiar structure of rule was discarded, with the emperor remaining as a mere "symbol" of Japan's national integration, which gave rise to what can be called a "network state," though here, too, the bureaucrats did inherit, and even strengthened, the role of caretakers that they had played under the Meiji state, this time entrusted to them by the Diet, which is to say by the people themselves.

Perhaps Kakuei Tanaka was astutely aware of the weakness of such a political structure in the network state of postwar Japan. He tried to establish a kind of informal government, the so-called "Mejiro machine," equipped with the real capability of making and executing prompt and effective decisions, though it did not last long.[69] Thus it still remains to be seen if and how Japan under the present constitution can avoid serious errors (of type 1, at least) in its national decision making when it faces a fundamental conflict of interests and a split of opinions internally.

Japan's Future Course

In Japan today, opinion is sharply divided concerning what future course Japanese society and the Japanese state should take. In the past several years, many voices have declared the necessity of *kokusaika* (internationalization) for Japan, leading to opposing voices warning of the dangers of too hasty or unthinking a move in that direction. And even though consensus may have been reached on the need for *kokusaika* in some form or other, it is by no means clear what exactly that would entail. As yet, therefore, no clear consensus has been achieved in Japan concerning either the direction or the speed of *kokusaika*.

One possible direction would be to try, by serious and active introduction of the institutions and even cultures of the developed Western nations, to make Japan more "homogeneous" with the West. However, opinion is divided as to how far such homogenization is either possible or, indeed, desirable.

Another possible course would be to go in the opposite direction: reevaluate the merits of Japan's traditional institutions and culture, strive to have foreigners understand the characteristics, especially the strengths, of Japanese civilization and culture, and thus persuade them to accept and coexist with it—even actively propagating things Japanese abroad. Here, too, however, there is no agreement. What is typically Japanese? What is especially valuable about things Japanese? How far is it possible, or even desirable, to disseminate these things abroad?

In my opinion, these two courses do not necessarily contradict each other, especially considering the sociotechnological changes now occurring all over the world and recognizing that every society has its own strengths and weaknesses. Today's rapidly developing information-processing and telecommunications technology has great potential, too, for reactivating the networking movement that began in the United States in the 1960s, and in Japan, as Ken-ichi Imai's essay in this volume indicates, the *ie*-type organization, the key postwar business structure, may finally be evolving into a more genuinely network-oriented form. This may signify the beginning of real convergence between the Japanese and American branches of modern civilization.

Another factor the Japanese should bear in mind is that, with Japan having accumulated such huge economic potential, their actions now have a powerful and inevitable impact on the external world, whether or not the Japanese are aware of them or actually intend them. Once Japanese are fully aware of these changes, they will also have to realize that they can no longer confine their social networks to their own national or cultural borders.

In light of these factors, two urgent tasks emerge: (1) to study, as objectively and thoroughly as possible, the comparative characteristics of the different societies of the world, and, at the same time (2) to analyze closely the direction and nature of current global environmental changes, sociotechnological as well as natural. This will set the stage for different nations jointly to design a prototype of the social system most suitable for propagation throughout the future world. Then, on the basis of such a model, each nation can work to apply it to its own society without losing sight of its own unique traditions and culture. I would call such an attempt the "globalization" of social systems.

In such an attempt, network organization and the societal network may perhaps be chosen as promising prototypes for the universal social system of the future. Indeed, the formation of a global network overcoming the barriers of distance and language will be facilitated by the combined impact of the revolution in human consciousness now evident in the networking movement and the revolution in information technology. I hope such an attempt will also, on the one hand, encourage better understanding of Japan by other peoples, and, on the other hand, help the Japanese overcome some of the negative aspects of their system by pinpointing whatever reforms need to be introduced, thus facilitating the process of consensus formation toward such reforms.

Masahiko Aoki

Decentralization-Centralization
in Japanese Organization:
A Duality Principle

Analyzing the interaction of cultural, historical, efficiency, and planned factors in the formation and workings of social organizations, particularly business firms, from a comparative perspective is extremely complex. It may be fair to say that few attempts to do so have ever succeeded. In general, scholars have chosen to focus on one, or at most a few, factor(s) they consider dominant. This has led to the formation of the following prototypical views, which are not entirely mutually exclusive, of the Japanese organizational mode:

1. *The culturalist view.* The Japanese organizational mode is culturally unique and therefore distinct from its Western counterpart.

2. *The historicist view.* Differences between the Japanese and Western organizational modes have been conditioned by the different historical processes through which they have been formed.

3. *The universalist view.* In any given environment, there is a specific organizational mode that is most efficient. Therefore, similar organizational modes tend to be selected in Japan and the West for the same environment.

4. *The institution-designer's view.* Some aspects of the Japanese organizational mode are superior to its Western counterpart and vice versa. Therefore, both Japanese and Western organizations could, and should, emulate each other in those aspects in which they themselves are inferior.

I emphasize that these four views are only prototypical, in that sophisticated scholarly works normally combine more than one view, either explicitly or implicitly. It is not difficult, however, to identify well-known works that have one or another of these views as a dominant theme. For example, an early statement of the culturalist view is found in an influential 1958 anthropological study by James Abegglen, who concludes his pioneering study of personnel practices in Japanese factories by remarking: "If a single conclusion were to be drawn from this study it would be that the development of industrial Japan has taken place with much less change from the kinds of social organization and social relations of preindustrial or nonindustrial Japan than would be expected from the Western model of the growth of an industrial society."[1]

Abegglen did not, however, regard Japan as being at that time at the midpoint of development toward the Western model of the growth of an industrial society. Rather, he observed, "the Japanese system is on the whole self-consistent."[2] This system was capable of assimilating modern technology in a manner consistent with the historical customs and attitudes of the Japanese. Therefore, one might say that there are two distinct systems, Western and Japanese. One of the reasons for the immediate impact of Abegglen's work was his introduction of the new notion of the Japanese system as "consistent" and "rational," paralleling that of the West rather than being transitional toward a more advanced system idealized by the West. This latter historical view was espoused in Japan by modernists as well as Marxists throughout the 1950s.

Later, in the 1970s, a new version of the historicist view was advanced by Ronald Dore. In an in-depth field study comparing organizational practices at English Electric and Hitachi, Dore found a "sufficient consistency" in the differences between the British and Japanese employment systems, based on market-oriented and organizational-oriented principles respectively.[3] He proposed, however, to distinguish differences resulting from cultural tradition from those attributable to employment system characteristics. In examining the historical development of the Japanese employment system, he discovered that some, but on the whole very few, features were the result of unconscious habits related to certain patterns of traditional behavior or conscious adaptations of earlier employment patterns. Rather, many features were consciously borrowed from abroad or wholly indigenously invented (some element of the institution-designer's point of view). For example, the system of seniority pay was devised as a management response to the excessive mobility of skilled workers in the early twentieth century.

Dore maintained that adaptations of the employment system to the emergence of giant corporations and the extension of democratic ideals to the workplace were exigencies that all advanced societies face. However:

The Japanese have got there ahead. They made that adaptation earlier than Britain did, first because—a characteristic of late development—the larger corporation set the pace in industry from the *beginning of industrialization*, and second because the great post-1945 flood of egalitarian ideas hit Japan (backed with the full authority of an occupying army) *before* union-management relations had acquired any institutional rigidity.[4]

Because the Japanese system adapted itself more to conditions of late capitalism, if there is any convergence between the Japanese and British systems, such a change "might be characterized, however loosely, as in a Japanese direction."[5] Thus, he reversed the order of leader and follower that had been held in the historicist view by modernists and Marxists.

The 1970s also saw a rise in the universalist view, following the wide acceptance of universalistic neoclassical analysis of the Japanese economy in the 1960s.[6] A strong indicator of this new trend, specifically in connection with the Japanese organizational mode, was a series of works by Kazuo Koike comparing U.S. and Japanese labor practices.[7] Koike emphasized that a set of apparently unique work practices in large Japanese firms provided a rational system for the development of workers' skills. Long-term employment, a wide range of job experience (through job rotation), and internal promotion were conducive to the development of broad skills among employees. Such skills in turn generated an economic value by enhancing the shop floor's ability to adapt to continually changing markets and work environments. Enterprise-based unions provided workers with an appropriate institutional framework in which to voice their interest in developing skills within the firm and sharing the resulting economic gains. Although Japanese firms might have developed an employment system conducive to in-house career development in a more conscious way, Koike argued, the internal labor market of Western firms and the enterprise-level bargaining prevalent in U.S. manufacturing industries function in essentially the same way.

The organizational characteristics described by Koike may have contributed to Japan's superb efficiency in manufacturing, but one wonders whether the same characteristics are found in other spheres, such as the Japanese bureaucracy and R & D organizations, and, if so, whether the same efficiency and/or desirable performance characteristics can be attributed to these organizations as well. One hint is found in the organization theorists' version of the universalist view, the contingency theory, which is relevant to the discussion below. According to this theory, an efficient organizational mode may be dependent on its environment (markets, technology, etc.). For example, an organizational mode that can mobilize organizational resources in a centralized manner may be better suited to an environment subject to sudden, drastic changes, while one with decentralized decision making may adapt more flexibly to a steadily changing environment. A viable, efficient organizational mode is therefore contingent upon its environment. Accordingly, as world markets connect national economies ever more closely, they ought to exhibit similar arrays of organizational modes, distinguished only by national resource endowments. If such arrays of organizational modes are not, in fact, observed, and the prediction of contingency theory thus does not hold, the cause may be traced to historical and/or cultural factors.

If differences in organizational modes are attributable to historical factors, one might be optimistic about mutual learning. Through competitive selection and conscious modification of outdated existing organizational modes, the contingency theory will in the future come to hold true. But if cultural factors are the cause, then mutual learning is difficult, and the institution-designer's task is compounded. An optimistic institution-designer's view, in which the adoption of Japanese industrial policy, management and employment systems, and so forth by the West was recommended to improve industrial efficiency, was advanced in popular books in the late 1970s and 1980s. William Ouchi's Theory Z and Ezra Vogel's "Japan as Number 1" proposition are examples.[8] To these authors, the cultural factor did not seem particularly detrimental to the recommended Japanization of the Western system.

But Dore, who modified his theory of the late development effect for the preface to the Japanese translation of his *British Factory, Japanese Factory*, has recently cast doubt on such optimism. He admits that "in analyzing the emergence of the Japanese employment system and the condition of its continuing existence, I underestimated (although of course did not neglect) the importance of the role of value and cultural tradition."[9] Japan is not the only country that experienced late development. Examining employment systems in large firms in Mexico, Sri Lanka, and Senegal, Dore found characteristics of late development, but poor efficiency. "I have come to recognize the importance of not only the institution of organizations, but also the values, ethics, and cultural traditions brought into organizations," he observed.[10]

Dore now faces the more difficult institution-designer's task. In his recent book *Taking Japan Seriously*, he attempts to tackle this task.[11] He analyzes how some superior aspects of the Japanese system, such as the development of intrafirm training programs, might be emulated in England in spite of that nation's individualistic tradition. He suggests that cultural differences between Japan and England could be overcome by carefully designing legal and institutional measures that would be workable and effective in a market-oriented system, yet could simulate superior aspects of Japanese practice. To finance in-house training, for example, he proposes a public loan scheme (employee training loan program) providing for loans to be repaid jointly by employee and employer, with the latter's share being shifted to the new employer if the employee changes jobs. Under such a scheme, employers might be motivated to provide more opportunities for in-house training without fear of capital loss owing to post-training exits of employees. Dore examines the feasibility of this and other measures and concludes that the Japanese recipe is worth emulating in England, although he remains skeptical about its feasibility in "individualistically ruthless" America.

These summaries are admittedly oversimplified and may have overlooked subtleties in each author's point of view. By concentrating on one or a few of the cultural, historical, efficiency, and planned factors, these studies have given insight into the nature and workings of Japanese organizations from various angles. Yet a broader picture of the Japanese organizational mode may be gained only by looking explicitly into the interactions of these factors. For example, one cannot possibly deny that history matters in understanding the formation of an organizational mode. But, as international interaction and competition intensify, inefficient organizations are bound to be selected out without the insulation of protectionist institutional barriers. To survive the competition, each organization must learn the superior aspects of other organizations. However, if what is learned is not carefully incorporated into a historically molded organization in such a way that the designed mode is consistent with cultural values and prevalent behavioral patterns, the efficiency and effectiveness of the organization may not be assured.

Culture, history, efficiency, and learning all play roles in organizational dynamics. This is hardly an astonishing statement, but it is no easy task to pinpoint the interactions of these factors in an empirical work. In the following sections, I take a partial and somewhat idiosyncratic approach to examining the interaction of cultural and efficiency factors in Japanese organizations (business firms and bureaucracies) from a comparative perspective. The first section adopts a purely theoretical institution-designer's point of view. Its purpose is to derive a principle, termed the *duality principle*, that effective organizational modes must satisfy. This principle describes how centralization and decentralization ought to be combined in organizational information systems and incentive schemes. Then I derive two prototype organizational modes that hypothetically satisfy this principle and compare the efficiency of the two. Since the efficiency of the prototype modes turns out to depend upon parameter values defining organizational environments such as markets and technology, if one attempts to explain viable forms of organizations solely in terms of the efficiency factor, it should be possible for two modes to coexist in one society, with one mode prevailing over the other contingent upon the environmental conditions of an individual organization (the so-called contingency theory).

The second section argues that, contrary to the prediction of the contingency theory, typical Japanese business organizations (firms) tend to cluster toward one end of the prototype modal spectrum relatively independently of their individual environments, while typical American business organizations tend to cluster around the other end, also independently of environments. I also discuss the ways in which some individual ministries in the Japanese bureaucracy are characterized by an organizational mode isomorphic to that of the Japanese firm, although the principle of organizational effectiveness (the duality principle) fails to hold for bureaucracies as a whole. Based on this observation, the potential malfunction of the Japanese polity in certain environments will also be discussed.

The fact that Japanese and U.S. business organizations are typified by different organizational modes independent of environmental conditions may imply two things: (1) the efficiency factor alone cannot explain the genesis of a dominant organizational mode in one society (i.e., the contingency theory does not hold), and historical inertia, cultural values, and/or behavioral patterns may play certain roles in defining a dominant organizational mode in one society; and (2) the comparative performance of a typical American firm vis-à-vis a typical Japanese firm may be relative and contingent upon organizational environments (e.g., it is stronger in certain industries and a certain type of innovation, but inferior in others).

These two implications pose a problem for mutual learning. Is it possible for an organization in one society to learn the superior elements of an organization in another society in spite of cultural differences? This problem is too fundamental and broad to discuss fully in this essay, but I shall touch upon a few related issues, namely, the role of the *mura* and *ie* principles in large modern Japanese organizations. Anthropologists, such as Abegglen and Chie Nakane, and socioeconomists, such as Yasusuke Murakami, attribute great significance to these cultural principles as fundamental driving forces in Japanese organizational dynamics. While small-group-ism (the *mura* principle) has been a significant contributing factor to organizational efficiency in Japan, it is neither sufficient to make large Japanese organizations effective nor necessary in order for non-Japanese organizations to emulate certain superior aspects of the "Japanese-type" organizational mode. In view of the duality principle, I maintain that a more fundamental issue confronting Western organizations is how to modify their market-oriented incentive scheme and make it compatible with the adoption of certain elements of Japanese-style information-processing within an organization. I speculate on the possibility that future development of technological and human capabilities will lead to a fusion of Western and Japanese modes in spite of cultural differences.

The Duality Principle

This section adopts a purely theoretical institution-designer's view to constructing two prototype modes of organization having certain desirable performance characteristics. Following a conventional notion in the organizational science literature, let us say that an organization is effective if it achieves its goals (such as producing high-quality goods that can be profitably marketed). However, there may be multiple ways to organize the activities of organization members toward collective achievement of organization goals. Therefore, we also need criteria to compare the performance of various organizational modes.

Recent literature on comparative economic systems, largely inspired by the pioneering work of Leonid Hurwicz,[12] has focused on two important aspects of organizations, the cognitive and motivational, and developed two corresponding criteria to compare the performance characteristics of large organizations: informational efficiency and incentive compatibility. To these basic notions, I shall add more concrete content that is specific to the analytical task at hand. I then design two prototype organizational modes that may satisfy the above two criteria. These prototype modes are used in the next section to compare characteristics of Japanese and U.S. organizations.

To visualize the cognitive aspect of an organization, suppose that it is simply composed of a center that sets strategic goals and many work units that operate to achieve these goals. The center and each work unit systematically process information within their jurisdictions, communicate according to the rules and conventions of the organization, and make various decisions affecting organizational activities. It is desirable for such an information system to be efficient in terms of time and resources. Furthermore, it must be compatible with the scheme of incentives provided to members, so that the efficient use and development of skills required by the information system is properly motivated by the corresponding incentive scheme. If participants are motivated to deviate systematically from required tasks, even the best information system will not function as designed.

Let us attempt to design two prototype information systems that satisfy these two requirements. Organizations are surrounded by uncertain environments. It is impossible to design an all-encompassing information system that can process all information relevant to the achievement of organizational goals without any time lag or noise and coordinate all activities of work units accordingly. Therefore, the designer of information systems must make some compromises. Let us consider two contrasting hypothetical information systems to cope with the bounded rationality of an organization: centralized and decentralized information systems.[13]

In a centralized information system (CI), the center collects all relevant information for the achievement of organizational goals and coordinates operations and transactions among work units. The information available to the center is, of course, not perfect or precise, but let us suppose that the centralized plan is as rational and consistent as possible within these limitations. Let us assume, too, that the centralized plan is fixed for a certain period of time and that information obtained during this period (posterior information) is utilized only for formulating the next period's plan. Work units are required to implement the centralized plan. In order for this system to be efficient, it is desirable for all participants to develop specialized skills in their own jurisdictions. To improve planning, the center must increase its information-processing and decision-making capacity. Each work unit must develop expert skills for efficient implementation of the plan by developing job-specific information-processing capacities. CI is therefore characterized by two elements: hierarchical centralized coordination and job specialization.

The alternative is a decentralized information system (DI), in which a plan made by the center (which I shall call prior planning) only sets a general framework for activity during a certain period. As more relevant information becomes available during this period (posterior information), each work unit is allowed to respond to and act upon the information on an ad hoc basis. In other words, decision making is delegated to the place where on-site information is available. But the use of posterior information and ad hoc adaptation often necessitates modification of the prior plan beyond a single work unit and therefore requires coordination among work units. As need arises, work units communicate with each other and jointly modify the prior plan. In this system, therefore, information-sharing between work units and the center, as well as among work units, plays an important role. Accordingly, skills required in this system tend to be more general and versatile, enabling work units to cope with emerging events autonomously, rather than specialized expertise for performing a prescribed job efficiently. Generality is desired because decentralized ad hoc problem solving requires an understanding of the problem from a broader organizational perspective, so that solutions are kept consistent with organizational goals. The capacity to communicate with other work units in order to benefit from posterior information is also useful. In sum, DI can be characterized by two elements: nonhierarchical horizontal coordination and fluid job demarcation.

By making use of posterior information that is newer and more accurate than what is available to the center at the time of prior planning, DI can generate an added "information value" for the organizations. But its generation is not costless. The acquisition of information by, and communication among, work units may divert their attention from intrinsic operating tasks, sacrificing productive efficiency and the development of expert skills. If these costs are subtracted from the information value generated over time, we arrive at information rent for DI vis-à-vis CI.

Rent can be positive or negative, indicating the relative informational efficiency or inefficiency of DI over CI.

The magnitude of information rent in DI depends on the value of posterior information as well as the information-processing capacities of the organizational participants. I have analyzed the relative informational efficiency of the two systems elsewhere,[14] and one important analytical conclusion is that if the organizational environment is continually changing in a not-too-drastic manner, the information efficiency of DI is superior to that of CI. However, if the organizational environment is either stable or changing drastically, the opposite is true.

It is easy to grasp this intuitively. If the environment is stable, the value of posterior information is minute relative to what can be achieved with prior information, which is relatively precise under stable conditions. On the other hand, since it takes time for work units to learn from on-site information and to communicate with one another, it is not worthwhile to sacrifice productive efficiency when the environment itself "forgets" its past quickly. With moderate environmental volatility, however, the decentralized fine-tuning of prior planning by work units improves the outcome. If efficiency alone is important in determining the choice of an organizational mode, one may expect that information systems of both CI and DI types coexist in society contingent on environmental conditions. (I argue below, however, that this is not necessarily the case.) For example, one might expect centralized functional hierarchies to be more prevalent among business organizations (firms) in fairly stable oligopolistic markets for standardized commodities or highly uncertain markets for new products, while the less centralized flexible information system is more discernible among firms in continually changing markets, such as producers of small-to-medium quantities of many products.

Next let us consider the kind of incentive scheme compatible with each of the information systems described above. In the discussion so far, we have considered a simple two-layered organization composed of the center and work units. Now let us assume that information systems are differentiated into multilayered structures and call them *functional hierarchies*. In a centralized system, each level in the functional hierarchy may be distinguished by the degree of centralization of information and decision making.

Assume that superiors at each level in the functional hierarchy recruit and discharge immediate subordinates from among the internal and external labor markets, organized according to standardized job descriptions. From the point of view of personnel administration, this market-oriented scheme is decentralized, since employment decisions are relegated to the immediate superiors at each level of the functional hierarchy.

Incentives provided by this decentralized, market-oriented personnel administration (DP) are generally compatible with CI, which relies more upon specialized skills, because competition within similar job classes is conducive to standard evaluation and development of specialized expertise. Conversely, the development of standardized skills in CI induces the development of well-defined markets for these skills. Thus, CI and DP reinforce each other.

There is a further link between CI and DP: where well-developed markets for specialized skills exist, individuals are able to seek better opportunities among other organizations, and the authority of their superiors therefore has only a weak foundation. In this situation, organizational integrity and managerial authority may have to be reasserted by bestowing greater power on upper management through the centralization of decision making and the threat of market discipline (i.e., discharge).

An alternative method of personnel administration is to centralize recruiting, allocating, and training within the organization. Such centralized, organization-oriented personnel administration (CP) may be best served by an internal hierarchy in which organizational rank is determined by pay and status. Employees are given the opportunity for internal promotion in rank, but ranks are not necessarily associated with specific jobs. (In this sense, rank hierarchy is distinguished from the internal labor market.) Suppose that each participant is recruited at the lowest rank and competes for promotion over his career lifetime according to criteria centrally set by the organization. These criteria may be formulated in more general terms than those required for an evaluation of skills specific to a certain job. An individual who fails to meet the performance standard of a certain rank may be ousted from the organization and forced to seek a position of lower rank elsewhere because of damaged reputation. (An analysis of this type of hierarchy can show that theoretically such discharges will not actually occur and will remain only as a potential threat, because the system can effectively prevent individuals from shirking.)[15] Since rank is not associated with a specific job description, personnel may be treated as relatively malleable, and the centralized allocation and reallocation of personnel among work units is therefore facilitated.

CP can, then, be effectively coupled with a decentralized informational system (DI), because the centralized reallocation (rotation) of personnel among work units, rather than decentralized hiring at each level of functional hierarchy, can promote the accumulation of knowledge required for efficient operation of DI. Recall that the skills useful in DI are versatile and can cope with a variety of tasks as the need arises. Such versatile skills are developed over time through a wide range of job

experience coupled with formal training at regular intervals to systema-
tize intra-organizational experience. Individuals may be given incentives
to develop such skills by assessments of their learning achievements
across multidimensional areas over the long run. Under a system of rank
hierarchy, an organization can also provide effective intra-organizational
training without fear of capital loss owing to departure of personnel after
training.

There is a further link between DI and CP. In DI, each work unit, by
being delegated a wide range of autonomy, may develop its own unit-
specific interests (such as to "maximize group output," which may not
necessarily be consistent with maximization of organizational output),
and this may be wasteful of time and other resources in promoting such
local interests at the sacrifice of organizational goals.[16] One way to cope
with this problem is to rotate personnel regularly to restrain the development of localized collective interests.

Under a market-oriented incentive scheme (DP), individuals tend to
compete in a well-defined job category within, as well as beyond, the
organization in a way that is often incompatible with DI's requirement
of systematic development of versatile skills attuned to organizational
needs. Achieving organizational goals effectively also becomes problematic if there is no integrating force in both information-processing and
personnel administration. Hence, the match of decentralization in both
cognitive and motivational aspects (DI-DP) would not be effective. On
the other hand, the match of centralization in both cognitive and motivational aspects (CI-CP) may be overly stifling in business and bureaucratic organizations, though it may have some merit in military organizations in a drastically changing environment. It seems that the
organization-oriented, centralized administration of personnel needs to
be balanced by decentralized decision making and coordination, and
that centralized decision making needs to be compensated by a market-
oriented, decentralized incentive scheme in order to encourage individual initiative. In other words, for business and bureaucratic organizations
to be effective and incentive-compatible, only combinations of CI-DP or
DI-CP seem viable. The following is thus proposed as a working hypothesis, which I call the *duality principle*:

In order for an organization to be effective and incentive-compatible, it is
necessary that decentralization/centralization in the cognitive aspect (information systems) of the organization be coupled with centralization/decentralization
in its motivational aspect (personnel administration).

In examining the cognitive and motivational aspects of organizations
separately (although we considered their interactions above), we have
distinguished two kinds of hierarchies: functional and rank. In the
former, a specific information-processing and decision-making function

is associated with each level, while the latter is simply a hierarchy of status, associated with different levels of pay. In view of the duality principle, one organization may be more hierarchical than another in terms of the former, while the opposite may be true in the other. Some economists, such as Joseph Stiglitz, have proposed the term *vertical hierarchy* (corresponding to *functional hierarchy*) and *horizontal hierarchy* (corresponding to *rank hierarchy*) to make the same distinction.[17]

Yasusuke Murakami has proposed a three-way distinction between nonfunctional hierarchy, heterofunctional hierarchy, and homofunctional hierarchy. He defines a heterofunctional hierarchy as "a hierarchy which assigns a different particular function to each stratum in the hierarchy," which clearly corresponds to the functional hierarchy described above. Nonfunctional hierarchy seems to resemble the rank hierarchy described above, but, according to one of Murakami's examples ("a stratified clan such as the *uji* . . . based on the symbolic distance between the main blood line and the lateral lines"), it is a static concept different in nature from the dynamic concept of promotional rank hierarchy, which is an incentive device.[18] As we shall see below (and as Murakami seems to acknowledge),[19] the concept of rank hierarchy seems more closely related to his third type of hierarchy. Yet Murakami's concept of homofunctional hierarchy involves some ambiguity. "All strata jointly performed [a] well-specified function," but "a specific part of this function [is assigned] to each individual stratum."[20] On the one hand, specialization seems to be denied, and on the other, the difference between monofunctional and heterofunctional hierarchies seems to be ambiguous and only a matter of degree. If a classification is to provide an analytical framework for the comparative study of modern organizational modes, then one based on the cognitive and motivational domains of hierarchical operation may be more clear-cut.

The Japanese Firm and Bureaucracy

The Firm

The previous section assumes that pure centralized/decentralized systems are possible in both information systems and personnel administration. This assumption is, of course, far from realistic, and the description of centralized/decentralized information systems and personnel administration should be dealt with only as a prototype model. Any actual organization may incorporate both centralized and decentralized elements in its cognitive and motivational aspects. Given this caveat, however, I venture to propose the following stylized typification: Western, specifically American, business organizations tend toward the CI-

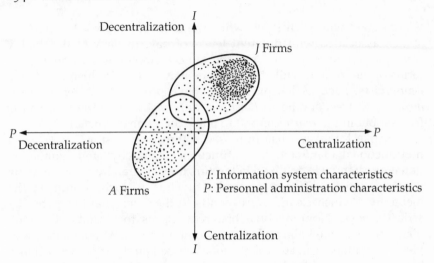

Fig. 1. Two types of organizational mode.

DP end of the organizational modal spectrum, while DI-CP is prevalent among Japanese business organizations. Figure 1 gives a schematic representation of this proposition.

I have provided detailed interpretation of empirical data to support the above typification of Japanese firms elsewhere,[21] and scholars such as Dore and Koike have also recently documented the fact that the Japanese work unit (i.e., the workshop or section) has developed relative autonomy from hierarchical control to direct operational activities.[22] Job demarcation among Japanese workers is much more ambiguous than in the West, and as Koike has emphatically argued, a wide range of job experience helps develop versatile skills to cope autonomously with changes, such as the breakdown of machines, absenteeism, and the need for rapid shifting between tasks.

Horizontal coordination of operations among work units without intervention by upper levels of the functional hierarchy is also relatively more developed in Japanese firms. The well-publicized *kanban* system is but one example of horizontal coordination in practice.[23] The *kanban* system was originally developed by Toyota and spread to other factories characterized by large-scale, intricate assembly work. In this system, neighboring units are connected directly through the circulation of *kanban*. Downstream shops periodically issue order forms called *kanban* to shops immediately upstream for the delivery of parts, in-process products, and so on, specifying quantities and delivery times during the day. These *kanban* are then returned to the issuer as a delivery notice with the delivery. Thus, they function as a device for checking the implementation of downstream demand. The automatic and periodic circulation of *kanban* is effective for fine-tuning prior production schedules, and the production system can generate information rents by reducing the time needed for interunit communication and negotiations, as well as holding to a minimum the buffer stocks of parts and in-process inventories under continually changing output market conditions. For this reason, the system is sometimes referred to as the zero-inventory method or the just-in-time system.

In terms of personnel administration, so-called Japanese management characterized by lifetime employment and seniority pay may be seen as an outcome of a rank-hierarchy incentive scheme. Its paternalistic character is overemphasized in the literature on Japanese management, but in reality the competition in a rank hierarchy is extremely intense. There is wide variance in the speed of promotion among employees. All new blue-collar recruits out of high school may start, for example, at the seventh level in promotional ranking. But the fast mover may reach the first rank at age 35 (subsequently continuing on to supervisory ranks), whereas the slow mover may reach the same rank only a year before mandatory retirement. A non-negligible proportion of white-collar employees even at large firms are separated from their initial firm before mandatory retirement either by being transferred to smaller affiliated firms by their original firms (*shukkō*), by being implicitly pressured to quit, or sometimes by being discharged.

The personnel department occupies a central position in the management structure of Japanese firms, administering recruiting activities centrally, keeping files on employees, deciding on periodic transfers of (white-collar) employees among different work units, running in-house training programs, and so forth. The strategic position of the personnel department is one of the most distinctive features of Japanese as opposed to Western firms. Thus, the DI-CP combination described by the duality principle seems to be an approximate characterization of the Japanese firm.

The nature of the centralization of personnel administration in Japanese firms warrants a note of caution. By *centralization*, I mean that personnel matters are systematically administered by a single office from a companywide perspective rather than delegated to individual supervisors in functional hierarchies. This does not mean, however, that the personnel department exercises authoritarian control over employees. Although the personnel department keeps records on employees and has discretionary power to decide transfers (even to subordinate affiliate firms), it cannot operate effectively by ignoring other opinions within the company. An employee's reputation among seniors, peers, and juniors is what matters most in determining the worker's opportunities.

In this sense, personnel administration at well-run Japanese firms is relatively free from the arbitrariness of individual supervisors, although episodes contrary to this generalization also abound.

One interesting illustration of the interaction between DI and CP within the Japanese firm is shown in the typical career pattern of engineers in manufacturing divisions. When recruited from engineering schools, they are relatively well versed in statistical methods, basic theory, mathematics, and so on, but not in specialized subjects.[24] During their first ten years or so, they are trained on the job by participating in various development projects and scanning relevant engineering and theoretical developments elsewhere. The main interest of the engineering department is to develop in-house engineering knowledge through the infusion of scientific knowledge, possibly with the aid of researchers at central research laboratories if necessary. The engineering department is usually located at the manufacturing site, and engineers have opportunities to interact with manufacturing personnel through participatory value-engineering and value-analysis teams. Engineers start to assume some administrative duties as project leaders in their thirties and may be transferred as line managers to the manufacturing site of new products they help develop. Later they may be promoted further in management. In fact, the presidents of important Japanese manufacturing companies predominantly have engineering backgrounds.

This brief description of a typical engineer's career involves all-important generic elements of the DI-CP combination and suggests certain implication for the R & D characteristics of the Japanese firm.[25] These are emphasis on better utilization of on-site information and on-the-job training (the focus of R & D efforts to develop in-house engineering knowledge); horizontal communication (value-engineering and value-analysis teams involving both engineers and blue-collar employees, as well as temporary transfer of divisional engineers to the central research laboratory to participate in commissioned research); and permanent transfer of engineers to manufacturing sites directed by the personnel department (which would make engineers more responsible for development and consequently make the transition from design to manufacturing smoother and less time-consuming).

All these factors suggest that the Japanese firm is relatively stronger in incremental process innovation than in the "conceptual innovation" that translates market/scientific potential into the conception of new products. It is consistent with the theoretical proposition that DI is informationally more efficient under moderately uncertain environments than under those that are highly uncertain. (It is to be added, however, that in the past ten years or so, central research laboratories engaged in more basic research have been gaining in importance in major Japanese firms, which may have important implications for the redirection of their research and development efforts toward more upstream-oriented innovation. In spite of such phenomena, personnel rotation remains to be utilized to facilitate communication between manufacturing divisions and central research laboratories.)

Bureaucracy

As I have demonstrated elsewhere, there is an important structural similarity between the industrial firm and the Japanese government bureaucracy in terms of the DI-CP combination.[26] In the bureaucracy, each *genkyoku* section of a ministry, in charge of specific jurisdictional spheres in the private sector, has a high degree of autonomy, similar to each work unit in a Japanese firm. Coordination among sections and departments within a ministry also involves a high degree of horizontal communication, as represented by the practice of *ringi*, the procedure by which documents are drafted at lower levels of functional hierarchies and then circulated from section to section, bureau to bureau, up and down the line, until they have gathered the required number of seals of approval. Each ministry administers its own rank hierarchy, in which bureaucrats compete for promotion until retirement, when post-retirement *amakudari* (descent from heaven) assignments to prestigious positions in the private or quasi-public sector are arranged by the personnel section of the ministry as final "prizes." The personnel section of the ministry is a powerful organ that directs the regular rotation of bureaucrats between sections and bureaus, preventing them from developing intimate ties with specific private interests and helping to elicit their dedication to the accumulation of political stock for the entire ministry.

Even when the Japanese bureaucracy is viewed as a whole, the DI element is still apparent. Cabinet control over the ministries is relatively weak. The ruling Liberal Democratic Party has been gaining influence by developing individual connections with particular ministries (the so-called *zoku* phenomenon) rather than through legislative control of the Diet. The essence of interministry relationships is the bargaining by relevant ministries and corresponding *zoku* politicians. Even centralized coordination by coordinating offices, such as budgeting by the Budgetary Bureau of the Ministry of Finance, may be modeled as a multiperson bargaining game, with principal players being *genkyoku* and the coordinating office acting as arbiter.[27] Recently, this "horizontal" tendency has been accelerated by the introduction of an automatic ceiling over ministerial budgetary demands, which has considerably narrowed the margin for discretion by the once-powerful Budgetary Bureau.

Thus DI in the bureaucracy gives a quasi-pluralistic nature to the

Japanese polity, with each ministry *genkyoku* acting as a quasi-agent of jurisdictional interests.[28] Similarities between the Japanese firm and the bureaucracy, however, stop at this point. In other words, CP is lacking and the duality principle fails to hold in the bureaucracy as a whole. Instead of a single rank hierarchy with centralized personnel management, parallel rank hierarchies are administered by the respective ministries. It is true that the Agency for Personnel Administration is responsible for recommending to the cabinet an annual revision of the pay schedule for various rank hierarchies within the bureaucracy of the central government based on an annual survey of wages in the private sector. However, important personnel decisions such as individual hiring, promotions, transfers, and *amakudari* assignments are administered by the personnel section of each ministry. In order to promote interministerial communication, the temporary *shukkō* (dispatch) of bureaucrats to other ministries is increasingly used, but the lifetime career of these bureaucrats depends on the personnel decisions of the parent ministries. Accordingly, their ultimate loyalty remains with the parent ministry.

As discussed in the last section, CP is an important mechanism through which individual compliance with organizational objectives is assured in spite of the wide-ranging delegation of decision making to lower levels of functional bureaucracy and nonhierarchical coordination. The practice of personnel rotation among functional units in the Japanese firm thus curbs inefficient assertion of sectarian interests. In contrast, there is no such safeguard in government bureaucracy as a whole. This may not be a serious problem as long as the political environment is fairly stable, so that interministerial coordination can be made routine. But when jurisdictional demarcation becomes an issue because of drastic environmental changes, the lack of any integrating element in the bureaucracy may result in fierce jurisdictional disputes and haggling among ministries, each seeking to expand its own jurisdictional sphere.

The tendency of diffused interest representation in the bureaucracy in a rapidly changing environment may also make increasingly difficult the formation and implementation of an innovative promotional policy that would hurt some constituents of a powerful ministry. Innovative reorientation of the industrial firm under entrepreneurial leadership may also undermine the interest of certain groups within the firm, such as workers with particular skills. But centralized personnel administration and emphasis on training in versatile skills may ease the burden of drastic internal reorganization, at least to some extent, by transferring and retraining affected workers. By contrast, in the government bureaucracy, each ministry administers its own incentive hierarchy and relies on specific interest groups for *amakudari* arrangements. Ministries are thus motivated to fiercely resist any policy change that might deprive them of vested power, such as regulatory power and discretionary grants to their constituents.

The quasi-pluralistic character of the bureaucracy and the inapplicability of the duality principle to it encourage intrinsic conservatism, which precludes radical policy innovation that may conflict with the interests of important political constituencies. We might refer to this tendency as *progressive conservatism*, in that it does not preclude, but rather promotes, incremental policy innovation that does not hurt important constituencies. Many fear that this conservative tendency has begun to manifest itself in the changing technological and international environments of Japan. One way for the bureaucracy to cope with this situation internally, rather than passively reacting to private and external pressures, would be to institute CI or CP to restore the duality principle.

CI could be introduced by strengthening the power of coordinating offices within the administration, and there have in fact been some attempts to do this. The September 1985 cabinet decision, based on a report by the Temporary Administrative Reform Council (Rincho), to reorganize the prime minister's secretariat and increase the role of the Management and Coordination Agency is an example. But the new coordinating offices in the prime minister's secretariat are primarily staffed by officials temporarily dispatched from various ministries, and it is doubtful that those offices can exercise autonomous coordination free from interministerial haggling. Even this modest attempt at functional centralization seems difficult to reconcile with incentives created by an administration of rank hierarchies dispersed among the separate ministries. Also, as the similarity between firm and bureaucracy in the decentralization of information-processing indicates, DI is a deep-seated characteristic of the Japanese social system, and there may be an intrinsic difficulty in switching to a CI-oriented system in Japan.

As an alternative to the introduction of CI, Iwao Nakatani has suggested the introduction of CP.[29] He argues that by means of unified personnel administration through a centralized personnel headquarters and the regular rotation of bureaucrats among ministries, the sectarian fusion of *zoku* politicians and bureaucrats could be curbed and the emerging conservative inertia of the bureaucracy overcome. It is said that a similar proposal was discussed in Rincho but never taken seriously. One problem with this proposal is that the bureaucracy may be too large for a single rank hierarchy. Further, even if it could be implemented, the centralization of bureaucratic hierarchy administration might create an enormous concentration of power within the headquarters. Episodes of the Tanaka era and experience with authoritarian organizations, such as various religious groups and the Japan Communist Party, indicate that the people who can control assignment of important positions can gain enormous personal power in the Japanese organizational context. This seems to be the inevitable consequence of the use of rank as a major incentive scheme.

If restoration of the duality principle from within is difficult, then the only hope for endogenously escaping the potential damage of bureaucratic conservatism in rapidly changing technological, social, and international environments may lie in the promotion of initiatives from the democratically mature private sector.[30] Until then, however, the lack of the duality principle and the consequent inefficiency and progressive conservatism may have to be accepted as the price for nontotalitarian pluralism.

Let me conclude this section with a brief comment on the relationship of my interpretation of the Japanese organizational mode based on the duality principle to two alternative characterizations. The first is that of Chie Nakane, based on the notion of *tate* (vertical) as opposed to *yoko* (horizontal).[31] Her vertical principle is the superior-inferior relationship among members of a group, and her horizontal principle is the competitive or collegial relationship developed across homogeneous members of the group. If the division of labor is sufficiently developed so that each occupational group cuts across various institutions (industrial organizations), the group becomes more homogeneous within, while clearly differentiated and autonomous vis-à-vis outsiders, so that the horizontal principle dominates. In contrast, if the division of labor is underdeveloped, the autonomy of occupational groups is absorbed into an institutional group comprised of many members with different attributes. The result is dominance of the vertical order in which the members of different attributes are related through a superior-inferior relationship.

Nakane claims that the vertical principle prevails in Japan, whereas the horizontal principle is predominant in the West. One can say that the former is related to our notion of centralized personnel administration (rank hierarchies), while the latter is related to decentralized personnel administration (market-oriented incentive schemes). She infers, however, that the vertical principle permeates social values in Japan, so that hierarchical institutional groups come to be ranked vertically themselves, culminating in the consolidated authoritative power of central administration. The source of the strength of this structure lies in "its effectiveness for *centralized communication* and its capability of efficient and swift mobilization of the collective power of its members."[32] From this statement, it appears that the *tate* principle also involves elements of CI. As we shall see below, Nakane qualifies this argument to a great extent by emphasizing the important role of group dynamics, but there is a danger that the monistic notion of the *tate* principle may lead to, or encourage, undue emphasis on the authoritarian nature of the Japanese social system.

In contrast, an emerging view stresses the "diffusive" nature of Japanese social organizations. One example of this is found in what may be called the "neo-Japanese management literature," distinguishable from traditional Japanese management literature by its emphasis on the "democratic" nature of the Japanese firm, rather than its "paternalism-loyalty" reciprocity. One of the outspoken advocates of this view, Hiroyuki Itami, argues that the Japanese firm is characterized by "the diffusive, decentralized, and egalitarian sharing of information, decision making, and value added among employees, combined with employees' control of the firm overriding the shareholders' sovereignty." He calls this institution *jinpon-shugi* (peoplism) as contrasted to *shihon-shugi* (capitalism).[33] While the diffusive sharing of information and decision making and the sharing of information rents therefrom are certainly important characteristics of the Japanese firm, I maintain that without a countervailing integrative force and profit-making discipline, the firm cannot be effective, efficient, or viable in the competitive environment.[34]

In my opinion, monistic theories, which try to characterize Japanese organizations with a single principle, centralization or decentralization, are one-sided and fail to capture the interesting organized array of both elements. I hope the duality principle can offer a simple comparative framework for a balanced view.

Is Culture an Invincible Barrier to Mutual Learning?

The reason I started this essay with the hypothetical institution-designer's point of view was to assess the impact of the efficiency factor in determining organizational modes in a way as free as possible from historical and cultural factors. The contingency theory was a plausible theoretical prediction: organizations facing stable or drastically changing environments tend to be of the CI-DP type, while those facing continual changes tend to be of the DI-CP type. In the last section, I argued that this prediction failed, however, and that Japanese organizations tend to be of the DI-CP type regardless of their environments, while their U.S. counterparts tend to be of the CI-DP type. A recent study by James Lincoln, Mitsuyo Hanada, and Kerry McBride comparing Japanese and American firms also refutes the contingency theory.[35] It found that Japanese firms have higher and more finely graded formal hierarchies (owing to the prominence of rank hierarchies), but actual decision making tends to occur at lower levels (DI factor), regardless of an industry's technological and market features.

Industrial developments in the postwar period are consistent with the above observation. In the 1950s and 1960s, U.S. manufacturing companies, led by the steel and automobile industries, dominated world markets. Large and stable shares in oligopolistic markets allowed these companies to rely on the mass production of standardized commodities; this in turn yielded considerable gains from narrow divisions of labor and detailed job specialization. (It may be recalled that job specialization is an essential element of CI.) But the oligopolistic dominance of those American manufacturing companies was gradually eroded in the late 1960s by the challenge of resurgent industrial powers in Western Europe and Japan. As competition in world markets intensified in the 1970s and later, success in efficient small- or medium-batched production of a variety of products that could meet continually changing market tastes, together with constant process innovation, which improved on product quality and cost efficiency, became crucial for global companies to gain a competitive edge. The opportunity for exploitation of oligopolistic rents became tighter in the increasingly competitive manufacturing industries. Instead, in the terminology used earlier, the generation of information rents had to compensate for the erosion of oligopolistic rents. It was at this time that Japanese global firms developed state-of-the-art practices in the DI sphere, such as regular job rotation on the shop floor, participatory value-engineering and analysis groups, the *kanban* system, and so on, which have contributed substantially to the generation of information rents.

Meanwhile, U.S. and other Western companies retain their dominance in industries such as petroleum refining and chemicals. These industries are characterized by process technologies; it is intrinsically difficult to add great information value at the shop-floor level after prior planning. A similar contrast seems to exist in the field of innovation as well. Although a bold generalization, one may say that conceptual innovation, which translates market/scientific potential into the conception of new products, has been relatively more noticeable in the West, while in Japan there has been relatively more improvement in design and manufacturing processes for existing products and technology.

These observations raise the following questions about mutual learning: Can Japanese and U.S. (Western) firms learn from each other? Specifically, can Japanese firms learn from U.S. (Western) innovative firms (or other organizations such as research institutes or universities) to nurture their own capabilities in conceptual innovation? Reciprocally, can Western manufacturing firms learn from successful Japanese firms to improve their manufacturing efficiency and process-innovation capabilities? These issues cannot be dealt with satisfactorily here, but let us examine this last question a little more closely. It boils down to the ability of Western firms to incorporate some aspects of DI in order to generate information rents at the lower levels of functional hierarchies.

The failure of the contingency theory may suggest that the comparative organizational characteristics of Japanese and Western firms are at least partially conditioned by historical and/or cultural factors. If the historical factor is primarily responsible for the comparative difference, in accordance with Dore's original statement of the "late development effect," the difference would be gradually narrowed to the extent that organizations would forget their past, so to speak, or that new rational organizations would be born. The future would come to resemble the predictions of the contingency theory through the process of competitive selection. But the history of the past two or three decades seems to indicate that the difference has not necessarily narrowed spontaneously. This may be taken as an indication that the cultural factor is not negligible in determining the comparative characteristics of organizational modes in Japan and the West. What then is the possible content of the cultural factor in defining the "uniqueness" of the Japanese organization? Is it detrimental to mutual learning?

Cultural values often referred to as operating behind the Japanese organization are, among others: small-group-ism, or the *mura* (village) principle, which emphasizes the value of a coherent group in which tasks and performance outcomes are shared in a relatively egalitarian way; and the *ie* (house) principle, an important characteristic of which is the high value attached to one's relative position in the group, combined with efforts to maintain group homogeneity and autonomy. The former is more closely related to the DI aspect of the Japanese organization, the latter to the CP aspect.

For example, Nakane qualifies her notion of the *tate* principle as describing the basic character of Japanese organizations in the following way: in the Japanese group, the *tate* relationship is actually no more than ranking based on seniority, and the functional distinction between leader and subordinates is often ambiguous.[36] The entire group becomes one functional body, in which all individuals are amalgamated into a single entity and subordinates often de facto carry the work of their leader.[37] Nakane argues that this undifferentiated role assignment in the Japanese group exhibits its strength in the group's flexibility to adjust its activities to changing situations. Individual jobs in the group may be redefined as new events require it to maximize its output. To aid this flexibility, work is assigned to a group, and gains from individual contributions are shared by the whole group. This system entails a somewhat unfair distribution of work and outcome, since an able worker tends to carry a greater burden without receiving a corresponding share in the outcome. In the absence of individual pecuniary incentives, it therefore becomes a crucial task for management to preserve and promote a sense of personal, emotional connection among members of the group. Successful mobilization of group dynamism along these lines is, Nakane claims, the driving force in Japan's industrial development.

No one can possibly deny that group orientation, exemplified by such practices as ambiguous demarcation of jobs and the sharing of responsibility and outcome within the small group, is a distinctive characteristic of the Japanese factory, and that this group orientation is reminiscent of the organizational principle nurtured and operating in the Japanese agrarian village (*mura*) throughout history. Economic development during the proto-industrial period in Japan was crucially dependent upon increases in the scale and productivity of rice farming.[38] But most Japanese land was not originally suited to rice cultivation. To make soil suitable for rice planting, collective control of the water supply was necessary, initially in the form of *tameike* (reservoirs) in flatland fields, and, at a later developmental stage, in the form of large-scale irrigation along river systems. Rice seedlings raised in nursery beds had to be transplanted to paddies at the right moment with a sufficient supply of water and concentrated labor input. This task required collective coordination and cooperation among villagers for allocation of the village's water supply. In the convention of *ageta* (paddy drainage), developed in villages in the Kinai plain at an early stage (dated as far back as the ninth century), the water supply was reduced equiproportionally across families during water shortages, and unirrigable land was converted to alternative uses, such as cotton cultivation.[39] As large-scale irrigation systems developed, flood control in the typhoon season before harvest time required collective, ad hoc responses to unpredictable climatic changes. In addition, weeding, insect control, and timing of the water supply demanded the constant care and attention of farmers.

There is no doubt that through centuries of such agrarian experience, extending up until as recently as a generation ago, the Japanese have developed the customs of cooperation, risk-sharing, and ad hoc and flexible adaptation to continual and incremental environmental changes through collective efforts and diligent work habits, and have endured the penetration of communal life into their private lives. All these are now viewed as characteristics of modern Japanese factory life. The important point, however, is that the group approach to work does not automatically assure an efficient work system in the context of a large organization. If the task of a work unit is carried out by a relatively egalitarian and cohesive work team, the team may tend to become autonomous and assert its own localized interests by taking advantage of its monopolistic position within the organization. Effective coordination between work units then becomes a problem.

This problem was not unknown even in the proto-industrial period. When the water supply was managed by the village in a self-sufficient, closed manner, a risk-sharing convention such as the *ageta* was able to solve the coordination problem fairly automatically. But the great leap forward in civil engineering in the Sengoku period (fifteenth and sixteenth centuries) made possible the development of large-scale irrigation systems across multiple villages. Tokugawa villages, which were organized as coherent, homogeneous user units of the irrigation system and were relatively autonomous from the control of castle towns except for tax obligations, often engaged in fierce disputes over the distribution of water resources. Those water disputes (*mizu arasoi*) sometimes led to bloody clashes among neighboring villages in times of water shortages. Elaborate arbitration schemes, agreed to as fair and equitable, had to be developed along the irrigation system to cope with this social conflict. The names of great agrarian leaders in the Tokugawa period, such as Sontoku Ninomiya and Chiyozaburo Mutsugawa, are associated with the organization and effective management of arbitration schemes that emerged from coalitions of neighboring villages.

The need for intergroup coordination and conflict resolution is no less important in the context of modern industrial organizations. As Thomas Rohlen has put it in his criticism of Nakane:

The total company situation is more complicated. While the nature of work groups is best approached from the question of their fundamental conceptualization, it is less likely that an ideology emphasizing small-group values will have the same significance for large organizations. Company leaders may be devoted to such values, but they are not in a position to unite the personnel of a company in the same immediate way group leaders are. . . . Companies have been able to elaborate a wide manner of activities of symbolic participation (such as ceremonies, gatherings or representatives, company-wide outings, and civic and charitable programs), but none of this will be sufficient to secure the sense of connectedness of individuals to the whole, a crucial matter to Japanese companies.[40]

As already emphasized, in order to control the self-interests of the small groups comprising work units, the Japanese firm has consciously designed and developed two important institutions: the semi-automatic coordination mechanism among work units, as exemplified by the *kanban* system, and the centrally administered rotation of personnel among work units. The *kanban* system was developed by the ingenious effort of industrial engineers at Toyota, who borrowed the idea of replenishing on-shelf stock from the American supermarket system and adapted it to the requirements of manufacturing coordination and inventory control. The introduction of the *kanban* system initially met resistance from workers on the shop floor, who held a strike. This incident suggests that its introduction was not entirely consistent with the interests of small work groups. The practice of rotation of personnel beyond work units was also centrally imposed. Although it may be considered simply a magnified version of job rotation on the shop floor, which began autonomously with the initiative of foremen and subforemen,[41] the interunit rotation was consciously designed and implemented by management and has been centrally administered by the personnel department. Thus, one may conclude that small-group orientation has certainly contributed to the emergence of Japanese organizational practices and that cultural influence may be traced to them, but small-group orientation in itself is not sufficient for the effective operation of the DI system.

Small-group orientation may also be unnecessary for DI to be workable in the future. Recall that what is essential for DI to generate information rents is autonomous problem-solving capability in constituent operating units. Such capability has certainly been nurtured by group-oriented teamwork in Japan. But what is essential here, as Koike has emphatically argued, is the development of the "integrative skills" of workers on the shop floor, which combines operating skills with problem-solving capacity. Such skills let them cope flexibly and autonomously with unusual local emergencies, with frequent shifts in task, and with the introduction of new technology, not groupism per se.[42]

Even in Western firms, integrative skills may be developed through a carefully designed intrafirm career-development program combined with a more flexible job-rotation scheme, although such a scheme would require more cross-jurisdictional interaction and cooperation among workers than is currently observed under the segmented job-classification scheme. If the incentives for such a career development program are possible (which I shall discuss shortly), as well as desirable from the perspective of individual development, the incorporation of DI elements into the traditional CI may become a viable alternative even in Western industries where quick, flexible adaptation to market pressures, as well as to continual technological innovation, is imperative for competitive survival. Indeed, various experiments in that direction have been attempted worldwide within the framework of management-labor cooperation.

The team approach to "integrative skills" in Japan may have been partially conditioned by the available state of information-processing and communications technology, as well as by the developmental stage of individual capacities. The ethnic homogeneity of the Japanese may have helped mutual understanding among workers through intense face-to-face interactions, and the cooperation of many individuals may have complemented the skills and talents of each. The fruits of the continuing development of information science, electromechanical technologies, and artificial intelligence will, however, become more readily available everywhere as aids to communicating more efficiently and enhancing the capacities of individuals rather than replacing them. Also, the possible redirection of education to develop more integrative and communicative individual capacities rather than specialize excessively in skills may also help develop DI elements without relying too much on coherent group dynamics. These possibilities also suggest increasing opportunities for Japanese firms. If fusion of human elements and developing technology is possible, Japanese group dynamism may become modified to allow more individual freedom from the conformist pressures of small groups. Such modification is desirable, not only in making established in-house career development more consistent with the needs of increasingly individualistic employees, but also in enhancing the organizational capacity of conceptual innovation.

Even if small-group dynamism, supposedly culturally unique to Japan, is thus not essential to the incorporation of DI elements into Western firms, and even if such incorporation is desirable practically for the revitalization of manufacturing industries in the West, the issue of incentive compatibility remains. Is it possible for Western firms to emulate some elements of DI without modifying the traditional market-oriented incentive scheme (DP)? Or can Western firms adopt some elements of CP in spite of alleged cultural differences? In view of the duality principle, this is a vital question.

I have stressed that Japanese rank hierarchies operate as a system to screen employees over the long run, using multidimensional criteria. One may argue, however, that such long-sightedness and relative ambiguity of ranking criteria are harmonious only with the rank-sensitive values of the Japanese. Murakami and his collaborators, Shumpei Kumon and Seizaburo Sato, note that there is indeed a marked parallel between aspects of Japanese management, such as the seniority wage and advancement system and high mobility between jobs within each firm, and the homofunctional hierarchy characterizing an essential element of the *ie* organizing principle. They argue that "the Japanese management system is clearly a variant of *ie*-type organization"[43] and maintain that the evolutionary development of the *ie* principle can account for the "unique" historical cycle of Japan since the eleventh century. If it is so unique, doubt may be cast upon the success of a "straightforward" transplantation of rank hierarchy as a principal incentive scheme into the individualistic and market-oriented West.[44]

Although a non-market-oriented, job-description-free rank hierarchy may be somewhat "uniquely" effective in the Japanese cultural context, I would maintain that the essential issue at hand is to provide incentives for the long-term, if not lifetime, association of employees with the firm, as well as to provide in-house training programs to promote and use employees' capacities to operate within firm-specific information systems efficiently and effectively. Inasmuch as the paternalistic and automated aspects of the seniority wage and advancement system have been unduly emphasized in the Japanese management literature, let me stress again that promotional rank hierarchy is a competitive screening device to motivate and sort out employees according to their learning achievements. This aspect of rank hierarchy may be emulated even in a competitive environment. For example, sharing of information rents with employees according to their achieved capacities, based on formal criteria, might limit their mobility between firms, while at the same time promoting intra-organizational competition.[45] For a systematic and consistent introduction of such a firm-specific incentive scheme, however, the function and authority of the personnel department must be strengthened. As an interesting study by Fred Foulkes suggests, there is indeed growing evidence that the personnel department is gaining importance in the management structure of well-run, nonunionized companies in the United States.[46] Also, from the policy perspective, proposals such as that by Dore for the establishment of an employee training loan program mentioned earlier, may be worth serious consideration as devices to mitigate the market pressure encroaching upon the effectiveness of personnel-training programs administered by individual firms.

Mutual learning by the West and Japan may eventually lead to the fusion of the DI-CP mode and the CI-DP mode: in other words, the phasing out of the duality principle. One class of organizations that approximates this tendency is the American research university, which forms the "most competitive industry" in the United States.[47] In such universities, professor-researchers are engaged in independent (DI without horizontal coordination), yet highly specialized (CP without centralized coordination), research. They are ranked by salary, professorial rank, and reputation, but are sufficiently mobile to seek better research opportunities and better ranking elsewhere, because universities compete for better researchers (DP). In spite of this competition, professor-researchers are fairly loyal to their institutions if they are well run, and the actual mobility of professors among top universities is not so excessive as to destabilize the educational and research atmosphere. This is so because such universities, in general, pay a great deal of attention to the research environment and to the mutual communication among and security of their own professors in order to maintain their "competitiveness" (some element of CP). These features of American research universities may suggest a future trend, however remote, in business organizations, since the generation of information rents, as well as conceptual and process innovations, is bound to become more like the generation of knowledge at research institutions.

One potential problem with American research universities, however, is the fairly rigid demarcation between disciplines institutionalized in the classic departmental organization. Although the high degree of specialization of researchers at American universities and their excellent analytical capabilities have made great contributions to the advancement of theories and applications in many fields, innovation in technology, and even in theory, may in the future come more from interaction among many different disciplines.[48] Innovative multidisciplinary research is possible only by cooperation and interaction among researchers highly capable in their own special disciplines. It is not yet known whether first-rate American research universities have the self-organizing capacity to meet such a challenge themselves, or whether other institutional interfaces, say between discipline-oriented academia and problem-solving-oriented industry, are necessary.

Until new knowledge production systems emerge, however, the West and Japan will learn a great deal from each other about their contrasting merits (e.g., the analytical approach versus the holistic approach and specialization versus integrative interaction) despite cultural barriers. It may be hoped that the symbiotic development of human capacity and technology will fuse cultural differences into a new, better hybrid.

The Japanese Enterprise as a Unified Body of Employees: Origins and Development

From the late 1960s to the early 1970s, Japanese management attracted attention both domestically and internationally. At its zenith, this interest brought on by the success of Japanese business was called "Japanese management fever."

Initially, the U.S. model had been regarded as a normative one, based on universal principles, and, in contrast, the "backwardness" of Japanese management was seen to be problematic. To overcome this perceived backwardness, Japanese managers studied the managerial skills of the United States after World War II, but what emerged as Japanese management has not converged with the U.S. model. Rather, during the learning process, a distinctive Japanese managerial pattern was created. From the 1960s to the early 1970s, during Japan's period of rapid growth, emphasis on the backwardness of Japanese management gradually lost influence, and new attempts were made to reevaluate it.

The initial focus was on institutional phenomena as an explanation for the vigor of Japanese management and emphasized lifetime employment, seniority-based promotion, and enterprise unions—the so-called "three treasures"—as the keys to understanding its power. Later, more sophisticated arguments were presented, and attempts were made to analyze the structure and functions of Japanese management, among other analyses, in relation to the values and behavioral patterns of the Japanese people.[1]

However, there were criticisms of the latter approach. Some accused it of narrowing its focus to particular features of Japanese society. Others argued that differences between Japan's managerial institutions and those of other nations, even if they existed, were a matter of degree. In response to such criticism, some began to investigate factors that lie beneath institutions in order to explain the strength of Japanese management within a general framework.

One of the leading arguments was advanced by Tadanori Nishiyama and Kōji Matsumoto, who concentrated on changes in the structure of stock ownership in explaining Japanese management's brilliant postwar performance. They asserted that the broad and rapid distribution of stock ownership in postwar Japan facilitated the "separation of owner-ship and control," a phenomenon seen in most major companies. Ac-cording to Nishiyama and Matsumoto, the separation of ownership and control changed the class structure of Japanese society by eliminating the distance between managers and workers and converted the Japanese company into a so-called "unified body of employees." This, contend its advocates, is the source of the vitality of Japanese companies.[2]

Although this idea is interesting, there are several problems with it. First, by concentrating on postwar developments, it lacks a historical perspective. Second, by emphasizing general factors, the idea neglects the influence of social and cultural factors. As a result, this approach cannot explain why the separation of ownership and control, a phenom-enon feared in the United States from the 1920s to the 1940s, produced different effects in Japan than those anticipated in America. Why would the same separation of ownership and control lead to diametrically different results? Is it because the phenomenon occurred at different times, because it had different implications for different developmental paths, or because of other factors? Such questions were not considered by this approach owing to the shortcomings mentioned earlier.

In this essay, I shall add historical and social perspective to the argument made by Nishiyama and Matsumoto, as constructive criticism, in order to overcome the limits of their analysis and to fully appreciate the potential of their idea.

New Perspectives for Analyzing Japanese Management

Post-Capitalism

Nishiyama, who has conducted detailed empirical research on the control structure of joint-stock companies in Japan, finds that throughout the postwar period, and especially during the rapid-growth period of the 1960s, Japanese society has seen the demise of large capital owners and the widespread emergence of managerial control.[3] The results of Nishiyama's extensive research on the control structure of the 1970s are shown in Table 1.

It is difficult to pinpoint exactly when the decline of capital owners occurred. For example, there are cases like that of the Mitsui family, in which the owners had disappeared from managerial activities before World War II, proving that a "decline" had occurred during the rapid

TABLE 1

Composition of the Control Structure of Japanese Joint-Stock Companies
(1970s)

	Number of companies	(%)	Total assets	
			billion ¥	(%)
Management control	296	(89)	104,746.9	(96)
Family control	23	(7)	2,433.7	(2)
Foreign capital	7	(2)	634.5	(1)
State-owned	2	(1)	284.4	(0)
Other	4	(1)	939.1	(1)
TOTAL	332	(100)	109,038.6	(100)

SOURCE: Tadanori Nishiyama, *Gendai kigyō no shihai kōzō: Kabushiki gaisha no hōkai* (The control structure of contemporary enterprise: The collapse of joint-stock companies) (Tokyo: Yūhikaku, 1975), p. 210, based on a sample of 332 companies, selected by their total assets.

growth of Japanese capitalism in the Meiji and Taishō eras. However, Nishiyama argues that participation and defeat in the Pacific War were decisive in this development.[4]

For the prewar *zaibatsu* conglomerates of Mitsui, Mitsubishi, Sumitomo, Yasuda, Furukawa, Asano, Ōkura, and Kawasaki, or the new *Konzern* combines of Nissan, Nichitsu, Nissō, Shōden, and Riken, a "revival of share-owners" did not occur after the postwar dissolution of zaibatsu. Moreover, most capital owners who managed to survive zaibatsu dissolution disappeared during the rapid-growth period. Nishiyama asserts that this completed the downfall of capitalist stockholders.[5]

To examine changes in the control structure, Nishiyama sampled 150 companies in 1920 and 800 companies in 1940, 1960, and 1980. His results are shown in Table 2. The decline of capitalist owners and the emergence of management power is far more developed in Japan than in the United States, and, as a result, many phenomena in Japanese society cannot be explained by regarding it as capitalist. Nishiyama argues that it is appropriate to call Japan a "post-capitalist society." Although it generates problems of its own, such a society is free of many of the problems seen in capitalist and socialist societies and is an advanced society that possesses certain advantages unavailable to either. It is free simultaneously of the lack of competition found in socialist economies and of "class conflict," the major fault of capitalist societies:

Since managers are not an agent of capitalist stockholders, there is no distance between managers and general workers. Managers share unity and homogeneity with the workers. The cooperativeness of Japanese trade unions, as compared to the militancy of their counterparts in other nations, the existence of total quality control [TQC], and the system of lifetime employment, all of which are considered major features of "Japanese management," are related to this structural characteristic of Japanese companies, and this characteristic is also closely related to the rapid growth of the contemporary Japanese economy.[6]

TABLE 2
Changes in the Control Structure of Japanese Joint-Stock Companies
(20-year intervals)

Change in control	1920–40		1940–60		1960–80	
	Number	%	Number	%	Number	%
C to C	100	93.5	97	18.4	28	7.0
C to NC	5	4.7	412	78.0	54	13.4
NC to NC	1	0.9	19	3.6	318	79.1
NC to C	1	0.9	0	0.0	2	0.5
TOTAL	107	100.0	528	100.0	402	100.0

SOURCE: Tadanori Nishiyama, *Datsu shihon shugi bunseki: Atarashii shakai no kaimaku* (Analysis of post-capitalism: The start of a new society) (Tokyo: Bunshindo, 1983), p. 143.
NOTE: C = capitalist control; NC = noncapitalist control. Combining the percentages for C and for NC within each period shows how the positions of the two types of control have been reversed across six decades:

C: 94.4 to 18.4 to 7.5
NC: 5.6 to 81.6 to 92.5

For purposes of comparison, let us examine the control structure in U.S. firms found by Robert Larner and David Kotz (see Tables 3 and 4).

The Theory of "Corporatism" (Kigyō shugi)

Since Nishiyama's main interest was to explain Japan's transition from capitalism to post-capitalism, he did not fully consider how changes in the ownership structure relate to the nature of Japanese management. The relationship between these two factors was taken up by Kōji Matsumoto. Following Nishiyama, Matsumoto wrote: "In Japan, under the shell of capitalism, a new kind of economic system has developed. Vitality, efficiency, and other characteristics of the Japanese economy—characteristics that distinguish it from the economies of other countries—are the effect or derivative of this system."[7]

Although a Japanese company may legally be a joint-stock corporation composed of stockholders, according to Matsumoto, this has become merely a formality. In reality, it is a "unified body of employees." The company is independent of the control of its stockholders, and it is the employees, through lifetime employment, who bear the risks and share the fruits of enterprise activities. The convergence of interests between the enterprise and its employees encourages voluntary participation in management.[8]

Matsumoto calls those who work under this new system "corporatists" (kigyō jin) and the system controlled by a collective of corporatists, which has emerged to replace capitalism, "corporatism" (kigyō shugi). In a company of corporatists, the homogeneity of its components is reflected in equal treatment. The enterprise is no longer conceived of as a "busi-

TABLE 3
Larner: Control of the 141 Largest
Nonfinancial U.S. Corporations, 1963
(excluding utilities)

Control category	Number of companies	%
Owner control	32	22.7
Management control	109	77.3
TOTAL	141	100.0

SOURCE: Robert J. Larner, *Management Control and the Large Corporation* (Cambridge, Mass.: Harvard University Press, 1970), p. 12; cited by David M. Kotz, *Bank Control of Large Corporations in the United States* (Berkeley: University of California Press, 1978), p. 117.
 NOTE: Kotz combines Larner's categories of private ownership, majority ownership, minority control, and control through a legal device under the title of owner control.

ness enterprise" of capital owners but becomes the "business concern" of all employees. This changes the concept of business responsibility. Labor unions become an association of corporatists and as such identify themselves with and feel responsible for the company.

In this sense, a Japanese company differs from either a Western capitalist or a socialist company. Western companies, whose management is restrained by both shareholders and horizontal labor unions, cannot keep their investment plans from being shortsighted or avoid great pain in dealing with the unions. By comparison, in the Japanese company, managers enjoy freedom, and the corporatist group is united in pursuing the growth of the company. Workers enthusiastically participate in managerial matters and base their activities on the criterion of "what is needed by the company."

This, Matsumoto asserts, is a highly advanced system because it is able to integrate management and labor, to encourage voluntary participation by workers, to develop their productive skills, to introduce organizational flexibility, and to facilitate the "humanization" of labor. The claim that large companies in Japan are no longer the "business enterprises" of their investors but have become the "business concerns" of their managers and employees is widely accepted, with the exception of a few obstinate economists. Many, including myself, have expressed similar ideas; the "management by all" philosophy advocated by Konosuke Matsushita, the founder of Matsushita Electric/Panasonic, is one example.

This idea also coincides with the frequent comment that Japanese companies exist to "feed their employees" and not to enrich their investors, and also with the fact that Japanese companies tend to emphasize

TABLE 4
Kotz: Control of the 141 Largest
Nonfinancial U.S. Corporations, 1967–69
(excluding utilities)

Control category	Number of companies	%
1. Financial control only	49	34.8
2. Both financial and owner control	8	5.7
3. Owner control only	19	13.5
4. Miscellaneous	5	3.5
5. No identified control	60	42.6
All categories	141	100.0
All financial control (1 + 2)	57	40.4
All owner control (2 + 3)	27	19.1

SOURCE: David M. Kotz, *Bank Control of Large Corporations in the United States* (Berkeley: University of California Press, 1978), p. 117.

increasing their market share rather than their profit rates. In Japanese society, a company's market share or size determines its social prestige, which, in turn, enhances the social prestige of its members.

Kōji Matsumoto has systematized some commonly perceived, but fragmented, ideas on Japanese companies. The following summarizes what Matsumoto lists as the major characteristics of corporatism:

1. *Stripping the joint-stock company system of its contents.* Major institutions designed to secure shareholder control have failed in Japan. Among such institutions are the shareholders' general meeting, the board of directors, the auditor system, and the CPA system. On the other hand, the importance of those at the apex of the company bureaucracy, such as the president, vice president, senior managing directors (*senmu*), and managing directors (*jōmu*), has increased, despite the lack of clear definition of their roles in the commercial codes.

2. *Independence of the company from its shareholders.* The stockholders do not control the company. Instead, the company controls the will of the shareholders. As a result, in a Japanese company dividends are regarded merely as a capital cost and the interests of stockholders do not have top priority.[9] Managers are freed from the restrictions of short-term perspectives and can set long-term goals.

3. *Change in the concept of the company.* The company has become dominated by the employee group, making the unified body of employees a social reality. According to the principle of non-dismissal, employees have come to bear the risks and receive the fruits of business activity. The staff of the company is homogeneous, and members enjoy equality in terms of treatment.

4. *Transformation of workers.* With the creation of the above relationship within the company, the interests of the company and its employees

start to coincide. As a result, voluntary participation by employees emerges. Instead of a worker being an external seller of his labor, the employee becomes a corporatist who shares the responsibilities of management. Labor unions become associations of corporatists.[10]

5. *Freedom of management.* In contrast to its Western counterparts, whose management is restricted by both shareholders and horizontal unions, the Japanese company enjoys freedom of management.

Although the arguments developed by Nishiyama and Matsumoto, as summarized above, have origins different from those of the traditional theories of Japanese management, they cut deep into the concept of what makes Japanese management truly Japanese. Furthermore, their arguments not only address the issues of Japanese management but also place the issues as part of a broader system. They have the potential of forming a grand theory.

The Introduction of Historical Perspective

The works of Nishiyama and Matsumoto shed light on an important aspect of enterprise activities since World War II. However, in emphasizing corporatism as a system, Matsumoto has tended to neglect its cultural premise.[11] The evolution he perceives can be summarized as follows. First, the company becomes independent from shareholder control owing to the latter's decline. As a result, employees, instead of stockholders, become the core of the company. With the dominance of the employee group, the principle of non-dismissal is established. Employees begin to bear the risks of company activities and workers become corporatists. Because employees are a homogeneous group, industrial relations become harmonious. Employees voluntarily participate in managerial activities. Numerous managerial characteristics seen in Japan can be derived from this institutional structure of the company without going into the mentality of the Japanese.

What requires further attention is Matsumoto's assumption of a mutually exclusive relationship between the mentality of the Japanese and the institutional structure of the company. As indicated by Matsumoto, the autonomy of the company is achieved by the decline in shareholder control. Without this structural development, it is difficult to understand how corporatism took its present shape. However, it is also difficult to explain the rise of corporatism solely in terms of the ubiquity of managerial control. Matsumoto's argument is problematic because he does not clarify the nature of the managers who assume control once the shareholders lose it. Loss of control by stockholders does not necessarily mean that the employee group, including ordinary employees, can take control of a company. Thus, there is no guarantee that employees will become corporatists or that the work force will become homogeneous.

The decline of shareholders' power might concentrate power in the hands of a small number of managers, allowing them to abuse that power. Managers might not only ignore the interests of shareholders but also sacrifice the company for their own interests. There is no guarantee that they will work hard to better the position of employees as a whole.

This topic was the focus of a controversy over managerial control in the United States. Even if such worries are unfounded, it is not realistic to assume that the decline of shareholders' power will result in a unified body of employees in the United States, as is the case in Japan. It is true that the separation of ownership and control was conducive to formation of a unified body of employees in postwar Japan. However, the former was not sufficient for the latter. Thus, it is necessary to explain the development path of Japanese companies that linked these two characteristics. The fact that it is unrealistic to assume that a unified body of employees suddenly emerged after World War II requires a careful look into prewar history.

The Development of Corporatism

The Starting Point

Several reasons can be offered to explain how the shareholders, or owners, of Japanese companies became excluded from managerial activities, and how firms then developed into unified bodies of employees. Such characteristics are seen in institutions of both the Tokugawa and Meiji periods.

House masters and employees in Tokugawa family businesses. As pointed out by sociologists and business historians, in the Tokugawa period the house was an entity that existed beyond the life spans of its members. Even the head of the family was merely the one who took care of the house estate and handed it down to his progeny. Thus family business was not an activity that belonged to the family head but was shared by other members, such as managers (*bantō*) and salesmen (*tedai*). All members bore the responsibility of maintaining and expanding the family business and expected to share the benefits of its prosperity.

Yasukazu Takenaka's description conveys the atmosphere of the times:

Merchant houses were enterprise organizations, handed down from ancestors to descendants, and had a kind of legal personality. The head of the family, who inherited the family business, had a duty to maintain, and if possible expand, the business and a duty to safeguard the house so as to hand it down to the next generation. These responsibilities of the family head were, without exception, emphasized in the principles of the family [*kakun*] and the rules of the shop [*tensoku*]. . . .

The merchant house as a business organization was never regarded as the private possession of the head as an individual. All the members of the business enterprise had a duty to receive the business from [their] ancestors and to pass it on. They also shared the benefits of prosperity. Thus, once the merchant house became established, as a so-called *shinise*, it institutionalized organizational devices to assist the family head, the so-called *tanakata seido*. Personnel were trained through this system, and at the same time managers and salesmen secured a strong say in managerial matters. The family head was the person responsible for managing and supervising the business. However, the actual execution of matters was left to managers and salesmen. It was established by custom that without their assent even the family head could not get anything done. Some shop rules explicitly stated that even if the family head affixed his seal to documents, the shop would not be held responsible if it was done arbitrarily. Also, there was a distinction between the shop and the family household [*oku*]. The family head was provided with his salary [*ategai buchi*], and his expenditures were limited. If he overspent, it was not at all rare that it was counted as the family head's debt to the shop.[12]

As Takenaka shows, the development of the *tanakata seido* caused the separation of shop and household. Thus, the separation of ownership and management progressed to a degree unimaginable in the modern notion of ownership. It seems that this separation of ownership and management resembled the separation of ownership and control. As a result, employees were regarded as part of the business enterprise.

In Tokugawa merchant houses, it was considered the duty of managers and salesmen to reprimand the master of the house if he engaged in activities not productive for the family business. If necessary, they could even force the master into retirement, with the consent of branch family (*bunke*) and "assumed" family (*bekke*) members. This shows the position of employees in the concept of family business. A similar idea of family business was seen in the early Meiji period.

Rizaemon Minomura's views of the company. The Meiji government promoted the Western capitalist system in Japan. Companies that had long traditions in the Tokugawa period had to adjust to the new times. In particular, those enterprises regarded as family estates had to be reorganized to fit the new system of capitalism. The ideas of Rizaemon Minomura, the head manager of the Mitsui family, were especially interesting. Minomura was recognized for his contribution in saving the Mitsui family business in its critical years at the end of the Tokugawa period and was appointed, in 1866, as one of the managers of Mitsui. Through his extraordinary talent, he led Mitsui's business activities throughout the turbulent Bakumatsu years and during the Meiji Restoration; he consolidated the base of what was to become the great Mitsui. The *ōmotokata-kisoku* (basic rules of Mitsui business), stipulated in August 1874 under his supervision, states in its first article that "the family property of the Mitsui-gumi [group] belongs to the Mitsui-gumi and is not the personal property of the Mitsui family. It is crucial that this distinction is made clear and the enterprise is not personalized. Both master and servant must bear this in mind and work hard so that they can reap the profits."[13]

Although the idea of the family estate lingered, it belonged not solely to the Mitsui family but to the Mitsui-gumi, which was engaged in the family business of Mitsui. The traditional view of family enterprise, including not only family members but even lowly salesmen, is vividly expressed.

Furthermore, when Mitsui Bank was established in 1876, its 20,000 shares, worth two million yen, were divided into three parts: 10,000 shares went to the house headquarters of the Mitsui-gumi, 5,000 shares were divided among the nine families of Mitsui, and 5,000 shares were divided among the 383 employees. The founding document, the *Mitsui ginkō sōritsu no taii* (The basic prospectus for establishing Mitsui Bank) states that "the master-servant relationship should be terminated and both should, as supporters of the company," cooperate and work hard together and should share the results.[14] This shows that in the transformation from family business to capitalism, the company had to clarify its investment relation and, thus, had to reincorporate its employees, who had implicitly been part of the family business, as shareholders. This was a measure to overcome the problems created by the collapse of the family business system and to reintegrate its members into the new system as investors in a joint-stock company.

This not only represents an attempt to adjust the traditional perception of the company to the new capitalist system but also marks the origin of the corporatist view of the company. It was based on the traditional view of the company rather than on the idiosyncratic ideas of Minomura. His ideas, still transitional, recognized employees as legitimate members of business activities. However, only a few Meiji firms inherited this tradition because, as is widely known, many of the great Tokugawa merchant houses went out of business during the turbulent times of the Meiji Restoraiton.

Of the four largest zaibatsu conglomerates—Mitsui, Mitsubishi, Sumitomo, and Yasuda—that enjoyed predominance in prewar Japanese society, only Mitsui and Sumitomo inherited the tradition of family business. Their systems of management by managers (*bantō*) was established during the Tokugawa period, and, as a result, family business owners were left with only indirect control over management. In the cases of Mitsubishi and Yasuda, which emerged after the Meiji Restoration, the owners exercised direct and powerful control over management.

The case of Seibei Fujimoto II. How the role of employees was redefined when family businesses reorganized into capitalist joint-stock companies like Mitsui sheds light on certain interesting aspects of Japanese family business. But what of cases in which family businesses did not go through capitalist reorganization but instead developed as "capitalist enterprises" from the very beginning? In this case, the capitalistic nature of business was strongly emphasized, as in Western countries, and the instrumental view of workers naturally spread in Japan. However, even in these "capitalist enterprises," the notion of employees as indispensable members of business activities started to emerge. The case of Seibei Fujimoto shows how the ideas of traditional family business were reflected in newly created modern capitalist enterprises in the Meiji era and suggests that Mitsui cannot be regarded as an isolated case with limited implications.

Seibei Fujimoto II was an influential entrepreneur who assumed executive posts in over 30 companies, including the posts of president of Fukushima Boseki (spinning) and Fujimoto Bank. In 1902 he started Fujimoto Bill Brokers, the present Daiwa Securities. The company grew rapidly, and in 1906 he converted it to a joint-stock company.

Fujimoto distributed shares of this company to his employees and selected some of them as the company's directors. The practice of promoting employees to directorships was seen in numerous companies thereafter.[15] Because the commercial codes of that period required that directors be stockholders, it became customary for employees who had been promoted to directorships to borrow stock from major stockholders and pay them back from their executive bonuses.

This idea of coexistence and coprosperity has shaped the perception of business in Japanese society since the Tokugawa period and survives in various aspects of Japanese business today. It marks a sharp contrast to the idea of business in a self-reliant society. It should be noted that the Japanese concept of business that refuses to regard employees as instruments but instead treats them as legitimate members of business activities—who share identical interests with managers—has its roots in traditional Japanese ideas of business.[16] It conflicts with the capitalist notion of business, and the tension between these two ideas is an important perspective for examining the history of Japanese business and the roots of the "unified body of employees."

The capitalistic transformation of the enterprise. Beginning in the 1890s, with the rise of Japanese capitalism, traditional ideas of business were overwhelmed by capitalist views. The fact that the Mitsui family repossessed the stocks of Mitsui Bank that had been distributed among Mitsui employees symbolizes the trend of the times. The idea of workers as dispensable things became widespread, and the wretched working conditions that resulted ignited violent industrial disputes.[17]

Some managers in major companies became concerned with the seriousness of the situation and deliberately tried to restore the traditional view of business. This resulted in the reconceptualization of business according to the idea of business-as-family (*keiei kazoku shugi*) or the ideology of company-as-family. Such ideas were widely diffused by World War I. Although such moves can be seen as deliberate and instrumental, they did harmonize with social morals deeply embedded in the traditional idea of coexistence and coprosperity. This is why, in my opinion, such ideas were accepted in the Japanese business community neither as means nor as understandings but as something in between.

The beginning of stock distribution. During the 1930s, the militarization of industries generated a vast demand for credit. In the face of such demand, the major zaibatsu, which had maintained a system of exclusive family stock ownership, had to offer their stocks to the public. The newly emerging combines called *shinkō zaibatsu* had rapidly established themselves by offering stocks, but in this period they faced the same financial problem as the older zaibatsu and were forced to rely more on the stock market.

Shōichi Asajima and his associates have compared the financial structures of the three great zaibatsu, Mitsui, Mitsubishi, and Sumitomo, and the new combines, Nissan, Nichitsu, and Riken, in the interwar period and examined how both groups went public for capital. Their findings can be summarized as follows.[18]

In the latter half of the 1920s, Mitsui still maintained a hierarchical ownership structure, in which the head office of Mitsui Unlimited controlled Mitsui Bussan (trading) and Mitsui Kōzan (mining), each of which headed a combine of its own. Faced with the need to increase their capital in the 1930s, the head office and the other two Mitsui conglomerates had to sell part of their stocks to "introduce capital from other sources, starting from peripheral subsidiaries," to reduce their financial burden, and to maintain the exclusiveness of ownership relations. In 1939, Mitsui Kōzan offered its stock to the public, terminating its exclusive financial relations and making way for further public offerings, although this was more in form than substance.

Mitsubishi & Co., Ltd., was the head company at the apex of a centralized zaibatsu. The company had been totally owned by the Iwasaki family, but during the years of wartime economy, to meet financial demands, "it had to transfer its burden by offering to the public the stocks of its subsidiaries and abandon its closed financial relations."[19] Ultimately, it even offered shares in the head company to the public. However, this was not enough to meet the company's needs. The family's share in ownership was kept at 50 per cent only through heavy reliance on loans.

Sumitomo's system was most centralized, with Sumitomo & Co., Ltd., fully owned by the Sumitomo family at the top. Since it was inactive in increasing equipment investment (mainly owing to its lack of strong involvement in militarization), "it was able to bear the burden of [generating] investment capital through the amount realized from the dividends of its subsidiaries."[20] Thus, it was able to cope with the situation by offering the public the stock of only three of its subsidiaries, while keeping its 100 per cent ownership of the head office's stock.

The Kuhara family attempted to expand its enterprises into a zaibatsu empire during the post–World War I boom by capital increases and stock premiums (representing the difference between the fixed price at which a stock is usually issued and the higher market price). However, during the recession after the war, it was dissolved under the control of the banks and eventually reorganized by Gisuke Ayukawa as the Nissan Konzern (Nissan combine). Nissan was composed of publicly financed companies and procured most of its capital by assigning stockholders premium stocks and quotas (stockholders are happy to assume the quota if the market price is higher than the fixed price they have to pay).

In the case of Nichitsu, the head office in principle held 10 per cent of its subsidiaries' shares, although the actual proportion varied by company. Ownership had been dispersed before World War II. Riken, in which companies' shares were mutually held within the group, had to rely on loans to raise capital and was eventually forced to reorganize. However, as Satoshi Saito points out, for Riken it was not entry into military industries but excessive diversification of its subsidiaries that caused the group's financial problems.[21]

As shown above, the major zaibatsu groups had modified their closed ownership structure by the time of World War II, and the newly established combines had to introduce outside capital rapidly, which further dispersed ownership.

The Critical Impact of SCAP Reforms

The economic reforms implemented by the General Headquarters of the Supreme Commander for the Allied Powers (SCAP)—zaibatsu dissolution, exclusion of excessive concentration, and the purge of top management officials—finally expelled the top owner-managers from business activities. As the result of SCAP policies, employee-managers established leadership in Japanese companies. The reforms thus forcibly imposed by the Occupation authorities completed the separation of ownership and control in most zaibatsu-affiliated companies.

One of the most important features of this process was the emergence of labor power. The labor movement, influenced by the threat of mass starvation, the initial policies of SCAP to promote labor unions, and the spread of Marxism, became radicalized to an extent that raised concern in SCAP. The power of the unions to defend the interests of their members and the rising resistance to employee dismissal established employees as a major factor in, not merely an instrument of, business activity to an extent unprecedented in the prewar years.

During this period it was not rare for companies to ask for the union's consent to nominees for company president. Most union leaders were graduates of prestigious universities assigned to middle-managerial posts; they were the junior officers of management. Indeed, some union leaders were later promoted to the presidency or other executive posts in their companies.

All the factors of the immediate postwar period cited above were mutually reinforcing and contributed to both the alienation of stockholders from business activities and the integration into them of employees. The "unified body of employees," to use Matsumoto's label for it, was thus established. As it gained momentum, this development was further promoted by the dispersion of ownership during the rapid-growth period of the 1960s, reflecting the cry for increased capital. With this separation of ownership and control in most major companies, with only a few exceptions, the system of corporatism neared completion.

We should note that this process was closely associated with the nature of the "contextual" society. In the contextual society, characterized by mutual dependence, mutual trust, and sanctification of human relations,[22] social relations within the workplace are much closer than where human relations are regarded as instrumental. On the other hand, investors, who barely maintain abstract rights as shareholders (who have little chance to see either employees or managers), are increasingly excluded from business activities. Thus, if investors are managers who work with employees (in this situation, the contextual society prevails), they maintain their position. However, once they leave the organization and become related to the company only as owners, they rapidly lose power over managerial matters.

With this sociocultural background, the separation of ownership and control developed rapidly in Japan and brought about the alienation of investors from business activities. As a result, companies became dynamic organizations of businessmen led by business wizards. In postwar Japan, business has not been an activity to profit investors but an activity to keep employees fed by maintaining and expanding the business itself.

Needless to say, in times of crisis the company is forced to lay off some of its members, but this is to protect its activities and enables it to keep "feeding" its high-quality employees. Reducing manpower is an operation that cuts the weakest part of the company and is not an act to defend the interests of investors.

In summary, many factors contributed to the rise of corporatism: the characteristics of prewar Japanese companies; the relationship between the Japanese people and their organizations; the drastic changes in the structure of ownership begun by the need to rapidly expand capital for militarization and completed during the rapid-growth period; the effects of the postwar reforms during the Occupation; and the paradoxical effects of militant labor movements. The disposition of the people in the contextual society facilitated this process. Thus, corporatism is not a sudden product of the postwar separation of ownership and control but has its historical origins in prewar management.

Social Background to the Development of Corporatism

There are three primary elements in the social factors that sustained the development of corporatism described in the previous section. I shall briefly identify each of them and then examine them in greater detail.

1. As mentioned above, the traditional Japanese notion of a company is different from that of the Western advanced capitalist nations. This is in part the result of the backwardness of Japanese capitalism but is also a reflection of social and cultural differences. However, paradoxically, it seems that the backwardness or incompleteness of capitalism has, in effect, facilitated the emergence of "post-capitalism" and corporatism in Japan.

2. One of the most important elements in the traditional view of the company was how the individual was conceived of in relation to the group. As will be examined in detail, in Japan this is not based on the self-reliance found in Western societies.

3. In Japan, there exist delicate checks on the exercise of power, preventing the abuse of business managerial powers.

The Company in a "Self-Reliance Society"

To depict how companies are typically viewed in Japan, it is necessary to provide for reference a model that explains the American case. According to Esyun Hamaguchi, the social relations of a "self-reliance society" can be summarized by three elements: the principle of egocentrism, the principle of self-reliance, and the instrumentalization of human relations.[23] In this type of society, people freely assert themselves within the boundaries of social rules that are clearly defined by laws and contracts.

Investors in this society act to maximize their profits according to the rules. If necessary, they will contract with capable managers and will try to get the most out of them. On the other hand, managers will also try to get the highest bid for their services. Thus, both sides regard each other as instruments.

When the company is a business enterprise of investor-managers, workers are merely instruments for the business enterprise and only receive rewards comparable to their contribution. They are excluded from the business enterprise's activities and do not bear any of its risks. Neither do they receive any share of excess profits: wages are based on job performance. This is the ideal of a company in a self-reliance society and is relatively close to the way the company is viewed in the United States.

What happens when changes occur in the ownership structure of the company owing to the dispersion of shareholders, and when managers are freed from investor control? In the relationship between capitalist owners and managers, it is natural that once managers gain power, they will use it to maximize their gains to the extent permitted by the law and contracts. This can be derived from the model of the self-reliance society. Once "managerial control" is established, capitalist owners are reduced to the status of mere investors.

This situation is widely feared in the United States, particularly since it conflicts with the classical notion of property ownership and the countervailing power attitude of Americans. Naturally, concern centers on the issue of the concentration of managerial power and the violation of shareholders' rights. This concern appeared in the mid 1920s and reached its height in the 1930s and 1940s, but it continues to appear in various forms today. The pattern of conflict in this new situation was investors versus managers.

The Concept of Enterprise in Corporatism

Companies are viewed in a fundamentally different way in a corporatist society. They are seen as bodies composed of managers and employees, where investors, as providers of funds, are an exogenous force.

In postwar Japan, except for a short period of confusion immediately after the war, the relationship between managers and employees has been that of partners in business activities, gradually developing into what Matsumoto calls a unified body of employees. It should be noted that the basic pattern of interest cleavage here is that of managers and employees versus investors. This pattern was the typical context for large and medium-sized postwar Japanese companies.

As discussed above, the assumption that this idea emerged suddenly after the war owing to the separation of ownership and control is problematic. My hypothesis is that company business activities have traditionally been conducted by a triumvirate consisting of investors, managers, and employees. Companies became unified bodies of employees when investors were alienated as the result of the separation of ownership and control.

Different Views of Business as Seen in Bonus Payments

In the United States, bonuses are still paid mostly to executives. Since workers are paid on the basis of their labor, except for special cases, they are not eligible for bonuses. In contrast, managers receive bonuses as rewards for leading a company to success, and these may add up to considerable sums.

According to Richard T. Pascale and Anthony G. Athos, only 500 top officials and field managers of ITT, out of its 350,000 employees, were considered eligible for bonuses.[24] These few were rewarded with bonuses whenever they exceeded their goals. Most employees, however, received no part of the company's profits, no matter how large they were. This is typical of the American view of bonus rewards. In Japan, even in the Tokugawa and Meiji periods, it was not unusual for even the lowest-ranked employee to be rewarded with a part of the company profits.

In postwar Japanese society, the bonus is not regarded as a reward for special contributions. Rather, it is considered a "conventional provisional salary" and reflects the annual performance of the company. Bonuses are paid not only to core members of business activities but also to the lower echelons of employees, such as janitors or guards, at the same rate.

When a Japanese company in California, which had adopted some Japanese managerial techniques, decided to pay bonuses according to the Japanese system, the reaction was extremely favorable despite the small amount. With this and other policies, the company was able to reduce the turnover rate of its workers from 75 per cent to 50 per cent.

By way of comparison, consider the case of an American friend of mine who took over the management of a company in crisis. He was appointed general manager and brought two competent people in with him, one as sales manager and the other as procurement manager. He made an agreement with the shareholders that 13 per cent of net profits would go to himself, 2 per cent to the sales manager, and 1 per cent to the procurement manager as bonuses.

My friend was very successful, and the company grew rapidly, generating a huge profit. His bonus thus grew larger and larger, reaching several million dollars. While he accumulated this huge fortune, ordinary employees received only their fixed wages. The treasurer and secretary received three-week paid overseas vacations as bonuses, but this was paid for out of the manager's pocket as a reward for their personal loyalty, not by the company. The approach was to secure the support, and motivate the personal loyalties, of able subordinates. This differs from the Japanese idea of bonus rewards, which are aimed at promoting the employee's loyalty to the organization.

A similar case in Japanese history had quite different consequences. In 1901, Toyoji Wada took over Fuji Bōseki, at that time in deep financial trouble, and with great effort and hardship made it one of the largest cotton-spinning companies in Japan. Since it had been decided beforehand that the executives could use 15 per cent of net profits as bonuses and entertainment expenses, Wada received a huge amount. To this point, the story is similar to the American case mentioned above.

However, in 1906 when the rehabilitated Fuji Bōseki merged with Tokyo Gassed Yarn and became Fuji Gassed Yarn, Wada voluntarily proposed to divide the 15 per cent executive bonus into thirds and to spend 5 per cent on bonuses for the executives, another 5 per cent on bonuses for white-collar employees, and the remaining 5 per cent on blue-collar bonuses. This new bonus plan was met very sympathetically by the board of directors and passed the general stockholders' meeting in July 1906. Thus, the situation moved in a totally different direction from the American case.[25]

The interesting point is that neither the board of directors nor the shareholders questioned the proposal but, instead, accepted it with "great sympathy." I suspect that such a proposal would be met with astonishment or suspicion in the United States, where shareholders constantly fear that managers will abuse their powers for private gain at shareholders' expense. In a society where employees are commonly regarded as part of the business enterprise, it is natural that Wada's proposal, although innovative, was accepted with favor. And if managers show such consideration, employees are bound to respond by zealously performing their duties.

The case of Fuji Bōseki occurred during the ascendancy of Japanese capitalism, when the traditional idea of family business had been rapidly transformed into the capitalist mold. It shows how the traditional perception of business prevailed despite the trend toward capitalism.

Development of the bonus system in Japan can be traced to records showing that as early as the merchant houses of the Tokugawa period, bonuses were paid to distribute profits. In the house of Mitsui, an ōkanjō (grand account settlement) was carried out every three years, when one-tenth of the profits were distributed down to the lowest-ranking apprentices (detchi), with all employees receiving part of the distribution in accordance with their services. This "reward" (hōbigin) was in principle saved by the shop and was given on retirement.[26]

The best-known case of bonuses in the Meiji era is that of Mitsubishi. Companies affiliated with Mitsubishi decided to distribute "profit money" to their employees in January 1876. Subsequently, bonuses were initially paid every December, and then, after 1897, twice a year (in June and December). At the beginning, the bonuses were about 20 to 25 per cent of the employee's monthly salary, and in 1888 they were increased to 100 per cent. From 1897 on, the biannual bonus payments added up to twice the amount of monthly pay.

A document written in 1879 explaining the bonus system supports my analysis of the Japanese view of the company. It points out that the achievements of business depend on the integrity and diligence of all employees and, thus, if a business is successful, its gains should be distributed. Unfortunately, the report goes on, during the early years of our company enterprise, this practice could not be afforded. However, in the previous year, because of the efforts of all, it had become possible to pay bonuses and it was hoped that this would encourage further hard work.[27]

So far I have traced fragmented but important cases. Systematic studies on how the bonus system took shape are still needed. It was a commonly shared view without clear research in Japan that bonuses were paid to white-collar workers as rewards for hard work but not to blue-collar workers. As seen in the Mitsubishi case, however, rewards for hard work were not limited to only a few individuals but were likely to be given to all (or most) employees. Records also show that bonuses were paid to blue-collar workers. If we consider the fact that bonuses were paid to all employees, and the fact that this practice was likely to increase when skilled labor was in great demand, it seems that the custom must have been more widespread than is indicated by available documents. The first volume of the first compilation of the *Nihon rōmu kanri nen-shi* (Yearbook of Japanese labor and management) reports several cases of bonus payment to blue-collar workers.

After World War II, with the change in managerial attitudes and the increase in labor's bargaining power, the bonus payment changed from a reward for hard work to a provisional salary paid to all permanent employees at a fixed rate. However, if we compare this idea of the bonus to the Western notion, it can be said that the inclination to treat it as a provisional salary was seen even during the Tokugawa, Meiji, and Taisho periods. It can also be said that this reflected the Japanese idea of giving employees a stake in the business enterprise.

Contemporary Views of Enterprises

Similar views were expressed by experts in these earlier periods. For example, Kamekichi Takahashi, a famous journalist who wrote a number of books on Japanese industrial history, deplored the degeneration of the joint-stock companies in the early years of the Showa period (the late 1920s) and proposed to separate shareholders from business activities and to secure legal status for employees. He pioneered the idea of what has flourished as corporatism since the war. It is worth noting that the separation of ownership and control had already been advocated among the most knowledgeable individuals of the time.

To prevent widespread corruption among company executives, Takahashi proposed the following rules (emphasis added):

1. Only those engaged in the everyday activities of the company should be permitted to become directors. *Only the auditor should represent the interests of the shareholders,* who are not involved in the normal operations of the company. The commercial codes should be revised so that directors can be appointed without being shareholders.

2. The selection of directors should be made at a *general meeting of the company,* composed of representatives of both employees and stockholders.

3. *At least half the directors should be chosen from among the employees.*

Takahashi also asserted that managers and workers should be allowed to participate in decision making in joint-stock companies and proposed that at the general meeting of the company, "the absolute power of the stockholder should be restricted, and the top managerial leader[s] . . . workers, and other employees should participate in business management by, for example, sharing one-third of the votes each."[28]

This explicitly states the idea that business is the combined activity of shareholders, managers, and employees. However, it is not clear who were to be included as employees. Presumably, temporary workers and female workers, with their high turnover rates, were not to be included as members of businesses. Nonetheless, it is clear that even before World War II—that is, even before the actual separation of ownership and control—there existed in Japan a unique idea of business, unique in the way it regards the roles of shareholders, managers, and employees, compared to the American system.

The Japanese view of business that portrays "business activities" not as "business enterprise" of investors and managers but as the "going concern" of a triumvirate that includes employees thus did not appear suddenly with the separation of ownership and control after the war. I contend that it originated in the business ideas of the Tokugawa era and has been developing among large and middle-sized small businesses in Japan ever since.

The Relationship Between the Company and Its Employees

So far, I have examined different ideas of the company by focusing on managerial principles. However, this is only one side of the story. For a complete view, we must examine the second of my three points, the relationship between the company and its employees—namely, the issue of group consciousness. This is important, because if employees consider their relationship with their company to be merely an instrumental one—that is, a means to secure a living—then they cannot respond to managers' inclinations to view them as partners in the business. This, in turn, will sour the attitudes of managers.[29]

In my opinion, the way the Japanese relate themselves to their groups is quite different from analogous relationships in a self-reliance society. Since I have already elaborated my ideas on this topic elsewhere,[30] I shall merely summarize the argument here to clarify my point.

The Relationship Between the Individual and the Group

Whenever an individual joins a group, there emerges, more or less, a tension between the needs of the individual and those of the group. In my view, in Western self-reliance societies, where the autonomy of the individual is stressed, people tend to avoid being too deeply involved in a particular group. Rather, they limit their relationship in a given group, in terms both of time and of function, and secure the right to leave. People satisfy their social needs and simultaneously secure their independence by being partly engaged in numerous groups. In contrast, in Japanese society the tension is resolved by the separation of *honne* (truth, or "is") and *tatemae* (principle, or "ought"). In normal situations, Japanese in principle (*tatemae*) accept the needs of the group as much as possible, while, on the other hand, they hide and repress their own needs (*honne*) and are only allowed to express them in limited situations. Since this psychological pattern is widespread in society, Japanese companies usually institutionalize occasions for people to air their grievances and frustrations.

In a "contextual" society (*aidagara shakai*), which is characterized by mutual dependence, mutual trust, and the sanctification of the personal relationship,[31] the maintenance of relationships has priority over individual needs, and this is why the problem is solved by separating *honne* from *tatemae*.

People in Japan have traditionally shown different attitudes toward the group than are found in Western societies (though some evidence suggests this may be changing, especially among young men). They usually ascribe the greatest importance to one particular group among the several that are of special importance to them—and they do so with

TABLE 5
Kind of Group Most Relevant to Employees, by City Size

	Real numbers			%		
	Neighbor-hood	Company	Hobby	Neighbor-hood	Company	Hobby
Small cities[a]	14	18	4	39	50	11
Big cities[b]	9	51	4	14	78	8
Osaka	0	36	2	0	95	5
Tokyo	3	48	2	5	91	4

SOURCE: Ryushi Iwata, *Keieitai no seichō to kōzō henka: Seichō purosesu moderu no tankyū* (The growth of business organizations and their structural change: A search for process models) (Tokyo: Bunshindō, 1986). See my analysis of interviews in chapter 3 on how strongly people in rural areas and small towns are rooted in their local communities and how difficult it is for group consciousness based on workplace groups to develop in such areas.
[a]Three provincial cities with populations under 150,000.
[b]Kanazawa, Okayama, Fukuoka, Kyoto, Nagoya, and Nagoya region.

few reservations.[32] The pattern of individual-group relationship seen in Japan can be described by the following:

individual → "particular group" → society affiliation

The Tension Between Local Groups and Occupational Groups

The deep involvement of the Japanese in a particular group has created competition between two socially and historically relevant groups: the local group and the workplace group. In rural areas and in small towns, where human relations are closely knit, allegiance to local groups tends to conflict with group consciousness based on workplace connections. Since people already have deep local ties in such areas, it is difficult for company loyalty to thrive. In contrast, the employees of major corporations located in large cities tend to be integrated into their companies and are less involved in the community activities in their residential areas.

My own research, conducted among 200 small and middle-sized firms, confirms this point. The results, shown in Tables 5 and 6, show that urbanization and increase in the size of the firm facilitate a shift in loyalty to the firm.

Managerial Principles and Group Consciousness

Employees of large urban companies tend to identify themselves with their workplace groups and are not satisfied with being treated merely as workers who relate to their bosses through a cash nexus or as instruments of their employers' business schemes. Employers quickly understand that in order to boost the morale of their employees, it is

TABLE 6
Kind of Group Most Relevant to Employees, by Company Size

	Real numbers			%		
	Neighbor-hood	Company	Hobby	Neighbor-hood	Company	Hobby
Tiny[a]	14	50	7	20	70	10
Small[b]	7	59	4	10	86	6
Medium[c]	3	44	0	6	94	0

SOURCE: Ryushi Iwata, *Keieitai no seichō to kōzō henka: Seichō purosesu moderu no tankyū* (The growth of business organizations and their structural change: A search for process models) (Tokyo: Bunshindō, 1986).
[a]Fewer than 70 employees.
[b]From 70 to 180 employees.
[c]From 181 to 500 employees.

necessary to regard them not as instruments but as partners. This idea is tied to the traditional principles of interpersonal relationships in Japanese management. When employers' managerial principles encounter the group consciousness of the employees, the idea of business by the combined triumvirate of owners, managers, and workers emerges. In my opinion, this was the dominant view of Japanese management even before World War II.

It is important that not all employees are considered part of the workplace group. There is a distinction between "proper members," who enjoy lifetime employment, and "semi-members," who do not have that privilege and are regarded as a buffer to protect the firm from the business environment. I call this the "dual structure of center and periphery in Japanese management." Before World War II, the center was quite limited and the incorporation of employees in management was underdeveloped. In prewar Japan, rural bonds were still strong and workplace ties did not enjoy their present predominant position.

After the war, owing to the growth of unionization, the stabilization of employment, the increase in company size, and the urbanization of business activities, workplace groups started to assume their predominant position. Employees established their status as legitimate members of management. This process was paralleled by the alienation of stockholders from business activities, which was caused by the dissolution of zaibatsu conglomerates, the dispersion of stock ownership, and the separation of ownership and control—especially during the rapid-growth period.

Employee Fidelity in Times of Merger and Management Change

The fact that most employees see themselves as integral to business activities, not merely as workers who receive wages for their labor, is most vividly expressed when the managerial staff is transferred because of takeovers or mergers. In Japan, it is not rare for takeover attempts or merger plans to be aborted by violent opposition from employees, and such failures are seen even when the majority of stock and ownership of a company have been acquired. This extreme difficulty in carrying out mergers without employees' consent is widely recognized by managers. (The best-known failed merger is that of Sumitomo Bank and the Kwansai Mutual Assistance Bank. This case, like those of the Takashimaya department store, Miyaji Ironworks, and Katakura Industries, is an example in which the merger did not materialize despite acquisition of the majority of the target company's stock. Employee opposition was the major reason the merger of the two banks was abandoned.)

However, this kind of reaction by employees did not coincide with the rise of post-capitalism after the war, as claimed by Nishiyama. It originated in the prewar period long before the emergence of corporatism. Let me provide a few examples to illustrate my point.

When Hikojiro Nakamigawa of Mitsui planned to take over Ōji Seishi (a paper manufacturing concern) and sent in Raita Fujiyama as executive director, tension mounted between Fujiyama and Heizaburo Okawa, the chief engineer, who was valued for his services to the company. (At the time, Mitsui owned more than half of Ōji's shares.) The tension exploded in 1898 when the engineers of the company, worried about Okawa's endangered position, mobilized the workers and organized a strike to support Okawa. Eventually, Mitsui's takeover was successful, but this case portrays employees' attitudes.

Another example is the case of the investor Hisagoro Suzuki, who acquired the majority of Kanebo's shares as part of his plan to take over the Mitsui-affiliated company. He planned to make a profit by issuing new shares in the rising stock market. These efforts were violently opposed by Sanji Muto, an entrepreneur-credited with the company's growth, but over half the shares were in the hands of his opponent. Muto concluded that he could not work under a person who endangered the foundation of the company and decided to resign. The employees united and announced that they would quit the company with Muto. Consequently, this takeover failed, demonstrating that a public company could not be managed simply by controlling its capital.

An interesting episode shows the different attitudes of Americans and Japanese on this subject. When a group of Japanese bankers organized a tour of U.S. companies, they asked how American managers, who face frequent takeover attempts, deal with employee resistance to takeovers. The American managers did not, however, understand the meaning of the question, which seemed obvious to the Japanese. The frustrated Japanese managers never ceased to blame the incompetence of the interpreter for this misunderstanding.[33]

Dore makes an interesting observation on the response of Japanese employees to takeover bids in his comparison with the British case: "It is unlikely that the Hitachi board would react as the English Electric board reacted initially to the Plessey takeover bid. A press release, posted on factory notice boards, concluded with a promise to keep shareholders fully informed. It made no mention of employees."[34]

What Checks the Arbitrary Use of Power?

Why have postwar Japanese managers not taken advantage of their power? Have they simply refrained from doing so, or have their powers been checked?

In my opinion, Japanese business organizations have indirect forces, rather than rigid accounting systems, that serve to check the arbitrary use of managerial power. In a Western organization, where clear lines of authority are drawn and defined, final authority is concentrated in the top manager, and a top-down pattern of control and order functions. In such an organization, the top manager does not necessarily need the approval and psychological cooperation of his subordinates, the members of the organization. This formal theory of authority has dominated American managerial theory. Needless to say, from an empirical point of view, even in Western organizations the authority of a superior rests on his acceptance by his subordinates, as claimed by the "acceptance theory of authority." However, the formal theory of the authority system still seems to function as the official ideology in the West.

In contrast, in Japanese managerial organizations, a different concept of authority and responsibility prevails. The authority system is kept vague and flexible. The sense of responsibility that members of the organization, including employees, feel toward the continuance and growth of the company generates enthusiastic commitment. Top managers have to recognize that they must win the cooperation of their employees to carry out their duties. Here the "acceptance theory of authority" is the formal ideology.

Most Japanese managers who have abused their powers have been expelled by their subordinates. In one famous such situation, the company president asked, "Why?" This shows his confusion of personal loyalty with the loyalty of subordinates toward the organization. When the loyalty of subordinates is directed toward the continuity and growth of the organization, any abuse of managerial power ignites rebellion in the most capable and trusted subordinates. In my opinion, it has been this pattern of power relations in Japanese managerial organizations that has checked the abuse of managerial power.

Under the numerous conditions examined so far, separation of ownership and control developed in the Japanese context into the unified body of employees. This process can only be understood by examining both developments in the ownership structure and the social and cultural background in which it took place. In this essay, I have examined the historical development and background of the Japanese company as a unified body of employees. I have made it clear that this system did not appear suddenly as a result of the separation of ownership and control that occurred in postwar Japan. As I have explained, the separation of ownership and control had a strong influence in the creation of the Japanese management system. However, historical background and sociocultural factors were equally important. Even today in smaller businesses (and in a few exceptional cases in big business), where ownership control has been traditional, the management pattern comes closer to the model of the unified body of employees than to the Western model. Similar trends can be seen in nonbusiness organizations such as hospitals and universities. These trends are related to the important role of historical and sociocultural factors in the diffusion of the concept of the unified body of employees. Even if it is the case, as pointed out by Dore, that Western companies are shifting from market-oriented forms of work organizations to organization-oriented firms, there still remains a considerable difference between Japanese and Western companies.

It is also necessary to address the question of whether Japan, as a late-developing capitalist state, became post-capitalist after fully developing its capitalist stage, or if it regressed into traditionalism because that stage was inadequate. My position, in accordance with Nishiyama, is that Japan had gone through the capitalist stage, even if the development of capitalism in Japan was not as full as in Great Britain, which is closest to the pure model of industrial capitalism, or in the United States and Germany, which are late-developing capitalist states. Japanese capitalism was not thoroughgoing, however, since it did not completely change the country's social relations and value systems into forms conducive to capitalism, and during the era of organized capitalism, traditional legacies functioned positively and expedited post-capitalist development.

It is well known that the classical idea of property, which was conducive to the early stages of capitalist development in the United States, evoked strong resistance there to the separation of ownership and control. Similarly, the same classical notion is one cause of the reassertion of shareholder rights. In Japan, however, where the classical notion of property did not fully penetrate, there was little opposition to the separation of ownership and control, and reassertion of shareholder rights never gained momentum. Lack of resistance hastened the progress of capitalism in Japan. Traditional elements, or the lack of modern elements, promoted the transition into the next stage of post-capitalism. This is not regression into tradition. The pattern of development should rather be understood as a spiral. This is one of the historical paradoxes often seen in the development of human society.

Conclusion: Problems Confronting Japanese Management

It is true, as asserted by Nishiyama and Matsumoto, that the system of corporatism that emerged in Japan as the result of the postwar separation of ownership and control has its merits. However, needless to say, this system also has its problems. For example, when industrial pollution became a major social problem in Japan, there was no criticism from within companies of the dumping of toxic chemicals. Rather, when fishermen demonstrated against a company in protest, employees usually clashed with the protesters and refused to make any comments that would hurt the reputation of their company. In other words, many employees opted to defend the interests of the company as against the requirements of social justice. Even the unions were uncooperative in solving such problems. Greater time and energy were required to solve industrial pollution in Japanese society.

The homogeneity and cohesiveness of managers and employees entails a convergence of interests. This has brought vigor into company operations in various ways but has led most employees to side with their companies rather than with the interests of larger society. The phenomenon of all employees uniting to fight the war of "excessive competition" can be explained by the same mentality.

Another interesting problem is the fact that the company as a unified body of employees now faces various challenges from the changing environment. With the end of rapid growth, the lifetime employment system (what I often call "long-term stable employment") and the pyramid-shaped age composition of the labor force have been distorted. As a result, there is a critical shortage of managerial positions that can be provided as significant incentives. Also, with the rapid development of advanced technology, the need for highly specialized technicians has increased. This causes tension in the unified body of employees, where marked differentiation in the treatment of workers is avoided.

The rapid changes in the technological environment also generate a problem that can be called a mismatch of manpower—that is, a discrepancy between the technology or skills needed by the company and those provided by employees. Radical changes in the environment have resulted in serious declines in mature industries. In many such industries, maintaining long-term employment relations has become increasingly painful, but without them, deep cleavages will emerge within the common interests of the employees, seriously damaging the workings of the Japanese company as a unified body of employees. At the present stage, most Japanese companies are trying to adjust to the situation by reducing the number of core employees to whom the longer-term employment relations apply, while introducing supplementary merit systems to modify lifetime employment and seniority rules.

The prevalence of long-term employment has, however, created a closed labor market, and the companies' adjustment plans would thus introduce meritocracy into a closed environment, making the workplace extremely uncomfortable. As a result, people will begin to identify themselves with other groups, such as those related to their hobbies or other leisure activities.

This might transform the Japanese company from a unified body of employees into something different. What will happen next is unclear. And whether the change is perceived as functional or dysfunctional will depend on the values of the observer.[35]

Ken-ichi Imai

Japan's Corporate Networks

The economic system is coordinated through both the "invisible hand" and the "visible hands" of large firms. In recent terminology, it is organized by the market and by hierarchies, two concepts denoting the typical mechanisms by which resources are allocated: prices and control by authority.

Economic Organization and Culture: An Analytic Framework

Cultural Elements in the Market and Organization

In theoretical economics, these two mechanisms are built on assumptions of information efficiency. In the real world, however, information transactions between economic agents, and information exchange within an organization and between people, are not purely economic phenomena and involve closely related cultural problems.

Even in a "pure" economic market, prices cannot convey all of the information required for coordination under conditions of endogenous technological change and uncertainty. Market economies depend on entrepreneurial activity and information networks to convey background knowledge surrounding prices. Entrepreneurship, which is especially important because its market function is to fill gaps in the knowledge of market participants, is not an impersonal, rational activity, and its character is embedded in the wider social and cultural system. Likewise, exchange of information within an organization is substantially influenced by social and cultural factors. As forums for communication that allow participants to transmit information among themselves, organizations have a special language, which is also an issue of culture.

Furthermore, resource allocation in the market arena is not only performed by market forces but is also carried out, to a great extent, by organizational decision making. And, to a certain degree, resource allocation within the firm is also based on the market principle, along with the organization principle. Two principles thus coexist in the market and the firm. This "interpenetration of market and organization" means that, in general, firms are related units, usually linked to one another rather than being freestanding, independent units, and their ties naturally lead to a group or network.[1] This pattern of linkages between units—people or firms—is deeply embedded in the social and cultural system.

In this essay, I investigate how Japanese corporate networks have evolved from *zaibatsu* to "business groups" to, most recently, "network industrial organizations." In a broad sense, corporate networks are the vital economic institution that has led Japanese economic development. The long history of coordination between firms may be a crucial factor in explaining the special adaptability of the Japanese economy. As an economist, I shall try to discuss the relationship between economic, institutional, and cultural elements within the framework outlined above. Three Japanese cultural elements are emphasized.

1. Learning is given high priority in Japanese society and was of particular significance for Japan's historical position as a late developer (as discussed in Thomas Rohlen's essay in this volume). The Japanese pattern of learning, which stresses "learning by doing," has influenced the way technology transfer, information exchanges, and organizational linkages have been executed.

2. As rice cultivators, the Japanese developed the habit of spontaneous cooperation among workers to cope with seasonal concentrations of labor. This has made the flexible division of labor easier for Japanese and has promoted spontaneous cooperation without detailed job specifications or legal contracts.

3. The pattern of Japanese knowledge is passive, in the sense that the Japanese strive to understand the meaning of a given circumstance and respond to it, rather than to manage the circumstance itself. This contrasts with the Western knowledge pattern, which is characterized by operationalism and activism. Passive knowledge offers special adaptability to crises because the Japanese can find a new context in a state of chaos without being constrained by the preceding concept. Unlearning is the other side of passive knowledge.

In this essay, I use the term *corporate network* in the broadest sense to mean interfirm relationships in general, including zaibatsu and business groups. A special type of corporate network representing recent Japanese interfirm relationships, discussed below, is designated by the term *network industrial organization*, sometimes abbreviated simply to *network* in the final section.

I agree with Shumpei Kumon's theoretical terminology (outlined in his essay in this volume) distinguishing between the market, the organization, and the network. He uses *network* to mean a "pure" network of information-sharing alone. This purely theoretical definition should be used with the concepts *pure market* and *pure organization* and is a useful tool for examining the real world.

My approach is to study interfirm relationships as a combination of pure "market," "organization," and "network," and also as a pattern of interpretation among the three. I use the special term *network industrial organization* because recent Japanese interfirm organizations include the "network" element, in Kumon's sense, more than other interfirm relationships.

Information and Interorganizational Linkages

To understand the actual working of the market economy and corporate behavior within it, it is crucial to consider explicitly how various economic actors are interconnected in the market economy and how information flows among them. Economic analyses developed to date are often based on unrealistic models of structure and information.

General equilibrium theory assumes the existence of a fictitious auctioneer who adjusts supply and demand at no cost. In the real world, however, every actor strives to communicate, obtain, process, interpret, and generate information through strong and weak ties with other actors. Although recently some types of information have been treated as commodities to be traded in the market, a major part of industrial information is still communicated among actors without explicit market transactions. This is why interorganizational linkages (such as groups or networks) are formed, and why the formation of such linkages is important to economic decision making. The network view, which gives explicit consideration to this linkage mechanism, provides an analytical framework more realistic than existing models.

The linkage mechanism includes not only economic but also social transactions. The sociologist Peter Blau has found that long-run transactions include such factors as trust, friendship, and power.[2] Economic transactions are settled by money transfer and are usually concluded in the short term. Social transactions are not settled in each transaction, however, but are part of a long-run reciprocal relationship. Usually some imbalances remain after a single social transaction, and they constitute the basis for continuing the long-term relationship. The meaning and content of information can be transmitted in such a long-term relationship.

Blau's framework for analyzing power structures or hierarchies within social transactions is important for an evolutionary analysis of the network concept discussed in this essay. At the same time, however, we need to understand how cooperation and trust evolve from a long-term social transaction. The sharing of information and mutual learning experiences create a basis of trust and commitment for maintaining such a relationship. The analysis offered below gives attention to these aspects of social transactions and cultural factors.

The Role of Entrepreneurs

The market process is the revision of the inconsistent expectations of various economic actors. To revise expectations, these economic actors must perceive the changing economic environment, have information about what others are doing, and, finally, decide what changes are desirable. Such abilities constitute at least part of the role of the entrepreneur, or "entrepreneurship." Creating a new product is a special case of the revision of inconsistent expectations. Joseph Schumpeter's "creative destruction" is a dramatic example of this.[3] I posit that creating a new context in inter- and intramarkets is the basic role of the entrepreneur. I define *context* as an aggregate of past and present relationships and experiences obtained through interactions. One viewpoint stressed throughout this essay is that a context is established in response to the economic environment, and that a period of crisis acts as a trigger for creating a new context.[4] In times of crisis, organizations must be renewed and restructured to meet present and future needs. In such situations, the cultural traits of a nation make their appearance.

The *Zaibatsu* as Corporate Networks

There have been three turning points in the process of Japan's industrialization. The first was the beginning of modernization, triggered by the Meiji Restoration, when the zaibatsu were bastions of the entrepreneurial spirit. The second was the period of postwar reconstruction, in which the main change was the dissolution of the big zaibatsu, with corporate groups engineering the process of rapid economic growth. The third turning point was the oil crisis, which brought the introduction and wide diffusion of technical innovations centered on electronics, motivated by the twin requirements of saving energy and labor. This last development transformed relationships between corporations and created the structure that is now known as the network industrial organization.

Market Failures and the Entrepreneur's Role

According to theories commonly held in the past, zaibatsu were monopolistic organizations of limited number, controlled by family ties and directing vast economic empires. As will be discussed later, it is true that with their consolidation from the late 1920s onward, the zaibatsu eventually developed these characteristics. However, the perception that zaibatsu were organized with the original aim of control alone is too one-sided. I would like to emphasize the viewpoint that the zaibatsu served as a source of genuine entrepreneurial activity with the advent of capitalism in Japan. These organizations were necessary for starting the engine of capitalism in the underdeveloped socioeconomic environment of the time. As has been pointed out by Keiichiro Nakagawa, a specialist in Japanese business history,[5] and more recently by Nathaniel Leff of Columbia University,[6] the appearance of "groups" in developing nations that to some extent parallel the Japanese zaibatsu suggests that the formation of such groups by business enterprises allows entrepreneurs to promote economic activity in an underdeveloped or immature market economy. That is to say, the zaibatsu can be viewed as organizations compensating for market failures during the development of an economy.

In the economies of developing nations, production factors such as capital and technological manpower are extremely scarce, and the market itself is immature. Furthermore, the information necessary for handling market capital or making decisions about investments is limited and available to only a small number of people. It is therefore necessary to create channels to compensate for this, to permit the flow of capital and information to the market as required. As mentioned above, entrepreneurship is required to fill gaps in the knowledge of market participants.

As Schumpeter emphasized, new entrepreneurs play a crucial role in formulating a new context in industrial society.[7] In the case of Japan, society before the Meiji Restoration consisted of four classes: warriors, farmers, manufacturers, and merchants. As the leading class in feudal society, warriors were educated and had the ability to find a new way of life. Naturally, some became new entrepreneurs. With government funding to support their new businesses, members of the former warrior class created relatively small companies and factories in light manufacturing industries (silk, paper, tea, sugar, matches, dying, pottery, and other miscellaneous manufacturing), as well as in projects related to agriculture. Such entrepreneurship started Japan in the right direction toward industrialization.

However, in larger-scale and more capital-intensive industries, such as mining, steel, and shipbuilding, the situation was more complicated than in the above cases of rather direct entrepreneurship. Of fundamental importance in these industries were the means to cope with uncertainty and risk in order to make decisions on large-scale investments. However, institutions to facilitate dealing with uncertainty and risk in the market had not yet been established. Consequently, business enterprises addressed this need by substituting intra-organizational systems and developing such means as vertically integrated production systems, in which input and output were coordinated within the group, and internal finance systems. Doing this required a combination of the capital of rich merchant families, the organizing capabilities of elite warriors, and the professional knowledge of university graduates. This was an essential reason for the birth of the big zaibatsu.

Thus, the zaibatsu as a large-scale, family-owned conglomerate represents the institutionalization of an organizational mechanism to compensate for the incompleteness of the market in developing economies. In addition, the role of zaibatsu can be interpreted as providing organizational innovation to retain internally the profits from mutually supporting and cooperative activities in an immature market.

At the same time, the formation of a group is an effective means of utilizing entrepreneurial ability, which is of limited supply in developing nations. Of course, the quality of individual entrepreneurs affects entrepreneurial performance, but studies of entrepreneurs published to date have focused too much on personality. Entrepreneurs, like everyone else, obtain information in the social context and make judgments on the basis of their interaction with others. If some kind of entrepreneurial group is established, it becomes possible to perform the entrepreneurial function without excessive reliance on individual personal qualities. For this reason, considering entrepreneurs within the context of a network may be a useful approach. Furthermore, the success of one zaibatsu will stimulate the success of others, and this will then play a pivotal role in starting the engine of capitalism for the entire economy. In Japan, about 80 zaibatsu, both large and small, appeared prior to the dissolution of zaibatsu after World War II.

The International Situation and Zaibatsu

The formation of zaibatsu was a development appropriate to the domestic and global economic environment of the period.[8] The world economy was entering the relatively long downward slide that followed the buoyant period begun by the industrial revolution. In general, restructuring takes place both intra- and interorganizationally as a countermeasure to the downward movement of an economy slipping into depression. Although new technologies are sought, the basic impetus for this countermeasure is the utilization of existing techniques in different fields in search of new applications and new markets. Social organization is generally restructured for this purpose. The developed nations, led by the United Kingdom, were squarely faced with the need for restructuring, i.e., with the task of transferring their technology internationally and exploring new markets in Asia and Africa.

It was at this time that the Japanese zaibatsu were formed. In the face of international industrial reorganization, Japan's best course of action was to design new industrial organizations appropriate to this international process. That is to say, it was desirable to seek aggressively the acquisition of international technologies and to master their techniques; to promote industries of strategic national importance; and, through the process of development, rapidly to create a domestic market. The task of the zaibatsu can be regarded as transforming large Japanese merchant houses based on the traditional *ie* system into organizations able to develop by learning from and following advanced foreign countries.

The most critical information such organizations needed was on new industrial opportunities, including actual technological knowledge and related know-how, acquisition and transportation of required industrial materials, and transactional skills in the sale and purchase of these goods. The required information existed in the advanced countries, and the agenda for Japan was to absorb and fully utilize it for industrial development. A zaibatsu's general trading company, such as Mitsui Bussan or Mitsubishi Shoji, became "a window to the world for a nation long isolated"[9] and served as a catalyst in providing such key information.

At the same time, procuring necessary resources and establishing and fostering markets were essential. Centralized purchases and sales and the development of organizations typical of general trading firms were of utmost importance. Also necessary was the proper control and allocation of capital. Furthermore, conditions for such capital distribution without dependence on the market required able entrepreneurs who could envisage the development of various industries through interdependence, while learning from the experiences of the developed nations. It was also necessary to grant these entrepreneurs basic authority in decision making and to provide them with the assistance of groups that conducted the required sales and acquisitions in world markets. These conditions were met in the zaibatsu. Japanese industry also produced independent entrepreneurs of outstanding creativity and personality, such as Ichizo Kobayashi and Yasuzaemon Matsunaga, but these individuals were not involved with the zaibatsu. These entrepreneurs who organized the zaibatsu, including Hikojiro Nakamigawa of Mitsui, Heigoro Shoda of Mitsubishi, and Saihei Hirose of Sumitomo, were organizational entrepreneurs and technocrats who could discern the world situation and conceptualize a path of industrial development based on capitalism.[10] New members of the business elite, graduates of Tokyo Imperial University, Tokyo Commercial University (now Hitotsubashi

University), and Keio University, gathered around these leaders, and with their assistance entrepreneurial networks were formed.

The role of these entrepreneurs in the zaibatsu's function of enabling the Japanese economy to take off deserves special mention. Had administrators of the zaibatsu concentrated, as is assumed in the usual "family and bank control model" of monopoly capitalism,[11] on making immediate profits and accumulating assets for merchant families, zaibatsu development would not have begun or sustained the historic development of the Japanese economy. In fact, the Konoike zaibatsu, which began as the largest zaibatsu, was unable to develop like the other four big zaibatsu because its management sought only the maintenance and development of the merchant family.[12] Several leaders of big zaibatsu had a strong sense of mission to develop Japan as an industrial nation. They tried to align the interests of the zaibatsu with the interests of the nation with a view to long-run benefits. Every developing nation has a leader who ardently promotes the national interest, but such leaders seldom succeed in causing industry to take off. A national strategy of industrial promotion succeeds only if it corresponds to the logic of industrial development. The leaders of the zaibatsu were not entrepreneurs who could understand development in theoretical terms or act as pioneers at great risk. However, they were skillful leaders well versed in what was taking place abroad and able to draw up a blueprint for industrial development by learning from the success of the United Kingdom and other developed countries.

For example, Table 1 shows the industrial structure within three major zaibatsu, Mitsui, Mitsubishi, and Sumitomo, each of which had special characteristics. Although these data are from the end of the consolidation of the economic power of the zaibatsu, we can discern the historical effects of initial leadership. In the case of Mitsui, Nakamigawa established an industrialization plan with Mitsui mining as the basic industry. Light industries such as Kanebo textiles and Oji paper were built on top of this, and Mitsui Bussan bought their input and sold their output. In the Mitsubishi zaibatsu, Shoda built up machine-making industries from a start in shipbuilding. Sumitomo was led by Hirose, whose leadership created a vertical industrial structure based on copper production (Bessi mining).

It is important that all of these industrial plans were envisioned and coordinated ex ante. From today's vantage point, they look like natural plans, but in those first days of Japanese industrialization, it was difficult to execute long-term plans that did not match the short-run profit incentive of "family" members. Serious conflicts often arose between Nakamigawa and Masuda (president of Mitsui Bussan), whose thinking was like that of family members. Shoda of Sumitomo was forced to

TABLE 1
Structure of the Three Big Zaibatsu

	Mitsui		Mitsubishi		Sumitomo	
	Honsha	Group	Honsha	Group	Honsha	Group
Number of companies						
Home	66	212	32	157	24	119
Abroad	9	61	9	52	5	16
Paid-up capital (million ¥)						
Home	2,452	3,061	2,054	2,704	1,074	1,667
Abroad	201	437	96	413	174	255
Paid-up capital (%)[a]						
Mining	16.7	15.6	13.9	14.3	7.4	7.1
Metal industry	9.3	9.2	8.4	6.1	48.8	37.8
Machinery and shipbuilding	26.1	26.1	45.9	40.3	22.7	36.1
Chemical industry	22.0	21.1	6.9	8.1	8.8	9.0
Other industries	10.4	10.7	1.5	3.7	0.6	1.6
Finance and insurance	6.4	4.9	7.4	5.1	5.2	3.3
Shipping	2.8	5.1	8.2	13.7	—	0.3
Trading	4.5	5.3	6.1	6.4	3.5	3.0
Miscellaneous enterprises	1.8	2.0	1.7	2.3	2.9	1.8
Percentage of shares or capital of honsha held or subscribed by zaibatsu families	63.8		47.8		83.3	
Percentage of shares of companies directly held by honsha and zaibatsu families	63.4		32.1		29.0	
Percentge of shares of companies indirectly held by honsha and zaibatsu families	47.4		18.4		13.1	

SOURCE: Mochikabu Kaisha Seiri Iin Kai (Shareholding Company Liquidation Committee), ed., *Nihon zaibatsu to sono kaitai* (Japanese zaibatsu and their dissolution), 1951; and *Shiryo hen* (Background material to Nihon zaibatsu to sono kaitai), 1950.
[a]Paid-up capital here includes home and overseas.

resign his position. The power politics involved were complicated. However, the visions and plans of the entrepreneurs clearly gave the initial boost for industrial development in each zaibatsu. They filled the knowledge gap of market participants and produced a new context for economic activities.

Control and the Quasi-Market

The dual dimension of zaibatsu was important. They served both as coordinating mechanisms and marketlike organizers of economic activities.[13] On the one hand, it is well known that they functioned as a control network, exerting direct control over their industries through holding companies and indirect control through related companies. The holding of stock, the dispatching of directors to subsidiary companies, and centralized purchases and sales were means for this control. However, on the other hand, the zaibatsu was also a marketlike organization. Even though there were no direct market connections, a similar mechanism was created within the zaibatsu.

There is much evidence that the controlled companies within a zaibatsu behaved independently and competitively. The Mitsubishi Economic Research Institute has summarized it as follows: "Controlled companies could and did operate independently in coordination with the *honsha* [central house]."[14] According to G. C. Allen: "A *Banto* (manager) who had been placed in charge of a firm where he enjoyed considerable freedom from control would be expected in an emergency to come to the aid of the parent concern. . . . Among the *Banto* themselves there are groups in rivalry, one with another."[15] They were controlled during times of crisis, but otherwise retained autonomous decision-making powers.

This relates to the way the zaibatsu exercised authority. It is certain that strong authority to control constituent companies existed in the central house. However, it was usually exercised as a catalyst to promote mutual industrial development and to adjust the inconsistent expectations of members. This coordination mechanism may have been the origin of the Japanese way of business that mixes organization and market, as will be explained below. It might be too hasty to discuss the cultural elements mentioned at the beginning of this essay as background reasons for this business style, but continuous learning and passive behavior adapting to changing circumstances were perhaps to some extent influential in creating this flexible coordination.

Thus, during the worldwide restructuring of industrial organization triggered by the depression of 1890, an industrial system that followed the pattern of industrial promotion in advanced countries was formed in Japan. This industrial system developed remarkably when the global economic boom began in about 1894. That is, Japan's zaibatsu organizations demonstrated their abilities by raising productivity and enlarging markets during this period of economic prosperity. This enabled them to advance in capital accumulation and to prepare for the second wave of technical innovation by creating capital-intensive industries as a source of profit within their financial empires. In this period, the merits of the quasi-market mechanism within zaibatsu conglomerates were brought into full play.

However, the character of authority and control determine the probable future. As the zaibatsu had grown and their profits increased, anti-zaibatsu feelings had gradually increased among Japanese citizens. Also, as new zaibatsu such as Nippon Sangyō (Nissan) and Nippon Chisso

(Nitchitsu) promoted heavy industrialization suited for military purposes and supported by the militarists and progressive bureaucrats,
criticism of the established zaibatsu mounted. The March 1932 assassi-
nation of Takuma Dan, the chief director of Mitsui Homei, by a terrorist
group of the extreme right was a symbolic event for the anti-zaibatsu
movement.

In this crisis, the adaptive character of authority in the zaibatsu organization brought untoward results. It was difficult to prevent the intrusion of political and military authorities in decision making, and the
zaibatsu themselves intensified their control within their systems. Thus,
the zaibatsu gradually transformed themselves into a monopolistic system while becoming tied more closely to the military. Monopolies were
gaining predominance throughout the world, and a structure of control
by a few zaibatsu was consciously and actively being created in Japan.
This process has been widely discussed elsewhere,[16] and I turn now to
the postwar period.

Postwar Business Groups:
Interpenetration of Market and Organization

*The Dissolution of the Zaibatsu and the
Change from Entrepreneurs to Managers*

Had the zaibatsu continued unchanged as systems of control, they
would have made the economic system completely bureaucratic. The
zaibatsu had formed internal organizations in accordance with the market within groups of business enterprises and had encouraged the
entrepreneurial function from the beginning of their existence. However,
with the rise of their economic and political power, they were eventually
completely isolated from movements of the market and inevitably became powerful hierarchical organizations. At the same time, the economic inequity and the suppression of business opportunities for others
caused by such a monopoly system resulted in social antagonism toward
the zaibatsu. Hence, in combination with government bureaucrats who
sought to resolve this social conflict and at the same time to utilize it as
a source of momentum to expand their own power base, the zaibatsu
had no other apparent option but to evolve into a bureaucratic economic
system. This is exactly the process of development discussed by Schumpeter, who dealt with monopoly and its strong relationship to the
entrepreneurial function in his *Theory of Economic Development*, although
in *Capitalism, Socialism and Democracy*, a work of his later years, his thesis
was that entrepreneurial functions themselves would become routine
and the industrial system would become socialized.[17]

In the case of Japan, the zaibatsu were unfortunately linked with the war economy. This was inevitable. However, the end result was an opportunity for regeneration when the zaibatsu were dissolved under the Occupation. The allied forces "called for removal of the *zaibatsu* families from their position of business power and a severing of the ties—ownership, personnel, credit, contracts—which bound the component corporations into combine structures."[18] Although the dissolution of the zaibatsu was forced on them, the severing of business ties that had grown too strong opened the way for democracy in the economy and established a basis for creating new industrial organizations. Since the dissolution of the zaibatsu has been discussed in detail elsewhere,[19] it will not be directly dealt with here. My emphasis in the context of this essay is the change in the character of Japanese entrepreneurship owing to the dissolution of the zaibatsu.

Not only was family control of the zaibatsu eliminated, but the January 1947 purge of the economic field also expelled the highest-ranking directors of 245 major Japanese companies. This extraordinary phenomenon severed human connections in the zaibatsu and changed the pattern of decision making. The posts of the highest directors and the decision-making role were transferred to men in their forties who were at the general-manager level and had grown up in the production-oriented and technology-oriented period of the 1930s and World War II. Many feared a weakening in decision-making bodies because of the loss of the central decision makers. According to Yoshitaro Wakimura, professor emeritus of the University of Tokyo and an administrator on the Japanese side of the dissolution of the zaibatsu, this fear was also shared by officials of the Occupation.[20] However, as Wakimura reassured the latter, graduates in economics from Tokyo Imperial University and from Tokyo Commercial University had already become members of the business elite and had secured positions as middle-level managers. There was thus no shortage of qualified personnel.

The outcome of the dissolution of the zaibatsu—namely, the appearance of a new breed of entrepreneurs and managers and the transfer of decision-making power to them—is a significant fact deserving renewed attention. Having replaced the entrepreneurial groups—that is, the small number of entrepreneurs who were capable of presenting a vision of industrial development rather than directly following the market, as well as the business elite entrenched around them—the new entrepreneurs in the postwar period found it necessary to promote the exchange of information, while at the same time they managed smaller firms than their predecessors. By necessity, they had to listen to the voice of the market and to emphasize economic principles, although remnants of bureaucratic regulations and controls still remained. According to the

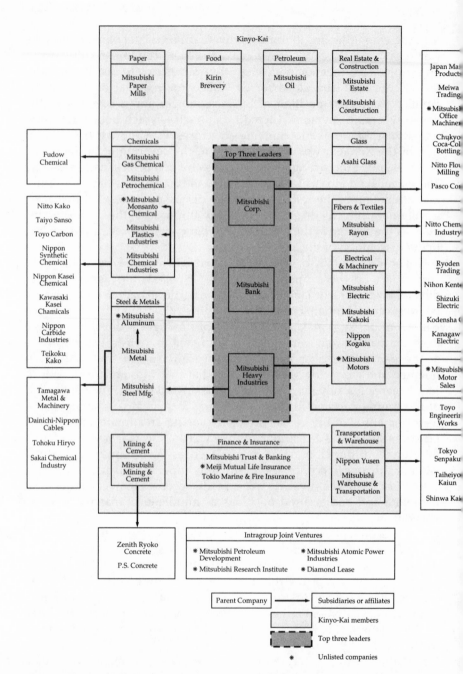

Fig. 1. The Mitsubishi group. Based on Dodwell Marketing Consultants in Japan, *Industrial Grouping in Japan* (Tokyo, 1984), rev. ed. 1984–85, p. 52.

economic thinking that prevailed then, the market mechanism was not capable of directing the economy. When young professors who had learned modern economics in the United States returned in the 1950s and emphasized the importance of the market mechanism, the fact that their ideas were received as new and original proves that such ideas had not previously been current among economic officials or the media. The entrepreneurs and managers who drove the postwar economy of Japan in the environment of drastic change following the dissolution of the zaibatsu strengthened their positions by making decisions substantially following market trends, and by the subsequent achievement of success. Although their behavior seems at first glance to have been strongly group-oriented, and although government policies seem to have provided them with strong direction, their organizational behavior was increasingly responsive to the market.

It is not off the mark to emphasize a cultural element in seeking to understand economic behavior in that era. The existence of an intensive information exchange within a specific industrial association and spontaneous, mutually supportive behavior was surely a reflection of the traditional *mura* (village) behavior in a rice-cultivating nation (which required cooperation among workers). However, despite such cooperation, people were becoming more sensitive to their own economic interests. Even if there was cooperation on the surface, underneath people were very responsive to small differences in wages and revenue. There was a conflict between cooperative behavior and individual interests. The best way to resolve the conflict was to increase total income by adapting to movements of the market. This produced a sense both of benefiting each member of the group and of competing aggressively with those outside the group.

The Character of the Business Groups

The dissolution of the zaibatsu thus created a competitive market system for Japan, but it cannot be said that Japan was able to begin from the ground up in its managerial development. Although weaker, the ties of the zaibatsu organizations remained between the related firms, and organizational principles rooted in ethnic tradition, such as the formation of networks among people, remained substantially intact.

The interaction of these forces produced what are known as the postwar business groups, which in the case of former zaibatsu (see Figure 1 as an example) had the following characteristics:

1. Periodic exchange of information and, occasionally, decision making among member businesses occurred in "presidents' clubs" at the core of the group.

2. Member firms maintained a considerable level of mutual long-term intercorporate holding of stock to prevent hostile takeover bids by outsiders.[21]

3. A large city bank operated at the center of the group, providing short- and long-term loans for member firms under slightly advantageous conditions, and in many cases was involved in the selection of companies' directors.

4. A general trading company at the core of the group engaged in information exchange between both buyers and sellers.

The decisive difference between these business groups and the zaibatsu was the extent of control. As previously mentioned, based on the strong connections resulting from mutual stockholding and the selection of directors, the zaibatsu had almost total control over the decision making of their subsidiaries. On the other hand, although both the holding of stock and selection of directors continued in the business groups, the connections were much weaker and of an entirely different nature and therefore did not substantially influence the decision-making process. Even if the "presidents' club" requested a particular change, it did not become an official prerogative of the association.

Organizations with such weak connections require a steady flow of information between member firms in order to function. Successful leadership requires correct decision making based on high-quality information, and changes are made on the basis of spontaneous coordination. Alternatively, when conflicting interests are allowed to arise among member firms, the organizational structure binding them is weakened and the group disbands.

Postwar entrepreneurs and managers aggressively engaged in information exchange. It was indispensable in compensating for the lack of experience of those who had assumed positions of responsibility at a young age, as well as for decreasing uncertainty and dispersing risk by obtaining information on other firms and thus making ex ante coordination (of production and investment) possible. Without a doubt, it was also advantageous for the firms themselves. The fact that these managers did not have the same personality traits as the zaibatsu entrepreneurs, with their unique and individualistic character, but rather were members of a business elite with the character of salaried employees, allowed the information exchange to be performed smoothly. Needless to say, relationships engendered by having attended the same leading universities contributed to the information-exchange network.

However, there is no certainty that conflicts of interest among member firms can be overcome by information exchange alone. In cases where two or more firms belonging to the same group enter a market, severe competition is possible, and this conflict becomes more evident as competitors' information is exchanged. If decisive confrontations are to be avoided, the role each individual firm is to play within the group must be established by a group leader. However, if the entire group ensures its continued growth through mutually dependent supply-and-demand relations, it can allow the coexistence of two or more firms in the same market. Growth thus enables adjustment of inconsistent expectations and conflicts among members.

The Growth-Promoting Effect of Business Groups

Information exchange within a business group is an effective means of reducing uncertainty. Moreover, exchanging information allows firms to estimate the growth in each other's demand and thereby formulate investment decisions. If mutually related firms make investments at about the same time as the result of information exchange, a sense of security is provided, investment decisions are simplified, and this brings about mutually dependent development and reduced risk. Since new business fields create not only complementary but also potentially competitive relationships in a group, information exchange also expedites investment decisions. Furthermore, since it gradually becomes clear that conflicts of interest can be resolved only by the growth of the entire group, as discussed previously, the incentive for growth intensifies steadily, and the growth of sales and related factors becomes an important indicator for evaluation among member firms. Thus, in general, a business group without the control of a leader becomes growth-oriented, and where such desire for growth is realized, the performance of the group advances.

In Japan, the influence of industrial policy was an important additional factor.[22] From the period of postwar revival to the early stages of the high-growth period, the level of fixed capital investment was allocated and adjusted by the Ministry of International Trade and Industry. Even where MITI did not have direct authority, entities with the function of performing such adjustments, called "cooperative conferences," were established by MITI leadership. No matter what method of adjustment was used, the principal criterion was, by necessity, actual production capacity or production volume. It was thus advantageous to announce as large a figure as possible for future investment plans. The simultaneous exchange of high-grade information combined with investment decisions within such a framework had a considerable promotional effect on investment. Since representatives of each group attended the cooperative conferences, competition among the groups was promoted there.

At the same time, business groups promoted growth by the widespread propagation of new technologies through the linkages between business enterprises. In the prewar zaibatsu, newly introduced technology was applied within the zaibatsu organization but was seldom transferred beyond its boundaries. In contrast, the boundaries of the postwar business groups were not fixed; rather, the number of members increased in response to the requirements of the time, and if we include associated companies in our analysis, the scope of the groups was even greater. In addition to the previous four leading zaibatsu groups and many other prewar smaller zaibatsu, numerous new groups were formed. The members of these groups were more loosely connected, and their territories continuously expanded. Technical innovations took place first within these groups and then moved beyond their borders.

Generally speaking, in the broader sense of the word, as used above, a group may be considered an "intermediate organization" between the market and the organizations themselves. That is to say, these groups exist somewhere between a genuine market, where entry and exit are free and prices are the basis of decisions, and a genuine organization, where membership is fixed to some extent and authority is the general principle. Thus, such groups have aspects of both the market and an organization. These intermediate organizations were formed to cope with shortcomings of the market and organizations.[23] In the case of technology, for example, market failure results from a lack of sharing and mutual accumulation of technical information between trading partners. On the other hand, the defects of organizations are manifested in their rigid structure and bureaucratic nature. The ability to maintain flexibility in response to the market is an advantage of the intermediate organization.

The intermediate organization, however, has a paradoxical character. It may overcome the failures of both the market and organizations, but, conversely, it may lose the advantages of both. In postwar Japan, the advantages were realized by the spontaneous mixing of the cultural traits mentioned above and rational economic behavior under the condition of rapid economic growth.

Strategic Industries Leading Industrial Growth

Let me now elaborate on the points raised above. The strategic industries that led the first stage of economic growth in postwar Japan were basic industries such as iron and steel, chemicals, and so on; whereas those of the second stage were manufacturing industries based on the assembly line, led by the automobile industry.[24] The development strategy of these basic industries, summarized very briefly, was to realize economies of scale by aggressive fixed capital investment. In such industrial fields as iron, steel, and the chemical industry, where economies of scale are significant, the basic business strategy was to achieve the advantages of mass production ahead of other producers, while simultaneously securing and strengthening ties with major end users. Business groups, which promoted investment decisions along with information exchange and thus created cooperative relationships through interdependent supply and demand, played an important role in carrying out this strategy.

Among the postwar entrepreneurs were certainly some Schumpeter would have called new entrepreneurs, those whose views were fundamentally different from conventional economic wisdom. These active entrepreneurs intuitively grasped the effect of demand springing forth at the early stages of economic development. However, many entrepreneurs and managers lacked this confidence at the start. They were not optimistic about the prospects for high growth, as is apparent from their statements at the time,[25] but their confidence was gradually strengthened as they learned from information exchanges with one another and with government agencies. This characteristic resulted in the trait known as "excessive competition," which often created overcapacity in several manufacturing sectors. There was a tendency toward simultaneous investment by many parties as it gradually became clear that investment in a certain direction was profitable and uncertainty decreased.

The success of a business strategy among primary (raw material) manufacturers depends largely on measures to avoid the risk of excessive fixed-capital investment and an unprofitable market situation. The Japanese method of organizing counter-recession cartels, with the entire industry bearing the cost of excessive investment, often proved an effective buffer for the enterprises concerned. Because the formation of cartels in general entails a sacrifice in social welfare in terms of reducing output and increasing prices, there was heated argument regarding the pros and cons of such cartels. Many feared that these industries would develop the disadvantageous side of group behavior. Illegal cartel behavior was, in fact, often discovered up to the beginning of the 1970s, until Japanese antitrust policy was gradually strengthened enough to limit such behavior. In addition, industrial development shifted from basic to assembly-line industries, which formed another kind of business group.

In assembly-line industries, the strategic industries of the second developmental stage, special characteristics of the business group contributed remarkably to the need for technology transfer both between and within enterprises. Vertically integrated groups such as Toyota and Matsushita played a crucial role in these industries. A rough organization chart of the Toyota group is shown in Figure 2. In these groups, the parent company actively provided subcontractors, subsidiaries, and associated firms with technical information and expected them to absorb and master such technologies and to accumulate technical know-how during the course of learning.[26] Cost reductions based on the learning

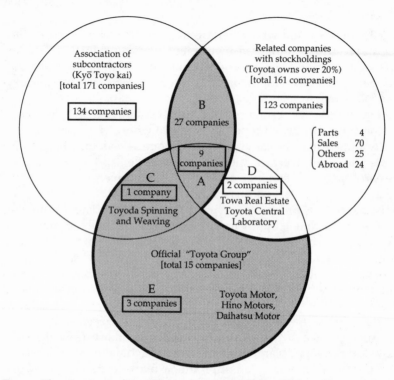

Fig. 2. The structure of the Toyota group. *A*: Nippon Denso, Toyota Automatic Loom Works, Aichi Steel Works, Toyota Auto Body, Kanto Auto Works, Toyoda Gosei, Toyoda Machine Works, Aisin Seiki, Toyota Tsusho. *B*: Fujitsu Ten, Tokai Rika, Aisan Industry, Takaoka Kogyo, Kyoho Mfg., Cyatara Kogyo, Taiho Kogyo, Aisin Light Metal Kogyo, Toyoda Tekko, Chuo Spring, Hosei Brake Kogyo, Chuo Precision Industry, Horie Metal Kogyo, Tsuda Kogyo, Yutaka Precision Kogyo, Koyo Seiko, Koito Mfg., Aisin-Warner, Kyowa Leather Cloth, Jeco, Kyosan Electric, Takashimaya Nippatsu Kogyo, Toyotomi Kiko, Toyota Chemical Industry, Central Motor, Gifu Auto Body, Arakawa Auto Body.

The structure of the association of subcontractors is as follows:

Percentage of sales to Toyota Company	Sales		
	Under 10 billion ¥	10–29.9 billion ¥	Over 30 billion ¥
70–100	24	15	12
20–69	21	15	15
<20	8	18	29

SOURCE: Kazuichi Sakamoto and Masahiro Shimotani, *Gendai Nohon no kigyo group* (Business groups in contemporary Japan) (Tokyo: Toyo Keizai Shimpo Sha, 1987), p. 58.

curve, as dictated by the core business strategy of the assembly-line industries, were thus realized for the entire group. Although the trading among companies in this phase was in the form of market transactions, they were long-term reciprocal transactions. When market conditions were unfavorable, the leading manufacturer might from time to time demand an unreasonably low purchase price for certain parts from a subcontractor. In return, the manufacturer would attempt to make up whatever loss the subcontractor might have incurred by giving it attractive margins when market conditions were favorable. There were no written contracts in this relationship, but rather a kind of "implicit long-term contract," or what has been called an organizational transaction.[27] Also, the degree to which information was shared among the parties and the fact that subcontractors were directly in contact with engineers in the major firms gave their relationships a similar character to those within a single organization. The market and the organization were interwoven.

This long-run relationship, as mentioned earlier, included not only an economic transaction but also a social transaction involving trust, loyalty, and power. Parent companies could have used their power to exploit subcontractors, but usually they did not; they used their power to strengthen the group as a whole. This helped to legitimize power within the group, and the parent companies' leadership was established.

However, implicit long-term contracts between a parent company and subcontractors do not imply fixed long-term relationships in a market without entry and exit. In the initial stage, a parent company usually orders rather simple parts from a subcontractor. This transaction is no different from any arms-length transaction in the market, except that it implies a screening process among potential competitors. If a subcontractor passes this test, the parent company gradually orders more sophisticated parts, and during this process mutual trust is created. Even at this stage, the subcontractor is still in competition with other subcontractors for such work, though the number of competitors will decrease. This long-term competition creates a highly reliable group of subcontractors. Moreover, the process of skill formation in large organizations is accompanied by a long-term competitive process among workers, in that a person who learns higher-level skills will get a better position. This long-term competition within the firm motivates Japanese workers to work hard.

Thus, Japanese vertical-group behavior is a mixture of long-term social relationships and long-term competition. However, it should be emphasized that it is under conditions of rapid industrial growth that an implicit long-term contract or long-term competition in the above sense becomes possible. Expected growth in sales was crucial for creating mutual trust between a parent company and subcontractors. Anticipated growth of income and future career advancement were indispensable elements motivating workers to participate in this long-term competition within the organization. Thus, the prototype of the Japanese industrial organization was formulated under the special condition of a mixture of Japanese cultural traditions and rapid economic growth.

The Network Industrial Organization

Technical Innovation and Network Specialization of Work Forces

The oil crisis may have been a blessing in disguise for Japanese industry, motivating it to explore new technical innovation. As changing climatic conditions in the sixteenth and seventeenth centuries had caused Europe to industrialize,[28] the depletion of oil and other natural resources drove Japan, a country with few natural resources, to technical innovation. In any era, efforts to solve problems of survival involve the exploration of new technologies and culture.

As shown above, the worldwide industrial reorganization that followed the recession of the 1880s contributed to the formation of the zaibatsu, while the dissolution of the zaibatsu, which was generally regarded as a crisis, produced the competitive postwar reorganization. Similarly, the oil crisis created a new industrial organization.

The oil crisis forced Japanese business enterprises to conserve energy by utilizing all available technologies, especially in the field of electronics. As a result, the specialization and division of labor associated with technological improvement advanced rapidly. Each company carefully studied its own rationalization techniques in pursuit of the highest degree of specialization. Major companies integrated these techniques and systematized them. Increases in specialization and division of labor were not a new phenomenon, but after the oil crisis, the way the division of labor penetrated and connected firms and industrial fields and multiplied horizontally, accompanied by the transfer of technology, exhibited a special character that may be called the formation of networks.

This specialization of the work force was different from both the isolated specialization of labor in the market and the planned variety seen in large business. In this type of work-force specialization, which may be called the "network specialization of the work force,"[29] units retain autonomy and yet remain closely interdependent. Unlike the hierarchical division of labor typical in automobile manufacturing, schematized by A in Figure 3, this type of specialization is characterized by self-organizing, as schematized by B. That is, a newly developed spe-

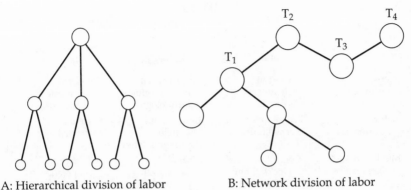

A: Hierarchical division of labor   B: Network division of labor

Fig. 3. Patterns of division of labor.

cialization, T1 for example, finds its own linkages with other specializa-
tions (T2, T3, T4) and creates its own demand or market.

This specialization of the work force has been noted by M. J. Piore
and C. F. Sabel of the Massachusetts Institute of Technology, who refer
to it as "flexible specialization."[30] They argue that this development has
created a second divide in the industrialization process, entirely different
from the conventional mass-production system.

At the same time, a more highly specialized work force necessarily
creates spontaneous linkages among firms engaged in related types of
specialized work. This is because when individual enterprises perform
highly specialized work in the age of system technology, they cannot
reach their full potential unless mutual progress is made as a network.
This requires a sharing of information among related firms that is beyond
the simple information exchange in the market. Hence, network activity,
or activity with consideration for one's "position" in the network and
"distance" from others, is the mode of action.

The specialization and improvement of technology thus results from
greater and greater specialization of the work force, and these specialized
technologies are closely linked by utilizing sophisticated market functions, enhanced by developing information technologies. They thereby
begin to function as what I call *network industrial organizations*, which are
described in the following section.

Characteristics of the Network Industrial Organization

The characteristics of the network industrial organization and a comparison with zaibatsu and business groups are set out in Table 2. There
are several important differences among the kinds of organizations. First,
in relationships between companies, emphasis has moved from such

TABLE 2
Evolution of Business Networks in Japanese Industry

	Zaibatsu	Business group	Network industrial organization
Nature of technology	Import of inventions, patents	Large capacity, mass-production technologies	Small-scale, small-batch engineering
Nature of information	Exogenous Special route	Endogenous Hierarchical Arbitrage-related	Creation Interaction
Interbusiness relationships	Control by stockholding, assignment of directors (strong ties)	Mutual stockholding, presidents' clubs, assignment of directors (strong and loose ties)	Affiliation, cooperation (loose ties)
Management	Control	Authority	Leadership and rules
Advantages	Concentration of decision making	Rapid growth	Dispersed decision making Creativity
Disadvantages	Financial control, suppression of entrepreneurial freedom	Groupism, cartels, excessive competition	Instability

formal systems as mutual shareholding between companies and the assignment of directors to informal relationships in which the exchange of information is of primary importance. Of course, mutual shareholding to prevent hostile takeovers is still important for core companies, but in general, human linkages based on mutual trust are becoming crucial for information exchange. Second, the handling of information has undergone a drastic change. In the zaibatsu, an organization received information on the affairs of the outside world, and, to use the jargon of the economist, information was *exogenous*. In business groups, however, it is *endogenous* in nature, in that internal transmission and processing of information is important, but, as has been typical in the conventional information activities of trading firms, arbitraging based on information has been the main activity and there has not been a high degree of information creation.

In network industrial organizations, information is created through interaction, and the creation of information becomes the driving force of business activity. "Creation of information" may sound like the activity of geniuses, or the creation of something from nothing. However, it here refers to the means of creating a new context in the process of normal decision making. (We refer to the aggregate of past and ongoing experience obtained through interactions—memories or the stock of information, and the emergent connections based on them—as *context*.) Context is the medium through which new information is generated, and it is the network that creates such context. The market fails in such activities. The network industrial organization provides a "place" for interaction between related actors, and each obtains positive externalities of created information.

To innovate, as Schumpeter says, is to carry out something new. To advance this concept further, one might say that innovation is nothing other than the creation of new information. Network industrial organizations may therefore be considered to be organizations that continuously execute incremental innovation based on on-the-spot information, which is obtained by a "man on the spot" in doing business in Friedrich Hayek's sense.[31] Japanese success in manufacturing has come from the continuous improvement of shop-floor technologies based on detailed information on the spot. However, this is different from simple skillful improvement, for which it is often mistaken. An essential point is the linkage between shop floors, marketers, machinery suppliers, and R & D personnel through on-the-spot information. The network industrial organization creates such linkage.

When on-the-spot information is used in the decision-making process, it naturally contains the subjective interpretations of its sender and receiver. The transmission of market price quotations, for example, is useful for decision making when the information is interpreted within a context agreed upon within the company. In this sense, all the people participating in a market or organization touch upon some sort of context. There must be many people, therefore, who have the experience of directly grasping changes while they are in contact with the actual spot or scene.

When an entrepreneur tries to advance things in a new way, he needs on-the-spot information to suggest the structural information from which he can grasp the new context in its entirety. This is the necessary qualification of an entrepreneur. However, even if an entrepreneur has grasped information that will enable him to discern future developments, he cannot begin work with that information alone. He knows only the direction of change for his immediate vicinity and does not yet have enough details to complete the whole job. For that purpose, he needs more information, which enables him gradually to identify the total structure of the new context. Entrepreneurs create a loop to obtain such information to match the situation at the moment. In abstract terms, they can be called information networks. The prewar zaibatsu formed networks that exercised dominant purchasing and selling power by virtue of their centralization of information. After World War II, information-exchange networks among entrepreneurs and managers were set up, but these tended to become looser than the prewar networks as the links between firms gradually weakened.

Since postwar entrepreneurs had to start from nearly ground level, they began on a small scale and could not take advantage of existing organizational structures to conduct their business. Even those who had been managers of relatively large firms, as high up as company president, virtually became operators of small firms once again. They confronted this situation directly, absorbing on-the-spot information. They did not see the course of development from the outset, but came to understand its path while proceeding in the initially determined direction. During the learning process, an important role was played by information exchange along the human networks that had emerged spontaneously. Since on-the-spot information is flexible and not closed like an established concept, links can grow between people through technical discussions and exchanges of market or financial information.

The fact that the numerous entrepreneurs who made possible Japan's postwar economic growth—from company president down to section chief—began what subsequently became leading firms as small enterprises or as a small section of a larger enterprise is an extremely important point in considering the characteristics of Japanese firms today. It resulted in a style of management in which the manager pays close attention to the details of on-the-spot information. While prevailing upon his workers to accept what he has discovered, he values and rewards highly the behavior of workers who grasp the meaning of such information and who try to improve their work on the shop floor. This background has also given rise to the sense that one should always strive to make incremental innovations, since technology is a ceaseless flow, and to perceive the market as a process of long-run adjustments.

Continuous incremental innovation provides the fundamental advantage of network industrial organization. In the zaibatsu, only innovations such as a great discovery or its patenting, things that occurred infrequently, were imported and dealt with. In later business groups, the nurturing of major technical innovations, accumulated over a very short timespan owing to the great advances in science and technology in the 1930s, was of major importance. Network industrial organizations, however, link various improvements and innovations of large and small scale and attempt to maintain a constant flow of innovation. The character of a new industrial society is one of continuous innovation by linkages across, rather than within, the borders of specific industries. By carefully combining internal and external business networks, Japanese industries and business enterprises have steadily advanced innovation across the spectrum of industry and have formed what can be termed network industrial organizations.

Self-organization and Network Structure

As already mentioned, the organizational principle of networks is self-organization. This means that an independent actor spontaneously establishes linkage with other actors and a mutually binding relationship among actors—that is, an "organization" in the most general sense—is thus formed. In the market, a kind of self-organizing system, each firm undertakes mergers, joint ventures, or information exchanges with other firms on the basis of its own decision, without control from above. In this case, however, the boundary of the firm is considered "fixed." The boundary will, of course, change with a merger, for example. But if two companies merge, the new company's boundary becomes "fixed" as an element of the new market structure until the next change takes place. However, in the network view, the basic unit is not the firm as a legal entity but as an economic actor that can make decisions independently or quasi-independently. Sometimes it may be a person, sometimes a section or a division of a company, and sometimes a whole company. Actors within many companies establish linkages with each other through strong or weak ties according to the needs of business. The boundary of the firm or corporation therefore most often changes continuously rather than sporadically. Such linkages are spontaneously formulated, and this spontaneous linkage is the first meaning of self-organization.[32]

Self-organizing in this sense is self-evident. The problem is whether self-organizing creates an organization with a better chance of survival in the economy. The second factor is controversial. Generally speaking, for an actor to have the ability to self-organize in this second sense, the conditions of autonomy, self-transcendence or self-reflection, and hybridization must be satisfied.[33]

Autonomy literally means the ability to make decisions independently. As the transition from zaibatsu to business groups took place, the autonomy of companies increased, while in network industrial organizations most companies have complete or quasi-complete autonomy. This autonomy, combined with direct interaction in the market, allows freedom for trial-and-error experimentation. Large Japanese corporations are now in fact decentralizing authority by creating smaller, autonomous decision-making units within the firm and, furthermore, establishing them as separate smaller companies (*bunsha*).

The second ability of self-organizing actors, transcendence, is a difficult term to define. It is the act of moving beyond one's past and, in the process, going beyond purely selfish activities and attempting to grow through mutual understanding. In spite of the fact that each unit is autonomous, an attitude of connecting with other units and consideration of the whole entity is made possible by self-reflection. The identity of an actor is expanded by information-sharing, and this attitude of self-reflection allows adaptation to a new environment. This thus becomes the mechanism for organizing.

The third condition, hybridization, means that in order to produce creative information, it is necessary for each autonomous unit to make connections with units different from itself, which also leads to self-reflection through the contrasts produced. Thus, autonomous behavior with freedom of action, an attitude of self-reflection coupled with information-sharing, and the creation of new information by hybridization are the essential elements of the self-organizing mechanism in the second meaning.

The movement toward the divestiture of a company's various divisions, which has been attracting attention lately as the organizational principle of some big businesses in Japan, is a movement toward creating autonomous decision-making units that can adjust more quickly in the changing economic environment. The division that becomes independent from a parent company leaves behind the restrictions of the past, attempts to make its own linkages with companies of different categories, and establishes interbusiness relationships in the process of self-organization. Even in places where such divestiture is not carried out, the management practice of forming quasi-autonomous work units (e.g., project teams) within a company, which function as small independent companies, has been adopted. They, too, form linkages in a self-organizing manner with personnel of other departments within the company and also with other business enterprises.

It is important to note that self-organizing does not occur in a vacuum; it proceeds within a framework or structure already established, and the characteristics of this structure influence the nature of the self-organization. Although the transition from zaibatsu to business groups was brought about by the intentional dissolution of the zaibatsu, the subsequent formation of business groups included a considerable element of self-organizing. However, the direction and extent of self-organization was still influenced by the traditional structure inherited from the zaibatsu. In the change from business groups to the recent network industrial organization, the initial phase of self-organizing was completed on the periphery of business groups. The linkages thus formed gradually and expanded into spontaneous interfirm organizations in search of new information; some of them have evolved into wider networks with linkages radiating in all directions.

Thus, the process of self-organizing involves the determination of a subsequent structure as well; that is, when self-organizing progresses within a certain structure, the scope of that structure is broadened and the structure itself changes until soon a new structure is established. Self-organizing then begins again with the new structure as its initial framework. In abstract terms, the process of "structure → self-organizing → structure" is what I perceive as the organizational evolutionary process.[34]

The existence of some kind of structure controls and sets the direction for self-organization. Without structure, self-organizing would be blind and could only lead to chaos. Therefore, as in the case of zaibatsu, structure is intentionally planned and designed at the outset, and the evolutionary process is then begun, its form depending on needs at various points in time. When a configuration begins to appear through the process of self-organizing, the structure is again intentionally adjusted by leading firms or government policy (e.g., deregulation) in accordance with the new economic environment. The dissolution of zaibatsu provided a new business-group structure. From that basis, network industrial organizations are now evolving. Therefore, today's networks of firms are combinations of "business groups" and "network industrial organizations" in various degrees. However, I would like to emphasize the new dimension of information-sharing in network industrial organization, as I believe it will become a new business framework.

Let me cite some examples to show the current trend of corporate networks in Japan. Network-type organizations are everywhere in the modern Japanese industrial scene. Examples include (1) horizontally and vertically integrated groups like the Hitachi or NEC groups, (2) heterogeneous R & D networks comprising several competing companies and government agencies, such as that for very large-scale integration (VLSI) or fifth-generation computers; and, (3), a multifaceted network among manufacturers, wholesalers, and retailers in the household goods industry.

Organizations like those under (1) represent an evolution of the "business group." As shown in Figure 4, which represents the essential character of the recent NEC group, they are actually a combination of a business group and a network. Recently, however, the importance of the network in the group has gradually been increasing to cope with software production.

The special networks under (2) are for R & D purposes. Although relationships are set up in the sense that business groups or big companies contribute to such networks through funding or by providing researchers, each network is a separate entity for a specific R & D purpose. These networks are sometimes transitory, and some parts of them may achieve only very weak performance. However, several are playing the role of engines pulling the Japanese information society.

The typical network industrial organization is found under (3), so let me elaborate on its basic characteristics. An example of a typical recent

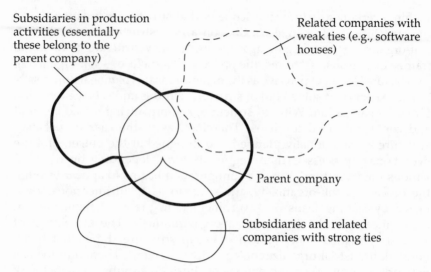

Subsidiaries in production
activities (essentially
these belong to the
parent company)

Related companies with
weak ties (e.g., software
houses)

Parent company

Subsidiaries and related
companies with strong ties

Fig. 4. Conceptualization of the NEC group.

network organization is sketched in Figure 5. Eight household goods manufacturers, including Lion, Unicharm, and Shiseido, were joined by Intec, an enhanced telecommunications service supplier, to form a communication network consortium called Planet. Planet also includes hundreds of independent wholesalers, and the members exchange data on business transactions through Planet. The consortium also functions as a code center; computer software is developed through joint efforts at Planet. This is a synergy-creating process within the network.

An important thing about this network is that Planet acts as an information infrastructure, so that its members are able to self-organize various kinds of subnetworks without worrying about basic communications facilities and service. Such subnetworks include Corenet, Act, Gruppe, and Soryu Forum, as shown in Figure 5. These subnetworks are various combinations of manufacturers, wholesalers, and retailers. For example, Corenet is a small group of wholesalers and retailers, and Soryu Forum is a voluntary study group, consisting of Unicharm and several wholesalers, that discusses collaboration between wholesalers and manufacturers and joint retail support. Membership in a subnetwork is very fluid, even allowing some overlapping, and entry to subnetworks or Planet (an infranetwork) is free, but information is shared among network members.

An interesting feature of structuring networks is that the addition of a new factor to the network causes unexpected linkage, and the synergy thus activated results in the entity undergoing drastic change. When

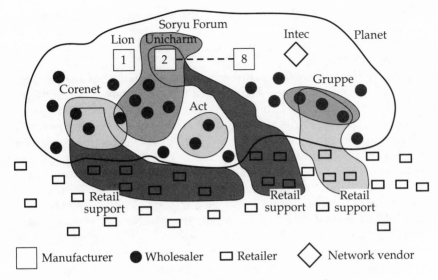

Fig. 5. A multifaceted network in the household-goods industry.

this progresses beyond a certain threshold, the commitment of the members changes fundamentally, and this in turn results in the formation of a new structure. The process of "structure → self-organizing → structure" thus begins to operate. The process is essentially a method of creating something entirely new by using the same components but changing the combinations.

Network Industrial Organizations and Entrepreneurs

From these observations about the characteristics of network industrial organizations, it can be concluded that an entrepreneur who can make such an organization work will also have the ability to "edit" the networks just discussed. Such a person would not be like a representative entrepreneur in a zaibatsu able to lead his organization with great vision in activities such as the allocation of resources in the marketplace; nor would he resemble the average entrepreneur in a business group who attains group accomplishments based on information exchange. Rather, he is an entrepreneur who, while measuring his position and distance within a network relative to others, can direct self-organization by making new linkages between autonomous units. It is also possible to interpolate that he is not a "creative destroyer" as described by Schumpeter but an entrepreneur who discovers unexplored opportunities and linkages. In the sphere of demand, he will find business opportunities that link those hitherto separated, while in the realm of supply, he will make networks of new combinations and will then coordinate supply and demand as described in Israel Kirzner's theory of competition and entrepreneurship,[35] which may be regarded as the modern version of Schumpeter's theory.

Thus, in recent network industrial organizations in Japan, the characters of both information exchange and the entrepreneur are substantially different from those in business groups. We cannot predict what kind of entrepreneur will play a leadership role in the coming network industrial organization. One possible prototype is Ichizo Kobayashi, who pioneered a new entertainment business in Japan. He was an organizer of different and heterogeneous talents, and his character was quite different from the entrepreneurs who led Japan's success in manufacturing by concentrating on their own businesses. According to Masakazu Yamazaki, Kobayashi's character recalls the Muromachi period (1392–1573) and its splendid cultural achievements. It is misleading to define the Japanese character in set terms like *group-oriented* or *homogeneous*. It is more reasonable to suppose that there is a range of diversified characters among the Japanese, and that those individuals best fitted to the time play a leading role as entrepreneurs in each period.

Summary and Implications

1. Japan is here characterized as a network society with extensive information-sharing among its people, a concept Shumpei Kumon also puts forward in his essay in this volume. This character also applies to a greater or lesser extent to other countries. According to Chie Nakane, many Asian countries can be characterized as network societies.[36] What distinguishes Japan is that its networks are strongly institution-oriented rather than individual-oriented. Japanese networks are built on the experiences people share by working in the same place or attending the same school. Relationships in such a network are linkages mediated through "place" in this sense. At the core of the overall network of Japanese society, and typical of it, are Japanese corporate networks.

2. Japanese corporate networks have evolved from zaibatsu to business groups and further to the recent network industrial organization. This evolution is seen as a gradual loosening of the intercorporate linkage and blurring of corporate boundaries. It has also been a process of adaptation to turbulent social and economic environments. Such adaptability is one source of Japanese economic vitality.

3. The network view is a process view, in which the basic unit is not the firm or any other economic agent acting in isolation but rather various economic agents acting in relation to one another. A dynamic market

process is one in which the inconsistent expectations of economic agents are adjusted through an interactive information exchange among them. Markets and organizations interpenetrate each other.

4. The entrepreneur is a key actor in this network view, and the role of the entrepreneur has changed in the evolution of Japanese networks. In the zaibatsu, the entrepreneur's role was to design a blueprint for industrial networks, in which power was centralized, by learning from the experiences of advanced countries. In business groups, the entrepreneur's role was to guide group behavior by establishing ex ante coordination. This was achieved through sharing of information among group members, related firms, and government bureaus, and thus promoted economic growth as a whole. In the recent network industrial organization, the entrepreneur is expected to play a new role as a network organizer. In each phase, entrepreneurs have been new men (in a Schumpeterian sense) who were freed from the constraints of the old paradigm and thus opened up a new context in Japanese industrial society.

5. Information exchange is a key variable in the network view. The handling of information has undergone a drastic change during the evolution of corporate networks. Information was exogenous in the zaibatsu and it was transmitted through a hierarchical network. In business groups, information became endogenous, and the exchange of information became a primary function of the group. In the network industrial organization, information is created through interaction, and the creation of information has become the driving force of business activity. However, in every phase, actual on-the-spot information rather than abstract concepts has been utilized, and this concreteness has helped maintain the dynamism of Japanese economic networks.

6. A network is regulated by a micro-macro linkage of information. In a network with strong ties, this linkage becomes a mechanism of hierarchical control. In a network with weak ties, it induces network behavior that takes into account one's "position" in the network and distance from others.

The Japanese economic system, for example, was helped out of the oil crisis by the network behavior of trade unions. Unions moderated wage demands based on knowledge, gained through a micro-macro information loop, of the likely repercussions of wage increases (see Haruo Shimada's essay in this volume). The economy is again coping with severe structural change, this time brought on by the sharply rising yen, by using information loops to take into consideration the macro effects of each company's exports.

This type of decision through a micro-macro information linkage, however, is accompanied by a specifically Japanese feature: people reach a final decision only after a macro image has emerged. In other words, there is a tendency to decide things at the eleventh hour, and this produces some nervous behavior when trying to keep in step with others. This is a source of friction with foreign countries, especially during negotiations.

7. Why have the Japanese succeeded so well in adapting their networks to the needs of the day? What is the cultural basis for this? There are various explanations: the Japanese organizational traditions of ie and mura; mutually supportive behavior and information exchange in a rice-cultivating nation that has traditionally required cooperation among workers because of the seasonal concentration of labor; learning behavior, as discussed by Thomas Rohlen in his essay in this volume; and the way of thinking of most Japanese, who are in the main passive and conform to the stream of time and circumstances, in contrast to the Western knowledge pattern, which is characterized by operationalism and activism.

I have given special attention to the last three points and explained their implications for the evolution of Japan's corporate networks. As a whole, their evolution has been a long-run learning process through understanding the meaning of given circumstances and responding to it rather than managing the circumstances themselves. Information exchange among firms and people has played a crucial role in this process. Modern economic organization is essentially a system of creating and processing information. Its evolution is a process of interaction among constituents. The pattern of their learning and of "editing" and transmitting information to other people shapes organizational structure and the network configuration of the economic system in each period. My basic theme throughout this essay has been an understanding of Japanese corporate networks as a system of learning and information exchange and their implications, in a nutshell, for other nations.

Thomas B. Lifson

The Managerial Integration of
Japanese Business in America

In February 1872, five youthful members of Japan's Mitsui family set sail for the United States to learn the ways of American business, eventually studying the textile mills of Lowell, Massachusetts.[1] A few years later, some of these first Japanese businessmen to arrive in America founded Japan's first multinational corporation, the prototypical *sogo shosha*, Mitsui & Co., Ltd.[2] One hundred one years after the arrival of Mitsui family members in America, Mitsui & Co. became the first Japanese firm ever to acquire a major equity share in a large U.S. corporation, buying half of an integrated aluminum producer.[3] The purchase attracted much notice and comment in Japan, but was comparatively ignored in the United States.

A scant 15 years later, Mitsui had plenty of company, and Americans had begun to pay attention. The upward valuation of the yen versus the dollar, which began in 1985, unleashed a torrent of Japanese foreign direct investment (FDI) in the United States. In 1988, yearly foreign direct investment inflows from Japan were greater than those from any other country save Britain.[4] In total cumulative investment, Japan ranked number three, following Britain and the Netherlands, though it appeared likely that it would rank number two by the end of 1989 and might possibly surpass Britain in the 1990s (see Figures 1 through 3). Although the quality of the statistics measuring Japanese FDI is so low that a leading scholar on the subject has termed them "full of errors and pitfalls,"[5] they are still a good relative indicator of the level of growth of Japan's U.S. economic apparatus, and they show that during a time of substantial overall growth in FDI investment in the United States, Japan's absolute and relative status as a foreign investor in the United States rose substantially during the 1980s.

During a period when the United States became the site of rapidly increasing numbers of subsidiaries of multinational corporations based

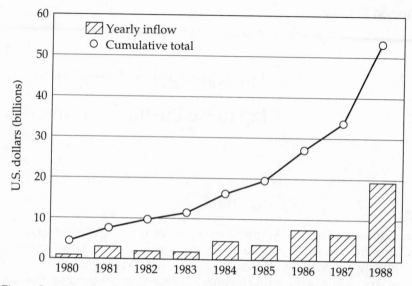

Fig. 1. Japanese FDI in the United States, 1980–88. From Association for Foreign Investment in America, *Periodic Review of Selected Statistics on Foreign Direct Investment in the United States, 1980–88* (Washington, D.C., 1989); and U.S. Department of Commerce, *Japanese Direct Investment in U.S. Manufacturing* (Washington, D.C., 1990).

in major trading partners, Japan's arrival in force has aroused a dual, if not schizophrenic response from American politicians. On the one hand, a majority of the states have established offices in Japan to promote investment in their jurisdictions. On the other, Washington voices have expressed uneasiness, if not hostility toward further Japanese investment, evoking the loss of national autonomy, or even some form of subordination to Japan. A congresswoman from Ohio, the site of Honda's major automotive manufacturing complex, accuses the Japanese of running "a completely closed system" and establishing "what amounts to colonies" in the United States.[6] Senator Alfonse D'Amato (R-N.Y.) predicts, "If we don't fight now, . . . we'll be like serfs working for the Japanese."[7] Senator Tom Harkin (D-Iowa) somewhat more thoughtfully notes that "over time, as ownership of our assets is transferred overseas, so is the authority to make important business and economic decisions affecting the prosperity and independence of our nation."[8]

  The United States is not yet used to being the host country for foreign multinational corporations and is generally more wary of Japanese than of the much larger British or collective European Community investments. U.S. governmental intervention prevented a Japanese corporation, Fujitsu, from completing the proposed purchase of Fairchild Instru-

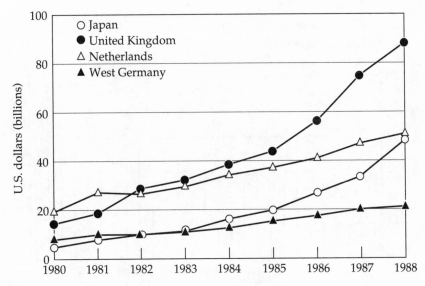

Fig. 2. Cumulative FDI of four leading countries, 1980–88. From Association for Foreign Investment in America, *Periodic Review of Selected Statistics on Foreign Direct Investment in the United States, 1980–1988* (Washington, D.C., 1989).

ment, a producer of semiconductors, which was forbidden upon review by the Department of Defense on the grounds of national security, despite the fact that the current owner was itself a French multinational firm, Schlumberger.

The growing number of corporations operating in the United States under Japanese ownership or control in the 1990s will be at the center of a spotlight of concern. Their responsiveness to American interests and sensitivities will be tested. They will need to bring together American and Japanese managers in creative and effective organizations. They must integrate high-performing, highly motivated American minds into a Japanese superstructure. As Japanese influence over sensitive industries increases, the roles played by American managers in Japanese-owned U.S.-based assets will come under increasing scrutiny. To what extent will Japanese corporations, rooted as they are in the political economy and culture of Japan, be able to walk the delicate tightrope of multinationalism, serving and being perceived as serving the economic interests of the host country, its citizens, and its local employees, while playing a coordinated strategic role in an enterprise centered elsewhere?

This chapter examines the integration of Americans into the emerging economic apparatus created by Japanese FDI in the United States. Foreign direct investment may be defined as any form of long-term capital movement for the purpose of productive activity and accompanied by

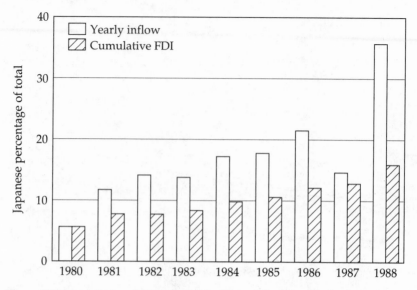

Fig. 3. Japanese share of total FDI in the United States, 1980–88. From Association for Foreign Investment in America, *Periodic Review of Selected Statistics on Foreign Direct Investment in the United States, 1980–88* (Washington, D.C., 1989).

the intention of managerial control or participation.[9] A basic distinction must be made between seedling organizations with managers sent from Japan, the way most Japanese investment took place prior to the late 1980s, and mergers and acquisitions (M & A), the buying of operating facilities and organizations. M & A activity by Japanese corporations in the United States did not become notable until 1987, but accelerated rapidly. In M & A investments, it is possible for integration to be gradual and less visible, with finance and capital budgeting often among the first areas affected. But if a U.S. company has been purchased by a Japanese company for strategic reasons rather than for speculative profits, as has nearly always been the case, then eventually there will be more integration with the parent's global operations over time.

The main body of experience in combining Japanese and American managers is in subsidiaries founded by Japanese multinational corporations. To understand them better, this essay will describe the evolution of Japanese investment in the United States in the postwar era. It will describe the issues surrounding American blue-collar workers in Japanese-owned factories. Difficulties surrounding the inclusion of Americans in the decision-making process constitute its major focus. Basic contrasts in assumptions and beliefs about the nature of work and organization are at the heart of problems in integrating Americans into

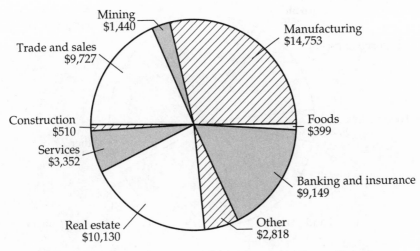

Fig. 4. Japanese FDI in North America in 1988, U.S.\$ millions. From Japan Economic Institute, *JEI Reports* 23B, June 17, 1988, p. 13.

a Japanese managerial structure. In particular, the role of interpersonal networks in information-gathering and influence processes will be seen as an important obstacle. The logic, formation, use, and utility of a particular form of network, the "administrative network," will be presented. The difficulties being experienced by Japanese multinational companies in incorporating Americans into their management structures and processes will be described. A final section will outline some of the approaches available to Japanese firms seeking to include Americans in important decision-making functions.

Postwar Japanese Investment in the United States

As a defeated nation, Japan had no foreign investment in the United States following World War II. The growth in the dollar volume of Japanese investment in the United States has been matched by a proliferation of actors establishing an organizational presence, industries being represented, functions performed, and motivations for investing. Figure 4 shows a sectoral breakdown of Japanese investment in North America, as of March 31, 1988. Figure 5 subdivides manufacturing investment by sector.

Among the first Japanese companies to establish a postwar presence in the United States were firms specializing in trade, shipping, and finance. In terms of business volume and number of personnel deployed from Japan, the *sogo shosha* were the largest operations.[10] The companies behind this first wave of Japanese investment were intermediaries,

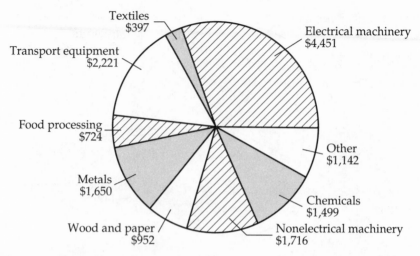

Fig. 5. Japanese FDI in manufacturing by sector in 1988, U.S.$ millions. From Japan Economic Institute, *JEI Reports* 23B, June 17, 1988, p. 13.

connecting Japan's economy to the richest nation in the world, a source of vital raw materials, markets, capital, and technology. Although their U.S. operations were small, these pioneering outposts had great visibility in Japan, because of the importance attached to the U.S. market. Many of the companies and managers who would subsequently start up U.S. subsidiaries passed through the American offices of banks and trading companies on their first forays to the United States.

In the mid 1970s, I had the chance to interview both American and Japanese veterans of these early years. According to them, the management environment was very different then.[11] Public consciousness of Japanese investment was almost nil, and few highly credentialed Americans were interested in working for a Japanese corporation. The cadre of expatriate managers was relatively small and often composed of some of the "best and the brightest" of the elite parent corporation's staff. An assignment to the United States was considered prestigious, and important to the company, and indeed to the entire Japanese economy. The scope of work performed was broad, and the opportunities to distinguish oneself within the parent organization comparatively abundant. In those days of the weak yen, dollar costs for local employees seemed enormous compared to employment costs in Japan. It made economic sense to confine Americans to those roles in which they were essential. Americans operated as secretaries and clerks, and in functions where public interface or specialized knowledge or resources were needed. The management was dominated by the expatriate cadre, hard workers and high performers, who kept in close touch with headquarters. Virtually no efforts were made to recruit, train, or develop Americans to assume managerial roles that would involve them with headquarters.

As expatriates returned to Japan, these attitudes spread and became institutionalized. Because the pioneers dealt with so many other firms who would eventually themselves establish outposts in the United States, often advising them about how to do so, the attitudes were spread even further. A vicious circle developed: the expectation that Americans would not or could not handle important affairs led to recruiting lower-quality personnel and to the departure of those with higher capacities. This process reinforced the very attitude causing the problem.[12] Thus, the most experienced Japanese firms in the United States inherited and transmitted a legacy that was decidedly unfavorable in its impact on the ability of other Japanese firms to localize their organizations by thoroughly involving Americans in decision making.

Through 1969, Japanese firms wishing to undertake foreign direct investment had to go through a strict screening process for the use of foreign exchange.[13] Outward FDI was liberalized in stages from 1969 to 1972.[14] From the 1960s onward, increasing numbers and types of Japanese firms established organizational bases in the United States. Manufacturers increasingly built up their own marketing and service organizations, independent of trading company intermediaries, in order to establish direct ties with distributors, retailers, and customers, and to create brand franchises of their own. In some cases, firms such as television and other electronics manufacturers entered the market via original equipment manufacturing contracts with mass-market retailers to supply private-label goods, and subsequently set up marketing organizations to enhance their margins, while building a brand name. With the growth in the physical and financial volume of trade came increasing numbers of banks and other financial intermediaries, marketing and logistics organizations, purchasing and technology-acquisition operations owned by manufacturers, liaison offices of manufacturers marketing through trading firms, and other comparatively small establishments.

There are often multiple motives involved in coming to the United States. Among the principal motivations behind many Japanese investments:

1. *Bypassing import restrictions, new or feared.* Examples include color television factories established by companies such as Sony, Mitsubishi, Matsushita, and Sharp, and auto assembly plants such as those of Honda, Nissan, Toyota, and others. Initially most components are imported from Japan, but local sourcing and manufacturing may expand over time.

2. *Maintaining close contact with industrial or commercial customers.* Examples include ball-bearing manufacturers such as NSK and Toyo Bear-

ing, where thousands of different designs must be produced for specific applications, and technical liaison with customers at the design stage is vital. Kyocera's semiconductor packaging operations, begun in 1971, made it the first "hi-tech" firm to follow this path.

3. *Taking advantage of lower raw material costs in the United States*. The food industry, with Kikkoman's soy sauce brewery, various fish-processing plants, noodle factories, and *sake* breweries, is a prime example. Mitsui's investment in the aluminum industry took advantage of lower American energy costs to supply Japanese and overseas customers, while a variety of Japanese petrochemical facilities in the United States have capitalized on lower feedstock prices, producing items such as polyvinyl chloride hose.

4. *Providing a captive outlet for semi-finished products* manufactured in Japan by establishing downstream processing facilities in the United States. The most notable examples are steel-product-finishing operations, using steel from Japan. Conceptually, these are quite similar to the assembly operations described under 1. Often these operations have been owned by consortia including the materials suppliers and *sogo shosha*. In the steel industry, every major Japanese producer has entered into joint venture arrangements with an American steel company to make advanced-technology products such as cold-rolled steel in the United States.

5. *Obtaining technology, products, or services* incorporating unique technology, or providing a technology-monitoring capability for the Japanese parent. The Seiko Hattori group's 1973 purchase of a majority interest in Micro Power Systems, Inc., of Santa Clara, California, an integrated-circuit producer, is an early example. In the late 1980s, service industries came to be prominent in this category. Examples include Sumitomo Bank's purchase of a 20 per cent share of Goldman Sachs and the retailing chain Taka-Q's purchase of a controlling interest in Wilkes Bashford, a San Francisco retailer of high-fashion menswear, whose buying skills are being used to supply its Japanese outlets. In a similar vein, several of Japan's leading automakers have established design studios in California, not only to produce cars particularly suited to American needs, but also to keep their fingers on the aesthetic pulse of worldwide automotive trendsetters.

6. *Providing parts or services to large Japanese customers*, who are themselves establishing operations in the United States. By far the most important example is the automobile industry, where scores of parts producers have established or are planning American facilities to meet the "just in time" delivery needs and exacting quality specifications of the Japanese-controlled U.S. assembly plants. Once established in the United States, such suppliers are often in an advantageous position to

compete with U.S. parts makers for the business of U.S. auto firms. With newer facilities and younger work forces, and often benefiting from local development incentives such as job-training funds or land and facilities development grants, these so-called "transplants" are perceived as a serious threat by their American counterparts.[15]

Of course, in many if not most cases, more than one motive has contributed to a company's decision to establish an American presence. Particularly important in many industries is the phenomenon of "competitive matching."[16] When one member of an industry takes a pioneering step, such as establishing an operation in the United States, then its domestic rivals, fearing that a potentially important competitive advantage they will not be able to duplicate will accrue to the pioneer, undertake similar ventures, almost regardless of the financial returns. Competitive matching is a risk reduction strategy for a company vitally concerned with its status relative to other industry members. Since the benefits the pioneer might gain cannot be calculated in advance, the risk of not matching is perceived to be great. The downside risk of matching the pioneer, on the other hand, is finite, since both competitors will suffer similar consequences, leaving their relative competitive status unchanged. Thus it is that in ball bearings, color television, fish processing, and automobiles, to name just a few industries, a whole series of ventures followed rapidly, one after another.

Competitive matching in FDI in the United States runs the risk of provoking public apprehension, as the rush to duplicate industry leaders may leave the impression of an endless stream of richly financed Japanese coming to devour their American competition. Of course, those who profit from the transactions necessary to carry out FDI constitute an institutional support structure encouraging just such behavior, which includes both U.S. and Japanese concerns.

On the American side, a large and powerful group of investment bankers, business brokers, securities sales syndicates, and specialists in the mergers and acquisitions (M & A) business gained in visibility and profitability during the boom in leveraged buyouts and corporate raiding that took place in the 1980s. As the overall leverage of corporate America increased and the number of large firms decreased because of the large numbers of mergers and acquisitions, this lucrative business threatened to decline. For such transaction-dependent intermediaries, the appearance of asset-laden Japanese companies on the horizon was a godsend.

On the Japanese side, banks in the late 1980s were brimming with financial assets, in desperate need of creditworthy borrowers to originate loans. Many of their industrial and service-sector clients in Japan were generating large cash flows and had little need to increase their indebtedness. Banks and other intermediaries, such as securities houses and *sogo shosha*, found that international projects, especially mergers and acquisitions, could generate both fee income and loans or other forms of financing, particularly in the case of smaller Japanese firms with limited international experience. Smaller firms with less international experience would be more reliant on the intermediary for both transaction assistance and ongoing business-generating services. Because of the Japanese land and stock-market booms of the time, some relatively small Japanese companies with fortuitously located facilities or good portfolios had collateral in Japan sufficient to obtain loans with which to purchase sizable assets or companies in the United States, even without the creative use of financing options available in America. For such companies, the argument that their domestic competitors were likely to go overseas and thereby gain access to cheaper land, energy, raw materials, or labor, or better technology, design, information, political connections, marketing capacity, scale merit, or other factors, was often persuasive.

A new breed of foreign investor from Japan has thus appeared. No longer is it only the giants of Japanese industry and relatively sophisticated internationalists who are buying into the United States. Entrepreneurial companies, subcontractors, and other neophytes at multinationalism are being thrust into the complexities of FDI, which promise to test their managerial resources. Moreover, the growth in scope of the operations of well-established investors means that expatriate personnel are drawn from a far larger stratum than the small group of managers who comprised the overseas cadre of an earlier era.

The Blue-Collar Work Force

As can be seen in Figure 4, just over a quarter of all Japanese FDI in the United States has been in manufacturing. There are no good data on the number of Americans working for Japanese firms in the United States, but 250,000 was the number most frequently repeated in 1988, a number seen as likely to double in the 1990s. Most are blue-collar workers.

Whatever the total number of Americans involved, and whatever their relative distribution between blue-collar and white-collar jobs, the overall experience of the two basic groups of workers has been dramatically different. In general, American industrial workers in the employ of Japanese-owned concerns have responded rather favorably to their workplace experiences, whereas white-collar workers, especially managers, have not. A number of explanatory factors for this positive experience with industrial labor can be adduced:

1. Japanese attitudes toward blue-collar labor contrast favorably with

common American attitudes from the workers' standpoint. The absence of such symbols of labor's second-class citizenship as executive parking spots and dining rooms is an important start. When management invests in extensive training of workers and then implements a policy of soliciting and acting upon workers' suggestions, positive reactions are frequent. Sometimes there is also an implicit or explicit policy of no layoffs of the industrial work force. Treating blue-collar laborers as human beings with creativity and energy to contribute, rather than as interchangeable parts capable only of using brawn not brain, is a frequent practice of Japanese manufacturers in the United States, which has led to favorable outcomes, including high morale.

2. In the case of start-ups, Japanese factories have generally been very careful to screen their applicants for positive work attitudes, frequently employing psychological testing. Because many Japanese-owned factories are located in regions with few high-paying alternative sources of employment, they have had a large universe of eager would-be employees to choose from. The workers may consider themselves to be quite fortunate compared to other members of the community and identify their good fortune with the company's continued prosperity.

3. A new company often enjoys a "honeymoon effect" of goodwill for bringing new opportunities and experiences to its workers and community, although this diminishes over time, especially if growth does not provide opportunities for workers to improve their lot.

4. The nature of factory work is usually more tangible and quantifiable than managerial work. Thus, Japanese trainers, foremen, and factory managers are able to explain and demonstrate their intentions, desires, and requirements more effectively than can some executives, who often deal with intangible, complex, and changing realities. Similarly, the interdependence of the work of the American factory with the Japanese home organization is more visible and easily understood than the realities of a managerial organization.

5. Japanese factories are often located in smaller communities. The Japanese staff thus have far more contact with their American associates off the job than do their executive counterparts in cities such as New York and Los Angeles, which have Japanese restaurants, bars, country clubs, and residential enclaves. Moreover, the arrival of a new source of employment in many towns is greeted with great enthusiasm, which often results in efforts to "reach out" and involve the Japanese staff and their families in community activities such as Little League, clubs, charities, and the like.

6. The staff sent from Japan to the factories are usually technically extremely competent. Their competence, rooted in tangible equipment and products, is highly evident to and appreciated by their American

associates, whereas the managerial skills of a Japanese executive are less visible to American staff, and may even aggravate them. Consider two common situations:

(a) *A production machine malfunctions.* A Japanese supervisor spends most of the night working on it to ensure that production resumes in the morning. His skill and dedication are obvious and impressive to Americans in the plant, who may be motivated to higher levels of performance.

(b) *A new budget is being prepared.* American managers submit their plans. During the night, a Japanese manager spends several hours on the telephone, fax, or telex, negotiating with colleagues in Japan to gain acceptance. As a result of this night work, he revises the Americans' plans to incorporate home office views, politics, and strategies. When the American managers come in the next day, they resent having their work altered, in part because the manager is unable to explain the reasoning behind many of the changes satisfactorily.

Japanese industrial investment is by no means without its problems, however. With some exceptions, Japanese manufacturers in the United States have preferred to have a nonunion work force. An extremely negative view of the contentiousness and inflexibility of American unions is quite common in Japanese manufacturing circles. Unions react unfavorably to this view and, more important, against the prospective weakening of their bargaining clout through the growth of nonunion Japanese plants in heavily unionized industries. The United Auto Workers, for example, has publicly declared its intention to unionize Japanese-owned auto assembly plants, but to date has had no success, other than in joint-venture facilities (General Motors–Toyota, Ford–Mazda, and Chrysler–Mitsubishi), where the American partner insisted on union recognition from the beginning.

So long as prospects for growth remain strong, workers at industrial facilities can feel secure in their jobs and generally expect promotions and rewards commensurate with their efforts and abilities. The wave of favorable publicity about Japanese management, which began with best-selling books and has permeated other media since the early 1980s,[17] has created a favorable climate for recruiting and an expectation among workers of being treated well. But these expectations are a double-edged sword for Japanese firms. Exaggerated expectations may be very difficult to live up to in the long run, and a disenchanted work force is capable of bitterness and retribution. Yet Japanese companies, anxious to hire capable workers, proud of their favorable image, and unschooled in the intricacies of such American concepts as the "implied contract," may do little or nothing to disabuse potential employees of their unrealistic expectations. If growth does not materialize, or worse, if an industry downturn requires cutbacks, workers' assumptions about no layoffs or rosy career prospects may in some cases prove to have been illusory.

A dramatic instance of these dangers is provided by Emcon, Inc., an electric-capacitor manufacturer acquired by Kyocera in 1980. By 1988, accumulated losses of $8 million were cited by Kyocera as a reason to close the entire plant. More than 130 former employees sued, claiming they had been explicitly promised lifetime employment. Although lower courts ruled in the company's favor, citing the large losses as justification for closure, the case has been appealed.[18]

Racial, gender, and age considerations in hiring policies are another area of danger for Japanese manufacturers. In Japan, race, gender, and age are widely used employment criteria, in ways that are illegal in the United States. There is also the widespread perception among larger firms in Japan that it is better to hire younger workers and train them in company ways throughout their years of maximum energy and flexibility (see Thomas Rohlen's essay "Learning" in this volume). Older workers are seen as less desirable.

Although Japanese companies, managers, and the public in general are becoming more knowledgeable about American sensitivities in these areas, consciousness of affirmative-action issues and their corporate implications is quite different in the two countries. Deeply entrenched Japanese attitudes may well find their way into Japanese hiring and promotion practices in the United States, with serious consequences. At minimum, there will have to be an explicit effort on the part of companies to enact specific policies to guard against overt as well as inadvertent discrimination, or at least the perception of such by the legal system and segments of public opinion.

Honda of America, which has received much favorable attention as an industrial employer, paid a $6 million settlement in 1988 as a result of a federal discrimination investigation of alleged bias against black and female applicants. In addition, jobs were offered to over 370 individuals previously denied employment.[19] The previous year, the same company had paid nearly half a million dollars and agreed to employment and seniority adjustments for 85 people over the age of 40 who had applied unsuccessfully for jobs between 1984 and 1985 but were subsequently hired prior to the settlement.[20]

In a rare action filed directly by the vice chairman of the U.S. Equal Employment Opportunities Commission (EEOC), rather than by an aggrieved party, a U.S. subsidiary of Japan's Recruit Company was accused of "blatant" employment discrimination. Interplace/Transworld Recruit, 50 per cent owned by Recruit and 50 per cent owned by a Recruit veteran, has been accused of systematically using a disguised code on internal job orders to channel Caucasians, Blacks, Japanese, Hispanics, men, women, and specific age groups to various positions for Japanese companies hiring in the United States.[21] Regardless of the outcome of this particular case, it is clear that attitudes about the relevance of these categories for hiring decisions vary greatly between Japan and the United States, and therein lies great danger of legal complications and public outrage.

Even if no overt bias in the hiring process itself can be shown, the overall impact on Blacks of the growth of Japanese factories in the United States has been criticized. Robert Cole and Donald Deskins of the University of Michigan found in a study of 7 Japanese auto assembly plants and 91 auto parts plants that they tended to be sited in areas with very low Black populations and were thus able to remain within EEOC guidelines, while in effect excluding Blacks.[22] Given that newer facilities are more efficient than older ones, and that the two million additional units of Japanese-managed assembly capacity are unlikely to be matched by any equivalent increase in primary demand, older plants owned by General Motors, Ford, and Chrysler are likely to close as a result of Japanese FDI. American Blacks are employed in Big Three plants well in excess of their proportion in the U.S. population. Thus, the authors argue that the net result of Japanese investment in the U.S. auto industry will be a reduction in employment opportunity for U.S. Blacks.

Regardless of intent, a pattern of geographical distribution of facilities, combined with a tendency to hire certain groups out of proportion to their number, is certain to arouse controversy and make enemies in the United States. This will create further suspicion that the power wielded by Japanese business in the United States is excessive or unfavorable to American national interests.

As industrial operations mature, skill development, career issues, and the management of change become more important. Issues of racial and gender balance in the selection, development, and rewards required to raise the level of blue-collar employees' functioning will become prominent. Dead-end jobs, the dominance of high-paying jobs by Japanese nationals, and limited upward mobility for various categories of Americans will predictably become the subjects of complaints and litigation. It will become more vital actively to manage internal mobility patterns among ethnic and age groups consistent with the requirements of American legal and public opinion. Japanese managers have, for the most part, little experience in dealing with such issues. A complex process of organizational learning must occur to cope with them effectively.

The officials closest to the problem area will usually be American human-resource professionals. They will have to work through their Japanese colleagues to reach executives in headquarters. The authority and other resources necessary to achieve a broad range of affirmative-action goals do not reside in a subsidiary's human-resources department. The amelioration of local racial problems may not normally carry much weight in headquarters' investment decisions, unless officials see a connection to the company's welfare. The threat of litigation is one way of establishing such a connection, as is the effect on the firm's public image. But such arguments tend to lose their power if repeated too often.

For Japanese companies to avoid the shoals while navigating American racial straits will require a concerted management effort, using the services of both American and Japanese human-resource professionals as well as line managers. Individual attitudes must be changed sometimes in the face of resistance. Policies, structures, and procedures must be designed and implemented in a coordinated way at both the local subsidiary and headquarters. These are difficult and complex goals to achieve and will require the assent and active collaboration of many. Influence processes, as much as the formal tools of organization, will be central to attaining the requisite understanding and cooperation. Because American operations tend to have high visibility at headquarters and may be regarded as the precedent-setting bellwether of the internationalization or globalization of the parent, the parameters of the problem are not limited to the boundaries of the U.S. subsidiary. Japanese and American staff members must work together closely on the issues. To be effective in integrating the industrial work force, the American managerial work force dealing with EEO-related matters must in some degree itself be integrated with the parent company's decision-making, information-processing, and political systems.

Integrating Management

Racial and gender issues also have been at the forefront of visible concern in the area of white-collar and managerial employment for Japanese companies in the United States. But in contrast to the industrial labor force, it is failure to delegate authority and promote, more than failure to hire, that has been at the heart of the most prominent legal actions. And, notably, Caucasian males and women rather than members of racial minorities are the primary aggrieved parties.[23]

Employment rights litigation by U.S. management personnel is usually related to much deeper issues of organization than industrial lawsuits. The substance of information flow, power and influence, recognition and reward, and other fundamental tools of management is rooted in human relationships as much as in formal organization. Culture plays a major role in defining these concepts and in structuring and giving meaning to human relationships.[24] Nothing illustrates this better than a phenomenon in Japanese subsidiaries often called "the shadow organization." As explained by one observer of Japanese management in the United States, "from the outside, you can only see the American organization. But there is a shadow organization behind it. The final decisions are always made by Japanese. Americans must always consult with Japanese, and Japanese with Japan. It's inefficient and frustrating."[25]

Feelings of frustration and powerlessness, of being cut off from the real substance of power, are extremely widespread among American managers working in Japanese subsidiaries in the United States. In the course of research and consulting, I have spoken to hundreds of such managers in over a score of firms. Of course, not all are vehemently dissatisfied by any means. But it is fair to say many have the feeling that the real authority and access to information they possess is less than either the formal authority and information they expected to have or the information and authority they deem necessary to do their jobs well.

These complaints are illustrated by a lawsuit filed against NEC Electronics, Inc., by two Americans who were once its highest-ranking local employees. The two assert that they were given assurances they would have wide latitude to run the corporation's U.S. operations. But over their objections, more and more Japanese executives were sent in, and virtually every aspect of the company ended up being run from afar, by headquarters. Frustrated with their powerlessness in the face of failure to make good on promises of positions carrying real authority that they felt had been made, the two men sued. The company denies the charges.[26]

Although no formal statistical documentation exists, it would appear that Japanese multinational corporations do use expatriate managers in much greater proportion to local staff than their American multinational brethren. Moreover, the volume of telecommunication and travel linking subsidiary and headquarters also appears higher. "In almost all Japanese MNC's, the core of the decision-making process remains almost purely Japanese,"[27] two leading observers of the multinational corporation have stated.

Without referring to the merits of any particular legal action pending, the fact that American managers' complaints are so frequent and widespread, and bear so much resemblance to one another in their themes, makes it clear that systemic differences in approach to the challenge of managing a multinational corporation are at issue. There are many ways in which modal American and Japanese assumptions and beliefs differ about the nature of work, organization, authority, communication, and other factors. The shadow organization is not a racist plot so much as a reflection of the tendency of Japanese bureaucracies to rely on self-organizing networks of interpersonal relationships (*kone, jinmyaku,* or *tsunagari*) as an important element of the management process. In Japanese bureaucratic organizations, particularly in nonroutine matters, information, resource allocation, and decision making rely on networks of personal relationships as instruments of their process. Of course, human relationships are important in any hierarchy, Japanese or not, although many Japanese make a point of stressing how important they are in Japan. What distinguishes Japan is the robustness of relationships as a vehicle or channel for bureaucratic processes. By this I mean that both the frequency with which relationships affect the performance of bureaucratic actions, and the degree to which they do so are relatively high, especially in comparison with the United States, where the use of relationships to obtain something of value is often seen as questionable or even illegitimate. It is often said to foreign businesses seeking to sell in Japan that before one can do business, it is necessary to build a relationship. The same holds true within bureaucracies. It is difficult to work with someone or some part of the organization before establishing a good personal relationship.

The tendency of Japanese bureaucracies to use relationships must be examined from a functional standpoint. If a preference for relationships is a mere prejudice, then it can be viewed as an obstacle to internationalization, harmful to foreign employees of Japanese multinational firms, and an obsolescent vestige of an isolationist past. If, on the other hand, there is functional logic to the use of relationships, then they must be carefully considered before being discarded. Their role in internationalization may be subject to trade-offs, for they must be replaced by some other means, at some other cost, with some other level of effectiveness.

Other essays in this volume use the network as an explanatory concept. Each author is making a different point, and therefore uses the term with a different nuance. Here I use the term *administrative network* to delineate the phenomenon of which I speak. An administrative network may be defined as a set of relationships existing among managers that enables them to contract with one another for the sharing of information, influence, or other resources without invoking formal organizational procedures. Administrative networks serve as an informal, but highly significant, information-channeling process within (and between) large Japanese firms. Although anecdotal accounts exist of the importance of human relationships in Japan, little systematic analysis exists of the formation, operation, and implications of network-based management systems.

The Utility of Administrative Networks

Administrative networks exist in many firms, though their comparative degree of development and use differs with circumstances. Administrative networks are most useful in situations with a high degree of change and uncertainty, and a high level of complexity and interdependence, where speed is important. These circumstances increasingly characterize many of the large global industries in which Japan is competitive. In sectors such as electronics and automobiles, the pace of innovation (both technical and nontechnical) is increasing. So, too, is the pace of the diffusion of knowledge. Thus, innovations appear more frequently, but innovators enjoy a shorter period of monopoly before competitors are able to duplicate their offerings. This creates a double squeeze: costs to undertake the higher volumes of research and development or other efforts necessary for innovation rise, while the time during which superior profit margins can be earned (to pay back the costs of innovation) is decreasing. Once imitators arrive in the market, they typically cut prices to gain market share from the innovator, so profit margins decline once exclusivity is lost.

The firm that is able to innovate quickly and efficiently has a competitive advantage. These innovations need not be merely technical product improvements in the narrow sense, but can extend to distribution, aesthetics, manufacturing process, product positioning, and many other aspects of operations. Fundamentally, successful innovation requires integrating information derived from a variety of sources and making decisions based on analyses of the data. Thus, the processes by which information is created, channeled, and used in making decisions is of fundamental importance.

I have previously examined the role of administrative networks in a study based on research into several *sogo shosha* trading companies.[28] These firms, professional intermediaries straddling countries, industries, and markets, are perhaps the purest and most extreme cases of administrative networks as a management system. They must combine information originating in different industries in many locations, and make decisions rapidly, under the discipline of rapidly changing markets and low margins. Manufacturing and many service firms face a task that is simpler in some respects. Information flows and decisions may fall into more predictable categories, and the relationship of effort to output may be clearer than in the case of the *sogo shosha*, so that fixed bureaucratic structures and procedures play a stronger role relative to administrative networks. But, nonetheless, most Japanese firms that are globally competitive (and therefore active in the United States), that share a broad set of assumptions, practices, and structures, and that are in dynamic circumstances rely on administrative networks to some degree.

The Basic Theory of Administrative Networks in Japanese Firms

Many of the most important managerial processes of large Japanese firms, such as gathering and evaluating information, consensus building, decision making, resource allocation, and certain key human-resource issues, are not rigidly conducted according to a highly structured bureaucratic protocol. Instead, these processes tend to be dependent on the character and use of specific relationships among key managers involved.

A simple example will illustrate. Because of the heightened importance of innovation, monitoring technological change is a prime concern of many Japanese firms, anxious as they are to keep their own technologies ahead of the field and to anticipate changes in their suppliers' or customers' technologies that might have an impact on their own operations. Formal processes exist to monitor sources of information about technological developments regularly. But in addition to this, a great deal of informal "opportunistic" scanning of technology may occur. A manager (whom we shall call Suzuki) working in one arm of a firm may come across a development that might affect another part of the firm. If Suzuki has an established relationship with someone in the other arm of the firm (call him Kato), they may have previously discussed Kato's operations. Thus, Suzuki will understand the potential impact of the development he has uncovered, and he may be motivated to make some effort (over and above anything required of him in his current position) to communicate the development to Kato.[29]

Such "ad hoc" or "opportunistic" action, over and above the formal, bureaucratic, mechanistic linkage processes designed into an organization, is highly useful in helping a firm to cope with change. Of course, such acts rest on a foundation of generalized commitment to an organization and an acceptance of responsibility by each (or most) of its members for its overall health and progress. Such general factors are a necessary but not sufficient explanation of the type of behavior just outlined. Because there are infinite possibilities for action facing any manager with a generalized commitment to the firm, over and above those formally designed into that position, there must be a mechanism for prioritizing and channeling activity. The structure and dynamics of a network system provide such a mechanism. We shall return to the above example in explanations below.

The basic principle governing the process of a network is the norm of reciprocity—along with the incest taboo, the most universal rule in human culture.[30] When Suzuki took the trouble to investigate and communicate his finding to Kato, he began to create an obligation that would be owed to him by Kato. If the Suzuki-Kato relationship is to continue

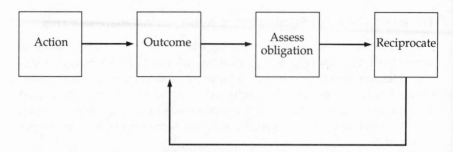

Fig. 6. Stages of a network transaction.

into the future, Kato will have to acknowledge the obligation, implicitly both will put a value on it, and eventually Kato will reciprocate. Thus, for any network process, there are actually at least four stages, as shown in Figure 6.

The assessment of the value of an obligation created is often a long-term process, for there are two components of value: the effort put into the action by Suzuki, and the value of the outcome to Kato. In most cases, Suzuki's effort may be rather readily known, but there may be complications. For example, Suzuki may have incurred some obligations of his own in obtaining the data, or Suzuki may have had to put aside other work to do it, which could create future problems for him. But in most cases, it is the assessment of the value to the receiver, in this case Kato, that requires the most time and judgment. If the information Suzuki supplies to Kato enables Kato to suggest actions by the firm that ultimately prove important, Kato may benefit powerfully in terms of his own career progress. One form of reciprocation might then involve sharing credit with Suzuki openly. Or, if sharing credit is not feasible or desirable, reciprocation may involve employing Kato's influence to obtain some kind of decision favorable to Suzuki's interests at some point in the future.

Reciprocation is an event that itself requires an outcome and assessment. Thus, there is a feedback loop from the last of the four boxes in Figure 6 to the second. In reality, it is impossible to draw an end point within the chain of favors and reciprocation that links two individuals who enjoy a solid, continuing, important network relationship. And, in reality, there is no "zero balancing" within a healthy relationship. In fact, the squaring of accounts (*karikashi nashi*) is really a way of distancing oneself. Rather, in a satisfying relationship, each party strives to maintain either an approximate equilibrium of obligation owed between the two, or perhaps a slight positive balance in his own favor. Thus, each party is constantly thinking of ways in which to add (at minimal effort to himself) obligation of the highest ratio of value-added in the other's "accounts payable" obligation column.

Although Suzuki and Kato may occasionally keep the depth of their relationship secret, or may sometimes choose to conceal its use in certain instances, a dyadic relationship such as this does not exist in isolation. It must be understood in the context of the other relationships Kato and Suzuki maintain. Context impinges on the dyad in several important ways:

1. Kato and Suzuki may need to rely on others, especially mutual associates, to help them measure obligation owed and discharged.[31]

2. Mutual associates constitute an implicit enforcement apparatus to ensure that obligations are fully discharged. If Kato refuses to satisfy Suzuki, and others side with Suzuki, then Kato's reputation, and ability to call on others for their help, will suffer. In a system where formal sanctions are few, and job responsibilities and authority are kept to a low level of specificity, this can be a fatal disability. Formal authority of position can become all but meaningless if members of the firm refuse their support.

3. Third parties can provide a supple currency for balancing obligations:

(a) By making Suzuki's meritorious deeds known to others, Kato can add to Suzuki's prestige and credibility easily. This is more than an abstract consideration, for it improves Suzuki's ability to form new relationships and to call on others' help readily.

(b) Kato may go a step further, and actually introduce and recommend Suzuki to a third party, say, Ikeda, when Suzuki is in need of a resource over which Ikeda has discretionary control. In so doing, Kato stands as a guarantor of Suzuki's ability to use Ikeda's resources well, and of Suzuki's ability to discharge any obligation that might be incurred toward Ikeda.

(c) Alternatively, Kato may have a store of obligation owed to him by Ikeda, and may realize that Suzuki, to whom Kato owes obligations, could use Ikeda's resources. In this case, Kato may act as a "broker" or reticulator, simultaneously collecting obligation owed by Ikeda and discharging obligation owed to Suzuki.

4. Inevitably, rotation policies mean that Kato and Suzuki will transfer to new positions, and the institutional component of their relationship will devolve onto others. When personal or organizational relations are strained, rotation may be a welcome means of avoiding or escaping from obligations, though there may be a reputational price to pay. But in most instances of satisfactory relationships, the personal component of the obligation balance between Kato and Suzuki must be correlated with an institutional or positional component.

The definition of a particular action, and the obligation that results from it as personal or as institutional, is a matter of signaling among the actors involved in a transaction and those around them. For instance, if Suzuki consulted with others, or sought his superior's sanction for devoting time to his search for information, the obligation would probably be more in favor of the unit than of Suzuki. Kato's actions also help determine who owes the obligation, himself or his unit. If he keeps himself centrally involved in using and dispersing the information, he will tend to receive more personal credit for benefits that occur in the future and owe more personal obligation. On the other hand, if he involves others in his unit early on, or if his activities receive other resources of his unit early on, then the obligation accrues to the work unit.

Shumpei Kumon's distinction (see his essay "Japan as a Network Society" in this volume) between networks based on the spontaneous offering of information and exchange systems based on reciprocity is helpful here. Interaction within a *network*, as he uses the term, is based not on the expectation of something eventually being given in reciprocation, but on sharing without direct return. Rather, what the giver receives is "priority," an acknowledgement of his or her forward position in the information chain. Eventually an accumulation of "wisdom"—a generalized ability to persuade—follows repeated acknowledgment of priority.

To the extent that a particular action is open and public, it tends to be a network rather than an exchange reciprocation. Similarly, to the extent that an act is seen as benefiting the entire firm, rather than certain subunits or individuals, it is network rather than exchange in nature. Network interaction requires no reciprocation.

Administrative networks are not pure networks in Kumon's sense. They are relationships that can be used for both spontaneous sharing of information and for reciprocal exchange of obligation. In most instances, both modes of action are present, but in differing relative degree. A spectrum might be envisaged: at one extreme, managers who privately help each other in a reciprocal way; at the other extreme, Kumon's pure network activity, where managers interested in advancing the overall welfare of the company publicly offer each other the most valuable information they possess. In the middle would be situations where managers expect both some degree of reciprocation and some degree of recognition for their access to valuable information. In most real situations there is probably some mixture of public and private motives, and some degree of tension between the two is at least latent.

Administrative Networks and Japanese Culture

The behavior of individuals in administrative networks is learned behavior, and so is obviously related to the culture within which the individuals are socialized. The behavior of such actors cannot help but be saturated with the values, symbols, forms, and other aspects of the culture of which they are part. But to say this does not necessarily imply that administrative networks are a uniquely Japanese phenomenon. After all, marriage is also permeated in equal degree by the surrounding culture, and no one would describe it as a uniquely Japanese institution.

In fact, nothing that has been described here is necessarily peculiar to Japan. Indeed, I believe that the mechanism so far described is a universal one, which operates in business systems where membership is important and the sanction of ostracism is a real possibility. Examples would include most ethnic business communities, such as Indian and Chinese traders in Southeast Asia, Lebanese in Africa, and various groups in America. There are a number of important commodities whose trade has been handled by systems with a large component of network-based obligation exchange: wholesale diamonds, certain metals, West Texas oil, and some aspects of investment banking. There may even be certain elements of this system present in university faculties.

Ostracism is a particularly potent sanction in the Japanese tradition. In pre-Meiji Japan, expulsion from the village (*mura hachibu*) was the most serious punishment a villager could receive for misconduct. Today, for workers in large companies, ostracism is also a very meaningful punishment. Japanese large companies rarely, if ever, hire someone other than recent graduates as entrants to their core staff.[32] So it is impossible to find an equally rewarding and prestigious position elsewhere if one is ostracized. Ostracism does not mean being fired. It means simply that others in the firm refuse to do anything the victim of ostracism asks for, other than what is explicitly required by the formal system. Powerless within the firm, and powerless to escape, the object manager lives in a kind of hell.

In smaller, less prestigious firms, the sanction of ostracism may be less potent, since there is considerable job mobility in this sector of the Japanese economy. It is accordingly likely that internal administrative networks are much less prevalent and important outside the large corporate sphere of activity in Japan. However, for the owners and top managers of such firms, their personal contacts with other companies are no doubt very valuable tools of management.

The sanction of ostracism does work in Japan in a specially powerful way, for networks are more extensively used as a basic mechanism, on a larger scale and with more regularity, in Japan than any other large country. The pervasiveness and scale of the use of administrative networks in Japan is related to the congeniality of certain aspects of Japanese culture to their efficient functioning. Japanese culture affects the use of administrative networks in the following two general ways:

1. Culture conditions the process of exchange among managers within an administrative network. The language, symbols, values, forms, and other expressions of and influences on their interaction derive from their culture.

2. Culture influences the organizational and environmental context within which the administrative networks function. The choice of a formal organization design of "lifetime" employment for managers, promotion by seniority, attaching rank to individuals rather than to jobs, and other practices common to large Japanese firms is influenced by Japanese culture, albeit not in a simple deterministic way. Similarly, concepts of authority and leadership are also heavily influenced by both national and corporate culture.

It is important to note that although we may speak of Japanese culture as if it were a uniform entity (it in fact has significant variations), large firms in Japan differ significantly in their corporate cultures. Local values, symbols, myths and sagas, guiding principles, common understandings, and shared experiences can be extremely important factors differentiating companies from one another.[33] Administrative networks are inward-looking. It is hard for outsiders to break in, even if they happen to share a common Japanese national culture. The difficulties non-Japanese managers working for the firm overseas experience in relating to administrative networks in Japan is different only in degree, not in kind.

Administrative networks rest on a basis of obligation and its discharge. Japanese culture supplies strong concepts around this set of values.[34] From the frequency of sayings about obligation to the perennial popularity of the story of Chushingura,[35] the consciousness of the Japanese people is drenched in reminders of how important it is to carry out one's obligations to others. There is also a strong tradition of the intermediary as a respected figure, providing an important function. The flexibility of administrative networks to reach beyond already-established dyads and incorporate new relationships is heavily dependent on skilled reticulators. Japanese culture accords great prestige to intermediaries, and the seeking out of go-betweens is second nature to most Japanese. The persistence of the formal marriage intermediary (nakōdo) is only the most obvious manifestation of this. Similarly, the widespread use of mediators and other forms of third-party conciliation in place of judicial proceedings may also be cited.[36] Thus Japanese culture provides an abundance of values and forms supporting intermediation roles. These intermediaries are vital to the construction and maintenance of large-scale, flexible administrative networks.

The high value placed on affiliation in Japanese culture is another contributing factor to the spread and utility of administrative networks. As Merry White notes in her study of Japanese primary schools: "For the Japanese, the most highly valued qualities are those which make a child *ningen-rashii*, "human-like," and the most valued among the qualities is an ability to maintain harmony in human relationships."[37] A Japanese person's administrative network, like other human relationships, is not merely a means to an end, it is an end in itself. Although skillful building and use of an administrative network may be rational in terms of economy and career, practitioners are not motivated solely by such narrow considerations. On the other hand, the Japanese preference for affiliation does suggest that relationships may be a favored means for the satisfaction of a wide variety of ends, including coldly rational self-interested ones.

The Japanese language itself may contribute to the use of administrative networks. Because of its many possibilities for signaling a change in status or affect between two speakers, it provides a subtle and supple medium for signaling nuances of change in a relationship. A back-and-forth exchange of valuation can take place without either party having to acknowledge it formally.

Moreover, because of the inherent vagueness and the importance of nonverbal cues in Japanese, it takes quite an investment of time for any two persons to establish a solid basis for communication. Taking the extra time and effort to understand each other, especially going beyond the requirements of the immediate situation, is a signal that the relationship has a longer-term significance. Extending the relationship to the social sphere through the rituals of drinking and eating, golf, mahjongg, or other such interactions further solidifies the basis for future interaction. This activity could be considered an investment in the establishment of a new relationship. Once it is in place, and becomes a sunk cost, there is a natural tendency to use it, rather than seeking information from alternative sources, with whom another "fixed cost" investment would have to be made.

The second avenue of influence of culture on administrative networks is through organizational and other institutional forms. There are specific widespread structures and practices of Japanese bureaucracy that contribute to the use of the network mechanism. The oft-noted clanlike elements of large Japanese firms,[38] with their emphasis on membership, and many other elements of the employment and corporate systems have evolved so that they structurally support the use of networks.

For managerial staff in a Japanese corporation, membership is a key concept, far more so than merely an employment relationship. New recruits are inducted into the company as a whole before receiving any specific assignment to a subunit. This symbolizes the primacy of their membership in the whole, over any of its subdivisions and produces a generalized commitment to the firm, its overall welfare, and to learning as much as possible about all its key aspects. The specific content of the new employee's work assignment is faced only after the high symbolism of entry to the whole, often accompanied by rites of passage during an orientation retreat.[39]

Concepts of authority, and the formal structures allocating it, create a large volitional element in the efforts of most Japanese managerial workers. Detailed assignments of exclusive authority to individuals and detailed formal measures of the individual's impact are rare. Rather, interdependence and collective results are assumed. Initiative and energy are highly prized. The levels of activity formally required by a particular job are only the beginning of the expected level and range of work for a manager. A good leader is expected to capture the active support, not merely the passive compliance, of others in order to be an effective manager.

The human-resource systems of large bureaucracies in Japan have evolved to provide extensive support and encouragement to the development of networks. The career-long employment commitment not only makes exclusion a devastating sanction, it also provides a stable context within which it is possible to take a long time to develop a consistent set of network relationships. Seniority-based promotion during the first half of a career reduces the incentives to grab credit for oneself prematurely. End-game strategies are not feasible.[40] There is no possibility of enacting a quick fix, being promoted out, or hired away and leaving others to pick up the pieces. By stretching out the time horizon of formal reward, Japanese companies allow a more leisurely pace of reciprocation and the gradual emergence of a broadly shared consensus about individuals' capabilities and credibility. With this pace, the likelihood of being able successfully to evade reciprocation without consequences is reduced.

During the first half of a managerial career, the dominant work context is that of a *ka*, or section. Within the *ka*, most members' job responsibilities are often formally undefined—that is, left to the discretion of the *kacho* or his delegate. This creates the necessity for the *kacho* or his delegate to monitor the work performance of junior members closely. The most efficient way to do this is to check with a network of those associating with the junior member in his work. Thus, from a very early stage, a new recruit into a company begins to see that the credibility he is generating through his work with others has direct consequences for his job responsibilities. If he impresses and works with others well, the *kacho* is likely to delegate more and more significant responsibilities to him over time. These increasing responsibilities will have a largely positive effect on his ability to be of use to others in his network. A self-reinforcing cycle is begun.

The daily work of a young section member provides many object lessons in obligation and its discharge. Because he is usually dependent on one or more *sempai* (older colleagues) for help in learning new duties or in performing existing ones, it is inevitable that the younger section member incurs obligation. The *sempai* for their part have a direct personal interest in encouraging the younger member to understand the depth of his obligation and the importance of its discharge. They seek to delegate as much of their "old work" (tasks they have already mastered) to free up their time and energies for "new work" (broader, more important tasks, which they seek to be delegated by more senior managers). This is how one rises in a Japanese bureaucracy, gaining recognition and a track record.

Ambition is one driving force behind the dynamics of administrative network construction and use. Members of an entering class of recruits are acutely aware of the fact that only a few of them will rise to top levels of rank and responsibility by the time of retirement. This provides a general motivation to perform well and be valuable in the eyes of others. While formal differentials in promotion will not appear until approximately the midpoint in a career (usually at the time when the first members of a class are promoted to *kacho*), some evidence suggests that in many companies less formally obvious distinctions begin quite early in career paths.[41]

A relatively small group within a cohort may be selected for a "generalist" rotation pattern, moving relatively swiftly through a large number of units of the firm. Those on the generalist track are widely perceived over time, if they are successful in their postings, as the emerging "stars" of the cohort. This is partly because their emerging broad range of contacts within the firm enables their reputations to grow. It may also be partly owing to the fact that, having been chosen for an elite track, they are given more opportunities to exercise higher-level responsibilities. These generalist stars not only provide a demonstration of a broad network's power, they offer an education in the importance of network selectivity.

Affiliation, the need to have a close group of associates, is another driving force in the construction of administrative networks. It is rewarding to have a group of trusted colleagues with whom one can share thoughts, feelings, perspectives, fears, and hopes. Yet the structures of corporate life and the ambitions of colleagues are not totally consistent with this intimacy. Most Japanese companies place great importance on the concept of harmony. The amount of attention is usually directly proportional to the need—that is, to the tendency of the parties involved to feel a keen sense of rivalry or latent conflict with one another. Because promotion is the chief means of distinguishing oneself and achieving higher levels of monetary and symbolic rewards, and because promotion is constrained by seniority, managers of the same age cohort and similar rank are locked into a conflict over promotion opportunities. The slower the growth of the firm, the fewer new positions will be created in the upper reaches of the hierarchy. In these circumstances, the competition for promotion becomes nearly a zero-sum game.

Most firms take care to avoid having managers of the same seniority working within a section. Thus, one's rivals for promotion are working for different sections. The sections (or other units of higher aggregation) need to cooperate with one another to accomplish their tasks, but they are also competitors for the organization's resources. There is thus an inherent tension in the organization between ideals of harmony that reinforce cooperation, on the one hand, and the structures of measurement and reward, which reinforce rivalry, on the other. The lack of escape mechanisms and the certainty of retaliation for illegitimate behavior represses conflict. The very underlying fact of the possibility of retaliation paradoxically creates the circumstances most favorable for trust. Within the comforting boundaries of such groups, the affiliation needs can be met.

Construction of an administrative network is one way a manager is able to handle the internalized consequences of this tension within the organization system. As his responsibilities begin to extend beyond the section, the young manager finds others with whom he is able to communicate comfortably and efficiently. These may well be people with whom he went to school or others who would share mutual acquaintances with him. He knows that anyone who shares mutual contacts is less likely to take advantage of him, for he can damage their reputation in their mutual social circle if they do so.

The spontaneous information offering of Kumon's networks is most closely related to affiliation needs. The retaliatory aspect of the administrative networks described here is related to achievement goals in a zero-sum situation. The structures and culture of most large Japanese companies embody a balance or a tension between the two forces, producing behavior that is driven by both motives.

Selectivity

Any manager, even a young one, is faced with the necessity of selectivity in the formation and maintenance of a network. His time is, after all, finite, so that by choosing to maintain one relationship, the time available for others is diminished. Priorities must thus be set, even if subconsciously. Over the long term, the most valuable network will be comprised of managers who are in important positions throughout the firm and whose ability to draw on others, through their own ample store of obligation, is highest. From a coldly rational, calculating point of view, it makes sense to invest one's time in establishing relationships with those young managers who are likely to rise the highest and to perform the most activity of a value-adding nature. If Suzuki is such a manager and Kato has previously established a relationship with him, then Kato has the good fortune to have potential access to Suzuki's large and valuable network of resources in the future. As Suzuki progresses, his obligation takes on a higher value to Kato than it previously had. This might be termed the "catch a rising star" effect.

Suzuki, meanwhile, finds himself at the center of a virtuous circle. As his network expands, he is in a position to pay back obligations faster through his ability to call on more diverse resources than most. Moreover, the value that others, such as Kato, place on Suzuki's obligation to them is rising. I call this valence applied to a manager's obligation his credibility. As more people are attracted by the reputation of a high-credibility manager, they become interested in bringing information and other resources to him, in the hope of establishing or reinforcing a network relationship. The fortunate Suzuki thus has even more resources at his disposal.

Suzuki's credibility in this case is closely analogous to the price of a commodity in short supply. But it is a market based on reciprocation over time rather than on immediate exchange. In fact, the entire reciprocity system of obligation accounting bears close comparison with a market system. I would contend that over time, through the credibility mechanism, quasi-market prices are established for the obligation of managers, and that these prices closely reflect the real executive worth of individuals. As one rises up the hierarchy of any organization, but especially so in a Japanese firm, the executive positions are more and more concerned with coordination, planning, relationship maintenance, and other skills that tend to draw heavily on a network such as the one described. Of course, the same sorts of market imperfections, especially those around imperfect information, apply to this system, as well as to economic markets.

Efficiencies of Administrative Networks

Administrative networks are important more for the kind of interactions they facilitate than for the volume of interaction that may take place through them. They are useful in managing the most difficult kinds of situations, where quick change is necessary and new paths must be explored, when a whole series of "what if?" questions have to be worked out and efforts, rewards, costs, and efficiencies balanced among different units. In stable and familiar circumstances, decision rules, formal procedures, and other tools that can be written down in the organizational manual may be utilized to provide the appropriate coordination of behavior. In somewhat more complex situations, marketlike mechanisms such as profit centers and transfer pricing provide flexibility and decentralization. In fact, most managers in most companies in most situations could get along without administrative networks as a tool if they had to. But innovation and coping with change require the ability to rise above ordinary procedures, to take account of information not routinely reportable and perhaps not quantifiable, and to mobilize resources in portions of the organization over which the relevant manager may have less than full authority.

The basic efficiency of administrative networks is thus threefold:

1. *Speed.* No adjustments to or constraints arising from the formal procedures are involved.

2. *Lower costs.* No new procedures have to be established formally, and the people involved already communicate efficiently. The establishment and maintenance of an administrative network is by no means a costless endeavor. Lower incremental costs are balanced by high fixed costs. But once the infrastructure is present, the incremental cost of a transaction is low, encouraging more thorough communication and weighing of various factors.

3. *Quality.* The surveillance is thorough and constant, and the incentive signals are not perverse. Not only the two parties to the transaction but others around them are monitoring outcomes.

Among the Japanese companies in the United States, those with the greatest need for administrative networks are the *sogo shosha* trading firms, other sophisticated service providers such as those in the finance and information sectors, and companies in rapidly changing industries, such as computers, telecommunications, microelectronics, new materials, and biotechnology. Not surprisingly, *sogo shosha* have faced the greatest number of civil rights actions from American managerial employees of all sectors of Japanese business in the United States.

But even in industries changing more slowly, it is the responsibility of upper levels of management to cope with uncertainty and change.

The ability to build and use an administrative network is thus virtually a prerequisite to effectiveness at these levels, even in more stable industries, where a significant portion of Japanese investment in the United States is concentrated.

The boundaries within which an administrative network is unnecessary for managerial effectiveness are the following:

1. The issues must not involve complex interdependence with other units of the company. If they do, discussion and negotiation are likely to take place using the administrative network of a Japanese manager on the spot.

2. The scale and risk involved should be small enough so as to avoid the possibility of surveillance and interference from elsewhere in the firm.

3. The urgency must be such as to permit the operation of formal channels.

Facing the Dilemmas of Managerial Integration

Japan and the United States have a mutual interest in finding ways to integrate Americans into the management structures of Japanese businesses in the United States effectively. For Japanese companies, it is not merely a matter of legal responsibility, public relations, and political liabilities, as serious and potentially explosive as these factors may be. A multinational company that denies itself the best possible access to information and decision-making linkages to its overseas environments will be a less effective competitor, with serious consequences for its longer-term global position, and even for its survival. Expatriates can never be as skilled as locals in reading the overseas environment and translating its opportunities and threats into appropriate action. Moreover, a shadow organization is expensive, cumbersome, and demoralizing to all involved, Japanese and American, when a charade takes place of having Americans perform work, only to have Japanese re-do it.

The Americans who at present or in the future are employed in Japanese companies have a direct stake in the ability of their firms to include them in high-level organizational processes. But so does the United States as a whole. Americans exposed to the cutting edge of a Japanese company's operations will become a vehicle of "technology transfer" in the broadest sense, teaching other Americans valuable lessons that they and their companies have learned. Japanese management is neither a homogeneous nor a static body of practice. The experiments and experience of companies from Japan in managing their businesses is a valuable resource for Americans to learn from. The more Americans who are more deeply involved in managing Japanese companies, the quicker the learning will be diffused.

The worst-case scenario would be for Japanese companies in the United States to make little or no progress toward managerial integration and, as a result, gain a widespread reputation of being closed to Americans at all but the lowest levels. With capable Americans staying away, Japanese managers would become entrenched in their view that Americans just can't handle the job. Lawsuits would proliferate. The companies would make mistakes owing to their misreading and misunderstanding of the business environment, and encounter economic, political, and public-relations problems. The buildup of problems would convince the parent companies to disinvest, pulling back from the current posture of aggressive investment. Jobs would disappear, the U.S. balance of payments would suffer, and the overall U.S.–Japan relationship would deteriorate significantly.

What, then, can be done to prevent this scenario, or some less apocalyptic version of it? There are only two long-term solutions: either lessen dependence on network-based systems or truly integrate Americans into administrative networks. The only realistic solution is to incorporate both approaches. A number of Japanese companies in the United States have launched "Americanization" or "localization" efforts aimed at managerial integration and incorporating both approaches. Based on research and consulting at over two dozen firms, and less formal contacts with many others, the following general guidelines for the process are offered:

Headquarters support and involvement are essential. The changes involved are systemic and cannot be achieved by the U.S. subsidiary alone. Various interested managers and groups in headquarters and elsewhere in the world may be reluctant to let go of power and prerogatives currently theirs. Defining and then respecting larger spheres of autonomy for American subsidiaries and American managers may harm their perceived self-interest. It may also seem to them risky from the company's standpoint, because a "check and balance" (their influence) is being diminished. Despite these reservations, such devolution is necessary and must be carried out steadily. Grandiose pronouncements of intention do more harm than good. What is needed is hard-nosed consideration, area by area, of decisions that do not require consultation or approval by headquarters, and then consistency in respecting the turf delegated to the American organization. All involved should understand that a track record is being compiled, which will become the currency of future power and other resources.

Particularly in an era when the Japanese economy has done so well, and the U.S. economy relatively poorly, the logic of delegating more power to Americans and adopting more American-style methods of management may not be completely persuasive. Ultimately, the success of localization efforts will depend on an internal political equation favoring "internationalists": those who understand and support localization efforts. Leadership, including clear and consistent support from the top, is an essential ingredient in such a balance. If top management is primarily composed of executives with little experience overseas, or who are lacking in exposure to the issues of multinationalism, it will be far more difficult to sustain success. To the extent that American managers become involved in reinforcing the maintenance of a coalition favoring devolution and network outreach, the long-term effort will gain in momentum. The process has inevitable political dimensions.

Replication of network socialization experiences for Americans is important, insofar as possible. Recruiting capable young Americans and posting them to headquarters to work with their Japanese peers for substantial rotations is the only way, long-term, to build a cadre of non-Japanese executives able to use the organization's resources fully and in turn be fully utilized themselves. Japanese language skills would be extremely useful for members of this cadre, and a posting to Japan could help them along in the difficult process of language acquisition. Even more important than language skills, however, are enlargement of their strategic perspective and exposure to the process of sharing information and building relationships. Exposure to key operations, functions, and people is essential to creating non-Japanese generalist stars.

Nurturing the ability of Americans to build strong and extensive administrative networks will require creative approaches. Some form of "buddy system" should be encouraged, both formally and by atmosphere and exhortation. Linking headquarters personnel likely to rotate overseas with non-Japanese staff posted to headquarters is one obvious possibility. Joint responsibility for certain tasks, joint evaluation, and some forms of shared reward might be considered. The headquarters experiences can be extended to life back in the subsidiary. Bicultural teams, joint responsibility, mentoring or buddy-system arrangements, and evaluation criteria adjustments are all feasible. Joint stakes must be created.

One key problem is that Americans exposed to these opportunities may become very hard to retain in the company, for their skills and experiences will make them valuable to other potential employers. However, if there are clear career ladders leading to attractive rewards, retention levels can be enhanced. Some form of vesting of long-term financial rewards could also be developed. The United States is rich in methods of creating "golden handcuffs," and there are many large U.S. companies that enjoy low managerial turnover. Those managers who do leave the firm should not be regarded as disloyal pariahs, but rather treated as alumni, who might someday do business with the company, recommend it to others, or possibly even return. Spinoffs of subsidiaries in which key Americans might hold a minority equity stake may be appropriate. U.S. accounting and consulting companies often cultivate their former professional employees as valuable resources. Given the value of the American employees with administrative networks, it would be a waste to shun them.

Another key problem could be resistance among Japanese managers. If the Americans sent to headquarters are perceived as receiving better treatment than their Japanese peers, if their "golden handcuffs" appear to be too generous, or if their career opportunities are perceived as coming at the expense of limiting the opportunities of Japanese staff, fatal resentment is sure to develop. Sensitivity to these and other reactions must be combined with clear vision and commitment to the changes. It is a delicate balance to maintain.

Education has an important role to play. Beyond just imparting an understanding of the need to localize overseas operations, management education has many other uses. Joint management-development sessions, with Japanese and American managers tackling tough decision-making exercises, can be used to build respect and understanding of each group's and individual's unique and valuable resources. Getting away from the atmosphere of the office, being exposed to new ideas, and undergoing shared experiences designed to offer challenges and accomplishment can open up minds to new possibilities. Japanese and Americans can become involved actively in the challenge of transforming the firm into a new form of multinational organization, but they have to be exposed to the dimensions of the problem and be asked for their ideas.

Communications issues must be continuously managed. Americans can readily become excluded from the Japanese-language communications loop, so constant efforts must be made to overcome this problem. Language training for Americans may never be adequate to resolve the problems created by this tendency. As much as possible, English should be used in the American operations. One of the most common complaints of American managers in Japanese subsidiaries is that during meetings the Japanese managers begin talking among themselves in Japanese. Although a natural human tendency, this must be seen for what it is: harmful to the interests of the organization. It is helpful for those involved to develop a gentle but meaningful reminder, such as a slogan, nickname, or other special term, to remind Japanese managers of their company's commitment to eliminating the practice.

Because of differences in time zones, much of the volume of telecommunications traffic between headquarters and the United States takes place at night. It is highly destructive to have only Japanese managers present during these hours, monopolizing contact with the home office. Rotating shifts, or some other means of ensuring that Americans are present for communications participation, must be developed. Combining greater autonomy for the subsidiary in specific areas with insistence on joint participation in the telecommunications traffic should cut down on the volume of such communication in the long run. Similarly, Americans must participate in travel to headquarters and other overseas locations.

Face-to-face communications between Japanese and American managers are also problematic, even when language skill are adequate. The most critical area is feedback, including both informal and formal performance evaluation. Even within a cultural group, providing critical feedback is a stressful, difficult task, which most people prefer to avoid. When cultural differences are present, and confrontation is seen as undesirable, the likelihood of ineffective feedback is great.

Cutting off the feedback loop for American managers produces a predictable cycle of mutually reinforcing frustration. Japanese managers are critical of their American colleagues. The most frequent complaints are "lack of initiative" and "failure to consider the relevant dimensions of the problem," or other criticism based on unfulfilled expectations. Americans feel the lack of feedback acutely and often construe silence as indicating disapproval or at least remoteness. This has the effect of diminishing their incentive to take initiative, which then directly feeds the Japanese prejudice.

It is possible to implement programs to teach the skills of face-to-face cross-cultural communication and feedback. Some combination of classroom learning and experiential exercises is most effective. But, once again, without thorough commitment and consistency of support throughout the organization, the effort cannot be effective. Role modeling on the part of management is an extremely useful tool.

Visible American role models must be given the support necessary for success. A number of Japanese subsidiaries have appointed Americans as president, including Matsushita Electric Corp. of America, Seiko Instruments USA, and Okuma Machinery, Inc.[42] Probably the first sizable American subsidiary to be headed by an American was Sony America. Harvey Schein, its president, resigned after five years, reportedly leaving behind him "an organization system and management process that isolated it and inhibited its relationship with Japan." Undaunted, Sony has appointed two foreigners, an American and a European, to the board of directors of Sony Corporation of Japan.[43] Schein's experience points out the delicacy of the task. If an American president becomes a figurehead, the shadow organization is reinforced, leading to cynicism and isolation of American managers. If, on the other hand, the American CEO is given too much autonomy, the subsidiary can drift apart from the global organization and become less than optimally effective.

The support necessary to steer a course between these hazards is both organizational and personal. Defining spheres of clear autonomy, partial autonomy (i.e., consultation is advisable), and interdependence with the parent is a start. But such determinations inevitably fail to anticipate the changes that regularly occur in dynamic industries. In the end, such American managers must be prepared to negotiate their relationships with top management in Japan on a continuous basis. They need a lot of support in doing so. First-class Japanese assistants who recognize their responsibility to help develop their boss's communications channels, skills in reading the parent organization, and clout are desirable (though such positions are potentially risky for the Japanese involved— the boss may resign or fall out of favor). Access to information is important. So, too, is the control over resources the American managers can offer the rest of the global system.

In the end, the personalities and interpersonal skills of people at the top of the U.S. subsidiary and the Japanese organizations make a big difference. Ironically, the very qualities that sometimes propel an American manager to prominence in an industry, making him an attractive candidate to be recruited for a top position by a Japanese subsidiary, may not serve the manager well in his relationship with the Japanese parent. Vision, dynamism, and a forceful and charismatic personality can make an American manager a problem-solver in the U.S. context, but unchecked by sensitivity to nuance, subtlety, and perceptiveness across cultural boundaries, these qualities can become liabilities.

Alas, there are no simple solutions. In the end, compromise and balance will be as useful as boldness and vision in integrating Japanese managerial bureaucracies. The 1990s will see these issues played out in the marketplace, the media, the courts, and the executive suite. Goodwill and the desire to learn and grow are probably the best hope for all involved.

Haruo Shimada

Japan's Industrial Culture and Labor-Management Relations

Appraisals of Japanese labor unions are mixed. During the process of vigorous industrialization in the postwar period, Japanese unions were an important and indispensable partner to management in promoting industrial production by fostering and maintaining cooperative labor-management relations. The question today, however, is whether Japanese unions can focus their perspective and activities beyond individual enterprises in order effectively to promote the social reforms needed to improve the economic welfare of the working class in contemporary Japanese society.

Since the mid 1980s, the social symptoms of the Japanese economy's misallocation of resources in the changing international environment have grown increasingly conspicuous. Such symptoms include the widening disparity between nominal income and its real purchasing power, unameliorated discrepancies between unfulfilled demand for and underutilized supplies of labor; enormous inequality in asset holdings, particularly of land; and inequitable tax burdens on workers. These growing symptoms reflect serious concerns that the healthy linkage between work and reward is being destroyed.

Restoring the desired linkage, however, would involve major reforms in the social framework by which resources are allocated. The full task is obviously beyond the realm and capacity of labor unions alone. Nevertheless, as a pressure group in the Japanese political system, unions are potentially one of the most powerful and resourceful institutions for initiating and promoting social change. Union leaders, particularly in organizations at the industry and national levels, are well aware of the desirable directions of their policies and the potential role of unions, as shown by their recent policy platforms. The question is whether they will carry these out. How seriously they will mobilize their human, monetary, and organizational resources to realize stated policy goals remains to be seen.

Thanks to success in postwar economic development and overcoming the oil crises of the 1970s, both Japanese management and unions seem firmly confident of the validity and productive power of their enterprise-based labor-management relations. Inasmuch as they confine their perspectives to individual corporations and focus on cooperative relationships within enterprises, their modes of thinking and behavior tend to be bound by a peculiar "industrial culture."

Both unions and management know that workers and corporations alike are trapped in a contradiction in which increased work will not improve real economic well-being, and they recognize that this situation is closely related to the institutional and structural arrangement of Japan's political economy. Reforms would be to their mutual benefit, but they have thus far been unable to take effective action to achieve them. Instead, they simply work harder to promote more efficient production. The dominant values, principles, and patterns of behavior developed and reinforced in the postwar Japanese enterprise community—the critical factors of industrial culture—may have their origins in prewar industrial society. These factors, which have potentially strong staying power, may well aggravate tension and friction in the process of institutional change in adapting to contemporary changes in environments.

In this essay, I review the formation and establishment of this industrial culture in Japanese industrial society, analyze its meaning and role in industrial relations, and assess the implications for future developments.

The Concept of Industrial Culture

In any industrial society at any point in time, there exists a set of values consistent with the norms and principles of people's behavior. This dominant set of values is *industrial culture.*[1] Japanese industrial culture, whose implications I explore in this essay, was formed and established during the historical process of industrial development, particularly in the postwar period.

How is a set of values that dominates the principles and patterns of people's behavior formed? It must be built upon the shared experiences of members of society, confirmed by repetition, accepted gradually as a pattern of practice and response, recognized eventually as a set of rules, and then institutionalized. To the extent that it takes time to accumulate widely shared experiences whose legitimacy is recognized and reconfirmed, it takes time for a dominant set of values built on such experiences to develop and become established.

Once established, these values naturally change only gradually. The dominant values in a society are often tied to people's expectations, vested interests, and the institutional rules and structure of the society; a change in such values means change in all these elements. When environments change, the economic, political, or social response to a given action will change. The people and institutions concerned will perceive such changes and their patterns of response will change. This will lead to changed behavior and desires in certain interest groups and will inevitably bring conflict among interest groups. In time, the distribution and structure of the interests among different social groups will change. The dominant values in a society will change only after experiences have been repeated and shared and their legitimacy reconfirmed through this process. When the dominant set of values is influenced strongly by widely shared historical values, the inertia operating against change may become stronger and the scope of possible changes more narrowly limited.

In an attempt to understand the issues confronting Japanese trade unions and the meaning of their responses, I would like to analyze and interpret the experiences of the unions by applying this concept of industrial culture. This will allow examination of the evolutionary nature of Japanese trade unionism in historical perspective and also, it may be hoped, suggest clues for assessing future developments.

The Historical Formation of Japanese Industrial Culture

Legacies of the Prewar Period

In examining the industrial culture that emerged during postwar industrial development in Japan, one should not overlook the effects of legacies from the prewar period. For example, the tendency of Japanese workers to commit themselves to the enterprise community has critical historical elements inherited from the prewar experience. Today's industrial culture appears to be deeply related to a corporate culture predominant in the Japanese enterprise community. The enterprise offers employees a place to develop social relations, share and commit to common interests and goals, and accept undefined roles as members. Inward-oriented labor-management cooperation for the purpose of improving corporate productive efficiency, a central feature of industrial culture, seems to be highly compatible with this type of corporate culture.

Traditionally, a number of hypotheses have been offered to explain the origins of this undefined commitment of employees to the Japanese corporate community.[2] Some attribute this to the traditional *ie* system.

Others seek its origins in the ethos of the agrarian village community, and still others suggest the commercial family system or even feudal government bureaucracy as its origin.

In contrast to these cultural and institutional explanations, economists have tended to offer economic explanations that may be summarized as the latecomer thesis. The fact that Japan joined the race toward industrialization as a latecomer had important implications for Japanese industrial society. Japan was able to take advantage of the latest technologies without bearing development costs. At the same time, however, Japanese enterprises had to train the work force needed for the newly introduced technology quickly.[3] The strategies for developing human resources adopted by many corporations to achieve this goal resulted in the formulation and development of management rules and policies that emphasized internal training and promotion and encouraged the commitment of workers to the enterprise.[4] Some economists explain the commitment of Japanese workers to the enterprise community through this historical process of human-capital development.[5]

Labor Turmoil and the Preparation of the Postwar Framework

The ten years after the end of World War II marked both an era of labor turmoil and an important period in the development of basic elements that directly and indirectly gave subsequent rise to the emergence of industrial culture. The most important of these elements was the formation and rapid diffusion of enterprise unions. With the legalization of the labor union movement, supported and encouraged by the Supreme Commander of the Allied Powers (SCAP), unions were rapidly organized throughout the country. The percentage of paid employees in organized labor unions climbed sharply from nearly zero to more than 46 per cent in about two years.[6] Strikingly, most unions were organized on the basis of individual enterprises and combined both blue- and white-collar workers in the same union.

Several hypotheses have been proposed to explain this pattern of union organization, unusual among advanced countries. Some point to the fact that many unions were organized within a very short period after the end of the war, which did not allow workers sufficient time to foster industrywide or craft union organizations. Workers had just previously organized themselves within enterprises under the Sampō (Labor Front for the Nation) campaign, and this experience allegedly helped them to conceive enterprise-based unions as the most practical alternative.

This hypothesis is weak, however, in explaining why enterprise unions remain the dominant form of organization long after the initial surge in union development, especially in view of the fact that many leaders and advisors within the labor movement criticized enterprise unions as a premature form of union organization and advocated the need to organize industrial unions. Perhaps the main reasons enterprise unions have prevailed throughout the postwar period is that the enterprise itself is the most common denominator for Japanese workers, a place where they find common interests, a source of income, and the opportunity to learn new skills.[7] This structural feature, as noted earlier, originated in prewar industrial development.[8]

A second element that ultimately contributed to industrial culture was the fierce labor struggles that characterized Japanese labor-management relations following the end of the war. With the destruction of productive facilities, paralysis of economic activities, shortages of food, and rampant inflation, workers' spontaneous labor struggles demanded higher wages and sometimes even workers' control of production facilities. Most firms suffered from serious labor disputes. For five years after the war, work stoppages resulted in an average of 4.6 man-days lost per 10 employees per year.[9] In the early spring of 1947, organized workers attempted a general strike led by a communist faction.[10] This attempt was banned by a special emergency order from General MacArthur. Although the labor camp no longer had SCAP's unlimited support, especially under growing fears of a cold war confrontation, Japanese labor unions continued to organize radical and at times violent strikes under the strong influence of Sanbetsu (Confederation of Industrial Unions) leadership. Sōhyō (General Council of Japanese Labor Unions), a national labor confederation formed to create a countervailing force to the communist labor movement, quickly drifted to the left.[11] In spite of increasingly harsh reaction from management and the cautious and even hostile attitude of SCAP and the government, labor unions continued to struggle, even at the expense of defeat in disputes and the division of their organizations.[12]

A third element that evolved in the early postwar period was management's efforts to regain the initiative in labor-management relations. Suffering from the labor turmoil in the wake of the war, management was left at a disadvantage. The dominant mood in society denied or even condemned the authority of management, based on the perception that SCAP was encouraging the labor movement to counteract management's power and to foster a "democratic" society. The destruction of productive facilities also hindered management attempts to build control and establish confidence.

However, as labor turmoil deepened and grew increasingly radical, and as the attitude of SCAP and the government changed, management began to regain control in the workshop and to restore its authority and power. Nikkeiren (the Japan Federation of Employers' Associations), organized in 1948, launched a series of studies of new labor-management policies and strategies.[13] A major amendment to the labor union law was enforced in 1949, a delayed effect of the Taft-Hartley amendment, which constrained the power of unions vis-à-vis management.[14] Management was increasingly stiff in its reactions to union demands and labor disputes.

The lessons Japanese management learned during this period of labor turmoil, and the basic principles and strategies it started to develop, were, I believe, to have significant effects on management's attitudes and policies toward industrial relations in the subsequent period, which saw the formation of industrial culture.

The Formation of Industrial Culture

After a decade of labor turmoil, the tide changed clearly in the mid 1950s, and the ground was laid for subsequent industrial growth by the mid 1960s. Three features were particularly important in the formation of industrial culture: the reform of the labor movement, an emphasis on quality in production, and the development of information-sharing systems.

The postwar labor movement, initially characterized by strikes and other disputes led or influenced by militant and revolutionary labor leaders, began to change gradually. The defeat of the militant labor movement was one that promoted this change. Labor unions led by radical and militant leaders fought prolonged battles against the management of many industries, such as steel, shipbuilding, automobiles, electric equipment, and coal mining. In many cases, however, they were defeated after long struggles, partly because of unfavorable general economic conditions and partly because of strong resistance by management.[15] With repeated defeats and the economic and social hardships of family life after prolonged disputes, skepticism grew among the rank and file about the political and revolutionary aims of leadership. In many companies, second unions were formed and organized the workers dissatisfied with the leadership of the primary union.[16] Management in many companies backed these second unions, seeing them as an effective organization to counteract the radical incumbent union and provide a place for the increasing number of workers who sought economic security within a company rather than adherence to the political and social goals of radical leaders. Although second unions received various forms of assistance from companies, they probably would not have grown as they did without the popular, spontaneous support of the working population.

Cooperative labor-management relations began to develop in workshops with joint problem-solving practices between supervisors and shop-committee members of the union. A joint labor-management consultation system was introduced in many companies around the end of the 1950s and became increasingly prevalent in the 1960s.[17]

At the national level, there was a major shift in the leadership and goals of the labor movement. Leaders who advocated militant or even revolutionary struggles at each locality by working with farmers were replaced by new leaders who promoted business-oriented union activities seeking to obtain economic gains from corporations.[18] The latter became known as Japanese unionism. In the mid 1950s, several industrywide federations of unions organized a concerted wage offensive in the spring, a practice that prevailed in subsequent years, known as Shuntō (Labor's Spring Wage Offensive).[19] This was a concrete expression of the new Japanese economic unionism. Also at the national level, the Japan Productivity Center was a catalyst in the development of cooperative labor-management relations and focused on the organizing principles of the productivity movement.[20]

A second feature of the changing postwar environment was the increasing concern by the 1950s of Japanese corporations, particularly those oriented toward exports, with improving the quality of their products.[21] Corporations recognized quality as a critical factor in the success of their products in the world market, and the government, which planned to use exports as the primary means for reconstructing the Japanese economy, supported corporate efforts to improve quality in many ways. Japanese corporations vigorously introduced technical know-how for quality improvement from the United States and other advanced countries.[22] Major investments were simultaneously made in key industries such as steel, shipbuilding, and electric power, providing facilities for the effective implementation of new technologies.

It is noteworthy that modernization and rationalization were achieved not only in the sense of introducing foreign know-how and building new plants but also in technological innovation, particularly in production control, process innovation, and management of human resources, in many industries. Examples include the Toyota method of production and widely used quality-control (QC) activities.[23] During this period, many major corporations had developed the preliminary form of an industrial system in which technological, economic, and organizational resources were integrated and mobilized to improve the quality of products.

An important consequence of this campaign for quality improvement was the particular patterns of behavior, response, and even thinking developed by employees, each pattern geared toward quality improvement and based on a fundamental grasp of technological knowledge and recognition of organizational implications.[24] This organizational transformation prepared the technological and organizational groundwork for industrial culture.

A third important development in the 1950s was seen in the information-sharing systems within organizations through which management, the union, and employees could communicate and share relevant information at various levels of the corporate organization. Let me mention three notable elements of this system still in use today.

1. The management-labor joint-consultation system facilitates information-sharing between management and unions. Topics dealt with in consultation are broad in scope, ranging from working conditions to such subjects as business prospects and long-term corporate plans. Consultation is a forum, not for bargaining between management and labor, but rather for sharing information, although often the system serves the purpose of selecting and identifying issues for collective bargaining. The Japan Productivity Center has advocated this system since the late 1950s.[25] The number of companies adopting this system increased steadily in the 1960s and 1970s, and currently the majority of Japanese companies have some type of joint-consultation system.[26]

2. As part of management's effort to restore authority and control in the workshop, many corporations introduced the foreman system. In the steel industry, for example, the Yawata and NKK corporations introduced the foreman system in 1956 and 1959 respectively, learning from the system of the Armco Company in the United States.[27] In Japan the practice emerged of selecting foremen from among the most experienced senior workers, unlike in the United States, where foremen are selected primarily in accordance with test scores of knowledge and skill. The Japanese practice made the foreman not only the first-line supervisor representing management but also the de facto representative of the worker group in the workshop. Because of this dual nature of Japanese foremen, they played a critical role in relaying information, not only from management to labor, but from labor to management and between workers themselves.[28]

3. Small-group activities in the workshop, such as QC circles, were also important devices for sharing information. The primary purpose of the QC circle or other small-group activity was to learn through experience and mutual education the skills and knowledge necessary to improve the quality of products and the efficiency of production. However, such activities also had the important effect of making workers share relevant information within operative terms.[29]

Many other organizational devices contributed to enriching the broad and intensive corporate information-sharing system. This system was highly instrumental in the development of industrial culture in the corporate community.

Establishment and Reinforcement of Industrial Culture

Rapid Economic Growth and the Establishment of Industrial Culture

From the mid 1950s up to the early 1970s, the Japanese economy experienced a period of remarkable growth, with an annual average rate of more than 10 per cent in real terms. In this "successful" economic growth period, some notable developments fortified the institutional framework upon which industrial culture grew.

In the process of rapid economic growth, many Japanese corporations expanded and consequently developed into large, well-structured organizations. Each corporation provided education and training programs for its employees and developed elaborate rules and policies of personnel evaluation, promotion, and allocation.[30] Such a well-structured human-resource management system offered an institutional and organizational basis for the development of industrial culture. This system also reinforced the value of intrafirm labor-management cooperation through education and training programs on the one hand, and, on the other hand, strengthened management's control over the workshop through personnel evaluation, promotion, and allocation tied to individual and group performance.[31]

Management's control over personnel was enhanced by the development of human-resource management systems, and its control and influence also increased in the sphere of labor-management relations. Close labor-management cooperation within a corporation and the maturation of the enterprise union as an indispensable partner to management meant a simultaneous and substantial increase in management's influence in industrial relations.[32] Unions' external linkage and coordination with other unions developed through such routinized activities as the Spring Wage Offensive (Shuntō), and intrafirm labor-management relations became increasingly strong within each corporation.

Enterprise unions spend most of their revenues from membership dues for activities at the enterprise level, such as paying salaries for union officers, organizing conventions, and printing documents, and contribute only a very small fraction to higher organizations such as industrywide federations of unions or national confederations. Management keeps a very close eye on the process of electing union officers, most of whom in the private sector serve the union as part of their long-term career plans, usually confined to one corporation. Most union officers in the private sector maintain employee status and return to the payroll of the company after retiring as union officers.[33] This practice, institutionalized during the period of rapid growth, helped fortify management's influence and control over labor-management relations.

With rapid and sustained increases in productivity in this period, wages also rose, and real wages kept rising. After the mid 1960s, wage increases tended to surpass productivity increases, thereby causing some domestic inflationary pressure. Nonetheless, since productivity growth was high enough, the standard of living improved continuously. Also, with vigorous expansion of aggregate demand, employment opportunities kept growing even in the face of substantial productivity growth. In other words, people were able to enjoy increases in income, security of employment, opportunity for promotion, and enrichment of the real standard of living during this period. All this was made possible primarily by vigorous increases in productivity and a remarkable improvement in product quality in the manufacturing sector, especially the export-oriented segment. This economic success convinced people of the legitimacy of the industrial system tied to industrial culture that was established during this period.

Economic Adjustment and Confirmation of Industrial Culture

Sustained rapid growth and people's expectations of future growth were shaken dramatically by the first oil crisis in 1973. Through the adjustment process following this and the second crisis at the end of the 1970s, it became increasingly clear that the era of sustained rapid growth had ended and that the Japanese economy had entered a new phase.

The quadrupling of crude oil prices in the first oil crisis triggered domestic inflation, which depressed the Japanese economy and dampened the yen exchange rate. Corporate profits were lost and investment curtailed.

In contrast, the performance of the Japanese economy during the second oil crisis was much more stable, despite the fact that the economic impact was no less than in the first oil crisis. One reason for lower inflationary pressure and its stagflationary consequence in the second oil crisis was a much larger GNP gap, or slack in the economy, than at the time of the previous shock.[34] Other powerful factors also helped the Japanese economy absorb the shock and restore stability much more quickly. One was the rapid increase in productivity. In the latter half of the 1970s, productivity increased on average at an annual rate of more than 10 per cent.[35] This dramatic productivity increase or equivalent reduction in production costs helped stabilize output prices and contributed to an increase in the international competitiveness of industries, which in turn helped to restore the yen's exchange rate.

Another factor was the moderation in wage increases. In the Spring Wage Offensive of 1980, the wage round following the second oil crisis, negotiated wage increases were settled at a rate of 6.7 per cent, whereas the economy grew in real terms by 5.3 per cent in 1979 and 4.0 per cent in 1980, and the consumer price index (CPI) increased by 10.4 in 1979 and 9.5 in 1980. In other words, organized labor accepted a substantial reduction in its relative share and a consequent decline in real wages.[36] This remarkable wage moderation helped the Japanese economy to absorb the shock of the second drastic increase in oil prices and quickly to restore a stable economic balance.

The significant productivity increases during this period were accomplished, not by the large-scale investments in pursuit of economies of scale seen during the rapid-growth period, but by rigorous application of cost-saving measures and promotion of cost-saving investments and innovations. The most notable types of investment were for conserving energy both in the production process and in products. The adoption of a continuous casting system in the steel industry and microcomputerized industrial and home products designed to minimize energy consumption were examples of such innovations. Many industries vigorously pursued cost reductions by various types of rationalization. In the automobile industry, the well-known Toyota method of production attracted keen attention for its outstanding cost savings through minimizing buffer stocks, utilizing a small-lot approach, realizing an even flow of production, and so on.[37] Similar cost-minimizing practices spread rapidly among other Japanese manufacturers after the first oil crisis.[38]

An important aspect of cost reduction was adjustment in the number of workers employed. A large part of the increase in labor productivity during the last half of the 1970s was owing to a reduction in labor input. Indeed, the employment index of the manufacturing industry as a whole dropped by 10 percentage points during this period. In structurally depressed industries, the reduction of employment was much greater, ranging from 30 to 60 per cent.[39]

By reallocating workers as much as possible and avoiding layoffs, abrupt reductions in employment were minimized. Unavoidable reductions were made carefully, allowing sufficient time in the adjustment process to minimize friction. A typical sequence of steps was to reduce overtime hours by flexibly reallocating the work force; reduce profits and dividends; reduce or stop new recruiting and wait for attrition; transfer and loan members of the work force; sell corporate assets; cut executive bonuses and salaries; ask for wage moderation; solicit voluntary resignations; and, as a last resort, lay off workers.[40] This process of employment adjustment is time-consuming and costly in the short run, but it is important in that it keeps up employees' morale in the face of economic hardship by giving workers sufficient time to make their own choices and adjustments. Moreover, it impresses workers with management's intention to share the cost of adjustment and to minimize the burden passed on to them. Such management behavior is probably less accepted in American industrial society because there priority is always given to investors rather than employees in making corporate decisions.

Wage moderation also played an important role in the process of adjustment. Unions probably accepted wage moderation in return for commitment by employers to an employment-security policy. Shortly after the first oil crisis, the leader of the Japan Federation of Steelworkers' Unions advocated "economic rationality" in wage determination.[41] This meant that the unions should be prepared to accept wage moderation if it helped to secure employment opportunities. After the first oil crisis, unions demanded high nominal wage increases to at least make up for increased prices, and this contributed to persistent stagflation. As a result of the lessons of this bitter experience, a multi-tier information-sharing network among management, unions, and government agencies now allows sharing of relevant economic and other information quickly and effectively.[42] In the second oil crisis, this information network helped wage negotiators and other influential parties quickly to reach a socially desirable wage settlement, in which labor absorbed part of the shock, enabling the economy to restore the balance.[43]

Japan probably suffered more than the other advanced industrial nations from the destructive and inflationary effects of the oil crises, but after the second crisis, it nonetheless managed to demonstrate the most stable and vigorous performance among the advanced economies with respect to movements of prices, national income, productivity, and the exchange rate. Behind this miraculous recovery was an efficient and powerful industrial system in which management, workers, and government worked vigorously and cooperatively to achieve desired goals. Japan's success in overcoming the crises proved the viability of this system. People's confidence in the system was fortified, and the system and its governing culture were reinforced.

In the labor movement, the loss of power and popularity of the leftists, concentrated largely in public-sector unions, accelerated, particularly after the defeat of the National Railway Workers' Union's eight-day strike in 1975; in contrast, the influence of private-sector unions affiliated with the International Metalworkers' Federation–Japan Council (IMF–JC) increased.[44] It is interesting that the leading unions of the IMF–JC were mostly organized workers in export-oriented industries such as steel, auto manufacturing, shipbuilding, and electric equipment. The highly efficient production system tied to industrial culture was most firmly established in these industries.

Given their success in overcoming the severe crises of the late 1970s, it is not surprising that management, unions, workers, and other actors in Japanese industrial society all spontaneously resorted to the same strategy of working hard together within the corporate production system supported by industrial culture when a new crisis broke out in the mid 1980s, marked by a sharp rise in the value of the yen.

A New Economic Environment and the Influence of Industrial Culture

Currency Realignment and the Subsequent Performance of the Japanese Economy

After the G5 meeting in New York in September 1985, the value of the dollar, which had been kept unduly high, started to fall sharply and, in contrast, the value of the yen began to rise rapidly. This drastic realignment of exchange rates produced dramatic results for the Japanese economy; these changes may be described in three phases: Phase 1, September 1985 to July 1986; Phase 2, July 1986 to June 1987; and Phase 3, June 1987 to spring 1990. Let us review briefly the notable economic changes in each of these subperiods.

Phase 1. During this phase, the exchange rate of the yen jumped from 240 yen per dollar to the 150-yen level, a remarkable change of as much as 60 per cent in only ten months. This chaotic situation brought a sense of crisis to Japanese industrial circles because of pessimistic perceptions of the prospects for Japan's exports, particularly to the United States.

In order to maintain the level of exports, managers and workers alike worked hard to cut costs, improve productivity, and sacrifice profits. Owing to the J-curve effect, and to some extent to these strenuous efforts in Japan, the U.S. trade deficit, which was the primary cause of the dramatic realignment of exchange rates, showed no signs of decline. Facing harsh criticism from the international political and economic community, the Japanese government published the report of a special advisory committee, which became known as the Maekawa report. The report recommended that Japan make maximum efforts to restructure its economy to open its markets to free international competition and expand its domestic demand.

In spite of efforts to sustain exports, quantities began to diminish in the face of the enormous price disadvantage that had suddenly emerged. Consequently, domestic production became stagnant, employment reductions became more frequent, and the unemployment rate began to soar. Phase 1 may be summarized as a typical acute recession in the wake of an abrupt and large increase in the yen's value.

Phase 2. From mid 1986 to mid 1987, the exchange rate moved from 150 yen to 140 yen, although it was for a short time at 160 yen. In other words, despite the common perception of unstable exchange rates, the yen rate was remarkably steady during this period.

With the passage of the storm, corporations developed more realistic views about international and domestic competition. Realizing the futility of continued export drives, corporations began to shift their resources and activities toward the Japanese domestic market. Restructuring of this magnitude required a huge amount of money, and many corporations that had real estate in Tokyo and other major cities received enormous gains in the market value of their assets owing to an incredible increase in land prices.[45] This gave many corporations a greatly increased capacity to borrow funds from financial intermediaries. The staggering boom in the stock market also helped corporations finance such investment projects.

Imports increased steadily because of the revalued yen, which brought Japan enormous gains by saving import costs of more than 10 trillion yen during this period.[46] When the follow-up version of the Maekawa report was made public in spring 1987, the Japanese economy had already begun a cycle of vigorous recovery, taking advantage of the high value of the yen. The unemployment rate, which is a delayed indicator of the business cycle, peaked in May 1987. This coincided with the beginning of the powerful recovery of the Japanese economy.

Phase 3. After June 1987, the yen exchange rate for U.S. dollars increased from 140 to 120 yen, with some fluctuations in between. This period was also one of a relatively stable exchange rate. The economy began to grow vigorously, taking advantage of powerful domestic demand. In consumption patterns, the wealth effect appears to have been realized on a massive scale. Consumption increased remarkably, and yet the savings ratio increased rather than declined. The liquidation of inflated stock seems to have begun gradually. Based on increased investment and consumption, production and consequently employment increased, which increased earned incomes, which will in turn give rise to even greater consumption. The Japanese economy has thus entered a phase of strong growth led by the expansion of domestic demand, which absorbs an increasingly greater amount of imports: the rate of real GNP growth for 1988 was greater than 5 per cent.

Remaining Structural Problems That Undermine the Well-Being of Workers

Despite the Japanese economy's remarkable recovery and marvelous macroeconomic performance since the spring of 1987, the structural problems under which workers suffer have not been resolved. Beneath the surface of this brilliant macroeconomic success, there remain a number of serious structural problems that erode workers' economic welfare. Let me mention four.

One problem is the large disparity between the nominal income of a Japanese worker and its real purchasing power. Thanks partly to increased values of the yen in the international money market, the nominal wage rate of a Japanese worker is said to have reached a top rank among major nations by 1987.[47] However, when evaluated in terms of parity of purchasing power, these wages shrink to about two-thirds of their nominal value.[48] This is because of the extraordinarily high prices of goods and services in Japan relative to other countries and implies that the high value of the yen has not been passed on to the Japanese people in terms of enriching their economic lives.[49] While Japanese workers' efforts are reflected in the high value of the yen in the international money market, workers cannot enjoy the rewards of their efforts.[50]

The basic reason for high-priced commodities and services directly pertaining to people's lives is low productivity in agriculture, distribution, construction, and various service industries. Important factors perpetuating the low productivity in these sectors are strict government regulation and protective commercial practices that prevent international competition from penetrating the Japanese market. Extraordinarily high domestic prices, which lower the real standard of living of the Japanese people, are one reason Japanese workers work longer hours than their European and American counterparts in spite of their high nominal incomes.[51]

A second structural problem affecting workers is the uneven distribution of employment opportunities. Despite the fact that aggregate employment conditions have improved remarkably over the past few years, the distribution of employment opportunities is highly distorted and segmented between different regions, age groups, and occupations.[52] Urban labor markets, particularly in the Tokyo area, are booming, but rural labor markets lag far behind. The supply of young workers is short relative to demand, but older workers suffer from a scarcity of demand.[53] Workers equipped with skills in information technology are sought after, but workers with conventional skills in "heavy" manufacturing industries suffer from underemployment. In other words, the Japanese labor market is now suffering from serious mismatches between supply and demand. Demand is concentrated in and around Tokyo and is mainly for young workers with information-technology skills; older workers skilled in conventional manufacturing industries such as metal processing and fabrication, located particularly in rural labor markets along the coast, constitute an important core of organized labor but suffer from unstable and insufficient demand.[54]

The skyrocketing prices of land are a third structural problem. During the past few years, the price of land in urban areas, especially in and around Tokyo, has risen drastically (on the order of more than 100 per cent).[55] Although this increase has mainly hit people living in the greater Tokyo area, including some neighboring prefectures, it has made it nearly impossible for a large number of urban workers to buy homes within reasonable commuting distance, using earned income, during their lifetimes. Although good statistics are not as yet available, it is obvious that this increase in land prices enormously widened the gap between those who have urban real estate and those who do not.[56] The large increase in land prices had some merit in that it increased the assets of corporations that owned urban real estate and consequently increased their capacity to raise funds for investment, as mentioned earlier. However, in addition to prohibitively increasing the price of housing for urban workers, who already suffer from high urban prices in general, the excessive concentration of economic and other resources in Tokyo, as reflected by abnormally high land prices, tends to aggravate the "hollowing" of other regions of the Japanese archipelago, which undermines employment opportunities for workers tied to such local labor markets.

Yet a fourth structural problem is tax and income distribution. Since, in the face of sizable government deficits, income taxes had not been reduced much until recently, workers' disposable incomes did not increase in proportion to their nominal incomes. This problem of a concentrated burden on wage earners will be deepened in the long run by the gradual relative shrinkage of the tax base under the current system, which relies largely on individual and corporate income taxes for its revenues. The burden of the direct income tax will be increasingly concentrated on wage and salary earners of prime working age, who are the main components of organized labor. This is because of a range of economic factors: a decline in the economic rate and an increase in the number of deficit-making corporations in depressed industrial sectors; an increase in tax-evading global corporations; an increase in the number of the elderly who pay no taxes; the large numbers of tax-evading self-employed workers such as farmers, physicians, small family businessmen, professionals, and so on.[57] Although this problem of inequitable burden-bearing by prime-age employees may be mitigated somewhat in the near future by means of the consumption tax introduced by the 1988 tax reform, the current tax system will have very little effect, if any, in preventing the vigorous expansion of both income and asset differentials accruing from capital gains.[58] In other words, the current tax system will allow the "new stock rich" to become ever richer by gaining from investments in stocks, real estate, and other financial assets and the "new working poor," who lacked significant assets to begin with, will become increasingly poorer in relative terms.

Tasks for the Union Movement

These structural issues are broad and far too complex for the unions to handle alone. However, because these issues pertain directly to the economic well-being of organized workers, unions must play a part in tackling them. I shall briefly examine the specific policies needed to tackle these issues and how unions are involved.

First let me address the issue of disparity between nominal income and its real purchasing power. As mentioned earlier, the main reason Japanese suffer from high domestic prices for basic commodities and services is low productivity in the relevant industries. There are several approaches to increasing the productivity of these sectors. One obvious course is to encourage private initiative to improve the efficiency of businesses. Assistance by the government or outside organizations may help, but the most powerful stimulus is usually the menace of competition, particularly from external competitors. The second course therefore, is to open markets to international competition. This has been sought in recent years by government policy and encouraged by spontaneous market forces.[59] The third course is to squeeze out redundant labor in the sectors concerned by increasing productivity.

How are Japanese unions involved in these policy issues? Lowering domestic prices by opening markets, abrogating government controls, and introducing foreign commodities are aims commonly accepted and adopted in general terms by trade unions.[60] However, once the issue is reduced to specific commodities and items, union voices become highly diverse, low key, and hardly effective. By reason of the basic organizational nature of enterprise unions, each union is inevitably bound by the economic interests of its own industry and companies, which naturally conflict with those of unions in other industries. Moreover, political parties, which unions support as their political agents, do not effectively represent the desires of union members. Rather than promoting efforts to open domestic markets to international agricultural competition in line with the desires of organized urban workers, for example, opposition parties often resist such opening. However, this may be unavoidable because opposition parties do not secure enough seats in, say, the Tokyo district, where a large proportion of organized workers are concentrated.[61] Unions hardly touch upon the issue of taking care of the large numbers of redundant workers likely to result from rationalization, partly because the issue is a serious life-and-death problem for them and partly because neither enterprise unions nor their industry federations have effective instruments to deal with such multi-industry restructuring.[62]

A second issue for unions is the problem of the mismatch between the supply of and demand for labor. The key to easing this problem is to increase or create employment opportunities in "hollowed-out" rural labor markets. The basic strategy is to develop economic activities in these regions. On this, there is no disagreement among the actors involved.[63] However, when it comes to formulating and promoting specific plans, unions are faced with a huge obstacle: firm control by central organizations in Tokyo, both in government and private corporations.[64] Generating regional development would inevitably involve interregional coordination of the allocation of resources by the initiative of local actors. This kind of action, however, can hardly be permitted in practice under the current administrative system.[65] This is true not only of government but often also of large private corporations. To the extent that unions are compartmentalized within each agency or company, it is difficult to integrate their forces across such organizational boundaries and to work toward reversing the order of control.

Third is the problem of high land prices. As noted, urban land prices have skyrocketed in the past few years, partly for short-run monetary reasons and partly for long-run structural reasons. Setting the monetary reasons aside, the long-run structural problem of excessive concentration of demand in the Tokyo area can basically be handled by two types of policies. One is to increase the supply of land in the Tokyo area; the basic measure to promote this is to reduce the income tax for selling land and to increase the real estate tax for holding land.[66] The other policy is to shift or redirect demand out of Tokyo.[67] Perhaps the most powerful measure to achieve the latter would be to construct a new capital city to absorb the administrative functions of Tokyo.[68] Obviously, these policies are somewhat beyond the scope of the union movement, although unions have a definite stake in them. Here again, the union movement faces formidable resistance and barriers stemming from the power of the central government and the great influence of the companies in which unions are organized.

Taxes are a fourth issue unions need to address. The tax reform of 1988 was historic: reforms of comparable scale may be made only once every few decades. The main thrust of the reform was to introduce a new, large-scale consumption tax. Unions obtained some gains, but they lost the opportunity to win further-reaching correction of inequities in the treatment of different groups, perhaps at least partially because they failed to unite their voices and energy. The principal gain was the introduction of the consumption tax, which is expected to reduce, at least theoretically, the tax burdens of organized workers relative to other groups less liable for direct income taxes. Even on this relatively simple issue, unions were split, partly for ideological and tactical reasons, and partly because of the different interests associated with the different industries and companies they organize. This split in attitudes obviously weakened labor's voice, preventing unions from applying the pressure necessary to realize the desired reforms with respect to capital gains and correct inequities.[69]

The present involvement of Japanese unions in these struggles appears to be much less effective than it might be. It is undeniable that unions fail to pinpoint strategically important targets, set common priorities, and mobilize their organizational resources to maximize their political pressure. Why are they unable to maximize their potential political resources? First, Japanese unions are organizationally segmented and confined to individual enterprises; they thus tend to be bound by the immediate economic interest of the enterprise. And, second, they are mentally restricted by the narrow scope of enterprise-level labor-management relations. In other words, they are the captives of industrial culture both organizationally and mentally. In the next section, I discuss the implications of the nature of Japanese industrial relations at length.

New Challenges for Japanese Unionism

Policy Targets and Political Strategy

Most of the issues raised in the previous section are essentially political in nature because they all require major changes of policy and administrative reforms. Obviously, there is not much unions can do directly here, and most of the work will have to be done by the government, legislature, politicians, and political parties. Furthermore, most of these policy issues involve sectors such as agriculture, distribution, construction, and personal services, which are largely ununionized. Labor-management relations in the modern industrial sector, which is the main territory of Japanese unions, are only indirectly related to these unorganized sectors. Japanese unions are not unaware of the nature of the issues they are confronting, and this is one reason they have recently been increasingly vocal in emphasizing the demand for new government policies and administrative reform.[70]

Although unions cannot change administrative systems or government policies directly, this does not mean they are powerless. On the contrary, unions can play a significant role as a pressure group to influence decision making in the legislature and government. In fact, unions are potentially among the most powerful pressure groups, as well as reliable support organizations of political parties in the Japanese political system.

Traditionally, Japanese unions have maintained close ties with opposition parties through a fixed and interdependent relationship: unions have supported political parties in financing, election campaigns, and organizing votes for elections, and in return political parties have provided seats for retired union leaders and worked with unions to relay their voice into political debates. In other words, Japanese unions have had formal political representation in national and local politics through their ties with opposition parties, such as those of the Japan Socialist Party (JSP) with Sōhyō, the Democratic Socialist Party (DSP) with Dōmei, and other arrangements.[71]

Despite such formal ties between Japanese unions and opposition parties, their relationship has been somewhat strained recently for various reasons.[72] Unions have increasingly demanded liberation from traditional ties of support for particular political parties. Historically, communist factions were most vocal in making such demands, hoping that the breaking of these ties would enable the Japan Communist Party (JCP) to compete with the Socialist parties, but recently the trend has been for an increasing proportion of union members to vote for the Liberal Democratic Party (LDP) and other parties, not the JCP. Many union members are disenchanted with the rigidity of the opposition parties and their impotence in formulating and materializing policies. Political parties also recognize that they cannot be totally dependent on the putative support of unions for their survival.

Possibilities and Opportunities

A critical question for unions, if they are seriously dedicated to the reform of policies and administrative systems, is how to utilize their potential political power most effectively in influencing national and local policy decisions. Time and again, traditional opposition parties have not been as effective as supporters wished in formulating policies and realizing them in the interests of workers. This is partly because the rigid internal structure of opposition parties, which prevents them from adapting flexibly to the changing political environment, makes it difficult for them to unite on specific issues.

If unions hope to realize their policy goals through the Japanese political system, they must free themselves from their ties to the opposition parties. Instead of supporting a political party as a whole, regardless of its policy platform, unions should base their support on specific policies. In other words, unions should provide money and organizational support only to the extent that a political party or political faction acts effectively as a political agent to realize union policy goals. Adherence to this approach will contribute to a realignment of political parties along the lines of policy goals and strategies, especially among opposition parties.[73]

If unions are to mobilize as support and pressure groups to effect desired policies, they could be influential and powerful: Japanese unions have about 12 million members; membership dues total 550 billion yen every year; among those they organize are talented and skillful professional workers capable of carrying out policy studies; and, above all, unions are potentially combative organizations and can organize strikes once a decision is made democratically.

The November 1987 unification of private-sector unions under the flag of Rengō (the Japan Private Trade Union Congress) may have been an important step in this direction. Unification of 5.6 million private-sector union members in a single national confederation suggests interesting and serious implications as well as challenges for Japanese trade unionism. The unification of union organizations inevitably implies consolidation of the relationships between unions and political parties in the long run. If Rengō is unable to unify or reorganize such support into a united political voice, however, and simply lets traditional political relationships remain intact under the new name, union influence on local and national policy decisions will be minor and insignificant. While this kind of supportive relationship may provide second employment opportunities for some retired union leaders as temporary politicians, the failure to mobilize the unions' political resources for social reform may have self-defeating consequences for union members in the long run.

On the other hand, if Rengō can effectively begin to implement political support based on policy, even without achieving total unification, unions' political influence would grow significantly. Theoretically, in such an approach there would be no boundary between the so-called opposition parties and the party in power; from the unions' point of view, any party or political faction would have an attraction to the extent that it was powerful and effective enough to realize desired policies for the benefit of union members. If this type of approach could be achieved, the Japanese labor union movement could open up new possibilities of social reform.[74]

Challenges for the Union Movement

Another important key is held by local labor movements, particularly enterprise unions, which have been much slower than the national labor movement in changing. National union leaders are well aware of the need for social reform and are quite vocal on the subject, but enterprise unions do not respond either as quickly or as effectively as national leaders urge them to. In fact, as discussed earlier, local leaders and workers still seem to be under the spell of industrial culture.

Two organizational or institutional elements in particular tend to make Japanese unionism particularly susceptible to industrial culture: allocation of funds and the psychological dependence of union leadership on management.

Each union member pays around 2 per cent of monthly take-home pay as regular dues, which amounts to 3–5,000 yen a month for the typical industrial worker.[75] Out of these dues, only a minor proportion goes to the industrywide federation. Even less is contributed to a national confederation—only 25 yen, or half of 1 per cent of an average worker's monthly pay, in the case of Rengō, for example. Although funds alone may not determine a union's vigor, this small budget obviously limits the extent to which the national confederation can formulate a policy platform based on its own policy research or organize campaigns to disseminate ideas and secure popular support.

This lopsided allocation of funds in favor of enterprise unions vis-à-vis industrywide and national organizations seriously limits the capacity and influence of the latter as leaders of the labor movement. Because of this pattern of fund allocation, the momentum of the movement remains with the enterprise unions, which are susceptible to direct influence and control by management and are easily caught up in industrial culture.

The leadership of many unions tends to be psychologically dependent on management for institutional reasons. The fact that they are organized mostly on the basis of individual enterprises does not by any means imply that Japanese unions are directly dependent on management. Unlike "company unions" in the American labor movement of the 1920s, Japanese enterprise unions are organized by the free choice of workers, and the proportion in which unions pay the salaries of union officials is among the highest in advanced industrialized countries.[76] Formally speaking, therefore, Japanese enterprise unions are bona fide independent unions.

However, most union leaders in the private sector retain employee status up to the retirement age of the company to which they belong, and they are therefore eligible for company pension plans and other fringe benefits after retirement.[77] Furthermore, many of those who serve in union offices for long periods see those years as an important part of their career plans within their companies. Given this economic dependence and institutional congruence, one may question whether union leaders can really be psychologically independent of management. Can they develop an independent perspective? Social reform may sometimes conflict with the interests of individual corporations. Can union leaders, when necessary, pursue social benefits contrary to the interests of the company they work for? In other words, with this institutional reliance of union leaders on the company, can they be free of industrial culture? Thanks to many years of peaceful labor-management relations, many enterprise unions have now accumulated sizable funds, which they are eager to increase even further through financial management. Have unions guaranteed the incomes after retirement of union leaders who terminate their employee status and become genuinely independent of the company? Has the union simply not attempted to do so, or is it that the company does not want the union to do so? In any event, the fact that most unions do not have programs ensuring the economic security of retired union leaders who have terminated their employee status, and that most union leaders in the private sector maintain employee status and enjoy company retirement benefits and income security after retirement, suggests that the institutional basis of industrial culture is still firmly in place.

If enterprise unions cannot move away from industrial culture and provide strong support for the social reforms advocated by national labor confederations, their raisons d'être will eventually be called into question, because it will come to be recognized that those unions have not effectively pursued the interests of their members.

Challenges for Management

In the face of changing environmental and policy issues, will management change? Japanese management has so far concentrated its efforts on developing and reinforcing the enterprise labor-management relations organized along the principle of labor-management cooperation. Management has worked hard to restrict each union to a single enterprise, to prevent unions from developing interests and activities in the outside world, and to shut out external influences.

Japanese management is not unaware of recent policy issues and recognizes the vicious circle mentioned earlier and the disparity between the micro logic of corporate survival and the macro logic of structural reform. At the national level, there are some signs of change. The attitude of Nikkeiren (the Japan Federation of Employers' Associations) appears to have shifted from one of confronting the labor camp to one of recognizing the need for working together with unions to tackle policy issues of structural reform.[78] Although management has not yet taken steps to organize joint consultation with labor at the national level, it has started periodic discussions with labor leaders.[79]

In contrast, however, the management of individual companies, particularly small firms, at the local level is still strongly against social activism on the part of enterprise unions and reluctant to approve of those unions' independence from management control. In this sense, management is strongly bound by industrial culture. If both management and unions continue to be trapped in industrial culture and fail to reform the economic and social framework so as to restore a healthy linkage between work and reward, misallocation of resources may in the long run not only disrupt the market conditions in which Japanese firms might enjoy further growth but also give rise to a radical social movement that could destroy peaceful labor-management relations.

Concluding Remarks

The economic, political, and technological environments surrounding Japanese unionism have changed drastically since the mid 1980s. The rapidly rising value of the yen has distorted the normal linkage between the labor of workers and their reward. Greater efforts by workers to increase the competitiveness of their companies sometimes erode the quality of their working lives. For instance, employment opportunities are eroded by employment adjustment in structurally depressed industries on the one hand and by direct overseas investments by export-oriented industries on the other. Both these industry groups suffer from the drastically increased value of the yen, which was caused in part by workers' efforts to increase competitiveness. Despite the ever-increasing value of the yen, its real purchasing power in domestic markets has not increased proportionately owing to the closed nature of domestic markets for consumption goods and services; the skyrocketing price of urban land makes it almost impossible for workers to purchase their own houses with their earnings; and the tax burden is increasingly and inequitably concentrated on those of prime working age.

All these issues must be tackled by political measures and government policies. Unions have the potential to exert a powerful influence on policy decisions. Will Japanese unions assume such a role effectively in the Japanese political system?

Japanese unions and management both seem trapped in the industrial culture fostered during postwar industrial development, which dictates the values, behavior, and way of thinking of the people in Japanese industrial society. Since past experiences with industrial culture have been so favorable, it is hard to criticize it and call for a change. Its efficiency has been demonstrated and its power witnessed time and again during periods of economic growth and adjustment. Unions are thus reluctant to take on the role of promoting social reform. Management is reluctant to recognize a societal role for the union. In this sense, both management and unions are victimized by industrial culture.

There are some signs of change, however. The parties concerned increasingly recognize the nature of contemporary issues. Union leaders at the national and industrywide levels express their concerns vocally and formulate their policy platforms for structural reform accordingly. Some enlightened leaders of employers' associations at the national level admit the need for cooperation between management and labor to achieve social reforms. Opportunities are unfolding in this direction. The unification of private union organizations under the flag of Rengō in 1987 and the total unification of labor organizations, including Sōhyō, in 1989 suggest the possibility of creating the powerful voice of a unified labor movement. The national employers' federation also acknowledges the value of joint consultation at the national level.

At the local level, however, such developments generate skepticism and reluctance. The leaders of enterprise unions still seem trapped by industrial culture. Working closely with management, they submit to long working hours, accept only moderate wage increases, depend psychologically on management, and leave few resources for organizations at the industry and national levels to spend. Managements at individual companies try to lock unions into the "cage" of a given enterprise and to prevent them from developing outside connections, thus reinforcing the spell of industrial culture.

As long as management and labor follow the traditional pattern of behavior dictated by the logic of corporate survival and do not reorganize and concentrate their resources on social reform, they miss the great opportunity of contributing their strength and wisdom to promoting comprehensive structural reform of the Japanese political economy in response to both domestic needs and international demands. Together, they could reorganize Japan into a genuinely advanced, open-market economy where both corporations and people would enjoy new opportunities for further development and well-being.

Robert E. Cole

Some Cultural and Social Bases of Japanese Innovation: Small-Group Activities in Comparative Perspective

The subject of the role of borrowing in Japanese economic development has a long and venerable history in the Western literature on Japan. Much of the treatment has focused on the ability of late developers to borrow technology from more advanced industrial nations, thereby permitting them to leapfrog stages of development or develop new and successful approaches.[1] Kazushi Ohkawa and Henry Rosovsky have discussed the "social capability to import technology," suggesting that Japan has displayed some distinctive capacities in this area; they also describe the rise of institutions such as *zaibatsu* and *shūshin koyō* (permanent employment) that have facilitated such outcomes.[2]

I am interested in examining Japan's receptivity to specific organizational technologies for what it tells us about the social and cultural bases of innovation in Japan. The organizational technology to be examined is what the Japanese themselves call "small-group activities" in industry (e.g., quality circles, self-managing teams, and team activity generally). I shall examine the evolution of these small-group activities between 1960 and the present, with particular concentration on the borrowing process. Borrowing is not a simple matter of copying, as commonly portrayed in popular discussions, but rather a complex process involving adaptation and the invention of new social practices.[3] Consequently, it is best to see the subsequent discussion in terms of learning processes.

To discover what, if anything, is distinctive about the Japanese approach, however, we need comparative analysis. Moreover, simple U.S.–Japan comparisons can be misleading, and therefore the comparison here will be expanded to include Sweden. This three-way comparison should enable us better to disentangle the impact of political, economic, and social factors. The political factor on which I focus principal attention is the national power distribution between management and labor. The economic factors are primarily the role of international competition and the economizing benefits associated with small-group activities. The social factors to be examined include shop-floor authority relations and, more generally, the social values regulating shop-floor relations. Underlying all these is the question of how culture interacts with the three sets of factors.

In focusing on small-group activities, I proceed differently from past analyses in the Japan field that have looked for cultural effects in the origin and performance of distinctive institutions (e.g., *shūshin koyō, zaibatsu, nenkō* [reward by length of service and age], *shōsha* [trading companies]). Rather, I seek the cultural effects in the energizing principles of ordinary aspects of economic organization.

General Motivational and Definitional Aspects of Small-Group Innovation

Why focus on small-group activities as our organizational technology? Over the past 30 years in most of the advanced market economies and even among some present and former command economies, a movement has grown for building small-group activities among production and office employees. Small-group activities refer to workshop or office-based work groups that are given a greater opportunity to exercise direct control over everyday work decisions and the solving of workshop problems. I use the term *control* here in the sense of workers being given relative autonomy to solve their own workshop problems. In the United States, the rise of quality circles (employee involvement groups) and, of late, self-managing teams has come to symbolize this movement. I focus on direct participation because, first, direct participation represents an area where the Swedes and the Japanese have been most innovative. Second, scholarly research suggests it is the area that matters most to workers.[4]

These developments have been associated in varying degrees and ways with a broader movement for the expansion of employee participation in managerial decision making. In many countries, this movement arose as a response to a crisis in management confidence that, in turn, derived from a need to respond to a threatened or lost competitive ability. The idea was to find a more effective way to recruit and make better use of employees to achieve organizational goals, while satisfying the need of individual employees for control over their immediate work environments. There were significant national variations in this regard, and indeed such variations are the subject of my analysis.

Implicit in statements about a "crisis in managerial confidence" is the view that small-group activities can have a positive impact on economic performance. Since this book is intended to clarify the relationship between economic performance and social and cultural factors, I need to comment further on this linkage. Fortunately, Masahiko Aoki's contribution in this volume is devoted to a great extent to clarifying this connection. Drawing particularly on the work of Kazuo Koike, Aoki stresses the role of the operational unit (read "small-group activity") being authorized to respond to emergent events and problems autonomously, utilizing on-the-spot information, while communicating with peers in both the same and related work groups and departments.[5] Such a system is seen as economizing on the time and resources needed for organizationwide communication and as particularly effective in responding to rapid change.[6]

Such rapid changes are growing in all sectors of the economy as the new technologies of flexible manufacturing and microelectronics spread in the context of the globalization of competition. These heightened pressures, combined with more volatile and sophisticated consumer tastes, lead to greater stress on producing more custom-made, high-quality goods and services. This increases the economic payoffs for decentralized operational decision making by small groups based on improved teamwork and autonomous problem solving. In summary, flexibility, speed, economizing on resources, and decisions based on accurate information are the major economic benefits of small-group activity.

There are, however, still other, more subtle economic benefits that are nevertheless substantial, especially in combination with other practices. Small-group activity focusing on on-the-spot problem solving can be linked with workshop presentations of problem-solving techniques and solutions so that all in the workshop are exposed to these outcomes. In this fashion, small-group activities can contribute to the rapid diffusion of generic problem-solving techniques and solutions. This learning process can have powerful economic benefits. Consider the case of the Japanese company NEC in the area of software development. It adopted small-group problem-solving activities for engineers and programmers in the early 1980s, partially to reduce the number of bugs appearing in the development of new software.[7] Instead of simply aiming to eliminate bugs as they appeared, a typical response in the past, NEC used small-group activity to get each group of 6–8 employees to address the question of why a bug appeared in the first place and then to seek to eliminate the conditions that gave rise to the bugs. The members of the small groups conducted frequent workshop presentations of excellent solutions combined with companywide competitions for the best problem-solving activities. These presentations had multiple functions: they highlighted management commitment, they stimulated workers' motivation to participate in these activities, and, for our purposes most important, they contributed to a rapid diffusion of best-practice techniques and solutions in the workplace. The economic benefits of such rapid diffusion to prevention of future error and elimination of costs associated with scrapping and redoing work should not be underestimated. This description accords well with Thomas Rohlen's observations in this volume about the pervasive extent of learning activities in Japanese firms. Indeed, it raises the issue of whether we need to think about the "culture of learning" and what might be involved in that construct.

Although the economic benefits of small-group activity have been highlighted here, it is important to keep in mind that in some countries public discussion of the benefits of small-group activity has focused on its contribution to individual empowerment by enabling employees to achieve greater participation in organizational decision making. Taken still further, the public discussion in some countries has stressed the role of small-group activities as a strong democratizing force that finally brings the benefits of political democracy into the workplace. Notions of self-governance and self-determination underlie this perspective.[8]

Before proceeding further, we need to clarify the unit of analysis, *small-group activities*. If we say that we are trying to explain the spread of direct shop- and office-floor participation in decision making in the three countries, what are we actually comparing? It is hard to "get your arms around" the concept of participation in decision making. This is because participation can occur in many work domains and in different parts of the decision-making process. It is possible to have small-group activities with greater or lesser degrees of employee participation. Thus, I chose *small-group activity* as a generic term that would not be weighed down by the high value loading of *direct participation*. Use of the neutral term *small-group activity* makes it possible to examine the processes operating in the three countries with less likelihood of attributing values and intentions to actors that do not apply.

My focus, then, is on the introduction of small-group activities at the workplace. Specifically, I examine quality circles in the United States and Japan and semi-autonomous work groups in Sweden.[9] The term *quality circles* refers to small groups of employees who belong to the same workshop or office and voluntarily engage in problem-solving activities, typically focusing on improving quality and reducing obstacles to effective work performance. By the terms *semi-autonomous work groups* and *self-managing teams*, I refer to a higher level of participation, in which the work group collectively makes its own decisions regarding work allocation, recruitment, planning, budgeting, production, quality, maintenance and purchasing. The small-group activities represented by these labels vary in structure and process across the three nations and, indeed, over time in a given nation.

The Language of Small-Group Activity

Consider the following: In Japan, the key term managers and scholars used to explain the innovation of small-group activity as it began to be applied was decentralization of responsibility. By *decentralization*, the Japanese generally mean, not delegation of authority to offices down the hierarchical structure, but rather the taking of responsibility for objectives by large numbers of people.[10] Generally, the Japanese simply talked about small-group activities (*shōshūdan katsudō*), which were commonly introduced as part of a corporate strategy to mobilize all the resources of a firm to overcome foreign and domestic competitive threats. In this sense, management sought to make participation a responsibility, an obligation, of each employee. Participation was not seen as providing an opportunity for employees to express their individual talents or self-actualize, California-style. Moreover, the term *democratization* was seldom heard. It was not until the late 1970s that one began to find a stress on participation in management (*keiei sanka*) in a sense even approximating how Americans use the term. Instead, the focus initially was on engineers aiming to solve quality and cost problems at the workplace; many of the more uplifting themes were afterthoughts that only came to be explicitly discussed many years later.

One of the earliest scholars to talk about small-group activity in the context of participation was Toshio Ueda. In their 1975 book, he and Kimiyoshi Hirota discussed the newly raised expectation that small-group activities might be a good path toward achieving greater participation (*sanka*).[11] This was some 13 years after the first quality circles were formed. The increasing tendency of interpreters of the movement to link it to participation occurred partly in response to positive American definitions of what the Japanese were doing. Prior to this time, and even to a great extent today, when the Japanese speak of *keiei sanka* and democratization of management, they are not thinking of small-group activities. Rather, they are thinking primarily in terms of systems of indirect participation, such as the widely diffused labor-management consultation system. For the Japanese, thinking internationally, the term *keiei sanka* conjures up images of the German co-determination system and other formal representational approaches in continental Europe.

Another sense in which *participation* has been used by the Japanese is quite revealing. This usage refers to the *necessity of the act of participation* in small-group activities. Shoji Shiba summarizes this perspective well:

Every worker participates in the same workshop. Let us say that there are seven workers in the workshop who work together on the same production line. All seven workers have to participate in the circle activities. Isolation of workers in the workshop is not allowed. Small-group activity with the participation of every worker is aimed at improving the work in which they are engaged. QCC [quality-control circle] activity is not an activity for amusement but is an activity for the improvement of work.[12]

We see clearly here just how the use of the term *participation* focuses on the behavioral dimension of all-employee involvement rather than the volitional dimension. Although some of the initial introductions of quality-circle activity had a spontaneous voluntarism, most of the follower firms adopted a policy of top-down installation. Hirota and Ueda report a 1973 survey by the Employers' Federation of Saitama Prefecture of 46 leaders of small-group activities in different firms. Fifty-six per cent reported that the groups were started on orders from superiors, while only 15 per cent reported that they were started by voluntary self-organization (21 per cent checked "other" with reference to such explanations as "I succeeded the former leader of the group").[13] The sample is small, but these results accord well with other discussions of the quality-circle phenomenon. While such findings clearly cast doubt on a simple interpretation of quality circles as worker participation, as commonly understood in the West, one should nevertheless not conclude that this is a simple case of coercion.

Coercion as an explanation, while appealing to neo-Marxist scholars, underestimates both Japanese management and workers. It underestimates management's understanding that workers must desire the outcomes sought by management or they will not occur. As one small-group leader replied when questioned on the merits of small-group activity, "It is possible to resolve issues only based on each member's *positive* participation" (emphasis added).[14] One of the major achievements of Japanese management has been to get increasingly well-educated workers to participate in their own job design through small-group activity, thereby tapping powerful motivational forces by challenging workers' individual abilities and giving them a limited sense of control over the workplace.[15] Management supplements these intrinsic rewards for learning and application of this learning to workshop problems by taking participation in small-group activities into consideration when making semi-annual and annual assessments of worker performance. Thus, small-group activity performance feeds into the wage and promotion system, providing additional incentives for workers to learn and participate in small-group activities. Viewed from still another angle, the coercion explanation underestimates the ability of workers to manipulate management directives to serve their own purposes. They are skillful in phrasing the solutions they want in the workshop in the language of management.

I mentioned above that follower companies often imposed small-group activity by top-down directives as opposed to the spontaneous development experienced by many of the early adopters. Many companies also, however, experienced an internal life-cycle effect. As workers became familiar over time with the tasks associated with small-group activity, management found that small-group activities were gradually taken over by workers. Kenji Okuda refers to this as the self-organizing principle and sees it as a theme (though not a dominant one) that has roots in the prewar period.[16] One company I studied in the mid 1970s reported that circle members were subject to monthly quotas for suggestions; this system had been in effect since circles were begun in 1964 at the strong request of a major customer, a large industrial firm. This hardly suggests voluntaristic participation. By 1980, however, the company reported that the monthly quotas had been dropped because the activity had become so well institutionalized.

Still, one should not overemphasize the self-organizing principle stressed by Okuda. Many companies have targets for the number of suggestions to be submitted per person and the number of themes a circle should complete (problems identified and solved) in a year. For example, Aishin Warner, a Japanese maker of transmissions, has targets of 120 suggestions a year per member and 8 themes a year per circle. One can be sure that there is implicit and often explicit pressure brought to bear on those well below the target to raise their output. Such pressures can be expected to increase the number of pro forma suggestions and ritualism as workers do what is necessary to get management off their backs. At the same time, one should not assume that learning and improved performance cannot occur except under conditions of pure intrinsic motivation. In other words, such pressures can be quite effective from the company point of view.

One last note on the language of small-group activity in Japan: the epitome of small-group activity has been the quality-control circle, and the Japanese specifically used the English term, QC sākuru, to denote this new activity, thus publicly recognizing what they saw as the organic link between small-group activities and the quality-control movement.

In the United States, *participation in management, quality of work life*, and *employee involvement* are terms often used by managers to explain what they are doing.[17] The term *democratization* (and *humanization*) of the workplace has been used—and often confused—in the United States to a greater degree than in Japan. Nevertheless, it is a rather subdued theme relative to other terminology. "I used to use the term *democratization*, but I don't anymore because I find it gets in the way of operational objectives," one leading academic QWL (quality of work life) consultant explained to me in 1985. There appears to be considerable confusion about what is meant by the terminology used in the United States. A 1982 study by the New York Stock Exchange on the concept of QWL and human-resource investment defined QWL as "the effort to encourage employees to participate in the key decisions that affect and determine day-to-day work patterns."[18] Its authors saw quality circles as the primary manifestation of this approach in the early 1980s.

The concept of participation appears to be central to how most American managers have understood what they are doing. Through participation, management sees itself as developing tools to tap unused human resources. The motivational consequences in terms of job satisfaction and worker morale are commonly highlighted. A strong element of voluntarism in these initiatives, at least for lower-level employee participants, ran through U.S. managerial thinking. However, by the mid 1980s, managers were talking about a "second generation" of team production taking over from the voluntary circle activity. Team production meant building small-group activity into daily operations, and, as such, small-group activity was simply part of an employee's job.

Finally, American managers consistently preferred the term *quality circle* over *quality-control circle*, thereby uncoupling the movement from the quality-control discipline, avoiding some of the negative popular connotations of the word *control*, and minimizing the connection with Japan itself. The quality-control discipline tended to have low status in many U.S. firms, and proponents of the new movement did not want to be associated with it. Many firms sought to remove any connection with the well-known quality-control circles of Japan by choosing other names, such as *employee participation group*.

In Sweden, unlike either Japan or the United States, the early movement was strongly punctuated by expressions stressing joint influence and democratization of the workplace. In an influential book in Scandinavia entitled *Form and Content in Industrial Democracy*, Fred Emery and Einar Thorsrud argued that the objectives of industrial democracy cannot be fulfilled by worker representation on boards of directors alone. Rather, such representation must be supplemented at a level where "a large proportion of employees are both able and willing to participate."[19] They had in mind, of course, direct shop- and office-floor participation. The Swedes stressed changing power and authority relationships between managers and employees at all levels. As one Swedish commentator noted, even when North American advocates talk about workplace democracy as a goal of new work structures, they commonly have in mind "democratic leadership styles" rather than a transformation of structural relationships, as was envisioned by many Swedes.[20]

The popular symbols and choice of language used to characterize a social movement tell us a great deal about the motivation of actors and the kinds of constraints they impose or have imposed on them. In the case of Japan, focusing the debate on *decentralization of responsibility* tells us that management was pretty much in charge and could impose its own categories and labels on developments. In the case of Sweden, the focus on *industrial democracy* tells us first that management did not have full control over the agenda. Moreover, the Swedes had a highly centralized labor-management decision-making system. This meant that advocates of semi-autonomous work groups within labor, management, and academic circles could argue forcefully and believably that there was something missing at the shop- and office-floor levels in terms of democratic decision making, and that semi-autonomous work groups could fill that vacuum. In the United States, unlike in many Western European countries, the labor movement had an active shop-floor presence, at least in the unionized sector. This to a considerable extent preempted the theme of industrial democracy, and instead there has been a rather more modest focus on *participation and employee involvement*, with the motivational consequences being given great emphasis.

The major implication of this extended discussion is that inevitably there is an element of comparing apples and oranges when we examine small-group activities in the three countries. Small-group activities are not really the same compared across nations. Rather than trying to eliminate the differences completely in what is being compared—which I judge to be a futile exercise—the strategy adopted here is to acknowledge those differences. The task is then to try to develop some plausible explanations for why these differences exist and their effects.

Search, Discovery, and Transmission

Let me turn now to the source of the ideas that formed the basis for small-group activities in each of the three countries. As I began investigating small-group activities in the three countries, I was soon struck by the importance of the flow of ideas across national borders. How this process operated and its significance became the subject of further investigation. This in turn led me to examine the nature of the search process used by the national actors at different phases of the diffusion process. Doing so shed further light on the nature of the decision-making models in use by the various social actors.

In this connection, it is important to clarify the way one thinks about the diffusion of ideas and organizational practices across national boundaries. My approach to this matter is to see the cross-national transmission of ideas and organizational practices such as small-group activities as an issue of technology transfer, not so different fundamentally from the transmission of, say, steel-making technology.

Swedish Developments: The Paradox of Success

The ideas adopted by the Swedish employers during the early 1970s can be traced to a small degree to the contributions of American behavioral science, and particularly to the work of Abraham Maslow, Douglas McGregor, and Rensis Likert.[21] The central line of influence, however, derives from developments at the Tavistock Institute in England.[22] The Tavistock researchers were strongly influenced by group dynamics and particularly by the research of Kurt Lewin,[23] who did pioneering work in the areas of the determinants of group decision making, the productivity of groups, and the influence on individual behavior of participation in group discussions and decisions.

The first social-science experiments to display a direct lineage with the early 1970 Swedish efforts to adopt self-steering groups were conducted by Tavistock researchers in the early 1950s. These efforts began in a study of English coal mines and involved systematic comparisons of different kinds of work organization and wage systems and their impact on work performance. They led the researchers to conclude that "composite" forms of work organizations with a holistic approach and stressing group work and responsibility were superior to conventional approaches. The aim was to develop small work groups that maintained a high level of independence and autonomy. This involved high levels of group-oriented work processes and group decision making. As a consequence, it was expected that jobs and learning possibilities would be enriched and individual responsibility increased. All this was to be achieved without any loss in productivity compared to conventional work organization.

English employers were slow to adopt these ideas, but the ideas were carried to Scandinavia—especially to Norway by Einar Thorsrud, a charismatic and visionary Norwegian scholar.[24] The ideas came to Sweden from Norway through the work of scholars such as Eric Rhenman,[25] a researcher associated with the Swedish Employers' Confederation, and Reine Hansson, a Swedish scholar who conducted studies on work motivation in the late 1960s.

The sociotechnical approach is a diffuse package with far-reaching implications for the firm's organization. This diffuse quality, deriving from ambiguous operational goals and technology, undoubtedly slowed the diffusion process. It was not the packaged solution with known costs and outcomes that management preferred. "Management wants balanced change where you know that will happen—where you can manage change—and therefore it is good," Pehr Gyllenhammer, the president of Volvo, remarked in a 1984 speech at a Volvo workshop entitled "Production Technology and Quality of Working Life."

In addition to this diffuseness, I noted earlier that the sociotechnical package had strong democratizing overtones. The books of Thorsrud and his collaborators typically focused on the theme of industrial democracy and democratizing the workplace. They offered a strong challenge to the traditional hierarchical control structure. The notion of autonomous work structures was linked explicitly with the freedom of workers from oppressive and arbitrary management controls. Thorsrud was known in the early days of the movement in Sweden as "the foreman killer." His challenge to conventional management emerges in the early descriptions of "psycho-social job design criteria" that he and his collaborators set down in the early 1960s. They assume that acceptable standards for income and job security have already been achieved. The criteria they set down were expressed somewhat differently from publication to publication but basically included the following:

1. Freedom (for individual workers) to make decisions about how to work

2. A meaningful set of tasks offering some variety and some free space to develop the job over time

3. Opportunity for learning on the job and to continue learning on the basis of feedback of results of one's work and future needs

4. Freedom to give and receive help on the job and to establish mutual respect between people at work

5. Recognition outside the workplace for doing a useful job and gaining social respect for it

6. Some form of desirable future in the job, not only in the form of promotion[26]

While a number of these criteria seen in isolation might be supplied by management action, the very first, "freedom to make decisions about how to work," sets the tone for the whole approach to work design in a way diametrically opposed to the control system of traditional bureaucracy. These criteria were widely discussed in Sweden during the late 1960s and early 1970s.[27]

This initial discussion in Sweden, however, was followed by a gradual diminution of the democratic theme as the concept was applied by management over time. That is, there was a sanitizing of the originally radical concepts as management tailored the implementation process to its own needs. In the late 1960s and early 1970s, the concept of "democratization of the workplace" was much in vogue, particularly among trade unionists, scholars, and the mass media. But gradually as management took over the implementation process, the theme of democratization diminished in importance, at least insofar as management applied the concept to small-group activity on the shop and office floor. Nowhere was this seen more clearly than in the shift in the language describing what managers thought they were doing. The term *autonomous work groups* (literally, "self-steering groups" in Swedish) fell rapidly into disuse by management in the early and mid 1970s. Increasingly the term *production groups* came to be used. By 1974, the Technical Department of the Swedish Employers' Confederation could write in a summary report: "Autonomous groups became for a time somewhat of a fad—today this term is less common and one now speaks most often of production groups, which better describes what it deals with."

As one management official explained to me, the term *autonomous work group* was not helpful "because it raised political expectations." Management talked rather about "group work" or "group organization" as one part of the creation of "new factories" characterized by small independent production units, untying of employees from machine-pacing, jobs with more personal involvement, and fast and reliable production systems.[28]

Concerns about democratization of the workplace were replaced in the early 1980s by a strong focus on improving productivity and quality. It was no longer enough to adopt small-group activities in a way that did not lose productivity; these activities were now expected to contribute strongly to productivity and quality improvement. At a workshop held at Volvo's Skövde engine plant in 1984 for foreign and local experts to see and discuss the current status of group work and new directions in work organization at the plant, Rolf Lindholm, a major formulator of the Swedish Employers' Confederation policy in the 1970s, commented impishly to the plant staff: "When I talked with managers in the early 1970s, it was a concern to meet the needs of human beings that drove change forward, but today it has the smell of business."[29]

Much of the discussion in the late 1970s centered around the kind of understanding that labor and management would reach regarding the implementation of the new co-determination law. But by 1984, the leading Swedish newspaper, *Dagens Nyheter*, reported that unionists and management were no longer talking about co-determination but rather about "development" which they defined as "local solutions for local problems." Furthermore, "the new slogans 'change' and 'development' belong together with service, efficiency, and all that is now called 'management.'"[30]

What we see here is the conversion of a blossoming mass movement stressing democratic principles into a much narrower business tool. In the course of this transformation, a good deal of the enthusiasm and motivation that drove the original changes evaporated. The initial conversion of radical scholarly theories to practical management knowledge may well have been necessary to ensure managerial acceptance. But this very narrowing, in dialectic fashion, seems to have limited the potential for more widespread diffusion and acceptance by employees and the powerful union movement. It is not surprising, therefore, that when I met Thorsrud and Hansson in late 1984, not long before their deaths, they both expressed considerable disappointment at the direction developments had taken.

Japanese Developments: From Elitism to Mass Movement

In the case of Japan, we see initially a similar cross-national diffusion process, but the source of the ideas was primarily the United States. American behavioral scientists' research is well known in Japan. It was part of a broad postwar "management boom," beginning in the 1950s, in which ideas of American management in all fields, especially personnel administration, achieved an especially exalted position among Japanese management officials. The United States was unquestionably the most advanced industrial nation in the early postwar period, in addition to being Japan's conqueror and occupying power, and thus it was not surprising that the Japanese were willing and eager to study American management techniques. Generally, the Japanese were willing to assume that American management techniques were the most advanced, independent of any objective confirmation. They soon found, as in other areas in which they borrowed, that they had to adapt these ideas to fit Japanese environmental conditions.

In the area of small-group activities, as in Sweden, the research of McGregor, Maslow, Likert, Chris Argyris, and Frederick Herzberg, to name a few key individuals, is particularly well known in Japan. This is a function of an almost instantaneous translation of books and articles, a steady stream of Japanese students to the United States (many of them are and were company employees doing graduate work), and invited lecture tours of American experts to Japan. It would be rare to find a personnel head of a major firm who was not well versed in the various ideas of leading American scholars in this area. These ideas, combined with and adapted to indigenous values and practices, formed part of the foundation of the Japanese effort in the area of small-group activities.

We can see these processes in the work and influence of Juji Misumi, a noted social psychologist in Japan. He studied at the University of Michigan in the mid 1950s and came under the influence of many of the students of Kurt Lewin (e.g., Ronald Lippitt, Alvin Zander, Dorwin Cartwright).[31] Based on these understandings of group decision-making processes, he conducted research in Japan upon his return that led him and his co-workers to stress the importance of small-group discussions conducted prior to individual or formal group decisions. In 1963 he began work with a large bus company, stressing a series of small-group meetings to devise strategies for accident reduction. These activities were quite successful and the company expanded them throughout the entire bus department in 1969.

At the same time, the firm merged the Misumi-derived programs with the zero-defect (ZD) program in vogue in Japan at that time.[32] The ZD program was also a U.S.-originated program, begun by quality-control personnel in the Martin Company in connection with its contract for the Pershing Missile System for the U.S. Army in the early 1960s.[33] ZD became identified as a motivational campaign for workers, aimed at zero defects in production. The program was modified by the Japanese to stress small-group processes and subsequently merged with the quality-circle effort in the eyes of most Japanese managers. We see in microcosm here the process by which Japanese students of American social science and organizations incorporated their new ideas and modified them in the course of applying them to Japanese work organizations. We also see how they merged with the different streams of development arising from the quality-control discipline.

These streams also merged with traditional approaches to group activity in industry. In the interwar period, Japanese firms carried on discussion and study practices among work teams.[34] Moreover, these ideas had the implicit support of the government through the Ministry of Commerce and Industry's setting up of the Deliberation Committee on Industrial Rationalization (Sangyō Gōrika Shingikai) in the early 1930s. This committee spawned a subcommittee of industrial engineers called the Production Control Committee (Seisan Kanri Iinkai). The head of the subcommittee was Okiie Yamashita, an influential National Railways official. His subordinate was Kodama, who along with Yonekichi Wakabayashi of the Postal Service Ministry and Kōichi Kanda of the Japan Tobacco Public Corporation, was among the most influential interpreters of scientific management. They modified the conventional theory of scientific management by stressing the need for workers' cooperation. Specifically, they promoted the importance of establishing mutual relations between workers and management, treating workers as collaborators in research (e.g., involving them in time and motion studies) and accepting workers' suggestions such as those forthcoming from joint research groups.[35]

Thus, Japanese managers—and workers, for that matter—had in their behavioral repertoire (tradition) experience with small-group activities, albeit on a more authoritarian model, with a clearly controlled management agenda. Still another development stream that supported such small-group activity was the idea of increasing efficiency through the promotion of positive mental and spiritual attitudes among workers. This motivational emphasis, with its implicit assumption that workers'

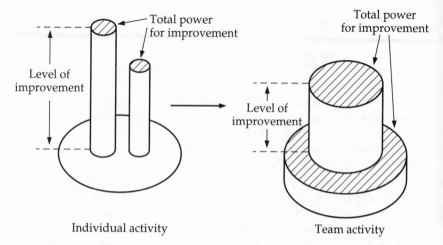

Individual activity   Team activity

Fig. 1. Relative contributions of the all-employee involvement system. Adapted from Bridgestone Tire Company training materials.

efforts can make a difference in managerial success, has a long history in Japan.[36] It was perpetuated during World War II by a government edict and subsidy for employee training (dropped in 1943 because of labor shortage).[37]

Underlying these experiences is the belief that many small improvements will be superior to a few large-scale initiatives. At one level, this view may derive from perceptions of Japan as a small, poor nation that has to make the most of its limited resources. However, Japanese managers do firmly believe that blue-collar workers can make a major contribution to their organizational objectives. These culturally based ideas are represented in a diagram developed by the Bridgestone Tire Company and used in its training activities (see Figure 1). The message is that the contributions of team activity provide a broad-based platform that surpasses selected individual contributions, however excellent they may be. General Motors gets some great suggestions from a few highly motivated shop-floor employees. These are far outweighed in its Japanese counterparts by thousands of suggestions for modest improvements through the mass participation by individuals and small workshop groups.

We can pursue the contribution of the quality-control discipline in Japan to small-group activity through an analysis of the evolution of quality circles. This will also give us a sense of the capacity of the Japanese to borrow and adapt Western organizational technology to their own needs. Quality-control circles are the essence of the Japanese approach to small-group activities and a prime example of the creative process of borrowing and adaptation in the personnel policies of large Japanese companies.

Before 1945, Japan had only modest experience with modern methods of statistical quality control. The Japanese Union of Scientists and Engineers (JUSE) was established in 1949 and became the focal point of efforts to introduce modern quality-control practices and, later, quality-control circles in Japan. An early postwar effort to improve quality was organized by Occupation officials seeking to restore basic services such as telecommunications, who helped arrange for American statisticians to go to Japan and teach American wartime industrial standards to Japanese engineers and statisticians. Prominent in this early effort was a series of postwar lectures beginning in 1950 undertaken by William Edwards Deming to teach the Japanese statistical quality-control practices (e.g., control charts and sampling inspection).

Initially, the Japanese implemented statistical quality control (SQC) in a rather bureaucratic fashion, consistent with the principles enunciated by Frederick Taylor, the founder of scientific management. That is to say, the planning department was supposed to design quality, the production department was responsible for strictly enforcing these designs and standards in the course of production, and the inspection department, a separate unit, was to monitor the performance of the production department. The new system failed to produce the desired results and fault was increasingly found to lie in the assumption that workers' behavior could be controlled through checking by a third party.

In 1954, the noted quality-control expert Joseph Juran arrived in Japan for a series of lectures. He emphasized a newer orientation to quality control, stating that it must be an integral part of the management function and practiced throughout the firm. Armand Feigenbaum's book *Total Quality Control* (1960) was also influential.[38]

These ideas spread rapidly in Japan from the mid 1950s through the early 1960s, but there were some critical innovations (adaptations) on the part of Japanese firms as they began to adopt them in their daily practices. In the Japanese reinterpretation, each and every person in the organizational hierarchy from top management to rank-and-file employees was to study quality control concepts and take responsibility for their implementation. As they began to teach foremen the concepts of quality control, the idea evolved of creating study groups at the workshops composed of the foreman and his subordinates as a means of getting workers to take more responsibility for quality.[39] In particular, these study groups were seen as a solution to the problem of how to make the workers read the materials on QC that were being prepared. Group activity would encourage those to read who were otherwise not so inclined.[40] Gradually, the bureaucratic approach to SQC was replaced with the practice of relying on self-inspection by workers as operation-alized through the development of work teams.[41]

Such developments, in turn, evolved into the quality-control circles of today. An examination of the first issue of *Genba to QC* (The workshop and QC) published in April 1962 by JUSE reveals a conception of work-shop activity relating to quality that was still somewhat removed from the actual operation of quality circles today. The focus was on training foremen to work with their employees to get the employees to accept and maintain work standards so that quality objectives would be met. Getting workers more involved in taking responsibility for setting and revising work standards was the strategy advocated.[42] The circles devel-oped as a rather spontaneous adaptive process as management began to extend the new ideas of quality control. Gradually, these ideas growing out of the quality movement merged with the ideas of decentralization of authority and group decision making.

Not only were all employees from top to bottom to be involved in taking responsibility for quality, but all functions of the organization from marketing and design to purchasing down through sales were also to take responsibility for quality in the new Japanese reinterpretation. Unlike Feigenbaum's narrow conception of total quality control (TQC), which still left responsibility for quality assurance with the quality-control department, the broadened Japanese conception stressed that all departments had to take responsibility for quality control through coor-dinated action. In a similar fashion, the Japanese developed creative strategies for coordinated departmental action through incorporating customer demands into the product design and production cycles.

In summary, during the course of their introduction and adoption in Japan, Western ideas on quality control were dramatically adapted. Of particular significance for the discussion below was the Japanese con-version of the American elitist-anchored system of specialists in quality control taking responsibility for quality in accordance with Tayloristic principles to a mass system in which all employees and departments were expected to take responsibility for quality.

It is in the sense of mass participation that we may speak of a "de-mocratization" of the elitist American approach to quality control. Simi-larly, when the definitive history of the quality-control movement in postwar Japan is written, it will include a strong emphasis on the role played by the "democratization of statistical methods." The development by Kaoru Ishikawa (the leading quality-control "guru" in Japan) of a simple cause-and-effect diagram allowing workers to display all the potential causes of a problem was one important development. Another was the shop-floor workers' utilization of Pareto diagrams (vertical bar graphs ordered according to importance of measurement values) to identify the variables causing most problems and allocate their problem-solving efforts accordingly. These and a variety of other applied statistical techniques became commonplace tools used by high-school-educated workers to deal with workshop problems, making it possible for ordinary employees to participate in organizational change. This was exactly the opposite of the process that took place in Sweden, where the democratic ideas of the Tavistock researchers were sanitized to make them acceptable. Again, this is not to say that the Japanese adopted a Tavistockian perspective on democratization. For the Japanese, democratization in this context meant mass participation rather than expanded autonomy for individuals and groups of employees at the expense of the system of hierarchical control.

Many of the Japanese innovations arose in incremental and spontaneous fashion as managers and workers extended Western ideas to their logical conclusions in ways totally unanticipated by the American experts and often not even by the Japanese leaders. Taking Western management strategies developed for use by and on management personnel and applying them to blue-collar workers has been a characteristic practice in postwar Japanese corporations. Thus, the evolution of quality circles fit a more general borrowing pattern reflecting egalitarian trends in the postwar period that broke down the barriers between white- and blue-collar workers.[43]

In the early postwar period, under the slogan "democratization of management," unions sought to abolish discriminatory treatment of blue-collar workers, and they had remarkable success. The extension of monthly pay systems and bonuses to blue-collar workers in the postwar period was one manifestation of this egalitarianism. Pay differences between white- and blue-collar workers were also significantly narrowed. Still another example is the transfer of American ideas on career development to Japanese firms. Managers moved in this direction even when not under pressure from the unions. For example, ideas on the importance of developing careers for employees and associated policies were developed in the United States and designed for application to managerial employees. The Japanese characteristically borrowed many of these ideas and extended their application to blue-collar employees.[44]

As one reflects on these various developments, the cultural theme underlying much of this behavior appears to be managerial belief in the benefits to be achieved by empowering blue-collar workers. Small-group activities were one vehicle for teaching a set of specific skills, especially problem-solving skills. The workers acquiring these skills were then given the autonomy to use them in a limited operational sphere. In so doing, the firm reaped great rewards in the form of improved economic performance. The origins of such managerial views reflect the prewar legacy discussed earlier, but also the coincidental reinforcement resulting from the pressures of postwar unions and more general postwar egalitarian trends. As Thomas Rohlen shows in his essay in this volume, these developments in turn depended on an effective general educational system capable of transmitting increasingly higher levels of knowledge even to those who were to become blue-collar workers.

Limiting Factors in the United States

To appreciate the different trends in the United States at the very time the Japanese and Swedes were moving rapidly toward adopting small-group activities, we turn to a consideration of the contributions of Charles Kepner and Benjamin Tregoe. The comparisons take on added meaning in light of the aforementioned propensity of the Japanese to extend Western ideas developed for management personnel to blue-collar workers.

Kepner and Tregoe were influential in American management circles in the 1960s and 1970s with the introduction of an approach to problem solving and decision making for individual managers. At the time that the Japanese were developing quality-circle methodologies for ordinary workers, these researchers were crystallizing their approach for teaching individual managers how to solve problems systematically. In *The Rational Manager* (1965), Kepner and Tregoe claimed to have put 15,000 American managers through their courses.[45] An examination of their text leads to a number of interesting observations. First, the techniques espoused for identifying, prioritizing, and solving problems for managers were not so fundamentally different from those being taught to blue-collar workers in Japan. In some respects, the Japanese techniques came to be more sophisticated! For example, the Japanese took another American development, value engineering, developed for engineers to assure that essential functions are provided at minimum overall cost, and introduced it for use among circle members. Interviews by Peter Arnesen of American engineers active in trying to promote value engineering in the 1960s yielded the impression that many nontechnical managers were uncomfortable using these techniques, finding them "too technical."[46]

It is also a minor irony that in the late 1970s and early 1980s, a number of major U.S. corporations explicitly absorbed some of the features of Kepner-Tregoe training into their quality-circle training materials. It was not, however, until their 1987 workshop schedule that Kepner and Tregoe announced that their new materials included "a totally new approach to statistical process control which permits this powerful tool to be used not only by managers but other key shop floor workers and specifically develops trouble-shooting skills enabling them to participate in quality improvement opportunities." Perhaps they might someday get to the point of developing materials that not only key shop-floor workers could use, but all shop-floor employees!

Second, in their discussion of the research of the noted organizational specialist Rensis Likert, Kepner and Tregoe criticize his advocacy of group action and participative management for lacking problem-solving and decision-making techniques. In retrospect, we can see that what was required for the emergence of the equivalent of small problem-solving groups at the shop and office floor would first have been a combination of Likert's ideas on group action with Kepner and Tregoe's ideas. It would also have required managers to have had the imagination to recognize that these ideas could apply to employees at all levels of the firm. The proprietary nature of the Kepner-Tregoe materials limited those opportunities. Even more important, the historic emphasis on the individual and on the decision-making authority of the manager, growing out of Tayloristic principles separating planning from execution, blinded American managers and researchers at this time. They were incapable of seeing the advantages of group problem-solving action at the shop- and office-floor level.

In the history of technology transfer, the inventors of a technology are commonly not its commercializers. The jet engine, for example, was invented in England but successfully commercialized in the United States.[47] The causes of this disjunction become the basis for an interesting intellectual inquiry.

Why has American management been so slow in this area in adopting the ideas of American scholars in contrast to the interest shown in their work by foreign scholars and practitioners? I have already suggested some explanations through analysis of Kepner-Tregoe contributions and why they took the form they did.

At another level, Japan and Sweden are oriented to the outside world to an extent that is hard for Americans to understand. Both perceive themselves as relying heavily on export industries to sustain their standards of living. Some one-third of Sweden's GNP is accounted for by exports. The Japanese have a sense that only by adding value to imported raw materials and then exporting the product are they able to secure the basis for national survival. As a result, in both cases, they believe that their success—indeed, their very survival as nations—depends on their ability to search out and absorb ideas from abroad rapidly and efficiently. In both countries, if a solution to a problem is not immediately at hand, it comes as second nature to management in large firms to look for solutions beyond national borders. To succeed in foreign markets, they have learned to be open to different cultures.

In Japan, this stems in large part from the "catch-up" mentality that has dominated the thinking of industry and government officials for over 130 years. To catch up, you had to be prepared to adopt the better ideas developed in the more advanced Western nations (see the Rohlen essay in this volume). Moreover, the loss to the United States in World War II and subsequent occupation by a foreign power for the first time in its long proud history had a profound, humbling effect that is hard for foreigners to understand. In the case of Sweden, the humility necessary for strong receptivity to foreign ideas seems to derive from the small size of the country. As one industry official explained to me: "Swedes believe that there is always something better somewhere else. It is inconceivable for them with only eight million people and such limited resources to think that they have arrived at the best solution to a given problem. Therefore, they are always looking for ideas from abroad."[48] The net result is that for diverse reasons mapping the foreign environment in a systematic fashion is a well–institutionalized practice in both countries.

The situation of the United States is very different. Throughout the post–World War II period until the 1980s, Americans have appeared confident of their own managerial abilities and technology. American companies have not been very attuned to learning from foreign technology and have maintained few listening posts in Japan relative to the size of the Japanese effort in the United States. Indeed, even with all that has happened between 1970 and the late 1980s, it can be said without the slightest fear of contradiction that U.S. monitoring of global developments in technology is woefully inadequate. Yet increasingly our firms operate in an environment where new developments in management and technology are occurring outside U.S. borders.[49] To take the example of organizational technology, few American managers are directly aware of the contributions of Emery, Trist, and Thorsrud; the same can be said to an even greater degree of their awareness of the Japanese gurus of small-group activity. With a vast domestic market, the U.S. economy cannot be said to be export-oriented to the extent of Japan or Sweden. In the post–World War II period, American managers were accustomed to being on top, with a vast internal market as their preserve. Under these conditions, there was not the same incentive to learn from others.

All this contrasts sharply with the United States of the first quarter of the twentieth century. That was a time of rapid American growth and absorption of foreign ideas. Immigration played a major role in this diffusion process. Many of the things Americans write enviously about the Japanese today, such as the rapidity of commercializing foreign ideas, were exactly what the British were writing about the Americans one hundred years ago. In an evolutionary process that has been played out many times in history, however, American success led to a hardening of vested interests in existing institutional arrangements. That in turn led to the kind of arrogance and insularity that has characterized much of post–World War II management. We may be witnessing a similar growth of managerial overconfidence in Japan as the Japanese increasingly come to regard themselves as the dominant economic power. The competitive pressure posed by the newly industrializing economies, however, has not allowed them the luxury of relaxing in a way that American management seems to have done after the devastation of the world economy in the immediate postwar period.

To return to the original question, the ideas put forward by American behavioral scientists seemed to fit much better with existing organizational practices in Japan and with their prevailing managerial philosophy than they did in the United States. The Japanese scholar Shin'ichi Takezawa caught the sense of this in the following remarks:

The behavioral science model of management, however, is not perceived as an anthithesis of the organizational reality as it might be in the United States. Instead, Japanese managers tend to accept the model as an idealized goal which essentially lies in the same direction as their own behavioral orientation. Often, they are puzzled to find out that American management in practice fits the scientific management model far better than that of the behavioral sciences.[50]

Rather than a separation of planning from execution as postulated in the scientific-management model, the behavioral model stressed that cooperation between management and labor was necessary for success. These kinds of differences provide an explanation of why these ideas were so eagerly received in Japan. Similar judgments could be made in comparing the Swedish management response with the American one.

In the United States these same ideas did not lead to a "choice opportunity"; rather, they were seen as threatening by many managers and union leaders. The prevailing adversary relationships between managers and workers and between managers and unions constitute a formidable obstacle to the adoption of new ideas about organizing work in a cooperative fashion. The notion that workers' loyalty and cooperation can lead to significant improvements in productivity tended to be seen as either trivial or unrealistic. Union leaders saw small-group activity as threatening to collective bargaining practices and as an attempt to bypass the union altogether. In short, the gap between existing practices in American industry and the new managerial philosophies has been so great as to make search for new approaches and their adoption problematic. Small-group activities were simply not on the agenda of solutions for most American managers in the 1960s and 1970s. Nor was the issue the province of any particular managerial level or department. Even if union leaders had been interested in small-group activities, the prevailing power of U.S. management and its lack of real interest in the subject did not allow a serious hearing. It is no wonder, then, that Japanese and Swedish managers acted more quickly than American management in searching out, adopting, and transmitting ideas about small-group activities. Without top management commitment at the senior level as occurred in Japan, and initially in a number of major Swedish firms as well, the pace of diffusion of small-group activities in the United States was bound to be slower.

To say that American managers have been slow to adopt small-group activities relative to Sweden and Japan is not to say that they will not eventually adopt small-group activities. The 1980s produced a burst of experimentation with small-group activities by U.S. firms. Both management and labor have been forced to reexamine the contributions of small-group activities, inspired in part by the rapid internationalization of the economy and in particular by the powerful competitive threat posed by the Japanese. Moreover, although cautious at first, a number of Japanese firms that have established manufacturing operations in the United States have introduced quality circles in their operations and are claiming that these are functioning quite well.

Still, the fragmentary national-level data that do exist suggest that quality circles have not been widely institutionalized in American corporations. Many enthusiastic start-ups have quietly been abandoned after a few years. Despite the initial excitement over circles in the early 1980s, by the mid 1980s the amount of attention devoted to them in the business press and management journals fell off dramatically. They are now publicly described as a fad, with discussion focusing on what will succeed them.[51] For many companies, self-managing teams are the new game in town. It is too early to predict final outcomes, but there is ample basis for questioning whether small-group activities will become as widely diffused among U.S. corporations and as deeply embedded in their operations as has been the case in Japan. Vested interests in existing arrangements by U.S. management and labor, reinforced by the prevailing values and authority relations, are powerful impediments to giving freer rein to participation by workers in small-group activities. Indeed, even those American managers in the late 1970s and early 1980s who supported circle activity saw circles at best in terms of providing good suggestions for improvements; they evidently never considered the more profound role for them of giving workers a major say in designing their own jobs and redesigning the workshop, as occurred in Japan.

Cultural Aspects of Borrowing and Adapting
Small-Group Activities: Concluding Observations

What, if anything, about the Japanese experience with small-group activities in the past 30 years suggests a distinctive and important role of national and/or organizational culture in their achievements? At the national level, the attitude and behavior of the Japanese as regards borrowing come immediately to mind. There is no hesitation about recognizing backwardness in economic and overall organizational performance, but rather than accepting that status, they exhibit a fierce determination to overcome obstacles, borrowing whatever and from wherever is necessary. This contrasts sharply with the "not-invented-here" syndrome—the tendency to shun solutions arrived at by others—that one often finds among American engineers, especially those who see themselves working at the cutting edge of new developments.

The catch-up mentality associated with Japan's late-developing status is paramount. Related to this mentality is the sense that existing institutions and rules are only temporary. Change and innovation are the norm. One cannot emphasize the significance of this point too much. As I watch American workers and managers struggling against the glue of past practices and ways of thinking, the sheer difficulty they experience in conceptualizing alternatives, much less implementing them, becomes overwhelming. One can only marvel at the irony of that nation of "can-do Yankees" that so captured the world's imagination in the early twentieth century now being surpassed by a nation allegedly steeped in traditional culture. This is not the first time, however, that cultural stereotypes have failed to keep up with realities.

What the Japanese borrowed from abroad was typically combined with indigenous ideas and practices to produce something new. The "new things" were often organizational inventions such as quality circles and systems that operationalized the idea that every employee, regardless of status, and every department has a contribution to make to organizational performance (TQC).

The cultural element in this borrowing process arises from Japan's experience of contrasting itself to technologically superior nations throughout much of its history—first China and then the West. Out of those interactions developed an almost instinctive tendency to look abroad for solutions nearly as readily as one searched for domestic resolutions. One cannot help but contrast this with the insularity of American management, its slowness in recognizing the international economic challenge and in responding with intense study of the Japanese experience. There was a vogue for studying Japan in the early 1980s, but for many it was soon followed by the reaction "I can't bear to hear anything more about the Japanese." The Japanese by contrast have been studying the United States, its institutions, and practices for some 130 years. Although there have been moments of xenophobia, they seem not to have tired of the effort, even now when they are acknowledged to be leaders in many areas (see the Rohlen essay in this volume).

While the same ability to borrow from abroad can be seen among the Swedes, it is not associated with that same aggressive catch-up mentality and does not give rise to the same level of adaptation in creating new organizational inventions and the same ability to implement innovations. In the case of small-group activities, despite the image of Sweden as a pragmatic society, the rhetoric of democratization and management's foot-dragging reactions ultimately reflected the strong hold of a class society, where neither side in the labor market was prepared to give up its vision. We can summarize the Swedish and Japanese experiences to date by saying that Sweden is a society that tried more and accomplished less in this arena, while Japan is a society that tried less and accomplished more!

None of these above observations allows us simply to extrapolate current and past trends into the future. It is unlikely, for example, that the Japanese will be as capable of learning effectively from the Koreans and Southeast Asians 20 years from now, given their historic tendency to look down on these peoples.

What about the focus on all-employee participation in achieving organizational improvement? Clearly, the idea of cooperation and participation of all employees in achieving organizational goals does have cultural roots, and I have discussed these. Yet it is also true that prewar Japanese organizations were noted for their autocratic style. Defeat in World War II discredited those prewar and wartime autocratic leaders and opened the way to new talent and a stress on all-employee participation.

The breaking down of barriers between white- and blue-collar workers was particularly important. It meant that Japanese management displayed less of a tendency than management in either the United States or Sweden to tailor new job opportunities, compensation systems, and human-resource programs to one or the other group. In avoiding this differentiation, Japanese management minimized the construction of two classes of citizenship, with all the negative implications of that for management-worker cooperation. We have seen in discussion here the contrast between the Japanese stress on the contributions of blue-collar workers through problem solving in small-group activities and the limited application of Kepner-Tregoe materials in the United States. If not a part of national culture, openness to utilizing human talent is at least a major feature of the organizational culture of large Japanese firms—certainly among regular male employees.

To be sure, there are variations in firms' performances on these dimensions. Upstart newcomers such as Honda and Sony have excelled in this domain relative to their older, more bureaucratic counterparts. But overall, the performance of Japanese companies in this regard has been strong, perhaps because, viewed from the perspective of the world economy, they have all been upstart companies. In the same connection, the stress on small incremental changes adding up to big contributions can be said to be an integral part of the Japanese cultural inheritance. It underlies the focus on mobilizing all-employee participation in small-group activities.

Whereas many Westerners seek to stress cultural continuities in Japanese economic success, many Japanese who were involved in forging the new postwar organizational systems are likely to stress the enormous efforts made to transform organizational practices and culture. Company histories and management recollections are full of melodramatic scenes of crisis as the protagonists seek to turn around their organizations against all odds. Many of the practices that we identify as culturally distinctive in large Japanese private-sector firms such as lifetime employment can be seen as impediments to change. These impediments are seen as being overcome by the same strong dose of top management commitment, vision, and follow-through that students of Western organizations stress. Group activity may have a long history in Japan, but there is nothing in that cultural tradition that guarantees a task orientation to organizational improvement. Firm managerial leadership was necessary to move in new directions.[52]

Yet in the end it must be said that Japanese managers in the postwar period have shown great ability to maximize employee potential without losing their sense of organizational purpose. The focus has been on decentralization of responsibility, with particular emphasis on quality improvement. In the immediate post–World War II period, Japanese leaders saw quality improvement as a critical hurdle to be cleared in successfully promoting the exports that seemed so central to Japan's survival. (It was not until much later that they began to see quality superiority as a competitive strategy.) They came to the conclusion that they could achieve their quality goals only with the help of all-employee participation. One major virtue of the quality focus is the motivational appeal that quality improvement has for workers relative to the threat often seen as posed by cost-reduction and productivity-improvement programs. Western managers have been slow to grasp the significance of quality as a mobilizing force.

Ultimately, these kinds of choices by Japanese managers, and their ability to make them stick, rest on powerful cultural constraints, rooted in traditional authority systems. Once management power was reasserted and the militant unions in the private sector were broken in the early postwar period, there was little fear on the part of management that their movement toward decentralization would lead to a challenge to their authority.[53]

Such confidence was and is far less apparent in the United States and Sweden. Instead of decentralization, other themes thus predominated there. In the case of Sweden, power was more evenly divided between management and labor. Indeed, with the social democrats in control of the machinery of national government for most of the past 50 years, labor may be said to have had the upper hand. In this context, it is not surprising that there was a focus on industrial democracy as the small-group activity movement unfolded.

In the United States, the power of organized labor is far more of a factor than in Japan, but far less of a factor than in Sweden. Moreover, different conditions prevail in the unionized and nonunionized sectors in the United States, although it should be kept in mind that fear of unionization is often a significant determinant of working conditions in the nonunion sector. The greater ambiguity surrounding power and authority in the United States as compared to Japan and Sweden has led to an emphasis on the more ambiguous concept of participation. Participation as a concept does not necessarily connote a major challenge to managerial authority, as democratization focus in Sweden did. Yet participation as a concept is also not a narrowly focused management tool, as is the case with the concept of decentralization in Japan. The three different emphases can thus be said to reflect the different distributions of power and authority in the three societies. These distributions in turn rest on the accumulated reservoir of characteristics associated with national cultures.

Part III

Trends

Thomas P. Rohlen

Learning:
The Mobilization of Knowledge
in the Japanese Political Economy

At the foundation of industrial dynamics is the human and social capacity to learn. The crux of the matter is the interface between technology, organization, and human resources. Change and development of productive capacities are generated when people in organizations learn more efficient ways of doing things. Education, information, diffusion, training, problem solving, invention, and innovation are all aspects of learning. All involve the generation, sharing, and utilization of knowledge, which cumulatively affects economic growth.[1]

Learning, however, is not simply a matter of human psychology or of universal economic laws. Rather, the cultural and social environment shapes what learning means and defines its character and dynamic. What parents, teachers, managers, and political leaders take to be true about learning has a profound impact. In industrial society, for example, we take it for granted that the encouragement of technical change is proper and good, but this basic assumption makes little sense outside of an industrial context. Between industrial nations, too, cultural differences can be notable. Study of the place of learning in the Japanese political economy involves initial recognition of this fact.

Learning processes are complex and difficult to discern, since they occur at what might be termed sub-micro levels of economic activity. The contributions of education, of management systems, and of individual talents are difficult to separate from one another. However crucial to macroeconomics, furthermore, the subject of learning is inherently difficult to define in a scientific sense. It is relatively easy to delineate fundamental breakthroughs and show how new technology has changed economic patterns, but very difficult to isolate the contribution of incremental improvements as they accumulate over time in existing technologies and organizations. The typical economic analysis of learning curves seeks explanations in more quantifiable and better documented factors such as investment and scale. This obviously does not go far enough. Yet, the problems of disaggregation and broad comparison have been so great that the contribution of human learning has been relegated to the status of a vacuous residual category. In the case of the Japanese political economy, this residual category, too important to ignore, is what we seek to understand better.

This essay is about the distinctive qualities of Japan's approach to learning. The argument is that the country's economic dynamic cannot be understood without recognition of the underlying significance of this general process and its relative vitality in Japan. Capacities for particular kinds of learning vary from society to society. In the Japanese case, the capacities for adaptive borrowing, broad knowledge promulgation, and continuous learning are particularly significant. They have allowed the nation to industrialize very rapidly. Furthermore, the level of learning that occurs in Japan today, both in schools and in companies, is arguably greater than in any other industrial nation. Such statements should not, however, disguise the equally significant fact that there are serious limitations to the Japanese pattern. These limitations are especially evident now that Japan is shifting from a position of technological catch-up to one of international leadership.

Obviously, the context for these remarks is comparative. It is in the light of other nations' achievements and failings in the area of learning that Japan stands out. It is a thesis of this essay that the Japanese pattern derives from a distinctive (but not unique) social and cultural foundation.[2] And while the Japanese approach has proved itself to be particularly suited to industrial catch-up, Japan's present global position presents large, new challenges that can only be effectively met by major changes, especially in higher education and in the very conceptualization of education's goals.

Learning is a particularly dynamic aspect of society. First, as economists have noted, unlike other economic inputs, it is inherently irreversible. It creates knowledge that does not fluctuate like other economic inputs, but rather is essentially cumulative in nature. In addition, the skill of learning is generalizable from one situation or problem to another. Learning is a habit that encourages further learning. Thus, learning processes can be said to have a momentum of their own. Nations, firms, and individuals can lose knowledge, of course, but only as the result of degenerative processes that are markedly pathological. Except for the outcomes of formal education, however, social rates of knowledge accumulation and transfer have never been measured comparatively or historically. We have no precise way of knowing how societies differ in this regard. Typically, we make comparisons by such crude measures as literacy rates or the years of schooling of the average citizen or the percentage of a population graduating from some particular level of education. These measures are but crude indicators of a far more complex totality.

Nevertheless, it is commonplace to assume the importance of this subject and to see it as central to the whole question of the "human factor" in comparative work. Today, for example, Japanese education is frequently pointed to as a key consideration in explaining the nation's economic success, and participative management techniques are credited with helping Japanese companies succeed in generating more efficient manufacturing processes. Similarly, in everyday thought we typically credit successful companies with acquiring, creating, and applying technology more effectively than their less successful competitors. Despite its diffuse and elusive qualities, in other words, there are few who would deny the centrality of learning to an understanding of economic dynamics.

For all of its assumed benefits, however, the encouragement of learning is not to be taken for granted. Learning involves change. For this reason it is often resisted as a threat to the prevailing order. Processes comparable to xenophobia operate at many levels to impede the acquisition of knowledge. One fundamental rule of social organization is that any existing system is inclined to routinization and standardization, and new knowledge typically represents a challenge to this status quo. Learning thus requires considerable effort to overcome the inertia of established patterns. Families, teachers, managers and governments all make a significant difference, then, by their tolerance (or intolerance) for change and their encouragement (or discouragement) of effort. This is particularly to be seen in their capacity to build institutions that routinely sponsor learning.

In recognizing the importance of institutions, we must distinguish the more obvious and discrete forms of learning, such as education and formal training, from the less obvious, but equally important, forms that occur as part of normal work processes.[3] Learning by doing (for example, on the job) is minutely incremental and interactive and thus especially difficult to grasp for analytic processes. Yet it is important not to equate "human-capital formation" simply with formal education. The fit between work and schooling is never easy to begin with, and over time the content of formal education often grows obsolete. What occurs at the company and shop-floor level is also of great importance. In school, the text is largely fixed and the task is to master it, whereas on the job, the text is being written and rewritten almost daily.

The Historical Perspective

Why was Japan able to catch up with the advanced industrial nations of the West with such alacrity when so many other non-Western nations (with equal or better opportunities in terms of access to resources and technology) failed?[4] This is not a new question to be sure, but it is one we should begin with because of what it reminds us of about Japanese learning. In the mid nineteenth century, Japan had few technical or material advantages. It was hardly the nation one would have expected to succeed best in mastering Western technology. Areas with much greater familiarity and contact with Europe, for example, were more likely candidates for successful industrialization. Theories about why Japan succeeded despite these disadvantages are numerous, and rightly so, but none deny the fundamental necessity of persistently learning at a very fast rate.[5] The term *catch-up* implies just such an effort, one that of necessity enrolled an increasingly large proportion of the population. The fundamental question, "How did the industrial sector borrow and put to practical use massive inputs of foreign technology?" can only be answered by examining those processes themselves.

The Japanese had long demonstrated a talent for borrowing knowledge. Centuries of periodic apprenticeship to China and Korea established fundamental patterns that placed a high value on the capacity to master foreign knowledge and techniques. Painstaking imitation, followed by careful examination and criticism, leading increasingly to greater independent innovation describes the typical process, whether we consider the seventh and eighth centuries or the nineteenth and twentieth. For example, in the sixteenth century, European musket technology, picked up by remote Japanese islanders and studied intensively there, spread with amazing rapidity through the entire country in a matter of a few decades, changing the nature of warfare and ultimately contributing to the formation of a new political structure. Foreign technology has always diffused rapidly in Japan once its practical benefits have been demonstrated. The Japanese also have long shown a keen interest in scanning the external environment for useful knowledge. Even during the Edo period, when the country was essentially closed to foreign commerce, the government maintained a regular system for picking up foreign commercial and technical information. At Nagasaki, the officers of foreign ships were routinely questioned about Chinese agriculture and silk-production technology.[6] The practice of quickly replacing highly paid foreign technical advisers with their Japanese students during the Meiji period illustrates how the Japanese drive for independent mastery was combined with intense borrowing. Massive borrowing and a heavy reliance on foreign teachers did not lead to permanent dependence on foreign sources. It was a matter of national pride to complete the process of borrowing as rapidly as possible.[7] Borrowing and imitation themselves brought no humiliation; rather they were necessary foundations for extended efforts aimed at demonstrating Japanese competence. Humility, not humiliation, was a crucial first step toward ultimately achieving autonomous strength.

In reviewing the historical record, it is important to look also at Japan's domestic resources prior to Westernization. At the time Japan opened its doors to commerce with Europe it was already in many respects among the most advanced nations. The Japanese literacy rate in the eighteenth and nineteenth centuries is judged to have been comparable to European levels, and the high standards of achievement in crafts and traditional manufactures greatly impressed the first Western visitors. Most fundamental was the fact that Japanese civilization was highly evolved as far as the place of learning was concerned. Literacy was a requirement for holding power, the basis of administration, and central to almost all aspects of cultural creation. The merchant class participated in this pursuit of learning, and among well-to-do farmers and artisans, there were some who acquired fame or power on the basis of their scholarly achievements. Many kinds of skills and arts were organized on the basis of intensive apprenticeships or formalized learning schemes (*michi*) that wedded status, ambition, and personal development to the acquisition of practical skills. In essence, study was an important prerequisite of getting ahead throughout Tokugawa society.

Nor was learning only a matter of scholarly pursuits among the elite. Practical studies were common. Manual skills and workmanship were much appreciated. In a wide range of crafts, high levels of efficiency and quality were encouraged by competitive markets. The literature and biographical material of the time, not to mention the neo-Confucian ideology, attest to the dynamism of learning prior to the start of the Meiji period. This foundation then needed only to be oriented to Western technology for the nation to begin the process of industrialization.

Imitation is an important initial form of learning, and the Japanese relish for careful imitation must thus be seen in this context as a social capacity of note. Rather than disparaging borrowing, the Japanese have long stressed its practical virtue. For a nation catching up, the capacity and enthusiasm to learn foreign industrial skills proved crucial in establishing a base of experience and knowledge, upon which innovative achievements ultimately became possible. To the swift at learning from abroad often went the greatest rewards.

The Japanese tradition of very demanding apprenticeship deserves close attention as a model of this kind of imitative learning. Training in traditional arts and crafts has long emphasized strict emulation and the repetition of rigidly defined essential forms to the point of exaggeration. Apprenticeships were long, ten years by legal fiat in the seventeenth century.[8] The unquestioning acceptance of the teacher's authority and the humble compliance of the student were regarded as essential ingredients of the pattern. If we see that Japan's posture to the West has been, until very recently, essentially that of an apprentice in matters of technology, the roots of Japan's competence in importing knowledge can be understood as founded on this tradition. A successful apprentice is one who finds the best teacher, learns diligently all there is to know, and ultimately surpasses the master's skill. This process is well understood in Japan even today, and it is imbued with great emphasis as a model not only of learning but also of virtue.

In spoken Japanese, the term *narau*, "to learn," also means "to imitate." The assumption underlying all traditional learning is that extensive copying of correct models is basic and necessary. The place of originality is properly found at the end of the apprenticeship, when mastery is attained. As Japanese accomplishments in traditional arts and crafts attest, such delayed creativity can come in abundance. This paradigm cannot, however, guarantee creativity or solve the question of how to nurture exceptional talent. Rather, the highest priority in the formative stages is given to discipline and subordination of the student to the master and the craft. Such a strict approach can be poorly adapted to times of very rapid change. Even much of formal education today in Japan echoes the traditional values of apprenticeship, and it is these very problems that seem so intractable to schools and policymakers. If apprenticeship was a particularly apt model for Japan's adaptive learning from the West over the past century, it is increasingly problematic today.

Successful borrowing also depends on what might be termed "alert objectivity." If learning is ultimately valuable because it makes for a better adaptation to some external reality (e.g., industrial markets), then the ability to scan the external environment objectively is especially important. Effective borrowing and adaptation, in other words, rest on a capacity to grasp the essence of other social and technological orders. Yet cultural and religious self-absorption present immense barriers to understanding other social and economic systems. It is typical in the early stages of intercultural borrowing, for example, for foreign items to be exaggerated and distorted, rejected, or blindly misunderstood.

Some of this kind of confusion certainly occurred in the course of early industrial imitation, but what stands out is the talent of the Japanese for "alert objectivity." On the whole they seem to have met Western technology and modern institutional forms with as pragmatic a frame of mind as the Europeans who developed them.[9] The religious aspect of Japanese culture, for example, never proved a significant barrier to practical learning. Cultural blindness or intolerance was rarely a Japanese problem when it came to learning from the West. The high status Japan granted to European civilization probably explains this to a large degree, since in dealing with low-status Asian neighbors, the Japanese were as prone to cultural prejudices as any.

We might also distinguish between societies preoccupied with expressing their own "reality" to the rest of the world and those oriented toward perceiving carefully what lies outside. In Japan's case, the accommodative inclination has been dominant. However simplistic, this distinction is quite important, for, comparatively speaking, the act of sending information involves much less new learning than the act of receiving. While some nations perfect the art of communicating their own virtues and worldview for political or religious reasons, Japan has emphasized listening and detailed observation. The quiet visitor taking notes and photographing everything is a much-derided stereotype of the Japanese businessman abroad, yet it was precisely such seemingly enigmatic visitors who, upon returning home, applied their carefully gathered information to produce technological advancement. This is not to deny that there have been obvious lapses when Japanese leaders lacked the capacity to perceive international realities.

This "objectivity" starts, I think, with a basic cultural disposition to an adaptive posture and with a fundamental epistemology that emphasizes exterior rather than interior truth. The "other" orientation and context-specific qualities of the language and of Japanese social relations are relevant here, just as is the generally nonproselytizing nature of the Japanese approach to religion.[10] That is to say, the fundamental character of the Japanese cultural pattern is strongly oriented to learning from others. Although far from always true, this inclination has definitely shaped the nation's response to situations in which technological superiority is a foreign possession.

Borrowing, however, introduces disruptive new knowledge. This fact was commonly recognized in Meiji Japan, and there was always serious opposition to foreign influence. How borrowing was legitimated is thus of particular interest. Japan's apprenticeship to the West was frequently defined by the appealing metaphor of teacher and student, one that provided a rather complete prescription for Japanese conduct. An inflow of ideas, institutions, and practices that continually threatened the status quo was made comprehensible and even normal within this conceptual framework. The authority given things foreign by the humble student powered a system of radical social change. Crucial here was the common acknowledgment of Western technological superiority. What appeared to outsiders to be "slavish" imitation was actually revolutionary in its impact. Yet this revolution was conducted within a framework of traditional values centering on learning. The legitimation of change by citing a foreign precedent, as the apprentice defers to the master, became a classic aspect of Japanese social innovation.

The reigning political ideology of premodern Japan was essentially neo-Confucian in nature. Among other things, this meant a high regard for education and self-cultivation. The social order, prosperity, and the richness of civilized living all hinged on study and personal development.[11]

That human nature is highly perfectible is one of Confucianism's basic tenets. Without this crucial assumption, the encouragement of learning is forever condemned to a kind of anemic state. Furthermore, because it is essentially a secular and practical philosophy, Confucianism has traditionally seen as much virtue in civil engineering as in ancestor worship. Societies influenced by Confucianism stress the ideal of a meritocratic social ladder, centering on competitive exam-taking. Indicative of the influence of Confucian values in Japan is the story of Sontoku Ninomiya. A studious reformer of agricultural practices and a believer in the common man, Ninomiya was used as a model for students in prewar Japan, much as Abe Lincoln was made a model in American schooling. Thousands of schoolyards throughout the country displayed large statues of this ideal individual. Inevitably these showed him as a young boy reading a book as he struggled along a rural path bent over under a heavy load of wood. The image is a dramatic and memorable one of struggle to achieve learning under impoverished conditions. A Confucian figure of virtue, Ninomiya became the ideal for modern Japanese education during most of its formative period.[12]

What does learning mean in the Confucian tradition? Put very simply, self-cultivation through the disciplined pursuit of knowledge is the path to human perfection. Spiritual fulfillment comes as the result of continuous study within some defined path of knowledge. The superior person is thus a learned person. In a world prior to the narrowed meaning of learning brought on by universal schooling, virtually all skills and forms of study were accorded dignity by this perspective. Self-development is a lifelong opportunity, and since wisdom grows with experience and study, age, knowledge, and authority are positively correlated in the Confucian conception. Society and the state are best led by people of learning. According to this ideal, political power, social order, prosperity, personal fulfillment, and virtue are all bundled together with learning. No wonder that study, schooling, and the written word have had enormous influence in China, Korea, and Japan for centuries. The resulting tendency to mandarinism contrasts notably with today's ruling ethic in these countries, but its legacy is still very much alive.

In England and the United States during the late eighteenth and nineteenth centuries, utilitarian thought also emphasized the importance of learning and education.[13] But thinkers such as Adam Smith and John Locke conceived of its value as lying in the creation of greater opportunities for individual rational choice and the achievement of personal wealth, whereas the sociocentric emphasis of Confucian morality portrays the benefits of study as essentially spiritual and communal. Without wishing to oversimplify, it appears that the key metaphors in utilitarian and Confucian thinking—namely, the market and the family—provide two rather distinct intellectual contexts for the conceptualization of learning and education. In the Anglo-American tradition, the individual invests in education for personal gain. Providing this opportunity is a legitimate responsibility of government, but only as long as education provides the citizen with the basis for independent political choice. Despite an emphasis on merit and an orientation toward secular practicality, Confucianism embraces neither individualism nor democracy. These differences continue to be of significance.

The impressive economic performance of other Asian nations with a Confucian heritage like Korea, Taiwan, Hong Kong, and Singapore naturally raises the question of Confucianism's role in encouraging industrialism. It makes sense to argue that at least as far as education goes, this influence has been significant. Like Japan, all have school systems that produce outstanding results according to standard international tests. Still, the common emphasis on human resources in the economic development of all these countries can be argued to be the result of necessity rather than cultural disposition. All the same, policies alone could hardly guarantee the enthusiasm for educational achievement and the recognition of merit that also distinguish these societies. As far as learning is concerned, what is notable is the congruence between economic necessities, development policies, and traditional values in both Japan and the Asian newly industrialized countries (NICs).

To conclude this section, among Japan's greatest assets at the start of industrialization were a strong orientation toward learning and an already talented populace. When the government in the 1870s began to implement an educational system modeled on Western examples, the ambition to catch up with the West via a process of rapid and massive borrowing and adaptation crystallized these strengths in a national learning effort that marks the entire modern period and distinguishes Japan from the numerous other non-Western nations with similar ambitions.

The Character of Japanese Education

Value-added development strategies depend on advances in education. What is notable about Japan is the relatively rapid gains it achieved in implementing a universal system of compulsory schooling and in orienting the entire nation to the task of absorbing foreign knowledge. The strategy was one of persistently upgrading human talent throughout the population. This strategy characterized both public education and the management of private enterprise. Only recently can this effort be said to have reached a plateau.[14]

To enroll the populace in the process of change, to equip everyone with the capacity to learn, and to disseminate imported knowledge, a system of universal education geared to technological processes was needed.[15] As early as 1872, only three years after the Meiji Restoration, we find one of the country's most influential leaders, Kido Takayoshi, writing home during a tour of the United States:

A long-range program for the stability of our country will never be attained if we have only a small number of able people; we have to develop universal adherence to the moral principles of loyalty, justice, humanity and decorum. Unless we establish an unshakable national foundation, we will not be able to elevate our country's prestige in a thousand years. The creation of such public morals and the establishment of such a national foundation depends entirely on people. And the supply of such people in endless numbers over a long period of time clearly depends on education and on education alone. Our people are no different from the Americans or Europeans of today: it is all a matter of education or lack of education.[16]

A month later the newly emergent nation-state announced the creation of a system of universal compulsory education for the capital, which was extended eight months later to the entire nation. The radical character of these steps is lost on us today, but at the time it not only meant that the country's young leaders were ready to pursue extraordinary new directions, but that Japan was committing itself to compulsory education ahead of many European countries.

Despite popular resistance in some quarters and a lack of public resources, Japan advanced very rapidly in the creation of a public school system. After just a quarter of a century, compulsory education was virtually as advanced as in any Western country. In no other non-Western nation did such rapid change occur.

Literacy rates also advanced steadily, and universal literacy was attained early in the twentieth century. School enrollments at all levels showed steady upward trends. The government also pushed curricular standards upward at a notable pace. The steady progress of education is a noteworthy parallel to the pace of economic growth throughout this century. In effect, the human-resource base of the economy advanced at rates at least complementary to the nation's economic advance in general.[17] All the same, the emphasis was not on higher education or on the independent development of basic science or advanced technology.

Rather, the crucial focus was on raising the general common denominator within the population as a whole. Advanced knowledge was more than abundantly supplied by the outside world.

Japan's system of education was founded on the assumption that the country was technologically apprenticed to the West. It therefore focused on transferring already-proven, primarily imported knowledge to the majority of the population. Practical learning was the dominant goal, and this led to an emphasis on teaching the basics. Standards learned from the more elite-oriented elements of European and American systems were gradually applied to the entire system, with the result that knowledge acquired by the average Japanese student gradually closed the gap with Europe and North America. In the postwar period, as we shall see, the Japanese pushed past their mentors in the West.

Nor was it assumed that Japan could develop early scientific and technological independence from the West. Typically, academic leaders functioned as talented conduits of foreign learning. Since the emphasis was on taking in knowledge from more advanced nations, the ability to read foreign languages received great attention and mature students were encouraged to go abroad in search of advanced information and training. Foreign works were translated in great numbers and still are. It is not surprising, then, that legitimacy in scholarly matters very often depended on congruence with foreign scholarly opinion. The results for higher education were not always felicitous, as can be imagined. This is not to deny the existence of independent currents in Japanese science and technology, but to point out that these were exceptions to the general rule. Japan's development strategy did not count on a mature scientific or technological infrastructure. Nor did the training provided orient students to paths of research independent of foreign influence. The one marked exception was the decade of radical nationalism from 1935 to 1945.

As is well known, the government also made serious efforts to monitor disruptive foreign cultural influence in the schools—to sort out useful technology from the culturally unsuitable in the borrowing process. Thus, despite the fact that Japanese education has very largely been modeled on Western institutional examples, its moral orientation and fundamental values have remained distinctively Japanese.[18] This, in turn, has served to confirm a pedagogical regime that was and remains quite hierarchical, with the authority of the teacher and the Ministry of Education firmly fixed and central. From the 1880s on, public institutions dominated the school system at all levels. The Ministry of Education effectively guaranteed its own centrality. The initiative has long rested with the central government.[19] Even the heavy dependence on rote memorization, so much the target of criticism these days, is congruent with this authority structure, since national textbooks and teacher-centered instruction encourage this pattern.

National policies thus assured that human resources would play a dynamic role in economic development, while containing the disruptive potential of foreign examples.[20] The clear recognition of a legitimate relationship between the government and all aspects of education thus became a key characteristic of the Japanese political economy. High levels of centralization and bureaucratization accompanied this orientation. Centralization has also meant that great resources have been available to policymakers for the execution of ambitious plans. This remains largely true today, despite the decentralizing intentions of the reforms of the Occupation. The Japanese educational system continues to be characterized by strong national authority in such areas as the setting of standards, the channeling of resources, and the determination of new directions.

Education in Japan is almost never influenced by local conditions. In contrast to the system in the United States, for example, neither local elections nor local funding sources significantly affect the quality or direction of schooling. The postwar dominance of the conservative Liberal Democratic Party has also ensured that the great variety of educational opinion in the population as a whole has not greatly affected the conduct of public education. Changes have had to wait for a new consensus to form within ruling circles.

The postwar era has also witnessed a prolonged stalemate between the ruling party and the leftist Japan Teachers' Union, which is bent on opposing the Ministry of Education's authority, especially in respect to such highly politicized issues as nationalism, minorities, tracking, and entrance exams. Although the intensity of the strife has been declining for a decade, from 1950 to 1980 education was one of the most conflict-ridden of all Japanese public institutions. The then-powerful Japan Teachers' Union trenchantly resisted the Ministry of Education's every ideological and administrative move. This confrontation greatly stymied initiatives at the national level, neutralizing many conservative inclinations, on the one hand, and essentially paralyzing reform efforts, on the other. The philosophy of public education changed very little. Such a stalemate meant that exam pressures and escalating family ambitions (fueled by prosperity), not government policies, became the major dynamic forces. Politics rarely spilled over into the classroom, but neither was the classroom improved much by new ways of teaching or new subjects for study.

Let us note the characteristic results of this kind of system. It has excelled in the shaping of an entire citizenry to sound fundamental skills, orderly behavior, and diligent work habits. This has greatly facilitated social integration and laid the basis for a relatively egalitarian distribution of earned income.[21] The cultural and social homogeneity of the population, a significant factor in Japanese political economy, is to a significant degree the product of this kind of school system.[22] The system also fosters a politically compliant, somewhat apolitical population, oriented toward the ideal of the nation as a community. One finds, for example, very little American-style "education for democracy" in which outspokenness is encouraged.[23] Nor are moral or religious ideals critical of established authority taught in the schools. It must be granted that within this framework of authority, the government's control of the political content of textbooks has not been greatly misused. That is, it has sought to perpetuate political compliance mainly through omission rather than commission. Student protests, the critical (if rarely disruptive) posture of university teachers, and the acrimonious conflicts between the Ministry of Education and the Japan Teachers' Union that punctuate the otherwise purposeful order have not, in fact, led to increased political content in classroom instruction or shifted the emphasis in schools from practical learning to cultural politics.

Pedagogy, too, has remained largely the same. Consistent with the overall strategy for education, teaching has been characterized by carefully developed, tightly executed instructions standardized for the entire nation.[24] As schooling progresses, high levels of classroom order and decreasing individual participation are characteristic. Students are given very little choice by Western standards. What they learn prior to college is a fixed canon of facts and theories.

At a deeper level, the Japanese model has generally assumed that most individuals are not seeking portable credentials (ones to be traded on an open labor market), but rather that education will be used to enter into a long-term employment relationship, one in which further investment in training will primarily come from the company. While it is misleading to think that the majority of Japanese in fact fulfill this, universities and the majority of secondary schools offer a curriculum that fits this conception, and, furthermore, the pattern is most closely followed by male university graduates (who have the highest visibility). This assumption leads high schools and universities to seriously disregard the content of education when it is not of obvious relevance to the ultimate goal of university entrance and desirable employment. At the high-school level, this means exam-taking. At the university level, it means satisfying future company employers of one's value, a process that centers more on club memberships and affiliation with particular professors than on grades, breadth of learning, or other accomplishments.

Vocational education is an exception to this general rule. About one-third of the public schools center on technical or commercial training, and privately run vocational training colleges (*senmon gakko*) and schools (*kakushu gakko*) offer special skills to high-school graduates seeking practical training. While vocational high schools have a generally low reputation, vocational training colleges and schools are increasingly popular, especially for those interested in careers in new areas like computer software. Attendance levels for universities and junior colleges have been on a plateau since 1975, while the numbers going to training schools have increased fivefold. This increase has been largely among young men drawn to the possibility of better jobs in new technologies.

Japan also has a well developed program of national skill certification, in which there is wide participation. Most vocational education leading to skill certification is conducted by private organizations, and most recipients work in medium to small-scale industry, but larger firms also actively encourage their employees to study to qualify for national certification. In the past decade, this area of practical skill development has shown considerable growth.

The system, especially from middle school on, has always been very competitive.[25] Because universities (particularly elite ones) serve as powerful signaling devices in the labor market, competition to enter them is severe. Companies hire more on the basis of a school's reputation than on the individual's record, and this, coupled with the expectation of permanent employment among male university graduates, greatly increases the intensity of the competition. A further result is that the ranking of universities has been exceptionally stable. Changing the entrance-exam system has proven very difficult, since neither the interests of the leading schools nor the most diligent students would be served by doing so. The fact that the central bureaucracy is led principally by graduates of the leading universities further compounds the problem. Nor have companies been willing to change their hiring practices, upon which the whole ranking mentality rests. Homogeneous educational foundations are thus the grounds for severe competition within a meritocracy of sorts that rests on ranking universities, however questionable this might be in terms of actual instructional quality.

As a result, individual energies and private family funds are drawn into the educational race. Any final totaling of expenditures on learning would have to include the sizable outlays of the average Japanese family to buy some slight additional advantage for their children in preparing for university examinations. If we were to divide educational systems into those "pushed" by government and those "pulled" by private demand, the Japanese system would best be described as pushed by the government for the first two to three decades of the Meiji period, but since that time increasingly pulled by the ambitions of parents and students. The competitiveness stems from a policy of maintaining a

TABLE 1
Education Level of New Entrants to the Labor Force
(per cent)

Year	Middle school	High school	Junior college, technical college, university, and above
1950	86%	14%	<1%
1955	62	30	8
1965	42	47	11
1975	9	57	34
1985	4	45	49
1988	3	39	58

SOURCE: Ministry of Education, *Waga kuni no bunkyō seisaku* (National policy on education and culture) (Tokyo: Okurashō, 1988), pp. 486–87.

meritocratic system of rewards (in the form of admission to a ranked universe of secondary schools and universities) coupled with egalitarian opportunities (at the level of elementary education). One indication of the significance of privatized effort is the fact that virtually half of all ninth graders facing high-school entrance examinations today enroll in private cram schools (*juku*). Even at the first-grade level, one in ten students in Japan's largest cities is receiving parent-financed supplementary education.[26] So popular have cram schools become that the most successful have their own competitive entrance exams, and a new kind of cram school has recently sprung up to help prepare for these. Success in this expanding market has gone to companies that have utilized such things as cable TV, electronic mail, chain franchising, and overseas expansion. Educational competition is big business, especially with rising consumer prosperity, and the result is even greater magnification of the distortions exam-taking generates.[27]

As with all highly competitive education systems, private investment has increased over time and for an increasingly large part of the society. The proportion of the population going beyond compulsory education (ninth grade) has steadily increased, and (as shown in Table 1) the educational level of the labor force has risen dramatically. The number of public schools has long been insufficient to meet the demand at the high-school and university levels. This situation has both increased the competition to enter public institutions and caused many private preparatory and cram schools to be created. Most parents thus pay a high price for tutoring school and/or for private college educations in order to keep up in the race for opportunity and status.[28] Nevertheless, as the privatization of advantages has increased, differences in family income levels have increasingly appeared to relate to disparities in educational success. During the 1970s and 1980s in particular, correlations between national university acceptance and both family socioeconomic status and urban residence (most prep and cram schools are located in cities) have been increasing.[29]

Several points about this competitive arrangement are noteworthy. The average return to individuals for educational investment has been declining over time, and yet private investments have increased steadily.[30] What explains this counterintuitive trend? First, even if diminished in value, there is some return for increased investment. Second, since one's own children are involved, quibbling about the price is difficult and even beside the point. Furthermore, elite universities have a kind of monopoly at the top that maintains the inflated pricing of preparatory schools offering increased chances of success in the entrance exams of those universities. Unwarranted parental optimism (typically regarding sons) further underpins the escalating investment picture. Eighty per cent of families, for example, expect their children to attend university, twice as many as can actually be accepted. All of this can rightly be termed "excessive competition." Perhaps there are parallels here with a similarly labeled phenomenon well known in Japanese corporate investment, where careful calculation of anticipated returns is less the issue than keeping up with one's rivals.

Yet more is involved. Education is virtually the sole avenue to social status. Because it is a "one-chance" race for elite positions, parents naturally concentrate their resources on education. A mass competitive phenomenon (one is tempted to say frenzy) results, inspired as much by fear of being left behind or left out as by the promise of high reward. The outcome—"excessive" investment in cram schools; test-taking aids; private high schools; parentally supported extra years of study; and paying outrageously high tuitions to third-rate private colleges that provide little else but acceptable social status for the academically undistinguished—is logical enough given the social environment. The creation of systems of universal education during the past century has led to various unanticipated, but all the same monstrous, outcomes, and the Japanese variety differs only in its specific ailment, one that reflects the particularities of the country's social and cultural environment.

Yet by calculating the returns as a whole, we can arrive at a rational explanation for this phenomenon.[31] In essence, while only the winners benefit directly by recouping their investment, overall the result is a very highly educated population, without undue public investment or coercion, and a clear gain for the collectivity. The national mean level of education has been raised very high and the standard deviation kept comparatively small.[32] This simple portrait carries profound implications for the political economy, especially when we recall that Japan is already a racially homogeneous nation and one profoundly centralized in terms of information and communication.

We must also note that this system diverges from Western education in terms of gender outcomes. While formal sex discrimination is absent from public education, there is still a strong societal tendency for males to advance further, to be given greater supplementary education, and to be encouraged to compete harder. As a result, females constitute only about a fifth of the student population of the nation's elite universities, and but 30 per cent of the total university population. The proportion of women in the professions has remained minuscule. On the other hand, over 90 per cent of those attending junior colleges are women. In relation to the employment system, then, education contributes to a strong bias toward gender differentiation in career patterns and expectations. Yet given the considerably greater bias in the traditional construction of sex roles, education has actually been a factor for change. There is regularly an excess of qualified females compared to employment and career opportunities, for example, and this certainly encourages greater gender equality over time. Coeducation has furthermore been a force for changed attitudes. Much of the same situation exists, interestingly, among the Korean minority in Japan, whose achievements in the public school system have outdistanced job opportunities in the society at large.[33]

While no one characteristic listed above is unique to Japan, the combination and the intensity of focus set the Japanese system apart. It is particularly noteworthy that systems similar to the Japanese (both in terms of strengths and weaknesses) are found in the East Asian NICs, where a similar pattern of economic growth, political stability, and broad popular participation in the industrial process are also found. The model has arisen as the result of many historical and cultural conditions, but, just as important, it fits a strategy of leveraging human resources to achieve economic catch-up. A basic aspect of this strategy is to close the industrial skills gap with more advanced nations (in manufacturing especially) at a faster rate than the follower nation's wage advantage disappears. Just as competitive advantage comes to firms with a young population of employees among whom rapid learning is generating productivity gains greater in value than their rising wages, so, in a parallel dynamic, national competitiveness derives from an education strategy of rapidly rising standards for the population as a whole.

The development of higher education has been much less impressive. Very few Japanese universities today can be said to be oriented toward either world-class research or training. Compared to American higher education, for example, Japanese universities have proportionally one-tenth the graduate student enrollment (nearly half are in a single field, engineering). Put differently, whereas the ratio of graduate students to undergraduates is 32 per cent in England, 22 per cent in France and 17 per cent in the United States, it is but 4 per cent in Japan.[34] Furthermore, Japan spends a smaller proportion of its total public education budget on higher education than any other OECD country.[35] Undergraduate instruction is notoriously lax and uninspired. Elite universities are aspired to more for their status than their quality of instruction. Many Japanese have gone abroad for advanced training (sent by their companies, university mentors, or government offices), and companies often provide what amounts to excellent in-house "graduate" training for their R & D employees, but these are compensating mechanisms for the weaknesses of university programs. Nor have Japanese universities successfully addressed these problems. They do not offer positions to world-class scholars, for example, and all curricular reforms have proved illusory. This pattern, too, has deep historical roots.

University governance has always been something of a problem. Having created elite national universities as key agents of change and provided them with impressive resources, the government was frustrated by demands from the academic community (echoing the rights of Western colleagues) for autonomy from its control. Over time, this struggle has led to a long series of partial compromises that have left the administrative structure of the national universities a bizarre admixture of highly centralized and highly decentralized processes and entrenched conflicts over power among numerous parties. Significant innovation and reform have been made enormously difficult as a result. Being national, the top universities must conform to a set of legal and administrative limitations (produced by the Ministry of Education) that contribute to insularity and inhibit new directions. The autonomy gained from the government rests largely at the school and department level, and this has led to parochialism and destructive territoriality. The central direction of each university is very weak, and the opportunity for self-serving conservatism at the department level is strong. The ministry's budgetary and legal authority, combined with great departmental autonomy, has left Japan's elite universities with the worst of both worlds.

In some respects even Japanese companies appear to want universities to stay the way they are. There is considerable evidence that they do not wish to hire people with advanced degrees, preferring instead to take in generalists, who are regarded as more flexible and compliant. Those with graduate degrees, it is said, are harder to train to the companies' specific requirements, harder to integrate into the organization, and more difficult to manage. Lifetime employment has long provided a different perspective for companies, since it has been the basis for enhanced internal systems of skills and managerial development.

The government's failure to build world-class universities can also be explained by the long-standing orientation toward imported knowledge. Japan has depended relatively little on domestic institutions for fundamental research. Rather, as previously noted, the country's development has rested heavily on the adaptation and improvement of borrowed basic technology. This has occurred most typically in private corporations, rather than in universities. Although professors would deny it, the university system's essential role has been a combination of sorting talented recruits for companies and ministries and serving as an important conduit and legitimizer for foreign ideas. Furthermore, being public institutions and beholden to the Ministry of Education, the elite universities never perfected a role for themselves as providers of a significant alternative vision for society from that of the government (a role at least claimed by Western private universities).

Educating a population in the basics is one thing; the placement and utilization of the skills produced is quite another. We can imagine two societies with the same level of compulsory education, but with very different economic outcomes because skills are put to work in differing ways. The Soviet system, for example, is known for the way it fails to utilize a highly educated work force. Similarly, there is continuing debate about the economic value of military R & D in the United States, in part because it diverts elite talent to less productive endeavors. Of particular relevance, then, is the allocation of the highly trained and talented.[36]

Where is talent drawn to in Japan and how is it utilized? Political scientists have long pointed out the strong attraction of government service among Japan's elite students, a certain contribution to the effectiveness of Japan's industrial policies. Unquestionably, compared to the United States, the quality and prestige of the national bureaucracy is high. This means that in a network of influence and mutuality between government and leading private institutions, elite ties based on education are arguably important assets enhancing coordination. Japan is certainly not the only nation with an elite nexus formed by education, but it is noteworthy that this form of identification and connection plays an important counterbalancing role to the powerful centripetal forces of company and ministry loyalties. If heavy involvement in one's company is the weft of Japanese society, educationally derived social status and affiliation are the warp. Japan is not a class society in the classic economic sense, but educational ranking serves to provide considerable hierarchy and elite identification.

Just as notable is the allocation of talent to engineering. One-fifth of Japan's university students are studying engineering, primarily in the national universities. Thanks almost entirely to public policy priorities, Japanese universities thus proportionally turn out twice as many engineers as American universities.[37] The proportion of engineers in the total university population is also extraordinary by European standards, where graduates in medicine and natural science far outnumber engineers. This difference becomes even more impressive when we realize that very few engineers in Japan are working in the defense sector. That is, Japan's engineering talent is concentrated almost exclusively in commercial work. In effect, Japan may proportionally be putting as much as three times more engineering talent into commercial development tasks than the United States.[38]

Turning to other professions, the distinctiveness of the Japanese system is again affirmed. Japan has virtually no business schools. Educating future managers in accounting, finance, marketing, and so forth is essentially handled by company programs and on-the-job training. Some American wit recently observed that one way to solve the trade problem would be to help create business schools in Japan. Whatever wisdom there might be in this suggestion, the point is that, as with general engineering and with rudimentary undergraduate legal education, Japanese education does not emphasize the production of a professional class with portable skills, distinct status, and a guildlike ethic of autonomy within the system. Rather, professional skills are subsumed largely within corporate and governmental frameworks, making them institution-specific.

The import of this pattern is that one is not likely to find consultants, accounting firms, and lawyers much in evidence in the activities of business and government; rather, one inevitably finds career members of key institutions at the center of affairs. Matters of flexibility and communication between institutions assume a distinctive flavor as a result. Less is a matter of public record, and less hinges on formal procedures (laws, accounting norms, etc.). Institutional memories tend to be long, and institutional ties are typically more durable than in a world in which independent professionals play major intermediary roles. As a result, in Japan, the "particular" (institutional relationships) holds sway over the "universal" (legal and arm's-length commercial dealings) in a greater proportion of all interinstitutional transactions.[39] Commitments are stronger, and there is less short-term fluidity as a result. Other essays in this volume, and in the previous volumes in this series, emphasize networks and the importance of what might be termed "relational economic transactions." What they observe is clearly related to this deeper social pattern.

To summarize at this point, the distinctive characteristics of education in Japan, and what I have been labeling the Japanese model, derive largely from the early formative period, when mobilizing the entire population to master industrial technology was the preoccupation of government leaders. The system that emerged allocated distinctive roles to compulsory and higher education and to company-level skill development, all three of which reflected the nation's developmental strategy. Despite many faults and chronic weaknesses, the system succeeded admirably when measured by the goals of those early leaders. The nature of that achievement is worth noting in detail.

Contemporary Educational Achievement

One of the theses of this essay is that public policy in Japan has given unusually high priority to the development of human resources. This means, of course, a strong school system, one that greatly stimulates learning in the young and provides the basis for even higher levels of learning in work organizations. Educational achievement, in other words, should be measured in terms of both skills acquired and habits of learning.

It is rather well documented that Japan's system of public education today produces the highest average quality in the world. In the basics of reading, mathematics, and science, the average Japanese has learned more than his or her counterpart virtually anywhere else.[40] Were there international measures of achievement in social science and foreign languages, the Japanese would not be so outstanding perhaps, but even in these fields, the Japanese master a tremendous amount of information. Most observers would agree, for example, that in social science the Japanese are strong in the area of factual mastery, but weak in analytic skills.[41] In the study of English, reading and writing are relatively well developed, but the spoken language is poorly taught. Acknowledging these points, it is nevertheless reasonable to estimate that the average Japanese twelfth grader is comparable in basic learning to the top students (those in the highest couple of deciles) in Europe and the United States.[42]

The essential picture is of a school system generating superb human resources by international standards. The list of distinctions is long. A greater proportion of Japanese children attend preschools, nursery schools, and kindergartens than in any society, with the exception of France. The school year contains 60 days more a year than in the United States, meaning that by the end of high school a Japanese has had three additional years of schooling (by American measure).[43] Better than 90 per cent of all Japanese youth are graduating on schedule from the twelfth grade, considerably more than in the United States (about 75 per cent), or any country in Western Europe. About 40 per cent are ultimately receiving a higher education, a figure roughly comparable with the U.S. and German rates and higher than elsewhere in Europe. Another 20 per cent are taking vocational courses following high school, meaning that 60 per cent of all young Japanese are receiving between 15 and 18 years of formal schooling (measured in terms of an American school year) beginning at 4 years of age.

Furthermore, a very large percentage of young Japanese are receiving supplementary training in private institutions. More than half of all students will have attended a tutoring academy or cram school for at least several years. More than two-thirds also take private nonacademic lessons (piano and judo being the most common) at some point during their elementary school years. Roughly one-fourth of all secondary-school students receive supplementary entrance-exam preparation during their time in high school or during extra years of study for university entrance exams.[44] The picture is thus one of prolonged schooling for nine out of ten new citizens of an intensity that in other industrial nations is limited to the elite.

Matriculation figures, however, mean very little if, as is often the case in education, large numbers only mean lower standards. Quantitative achievements in Japan are reinforced by the more significant qualitative measures of accomplishment. Japanese students through grade twelve receive a very demanding education indeed. The curricular requirements for completing regular high schools are as high as those designed for European school systems that enroll only the academically talented. They are considerably higher than those in the United States. For example, it is expected that those graduating will have completed at least six years of a foreign language, two years of secondary-school science, and two years of secondary-school math. Most university-bound students will take science and math each year of high school. In the case of math, for example, algebra is a seventh-grade subject. Differential and integral calculus is an eleventh-grade subject, taken by approximately half of all students. In the United States and Europe, roughly 10 to 15 per cent achieve this level of math, typically at the university level.

Schools also do a very competent job of socializing students. Behavioral problems in Japanese schools, while worrisome to Japanese these days, are at low levels in comparison with those in the United States.[45] The very great majority of schools are extremely well run, orderly, and efficient in teaching the basics, and this despite very large class sizes. Various surveys also show Japanese students doing considerably more homework than their American counterparts. Between one-third and half of all Japanese high-school students do more than ten hours' homework a week; in the United States under one-tenth of all high-school students do that much work.[46] Interestingly, twice as many American students as Japanese at this age report parental supervision of homework.[47]

One key appears to be the early and thorough learning of orderly routines and the sensitizing of students to cooperative group processes.[48] Recent studies indicate that while Japanese nursery schools are characterized by relatively little direct teacher control, considerable emphasis is placed on teaching basic routines that form the basis of school activities up through high school. Highly standardized, these routines teach group coordination, attention to details, and conformity. Each year through elementary school, they are reconfirmed and supplemented until the school day is reliably under control, without great requirement for teachers to discipline students. It is interesting to note that many of the routines learned in preschools are utilized by adult organizations for the same purposes.

Social control is also effected by utilizing small-group processes that enhance peer pressure.[49] As early as the preschool level, observers find teachers sidestepping the need to exercise their authority directly. The technique is to introduce the problem issues to small-group discussions and encourage students to solve them among themselves. Again, what is most fascinating is the similarity of this approach—one that shifts responsibility to the small group—to what can be observed in Japanese society at all levels, from the national government to offices and factories.[50] Groupism is a learned pattern.

Numerous other factors help to explain Japan's academic achievements. Support at home from parents is stable and recognition of education's importance nearly universal. More Japanese than American high-school seniors can expect to graduate from a four-year college. Most notable is the difference between males in the two nations; 40 per cent of Japanese males, as against only about 25 per cent of American males, are receiving four-year degrees.[51] Effort, rather than innate intelligence, is emphasized by parents and teachers, with the result that expectations are not lowered for the majority of students at an early stage, as has been shown for the United States.

A number of careful comparative studies of elementary-level learning are also particularly relevant. Researchers have found the actual time spent teaching per hour of school to be considerably higher in Japanese classrooms than in American ones.[52] This difference alone greatly explains the fact that even in very early elementary education, a gap begins to grow in the accomplishments of the two student populations.

Shorter school vacations, more homework, cleanliness, attention to detail, less disruptive and antisocial behavior, little absenteeism, and greater persistence are all characteristics of the student population in Japan that have direct analogies in adult work behavior. The sources of this learning are certainly not limited to the school system, and yet it is in the schools that a high level of good conduct must be achieved and maintained for the standards to be fixed for society as a whole.[53]

On the other hand, the products of Japanese schooling today are deficient in some skills that are given greater emphasis in other nations. The way Japanese are taught emphasizes passive listening and rote memorization. Self-expression, argumentation, and creative thinking are not emphasized. The rhetorical foundations of Western education are missing. Nor do Japanese schools encourage independence of opinion or support idiosyncratic skill development. Large classes, the routines, the emphasis on group social controls, and the strenuous pace required for exam preparation all preclude much individualistic activity. Through eighth grade, furthermore, the system avoids tracking and self-paced teaching. There are no classes for exceptional students, and only by entering fast-track schools, via examinations, can the brightest students find a suitable place of learning. The consequence is a degree of overall uniformity and equality of opportunity that is admirable from an egalitarian perspective, but open to criticism for lacking variety, responsiveness to the individual, and attention to creativity.[54] Not surprisingly, this same portrait holds true for Japanese society as a whole. Earned-income distribution differentials are admirably small, but, on the other hand, in Japan the individual is more thoroughly subjected to the social order.

Another weakness in the present compulsory system is the relatively low degree of what, for lack of a better term, is called "international" learning.[55] Not that Japanese students do not digest large quantities of facts about other countries and stay up late at night putting to memory impressive amounts of English grammar and vocabulary. Rather, there is something very insular about Japanese society as a whole, and the educational system's efforts to overcome this insularity have been distinctly inadequate. Globally and historically speaking, Japan is a relatively remote archipelago, and the cultural and linguistic gap between it and most other industrialized nations is especially problematic with the country being propelled to center stage in the world system. Schools, to be fair, are quite limited in what they can do to "internationalize," but it is also true that, when given opportunities, few teachers and administrators respond to this enormous challenge with more than lip service. Spoken English has not been given much emphasis; there has been a conspicuous reluctance to employ foreign teachers; non-Japanese (e.g. Korean, American, etc.) schools are given second-class status; and textbooks have not attempted to teach other cultural points of view. Some of this has begun to change, but so far with very mixed results.

Higher education is unquestionably the least impressive part of the total schooling picture. The reasons for this have largely been covered in the previous section, but a closer look is in order. A pedagogical and motivational crisis is endemic to the private universities, where more than half of all students matriculate. Poorly endowed, overcrowded, dependent on government help, and generally unsure of their futures, the private institutions are clearly the most troubled. Their teacher-student ratios, research facilities, and faculty profiles all reflect the much weaker state of their finances compared with public universities. There are few pressures to study hard, and innovative teaching is rarely encountered. Grades mean little, students are not motivated to attend classes (typically about a quarter of those enrolled appear for lectures), and professors often spend much time moonlighting. The picture is hardly better as far as instruction at the national universities is concerned. One American professor, who has taught at three of Japan's top national and private universities, has labeled the instructional system a "charade" in which "exams and papers are given infrequently and almost never returned. Graduation is automatic, transfer of knowledge incidental, and accountability nonexistent."[56] Even in the best national universities, student clubs are the most vital aspect of the university experience for the majority of students. Exceptions to this are medical, science, and engineering departments in the top national and public universities. Since neither jobs nor research funding nor institutional prestige are affected by the quality of instruction, this pattern has been very stable. Whatever the ultimate explanation for the weaknesses, the result is that Japan has hardly tapped the educational potential of its university system.

It is worth noting that the Japanese case appears to repeat a pattern that has existed for some time in the West—namely, that great competence in basic science (measured by such things as Nobel Prizes) seems poorly correlated with vitality in applied technology and economic growth. Japan, as a follower (and "free rider"), has benefited greatly from the fundamental advances achieved elsewhere. Weakness in its higher education has not hampered progress in applied technology or limited economic growth. The allocation of resources to immediately useful forms of learning, rather than to basic science, for example, follows a pattern similar to that in the United States prior to World War II.

The issue of higher education is essentially one for the future, when foreign technology and basic science may not alone be sufficient to sustain Japanese growth and provide stimulus for leadership in key industries. The rest of the world, furthermore, is expecting Japan to apply more of its resources to the kinds of basic research that will have universal benefits.

To summarize, despite some increasingly conspicuous problems, Japanese education today is unquestionably a crucial ingredient in the country's vitality and general dynamic thrust within the global system. In the comparison of whole populations, the Japanese accomplishment stands out for its high average level of knowledge, for the skills and habits put in place by schooling, and for the general thirst to continue formal learning past the compulsory period.[57] This does not mean that Japanese schools are producing a greater percentage of brilliantly talented people. What is truly notable is the nation's success in raising the average level, particularly of realizing high standards for the middle and lower socio-economic portions of the population. It is as if Japan accomplishes for 70 or 80 per cent of its youth what American education is able to accomplish in its suburban public and elite private schools for the top 10 to 20 per cent.

This human-resource base is available to Japanese companies, not only in laboratories and executive positions, but on the factory floor as well. It is the foundation for a society of low crime, high savings, and generally stable living patterns. Similarly, whether we look at health statistics or traffic accident rates, absenteeism or false fire alarms, we are confronted with impressive social differences that in part are generated to Japan's advantage by the school system. One could argue with considerable validity, on the other hand, that it has been the Japanese family and the long-standing homogeneity of the population that has made possible the nation's educational achievements. Acknowledging these contributions, the crucial point is that the issue is not a chicken-or-egg one, but rather a matter of positive synergy, generation after generation, among national policies, schools, and families in emphasizing much the same goals for children.

Given Japan's educational accomplishments, it is interesting to note the general skepticism and impatience of Japanese business leadership with the educational system. To them, the schools are not doing an adequate job, the teaching profession is largely anti-business, and the universities are hopelessly out of step with the pace of change. In their view, companies are forced to shoulder a heavy burden of training and socialization in order to have the kind of human resources they desire. While these criticisms have some merit, the more interesting point is that such dissatisfaction has stimulated companies to further encourage learning among their workers.

Learning in Work Organizations

A school system offers general skills, but no matter how good, it cannot tie human resources directly to productive processes. This fitting together occurs in the workplace and is mediated by organization and management. The knowledge base established by education can easily go to waste in a work environment that inhibits its application or in which textbook learning is obsolete. More important, as the technology of production changes, skills on the job must keep up. The postwar story in Japan is one of extensive organizational innovation aimed at enhancing the acquisition and sharing of knowledge, especially on the factory floor, and including line workers. Often we label these "worker involvement" programs, as in the well-known example of QC circles, but in essence what has been perfected by Japanese management is an extensive range of learning systems centering on average employees. The dissemination and acceptance of new techniques in this area of management has been impressive, as Robert Cole's essay in this volume illustrates. As a result, a dynamic approach to learning and problem solving has been cultivated widely in most large Japanese firms.[58]

The immediate goals of enhanced efficiency and adaptability in production processes require both that workers understand the technical nature of their work in order to make intelligent decisions and that they acquire a wide range of skills so as to allow for greater flexibility. In seeking to enhance understanding and skills, Japanese managers have created new systems that have transformed workplace organization and raised the sense of participation of the average worker. Put another way, management has consciously focused on the task of reducing the vertical and horizontal barriers to communication and learning in organizations. The ultimate foundation of this very commonsensical effort is certain key attitudes. First, managers believe in the perfectibility of workers' skills and of organizational means to enhance learning. Second, workers by and large have been willing participants in efforts to improve their skills, even when there have been no immediate rewards or compensation for the extra effort. Third, underlying both management's optimism and workers' willingness is a shared assumption that the company's success will bring benefits to all. Thus, while the goals and means have been very pragmatic and hardly unique, what we might call the attitudinal (or cultural) context has greatly facilitated the effort.

In contrast, American and European systems of production management have been shaped by very different attitudes. First, individual skills are transferable individual possessions and thus appropriately gained at personal, rather than company, expense. In relating people to machines, managers have relied much more heavily on a static approach to workers' skills, depending more heavily instead on a professional class (scientists, engineers, and managers) to do the thinking and innovation. Influenced by economies of scale that arose with mass production, industrial strategies have called for large investments in equipment that requires little learning by hourly workers. The term *foolproofing* aptly describes the intent. High labor turnover, the availability of immigrant workers in many industries, and union rules have all further encouraged the development of this pattern, one often known as "Fordism." All of this, furthermore, has rested, until very recently at least, on a set of modern Western assumptions emphasizing inherent differences of interest and talents within companies between owners, managers, union leaders, professionals, and rank-and-file workers. This categorizing, fixed by contractualistic attitudes and periodically reinforced by adversarial activity, creates many very high barriers to shop-floor learning. In this classical utilitarian and mechanistic model of company organization, market mechanisms and individual incentives have been assigned a central role in the motivation of learning. As a result, both managerial initiative and workers' willingness have largely been inhibited. A situation in which all parties view their participation in company programs as tentative and conditional provides a very weak foundation for company-based systems of continuous learning. In the light of this comparison, it is not difficult to see how different Japanese cultural attitudes and different educational and company institutional arrangements have shaped a more encouraging environment for company-based continuous learning.

It is now well established that the two decades beginning in the early 1950s witnessed enormous strides in Japanese productivity in key large-scale industries.[59] Comparative studies, furthermore, consistently demonstrate the human and organizational strengths of Japanese firms in manufacturing and product development. In the period from 1955 to 1980, labor productivity in manufacturing in Japan grew at a rate considerably higher than in any other industrial nation, and throughout the 1980s, it has remained somewhat higher than in the United States and Europe. Technology and investment have played important roles, but the evidence points to a more fundamental strength in the organization of complex systems. That is, Japanese comparative advantage has centered on such industries as autos, electronics, and machinery, where the ratio of parts to finished product is high, where product cycles are short, and where the relationship of investment to scale efficiencies depends heavily on organization.[60] This advantage extends to many of the newest production technologies. In a recent study of Japanese and American adaptation and utilization rates of computerized machining equipment (the basis of flexible manufacturing), for example, the Japanese were found to be impressively ahead. "Japanese factories have 2.5 times as many CNC [computerized numerically controlled] machines, five times as many engineers, and four times as many people trained to use the machines," notes the author.[61] Within organizations, coordination, problem solving, and improvement rest on the application and development of knowledge, and while this sounds simple, it actually involves changes in such fundamental matters as control, decision making, and strategy.

Japanese management has been the leading innovator in these matters in the postwar period, and this has given Japan a competitive advantage in certain key industries.

In the first volume of this series, Kazuo Koike draws attention to the importance of on-the-job (OTJ) training in Japanese manufacturing.[62] He correctly underscores OTJ training as the bedrock of company training programs and notes that even small companies lacking the resources to conduct formal training have developed systematic means of advancing skills and knowledge via OTJ programs. Among the many methods that might be used as illustrations of this, Koike emphasizes job rotation in work teams. He notes how common this is in Japan, and how it results in extensive skill enhancement, as well as greater teamwork, flexibility, and job satisfaction.

Before considering systems, let us note the basic organizational dynamic established by enhanced learning, such as that which occurs through job rotation. In addition to multiplying an operator's particular job skills, rotation results in a wider and more detailed understanding of the overall production process. This in turn makes participation in problem solving more possible, since most problems involve such things as work flows, communication, and quality, which occur within the process as a whole. Participation in problem solving in turn facilitates further learning, both specific and general. Broader knowledge, skills, and participation lead to greater group flexibility of response to change. This learning-participation link is a dynamic one that gradually restructures the role of management from being authoritative and directional to being facilitative and inclined to delegation. When the learning capacities of the lowest level of a system are activated in this manner, supervisory management can spend less time on control and on immediate problems. As the delegation of routine problem solving increases, each level of management comes to have more time to focus on larger issues, strategic and external to its immediate responsibilities.

Comparative studies have found, for example, that the depth and breadth of Japanese managerial job descriptions are greater than in comparable American circumstances, and this extra latitude stems from the capacity of Japanese organizations to handle greater degrees of delegation effectively.[63] A well-educated work force at even the lowest levels is a prerequisite of extensive delegation. That is, how learning is viewed by workers and how human potential is viewed by managers, together with the actual learned capabilities of the work force, combine to shape management style.[64]

As is now well known, it is common for large Japanese companies to hire new employees directly from school and to expect the males among them to stay with the company for a very long time. Some turnover among regular employees occurs, of course, especially among younger blue-collar workers, but the crucial point about Japanese "permanent" employment is its fit with a managerial focus on learning. The company both enjoys greater returns from improved human resources the longer people stay and must pay a higher price for its failures to train or motivate workers. As mentioned, large companies prefer to hire general skills, and this "blank page" approach puts a premium on teaching the employee company-specific skills. This, in turn, requires a long-term perspective, one that applies to all new (male) hires, and not just to future managers. Large companies generally give new recruits intensive introductory training, both to provide an information base and to socialize them to the company community.[65] Programs last from several weeks to several months and are characteristically followed by at least a few years of on-the-job training in the company's basic operations. Honda male employees, for example, high-school and university recruits alike, begin their careers with a period of months on the assembly line. "Spiritual training" exercises, such as marathon walks and Zen meditation, and exercises reminiscent of summer camp are often added to the initiation process for the stated reasons of group bonding and character building.

The point is that Japanese firms have creatively sought to develop intensive means for shaping their new workers' attitudes and skills, the better to integrate them into the firm. The process is hardly casual, for it defines the moral relationship of the individual, his fellow workers, and the company. Interestingly, this attention to building a firm base of socialized habits and attitudes is very similar to what has been observed throughout Japanese education, beginning with nursery schools. Everywhere, teachers initially spend an inordinate amount of time making sure of integration within the group (and the cooperative order it produces) before proceeding to regular instruction.

The recognized importance of human resources, of continuous learning, and of the role of organization give the personnel function particular prominence in Japan. All aspects of training and the careful tailoring of workplace learning systems are the responsibility of personnel departments. In American firms, regardless of lip service paid, personnel work is generally low on the management totem pole and rarely do personnel managers have the authority or the resources to innovate effectively. In Japan's case, the reverse is true. Personnel departments exercise authority and are very active in designing more effective organizations.[66]

One highly visible example would be quality-control circles. Cole's essay in this volume discusses their diffusion at length, and my remarks will be limited to their fit with the general cultural assumptions about participation, learning, and authority. To begin with, we should note that QC circles and suggestion systems are extensively developed in

Japanese firms. The numbers of participants and the number of suggestions per worker reported by large firms can be so staggering that one cannot help feeling skeptical. In my experience it is not unusual for large firms to record nearly 100 per cent participation and a rate of suggestions per worker that works out to one a week or better. The great majority of ideas submitted are about minuscule changes, but collectively they amount to considerable improvement each year. More to the point, according to managers, QC circles and suggestion systems encourage greater attention to details of the work at hand. They are also valued because they sponsor a sense of participation and give a voice to all employees. Asked what result is most important, managers typically stress morale. Yet in effect, both circles and suggestion systems are means for regularized learning around the most mundane and repetitive of work activities.

Why then did QC circles succeed so remarkably in Japan? Besides the reasons Cole offers, I would like to stress cultural ones. First, because the education level of workers is high, they have less difficulty grasping the formal principles of statistical analysis involved. Second, Japanese workers have been thoroughly socialized to small-group processes. Third, it is taken as normal for workers to contribute to their companies' efficiency in noncontractual ways. Fourth, Japanese managers are relatively secure in their authority, meaning that they see little threat in the prospect of worker involvement. Discussions of worker participation in European and American settings have tended to carry political overtones (participation implies a shift of power), whereas in Japan, social control and company unions make this perspective inappropriate.[67] These sociocultural conditions have combined to help make Japan fertile ground for increased worker participation.

Other examples of learning systems can readily be found in visits to Japanese companies. One of my favorites is the country's third-largest superstore chain, Jusco, which has an elaborate train-by-mail program built around each salesclerk's job. The trainees are mostly part-time salespeople, largely middle-aged housewives, whose turnover rate is high. Based on a detailed analysis of the kinds of product and sales knowledge involved in each specific department (e.g., women's wear would include understanding the laundering and stain characteristics of dozens of materials), the personnel department has created study modules similar to a Boy Scout merit badge system. Tests, small awards, and eventually promotions are geared to each step of advancement. The genius of this particular learning system is in its adaptive fit to a situation otherwise not conducive to on-the-job learning. At a low cost to management, thousands of salespeople participate virtually daily in improving their job-related knowledge and do so at their own pace.[68]

Westinghouse surveyed its major Japanese competitors in the early 1980s and found that, except at the executive level, the Japanese offered considerably more training to workers at all levels. Executive training at Westinghouse was greater.[69] This pattern corresponds well with the higher managerial salaries and greater executive prerogatives found in American firms and reflects another attitudinal difference. Management careers in Japan are not keyed to external courses or business schools. The career path is typically internal and slow-paced. Personnel and senior managers monitor careers over long time periods, and senior promotions are based on frequent evaluation over many years. Philosophically at least, managers are just average employees who have proven themselves to deserve more responsibility. It follows that investments in training would spread more evenly across the entire company work force in Japan. This fits rather neatly with the observed long-term orientation of Japanese human-resource strategies.[70]

Japanese firms do not analyze training investments using financial measures. Rather it is generally assumed that investments in learning pay off for companies that must meet the demands of dynamic marketplaces. This article of faith assumes long-term employment and long-term business strategies. Older workers, for example, receive less training. This is not to say that training receives unlimited funds or that funds are not cut in business downturns, only that in case after case known to me, the Japanese firm, compared to its American counterpart, dedicates more time, money, and attention to encouraging job-related learning at virtually all points along the career path, except among senior executives. The expectation of long employment tenure and faith in the potential of average employees seem to be the crucial reasons for this difference.

Nearly all Japanese companies pay homage to the centrality of human resources in their managerial philosophies. Such statements (which I have learned to take seriously) only make sense if taken as testimonials to the centrality of learning. No political ideal or religious principle inspires this perspective, although it is certainly consistent with the Confucian tradition. This approach to human resources itself has evolved, rather, as its potential for stimulating the involvement of workers has proved increasingly effective.

Has this made a significant difference to the competitiveness of Japanese companies? Overwhelming evidence suggests that it has done so in manufacturing. Numerous studies show that Japanese factory workers perform standard work significantly more efficiently than their American and European counterparts. It is also clear that they have played an important role in the processes leading to improvements. For example, in numerous separate manufacturing joint ventures in which the same production equipment is used in both the United States and Japan, the Japanese regularly show a higher output for the same amount of input. The explanations are quite similar, involving greater cleanliness, more reliable work habits, better operator maintenance, closer attention to details of machine function, and a greater capacity to make very small incremental improvements in the equipment and its surrounding processes. Whether the machines are producing soft drinks, microchips, band-aids, or auto parts, the story is consistently the same when the comparison is strictly a matter of the human factor.

Observation of the nature of innovation in manufacturing processes also indicates some relevant differences. In the American case, fewer engineers are responsible for larger shares of projects. American innovations tend to favor more technically complex and capital-intensive solutions.[71] The human factor is frequently seen as unreliable or static in its contribution. Related to this, process improvements tend to occur in larger, less frequent increments. And for these reasons, organizational adaptation to technical change often tends to be cumbersome and inadequate. The Japanese, by comparison, seem to have a larger percentage of the total work force involved in the change process, with more contact between engineers and operators. This is facilitated, of course, by the larger proportion of engineers in the work force. High-and low-tech solutions mix and evolve as part of innovative processes that are relatively continuous. Japanese capital investment is often very large, but it is more carefully integrated with human-resource capacities and with organizational changes. Historically, the American pattern evolved in an era characterized by economies of scale, in which the financial justification for capital investments in technology was dynamic and the quality of the labor force was theoretically of diminishing consequence. Japan's manufacturing strategy, evolving later, has focused much more on the positive contribution of the total work force (learning potential) and on the gains to be achieved from more flexible systems of production. The crucial point is that work-force learning has been an integral and often central aspect of technological innovation in postwar Japan. Machines alone hardly tell the story.

A parallel picture is emerging from a study comparing Japanese, American, and European auto design teams.[72] Essentially, the Japanese are capable of shorter cycle times in new model development. In general it takes Honda or Toyota half the time it takes GM to take a new design from the initial clay model to the dealer's floor. The central problem is the coordination of information, which in turn depends on communication of knowledge between separate elements of an extensive system of differing functions (from manufacturing and supplier relations through design to marketing and sales), each with distinct realities and points of view. Among the factors enhancing coordination is the degree of shared knowledge possessed by these elements. Contributing to this are such things as initial training, job rotation, and internal transfer from function to function. Again, the human capacity for learning, and the way management has structured the organization to facilitate information-sharing, are at the heart of Japanese capabilities. The Japanese firms studied, in essence, have lower barriers to information flows and higher levels of shared knowledge on which to base coordination.

We might also note the results achieved at the GM-Toyota manufacturing joint venture (New United Motors Manufacturing Inc., or NUMMI) located in Fremont, California. With roughly half the capital investment, the NUMMI assembly plant has reached twice the productivity of comparable GM plants. Among the many differences noted was the greater attention to human factors, especially learning, on the part of NUMMI's Japanese managers. After signing a contract with the United Auto Workers (UAW) that provided for great flexibility in cross-training and worker cooperation, the Toyota managers set about upgrading the skills of the work force. The head of NUMMI's UAW local remarked to me in 1987 that, in his two years under Japanese management, he had "learned more" than in his twenty years working in the same plant run by General Motors.

In sum, a major aspect of Japan's recent economic prowess derives from innovations in organizational learning that have been developed and diffused largely during the postwar period. These have bestowed advantages in manufacturing and product development that have, in turn, been crucial to export-led growth. Beginning with a well-trained work force, management has stressed the possibilities of wide participation in continuous learning processes. While these innovations can be adopted and adapted by non-Japanese companies, the fact that they have largely arisen and progressed so rapidly in Japan cannot be explained, I would argue, without recourse to fundamental cultural and social considerations.

Issues for the Future

Learning is an adaptive activity, and systems of learning, too, must be adaptive to remain effective. As the environment changes, prior adaptations become obsolete. Today, in part because of Japan's continuing economic success, the conditions that characterized the postwar world are disappearing rapidly, and Japan is being propelled into a position of global leadership that has no precedent in Japanese history. This emerging situation raises a fundamental question: can the patterns of knowledge mobilization that have served the country so well under other conditions be adjusted to meet the new challenges Japan now faces? Can the Japanese adapt to circumstances in which their country is no longer a net borrower of technology, no longer primarily a manufacturing island, no longer inclined to follow the lead of Western powers, no longer a youthful nation, and no longer able rapidly to improve its human resources by the expansion of educational opportunities? If intensive borrowing, very high educational standards, and advanced company learning systems have all played a role in generating momentum under prior conditions, will they be sufficient in an era of Japanese leadership?

To begin with, matriculation rates reached a plateau around 1975. The century-long trend of educational expansion thus came to an end over a decade ago. For the foreseeable future, the proportions of young Japanese going on to high school and university will not change significantly. If we assume that learning declines with age, then an aging population is one less oriented to learning. One cannot help but wonder whether as the population shifts from being one of the youngest in the industrial world in the 1950s and 1960s to being one of the oldest after the turn of the century, Japan will not lose its momentum as a learning society. Together, the matriculation plateau and aging population mean that the proportion of people in school or in the early years of employment (when learning is most active) is actually going to decline, reversing a century-long pattern. The upgrading of human resources from here on, in other words, must rest almost entirely on improvements in the quality of education. This underscores the importance of universities in the future, since it is in higher education that most room for progress lies.

Have Japanese company learning systems also reached a plateau? There is no statistical evidence available, but such key practices as job rotation and quality-improvement programs have inherent limits which are now being approached. Most innovations in managerial thinking these days point in a new direction, toward reducing the size of the permanent employee core and moving more routine processes offshore. This may imply that companies will focus their attention on an elite work force of managers and research personnel and away from trying further to increase the capacities of production workers. Whether the manufacturing work force, still certainly the world's best, can be counted upon as a key source of dynamic improvement in the future is a very real question.

Learning from Japan has become an international preoccupation, and should other countries achieve the same rates of learning in their factories, Japanese manufacturing leadership could lose its edge. Certainly, in industries unsupported by fresh technological innovation, catch-up on the part of other countries is widely evidenced. The Japanese are focusing attention heavily on efforts to develop greater and greater flexibility (small-batch production) and enhanced interfunctional coordination (reducing design-to-market time lags), and they are investing very heavily in advanced processes and new technologies, but the plateau issue remains. Furthermore, as the Japanese invest heavily in automation, and as they establish manufacturing facilities abroad, the relative advantages obtained from the organization of learning among production workers may decline. As the manufacturing gap in general closes, the role of new technologies becomes pivotal to the retention of comparative advantage, and this speaks to rather different organizational forms and patterns of knowledge mobilization.

Furthermore, the great advances in postwar productivity have come primarily in the manufacturing sector, where learning systems have had a major impact on the overall capacity to add value. Since the mid 1970s, however, the place of manufacturing in the overall economy has shrunk, while the service sector has grown. This raises the further question of whether in the enlarging service sector, learning systems can contribute as significantly to productivity gains. There is little evidence that the service sector in Japan has made great strides in terms of increased productivity.[73]

The key competitive issue, then, is the rate of learning in product development and global marketing. The evidence is that what has been true of manufacturing is also true of product development—namely, that the Japanese are particularly adept at this kind of learning. But for many Japanese companies, a shift from a manufacturing-based strategy to one focused on R & D, product development, and new technology carries many far-reaching implications. Shrinking the core of permanent workers, for example, makes sense if manufacturing is moving offshore. Rather than inclusive programs aimed at high morale, participation, and so forth, more specialist training, the purchase of outside skills and knowledge, and closer ties to research organizations of all kinds will be emphasized in the future.

As Japan prospers, the structure of status and rewards is also changing. Manufacturing and engineering, recently so attractive to young graduates, are reportedly declining in appeal compared to work in sectors such as banking, investment, and insurance. The abundance of capital and the rise to global prominence of Japanese finance now draws an increasing proportion of top talent. Such work is notably more lucrative, and this fact is redefining Japan's occupational structure, giving the management of money and its associated consumerist ideology a particular allure, one already common in Europe and North America. As evidence of this change nearly 10 per cent of the nation's engineering graduates in the past few years have been taking jobs in securities firms, banks, and related companies. Yet if there is a change away from the popularity of engineering, it should not be exaggerated. First, the contemporary factory is not an unpleasant work environment. Second, the large number of engineers produced annually in Japan are primarily the result of the large number of university places available in schools of engineering, and this will not change. Third, the attractions of innovative work in the new technologies remain high in Japan. And fourth, engineering is well integrated with careers in top management in most of Japan's leading companies. If money management is a flourishing new direction, and production engineering is less attractive, it is also true that more and more engineering graduates are staying on for advanced degrees in recognition of the central role of R & D in Japan's future.

Broadly inclusive learning programs and enhanced communication are fundamental to manufacturing success Japanese-style. But if the technology is largely borrowed, the time comes when R & D strength is vital. Japanese companies, it is often asserted, are good imitators, but poor innovators of new technology. If this were simply a matter of foreign "sour grapes," it would be one thing, but many knowledgeable Japanese worry about this as well. Everywhere the issue is made particularly poignant by the recognition that Japan's apprenticeship is over.

Two inferences might be made: (1) Japanese organizations are too group-oriented and hierarchical to encourage creativity, and/or (2) the nature of learning in Japan is too dependent on imitative foundations. Both schools and companies are paying attention to these assertions, but companies have made far greater progress in trying new directions. Many are experimenting with special arrangements to help stimulate creative work. Some claim to tolerate greater idiosyncratic behavior among young researchers than ever before, for example, and many are trying to find ways of protecting their R & D activities from the bureaucratic aspects of their larger organizations. The Ministry of Education is also very cautiously experimenting with the notion that Japanese education might develop a more creative pedagogical style and curriculum, but the results of the very localized attempts that are being made will not be known for a while.

Read the papers or listen to public discussion. "Creativity" is a burning issue. Many Japanese fear that their nation is not oriented toward fundamentally original work. The issue touches on much that we have considered in this essay, but at a profound level it asks the question of whether the national character itself is not too rigid and too conformist in its sensitivities to foster significant new initiatives. The historical dependence on borrowing, a highly standardized education system, strong governmental control, weak universities, and tightly organized companies are regularly construed as barriers to independence of thought and originality. These we have touched upon, but behind them lies a strong national inclination to close, frequently hierarchical monitoring of one another's behavior and to meticulous defense of established forms. In such a dynamic society, paradoxically, these constitute a kind of security blanket providing order and meaning in the midst of rapid change.

Given the rapid rise in Japanese corporate competence in a host of advanced technologies, however, one cannot help wondering whether concerns about "creativity" are not somewhat misplaced. First, the diversity of the population guarantees that some percentage of the people will always be relatively independent and productive of new ideas. Second, while there are undoubtedly aspects of creativity that are highly individualistic, and that in Japan are inhibited by organizational constraints, from a learning perspective, imitation, adaptive borrowing, and innovation are related positively in the staging of accomplishment over time. That is, the talents that make for succcessful borrowing prove useful for innovative work as long as the final creative stages are not inhibited by either unwillingness to change or a lack of crucial basic knowledge. Clearly, problem solving is common to all stages, as are willingness to change and a capacity to share information.

Learning skills applied to borrowing, in other words, are generalizable to circumstances of innovation. In a detailed study of technology borrowing within a U.S.–Japanese joint venture that I made in 1975, it was quite apparent that learning continued smoothly past the end of the borrowing stage and proceeded within a few years to the point where the American engineers who had originally supplied the knowledge were deeply impressed with the independent advances of their precocious Japanese colleagues.[74]

Such stories are not uncommon in many industries. The initial effort to learn a foreign technology often proves to be the most difficult of all stages, with innovation flowing rather smoothly from the process of continued problem solving.[75] This rather counterintuitive observation points to a bias in popular Western thinking that exaggerates the difficulties of creating new knowledge and understates the difficulties of learning and integrating borrowed knowledge. In contrast, the traditional understanding of apprenticeship as leading to mastery through imitation seems to be quite apt. By this perspective, there is very little evidence upon which to argue that Japan is beginning to flounder in terms of corporate innovation.

But correcting a pejorative view of imitation is only part of the story. Another issue is basic research. The infrastructure for such research in Japan is not well developed, for example, and new forms of organization suited to R & D may be necessary. Interchange with the international research community will have to be strengthened and Japan's best universities will have to be greatly improved or new research centers created, if the flow of new fundamental knowledge is to be guaranteed. This is, remember, an era of growing international resistance to perceived Japanese "free riding" in science and basic engineering. How Japan will adapt to a position of global research leadership is an important question.[76]

Today, the crucial issue is innovative research, and the Japanese agenda for change is lengthy. Past necessities dictated a school system preoccupied with the skills of knowledge absorption. Now this must be supplemented by an orientation to more independent styles of learning and exploration, especially in the secondary level. In Volume 1 of this series, Daniel Okimoto and Gary Saxonhouse consider the issue of institutional change in detail,[77] but its potential significance for the entire educational system is worth noting here.

More intractable is the bedrock character of the educational system. Major changes in a highly developed and complex system like Japanese education are very difficult under stable historical conditions. The two moments of truly radical change that the Japanese education system has experienced—namely, the early Meiji period and the American Occupation—both came under historical conditions of exceptional fluidity in all aspects of Japanese society. Both also involved extraordinary foreign pressure. In fact, the postwar period since the Occupation has been largely one of retrenchment following the radical changes brought on by American reformist impulse. This fact hardly bodes well for the prospect of Japan being able to basically reorient its education system in the near future to something more productive of a different national character. To successfully transform the universities, to undo the hold of entrance exams, and to end stultifying pedagogical practices under conditions of general prosperity, political equilibrium, and cultural continuity is hardly likely.

Recently, under Prime Minister Yasuhiro Nakasone, the idea of reform was raised to a high level of political visibility. A public commission reporting directly to the prime minister was established. Because Nakasone continually mentioned education, the topic received persistent public attention for several years. Yet, while there has been no scarcity of voices calling for change, the effort has had, so far, very moderate success, at best. Japan is a nation perpetually anxious about, and preoccupied with, its educational system. Nakasone raised expectations that something would be done about its fundamental character, but these expectations have not been fulfilled.

Unquestionably, there is consensus that the educational system should change, but little agreement about the direction to be taken. Since the various power-wielding entities cannot agree, the existing system, centered on entrance exams and a cram mentality, remains impressively entrenched. Reforming the schools means very different things to the electorate, to the Ministry of Education, to the political opposition, and to the many other actors on the educational scene. None of this bodes very well for fundamental reform.

If we accept, say, an American model, we would conclude that the heart of the problem is the leading universities. Great nations, it is assumed, need great institutions of higher learning. Perhaps, in catching up, universities have not been so central, owing to the possibility of borrowing technology and basic research. But occupying a leadership role in the global system implies strong universities that can exercise intellectual and scientific leadership. A world leader needs institutions that can generate basic knowledge and provide guidance. Can Japan's quite conservative universities be changed in directions that emphasize innovative basic research, meaningful instruction, and greater independence from government? Can they establish a fresh pedagogical vision that will change the nature of elite education and redefine what is of value in preparing for entrance examinations? Can the universities establish themselves in the international academic environment through imaginative hiring policies and aggressive support of new research? In many respects, unfortunately, the top schools and their faculties have much to gain from the continuation of the status quo. Even if they were to attempt major internal reforms, they would face certain opposition from a Ministry of Education that resists any diminution of its own power. In other words, the prospects for serious reform are not very good, short of creating new research institutions.

Watching on the sidelines are the nation's leading technology companies. From their perspective there are three complementary means to the generation of the necessary fundamental research. They can invest more heavily in their own R & D capacities and focus more effort on basic issues; they can invest in partnerships with foreign universities and research organizations; or they can lend strength to those Japanese universities that prove innovative. So far they have hedged their bets carefully, spending considerable sums on the first two options, while cautiously waiting to see if the universities at home will make the necessary transition. In the mid 1980s the government lifted many restrictions on private business funding of public university research, and some headway has been made, especially at Tokyo and Kyoto universities, but the ultimate significance of this relationship remains unclear.

There are great potential rewards for any university among the front-runners that can effect significant changes and thereby attract industry's support and the most talented faculty and students. Such a transformation could guarantee a leading role in research and teaching during the next century. Sensing this, might the top universities become competitive with one another in a kind of race to reform?

If not, will Japan become a nation characterized by a powerful R & D capacity in the private sector, but a weak and increasingly marginalized public R & D sector? Using partnerships with foreign institutions, Japanese companies may move forward with relatively little input of basic research from their own universities. Certainly, there is much evidence that Japanese firms are deepening their connections with overseas research and using such places as locations for advanced training and information gathering. And there is certainly evidence of a relative decline in the share of overall Japanese R & D activity conducted by its universities. If these trends were to continue, the implications for international policy would be great. Private sector R & D does not lead to much public information sharing, and partnerships with foreign institutions raise numerous political questions. Clearly, the dynamic of corporate R & D is so great these days that it overshadows the universities and drives the search for foreign alliances of all kinds.

There is an equally basic question to be considered: namely, if universities really do reform and as a result secondary education shifts away from entrance exam preparation, will standards come down as a result? The present system relies heavily on exam competition that, in turn, depends on a highly standardized curriculum. Independence of opinion and idiosyncratic learning have almost no place in secondary schooling. The high standards, in other words, appear to rest on a highly structured approach. If the top universities were to begin recruiting students by criteria other than objective tests, for example, the whole fabric of the school system might be so weakened that standards would fall.

Noteworthy here are the parallels between education and company organization in terms of the issues and problems raised by Japan's success. If catch-up is no longer the basic name of the game, then the kind of learning considered most desirable also changes. How to deemphasize formality and uniformity and sponsor greater differentiation of attitude and reward are central issues on the minds of managers and educational thinkers alike. Furthermore, fundamental changes toward greater flexibility are obviously dictated by the increasing premium placed on rapid response in a world whose rate of change seems to be speeding up. Companies, it appears, are making these changes much more successfully than Japan's schools and universities. This gap between rates of change in the private and public sectors will be worth following closely in the future.

If the great educational issues before the nation are no longer ones of apprenticeship, but rather ones of adaptivity, change, and innovation, then this fact alone makes Japan rather distinctive. Most other nations are simply trying to produce the results the Japanese now take for granted. Japan alone has largely solved the problem of constructing a mass-oriented school system with average attainments that are equivalent to elite education elsewhere. The Japanese must now figure out how to ameliorate and transform the results of their own success.

A parallel issue is the constantly mentioned "internationalization." Japan is unquestionably an insular society, but one that now has large foreign investments and a public goal of becoming cosmopolitan. This means that the society itself must open up much more to foreigners, and, as in the case of opening Japanese markets, change is very slow. In some respects the schools are leading the way, but in others, just the opposite can be said. For example, the massive importation by the government of young foreigners to teach English (the JET Program) has been partly neutralized by the way local teachers have limited its impact.[78] Internationalization implies a willingness to accept considerable diversity and independence, and here again is the rub.

But there is no question that more and more foreign students are coming to Japan, especially from nearby Asian countries. Japan's graduate schools are filling up with foreigners, and every year more government fellowships are announced. A third of the graduate students at Kyoto University are foreign, for example, the great majority from Korea and China. Gradually, Japanese higher education appears to be evolving toward a central role in the dissemination of applied technology in Asia. Thus, Japan is becoming an educational and cultural center of an increasingly interdependent Asia, but internationalization of this kind only serves to underscore the problems of Japan's universities. Research work in Japan involving students from other Asian countries is rarely world-class, and the role of the visiting graduate students at times resembles that of imported laborers.

What happens as Japan stops feeling itself to be in the humble position of an apprenticing student is another major question for the future. "Internationalization" may be a much-heard buzzword, but it is also true that the Japanese have been encountering more hostility lately. There is a real possibility that Japan will incline toward a self-confident insularity as the label of rich upstart begins to seem less and less fair. The rate of cultural influence from outside may begin to diminish as a result. Would such a worldview mean less stimulus for change? The historical precedents for this are numerous, and, in fact, Japanese history is often seen as a matter of cycles between periods of very active external orientation, followed by periods of nativism and consolidation. A diminishing of the nation's interest in identifying, learning from, and mastering the best international practice has serious implications, of course, and yet to some degree it is almost inevitable as the economic balance shifts.

The time may already have come, also, when Japan's success begins to blind it to the importance of foreign achievements, especially if they occur in neighboring nations viewed as being of lower status. Companies in Europe and the United States have certainly suffered from a similar problem vis-à-vis Japan during the past quarter century. How good, one wonders, will Japanese companies be at learning from the Koreans or the Taiwanese?

This chapter has essentially been an argument that Japan's capacity to evolve economically and to adapt successfully to an exterior world of superior technology and economic power has rested on an extraordinary capacity for learning, which, in itself, followed a pattern of apprenticeship, one rooted in traditional values and well established in contemporary education and work organizations. A highly educated population and a work force engaged in continuous learning make for impressive and regular gains in productivity. Such a population constitutes a strong platform for continued adaptive change. This capacity for learning is still today a major cause for optimism regarding the country's likelihood of successfully meeting the extraordinary challenges of the future. It is sobering to recall, however, that Japan has never before in history succeeded in being an international leader in cultural, scientific, or political terms. The challenges and contradictions ahead are truly momentous and should not be underestimated.

If we are to envision societies of the twenty-first century as powerful primarily because they can generate and utilize knowledge (compared to land or natural resources or geopolitical advantage, for example), then Japan still looks very well positioned indeed, for it has gone further in the creation of a learning society than any other, and it suffers less drag in generating a population capable of continuing along this path. While other nations are trying to overcome many fundamental socioeconomic barriers to engaging their entire populations in the learning process, Japan is attempting to move toward leadership in knowledge generation. This is a relatively enviable position to be in.

Takie Sugiyama Lebra

Gender and Culture in the Japanese Political Economy: Self-Portrayals of Prominent Businesswomen

Gender is an issue that warrants special attention in considering the political economy. It is a generally shared preconception that the two institutional domains, public and domestic, belong to men and women, respectively. But a gender-focused inquiry into the political economy, a main sector of the public domain, will show how the two domains in fact so interpenetrate each other as to challenge the male-female domainal opposition. In Japan's political economy, women's minority status is more firmly established than in the postindustrial West. However, there is a fundamental difference between women and other minorities. Women not only constitute half the total population but are partners with men in sexual attraction and the interdependence created by conjugal and familial bonding within the domestic domain. This difference does not necessarily give women an edge in redressing their inferior status and may contribute to its persistence and complexity.

This essay consists of two parts. The first takes a broad view of the position of women in the Japanese labor market, which is further contextualized against two general considerations: (1) models of gender ideology supporting and challenging gender asymmetry, and (2) the age-linked life schedule underlying the gender issue. This part, which draws largely upon secondary sources of information, provides a frame or context for the second part, in which the primary data are presented.

The second part depicts twelve prominent businesswomen as they recalled and portrayed their careers and experiences in interviews. These women are company presidents engaging in what is broadly understood as "entrepreneurial" endeavors. It is cross-culturally recognized that to establish one's own business is "a viable strategy" for women squeezed out of the organized labor market.[1] Entrepreneurship as a route to beat the system is thus likely to attract women who aspire to careers. At the same time, one can easily imagine the difficulties and obstacles that confront such women, precisely because of their organizational independence, in surviving in the competitive and male-dominated world of business. How they seized opportunities and how they encountered and managed obstacles illustrates the general discussion of the first part. The two parts are thus interdependent, the first at once contextualizing and being amplified by the second. While the first part offers an outward macro view of where women stand in relation to men, the second part takes an inward turn to look into the subjective microcosms of the individual women by listening to their narratives. Throughout, Japanese culture explicitly or implicitly serves as a sorter of information in diverse contexts.

The Labor Market, Ideology, and Life Schedule

Gender in Economic Dualism

In his pioneering study of the Japanese employment system, James Abegglen points out that the rigidity inherent in "lifetime commitment" is ameliorated by two buffer mechanisms.[2] One is the categorical distinction between insiders to the permanent system—namely, permanent or regular employees—and outsiders—that is, temporary or supplementary workers. The other is the system of subcontracting, in which the contracting "parent" firm can displace its own burden upon the subcontracting "child" companies attached to it. This mechanism involves a relationship between large and medium-to-small enterprises. The two buffers, which do not necessarily overlap, together constitute the "economic dualism" of Japan, although granted there is some variation in what is meant by dualism.[3] Duality here involves status hierarchy between employees or companies, subordination of one party to the other, and possible exploitation of one by the other. Asymmetry is thus an essential characteristic of this dualism.

Whether this widely accepted view is valid or not may be open to question. Hugh Patrick and Thomas Rohlen, for example, noting the increasing viability and diversification of small family enterprises over the past two decades, observe that *economic dualism* "has become an outmoded phrase."[4] Rodney Clark proposes the use of *industrial gradation* to replace *dualism* in view of "continuous variation" in size among firms.[5] Even the intrafirm dualism of tenured versus untenured workers, which seems much sharper than dualism in firm size, is no longer entirely certain, in that the lifetime employment system itself is threatening to break down, as is constantly reported in the media.

It is likely that the real economy reflects multiplicity or complexity rather than duality. I suggest, however, that when applied to gender, duality continues to be a striking feature. The above buffers find their gendered counterparts. Can we not say, for example, that women are to men what temporary workers are to permanent employees, and what small-scale subcontractors are to large-scale contracting firms?

This parallel is not merely a matter of analogy but involves actual overlaps. First of all, a large portion of employed women are in fact temporary, untenured, supplementary, peripheral workers outside the permanent employment system, which is quite literally "manned." Interlocked with the normative domestic career pattern, the woman employee's temporariness is typically demonstrated by her mandatory or voluntary "retirement" upon marriage or first pregnancy, full-time engagement in housewifery and motherhood until her youngest child enters school, and reentry into employment as a middle-aged part-timer. The overall distribution of women employees by age thus forms a skewed M-curve, the first peak being sharp and the second peak more gradual. As of 1985, the 20–24 age bracket (i.e., premarital or preparental stage) formed the left peak of the M with 67 per cent employed, the 30–34 bracket hit the bottom (35 per cent), and the curve began to rise again from age 35 on, reaching the right peak with 46 per cent employed at age 40 to 44.[6]

By international comparison, Japan stands out in the sharpness of its M-curve.[7] The term pāto (part-time) in the vernacular refers largely to the untenured, peripheral status of second-peak employees, who are not necessarily distinct from full-timers in terms of work hours. In 1983, 10.5 per cent of all employed workers were part-timers, and two-thirds of them were women.[8] The two peaks are totally discontinuous, in the sense that the second-peak workers do not return to their previous jobs but must find new jobs. And yet this two-stage employment career pattern, particularly second-stage employment, is attracting more and more women, reflecting the reality and anticipation of prolonging the postparental life stage further and further. From a woman's point of view, employment is largely an in-and-out matter, as indicated by a survey finding the percentages of women both entering and leaving employment to be twice those for men.[9]

Women are a significant half of the dual economy, not only as temporary workers but as workers in small-scale, family-based, and often subcontracting enterprises.[10] Women are concentrated in small factories, sales, and service industries, including "minuscule units of fewer than five workers."[11] In addition to being part-time and regular corporate employees working away from home, they manage their own businesses, join the work forces of family-owned enterprises, and do naishoku (piecework done at home, thus dispensing with the employers' need to provide a workplace).[12] Yōko Satō warns that as much as half of the census category of "self-employed" women may actually include *na-ishoku* workers, 60 per cent of them engaging in tiny-scale subcontracting in manufacturing industries.[13] Traditionally notable in agriculture, women's presence is now more important in sales and other service industries. Women come to head their family businesses as successors to their late husbands, and also when the male heads choose to work elsewhere as wage earners, leaving farming, family-owned retail shops, or other family businesses to their wives.

It is safe to assume, then, that women's labor is largely localized in the lower half of the asymmetric dual economy. In this sense, as pointed out by Frank Upham, women are no different from other "undesirables," such as *burakumin*, Koreans, and the handicapped.[14] Further reinforcing this point is the gender-specific repertoire of jobs and businesses. Professional women specialize in areas associated with housewifely responsibilities and their extension, such as the health professions (nursing, pharmacology, pediatrics, nutritional science, etc.), teaching and caring for small children (as nursery and grade-school teachers), and instruction in bridal arts such as flower arranging, the tea ceremony, and the like. Businesswomen, too, who start their own enterprises tend to stay within the traditionally or properly female repertoire, as exemplified by beauty shops, coffee shops, restaurants, bars, kimono shops, dress shops, and sales catering to women customers (e.g., cosmetics). This gender bias is confirmed by Barbara Ito's sample of "entrepreneurial" women engaging in a variety of businesses.[15]

The gender-specific repertoire is reflected in employment as well. In 1981, 83 per cent of all employers admitted that their firms have certain jobs in which no women are placed.[16] Most striking is the absence of women from managerial positions. Among the total of about 1,400 companies listed on the Tokyo Stock Exchange, as of 1979, women constituted only 0.1 per cent of roughly 300,000 managerial/policy-making personnel (*kachō* or equivalent and above), and even in service industries, where women supposedly predominate, they hold only 0.5 per cent of these leading positions.[17]

Young women employees of large companies, those at the first peak of the M-curve, theoretically with "permanent" status, are typically represented by the so-called "office lady" (OL), who may or may not have a college education, working as "a prelude" to marriage.[18] Lacking any prospect of promotion, the OL symbolizes the auxiliary, insignificant nature of work—simple, tedious, clerical—without authority or much responsibility, performed only to assist male bosses. Internationally notorious is her housewifely or servile role as an office waitress serving tea and cleaning ashtrays. The tea-pourers' rebellion that took place in the early 1960s at a division of the Kyoto City Office was unsuccessful, failing even to attract the attention of the union leadership as a legitimate labor issue, and the women resumed tea-pouring.[19] In the late 1970s, a company studied by James McLendon was training new women employees in such "women's work" as serving tea to male colleagues and guests and keeping the office area clean, as well as in talking politely to customers and male staff.[20] At parties such as *bōnenkai* (year-end celebrations), McLendon observed women workers waiting on men, because "no man should have to pour his own drink or serve himself rice."[21] Women seem to accept this role as a matter of temporary obligation until they relinquish their tenured-employee status and retire at 25 or so to attain their real goal in life, marriage.

In short, gendered duality in work status is thus indicated by women's concentration in small-scale enterprises; the part-time status of middle-aged women; the short-term employment pattern in contrast to that of men in the same age range, who benefit from the seniority rule;[22] gender-segregated job categories; inaccessibility of managerial positions; the insignificant, auxiliary nature of the tasks assigned to women; and so on. This qualitative inferiority of women's status is manifested in a quantitative discrepancy in wages. Women's average monthly pay amounts to roughly half of men's, and this discrepancy has not improved over the years. If we take men's monthly average pay as 100, women's pay peaked at 56 in 1976, but then dropped to 52.8 in 1982.[23]

Despite gender barriers, the number of working women has been growing. A 1982 survey by the Prime Minister's Office showed 49 per cent of women aged 15 or older to be working, a continuing trend that accounts for the termination in 1984 of an extremely popular TV drama series addressed to the daytime audience, that is, housewives.[24]

Full-time housewives, the category paralleling that of full-time urban male salaried employees, are a recent phenomenon associated with the high-growth period of the 1960s and the unprecedented affluence and enlargement of the "middle class." (In pre-affluent Japan, except among the well-off classes, families could not afford specialized housewifery: women worked as co-breadwinners side by side with their husbands or in-laws. This corresponded with that stage of social and economic evolution where work and family life were not as sharply bifurcated as at the later, fully industrialized stage.) It is customary to distinguish housewives from working women as if the former were nonworkers. Indeed, the media image of the housewife is that of a leisurely, privileged woman with *sanshoku hirune tsuki* (three free meals and a nap per day), devoting herself to aerobics and pursuit of her own hobby or pleasure. Accepting this image, some housewives appear embarrassed or apologetic about themselves, but a majority would be resentful and able to demonstrate that housewifery is full-time work, in fact more than eight hours a day.

Housework in Japan is more than just such chores as preparing meals, house cleaning, laundry, shopping, bookkeeping, or "home management" as a whole. The Japanese housewife is expected to be perpetually available to her children, husband, and aged parents or parents-in-law. Every morning, she prepares her children for school and re-energizes her husband for another day of overtime at his firm. Her presence at home is taken for granted during the absence of the daily commuters at school and workplace. Her mothering resumes when they get home; now her task is to provide relaxation therapy for the tired returnees. "If the wife is tired and unable to give the husband the soothing he desires, he will be annoyed and suggest that she cut down on outside activities," observes Anne Imamura. "Conserving her energies for the primary tasks of running the home, mothering, and comforting is the wife's major duty."[25] Even women interested in outside activities such as consumer movements feel "that a housewife must never participate in anything until she has taken care of her home and family," according to Imamura; one civic activist, she reports, never attended evening meetings because "it is not right that her husband should eat alone."[26]

It may be that this perfectionist image of a housewife is not so much actually lived up to as put forward to counter the popularized image of the idle housewife. It is indeed true that with the proliferation of ready-to-eat food products and automation of housework, the housewife today has more free time than before, particularly if she is left alone without a small child or elderly parent to look after around the clock. But it is not the kind of time she can control or schedule at her will. One of my informants, a doctoral candidate at the University of Tokyo who had to quit to become a full-time housewife, described housewifery as a role of "waiting" (*taiki*) for calls that could occur at any time, unpredictably. "It does not matter how much time the housewife has. The time is for waiting, not for planning."

The housewife's presence at home and care giving are part of a package in the employer's investment in her husband. The employer expects the employee to be well taken care of by his understanding, nurturant wife, so that he is ready to resume his work each morning with refreshed energy and single-minded dedication. The worst thing from the employer's point of view would be the wife's interference with her husband's work career and schedule. School is even more demanding. Mothering a schoolchild includes performing all kinds of tasks assigned by schoolteachers to parents, ranging from participation in frequent PTA meetings and activities, to supervising homework, to making a standardized cloth container for stationery or sewing the classroom cleaning dust cloth that each child must take to school. The school expects the mother to be ready, full-time, for educational collaboration, often competing with her husband and his employer for her time and energy. Even more pressing is the mother's responsibility for her child's performance in examinations, accounting for the common association between the housewife and *kyōiku-mama* (mother obsessed with her child's educational success).

With her total and exclusive involvement in a wide range of chores and tasks as a wife, mother, and homemaker, the housewife may develop domestic expertise, become adept in managing human relations, and acquire mastery, confidence, and autonomy within her realm. She may become a "professional housewife."[27] When she decides to work outside the domestic sphere, however, she realizes herself to be dreadfully unskilled, hence unable to find a job better than part-time kitchen work. On the other hand, the market for domestic expertise is wide open, and "housekeeping" is a professionalized job taken by supposedly unskilled "former" housewives.

Although full-time housewives are declining in number, I have discussed them at length partly in order to dispel the prevailing perception of a dichotomy between working women and housewives and partly to underscore the symbiosis of home, school, and workplace. Furthermore, few women workers, whether full-time or part-time, professional or unskilled, in the home or outside it, are completely free of their housewifely identity, whether as a matter of desire, obligation, ambivalence, guilt, or frustration. It is this identity that keeps women workers crowded into the lower half of the dual economy. One may well go as far as to say that the full-time housewife is one of the purest manifestations of gendered dualism in the Japanese economy.

Gender Ideology: Functional Complementarity or Egalitarian Justice

One way of explaining or legitimizing gendered dualism derives from the functional model. It may be argued that a woman's participation in the lower half of the dual economy is functional to the goal of a social unit, be it the woman herself as an individual, her family, the company employing her or her husband, or the national economy at large.

It is apparent that hiring a middle-aged woman as a part-timer is functional to her employer in terms of flexibility and low cost. A 1983 survey showed that, among nine reasons (which are not exclusive of one another) for choosing female part-timers, the undemanding nature of the work was indicated by 63 per cent of the responding employers, the lower cost of labor by 29 per cent, adjustability of labor supply to the amount of production or sales by 20 per cent, and seasonality of business by 18 per cent.[28] All these reasons imply labor-cost reduction and/or flexibility in hiring and firing.

Conversely, the woman, too, may find a part-time arrangement flexibly adjustable to her own and family needs and suited to her double life as a housewife and employee. "Many women favor part-time work in spite of its limitations because the hours, although sometimes nearly as long as those worked by regular employees, are more flexible, allowing women with family commitments to schedule working hours accordingly," says Ito.[29] If that is the case, part-time employment is solidly based upon functional complementarity between employer and employee. The growing number of part-timers among married women and mothers may attest to such functional complementarity between the two parties.

Similar complementarity may hold between a young woman employee who, despite her full-time, permanent status, accepts her work as a bridal apprenticeship or a premarital experiment, on the one hand, and her employer or boss, on the other, who wants to keep his regular female staff youthful. For the employer, women's early retirement kills two birds with one stone: it raises male workers' morale and cuts the financial burden that would accumulate with seniority if a full-time woman employee chose to stay on along with her male colleagues. Related to youthfulness, and killing still another bird, is the functional consideration of beauty. McLendon notes that the company's hiring committee paid special attention to looks because a woman employee's attractiveness would contribute to creating positive rapport between the company and clients and because these women were prospective brides for male workers.[30] And, for Japanese, feminine beauty is inseparable from youth.

There are indications that the M-curve pattern is functional not only from the employer's point of view. Over half (56 per cent) of a surveyed sample of women were found to prefer a two-stage work career, with an interval of home life as wife and mother, whereas only 16 per cent favored a continuous work career. The same survey revealed that 50 per cent preferred that their second-stage work be part-time.[31] The familiar M-curve seems to have stabilized.

In the case of participation in family business, there is a functional unity between the woman's domestic role and her work role, between the woman herself and the family as a whole. The home-site job, including low-paid *naishoku*, is preferred by those women who want to supplement family income without sacrificing their domestic responsibility. As subcontractors, these women in turn fit the needs and interests of small, local contractors that cannot afford workplaces, facilities, or job security. Even entrepreneurial women, as observed by Ito in Niihama, find their business activities well integrated with their family roles and identities as wives and mothers.[32]

Finally, role division between housewife and salaried husband in urban, middle-class Japan may be viewed as a culmination of functional complementarity at two levels: (1) functional interdependence between the wife as a full-time care giver and homemaker and the husband as a full-time or overtime employee and economic supporter of the family; and (2) reciprocity between the family that refuels the worker husband daily and the company that rewards the workaholic husband with job security, promotion, and pay raises. Thanks to such role division, the wife can also devote herself to bringing up her children, the next generation of workers and housewives.

Extending our perspective to the societal level, one may argue that women's contribution is indispensable to the strength of Japan's national economy precisely because they occupy the lower half of the dual economy. It is not surprising, then, that Japan's economic success offers one of the rationales for excluding women from the upper half of the dual structure. The growth of GNP owes, the argument goes, to men's total devotion to work, which in turn is made possible by women's support at home.[33]

In the functionalist argument, gender segregation in career tracks has nothing to do with gender discrimination, but is a natural way of self-fulfillment for both men and women. This kind of polemic reached a peak when a provocative article attacking the Equal Employment Opportunity Law (EEOL) appeared in a popular journal. That the author, Michiko Hasegawa, was a woman with a career apparently contributed to the sensational ripples it caused. In Hasegawa's view, the EEOL degrades the housewife as a nonworker, whereas she is in fact a full-fledged worker, performing daily absolutely necessary chores; "being" at home alone, while "doing" nothing, is an essential part of her work. The introduction of the EEOL, Hasegawa believes, will end up demoralizing housewives and replacing mutual appreciation and cooperation based upon the division of labor with competitiveness and animosity among invidious status-seekers. Hasegawa extends the functional model to the "ecosystem" of indigenous culture, which she predicts will be destroyed by this law of alien origin, externally enforced because of Japan's submission to international, "colonial" pressures.[34]

As best exemplified by the Hasegawa article, the functional explanation of the gendered dualism thus derives from and in turn reinforces conservative ideology. It is not at all certain, however, whether the gendered dual economy is in fact functioning well, serving the needs and goals of each social unit concerned. Do women really opt for employment in small-scale subcontracting firms? Do they want to work in their family business or do piecework at home rather than go out to work? If working outside the home, do they find their part-time status really suited to their personal goals? Is it functional to the young woman and her employer for her to quit her "permanent" job at age 25? In fact, many men and women alike deplore this early retirement phenomenon as a "waste" of human resources and investment, and in turn use it as a justification for gender discrimination in the hiring practice.

Gendered dualism as such can be challenged in terms of its dysfunctional implications and consequences. Women may be only submitting to, not choosing, what is available to them. Far from it helping them attain their goals in life, they may find the prevailing asymmetry frustrating; part-time status may be taken as degrading rather than fulfilling. The survey of women's attitudes toward work cited above, while indicating the relatively prevalent desire for an M-shaped life-course, also shows that preference for a continuous career nearly doubled between 1972 and 1984 (from 11.5 per cent to 20.1 per cent), and that the perceived desirability of quitting upon marriage or first childbirth dropped from 30.9 per cent to 21.7 per cent over the same period.[35] Two opposite conclusions can thus be drawn from the same kind of information.[36]

Contrary to Hasegawa's view of her, the housewife may be one of a frustrated, unfulfilled, demoralized crowd of women who are no longer content with the endless cycle of domestic drudgery and care giving. The "professional housewife" is more ideal than real. In reality, the housewife frequently finds herself under stress and may face serious crises in her life: perhaps her husband does not reciprocate her nurturant care giving, but instead becomes a mere "boarder" of the house; perhaps he has to live away from home because he has been transferred to a distant branch office (*tanshin funin*); perhaps his career has reached a ceiling below what she expected; or, worst of all, perhaps he has started womanizing. Economically helpless, unable to risk divorce, she reintensifies her commitment to the future of her child. There are reasons to believe that the *kyōiku-mama* is symptomatic as much of the mother's neurotic obsession as of her devotion to her child. Still, there is no guarantee that her child will grow up into a successful, filial adult as expected. Furthermore, the Japanese housewife is likely to outlive her role as mother, inasmuch as her life expectancy is steadily lengthening.[37] According to latest reports, Japanese women can on average expect to live for 81.4 years and men for 75.6 years.[38] Widowhood and divorce make the functional-interdependence thesis bankrupt.

Asked if they agreed with the idea that the husband should go to work and the wife remain at home, 71 per cent of women respondents indicated unconditional or conditional agreement in 1982, 12 per cent fewer than a decade before.[39] The increase in the number of part-timers who are married women may be a sign of housewives attempting to escape these dilemmas and to capture a sense of autonomy, although such women tend to justify their action in terms of supplementing family income rather than of their own fulfillment.

What emerges is the stressful, demoralizing, pathological, wasteful, dysfunctional aspect of gendered duality. If there is anything functional about it, the functionality is one-sided, not complementary. The male employer may believe in the functional advantage of gender division between regular and temporary employees, but his opinion may be rejected as a "top-down" view, not shared by those at the bottom looking upward.[40]

This asymmetrical functionality brings us to the idea of justice based on egalitarian ideology as another model for understanding gender dualism in the economy. This is a feminist point of view. In today's Japan, as elsewhere, the gender issue swings between the functionalist ideology and feminist ideology, the former seeing functional disaster in the latter, the latter finding an embodiment of injustice in the former. Self-proclaimed feminists are not the only ones trying to reform the gender asymmetry. The national government itself, not immune to domestic and international waves of feminism, is taking steps to rectify inequality and discrimination, and some progress has been made in the public sector. In 1975, out of 6,938 top-level administrative positions in the national government, 20 were occupied by women. Eight years later the number had increased to 47 out of 8,334, rising from 0.3 per cent to 0.6 per cent.[41] Feminists may groan over this persistence of overwhelming male dominance, but these figures can also be taken as an initial sign of change, at however slow a pace. The last male sanctuaries in the civil service, such as the defense force and police, have been opened up to women. In 1986, despite strong opposition by many Hasegawas, the Equal Employment Opportunity Law went into effect. A survey of about 7,200 private employers conducted ten months later by the Ministry of Labor indicates some movement toward equalization, especially among large-scale companies.[42] Once egalitarianism is embraced, functionalism comes to be seen as a mask for injustice and exploitation.

Controversy over these two ideologies goes on between men and women, the young and old, the privileged and underprivileged, the better-educated and less-educated, and so on. Nevertheless, the two models of gender ideology are not as far apart as claimed by the most vocal advocates of each. Nor is there consensus within each camp. In the feminist camp there is debate over the meaning of equality when applied to gender. If there is no way of denying sexual differences and complementarity between male and female or of "ungenderizing" society completely, the question is how this fact is to be made compatible with gender equality. One feminist, for example, might demand total abolition of the existing law protecting women workers in order to bring about true equality, while another might advocate expansion of services and facilities such as child-care centers at work sites for working women.

The revision of the Labor Standards Law, necessitated by the EEOL, is a product of compromise between such oppositions: retaining and expanding the mandate of maternity protection on the one hand, and removing and relaxing all other protection requirements. The question continues to pop up, "Isn't the law overprotective of working mothers at the expense of all other women, let alone all men?" The rationale for maternity protection is protection not only of the mother's health but of the next generation to be born and reared.[43] It is interesting that the strong mother-child bonding sanctioned in Japanese culture can be ideologically mobilized in opposite directions: to keep mothers homebound as full-time child-care providers, and to support mothers working outside the home without sacrificing their mothering role and time.

If multiple meanings of egalitarian justice generate controversy, the functional model has its own share of complexity. What is often overlooked about women's status is the fact that women are not always losers and men winners in the functional division of labor. The gender asymmetry inherent in the functional model can produce a reversed hierarchy, in that role division actually gives the housewife the exclusive privilege of dominating the household. Under extreme role opposition, domestic matriarchy goes in tandem with public patriarchy,[44] the essence of functional complementarity. Further, as a housewife or peripheral employee, the woman may be a winner in the "lifelong" run, as suggested, if not proved, by her longevity being greater than men's by six years. Men pay the price of male status in shorter, more stressful lives, and it is said that there are many men envious of women.[45] In the labor market, too, women's monopoly of pink-collar jobs (e.g., nursing, nursery teaching) is well justified in the functionalist perspective. Some men and women may see a reciprocal balance in this relationship, whereas others may find it an intolerable or unhealthy imbalance, whether in favor of men or women.

For Japanese, in my view, the two ideologies are linked by what I call the role complex, a system of meanings, values, and rules centering around the concept of role. I propose the role complex as essential to building and maintaining Japanese self-identity. A person "out of role" is in an identity crisis. The role emphasis becomes easily allied with the functional ideology that justifies women's role as distinct from men's, since a role is recognized as such only in differentiation from other roles, and gender is a readily identifiable variable to dichotomize roles. The pervasive idea that each person has a role to play underlies the conservative stance in gender issues.

But this is only one facet of the role complex. Role also entails the value of performance and thus involves a work ethos. This is why the leisurely way of life symbolized, fairly or unfairly, by a housewife watching noontime soap operas or attending "culture center" classes is belittled by both feminists and their opponents. Life as an uninterrupted work career is an ideal for men and women alike, as long as the work is within role bounds.[46] Furthermore, within the role complex one finds excellence in performance as a key standard of evaluation. Women can transcend their gender handicaps by excelling men in actual performance. There are reasons to believe that the small number of women who have established themselves in the top echelon of the national hierarchy have done so through their performance and competence, outdoing their male peers. Further, the role complex dictates that gender identity be superseded by the role the person has successfully obtained. True, gender for a woman is detrimental to entry into a male-dominated organization and to promotion to an administrative position, but once she gets in, she finds it easy to control her male subordinates because her positional role overshadows her gender.[47] In addition, the role complex allows one to take a surrogate role on behalf of another, as when a woman becomes a surrogate head of the family business when her husband is not available for one reason or another.

It is likely that the two models coexist within the same individual, the same mind, in varying proportions. Consequently, I believe most people, both male and female, in Japan as in other societies, are ambivalent toward gender issues. Emotionally charged opposition to feminism, expressed by a male executive or an older woman, is most likely to be an overreaction to awareness of the unstemmable liberationist tide. Conversely, the less hope an active feminist has of realizing her ideal, the more radicalized she may become. In both cases, there is an ambivalence, I think, in what is openly espoused. Otherwise, it would be difficult to understand the action taken by the well-known leader of the "pink-helmeted" feminist group. The group had been organized to demand legalization of oral contraceptives and attracted media attention by its idiosyncratic tactics in assaulting male complacency. The leader, after losing a Diet election, made a sudden turnabout to withdraw into home life, to the dismay of her admirers. It is my assumption that most middle-of-the-road Japanese handle their ambivalence by distinguishing *honne* (spontaneous, personal feeling) from *tatemae* (socially acceptable belief or opinion) and alternating between these two sides of their selves. What is needed is a third model that mixes or supersedes the models presented here, something like "neofunctionalism," "neofeminism," or "complementary egalitarianism."

Age and the Life Schedule

The M-curve that has frequently appeared in the foregoing has foreshadowed the significance of age in determining a woman's engagement in and disengagement from the labor market. Typically, a young woman at 20, upon graduation from junior college, finds regular, full-time employment at a company, works as an OL, quits working and marries at 24 or 25, bears and rears about two children, and reenters employment in her late thirties or early forties to work as a part-timer until her fifties, assuming she is not laid off earlier. This pattern is a manifestation of the overall age norm and age-linked life schedule, which is standardized culturally and embedded in the social structure.

Japanese, compared with Americans, tend to be keenly aware of and curious about one another's age. Age is a major topic in greetings and conversation, particularly among older people, but young people for their part are strongly conscious of slight age differences, even of less than a year. Cultural reinforcers abound: terms of address indicative of the addressee's age or relative age difference between addressor and addressee (e.g., elder sister/brother, uncle/aunt, grandpa/grandma, for addressing a stranger as well as actual kin), including the *senpai* (senior member of a group such as a school, an alumni club, a company) designation by a *kōhai* (junior member); speech levels differentiated by the relative age gap between speaker and listener; age-marking ceremonies throughout life, notably, the later-life celebrations beginning with the 60th year of age. In a broad sense, Japan is an age-graded society.

The prevalence of age awareness hinges upon the different life schedules and commitments for men and women in the following ways. First, age enters the seniority system but only insofar as one stays on in a single work organization continuously. Age is thus articulated with seniority increments in status and wages for men, but not for women, whose work careers are typically discontinuous in both time and space. In other words, gender discrepancies in benefits are wider among older than among younger cohorts. Managerial positions are held by older men as a matter of age-seniority articulation, while they are hardly accessible to women of the same cohort, partly because of age-seniority disengagement.

Second, age has bearing on the view of life as a standardized sequence of stages and transitions that inhibits dropping out of a stage, skipping a stage, or reversing the normal sequence. The completion of school education must precede taking a regular job, which in turn should, for men, precede marriage. Dropping out of school, marrying, working, and returning to school—a fairly normal sequence for Americans—would be for Japanese a deviation that spelled a hopeless future. To begin with, school reentry would be even more difficult than job reentry for an overage ex-student. The low rate of school dropouts may have much to do with this irreversibility of life-stage sequence.

Implied here is Mary Brinton's "condensed timing," in contrast to "diffused timing," over the life cycle for investment in "human capital." Diffused timing, characteristic of the contemporary United States, entails "multiple decision points," spread over the life cycle, at which to enter or reenter educational institutions and work organizations for human-capital development. Underlying this flexibility is a culturally sanctioned variation in life sequences. Condensed timing, which is institutionalized in Japan, involves structural rigidity with a few key points, strong age barriers, a fiercely competitive examination system, primacy of internal over external labor markets, and so forth.[48] Condensed timing and irreversible sequencing are two sides of the same coin.

In a given sequence, one stage becomes preparation for the next life-transition test, toward an ultimate life goal. For men, the goal is to succeed in entering the most desirable job market and move upward into administrative rank: one's prospects for attaining the goal are directly conditioned by the rank of one's alma mater. For women, both education and employment are preparatory to marriage, which is clearly demonstrated by the choice of a junior college with only mild competition and two years of attendance. As observed by McLendon, marriage is "the only appropriate life career for women,"[49] and postgraduation employment is undertaken to meet a marriage mate in the workplace, which is encouraged by the employer as well. The company office is "a way station" one is expected to leave in about four years, and this is when the condensed timing scheme is pressed upon women relentlessly in full force.

"Marriageability" peaks at 25, after which a woman is said to become like a post-Christmas Christmas cake, which cannot be sold. Still single at 30, a woman employee is no longer at a way station but in a "blind alley" with no prospect for a career job or felicitous marriage.[50] Marriage pressures during the few peak years of marriageability may be the female counterpart to the pressures put on boys for the few years before university entrance examinations. Each test must be passed as a necessary step toward womanhood or manhood. The sharp drop in the M-curve is an inevitable result for women of the condensed and irreversible marriage schedule.

Third, age awareness goes with the importance of age-linked social relations. It is well known that individual Japanese careers are the product of joint endeavors by a group of collaborators. (David Plath's term *convoy* and Brinton's *sponsor* come closest to what I have in mind.[51]) The collaborative team is age-linked in two contrasting ways: cross-age and same-age.

Cross-age collaboration is familiar from many works on Japan. Chie Nakane's notion of "vertical society"[52] sums up age hierarchy as a basis for the strongest bonding and patronage, such as between *senpai* and *kōhai*, *oyabun* (fatherlike boss or leader) and *kobun* (childlike subordinate or follower), *sensei* (mentor or teacher) and *deshi* (disciple or pupil). An individual begins to develop a career as a *kōhai*, *kobun*, or *deshi*, and, as he attains senior status, recycles his experience into the career development of juniors as their *senpai*, *oyabun*, or *sensei*. This vertical arrangement of collaboration affects the placement of a junior person in the job market as well as his promotion, which becomes competitive above a certain level of the bureaucratic hierarchy, replacing the seniority-based promotion automatically granted up to that level. The seniority system of a bureaucracy is interlocked with this vertical joint venture. Women are decidedly disadvantaged in this system, because such alliances are usually within the same sex and there are still too few female seniors, except in gender-segregated job markets, as potential patrons.[53]

Women's role in cross-age collaboration belongs elsewhere. As Brinton has noted, Japan is striking in its "intergenerational" sponsorship, and this is terminologically symbolized by *oyabun/kobun*.[54] Brinton pays special attention to the educational system, where intergenerational sponsorship looms large, involving parents and teachers around a child, and culminates in a series of "sponsored contests" in examinations. It is here that a woman becomes a major sponsor as a contestant's mother. After the first goal of marriage is achieved, it is motherhood that occupies a woman's time, energy, and mind.

The M-curve seems to indicate that a woman finds time for outside work when her youngest child enters school, but many mothers I listened to stressed and confirmed that infant care was nothing compared with the educational problems of a school-going child, a son in particular. Whether or not the woman regarded herself as a *kyōiku-mama*, and some did, she took her children's educational success as *her* heaviest responsibility.

It may be that with her last child's entry into school, a woman finds more free time in a physical sense, but becomes mentally busier. She has to expend more psychic energy, if less physical effort, and this mental preoccupation continues throughout the child's school career and climaxes at examination time. If so, a part-time job with a flexible schedule and monotonous work content, requiring little concentration, may be the best such a mother can afford.

Maternal identity does not come to an end upon the child's successful performance in examinations, but is lifelong. The child's marriage is particularly high on the mother's list of responsibilities, and a 30-year-old unmarried daughter would be the most painful source of guilt and shame for her. Intergenerational sponsorship thus reinforces condensed timing.

The *kyōiku-mama* commitment can be explained in terms of cultural psychology: it is an identity interchange in which the mother experiences her child's success or failure as her own. Often coupled with this, the *kyōiku-mama* syndrome may also, as noted earlier, be a way to shift one's focus of attention from conjugal frustrations and estrangement to something else. Brinton's hypothesis of intergenerational exchange offers a more rational, less emotive explanation, viewing parental sponsorship of a child's career development as an investment in exchange for security to be provided to the sponsor in her old age by the sponsored.[55]

Few mothers I have met articulate perceptions of this sort of reciprocal payoff, and many explicitly deny such expectations, stressing their lifelong economic security, guaranteed by one type of pension or another. Still, non-monetary payoffs are not ruled out. Emotional support and sympathetic nursing care for aged parents on their sickbeds (and deathbeds, too), which no money can buy, are what they want and what "only your own child can provide." Since nursing care falls into the women's job category, "your own child" means your daughter or daughter-in-law. The daughter is directly in debt, but the daughter-in-law is a vicarious debtor, expected to repay the obligation on behalf of her husband.[56] In either case, this is yet another aspect of cross-generational collaboration that keeps women at home and thereby barred from the organized sector of the job market.

The joint career venture is not confined to cross-age pairs. Even though Japan is better known for the prevalence of junior-senior solidarity, age peers also play a significant collaborative role. This is not surprising in view of the 14 preschool and school years up to high school in which children's social life is concentrated in classrooms and playgrounds with age peers. Peers, if placed outside an arena of rivalry, are indispensable helpers. In the work career, the same-year starters, called *dōki*, are also age peers because of the standard practice of hiring only new graduates at the same time of the year. Generally, *dōki* workers are placed in different sections so that rivalry is minimized and senior-junior solidarity is encouraged. The result is the formation of informal networks among *dōki* peers across sections; the importance of such networks for one's career is augmented with moves up the bureaucratic ladder. Here, too, reciprocal exchange takes place, although in much shorter cycles than in the case of intergenerational exchange. This is a story of men, and male solidarity is among the strongest barriers to women trying to share the job market.

Peer solidarity among women, which also arises among *dōki* entrants into the work force, is less articulated with their careers, for the good reason that for them the workplace is not a final destination but only a way station. As observed by McLendon, possible jealousy over marriage prospects in the company keeps women co-workers apart from one another. Paradoxically, a more stringent rule of seniority prevails among women than among men, bringing junior women under the strict supervision of senior women to compensate for the structural looseness of relationships among women.[57]

Classmate intimacy is carried over into the woman's postgraduation stage of life, as is the case with men. This tie is weakened through marriage and then selectively revived when women become "maternal peers" sharing the same interest and concerns about their children. In a provincial town, it was found that classmate ties survive and are strengthened among those women whose children are in the same school year and enrolled in the same school.[58] This relationship is double-edged in that, while strongly tied together as best friends, they compete with one another in their children's school performance. Again we are reminded that, for women, even age-peer solidarity is contingent upon mother-child bonding. Whether this relationship is really one of peers is questionable because it contains two sets of peers coupled intergenerationally.

Analyzing the development of gender personality, Nancy Chodorow suggests that "daughters are likely to participate in an intergenerational world with their mother, and often with their aunts and grandmother, whereas boys are on their own or participate in a single-generation world of age mates."[59] My analysis of the Japanese case goes against Chodorow's generalization as far as men are concerned; Japanese men are deeply involved in both intergenerational and peer solidarity. Chodorow's proposition holds truer of Japanese women, in that for them intergenerational (mother-child) bonding has primacy over peer solidarity. Furthermore, age-linked solidarity, whether between junior and senior or between peers, is articulated in jobs for men, while for women it is either unrelated to a job or feeds back to maintain separate life-courses for the two sexes, as when a mother devotes herself to her son's education and her daughter's marriage.

Career Recollections and Self-Portrayals of Twelve Businesswomen

As mentioned earlier, women have been running their own businesses, incorporated or not, without necessarily contradicting their gender role. And yet numerically, the number of women in business is only a small fraction of the number of men. In 1982 there were over 500,000 Japanese companies with capital of a million or more yen, of which about 17,500 were headed by women. The percentage of women presidents was 2.4 per cent in 1980 and 3.7 per cent in 1984.[60] These figures include those women who have assumed presidencies as part of their domestic responsibility, as successors to husbands who died, fell ill, or opted to work elsewhere for wages. Women have also established their own enterprises, sometimes joined by their husbands or other family members, as exemplified by Ito's sample.[61] But these tend to be in "female" businesses.

I chose to study a special category of businesswomen who do not fit the traditional type, and who instead received publicity in the news media precisely because of their novelty. These women have either entered male-dominated businesses or launched new enterprises whose character is not yet well known and thus may be regarded as neutral in gender. I assumed these women would personify a confluence of different ideologies and values, of tradition and a new era, of gender dualism and androgyny. The businesswoman operating within Japanese society must accommodate herself to the male-dominated business culture, but at the same time she is likely to identify herself as a leader of women partly because of the publicity she receives as such. She may champion feminism as expected by fellow women, but as an employer she may be more concerned with the functional efficiency of her employees than with justice. Is she more bound by the traditional dictum or more inclined to present a novel self? Where does she stand against the M-curve pattern and age-linked life schedule? It was hoped that the self-portrayals of these businesswomen would serve as a window to the present and future interrelationships between culture, gender, and political economy in Japan.

After consulting several people familiar with Japanese business-women, I contacted 20 company presidents in Tokyo in the special category described above and subsequently interviewed the 12 who responded favorably to my request to do so.[62] The interviewees varied widely in age (ranging from 39 to 75), marital status, education, the kinds of enterprises they had launched, and the number of years they had been president of their companies. (See Table 1 for a synopsis of background information.) All the companies belonged to the category of chūshō-kigyō (medium and smaller enterprises), and they had from 4 to 180 regular employees. The employees of six of the companies were exclusively or predominantly male, the employees of three were exclusively or predominantly female, and the employees of three were relatively balanced between the genders. All the sample companies but one were in service industries; the nature of their businesses is detailed below.

Two summer months in 1985 were spent in interviewing the women presidents and other data gathering. All the interviews took place in company offices, except for one woman, who preferred to meet me in

TABLE 1
Profiles of Twelve Businesswomen

Subject	Age	Education	Marital status now (then)	Child(ren)	Years of presidency	Staff size
A	75 +	C	M(M)	+	15 +	100 +
B	75 −	H	W(M)	+	35 +	40 +
C	70 −	H	D(D)	+	35 +	90 +
D	65 −	H	D(D)	+	25 +	15 − [b]
E	60 +	C	M(M)	+	5 − [a]	20 + [b]
F	55 +	H	S	−	20 − [a]	180 +
G	50 +	JC	M(M)	+	10 −	20 +
H	50 −	U	M(M)	+	10 −	15 + [b]
I	50 −	U	M(M)	+	15 −	5 +
J	45 +	JH	R(D)	0	5 +	5 + [b]
K	45 +	U	D(M)	+	15 +	25 −
L	40 −	U	S	−	10 −	5 − [b]

NOTE: The alphabetically coded subject women are ordered by age. Symbols for education: H = high school; C = prewar women's college; U = postwar university; JH = junior high school; JC = junior college. Symbols for marital status: M = married; S = single; D = divorced; W = widowed; R = remarried. Symbols in parentheses refer to the marital status at the time when the business was launched. In the column "Child(ren)" a plus sign means "has child(ren)," zero means "childless," and a dash means "not applicable."

The numbers for the three columns are given by intervals. For age and presidential tenure, five-year intervals are taken, and the closest numbers are given with plus or minus signs. Age 50 +, for example, means 50–52 years old, and 50 − means 49–48; likewise, 35 + for years of presidency means 35–37 years, and 10 − refers to 9–8. For the number of regular employees also, the interval of 5 is adopted: 20 + means 20–22 employees, and 15 − refers to 14–13.

[a]Cases where the women had years of entrepreneurial experience prior to undertaking the present business. The number refers only to the present business.

[b]Cases where temporary or part-time workers are hired in addition to the regular staff counted here.

her apartment. Some of the women could spare me no more than an hour, but others were more generous than I had asked, meeting with me for up to four hours, for example. I asked open-ended, suggestive, but not explicitly directive, questions about how they had become involved in their business careers and their experience as businesswomen. I tried to get each informant to tell me about herself spontaneously because I wanted to see what each of them would stress.

Communication was possible to the extent that my informants and I tapped the same fund of cultural information, the collective store of symbolically mediated and embodied meanings, values, and rules, to create rapport and understand one another. This fund also guided each of these women, I assume, in recalling and organizing her experience through self-reflection and in presenting herself in conversation with me. In this sense, the interviews were to capture the "culturally reconstructed reality," rather than the phenomenal reality, of the interviewees' careers, loaded with meanings, values, and rules that define, explain, and regulate action and experience.

At the same time, it must be acknowledged that culture, while a collective reservoir of meanings, values, and rules that potentially generates patterned responses from interviewees, also manifests itself only through situationally variable discourses where individual concerns and biases, of both interviewee and interviewer, enter. Furthermore, culture not only constrains the individual in organizing her experience and regulating her action and self-presentation, but also serves her personal ends as symbolic resources to tap, manipulate, and modify in the course of communication.

My professional burden of keeping my informants anonymous is doubled by their conspicuousness to the media, particularly in the area of business. Finding out that financial conditions were a sensitive matter, for example, I stopped asking about them, which left me dependent upon voluntary sharing of information. In the following analysis, only scattered segments of autobiographical narratives appear in context, but lengthy accounts are also given of individual cases when they illustrate an argument. When necessary, individual informants are identified by the letters A to L (see Table 1).

Entrepreneurial Launching and Commitment

All the women had had experience as employees or had been self-employed before undertaking their present businesses. I shall first characterize how they launched their present businesses and became committed. As each informant appears, the kind of enterprise she has launched will be also revealed. Let me begin with some cases.

Mrs. A, a housewife, belonged to a local Christian church, and when an American chaplain sent by the Occupation authorities preached there, she volunteered to interpret for him. She was a graduate of a women's college well known for its English teaching. Her performance was witnessed by a government official, which led to her accepting a government job created in connection with the resumption of Japan's overseas trade. It never occurred to Mrs. A, who was content to be a housewife, that this temporary job would open up a sequence of opportunities and finally lead to her collaborating with American businessmen in establishing an international enterprise. The business specializes in (nongovernmental) inspections of the quality of industrial products to expedite international trade. In the beginning, its clients were almost all Japanese, and orders were for miscellaneous products. But the business has expanded, and it now receives orders from as many as 40 countries. Many clients are foreign governments seeking to import Japanese products. Exporters also use this inspection system to certify their products. The reputation of the company is such that the emblem of its certification is required by many importers around the world. The products to be inspected have also become large-scale, such as an entire oil plant in a

Middle Eastern country, and some inspections take as much as two years to complete.

Although she was a co-founder and vice president of the company, Mrs. A, the only woman on the five-member staff, had to turn her hand to everything originally, including looking after a room heater, making tea, typing, interpreting, and sales. Then, to her great surprise, she was nominated to the presidency of the company to succeed the original American president. The company started as a branch of a firm in the United States, but with her assumption of presidency, it became a Japanese company, while the stockholders remain 100 per cent American. Under her presidency, the company has acquired over 100 employees, most of whom are internationally oriented engineers.[63] Success is apparent from the dazzling presidential office in a modern high-rise building at the business center of downtown Tokyo. Annual sales total one billion yen, actually a modest amount in view of the grand-scale contracts involved.

At the outset, the business was a hand-to-mouth operation, and Mrs. A did not think it would survive long or suspect it would expand so far. She took the job as a temporary one and continued to see it as such until she realized she had been with the company for decades. She is still spellbound by the unanticipated careers of both the company and herself.

In this tale, we are struck by the emphasis Mrs. A puts on *circumstantial forces* that moved her into a career track without her awareness. A subjectively set goal and the determination to pursue it are not part of the launching story. Instead, Mrs. A paints herself as a person who accepted whatever opportunities came by, and she marvels at what has in retrospect emerged as a business career. This style of self-presentation characterizes a majority of the autobiographies in their early phases and reaches an extreme with Mrs. I, who heads a company that produces and imports films and has other film-related business. As a child, Mrs. I loved to live in the world of fantasy created by movies, and upon graduation from university, she found a job at a small film-importing/producing company. She was perfectly happy to be an employee blessed with a variety of challenging experiences, relocating from the business department to the production department. But "every time a new assignment was given, I was placed in a milieu that nurtured and shaped me" toward a business career. "Step by step, I was pushed by natural forces into one opportunity after another. I yielded passively without resistance." Mrs. I cited her "fate" as responsible for her entrepreneurial engagement.

Both Mrs. A and Mrs. I portray themselves as receptors, not explorers, of chance and fate, pushed by circumstances, not by their own wishes or determination. Quite different in outlook from either, and not matching the stereotype of Japanese womanhood, Mrs. K nonetheless joins them in denying initial self-motivation. A successful free-lance journalist and writer, Mrs. K would not have gotten involved with a business career if her husband had not started a sort of stationery store dealing in paper products. Against her wishes, she was "forced" into taking over the entire business to rescue it from near bankruptcy. She transformed the business into her own, based on her novel idea that paper is a means of communication, as exemplified by greeting cards of the Hallmark type, an idea that was yet to hit the market. Her fame as a journalist carried over into the new business, and her name became attached to the products like a quality brand. Mrs. K has succeeded in bringing the business to solvency.

These three cases all play down self as the central agent in launching a new career, consistent with the generally accepted notion of Japanese personhood. No mention was made by any of the three women of a need for achievement, self-fulfillment, or independence. In contrast, American women entrepreneurs have been found to perceive "achievement" and "independence" as the strongest motivations for starting their own companies.[64] Striving for success, assertiveness, goal-orientation, and high energy are also part of the American entrepreneurial profile. American researchers have developed such motivational assumptions into checklists against which a woman may examine her own personality to see if she "fits" an entrepreneurial career.[65] Similar conclusions have been reached on the basis of a sample of British women entrepreneurs: more than half (ranging from 59 per cent to 76 per cent) find their motives in autonomy, achievement, or dissatisfaction with other alternatives.[66] From the Anglo-American point of view, the above sample of Japanese women might not be regarded as entrepreneurs. But I suggest that the two contrasting findings reflect the cultural biases with which career launching is interpreted and communicated, both sides probably exaggerating culturally sanctioned rationales.

The Japanese style of autobiographical presentation sketched above is generally consistent with my previous findings about professional women. Similarly, too, for ordinary women, in their recollections, marriage tends to lack bridal choice and decision, even in the case of "love marriages."[67] What surprises me is that launching an enterprise, which would seem to call for great commitment, is also recalled and presented in such a self-suppressing style. The inconspicuous status accorded to self may characterize both female and male Japanese autobiographies as a matter of cultural style, but the same principle is likely to be more rigidly applicable to women, who need extra justification for launching an unfeminine career to protect themselves from looking selfish.

This does not mean that these women remained uncommitted. As suggested by the above episodes, each woman became the fully committed leader of her company, taking overtime for granted, putting her entire fund of resources into the enterprise, and striving hard for success. Even Mrs. K, who is not sure of the fit between her personality and business career, shows a compulsion to succeed and admits she is having fun running her business. It may be that the woman president, once she sees herself in that role, takes it seriously and exhibits an entrepreneurial drive for achievement and success. Emphasizing the role of circumstances in the recollection of the launching phase in fact highlights subsequent performance and success. I might further postulate that a Japanese woman, trained in role compliance, does not have to be intrinsically motivated to assume a new role such as that of a businesswoman, since an inner fit is likely to develop subsequent to role assumption.[68] Such role commitment, apart from the initial lack of motivation, confirms what was said about the role complex of Japanese culture. It seems that once placed (or caught?) in the role of business leader, the woman's dormant potential awakens and is harnessed toward the realization of her individual self through a business career. Rather than always contradicting it, role assumption can thus trigger individuality.

If strongly motivated at the very beginning, the autobiographer tends to stress *social mission*, instead of self-interest, as the incentive for entrepreneurial engagement. After starting her work career as an "office lady," Miss F subsequently ran a small, one-woman retail dry-goods store, which yielded substantial profit. She then wanted to do something with the money to contribute to society. In collaboration with a senior man, Miss F established a company specializing in computerized information services. Among the services are designing, processing, and storing psychological tests beneficial to society, such as those for safe driving (because she was concerned with the increasing rate of traffic accidents) and for normal child development (because she was worried that young mothers today do not know how to rear children). In the first few years, the business was a continuous loss, surviving only by sacrifice of the president's personal savings and real estate, a condition one could not have tolerated unless driven by something more than self-interest.

Again, the altruistic emphasis is nothing peculiar to businesswomen, but is familiar from the biographies of male business leaders, and male-led companies play up societal, national missions as their mottoes. A nonconformist woman may be under heavier pressure to legitimize her action in altruistic terms, probably to assuage her guilt or to compensate for her "selfish" appearance. Mrs. A, too, expresses satisfaction at knowing that her business has contributed to Japan's postwar success as an exporter.

In the case of Mrs. B, the altruistic theme reflects an unresolved conflict between gender role and business career. She was a housewife until the end of the war, when her husband, a military officer, was arrested and imprisoned as a war criminal. Mrs. B first took a job and then opened a publishing company specializing in labor relations. It was a Christian mission, she explained, that motivated her to set up such a company. Through this business, the former housewife sought to restore harmony and love between labor and management, which were in confrontation with each other in the postwar era. Mrs. B is successful in running the company, which publishes and sponsors lectures and seminars, and she now heads a 40-member staff. At the same time, she insisted while talking to me that a woman's proper place is the home. Yet she could not explain why she continued to work even after it was no longer necessary for her to earn a living. It is quite likely that being trapped in this dilemma intensifies her Christian altruism. (It might be noted that three out of the twelve businesswomen I interviewed are Christian. This overrepresentation in the non-native faith may be suggestive of the cosmopolitan outlook in business, as shown below, characterizing the majority of the sample women.)

A third type of launching tale involves *gender barriers in employment*, which fits the more universal pattern in which starting a business is taken to be the only viable alternative for women blocked out of an employed career. Three cases stand out.

Miss L, a university graduate who had worked as a skilled employee for five years, saw no future in remaining with the company, since she was unable to share the prospect of promotion with her male colleagues. She sounded out friends for other employment, only to be encouraged, instead, to go independent. Even though she could not imagine herself running a company, she opened an office in a one-room apartment with a mere 100,000 yen in capital to launch a technical translation business, utilizing her previous experience. (Japanese manufacturers require technical translation of their service manuals and related documents illustrating their products into the language of importers.) Illustrating her success, her present modern office is located in one of the most expensive hillside areas of Tokyo. In addition to her in-office staff, she employs about 15 free-lance technical translators virtually on a regular basis.

Gender barriers are often imputed to the psychological complex of the male ego. As an employee, Mrs. E could not help reminding her boss of the errors and shortcomings in his decisions, which embarrassed, offended, and infuriated him. She realized she was more fitted to lead others than to be a follower and thus launched a successful multibusiness career. The latest addition, which has made her famous and is of concern to this essay, was to build and run a hotel-like care home for the elderly, comparable to an American luxury nursing home. While our interview was going on in the lobby, a number of old, frail, but apparently wealthy men and women were sitting around and chatting with visitors. The president, who was often distracted from the interview by her staff asking for her instructions, was undoubtedly a central figure in the whole setup.

Psychological confrontation between a male boss and a female subordinate also drove Mrs. G to start her own business in the travel industry. As a young junior-college graduate, she first took what she thought was a temporary job at a local travel agency, and then worked in larger companies. When her expertise came to be recognized, Mrs. G was promoted to a managerial position but found herself still subjected to the prejudice of male colleagues. "This is something inevitable in Japanese culture," she exclaimed. "The most stupid male is said to be equal to the brightest female." Her male colleagues—she was the only female manager—would replace her travel projects with their own or steal credit for a job she had accomplished. "A protruding stake is pounded down, indeed!" Another company invited Mrs. G to become its vice president, an extraordinary move in the male-dominated travel industry, but after bringing her in, the president, a newcomer in the field, behaved as if he would rather do without her, "probably because he was irked that people knew my name better than his." His masculine pride could not stand this humiliation. Mrs. G accordingly decided that "in order to work fully among men, you must be independent" and opened her own travel agency in a condominium.

In all these cases, gender inequality in employment practices in combination with circumstantial inducement compelled women to embark on entrepreneurial careers as the only avenue to get ahead. In other words, the presence of women entrepreneurs is not necessarily an index of women's liberation, but can be a sign precisely of discrimination. It is only natural that resentment was part of the entrepreneurial motivation for these and other women. Mrs. G is most articulate in expressing her indignation about the gender dualism prevailing in the labor market.

As we have proceeded from circumstantial involvement to social mission to gender barriers, assertion of the woman's self in entrepreneurial launching has come to the fore. The fourth and last type refers to the extreme pole of *self-assertion*.

Mrs. H, a law school graduate, found herself a frustrated housewife and irritable *kyōiku-mama*, and above all became impatient with her economic dependence upon her husband, saying to herself, "There is no money whatsoever that I am truly free to spend on my personal needs." Her stress peaked when her husband was diagnosed—actually misdiagnosed as was disclosed later—with cancer. With no hope of finding employment better than dishwashing, a typical middle-aged part-timer's job, Mrs. H set an entrepreneurial goal. Gender barriers in employment thus entered her decision.

Mrs. H tested herself by starting out with a short-lived coffee shop. In the meantime, while shopping around for a residential condominium (the Japanese housewife is responsible, often solely, for making decisions on such purchases), she noticed a big gap in information between salesmen and customers: the male sales staff were insensitive to the needs of female customers, who are *the* managers and buyers of their homes, while the latter were too intimidated to express their thoughts. As an expert housewife, Mrs. H became convinced that she could do a better job selling condos by providing the kind of information wanted by fellow housewives. She began to plan her career in real estate and took examinations to acquire the necessary licenses and desirable credentials. Gender and age barriers continued to block opportunities for Mrs. H, then in her late thirties, in the male-dominated real estate business, until she persuaded a man to accept her on a tentative basis as a temporary member of a previously all-male sales staff. Her employer accepted her proposal to sign a contract to sell condominiums, and this was the beginning of her independence and her successful career as president of a company specializing in housing sales and housing consultation, meeting the demands of both "users" and developers/contractors. She took over the company started by her husband and changed it into a new business, as in the case of Mrs. K, but in her case she was eager to do so. With an impressive record of accomplishments, Mrs. H now leads 16 regular staff members and about 180 part-timers, all women. Mrs. H is exceptional in stressing the need for "independence" as the primary goal, not just a means, of her launching her enterprise.

Although very different from Mrs. H in age, education, and many other aspects of her background, Mrs. C belongs in the same category. Her self-assertive launching of a business of her own deserves to be looked at in some detail. She had been deserted by her husband and was supporting her daughter and herself by buying silk and rayon from producers in a provincial city, having the material worked into embroidered souvenirs in another city, and wholesaling these to stores in resort towns. While on a business trip shortly after the Occupation began, she happened to hear from a fellow passenger on a train that American servicemen were interested in buying souvenirs, and she lost no time in locating the main post exchange catering to U.S. military personnel and their families in Tokyo's Ginza.

"Two MP's were standing in front of the PX building," she recalls. "In those days, we women were told to run away from Americans, but why should I? I did not know what to do, just stood there for an hour, and then went home. On my way home, I said to myself, 'I was not begging for things but for work.' So I went back the next day and found a Japanese employee. I explained why I was there, and this man welcomed me, saying the store had been looking for someone just like me! It was sheer chance or luck that an amateur like me got in so easily."

She was trusted at once, and the PX contracted to supply confiscated silk for her to have made into embroidered goods such as handkerchiefs and scarves. Being an amateur, she had to learn the technical details from the embroiderers, as well as how much profit she should charge. "I did try hard [*doryoku*], and worked seriously [*majime*]." She commuted all on her own between the PX and the manufacturers, carrying on her back a bundle of material and goods wrapped in a *furoshiki* (wrapping cloth symbolic in this context of a person trying to survive under the socially and economically formidable conditions then prevailing). Seeing this one day, a U.S. serviceman offered her a car ride. "All my effort was rewarded," she says. From this beginning, the business went on to produce a wide range of things, including slips and gowns. She now had to learn something about dressmaking herself, and she got a graduate of a dressmaking school to accompany her to lessons from a professional designer.

In the meantime, she was turning a good profit, primarily from leftover pieces of the material supplied by the PX. "To be honest with you, I had great fun making so much money," she says. Her own family joined her in the business (*kazoku-gurumi*), and by the time the Occupation forces left, she had succeeded in building up her credibility (*shin'yō*) and establishing her *jiban* (solid support base). Turning to the domestic market, she opened her own store selling baby clothing and consequently expanded her business to emerge as one of the first few successful women entrepreneurs in postwar Japan. Now she has several factories working for her as subcontractors, with about 800 workers sewing dresses designed by her full-time staff, and sells her products through prominent national department store chains.

Mrs. C tells this success story with no false modesty or hesitancy. She credits her success to her foresight, fearlessness and hard work. She believes her career had its roots in her childhood, explaining, "I was a shrew or tomboy." In talking to me, Mrs. C showed little feminine inhibition in her speech or demeanor. She said she was no different from a man and repeatedly stressed that there is no "male" or "female" in the world of business. For her, transcendence of gender meant a woman becoming manlike, however, which suggests that in her mind self-assertiveness is intrinsic to masculinity. "People say I am like a man," she told me proudly. "They say I talk crisply like a man."

For both Mrs. H and Mrs. C, economic necessity was the primary initial concern. The one sought to achieve financial independence, the other simply to survive. They are both sure that making a profit is the goal of business, and they show no sign of self-effacement or altruism. Underlying this attitude, which is more or less free from cultural and gender constraints, both had good reason to want to go beyond their domestic, wifely identities. Mrs. H got married while she was a university junior and jumped into full-time housewifery without any qualms about wasting her legal training. After years of compulsive homemaking, she came to realize that there was no sense of accomplishment to be gained from the endless cycle of housework—"making and unmaking"—or from the hobbies and studies she had tried. Overcommitment to the domestic role thus seems to have turned into unambivalent alienation from it. Mrs. C had to shed her domestic identity for quite another reason. Her husband left her to live with another woman and without her knowledge removed her name and that of their daughter from the house register by forging the family seal.[69] She quietly waited until after the war, when she sued him for damages and won. The bitter divorce engineered by her husband's betrayal and deception may have contributed to Mrs. C's surmounting her gender identity and ambivalence about self-assertiveness. She is different in this respect from all the other divorced women in this survey, for whom divorce was their own choice. It is interesting to note that marriage was a love match for both Mrs. C and Mrs. H. The latter's marriage in particular was a rebellious one, not blessed by her family, and her compulsive domesticity prior to launching into business may have been a way of justifying her rebellion.

Niches and Resources

Whatever the initial incentives, every entrepreneur, regardless of gender, must find or cut out a niche that matches her resources and expertise. How does womanhood function as a sorter in locating niches? In this section I attempt to identify the niches that my informants found or created and the resources they mobilized to adjust to those niches.

Of the twelve women, all but two found their niches in one aspect or another of *communication service*, centered around information to be searched out, produced, stored, organized, translated, printed, transmitted, or distributed. Included here, as we know from the above accounts, are technical inspection to certify the quality of industrial products for importers and exporters; publication and sponsoring of seminars; computerized data processing and storage; translation of Japa-

nese engineering manuals into foreign languages; and film production
and importation. The travel agency run by Mrs. G may well be understood as a communication service too, as may Mrs. J's marketing research
business, in which she and her staff use "group interviews" to elicit the
needs and demands of potential consumers. The advertising company
headed by Mrs. D is also a communications industry par excellence. The
most articulate about this feature of business is Mrs. K, whose business
is in the production and sales of what she calls "communication goods"
such as greeting cards.

I was told that companies under female management tend to assume
katakana names, usually derived from foreign words or at least giving
that impression. Indeed, eight companies in my sample have *katakana*
names,[70] and one of their presidents volunteered to elaborate on the
meaning of her company's name for my benefit. Six of the eight are
actually connected either directly or indirectly with foreign countries, as
clients, suppliers, or, in the case of international travel, as hosts. In other
words, the communication services typically involve *intercultural mediation* between Japan and foreign companies or governments—American,
European, Middle Eastern, Chinese, Southeast Asian. It is no coincidence that half of my sample informants were trained in foreign languages, either in school or elsewhere. Foreign languages give women
the most powerful resource to compete in the male world, said Miss L,
since "no man can do anything about women's language ability." The
best proof is Mrs. A, who really does not know the technical aspects of
her business and manages her company mainly through her ease in
communicating and negotiating with foreign clients. "In my business I
have never felt handicapped by being female," she says. "Quite the
contrary, as the only woman in the [otherwise] entirely male group, I
have been treated especially well. It may be because a foreign language
is used frequently in talking with our customers."

By mobilizing their linguistic or other communicative skills, these
women found their niches in areas bridging cultural borders. Mrs. A
again represents an extreme: she heads a company not only dependent
upon foreign clients but inherited from an American predecessor and
owned entirely by American shareholders. She credits the ease with
which she has been able to manage the company without being handicapped by her gender to this unusual background. Further, the original
models of this and some of the other businesses, such as marketing
research and greeting cards, came from abroad.

A communications business becomes possible when communication
gaps or "crevices" are perceived. The most alert to such crevices was
Mrs. H, who found her niche in filling communication gaps between
housing consumers and housing developers in the domestic market. She

calls hers an *interstitial industry (sukima sangyō)*. Most of the other women's information businesses are also interstitial and meant to fill gaps between vendor and customer, worker and manager, producer and audience, visitor and host, well-wisher and receiver (through greeting cards). In such businesses, as one of the presidents emphasized, feminine sensitivity is an advantage.

Femininity as a resource is best utilized by the luxury nursing home run by Mrs. E. Assisted by the all-female staff and part-timers, the president herself looks after the residents, providing care for the incapacitated. This is a woman's business, she declares, because no elderly person, male or female, would want to be touched by men, and no man would like to touch the bodies of the aged, male or female.

At first thought, there seems to be nothing in common between communication industries and the nursing business. However, both involve human communication, after all, either with words or by touching. I speculate that one of women's primary niches is in human communication and human relations, where they can be resourceful.

The "female advantage" is recognized by a whole range of women, from a conservative functionalist to an egalitarian feminist, in a sense broader than that proposed by George Murdock and Caterina Provost.[71] Mrs. E represents the functionalist view of the male-female division of role territory and makes a successful business out of this division. Others espouse the feminine contribution in opposition to such stereotypes of gender dualism. "Both male dominance and male-female dichotomy are out of date," Mrs. K says. "The economy, like everything else, is destined to change, and, in the future, feminine sensitivity ought to be learned and shared by men." Mrs. K, who has predicted an upcoming era of women in a book she wrote, is the most eloquent advocate of this feminist ideology. "From now on it is the female perspective that will open up new fields of business, because the male perspective has already been exhausted." The female perspective is symbolized as "soft(ware)" in contrast to male "hard(ware)," or as "heart" as opposed to "thing."

Heart versus thing and soft versus hard may be oversimplified polarities, but this calls attention to a single case in my sample that deals with "things." Mrs. C, as mentioned earlier, designs, manufactures, and sells dresses and appears uniquely masculine in speech and comportment. She characterizes herself as no different from men while at work, not like a woman whose speech is ridden with long-winded honorifics. She makes no apology about making a profit being the most important purpose of business, since "business is not charity work." She stresses that a company president, whether male or female, must always monitor how the business is going, above all by keeping track of "numbers." The measure for success or failure seems unambiguous: "how many pieces have been sold, how many are in stock, and how many returned." In no other case is the measure that clear and simple. Instead, the majority of my informants emphasized the importance of nonpecuniary profit such as trust and reputation, as will be touched upon later.

Styles of Management

This section is divided into external and internal management. Again, some of the remarks below are relevant more to Japanese culture, shared by men as well, and others more to gender, characterizing the female management style.

External management. External management refers to strategies for perceiving, evaluating, and handling the world outside the company, or people other than the company's own personnel. Included here are markets, clients, patrons, suppliers, banks, retailing outlets, business associations, the business community (*gyōkai*), rivals, and the general public. What is most emphasized by all is the benefit of *human relations* to business. A number of informants referred to human relations or networks as capital to draw upon or as profit gained through transactions. Particularly important are relations with corporate clients, but also mentioned were mentors, patrons, former employers, former bosses, and benefactors. These are predominantly male.

Starting from scratch, as most of my informants did, the first customer is all-important; if satisfied with one's work, he or she will in turn introduce a second and third customer, and thus snowballing takes effect. Mrs. I, the film importer and producer, describes her career as a cumulative expansion of her client network through introductions and word of mouth. She attaches importance to every kind of social gathering, and attends several, including a Buddhist class. Even Mrs. E, who is not shy about her native talent, ascribes her success to long, multiple chains of introductions. "Nothing could have started without introductions," she says.

Lacking organized sponsorship, these women built networks of sponsors by their personal sociability. It seems that men are willing personally to sponsor independent businesswomen, whereas within the organized job market they keep job-linked sponsorship to their own sex. This is in contrast to the organized resistance of financial institutions to women entrepreneurs encountered by some of my informants at the earliest stages of their enterprises. Banks have little trust in women, assuming their businesses to be no more than feminine pastimes. Only after a new business succeeds in creating its own market, as in the case of Mrs. K, do banks begin to rethink their male-centered loan policies.

Among my informants there is a tendency for human relationships, once formed, to last a long time. Social credit based upon *relational duration* is idiomatically expressed as "not the kind of people you got acquainted with only yesterday" (*kinō ya kyō no tsukiai ja nai*). Mrs. D, an advertising agent, has been receiving orders from a Mitsubishi company for 30 years. A regular, stable relationship with fixed clients is typical of my sample companies. "I deal with ten companies regularly, which is all I can handle," says Miss L. To ensure relational durability, one must socialize and chat with clients or participate in their social club reunions. In the publishing business, durability may be secured by long-term subscribers. Mrs. B singlehandedly recruited such members through personal solicitation.

The longer the relationship lasts, the more advantage accrues to it, since the person in the client company with whom one has been in personal contact will have risen up the organizational ladder. Older informants in particular refer to "old friends" who now, as executives of big companies, can do favors, and more substantial favors than before, more easily.

More efforts are made to retain and rekindle the customer network by those who are in established male industries, and thus are exposed to fierce competition with male rivals, than by those who are freer from competition because of the novel character of the industry. Among the former are advertising and travel agents. In the travel business, client relations are inevitably short, but Mrs. G tries to overcome this problem by her style of customer management. She goes out of her way to intensify interaction through pre-tour orientation classes, post-tour reunions, and follow-up correspondence, including sending birthday cards according to the computer-retrievable information on the clients' vital statistics. The trip itself involves elaborate interaction between the travel agency staff and travelers, resulting in the latter's complete dependence upon the former throughout. The customer's travel plan is perfected in advance, with an hour-by-hour schedule and instructional information on sites to be visited, all printed in diary form, and around-the-clock service is provided during the trip. All this reminds me of the "around-the-body care" provided by a nurturant wife to her babylike husband in the house.[72] The payoff has been customers returning to Mrs. G repeatedly over the years and bringing her the latest news on planned conferences or similar events requiring travel, whereupon she starts a travel plan before other agents catch on. Mrs. G's customer management exemplifies an extension of service above and beyond the bounds of a business transaction.

In order to create new relations and to maintain old ones, the president must be acceptable as a person, since her personal approach is crucial in a small-scale business. Her attractiveness as a woman counts, as I can infer from the good looks of all twelve informants. More culturally relevant is personally presenting a *low profile*. No informant is consistently self-assertive; even someone like Mrs. C, who is atypically self-assertive and masculine, referred to herself as an "amateur." A low profile was typical of the majority.

Humility and self-denigration are imbedded in the culture of reciprocal obligation (rather than reciprocal right) as represented by *on* (a moral sense of being in debt, which calls for acts of repayment). The history of a business that started with nothing whatsoever is a history of running into many benefactors whose help was indispensable for surviving and getting ahead in the ruthless world of business. A sense of debt and gratitude leads to humility and self-abnegation. Many of my informants look back on their lives in the light of this cultural formula of self-abnegation and gratitude in connection with their debts. The extreme is Mrs. D, who literally started from scratch, not only as a woman but as a postwar repatriate from China and a divorcée. She landed at an advertising company as an employee, which led her into contact with "many" clients who recognized her talent and encouraged her to start her own advertising business. These people offered to sponsor her switching from her employer and taught her how to manage the business. Soon she found herself flooded with orders. Now she runs a company with 14 male employees. Looking back, Mrs. D cites a long list of men, including a former prime minister, whom she calls *onjin* (benefactor) or *onshi* (mentor). Her published autobiography is a record of meeting such benefactors, who have enabled her to launch a career in the advertising business and to achieve a series of successful transactions. Crediting others for her success, Mrs. D denigrates herself and her company with extraordinary humility, calling herself a "fool" and trivializing her company down to "mere snot." If she speaks in that way to an outsider like me, who can be of no benefit to her business, she is likely to belittle herself with even greater hyperbole when speaking to business associates or clients. Humility is often associated with femininity, and some women extend it to female helplessness, especially in business. The helpless woman who "did not know right from left," who was "about to fall apart," evidently stimulated gallantry in the men who were around, even in potential rivals. In this context, too, the female advantage was stressed: thanks to her gender, the woman was able to present herself as helpless and to solicit help and advice from men.

In other words, women, while more constrained than men by the cultural norm of self-denigration, can also turn it to their advantage by using it as a strategy, particularly in transactions with men. My informants were cautious not to hurt the pride of the men they came across and decided that feminine humility and helplessness was the best strategy to boost it. "If a woman tries to do business on an equal footing with men, pretty soon she will be crushed under a hail of kicks and blows. So, I try not to stand in their way, not to be obtrusive. Yes, that's the way I behave. Otherwise I would be ostracized. . . . After all, this is a male society," Mrs. D says. Even Mrs. H, who betrayed no sign of self-abnegation, admitted that a woman, when she offers advice or a suggestion, must appear as if she were soliciting the other's opinion. Otherwise, "he would lose face, being instructed by a mere woman." Under these circumstances, the cultural value of humility is cynically manipulated in one's *omote* (externally presented) behavior, consciously differentiated from one's *ura* (hidden) thinking and feeling. Whether as a source of inhibition or as an object of manipulation, and probably as both, the theme of self-effacement appears central to women's business management, as well as in their launching stories.

The low profile further involves a defensive and passive, instead of aggressive, management style. Avoidance of aggressive strategies was mentioned by many, and this was often attributed psychologically and physiologically to their gender in contrast to male aggression. It was frankly admitted that the male physique and belligerence cannot be matched by women. Miss L, though the youngest, always anticipates the limits of her energy, she says. Mrs. J, a marketing researcher, is convinced that men are better fighters: "They are different in their bone structure. They are accustomed to fighting, born to fight, love games and warfare. I love games too, but need to take breaks to rest." The above finding, however, suggests that behind the physiological explanation lies the cultural preconception of aggression as incompatible with womanhood.

The *defensive strategy* means avoidance not only of getting involved in fierce competition but of taking risk, which counters our image of the "entrepreneur." Risk is avoided because, according to my informants, a woman, unlike a man, cannot afford a single mistake, since she will be unable to bounce back physically or socially, and because a woman president is too concerned with the security of her employees and their families to take risk. Consequently, the woman manager, I was told, instead of having herself recognized through quick, dramatic tactics, resorts to a more inconspicuous, slow tactic of waiting passively for her name to spread by word of mouth.

The aggressive management supposedly typical of men is exemplified by *settai gaikō*, extravagant dinner entertainments for clients, attended by geisha. The reason my informants preclude this familiar strategy from their repertory seems, however, to have little to do with male-female differences in aggressiveness. At a geisha party, there is a conspicuous role division between women and men: women are entertainers and waitresses, men are guests, entertained and waited upon. A woman president would be even more out of place amid this sexually charged dichotomizing than a wife would be.[73] To participate there comfortably, she would have to tailor her presence into the role either of a male client or of a female entertainer. That my informants stay away from such parties is understandable. One exception is Mrs. D, ironically the most self-denigrating woman of all, and her *settai* performance takes an extremely feminine form. Being a teetotaler and having learned to play a *shamisen* as a hobby, Mrs. D escapes coerced drinking by contributing a musical performance! Temporarily, she becomes a geisha.

Mrs. D is a good example of those who play distinctly female roles in managing external relations. One of her extra-business services is to act as a matchmaker for the sons and daughters of her clients and associates. She explains that this is "a small repayment" for the great favors she has received in business. "I cut down on sleep to work hard at something that has nothing to do with my business. Sometimes I think I'm stupid, but then I decide that this is a proper way to repay my debts, and that if I didn't do this, I would be unable to reach a nice place after death," she says. But although she cites moral obligation and religious sentiment as her motives in providing this extra-business service, it is easy to suppose that it pays off in business since, as she tells me, many renowned families in business and government have been among her marriage clients.

Avoidance of outward aggression is accompanied by a stress on inward discipline or *sincerity* as a clue to recognition and success. "Nothing is impossible," says Mrs. A from her personal experience, "if one tries hard enough with sincerity." Many informants share the optimistic conviction that one's sincerity in doing one's best will win over the toughest adversary. Sincerity is at the heart of the Japanese ideal self shared by both women and men, and yet it is often discussed as an inner strength compensating for outer weakness, such as the lack of aggressiveness presumed to be characteristic of women.

Internal management. Turning to internal management styles, we see the woman as an employer and boss, which is naturally quite different from our image of a woman as a job hunter, frustrated employee, or contract negotiator subject to male dominance and prejudice. Let us consider the criteria used by the informants for employee recruitment and reward. All the informants agree that ability is the most important consideration in hiring, and record of performance most important in determining pay increases and promotion, but not all of them adhere exclusively to *ability/performance*, several conceding to the seniority rule to some extent. The concession is explained either positively as an encouragement of companywide organizational identification and solidarity or negatively as acquiescence in the prevalent convention of Japan or as humane obligation. But all subscribe to the principle of ability and performance as a matter of *honne* or *tatemae*, and a majority practice it.

The primacy of economic considerations implied in this aspect of internal management may reflect the size of the enterprises more than anything else. Like most *chūshō-kigyō* (medium-to-small-size enterprises), including both female- and male-headed companies, the sample companies hire experienced/skilled workers when need arises, instead of hiring inexperienced college graduates at the standard hiring time. They simply cannot afford to train new employees. They can only employ "troops ready to fight" (*soku senryoku*). For the same reason, many rely on part-timers and external pools of skilled labor, including free-lancers employed on a contractual basis, thus minimizing regular internal staff. (It should be noted, however, that such contractual arrangements tend to be regular, fixed, and stable. Miss L hires the same external translators to work at home and consistently pairs each translator with a particular client to take advantage of his/her familiarity with the company's products and styles.)

Decisions on wages, bonuses, and promotion are made singlehandedly by the presidents, a clear indication that none of the companies has a union and that the owner-president has the financial basis for such autocracy.

Internal management further involves *gender issues*. All of my informants believe in gender equality, but only in the sense that competence and contribution are what count, regardless of gender. They are strongly opposed to legal protection for women in hiring practices. The newly introduced Equal Employment Opportunity Law (EEOL) referred to earlier was blasted by one informant as "disastrous to the Japanese economy." Another remarked, "All right! If you want equality, let it be equal in everything. Don't be ridiculous, demanding privileges and equality at once. Don't be spoiled." She dismissed the new law as relevant only to public institutions.[74]

"Spoiled" is my translation of being in a state of *amae*. This word was frequently used by several informants to characterize women employees. "What infuriates me most is a woman's *amae*," said one, a radical egalitarian who believes that there should be no division of labor by gender and that men should be free to be house husbands. Her severity in criticizing female employees comes precisely from her conviction of the need for equality. Less severe informants predicted with sympathy that the EEOL would be harder on women than on men. It was also felt that female workers were being overpaid, doing injustice to much more deserving male workers. My informants thus enunciate nonprotectionist egalitarianism, which joins with economic realism from the point of view of an employer. They are open and guilt-free in demanding this version of equality because they are aware of themselves as models ("I tell my women workers to 'look at me as a good example' ") whose achievements have resulted entirely from personal competence, performance, and effort.

As sex-neutral criteria, competence and performance, coupled with the immediate needs of the company, seem to end up revealing rather than burying gender differences and gender-bound assets or liabilities. This is reflected in the gender distribution of employees for the sample companies: six companies are exclusively or predominantly male, three are exclusively or predominantly female, and three have relatively balanced gender distributions. Nine out of the twelve are extremely skewed in favor of one sex, and the male bias is twice the female bias. Such sex-biased distributions were justified by my informants in terms of role fitness (*tekisei*). Further, the allocation of positions and tasks is equally skewed. One company employs 180 people, only 3 of whom are female; they are high-school graduates hired to serve and do simple clerical work—typical OLs.

Another company, with more than a dozen male staff members, recently dismissed its only female employee. "The OL has been replaced by OA [office automation]," said its president, meaning that "from now on men must do everything, including tea serving and toilet cleaning." When I visited her office for a second interview, a young man brought me a cup of tea. The discharged OL, the worst ever hired, "would not bother to pick up litter" lying around in the office, and when the president picked it up, the girl "did not even apologize." Earlier, the president had had better luck with women employees, but "they all quit to marry, and I myself arranged marriages for them." And "girls do not hesitate to move to any company that offers a penny more." The informant went as far as to say that she would welcome a woman determined to stay and aggressive enough to "hijack" the company.

Except for companies that are exclusively or predominantly female, administrative positions are nearly monopolized by men. Several presidents expressed their wish to hire more women and to promote more women and regretted that they could not afford to. One company makes no sex discrimination in its hiring policy and, in advertising job vacancies, does not indicate sex preference. Yet its employees are predominantly male, because "no woman has applied for an engineering job."

Although they impose rather severe standards in terms of ability, the women presidents resemble other Japanese managers in likening a company to a family. Idiomatic expressions like "eating together from the same rice cooker" were used by more than one informant. This particular expression, by the way, is not always figurative: in some cases workers do stay overnight at the office to meet a deadline and cook and eat there, as in the case of the film-producing company. Sharing the same cooker is always the case with Mrs. E, who runs the care-home hotel. She referred to herself and her employees as being "ready to die together [*shinaba morotomo*]."

Familylike management was identified as the Japanese style of management being learned by foreigners. "In my company, too," said Mrs. A, "I have a couple of foreign visitors studying the Japanese style of management. They are so eager to learn things Japanese and are becoming more Japanese than the Japanese."

The family image makes the woman president symbolic of *maternal nurturance*. This is best represented by Mrs. A, the oldest of the twelve, who sees a parallel between being the president of a company and the mother of a family. She feels she has been raising the company the same way she raised her children. Her maternal concern for her employees is evident in the pride she takes in being the first to detect signs of illness in them and advise them to rest or, "as a surrogate parent, take them to the company hospital. It is necessary to ensure that employees stick with you not only during a boom but in a slump as well," she observes. Such relationships can be built up only with a motherly approach.

Mrs. A handled a labor dispute in motherly fashion and managed the union toward voluntary disbandment. As she recalls, the company, then under U.S. management, faced the threat of strike, but the American president refused to meet the union leaders, as the latter demanded, without being accompanied by a lawyer. Mrs. A, then vice president, volunteered to substitute for him and met with a union leader by herself. Her sympathetic attempt at persuasion was successful, and the union gave up on striking and gradually dissolved itself. "In the family, the children, when grown up, begin to disagree with their parents. So do the employees. Conflict would only be aggravated if handled in a stiff confrontation."

For Mrs. A, mothering goes with sincerity in managing company crises. She was not afraid to meet with a union leader all by herself "because nobody would beat up someone who holds no hostility," she explains. "Facing him with whole-hearted sincerity [*seishin seii butsukaru*] was a breakthrough."

Naturally, older informants accept and play the role of mother more readily than younger women. (Two older women fed me during their interviews with their own cooking.) The feeling of maternal love for employees was expressed as *kawaii* (cute, lovable). Even young presidents admit they are expected to be maternal whether they like it or not. Female employees in particular, I was told, want the assurance of maternal support to heal the emotional injuries they suffer in the workplace from time to time.

Maternal nurturance is said to have nothing to do with the gender of the manager. In Japan, both male and female presidents are expected to assume a maternal, not paternal, role, according to my informants. If so, the label *paternalism*, commonly used to characterize Japanese management, should be replaced by *maternalism*. Both sexes thus seem to share what Hayao Kawai calls the "maternal principle."[75]

Paradoxically, Mrs. H, the former frustrated, compulsive housewife and mother, is again exceptional in that she does not see any sign of "maternal instinct" in herself. Maternal care for employees, in her opinion, is nothing but meddling. "I think the employer's interest is different from the employee's," she says.

All the informants, including Mrs. H, try to "teach" their subordinates the "know-how" of their business. For a relatively larger enterprise like that of Mrs. C, staff education includes management. Mrs. C wants to promote a woman to departmental chief, a position now monopolized by male staff, but not until the female managerial candidate learns to delegate some tasks to her subordinates instead of trying to do everything herself.[76] Again, our entrepreneurial women seem to follow the Japanese convention that expects a superior (*jōshi*) to assume a parental role to "bring up" his/her subordinates (*buka o sodateru*). In this respect, far from handicapping it, their gender facilitates a leadership role.

Sexual involvement between a female employer and a male employee, not uncommon in the United States, did not appear in my informants' conversations, except that two older women alluded to mild forms of erotic fantasy. One referred to a company dinner party where, because of her sex, her presence aroused excitement among the male staff in a way that a male president's would not have done. The other woman mentioned some men on the staff wanting to have affairs with her. Both women, however, appeared to take such fantasies as amusing and to handle them with motherly indulgence. I am tempted to speculate that maternal nurturance is a culturally available defense against sexual vulnerability on the part of both employer and employee. By taking a maternal role for herself and placing male subordinates into a filial position, the woman president can symbolically structure an otherwise unstructured, unpredictable sexual relationship. There are indications that maternal symbolism is a way of transcending sexuality and the gender issue itself. Mrs. C, whose demeanor is most masculine, is also maternal toward her subordinates and is confident that she can tell them anything she wants in order to discipline them "as long as you love them [*aijō ga areba*]." Needless to say, the "love" here is maternal, nothing sexual.

Internal management further involves the problem of *authority*. The president's authority derives from her exclusive power to hire and fire personnel and to determine wages and promotion; her privileged access to clients, banks, and senior leaders in the business world (this explains why human relations are cherished as property); and, in most cases, her ownership of capital. In addition, the novelty and scarcity of female presidents tempts the media to feature them in such a way that their individual personalities overshadow the organizational aspects of a company. Moreover, some of my informants are the authors of autobiographical or business-related books, which adds to the impression of an autocracy.

A closer look reveals another aspect of presidential authority held by a woman. Maternal nurturance often comes close to indulgence and leniency at the expense of managerial authority. Some female presidents find it difficult to assert their authority and to exercise leadership vis-à-vis male employees. The general strategy seems to be to not interfere with technical work. Responding to my question about what it was like to work under a woman president, a staff member of Mrs. B's publishing company said that, under Mrs. B, the staff are free to exercise their own creativity and to enjoy a sense of full participation. Mrs. B, on the other hand, confesses that she cannot assert her authority and is unable to give orders. As a result, she tends to perform tasks that should be delegated to the staff, including janitorial work. In the same vein, Mrs. G feels unable to demand that her employees put up with hardship unless she burdens herself with greater hardship. "There is absolutely no intention on my part to let them work hard and to exploit them. This, I think, is the weakness or strength of a woman entrepreneur who has lived in Japanese society." She wishes to free herself from this culturally ingrained gender bind.

Both age and education make a difference in assuming authority, but the latter seems more important: an old high-school graduate has more difficulty than a young college graduate in managing college-graduated men. Men are more difficult to handle than women. Egalitarian ideology is another variable interfering with the authoritative role. Mrs. K, well-educated and confident of the business as her own creation, found herself unable to refer to her employees, in speaking to an outsider, without the honorific *san* as demanded by Japanese speech convention, to express humility about her own employees. It took a long time before she began to use the *yobisute* (unhonorific) form. Underlying this is her general guilt associated with the hierarchy. She felt guilty, for example, about receiving a higher salary than her subordinates. Mrs. K attributes all this to her liberal, egalitarian ideology, which her friends claim disqualifies her as a top executive. From my observations, I think this egalitarian attitude is more characteristic of female than male leaders.

Maternal leniency is one way of managing the authority problem, as suggested by the self-portrayal of Mrs. D, who transmutes authority into joking relations. "You dumb fool [*bakatare*]!" or "drop dead!" she yells at her male staff. "Nobody takes me seriously, everybody makes a fool of me [*nameru*]," she added, again jokingly, in telling me this. The word *nameru* implies a total lack of respect and even a reversed hierarchy between employer and employee, but she really meant *amaeru*, as revealed by my questioning. This blurring of *amaeru* into *nameru* reveals that the desire for maternal indulgence may contain an element of disdain. Evidently, the staff enjoy this state of affairs. This can be inferred from the staff's reaction when Mrs. D had fallen ill, could not hope for a quick recovery, and invited in an acting male president with the intention of having him replace her eventually as formally titled president. The new administration "terrified" the staff, resulting in their joint resignation. Mrs. D had to return.

What has been said in this section seems to contradict my earlier remark about the authoritative role, once assumed, overshadowing the gender of its player. I had in mind the women in large bureaucratic organizations, typically government officials. Apparently, these women are protected from gender stigma by the rigid bureaucratic structure. Lacking an organizational wall of protection, our businesswomen may be more exposed to the uninhibited prejudice or forcefulness of men.

Managerial success depends upon the caliber of the second in command. Unless the staff is exclusively female, the vice president is usually male, and this reversed gender hierarchy may give rise to psychological tensions. Miss F, for example, is teamed with an older man who is more experienced than she is in the business. It was this male vice president who received me first and took me into an inner room where the president was waiting. They sat side by side in front of me, which made me ill at ease, unsure of whom to address my questions to. As I feared, the vice president kept talking, as if he were a Samoan "talking chief." Finally, running out of patience, the president interrupted to ask me if I was getting the kind of information I was looking for. This gave me an opportunity to emphasize my purpose of studying women presidents, which forced him into silence. The president, a smart woman, is well aware that she is heavily dependent on him to run her high-technology enterprise and generously acknowledges her debt to him in speaking to interviewers and writing for magazines. Talking to me, she credited their successful teamwork, devoid of the conflicts likely to occur under such a reversed hierarchy (the president is not only a woman but much younger than the male vice president), to the vice president's good character. Nevertheless, she appeared silently to resent his overplaying of the leadership role. This was my conjecture based on her behavior in reaction to the vice president's lengthy exposition: she betrayed irritation and impatience by yawning, looking outside, or leaning backward.

The situation looked like a functionally complementary but uneasy duocephaly. Interestingly, the vice president characterized his role as that of a wife, but this does not mean that his role is secondary, any more than a housewife is secondary as a household manager. The vice president meant that his role was formally secondary but operationally primary. In another analogy, he likened the president to the central actor on stage and said that when she succeeds in capturing the attention and admiration of the audience, he flatters himself that he has performed his role well. Quite clearly he considers himself the producer of the play. Another figure of speech he used places the president at the center of an unfolded fan, surrounded by her staff, and equates himself with the rivet of the fan. The generous use of such metaphors is indicative of the difficulties involved in duocephaly.

Duocephaly is part of the cultural idiom of Japanese politics, and the separation and complementarity between a symbolic, center-stage authority figure and an actual, backstage power wielder has been all too familiar throughout Japanese political history. Nor is the female-male duocephaly alien to Japanese tradition. What makes the above case different from the traditional model is the lack of a hereditary status that would unequivocally legitimize the woman's (e.g., the empress's) symbolic but supreme authority.

In two other cases what seemed to have been a duocephaly in retrospect resulted in the "right-hand man" attempting to take over the enterprise. The president of one of the two companies decided that having two company heads was unhealthy. Instead of reclaiming unicephalous authority for herself, Mrs. B withdrew into the role of a helper to the vice president. "A typical woman," she called herself. She was actually trying to practice within her company what she believed a woman should be doing, that is, provide *naijo* (backstage assistance), which means wifely support without implying wifely dominance. Here the wifely role is reversed from the previous case—an exemplar of the multiple, mutually contradictory meanings of culture-loaded terms like *wifeliness*. Giving up her presidential authority, Mrs. B refrained even from talking to her employees "for fear of interfering with the authority of the vice president," who was virtually the top executive. The employees, too, "would not dare to step into the president's office lest the vice president punish them." The vice president apparently took advantage of the president's trust to rally his faction in an attempt to oust her and "hijack" the company. Fortunately for the president, this attempted coup d'état met resistance internally and wound up with the exit of the usurper and his underlings. They tried, said the president, to set up their own company, stealing her ideas and projects, but failed. She became convinced through this incident that her business owed its success to her reputation and the social capital she has accumulated over the years.

The other case is not so poignant, but also involved an attempted "hijacking" by the vice president. As the president observes: "For a man it must be very difficult to be second to woman." The only way for a male vice president to sustain his ego under a female president was to reduce her to an ornament for outward display while he took over the real power internally. "That gives a man an excuse for working under a woman without losing his male pride," she explained. To leave the internal affairs to such a vice president was truly a mistake, she admitted.

It is obvious from the foregoing that the conventional gender hierarchy interferes with the authority of a woman president. The temptation, then, would be to hire women only, and some informants do so because women are easier to manage. Nonetheless, the gender distribution of employees in these twelve firms indicates a bias for men over women. This asymmetry is mainly because of the companies' needs for certain skills, such as engineering, supplied by men only. Nevertheless, that is not the whole rationale. I was told over and again that, despite the hierarchical problems, men are less troublesome.

If intersexual relationships are problematical, so are those between members of the same sex. Women employees are regarded by women employers as more emotional and irrational, more *amae*-prone, less businesslike. The employer must refrain from using harsh words in criticizing a woman for fear of "rain" (tears), while she has no such worry in scolding male employees.[77] Mrs. J, the president of an all-female company, confirmed this stereotype and illustrated it with the case of another company she knew. In that company, also exclusively female-staffed, the women support themselves by regularly praising one another.

Involved here is the problem of gender-related *sensitivity*. Obviously, women are just as sensitive as men, but the two sexes seem different in type of sensitivity. Male sensitivity seems focused on the ego or face to be sustained in the hierarchical order, whereas female sensitivity lies in unstructured interpersonal relationships. To borrow Victor Turner's typology, men's sensitivity may be more "structural" and women's more "liminal."[78] Another problem with women that was mentioned by several of the presidents supports this hypothetical contrast. A woman employee tends to admire and like her employer (in fact she may have applied for a job because she is a fan of the president), orients her work to the president's approval, is overly concerned with what the president thinks of her, and wants a dyadic intimacy with the president. "She is always looking up to me"; "women try to relate themselves directly to me, unable to see the organization as a whole." Thus, the presidents tend to be overloaded by the personal expectations of women employees, which are bound to be disappointed.

Domestic management. Finally, what concerns businesswomen much more than businessmen is the domestic realm. The following is an attempt to shed light on how a woman's entrepreneurial career tangles with her domestic career. The main issue here is how a woman can start and maintain a double career, an issue that brings to light the age-linked life schedule and condensed timing.

It is significant that of the twelve women, four were divorced either before or soon after they launched their enterprises; only one remarried, which she did much later. My sample also includes two women who have remained single. Half of the sample thus do not fit the stereotype of woman as wife and mother.[79] Husbandlessness impels a woman toward a nondomestic career for two different reasons: the need to make her own living and the freedom to pursue her own career. The former applied, at least initially, to the two pre-career divorcées with children to support. The latter motive, the desire for freedom, is most clearly embodied by Mrs. K. When she became fully committed to managing her business, she found herself running out of time and energy to maintain a smiling face as a good wife. She stunned her husband by proposing divorce. The woman who remarried—the only such case so far—does not live with her second husband: hers is a weekend commuter marriage. One of the single women said she has no desire to marry at the expense of the freedom she is enjoying now.

All this confirms my general view that a husband inhibits a woman's aspiration for or commitment to a nondomestic career, whether because of the economic security he provides or the domestic burden he imposes. The only exception to this pattern is Mrs. J, whose first husband, upon seeing her launch into business, lost his own motivation to work and began to indulge in gambling and womanizing. She divorced him and thereafter worked harder to start a new life. Domestic conflict triggered by the wife's launching of an enterprise may thus involve the husband slipping out of his spousal role, but this is atypical, since the average Japanese husband considers it his *ikigai* (life purpose) to be the sole economic pillar of the household (*daikoku-bashira*) in support of his wife and children (*saishi o yashinau*). Not being tied to a husband makes a woman free to build up cross-gender alliances and networks in business. Indeed, extensive and enduring networks were highlighted more in the autobiographies of the divorced, single, and widowed.

If we are to generalize that a nondomestic career tends to be incompatible with full-fledged marriage, then we must explain why other women have had double careers. Five of the six women in this category have had a career mutation, so to speak. Around mid-life, after having been full-time wives and mothers for years, they embarked on their entrepreneurial careers for the reasons discussed above. Invariably, they are proud of having spent enough time in rearing their children, and some are critical of today's young women who neglect their home duties and simply want to go out. "So, I tell young women to marry in their twenties, raise children, and thereafter be independent," says Mrs. E, a 61-year-old woman who has been in business since age 35. She terminated full-time wife/motherhood and began a business career when the younger of her two sons became a first grader. Another woman, Mrs. I, at 48, recalled quitting her job when she was in the last trimester of pregnancy and enjoying full-time motherhood before returning to work and eventually starting her own business in a related field. This case confirms the generally shared desire for the M-curve career pattern. All these cases of late launching or career interruption suggest that marriage is inseparably tied with child-rearing. All the late starters mentioned their children, not their husbands, as the reason for their mid-life careers. It is the flexibility of an entrepreneurial career that has enabled our informants to alternate two careers, domestic and extradomestic, in avoidance of role congestion.

Late starting and interruption are strategies to minimize the pressures of condensed timing by spreading the career role and domestic role over the life cycle. But this is not a solution for a divorcée with small children to support, as was the case with Mrs. C and Mrs. D. Likewise, the above option was not available to a woman who chose to start young and pursue a continuous career while married and having children, as with Mrs. G. It was the woman's natal kin who rescued her from the condensed schedule. Most important is the contribution of her female kin as surrogate home manager and mother. Mrs. C could not have had a continuous, full-time business career if her mother and sister had not looked after her daughter. "When my daughter needed intimate love, my mother, sister, and brother were there to keep her company," she says. "I haven't worried a bit about my family. You can't work this way while running a home." Her sister substituted for her at PTA meetings at her daughter's school, which she has never visited. Having been thus assisted early in her career by her mother and sister, Mrs. C is still a free businesswoman. Now she leaves all domestic responsibility to her married daughter, a skilled cook.

A similar course was followed by Mrs. D, another divorced woman with a daughter. "[My mother] stayed with me throughout for the sake of my daughter, even though she had three sons [with one of whom she should have lived according to the old Japanese norm]. My daughter grew up entirely under her care." When the daughter was going to marry, Mrs. D learned later, the parents of her husband-to-be were convinced by a detective's investigation that their future daughter-in-law was acceptable because she had been brought up by her grandmother, an admirable woman. Now the married daughter keeps house for her mother.

Mrs. G, the only married woman whose career began early and has been continuous, also benefited from her mother's presence. Upon giving birth, Mrs. G brought her mother, then separated from her father, to her house. "My mother took entire responsibility for caring for all the children, and for me and my husband. It was as if she had had so many children."

These cases confirm my earlier finding that many of the career women in elite professions had their mothers as surrogate or at least supplementary homemakers and child-rearers, allowing them to devote all their time and energy to their careers.[80] Probably, this is where culture enters to a large extent, as best illustrated by the American situation.

Among middle-class Americans, according to Katherine Newman, the autonomy of the nuclear family is so sacred that it is understood that a woman, upon marriage, will be cared for by her husband, precluding her continued dependence upon her parents. Symbolically, one cannot be both a daughter and wife at once. This creates a serious problem for a divorced woman. If she is young enough to have active parents, she may be able to retrieve her daughter identity and receive help from them, as frequently occurs in the contemporary United States. Yet the retrieval cannot be complete. As a once-married adult, the daughter maintains her autonomy, and support from her parents tends to be limited to financial or material aid. The incongruity in this situation seems somewhat mitigated by the presence of grandchildren. As Newman points out, grandparents may "exercise a culturally defined role as giftgivers to grandchildren without offending their daughters' sense of autonomy."[81]

By contrast in the Japanese case, the woman's supporting relative lives with her and assumes overall responsibility for home management as well as child-rearing. The cultural resource underlying this accommodation is a role complex expediting role surrogacy, in addition to the legacy of the extended family system.

The contrast may be an exaggeration.[82] Both the American ideal of nuclear-family autonomy and the Japanese extended family may well be dismissed as myths. Indeed, the former is becoming outmoded by the dramatic increase in single-parent families in the United States, whereas the latter is being replaced by the nuclear family as a normative pattern in Japan. Nevertheless, the American cult of each generation's independence embedded in the nuclear family scheme is likely to live on, causing an American divorcée to feel more hesitant about "dumping" her children upon her parents, or guilty if she does. Her Japanese counterpart, on the other hand, backed up by recapture of the old culture of intergenerational co-residence, may have much less resistance to throwing herself and her children into total dependence upon her kin. The difference is even greater, I think, when the working woman is still married, as in the case of Mrs. G, and the whole family, including the husband, comes under the care of her natal kin. It is more difficult to imagine an American family living in such arrangement.

Dependence is reciprocal. The businesswomen thus helped by their kinswomen as surrogate housewives in turn financially support them. In this sense, the full-time businesswoman replicates the role of the husband as a breadwinner interdependent with the wife as a homemaker, and thus establishes her career within the framework of functional complementarity. The only difference here is that the reciprocal exchange takes place between women, usually mother and daughter, rather than between husband and wife or man and woman. One might detect a duplication of injustice perpetrated against the surrogate housewife subjected to female chores. However, the asymmetry inherent in such division of labor may be reversed when the debtor has retired from her career by her looking after her aged, perhaps bedridden, mother, just as the latter had cared for her grandchildren.

The above pattern involving businesswomen's natal kin, particularly mothers, as surrogate housewives is predominant. But the woman's inlaws, her mother-in-law first and later her daughter-in-law, are not totally resistant to such collaboration. When a supporting kinswoman was unavailable, as in the case of Mrs. K, a live-in baby-sitter was hired. Child-rearing and homemaking is an around-the-clock job, so as the nuclear family becomes the dominant pattern, making relatives unavailable as surrogate mothers, working women have no alternative but to rely upon extrafamilial surrogates like day-care centers.

What is truly new is the husband's cooperation. The husbands of the younger informants do assist in housework or at least acquiesce in their wives' neglect or absence. When Mrs. I's business is at a peak season, she stays at her office for several days and nights, and the telephone is the only way for the couple to communicate. Mrs. H claims to have gradually succeeded in reeducating her husband, so that he has begun to do what he never did before, such as washing rice, making *miso* soup, and doing laundry.

The point here is that no "independent" businesswoman is truly independent, any more than an independent businessman. While enjoying the flexibility of being self-employed, both businessmen and women are assisted, supported, or "sponsored" by domestic collaborators, kin or non-kin. Freedom and equality are bought, in other words, by engaging in functional complementarity in a broad sense.

If a woman wants both a marital and an occupational career, she must manage her husband's mental and physical well-being, especially to protect his ego. Older women who were also late starters tend in particular to display their respect for their husbands. One informant called attention during her interview to the fact that she had never sacrificed her family for her career, that it was inconceivable for her to burden her husband with house chores. Her husband is a retired professor, studying at home.

Mrs. B, a widow, remains a firm believer, as described earlier, in the sexual division of labor, with the husband as the provider and the wife staying home and rearing children. Her emphasis upon Christian missions as her motive for staying in business may be compensation for the discrepancy between what she does and what she preaches.

In both cases, the traditional male-female distinction is played up. Whether this outlook comes from the women's convictions or has emerged as a necessary strategy to protect the male egos of their husbands is not certain. In an earlier study, I found that some professional women, more than housewives, exhibited compulsive domesticity, if only in talking.[83] Mrs. E presents a special case of rhetoric in traditional terms to legitimize the apparently incongruous relationship between herself and her husband. There is not much evidence of spousal respect on her part. In fact, she commented that her husband stays home and does nothing all day long, while she herself works as the top manager of the care-home hotel from morning till midnight without resting. Nevertheless, her husband is far from having fallen from the exalted status of a Japanese male: she describes him as a typical lord, *tonosama*, sitting still as a symbol of authority, leaving the real job of exercising it to his vassals. Mrs. E puts herself within the pre-Tokugawa feudal tradition of Japan, where, she claims, the lady, not the lord, actually governed the domain. (It may be noted here that the rhetoric of duocephaly is mobilized to justify as well as to disclaim female power under a gender-reversed hierarchy.) Before the Tokugawa period, "the wife was president, so to speak, and the husband was more like a vice president. It was the lady who had real ability. Men were busy fighting on battlefields, leaving the government and financial management to their wives. . . . Japanese women were smart indeed." In historical discussion, Mrs. E jumped back to the prehistoric age when matriarchy supposedly existed (obviously she was parroting the widely accepted belief that ancient Japan was a matriarchy).

Mrs. E thus devoted her limited interview time to Japan's history, which first disappointed me but then led me to conclude that she was trying to justify the status reversal in her marriage by projecting herself into the role of the first lady of a domain. Moreover, it turned out that her husband was indeed descended from a domain lord (daimyo). Here, invoking an age-old "tradition" characterized as "matriarchal" legitimized the woman's new role as an entrepreneur and provider.

Finally, my informants would like their sons to succeed them in the business as much as male presidents would. Of the five owner-presidents with sons, two already have their university-educated sons on the staff and hope the sons will eventually take over the presidency. Two others are still too young to think about their successors, and the last one, Mrs. E, has nominated her son's wife as successor because her business requires a female leader. Those who have only daughters rule out the idea of filial succession, but Mrs. C hopes her son-in-law will take over the company soon so that she can retire.

In no case is a daughter a successor-nominee. This suggests that the woman president reverts to the cultural rule of patrilineality despite herself, that she feels her married daughter irretrievably lost to another "house," headed by her husband (a daughter-in-law is different in this regard). Daughters, when discussed, appear as domestic managers and assistants, which the mothers find essential to their pursuit of business careers. Whether or not this is a sign that the career-woman mother tends to be a counter-model for her daughter is unclear. But my limited sample suggests that gender dichotomy is intergenerationally more reinforced than superseded.

It is not that succession by a son or son-in-law is a smooth one. Mrs. B could not hold out her son to her staff as her successor and even discriminated against him in the company. "'You, mama, would listen to the vice president only, not to me,' my son used to say. We Japanese tend to belittle our own kin. I am typically Japanese." She was actually a typical Japanese woman in being inhibited about openly asserting her son's privilege as heir to her career. On the other hand, a son may be overly self-assertive and more interested in innovating or totally changing than perpetuating the company his mother founded, if only to prove his autonomy. Educated at an American university, Mrs. G's son is not particularly interested in the travel industry but wants to start a new business, something like an international information service. Although on the payroll of his mother's company, he engages in business transactions with small firms in the United States and Japan, supplying information on each other's business practices. While he was discussing

his ambitious dream of "expanding the horizon of informational anten-
nae" far beyond the travel business, his mother, somewhat worried,
interrupted to say that such business is compatible with the travel
industry. The son wishes to make a lot of money and to renovate the
office with plush furniture in accordance with the American idea of a
"corporate image" so that workers will be proud of working there. The
mother warns him against "a phony image." She does so gently and
indulgently, far from challenging her son. In both cases it is clear that
the mothers are proud of and reliant on their sons.

Even though the business is established by a woman, it becomes a
family business, as observed by Ito in regard to her sample of women
entrepreneurs,[84] when it is joined by a male member of her family. In
none of my cases did the husband join his wife's business (whereas in
two cases, the wife took over her husband's company and transformed
it). Sons are another matter, and, although mother-to-son succession is
not unproblematical, as seen above, the intergenerational link (including
mother-in-law and son-in-law or daughter-in-law) may be more crucial
to stabilize a woman's enterprise as a family business. To what extent
such intergenerational stabilization *must* join hands with a perpetuation
of the gender dichotomy remains to be further studied.

Conclusion

The oral autobiographies of these twelve businesswomen confirm,
reinforce, replicate, or otherwise reflect the gendered dual economy in
many different ways. All the companies led by these women are small,
and most are family-owned. At one phase or another of their careers, all
the women were victimized by institutional gender barriers and disadvantages. We have seen how career-minded women found themselves
discriminated against prior to launching their own enterprises. Some
mentioned the difficulty, by virtue of their gender, of getting bank loans
at the initial stage of their enterprises. At a sociopsychological level,
there were pressures for women entrepreneurs to present themselves in
low profile in transactions with businessmen. Authority is another issue
stemming from gender inequality. We have seen cases where the woman
president was unable to assert or exercise her authority over her staff in
a straightforward manner, extreme cases where a duocephalous structure emerged and "hijacking" of the company was attempted by a "right-
hand man," and so on.

Gender handicaps such as the above are likely to be magnified by
cultural inhibitions in self-presentation. Women, more than men, must
be on guard against "sticking out" and appearing selfish (*wagamama*),
and therefore may be compelled to suppress their "selves" in shaping,

reconstructing, and presenting their careers. It is quite conceivable that this kind of cultural program steered many women to stress circumstantial pressures or altruistic missions in their stories. In Japan "individuality" is cherished but "individualism," even today, is not.[85] Dovetailed with self-inhibition is the role complex that allows self-expression within role bounds. Small wonder that initially unmotivated women soon became firmly committed to their entrepreneurial roles and began to actualize their selves through their business careers.

However extraordinary they are, the women entrepreneurs have thus not been immune from the dominant structure of gender stratification; they too have had to submit to gender-bound status inferiority. Nonetheless, their self-portrayals reveal much more than a picture of women as victims. Female inferiority was strategically manipulated and even played up in order to boost male egos, arouse gallantry in helping "helpless" women, or bring transactions with male clients to success. Feminine self-abnegation was a key, paradoxically, to transcending gender barriers, in that it expedited the ability of women to establish and expand cross-gender alliances and networks as solid support bases for their business careers. An extreme example was found in the woman who, in the tea-house entertainment of male clients, used her musical talent to simulate the geisha role, which only a woman can play. Most of my informants have thus put into practice the adage "Convert a misfortune into a blessing" (*Wazawai o tenjite fuku to nasu*), which I have frequently heard women leaders quote in Japan.

The conversion of the misfortune of female gender into a fortune takes a more positive form when women's superiority, rather than their inferiority, is brought into play. As newcomers in the male-dominated business world, the women had somehow to acquire a competitive edge against male rivals in existing trades or to carve out new niches for themselves. The majority of the women sampled came from an emerging group of women leaders who chose the latter alternative. Feminine sensitivity in human communication was captured as the greatest resource to be harnessed for communication enterprises. Women's linguistic facility in particular was singled out as a weapon in winning in international communications businesses. A former housewife harnessed her experiential understanding of other housewives' feelings and desires into a successful enterprise communicating between housing producers and consumers. We have also heard the feminist view that "from now on it will be the female perspective that opens up new fields of business, because the male perspective has already been exhausted."

The claimed female superiority can take a conservative overtone as well. As a management style, older presidents in particular stressed maternal nurturance. To be recalled is the woman who equated the president with a mother and the company with her child and claimed that her maternal approach had won over disgruntled male-led labor.

Gender does not always come to the fore as a political issue or as a matter of status inequity, but often is taken for granted or hidden behind the functional premise. This is especially true where the domestic career interlocks with the business career. Married women either started their business careers late or interrupted their careers in order to fulfill their domestic responsibilities or to enjoy a feminine identity as wife and mother. The M-curve life schedule as a way of mitigating the problem of time compression was largely taken for granted. One woman even embraced the idea that a woman's place is the home, an idea irreconcilable in her own mind with her entrepreneurial career.

The touchy problem of the husband's ego was handled in one case by a strong reassertion of the division of labor by gender. A more uneasy case called forth a justification of the woman's role as a president and sole breadwinner in terms of the Japanese tradition of functional dyarchy: the "matriarchy" was supposedly intrinsic to the feudal system in that the domain lord was a symbol of authority and his wife executed it. The husband's role in a woman's business career may well be inferred from the fact that half of the total sample were divorced, single, or widowed. As for the future prospects of the enterprise, the owner-presidents tended to expect their sons (and sons-in-law) to succeed to the business, while no daughter was considered for intergenerational succession. This looks like a reversion to traditional male headship.

In no case was the problem of time compression solved by the businesswoman alone, particularly when she had small children. It was necessary to mobilize her mother or another kinswoman as a domestic helper or surrogate housewife/child-caretaker. Upon a generational turnover, a daughter or daughter-in-law might take over domestic responsibility. Without such a surrogate, I was told, it would have been impossible to carry on a full-time business career. This seems to mean that functional complementarity was lifted from the gender opposition only to be reimposed upon two women, one specializing in a career, the other taking a housewifely role. The career woman, then, might be likened to a man assisted by his wife, except that she is more likely than he is to reciprocate later by looking after the former domestic collaborator. The autobiographies of businesswomen illustrate the fact that a career is the product of interdependence and teamwork even for an "independent" businesswoman or businessman.

Functional considerations cut across the domestic and public domains. As presidents of small enterprises, most of our businesswomen keep costs down by resorting to part-timers, temporary workers, and subcontractors. If both men and women are hired, a female president is no different from a male president in hiring more men in regular, technically higher-level, and managerial capacities, and more women as "office ladies" or for irregular employment. Except for the cases of all-female enterprises, there seems to be no way of superseding the gender dichotomy prevailing in the labor market.

Furthermore, the enterprises studied are largely complementary to, not competitive with, large-scale, male-led businesses. They either fill gaps in the latter or perform functions better served by women. The majority of those in the communications-service industry are directly or indirectly involved in international trade or contacts and thus contribute in varying degrees to export-oriented, male-dominated industries, and ultimately to the national economy of Japan.

How about the egalitarian ideology? There is something paradoxical in my informants' attitude toward the political issue of gender. All the women are openly egalitarian, but not necessarily feminist or liberationist. Their egalitarianism is based foremost on the gender-blind principle of ability and performance, which results in a paradox: the more egalitarian, the more severely critical one tends to be of female employees for being spoiled, emotionally problematical, professionally uncommitted, and so on. Furthermore, none of the employers can afford to relinquish the idea of role-fitness, which provides the rationale for an imbalanced gender distribution of employees. Keenly aware of their role as new women leaders, they wish to promote women's status, but admit they cannot embrace the Equal Employment Opportunity Law unconditionally. This dilemma is understandable because they are not ideologues but business practitioners, not leaders in the sexual revolution but caught up in the day-to-day operation of surviving and winning in competitive money-making projects.

It would be wrong, however, to say that these women are only reinforcing or replicating gender dualism. They have, after all, demonstrated that an entrepreneurial career is a viable alternative to surmounting gender barriers in the labor market. Their insistence on gender-blind equality is a natural result of their having made it in the predominantly male world through their personal ability and perseverance. The media publicity given their innovative businesses and extraordinary careers is most likely to impress the audience with women's creative capabilities and to induce young women to follow them as successful models. Our women found mentors, supporters, and "benefactors" only among men, but as the number of women leaders increases, younger-generation women will be able to find female *senpai*.

The careers of the twelve women thus suggest prospects for a new generation of career-minded women. The organized labor market may open up for women, partly under the influence of the EEOL, but entrepreneurial opportunities look more promising, given the widely recognized viability of small enterprises in today's fluctuating techno-economic environment, and the likelihood that a woman's personal strength, creativity, and sensitivity are best put to direct use by her own enterprise. The United States is witnessing an upsurge of female entrepreneurs, and it is possible that Japanese women will follow suit in the foreseeable future.

One of the industries receptive to women's talent and free from gender discrimination may be international communication, and this point was stressed and demonstrated by those informants who deal directly with foreigners. I believe women entrepreneurs will in future come to play an increasingly greater role in Japan's internationalization.

Another area of advance, I suggest, has to do with the life schedule. It is clear that the most common obstacle to women's careers is the burden of playing two roles, domestic and extradomestic, simultaneously. Men's participation in domestic chores, which is essential to equalization, does not seem likely to take place soon on any large scale. There seems to be no immediate solution, and to some extent this problem may persist indefinitely. But women's entrepreneurial vitality might well be channeled into enterprises that contribute to lightening the load of career-minded women. As the availability of kinswomen as surrogate homemakers dwindles, businesswomen can help other women by taking over domestic burdens and developing them into enterprises finely tuned to the needs of clients. Along with public institutions, there already exist private businesses, often run by women, catering to the needs of children and the elderly, such as laundry, house-cleaning, and meal-providing services, day-care centers, and so on. Much need is felt for improving this service industry in quantity, quality, and repertoire, and this is the area where I believe women's creative sensitivity can best be stimulated and harnessed.

Ideally, both men and women should be recruited to work in such settings, but realistically more women will be interested for the time being. The domestic industry serves, moreover, not only to help career women but to take care of the opposite side of the time-compression equation—namely, postparental women with time on their hands. This is not meant to reinstitute the M-curve and encourage middle-aged women to reenter the labor market as unskilled, low-paid part-timers. Women entrepreneurs may recognize these women's skills in caring for children, the elderly, the handicapped, and the sick, and in doing other domestic tasks, precisely when such skills are getting scarce, although in increasing demand. Promoting housewifely skill, efficiency, and experience to professional status and organizing it into a new repertoire may give domestic work new prestige.

This may perhaps sound like a dream, but it can confidently be predicted that the future will see the introduction of a flex-time system and/or employment at home to restructure the current rigid system. Women then will have more options to pursue careers, whether as entrepreneurs or employees, as full-time businesswomen or temporary workers. Women entrepreneurs may be expected to hasten this change.

Notes

Notes

Kumon and Rosovsky: Introduction

1. Hugh Patrick and Henry Rosovky, eds., *Asia's New Giant: How the Japanese Economy Works* (Washington, D.C.: Brookings Institution, 1976).
2. Nathan Glazer, "Social and Cultural Factors in Japanese Economic Growth," in ibid.
3. The term *political economy* was widely used as one way of describing economics—particularly of the applied variety—until approximately the 1940s. At that point, the profession started to prefer *economics*, which supposedly described a more scientific, rigorous, and "harder" discipline. The inevitable by-product was increasing formalism and declining relation to reality.
4. Glazer in Patrick and Rosovsky, eds., *Asia's New Giant*, p. 815.
5. Rodney Clark, *The Japanese Company* (New Haven: Yale University Press, 1976), p. 258. Cited by Chalmers Johnson in *MITI and the Japanese Miracle: The Growth of Industrial Policy, 1925–1975* (Stanford: Stanford University Press, 1982), p. 33.
6. See *Nikkei Bijinesu* (Nikkei business journal), Feb. 22, 1982, p. 193.
7. Of course, this is not the first time that the Japan Problem has been on the minds of foreign competitors. The problem arose as soon as Japanese exports started providing strong competition for those countries that had industrialized earlier. In the 1920s, Great Britain's cotton-textile industry was very vocal about the Japanese threat. Special rules in the form of protection were urged, and cheap labor was considered to be the principal problem. There was, at that time, far less emphasis on sytemic differences between Japan and the West, and access to Japanese markets was a relatively minor issue.
8. Advocacy of special rules and a new system designed to control Japan is most often associated with scholars and social critics who are rather unfairly labeled "Japan bashers." Prominent examples are James Fallows, *More Like Us: Making America Great Again* (Boston: Houghton Mifflin, 1989); Clyde V. Prestowitz, Jr., *Trading Places: How We Allowed Japan to Take the Lead* (New York: Basic Books, 1988); and Karel van Wolferen, *The Enigma of Japanese Power* (New York: Knopf, 1989). More optimistic views—espousing the possibility of harmonious relations between Japan and the United States without special rules—have been expressed by such well-known authorities as Zbigniew K. Brzezinski, "A Trans-Pacific Venture Called Amerippon," *International Herald Tribune*, Apr. 29, 1987,

and C. Fred Bergsten, "Economic Imbalances and World Politics," *Foreign Affairs*, Vol. 65, No. 4 (Spring 1987), pp 770–806.

9. Esyun Hamaguchi, "Nihon bummei no kihonteki seikaku" (Fundamental characteristics of Japanese civilization), in Hikaku Bummei Gakkai (Japan Society for the Comparative Study of Civilizations), ed., *Hikaku bummei* (Comparative civilizations) (Tokyo: Tōsui Shobō, 1986), Vol. 2, pp. 21–38. An analogy from biology may clarify the distinction between culture and civilization. Culture corresponds to organizing principles or genotypes; civilization produces the organized outcome or phenotypes.

10. See Ruth Benedict, *The Chrysanthemum and the Sword: Patterns of Japanese Culture* (1946; New York: New American Library, 1974) pp. 13, 14. Judging by Alfred L. Kroeber and Clyde Kluckhohn's large collection of definitions of culture in *Culture: A Critical Review of Concepts and Definitions* (New York: Random House, 1953), Benedict was ahead of her time. Most anthropologists in Kroeber and Kluckhohn's compendium were mainly interested in societal phenotypes—what some Japanese call civilization (*bummei*).

11. Edward T. Hall and Mildred Reed Hall, *Hidden Differences: Doing Business with the Japanese* (Garden City, N.Y.: Anchor Press/Doubleday, 1987), pp. xvii, 4.

12. *Nihonjinron*, perhaps best translated as the theory of the essence of what is Japanese, refers to a variety of writers—both scholars and popularizers—who have been concerned with allegedly unique characteristics of the Japanese people. In effect, these individuals are all, in one manner or another, attempting to describe aspects of Japan's "national character." See Fosco Maraini, "Japan and the Future: Some Suggestions from Nihonjinron Literature," in Gianni Fodella, ed., *Social Structures and Economic Dynamics in Japan up to 1980* (Milan: Institute of Economic and Social Studies for East Asia, Luigi Bocconi University, 1975), pp. 17–19.

Smith: The Cultural Context

1. A recent discussion is that by Aram A. Yengoyan, "Theory in Anthropology: On the Demise of the Concept of Culture," *Comparative Studies in Society and History*, Vol. 28, No. 2 (1986), pp. 368–74. The classic review of the concept, now almost 40 years old, is by Alfred L. Kroeber and Clyde Kluckhohn, *Culture: A Critical Review of Concepts and Definitions* (New York: Random House, 1953). Debate over the utility of the concept and its definition has continued unabated to the present. I have taken a more assertive stand in defense of the utility of the concept in this essay than I would adopt for an anthropological audience, with whom I would be more circumspect and certainly more tentative, for the simple reason that, like many concepts, this one clearly enjoys more currency in other disciplines than in the one that originated the idea. Some very sophisticated discussion has been carried on, and the misuses of the concept have been so thoroughly exposed that many anthropologists have abandoned it altogether. Such in-house debates seldom have much meaning for outsiders, so I have made use of the concept here in a way that I hope will have a salutary influence on analyses of political economy. For a hilarious, on-target presentation of developments that have affected the fate of the concept of culture in archaeology and anthropology, see Kent V. Flannery, "The Golden Marshalltown: A Parable for the Archaeology of the 1980s," *American Anthropologist*, Vol. 84, No. 2 (1982), pp. 265–78.

2. For a succinct statement of this position, see Roy G. D'Andrade, "The Cultural Part of Cognition," *Cognitive Science*, Vol. 5 (1981), pp. 175–95.

3. For that matter, so are the concepts and variables employed by students of the political economy. For a recent discussion of the relationships between culture and economy, see Vernon W. Ruttan, "Cultural Endowments and Economic Development: What Can We Learn from Anthropology?" *Econmic Development and Cultural Change,* Vol. 36, No. 3 (1988), supplement, pp. S247–71. Ruttan presents a "pattern model" of a broadly defined general-equilibrium framework, in which everything can change and affect everything else. He posits four interacting categories of variables that determine economic behavior and performance: resource endowments (the economists' standard variables of labor, capital, and natural resources), technology, institutions, and cultural endowments. These last two categories of variables are almost always excluded from economic analysis in the interest of parsimonious explanation of change over a relatively short period of time. Even the technology variables are often taken as a given. Contemporary economics, Western in origin, is itself a cultural product, insofar as it seeks to establish proximate causation. Cultural explanations place far less emphasis on proximate factors that shape economic behavior; they are also frequently concerned with long-term processes which often include changes in cultural variables as well. By denying any role to culture, economic models sacrifice broad explanatory power for parsimony and long-run explanation for the short-run. Admiration for parsimonious explanations is not a cultural universal found in all societies.

4. These are among the key elements of the utility function, which I understand to be a formal statement of what defines the economic goals of individuals. It is assumed that individuals are rational actors and seek to optimize their self-interest (which they have no difficulty in discovering), typically rather narrowly defined. As was pointed out during the January 1988 meeting of the Japanese Political Economy Research Committee, however, there are clear differences among societies as to whether the definitions of self-interest and utility also incorporate concern for the welfare of other members of the community, however defined. The degree to which societies emphasize the value of interpersonal relations—concern for the needs and welfare of others—varies greatly. I assume that it is more strongly emphasized in Japan than in the United States. However that may be, it is surely simplistic to assume that the utility functions of representative Japanese, Americans, Englishmen, or whatever nationality are identical.

5. The production function defines and attempts to measure the relationship between inputs—typically labor, land, capital, and technology, but in principle including cultural and institutional variables as well—and output. For example, Japan's high rates of personal saving and business investment in the postwar but not the prewar period resulted in a rapid growth of the amount of physical capital. Their willingness to devote long hours to schooling has increased the capabilities of Japanese workers (human capital). Similarly, pride in work, willingness to work more hours per year than is true of labor forces in most industrial nations, and the relatively high propensity to work at part-time jobs beyond the age of retirement are all Japanese behavior patterns with a strong cultural base. Moreover, both institutional and infrastructural arrangements are essential to the production process. In the case of Japan, these include the systems of labor management and industrial relations, and of business management—themes addressed in several of the essays in this volume.

6. For a sharply contrasting case, one need look no further than the modern state of Israel, where religious orthodoxy in matters of food consumption and the tensions it engenders continue to affect both political and economic behavior.

7. Daniel O'Keefe, *Stolen Lightning: The Social Theory of Magic* (New York: Random House, 1983).

8. Craig Calhoun, "History and Sociology in Britain: A Review Article," *Comparative Studies in Society and History*, Vol. 29, No. 3 (1987), pp. 615–25, reminds us that every historical monograph is not just a compilation of facts, but an argument: "As we are now acutely aware, there are no unproblematic, simply given accounts of actual historical reality in its fullness of content. Descriptions may be more or less rich, of course, but even the most straightforward narrative is a construct, an interpretation." Any reader of the many versions of the history of Japan must doubt that it has only one. The history of the development of labor relations in Japanese industry as written by management differs greatly from that written by labor. The Ministry of Education and Ienaga Saburo are in fundamental disagreement about the "real" history of modern Japan. Institutions, for their part, are no more concrete, no more real; the most cursory glance at the many interpretations of the nature of labor unions, the *uji*, and the Imperial House, to take only three disparate examples, should serve to lay that comforting thought to rest.

9. Andrew Gordon, *The Evolution of Labor Relations in Japan: Heavy Industry 1853–1955* (Cambridge, Mass.: Harvard University Press, 1985), p. 416.

10. Ibid., p. 417.

11. Ronald P. Dore, *British Factory, Japanese Factory: The Origins of National Diversity in Industrial Relations* (Berkeley: University of California Press, 1973), pp. 375–76.

12. Ibid., p. 376.

13. Dan F. Henderson, *Conciliation and Japanese Law: Tokugawa and Modern* (Seattle: University of Washington Press, 1965), Vol. 1, pp. 183–87.

14. Gordon, *Evolution of Labor Relations*, p. 413.

15. Ibid., p. 432. See also Thomas C. Smith, "The Right to Benevolence: Dignity and Japanese Workers, 1890–1920," *Comparative Studies in Society and History*, Vol. 26, No. 4 (1983), pp. 587–613.

16. Tadashi Fukutake, *The Japanese Social Structure: Its Evolution in the Modern Century* (Tokyo: University of Tokyo Press, 1982), p. 34.

17. Koji Taira, "Modernization, Uglification, and an Urban Revolution in Japan," *Asian Profile*, Vol. 6, No. 2 (1978), p. 141.

18. T. R. Rochon, "Review Article: Political Change in Ordered Societies: The Rise of Citizens' Movements," *Comparative Politics*, Vol. 15, No. 3 (1983), p. 356.

19. C. Scott Littleton, "The Organization and Management of a Tokyo Shinto Shrine Festival," *Ethnology*, Vol. 24, No. 3 (1986), p. 201.

20. Theodore Bestor, "Tradition and Japanese Social Organization: Instituional Development in a Tokyo Neighborhood," *Ethnology*, Vol. 24, No. 2 (1985), pp. 132–33. And see also Bestor, *Neighborhood Tokyo* (Stanford: Stanford University Press, 1989).

21. Eyal Ben-Ari, "A Sports Day in Suburban Japan: Leisure, Artificial Communities and the Creation of Local Sentiments," in Joy Hendry and Jonathan Webber, eds., *Interpreting Japanese Society: Anthropological Approaches*, JASO Occasional Papers, No. 5 (Oxford: Journal of the Anthropological Society of Oxford, 1986); Stephen P. Nussbaum, "The Residential Community in Modern Japan: An Analysis of a Tokyo Suburban Development" (Ph.D. diss., Cornell University, 1985); Jennifer E. Robertson, *Native and Newcomer: Making and Remaking a Japanese City* (Berkeley: University of California Press, 1991).

22. Robert J. Smith, *Japanese Society: Tradition, Self, and the Social Order* (New

York: Cambridge University Press, 1983), p. 22; Bestor, "Tradition and Japanese Social Organization," p. 133.

23. Ben-Ari, "Sports Day," pp. 220–21.

24. John M. Roberts, "The Self-Management of Cultures," in Ward H. Goodenough, ed., *Explorations in Cultural Anthropology* (New York: McGraw-Hill, 1964).

25. D'Andrade, "Cultural Part of Cognition," p. 180.

26. *Time*, July 1, 1985.

27. Whether one is tempted to assign a certain speciousness to Beethoven's involvement in the Japanese New Year observances depends in large part on the length of the perspective adopted. After all, the cultural historian will remind us that Takasago itself is a hybrid and that *kagami-mochi* (glutinous rice-cake) cannot pre-date the introduction of glutinous rice into Japan from the continent.

28. Kanae Kaku, "Are Physicians Sympathetic to Superstition? A Study of Hinoe-uma," *Social Biology*, Vol. 19, No. 1 (1972), pp. 60–64; "Increased Induced Abortion Rate in 1966: An Aspect of a Japanese Folk Superstition," *Annals of Human Biology*, Vol. 2, No. 2 (1975), pp. 111–15; and "Were Girl Babies Sacrificed to a Folk Superstition in 1966 in Japan?" *Annals of Human Biology*, Vol. 2, No. 4 (1975), pp. 391–93.

29. There are, of course, social and cultural factors of a more general kind that ought to be taken into account in making demographic projections, which often have clear economic and political utility. Allen L. Otten, "Why Demographers Are Wrong Almost as Often as Economists," *Wall Street Journal*, Jan. 29, 1985, concludes, based on interviews with several demographers, that they are so often wrong because they fail to anticipate the ways trends interact. Quoting William Alonso: "Changes take place at the same time in a number of areas and we simply must take into account the interrelationships of these changes." Why did demographers fail to foresee the exodus to the Sun Belt? Because it "resulted not simply from old people's desire to warm their aging bones, but also from developments that permitted them to fulfill that desire: a general weakening of family ties, the loss of small-town roots that formerly pulled retirees back to their birthplaces and transfer systems that could send Social Security and annuity checks anywhere." Reynolds Farley says, "We have a very elegant statistical apparatus, but we really don't have good ways of spotting changes in life styles or tastes." These last, which may be glossed as cultural and social changes, resist incorporation into elegant statistical operations.

30. See, e.g., Aurelia George, *Japan's Beef Import Policies, 1978–84: The Growth of Bilateralism*, Pacific Economic Papers, No. 113 (Canberra: Australian-Japan Research Centre, Research School of Pacific Studies, Australian National University, 1984).

31. Two recent books on the subject are John D. Donoghue, *Pariah Persistence in Changing Japan: A Case Study* (Washington, D.C.: University Press of America, 1978), and I. Roger Yoshino and Sueo Murakoshi, *The Invisible Visible Minority: Japan's Burakumin* (Osaka: Buraku Kaiho Kenkyusho, 1977). The classic compendium remains George De Vos and Hiroshi Wagatsuma, eds., *Japan's Invisible Race: Caste in Culture and Personality* (Berkeley: University of California Press, 1966).

32. Ronald P. Dore, *Flexible Rigidities: Industrial Policy and Structural Adjustment in the Japanese Economy, 1970–1980* (Stanford: Stanford University Press, 1986), p. 247.

33. Kittredge Cherry, "Translation or Transgression?" *PHP Intersect*, Vol. 3, No. 4 (1987), pp. 14–16; Donald Richie, review of *Long-Suffering Brothers and*

Sisters, Unite! The Buraku Problem, Universal Human Rights and Minority Problems in Various Countries (Osaka: Buraku Liberation Research Institute, 1982), *Japan Times*, June 12, 1982; Frank K. Upham, *Law and Social Change in Postwar Japan* (Cambridge, Mass: Harvard University Press, 1987), p. 242.

34. Viv Duus, "Protectionism: The Beef About Beef," *PHP Intersect*, Vol. 2, No. 11 (1986), p. 11.

35. Upham, *Law and Social Change*, p. 113.

36. Anonymous, "Two Austrian Trade Papers Carry Articles Libeling Burakumin," *Buraku Liberation News*, No. 11 (1982), p. 6.

37. Margaret M. Lock, *East Asian Medicine in Urban Japan* (Berkeley: University of California Press, 1980); Emiko Ohnuki-Tierney, *Illness and Culture in Contemporary Japan* (Cambridge: Cambridge University Press, 1984).

38. Edward Norbeck and Margaret Lock, eds., *Health, Illness, and Medical Care in Japan* (Honolulu: University of Hawaii Press, 1987).

39. Kyoichi Sonoda, *Health and Illness in Changing Japanese Society* (Tokyo: University of Tokyo Press, 1988); William E. Steslicke, "The Japanese State of Health: A Political-Economic Perspective," in Norbeck and Lock, eds., *Health, Illness, and Medical Care in Japan*, pp. 24–65.

40. Margaret M. Lock, "Introduction: Health and Medical Care as Cultural and Social Phenomena," in Norbeck and Lock, eds., *Health, Illness, and Medical Care in Japan*, p. 6.

41. Ibid., p. 10.

42. Ibid., p. 5.

43. William E. Steslicke, *Doctors in Politics* (New York: Praeger, 1973).

44. Steslicke, "Japanese State of Health," pp. 34–35.

45. Clifford Geertz, "Ideology as a Cultural System," in *The Interpretation of Cultures: Selected Essays* (New York: Basic Books, 1973), pp. 202–3.

46. Robert L. Heilbroner, *Behind the Veil of Economics: Essays in the Worldly Philosophy* (New York: Norton, 1988), pp. 47–48.

47. Dore, *British Factory, Japanese Factory*, pp. 51–53; Thomas P. Rohlen, *For Harmony and Strength: Japanese White-Collar Organization in Anthropological Perspective* (Berkeley: University of California Press, 1974), pp. 34–61.

48. Carol Gluck, *Japan's Modern Myths: Ideology in the Late Meiji Period* (Princeton: Princeton University Press, 1985), p. 3.

49. Ibid., p. 17.

50. Winston Davis, "Religion and Development: Weber and the East Asian Experience," in Myron Weiner and Samuel P. Huntington, eds., *Understanding Political Development* (Boston: Little, Brown, 1987), p. 47.

51. Smith, *Japanese Society*, p. 17.

52. Rob Steven, *Classes in Contemporary Japan* (Cambridge: Cambridge University Press, 1983), pp. 112–13, entirely rejects the utility of the concept of "false consciousness," which he dismisses as a *"deus ex machina* summoned by Marxists to fill the gaps in their analysis. Although schools and the media might put out ideas which account for some of the specific forms assumed by bourgeois ideology, none of this can explain why people find the ideas acceptable or why different classes do in different degrees." He adds the telling point that if we are to understand why people embrace an ideology, we must analyze their day-to-day behavior.

53. Otten, "Why Demographers Are Wrong."

54. Jerome B. Cohen, *Economic Problems of Free Japan* (Princeton: Center for International Studies, Princeton University, 1952), p. 84.

55. This passage was written long before publication of Prime Minister No-boru Takeshita's book *The Furusato Concept: Toward a Humanistic and Prosperous Japan* (Tokyo: Simul International, 1988). The word *furusato* has thus been thrust into unprecedented prominence and given some stunning new twists of meaning, as the following remarkable passage from the prologue of Takeshita's book shows:

I am confident we can find many of the answers [to Japan's problems] in an ideal I have held for many years: *furusato* creativity.

Furusato is a special word to the Japanese. For most of us it means our hometown, the place where we were born. But it is more than that. It also evokes the values of family ties and harmonious social relationships. The *furusato* is a home to the spirit as well as the body, the place where we instinctively know we belong.

By *furusato* creativity, I do not mean, then, simply developing Japan's national land or promoting regional economies. Rather, my vision of *furusato* creativity is a vision of the Japanese people, sure of their own identity, building a nation that provides a secure life and a solid basis for their pursuits. This means laying the foundations—social, cultural and economic—essential to ensure that future generations will have a *furusato* of their own wherever they live. And achieving this, in turn, means revamping the very concept of government from the ground up. It means engineering radical transformations in everything from Japan's industrial and economic structure to its technology, organizations, and social systems.

I believe that these efforts will yield the key to creating a Japan capable of living up to the expections of the world, an affluent nation, a cultural and economic state that the next generation will be proud to call its own. (p. 4)

It is no wonder, as I was told by a member of the Japanese diplomatic corps in the winter of 1987, that "we are having a terrible time trying to find a good English equivalent for *furusato*." They appear to have settled instead for the unhappy mystification of transliteration.

56. M. Paske-Smith, ed., *Report on Japan to the Secret Committee of the English East India Company by Sir Stamford Raffles, 1812–1916* (London: Curzon Press, 1929; reprint 1971).

Haley: Consensual Governance

1. George Eads and Kozo Yamamura, "The Future of Industrial Policy," in Kozo Yamamura and Yasukichi Yasuba, eds., *The Political Economy of Japan*, Vol. 1, *The Domestic Transformation* (Stanford: Stanford University Press, 1987), p. 430.

2. Richard Samuels, *The Business of the Japanese State: Energy Markets in Comparative and Historical Perspective* (Ithaca: Cornell University Press, 1987), p. 260.

3. Ibid.

4. H. L. A. Hart, *The Concept of Law* (Oxford: Clarendon Press, 1961).

5. Judith N. Shklar, *Legalism: Law, Morals and Political Trials* (Cambridge, Mass.: Harvard University Press, 1964).

6. See, e.g., Ronald Dworkin, *Taking Rights Seriously* (Cambridge, Mass.: Harvard University Press, 1977) and *Law's Empire* (Cambridge, Mass.: Harvard University Press, 1986).

7. Shklar, *Legalism*, p. 44.

8. David Danelski, "The Constitutional and Legislative Phases of the Creation of the Japanese Supreme Court," in R. H. Redford, ed., *The Occupation of Japan: The Impact of Legal Reform* (Norfolk, Va.: MacArthur Memorial, 1977), pp. 27–56.

9. Michael P. Birt, "Samurai in Passage: The Transformation of the Sixteenth-Century Kanto," *Journal of Japanese Studies*, Vol. 11, No. 2 (Summer 1985), pp. 369–99.

10. See Shuzo Shiga, "Criminal Procedure in the Ch'ing Dynasty," *Memoirs of the Research Department of the Toyo Bunko*, No. 32 (Tokyo: Toyo Bunko, 1974), pp. 1–138.

11. William P. Alford, "The Inscrutable Occidental? Implications of Roberto Unger's Uses and Abuses of the Chinese Past," *Texas Law Review*, Vol. 64, No. 5 (Feb. 1986), p. 955.

12. Ronald P. Dore, *Taking Japan Seriously: A Confucian Perspective on Leading Economic Issues* (Stanford: Stanford University Press, 1987), pp. 94–95.

13. Dan F. Henderson, *Conciliation and Japanese Law: Tokugawa and Modern* (Seattle: University of Washington Press, 1965), p. 25.

14. Dan F. Henderson, *Village "Contracts" in Tokugawa Japan* (Seattle: University of Washington Press, 1975), pp. 31–32.

15. See Jeffrey P. Mass, *The Kamakura Bakufu: A Study in Documents* (Stanford: Stanford University Press, 1976) and *The Development of Kamakura Rule* (Stanford: Stanford University Press, 1979); and Carl Steenstrup, "The Legal System of Japan at the End of the Kamakura Period from the Litigants' Point of View," in Brian McKnight, ed., *Law and the State in Traditional East Asia* (Honolulu: University of Hawaii Press, 1986), pp. 73–110.

16. See Henderson, *Conciliation and Japanese Law*, and Yoshiro Hiramatsu, "Tokugawa Law," *Law in Japan*, Vol. 14 (1981), pp. 1–48.

17. John Henry Wigmore, "New Codes and Old Customs," *Japan Weekly Mail*, Oct. 29, 1897, pp. 530–33; Nov. 19, 1892, pp. 617–19; Nov. 26, 1892, pp. 656–61; Dec. 10, 1892, pp. 722–26.

18. See Marius B. Jansen, "Tosa in the Sixteenth Century: The 100 Article Code of Chōsokabe Motochika," in John W. Hall and Marius B. Jansen, eds., *Studies in the Institutional History of Early Modern Japan* (Princeton: Princeton University Press, 1968), p. 100.

19. Hiramatsu, "Tokugawa Law," p. 6.

20. Johannes Seimes, *Hermann Roesler and the Making of the Japanese State* (Tokyo: Monumenta Nipponica, 1968), pp. 43–44.

21. Richard H. Minear, *Japanese Tradition and Western Law: Emperor, State and Law in the Thought of Hozumi Yatsuka* (Cambridge, Mass.: Harvard University Press, 1970), 73.

22. Civil Code of Japan, art. 449, quoted in Richard W. Rabinowitz, "Law and the Social Process in Japan," *Transactions of the Asiatic Society of Japan*, 3d Ser., Vol. 10 (1968), p. 22.

23. See John O. Haley, "The Politics of Informal Justice in Japan: The Japanese Experience, 1922–1941," in Richard L. Abel, ed., *The Politics of Informal Justice*, Vol. 2 (New York: Academic Press, 1982), pp. 129–30.

24. Ibid., pp. 126–27.

25. Robert P. Epp, "Threat to Tradition: The Reaction to Japan's 1890 Civil Code" (Ph.D. diss., Harvard University, 1964), p. 16.

26. Haley, "Politics of Informal Justice in Japan."

27. Nihon Bengoshi Rengōkai, *Shihō hakusho* (Tokyo, 1974), p. 19.

28. John O. Haley, "The Myth of the Reluctant Litigant," *Journal of Japanese Studies*, Vol. 4, No. 2 (Summer 1978), pp. 383–84.

29. Robert J. Smith, *Japanese Society: Tradition, Self and the Social Order* (Cambridge: Cambridge University Press, 1983), p. 33.

30. Frank K. Upham, "Instrumental Violence and Social Change: The Buraku Liberation League and the Tactic of 'Denunciation Struggle,'" *Law in Japan*, Vol. 17 (1984), pp. 185–205, and *Law and Social Change in Postwar Japan* (Cambridge, Mass.: Harvard University Press, 1987).

31. Smith, *Japanese Society*, p. 33.

32. Chalmers Johnson, "Japan: Who Governs? An Essay on Official Bureaucracy," *Journal of Japanese Studies*, Vol. 2, No. 1 (Autumn 1975), p. 16.

33. Steven R. Reed, "Confused Voters and Contentious Politicians: The Five General Elections, 1947–1955" (paper presented at the 39th Annual Meeting of the Association for Asian Studies, Boston, April 10, 1987); Seizaburo Sato and Tetsuhisa Matsuzaki, *Jimintō seiken* (Tokyo: Chūō Kōron-sha, 1986), p. 232.

34. Sato and Matsuzaki, *Jimintō seiken*, p. 232.

35. See Joel D. Aberbach, Robert D. Putnam, and Bert A. Rockman, *Bureaucrats and Politicians in Western Democracies* (Cambridge, Mass.: Harvard University Press, 1981).

36. See John O. Haley, "Sheathing the Sword of Justice in Japan: An Essay on Law Without Sanctions," *Journal of Japanese Studies*, Vol. 8, No. 2 (Summer 1982), pp. 265–81.

37. See John O. Haley, "Administrative Guidance Versus Formal Regulation: Resolving the Paradox of Industrial Policy," in Gary R. Saxonhouse and Kozo Yamamura, eds., *Law and Trade Issues of the Japanese Economy: American and Japanese Perspectives* (Seattle: University of Washington Press, 1986), pp. 107–28, and "Governance by Negotiation: A Reappraisal of Bureaucratic Power in Japan," *Journal of Japanese Studies*, Vol. 13, No. 2 (Summer 1987), pp. 343–57.

38. Haruhiro Fukui, "Studies in Policymaking: A Review of the Literature," in T. J. Pempel, ed., *Policymaking in Contemporary Japan* (Ithaca: Cornell University Press, 1977); Martha Ann Caldwell, "Petroleum Politics in Japan: State and Industry in a Changing Policy Context" (Ph.D. diss., University of Wisconsin-Madison, 1981); Steven R. Reed, *Japanese Prefectures and Policymaking* (Pittsburgh: University of Pittsburgh Press, 1986); Laura E. Hein, "Energy and Economic Policy in Postwar Japan, 1945–1960" (Ph.D. diss., University of Wisconsin-Madison, 1986); Samuels, *Business of the Japanese State*; and Michael K. Young, "Administrative Guidance in the Courts: A Case Study in Doctrinal Adaptation," *Law in Japan*, Vol. 17 (1984), and "Administrative Guidance and Industrial Policy: Participatory Policy Formation and Execution in Japan," in Kōichirō Fujikura, ed., *Eibei hō ronshū: Tanaka Hideo sensei kanreki kinen* (Collection of essays on Anglo-American law, in celebration of Professor Hideo Tanaka's 61st year) (Tokyo: University of Tokyo Press, 1987), pp. 569–88.

39. Samuels, *Business of the Japanese State*, p. 290.

40. See Thomas Roehl, "A Transactions Cost Approach to International Trading Structures: The Case of the Japanese General Trading Companies," *Hitotsubashi Journal of Economics*, Vol. 24, No. 2 (1983), pp. 119–35.

41. Jinpū Yoshida, *Nihon no karuteru* (Tokyo: Toyo Keizai Shimbunsha, 1963), p. 20; Keizo Fujita, "Cartels and Their Conflicts in Japan," *Journal of the Osaka University of Commerce*, Vol. 3 (1935), pp. 65–109.

42. William W. Lockwood, *The Economic Development of Japan* (Princeton: Princeton University Press, 1954), p. 250.

43. See Chalmers Johnson, *MITI and the Japanese Miracle: The Growth of Industrial Policy, 1925–1975* (Stanford: Stanford University Press, 1982), pp. 32–34; Takafusa Nakamura, *Postwar Japanese Economy* (Tokyo: University of Tokyo Press, 1981), pp. 14–20.

44. Jerome B. Cohen, *Japan's Economy in War and Reconstruction* (Minneapolis: University of Minnesota Press, 1949), p. 58.

45. Chalmers Johnson, "MITI and the Japanese International Economic Policy," in Robert Scalapino, ed., *The Foreign Policy of Modern Japan* (Berkeley: University of California Press, 1977), p. 231.

46. Ibid., p. 247.
47. See Reed, *Japanese Prefectures and Policymaking*; Upham, *Law and Social Change*.
48. See, e.g., Takeyoshi Kawashima, *Nihonjin no hōishiki* (Tokyo: Iwanami, 1965); Kahei Rokumoto, "Nihonjin no hōishiki saiho," in Reijirō Mochizuki et al., eds., *Hō to hōkatei* (Tokyo: Sobundo, 1986), pp. 279–306.
49. Upham, "Instrumental Violence and Social Change," p. 21.
50. Young, "Administrative Guidance and Industrial Policy."
51. See Uno et al. v. Ministry of Agriculture and Fisheries, 36 Minshū 1679 (Sup. Ct., 1st P.B., Sept. 9, 1982).
52. The four most widely cited pollution cases are: Komatsu v. Mitsui Kinzoku Kōgyō K.K., 22 Kakyū minshū 1 (Toyama Dist. Ct., June 30, 1971), affirmed on *kōso* appeal, Hanrei jihō (No. 674) 25 (Nagoya High Ct., Kanazawa Br., Aug. 9, 1972); Ono v. Shōwa Denkō K.K., 22 Kakyu minshū 1 (Niigata Dist. Ct., Sept. 29, 1971), the Agano River–Niigata Minamata Disease Case; Shiono v. Shōwa Yokkaichi Sekiyu, Hanrei jihō (No. 672) 30 (Tsu Dist. Ct., July 24, 1972), the Yokkaichi Asthma Case; Watanabe v. Chisso K.K., Hanrei jihō (No. 696) 15 (Kumamoto Dist. Ct., Mar. 20, 1973), the Kumamoto Minamata Disease Case.
53. See Kurokawa v. Chiba Prefecture Election Commission, 30 Minshū 223 (Sup. Ct., G.B., Apr. 14, 1976); Shimizu et al. v. Osaka Election Commission, 37 Minshū 345 (Sup. Ct., G.B., Apr. 27, 1983); Tokyo Election Commission v. Koshiyama, 37 Minshū 1243 (Sup. Ct., G.B., Nov. 7, 1983).
54. See, e.g., Kawashima, *Nihonjin no hōishiki*; Henderson, *Conciliation and Japanese Law*; Haley, "Myth of the Reluctant Litigant," n. 1.
55. See, e.g., Masao Ohki, *Nihonjin no hō kannen* (Tokyo: University of Tokyo Press, 1983); and Mass, *Kamakura Bakufu and Development of Kamakura Rule*.
56. Haley, "Politics of Informal Justice in Japan."

Murakami and Rohlen: Social-Exchange Aspects

1. Oliver Williamson's *Markets and Hierarchies: Analysis and Antitrust Implications* (New York: Free Press, 1975) and *The Economic Institutions of Capitalism: Firms, Markets and Relational Contracting* (New York: Free Press, 1985) are representative of recent conceptualization in the field.
2. A sophisticated version of the market-oriented approach is the introduction to Hugh Patrick and Henry Rosovsky, eds., *Asia's New Giant: How the Japanese Economy Works* (Washington, D.C.: Brookings Institution, 1976). For a portrait typifying the Japan, Inc., approach, see Eugene J. Kaplan, *Japan: The Government-Business Relationship* (Washington, D.C.: U.S. Department of Commerce, 1972).
3. Examples include Yasusuke Murakami, "The Japanese Model of Political Economy," in Kozo Yamamura and Yasukichi Yasuba, eds., *The Political Economy of Japan*, Vol. 1, *The Domestic Transformation* (Stanford: Stanford University Press, 1987); Ken-ichi Imai, Hiroyuki Itami, and Kazuo Koike, *Naibu Soshiki no Keizaigaku* (Economics of Internal Organization) (Tokyo: Tōyō Keizai Shimpōsha, 1982); Seizaburo Sato and Tetsuhisa Matsuzaki, "Jimintō chōchōki seiken no kaibō" (The anatomy of the super long-term LDP government), *Chūō Kōron*, Nov. 1984; Takashi Inoguchi, *Gendai nihon seiji keizai no kōzō—seifu to shijō* (The framework of the contemporary Japanese political economy: Government and market) (Tokyo: Tōyō Keizai Shimpōsha, 1983); Daniel I. Okimoto, *Between MITI and the Market* (Stanford: Stanford University Press, 1989); Richard J. Samuels, *The Business of the Japanese State: Energy Markets in Comparative and Historical Perspective* (Ithaca: Cornell University Press, 1987); Ronald P. Dore, *Flexible Rigidities: Indus-*

trial Policy and Structural Adjustment in the Japanese Economy, 1970–1980 (Stanford: Stanford University Press, 1986); Kenneth B. Pyle, ed., *The Trade Crisis: How Will Japan Respond?* (Seattle: Society for Japanese Studies, 1987); and Stephen D. Krasner, "Trade Conflicts and the Common Defense: The United States and Japan," *Political Science Quarterly*, Vol. 101, No. 5 (1986). The general groping for a vocabulary representing this intermediate area is evidenced by the kind of terminology being generated by the above authors, such as "compartmentalized competition," "canalized pluralism," and "reciprocal consent."

4. The classic statement of this assumption is Karl Polanyi, *The Great Transformation* (Boston: Beacon Press, 1957).

5. Peter M. Blau, *Exchange and Power in Social Life* (New York: Wiley, 1964), p. 91.

6. Ibid., p. 93.

7. In epistemological terms, a "complex system" of this latter type is similar in richness to the symbolic systems of a normal, everyday "living social world" (recall Edmund Husserl's *Lebenswelt*, Alfred Schutz's "life world," and Maurice Merleau-Ponty's *monde vécu*).

8. This "in time" framework for balance in relationships is discussed for traditional Japan by Ruth Benedict, *The Chrysanthemum and the Sword: Patterns of Japanese Culture* (1946; New York: New American Library, 1974). Her well-known discussion of the obligation to "repay *on*" is precisely about this time-dimensional quality.

9. Thus, whereas economic exchange is defined in what economists label *commodity space*, social exchange is primarily defined in what might be termed *player space*, the closest example of which is the "payoff matrix" in the theory of games. Certainly, the concepts of economic exchange and social exchange are relative: various mixtures of these two modes of exchange give rise to diverse intermediate cases. In fact, monetary exchange and ceremonial gift giving constitute polar cases. Monetary exchange is totally unspecified with respect to participants (any person can participate in monetary exchange) whereas ceremonial exchange is strictly specified in terms of participants and relationships.

10. Though social exchange and economic exchange are juxtaposed under the rule of classification offered here, this parallelism is of a limited nature. Exchange theorists often try—in vain—to find an equivalent of extrinsic utility in order to establish a one-to-one parallelism between social exchange and economic exchange. This effort is beside the point. The foregoing argument suggests that social exchange and economic exchange belong to very different kinds, not only of calculations, but of social experience. While economic exchange belongs to the level of *objects*, social exchange belongs to the level of *systems*, because human relationships play an axial role. Generally, a system is not subject to exact quantitative description. We must recognize that social exchange is more general in character than economic exchange. To summarize in the language of exchange theory, extrinsic utility is only a projection of intrinsic utility onto the space of objects, with other systemic components being given and largely taken for granted. This implies that from the generic viewpoint, economic exchange is a polar derivative of social exchange. Social exchange is not to be understood as merely an inaccurate or degenerate version of economic exchange. It is also worth noting, however, that the calculus of extrinsic utility is often one important component of an intrinsic valuation.

11. To be more exact, we are saying social exchange is *diffused* into an economy largely as an explanatory device. In long historical time and in the human life cycle, social exchange comes before economic exchange. Personal relations come

before impersonal institutions. Only late in historical time and in individual lives do we learn to calculate and value the logic of economic exchange.

12. Claude Lévi-Strauss, *Anthropologie structurelle* (Paris: Plon, 1958), chap. 8.

13. Peter M. Blau, "Interaction, IV: Social Exchange," in David Sills, ed., *International Encyclopedia of the Social Sciences*, Vol. 7 (New York: Crowell, Collier & Macmillan, 1968), pp. 452–57.

14. *Payoff matrix* is usually defined as referring strictly to only two players. For more than two persons, the term *payoff function* is used, signifying a multidimensional payoff matrix. We shall, however, use the former term for simplicity's sake.

15. See, e.g., Mancur Olson, *The Rise and Decline of Nations: Economic Growth, Stagflation and Social Rigidities* (New Haven: Yale University Press, 1982) and Masahiko Aoki, *Information, Incentives and Bargaining in the Japanese Economy* (Cambridge: Cambridge University Press, 1988).

16. See R. Axelrod, *The Evolution of Cooperation* (New York: Basic Books, 1984).

17. For an inclusive overview of this topic, see Robert J. Smith, *Japanese Society* (Cambridge: Cambridge University Press, 1983).

18. Francis L. K. Hsu in his *Iemoto: The Heart of Japan* (New York: Schenkman, 1975), for example, asserted that Japan is unique because of its tradition of "functional collectivity" in comparison to India, China, or the United States. See also Thomas P. Rohlen, *For Harmony and Strength: Japanese White-Collar Organization in Anthropological Perspective* (Berkeley: University of California Press, 1974) for an extensive discussion of this as regards corporate organization.

19. Yasusuke Murakami, Shumpei Kumon, and Seizaburo Sato, *Bunmei to shite no Ie Shakai* (*Ie* society as a pattern of civilization) (Tokyo: Chūō Kōron Sha, 1979).

20. Readers are referred to Taishiro Shirai, ed., *Contemporary Industrial Relations in Japan* (Madison: University of Wisconsin Press, 1983) for an extensive overview of this subject.

21. See Kazuo Koike, *Understanding Labor Relations in Modern Japan* (London: Macmillan, 1988).

22. See Masahiko Aoki, *Cooperative Game Theory of the Firm* (Oxford: Oxford University Press, , 1984).

23. See, e.g., Hiroshi Hazama, *Nihon no rōmu kanri-shi kenkyū* (A study of the history of Japanese labor management) (Tokyo: Diamond, 1964), and for a more specific case, see Mark Fruin, *Kikkoman: Company, Clan and Community* (Cambridge, Mass.: Harvard University Press, 1983).

24. The precise historical role of labor and of labor unions in the history of the Japanese system of industrial relations is much debated at present. See Thomas J. Smith, *Native Sources of Japanese Industrialization* (Berkeley: University of California Press, 1988) and Andrew Gordon, *The Evolution of Labor Relations in Japan* (Cambridge, Mass.: Harvard University Press, 1985).

25. See Michael A. Cusumano, *The Japanese Automobile Industry* (Cambridge, Mass.: Harvard University Press, 1985) for an account of the strike at Nissan.

26. In modern industrial economies, these financial transactions are indeed organized into financial markets in which, by institutionalized extension, a large or even huge number of people participate. Thus, uncertainties of return on financial investments quantitatively translate into different levels of interest rates by virtue of the "law of large numbers," so that financial transactions come to approximate ordinary economic exchanges. Venture-capital investment is a borderline case between social exchange and economic exchange, however, since it

is one of those economic activities where trust and evaluation matter greatly in the early stages of an enterprise. Financial investment is thus liable to assume the pattern of social exchange and to give rise to a social nexus.

27. David Landes, *The Unbound Prometheus: Technological Change and Industrial Development in Western Europe from 1750 to the Present* (Cambridge: Cambridge University Press, 1969).

28. Frederic W. Taylor, *Scientific Management* (New York: Harper & Row, 1947).

29. See Richard Pascal and Thomas P. Rohlen, "The Mazda Turnaround," in Daniel I. Okimoto and Thomas P. Rohlen, eds., *Inside the Japanese System* (Stanford: Stanford University Press, 1988).

30. The studies of Banri Asanuma are particularly revealing in this regard. See, e.g., "Japan's *Keiretsu* System: The Case of the Automobile Industry," *Japanese Economic Studies*, Vol. 13, No. 4 (1985), pp. 3–76.

31. Hugh T. Patrick and Thomas P. Rohlen, "Small-Scale Family Enterprise," in Kozo Yamamura and Yasukichi Yasuba, eds., *The Japanese Political Economy*, Vol. 1, *The Domestic Transition* (Stanford: Stanford University Press, 1987), pp. 352–53.

32. Yasusuke Murakami, "The Age of New Middle Mass Politics: The Case of Japan," *Journal of Japanese Studies*, Vol. 8, No. 1 (Winter 1982), pp. 29–72.

33. Abraham H. Maslow, *Motivation and Personality* (New York: McGraw-Hill, 1960).

Kumon: Japan as a Network Society

I wish to thank Henry Rosovsky, Joel Migdal, and Jan Walls for invaluable comments and suggestions that helped give this essay its final shape. Thanks are also due to all participants in the JPERC III conferences for stimulating discussions of this essay's earlier versions.

1. Representative examples of this viewpoint, aside from the great mass of books on the uniqueness of Japanese culture—*Nihonjinron*—published in Japan since the 1970s, are Karel van Wolferen, "The Japan Problem," *Foreign Affairs*, Vol. 65 (Winter 1986–87), pp. 288–303; id., *The Enigma of Japanese Power* (New York: Knopf, 1989); Stephen D. Krasner, "Trade Conflicts and the Common Defense: The United States and Japan," *Political Science Quarterly*, Vol. 101, No. 5 (1986), pp. 787–806; James Fallows, *More Like Us: Making America Great Again* (Boston: Houghton Mifflin, 1989); id., "Containing Japan," *The Atlantic Monthly*, Vol. 263, No. 5 (May 1989), pp. 40–54; and Leon Vandermeersch, *Le Nouveau Monde sinisé* (Paris: Presses Universitaires de France, 1986).

2. See Ezra F. Vogel, *Japan as Number 1: Lessons for America* (Cambridge, Mass.: Harvard University Press, 1979), and Chalmers Johnson, *MITI and the Japanese Miracle: The Growth of Industrial Policy, 1925–1975* (Stanford: Stanford University Press, 1982); for more recent examples, see William G. Ouchi, *The M-Form Society* (Reading, Mass.: Addison-Wesley, 1984), and Richard Rosecrance, *The Rise of the Trading State* (New York: Basic Books, 1986).

3. Van Wolferen, *Enigma*; Krasner, "Trade Conflicts."

4. See, e.g., Joyce Rothschild-Whitt, "The Collectivist Organization: An Alternative to Rational-Bureaucratic Models," *American Sociological Review*, Vol. 44 (Aug. 1984), pp. 509–27, Marilyn Ferguson, *The Aquarian Conspiracy* (New York: St. Martin's Press, 1980), and Jessica Lipnack and Jeffrey Stamps, *Networking: The First Report and Directory* (New York: Doubleday, 1982).

5. Alec Nove, *The Soviet Economy: An Introduction*, 2d ed. (London: George Allen & Unwin, 1968), p. 22, in talking about socialist and capitalist countries,

shrewdly warns of applying what is a model in one instance to a case in which it is effectively a muddle. I think the same observation applies to comparing different nations within the capitalist bloc.

6. Later in this essay I shall try to present, as briefly as possible, an example of just such a model of social systems having a higher degree of universality.

7. See Daniel I. Okimoto, *Between MITI and the Market: Japanese Industrial Policy for High Technology* (Stanford: Stanford University Press, 1989).

8. Johnson, *MITI and the Japanese Miracle*; Daniel Okimoto, "Power in Japan: The Societal State" (MS).

9. See, e.g., Frank Harary, Robert Z. Norman, and Dorwin Cartwright, *Structural Models: An Introduction to the Theory of Directed Graphs* (New York: Wiley, 1969).

10. See J. Clyde Mitchell, "Social Networks," *Annual Review of Anthropology*, Vol. 3 (1974), pp. 279–99, Ronald S. Burt, *Toward A Structural Theory of Action: Network Models of Social Structure, Perception, and Action* (New York: Academic Press, 1982), and Ken-ichi Imai, "Nettowākingu soshiki: Tenbō" (Networking organizations: A survey), *Soshiki kagaku*, Vol. 20 (1986), pp. 2–12, for surveys of social network research. Howard Aldrich and David A. Whetten, "Organization-Sets, Action-Sets, and Networks: Making the Most of Simplicity," in Paul C. Nystrom and William H. Starbuck, eds., *Handbook of Organizational Design*, Vol. 1, *Adapting Organizations to Their Environments* (London: Oxford University Press, 1981), pp. 386–408, provides an overview of network analysis of interorganizational couplings, and Noel M. Tichy, "Networks in Organizations," in ibid., Vol. 2, *Remodelling Organizations and Their Environments* (London: Oxford University Press, 1981), pp. 225–49, looks at studies of networks within organizations.

11. Edward J. Jay, "The Concepts of 'Field' and 'Network' in Anthropological Research," *Man*, No. 177 (1964), pp. 137–39.

12. Everett M. Rogers and D. Lawrence Kincaid, *Communication Networks: Toward a New Paradigm for Research* (New York: Free Press; London: Collier Macmillan, 1981), pp. 38, 63.

13. That is to say, he thinks and believes he is a goal seeker, even though, to the eyes of an objective observer, his behavior may seem to be full of miscalculations and errors.

14. There is no need, however, to think of an actor's worldview or sense of values as being constant and unchanging. These may be transformed by outside communications or learning, or partially revised by conscious effort or external influence.

15. I am tempted to call those traits the "civilization" of an actor or group of actors.

16. Augustin Berque, *Vivre l'espace au Japon* (Paris: Presses Universitaires de France, 1982), refers to "metaphor" as the core of culture; his metaphor corresponds here to the principle of interpretation (of the world). Examples of the principle of interpretation in Japanese culture are Berque's own situationality and the monism (as opposed to dualism) argued by Fosco Maraini, "Japan and the Future: Some Suggestions from Nihonjinron Literature," in Gianni Fodella, ed., *Social Structures and Economic Dynamics in Japan up to 1980* (Milan: Institute of Economic and Social Studies for East Asia, Luigi Bocconi University, 1975). An example of the principle for acts would be the "accommodative" (as opposed to the "dominating") type posited by Shumpei Kumon, "Dilemma of a New Phase: Can Japan Meet the Challenge?" in Kenneth B. Pyle, ed., *The Trade Crisis: How Will Japan Respond?* (Seattle: Society for Japanese Studies, 1987). The principle of organizing social systems is illustrated by the *ie/mura* principle in Yasu-

suke Murakami, Shumpei Kumon, and Satō Seizaburō, *Bunmei to shite no ie shakai* (The *ie* society as a civilization) (Tokyo: Chūō Kōron Sha, 1979), and by the formative principles of networks and paramarkets presented here.

17. But it is somewhat doubtful if it is really useful to introduce the concept of "cultural acts" here. As long as most of "culture" in our definition is a set of principles that are transmitted among people subconsciously, it sounds almost self-contradictory to talk about "cultural acts" whose intention is transmitting or educating culture.

18. For this trichotomy of ideal types of mutual acts as the organizing factors in social systems, see Kenneth E. Boulding, "Economic Libertarianism," *Beyond Economics: Essays on Society, Religion and Ethics* (Ann Arbor: University of Michigan Press, 1968), pp 43–54.

19. What I have referred to as "complex actors" can be thought of as being more or less identical to what are called "organizations" in business administration or organization theory. I shall therefore use both terms interchangeably hereafter.

20. We can then define a government as distinct from a state: when one part of a complex actor (especially a state) is structurally differentiated from the other parts and acts representing the actor as a whole, then we can call that part the *government* of that actor.

21. Needless to say, it will be impossible to manage an organization—that is, a complex actor—without the use of any coercion or threat whatsoever. With that caveat in mind, however, let us also recognize that there are organizational types that place relatively more importance on control by exchange/exploitation, or on control by consensus/inducement.

22. As is well exemplified by the modern sovereign state, coercion or threat is rarely seen in naked form even in organizations of the threat/coercion-oriented type. Often they are legitimized under the mantle of "law."

23. Another group of constituent members of the modern world market is the organization called "the household." While an industrial firm is an organization specializing in buying (the right to use) the factors of production and then producing and selling products, the household is an organization specializing in selling (the right to use) the factors of production and in buying/consuming products.

24. The most fundamental right in a social system may be called *actorship*, the right to exist as an actor. This fundamental right can be divided into many subrights and secondary rights. For example, on the basis of our model of an actor, we can divide an actor's acts as a whole into a chain of sub-acts: (1) internal information-processing (recognition, evaluation, and decision), (2) acts in a narrow sense—namely, using some means against an object, and (3) enjoyment of the resultant state, in which the actor's goal is or is not achieved. Let us call the respective rights in connection with these sub-acts *information rights, acts rights,* and *enjoyment rights.* An actor's acts can also be seen to have (1) the aspect of autonomous activity and (2) control over the states or things produced by such acts. Rights concerning the former can be called *personal rights,* while those concerning the latter can be termed *control rights.* On the other hand, once the actorship of an actor has been well recognized by others, secondary *prohibition rights* and *claim rights* will also be recognized, at least to a certain extent: that is, the right to prohibit acts by others that would infringe on the realization and enjoyment of an actor's basic rights, and the right to claim acts by others that would aid in the realization and enjoyment of such basic rights.

25. In modern society, each of these societal systems tends to become the arena for a certain type of competitive social game, with some of its constituent organization as players. For further discussion, see Shumpei Kumon and Akihiko Tanaka, "From Prestige to Wealth to Knowledge," in Takashi Inoguchi and Daniel I. Okimoto, eds., *The Japanese Political Economy*, Vol. 2, *The Changing International Context* (Stanford: Stanford University Press, 1988), pp. 64–82.

26. For analyses and reports of such new phenomena or a new social movement, see Rothschild-Whitt, "Collectivist Organization," Ferguson, *Aquarian Conspiracy*, and Lipnack and Stamps, *Networking: First Report*.

27. A pioneering work concerning such a development is Starr Roxanne Hiltz and Murray Turoff, *The Network Nation: Human Communication via Computer* (Reading, Mass.: Addison-Wesley, 1978). For more recent reports, see Jessica Lipnack and Jeffrey Stamps, *The Networking Book: People Connnecting with People* (New York: Routledge & Kegan Paul, 1986), and Robert Deward (Program Director) and Howard Rheingold (Managing Editor), *Electronic Citizenship* (Pacific Bell, Oct. 1988).

28. As long as individual actors retain some degree of actorship, even when they join a complex actor (organization), they will continue to maintain their own individual goals and not dare to sacrifice them completely for the good of the whole.

29. See, e.g., Mark Granovetter, *Getting a Job: A Study of Contacts and Careers* (Cambridge, Mass.: Harvard University Press, 1974) and the same author's "Economic Action and Social Structure: The Problem of Embeddedness," *American Journal of Sociology*, Vol. 91, No. 3 (Nov. 1985), pp. 481–510, as well as Stewart Macaulay, "Non-Contractual Relations in Business: A Preliminary Study," *American Sociological Review*, Vol. 28, No. 1 (1963), pp. 55–67, and Robert Eccles, "The Quasifirm in the Construction Industry," *Journal of Economic Behavior and Organization*, Vol. 2 (Dec. 1981), pp. 335–57, both quoted in Granovetter, "Economic Action."

30. It might be useful to provide generic names for threat/coercion–oriented systems (including states-systems and states) and exchange/eploitation-oriented systems (including markets and firms). For example, the former might tentively be called *power systems* and the latter *transaction systems*.

31. I have attempted to enumerate some of the basic element of contextualist world outlooks and values in Shumpei Kumon, "Some Principles Governing the Thought and Behavior of Japanists (Contextualists)," *Journal of Japanese Studies*, Vol. 8, No. 1 (Winter 1982), pp. 5–28. For a methodological discussion of contextualism, see Esyun Hamaguchi, "A Contextual Model of the Japanese: Toward a Methodological Innovation in Japan Studies," *Journal of Japanese Studies*, Vol. 11, No. 2 (Summer 1985), pp. 289–321.

32. The all-too-famous concept of *amae* presented by Takeo Doi in his *The Anatomy of Dependence* (Tokyo: Kōdansha International, 1973) refers only to one of the two complementary aspects of this most fundamental desire of the Japanese, or of all human beings for that matter, to identify with others. For a vivid description of the custom of caretaking in Japanese villages, see Minoru Kida, *Nippon buraku* (Tokyo: Iwanami Shoten, 1967), chap. 4. See also Hayao Kawai, *Bosei shakai Nihon no byōri* (Pathology of Japanese society based on the mother principle) (Tokyo: Chūō Kōron Sha, 1976), on the dominance of the mother principle in Japan (though this does not at all mean that Japan totally lacks the father principle, that of separation and distinction).

33. Let me here define *networking* as the formation, maintenance, and development of networks as social systems.

34. See Edward T. Hall, *Beyond Culture* (Garden City, N.Y.: Anchor Press, 1976), and Edward T. Hall and Mildred Reed Hall, *Hidden Differences: Doing Business with the Japanese* (Garden City, N.Y.: Anchor Press/Doubleday, 1987) for "hi-context" communication.

35. For example, one of the key phrases for the administrative reform the Japanese government has been attempting since the early 1980s is *henka heno taiō* (coping with change). Also, quite frequently, where some people in a group realize that its past acts have not necessarily been successful, they call for *hassō no tenkan* (thinking differently). See Akio Watanabe, "Foreign Policy Making, Japanese Style," *International Affairs*, Vol. 54, No. 1 (Jan. 1978), pp. 75–88.

36. For a distinction between two contrasting styles of mastery of computer programming discovered among American children, see Sherry Turkle, *The Second Self: Computers and the Human Spirit* (New York: Simon & Schuster, 1984), pp. 104–5. I think this classificatory scheme can usefully be generalized to characterize cultural types. For the "situational ethic," see the final chapter of Ruth Benedict, *The Chrysanthemum and the Sword: Patterns of Japanese Culture* (1946; New York: New American Library, 1974).

37. Murakami, Kumon, and Satō, *Bunmei to shite no ie shakai*. See, for a condensed English version, Yasuske Murakami, "*Ie* Society as a Pattern of Civilization," *Journal of Japanese Studies*, Vol. 10, No. 2 (Summer 1984), pp. 281–363.

38. Or it may be better to say that business organizations that were first established following the Western model gradually reorganized themselves, in an atavistic way, into *ie*-type organizations.

39. This is Nakane's position in her *Tate shakai no rikigaku* (Dynamics of a vertical society) (Tokyo: Kōdansha, 1978) where she introduces it to overcome a theoretical weakness of her famous book *Tate shakai no ningen kankei* (Human relations in a vertical society) (Tokyo: Kōdansha 1967), published in English as *Japanese Society* (Berkeley: University of California Press, 1970). In the earlier book, she could not fully explain how a society made up of such highly independent organizations could be integrated into a single whole, making tinkerer's attempts to introduce a strong centralized government as the deus ex machina. See her introduction to the 1978 book.

40. In such a hierarchy of concentric, circlelike, vertically divided network organizations, the one that occupies the bottom position is often called the *mura* (literally, village) and such a division of a larger "world" and formation of a corresponding bottom-level network organization, usually brought about through the initiative of the government bureaus concerned, is called the *mura-kubun* (division into villages). In a similar way, major political parties in Japan are divided into several factions called *mura*. In this case, too, both the political parties and their factions can be regarded, at least in a first-order approximation, as network organizations according to my definition.

41. Needless to say, in Japan, as in other societies, there are many other informal, semi-secret, and/or conspiratorial networks, of which one notorious example is the so-called *dangō* system in the subworld of the construction industry.

42. Shichihei Yamamoto points out in *Kūki no kenkyū* (A study of *kūki*) (Tokyo: Bungei Shunjū Sha, 1977) that this "group sentiment," called *kūki* in Japanese, is the single most influential determinant of network members' sentiments, decisions, and acts.

43. This trait corresponds well with what Takeshi Ishida calls the "synchronization-competition complex" and postulates to be the core of Japan's political

culture in *Nihon no seiji bunka—dōchō to kyōsō* (Japan's political culture: Synchronization and competition) (Tokyo: Tokyo Daigaku Shuppan Kai, 1970). His *synchronization* is "conforming with the dominant value-orientation and behavioral modes dominant in the group one belongs to, or, in other words, acting the same as other people." *Competition* refers to such acts executed by the members of a group who have a strong sense of loyalty toward their group and seek to contribute more than other members toward its development, thereby gaining a preeminent position (p. 33). In such a group, since there is a shared traditional view that "everything has to follow its own natural course" (pp. 62–63), any deliberate decision making tends to be avoided. At the state level, in particular, Ishida posits that even the procedures for determining goals are unclear (p. 117).

44. It is in this sense that I am tempted to call today's Japan a *sentiment-governed society* rather than a *law-governed state*.

45. A fine example of this can be seen in the news coverage of the incident in July 1988 in which a Self-Defense Force submarine, the *Nadashio*, collided with a fishing boat, the *Daiichi Fujimaru*, resulting in the sinking of the latter with much loss of life. Andrew Horvat, the new chairman of the Foreign Press Club of Japan, pointed out in an interview that the extremely emotional coverage by Japanese TV was "not reporting but one form of drama," the title of which was "Protest Against the Self-Defense Forces" (quoted in Kinko Sato, "Feā na baransu hōdō o: Sensuikan shōtotsu jiko to masukomi" [I want fair and balanced reports: The submarine collision accident and the mass media], *Sankei*, Aug. 23, 1988). Thus, before any coolheaded, thorough investigation of the causes of the incident could take place, the mass media fed "reporting" aimed at arousing emotion to the public, which then fed those sentiments back to the media.

46. Here I should reemphasize the fact that Japanese, not unlike other people, simultaneously belong to a number of often concentric networks, and that they compete as well as cooperate in each of them. In this sense, the "informational closedness" of the Japanese is a relative matter: foreigners are not the only people in Japan informationally insulated from networks of which they are not members.

47. This implies a strong likelihood that, if the members believe sharing information with others may be disadvantageous to their competition within a certain network, such sharing will not occur. In fact, there is a well-known tendency, perhaps not unique to Japan, for scholars and government departments, as well as firms, to monopolize information about their activities on the one hand and on the other hand to regard it as shameful for it to be pointed out that they are not capable of doing something by themselves or don't know their own business.

48. *Nihonjinron* is precisely the literature of this type of discussion in the nationwide societal network, Nihon. This sort of active information-gathering and information-sharing is, of course, not unique to Nihon. The members of the many smaller-scale networks making up the subsystems of Nihon also tend to possess a strong consciousness of being "special" or "unique"—different from those belonging to other "worlds." Thus they also tend to carry on unending discussions, often in a self-depreciating rather than self-assertive way, of how they are "special" and of how those in other worlds view and treat them differently, and sometimes even discriminate against them. They often strenuously gather information about the outside world as the data for such discussions. Such information—where we differ from others, which of our characteristics are distinct from those of others—often provides the most fundamental

ground for comparing and assessing their own members: the most typical member of the group is also its best member.

49. The term *unit-veto system* is taken from Morton A. Kaplan, *System and Process in International Politics* (New York: Wiley, 1957). Note that a unit-veto system is one in which a consensus (agreement of all qualified sub-actors) is necessary to reach a decision. In that sense it may also be called a "consensual system." Note also that qualified sub-actors can vary in their power to influence a collective decision. In other words, the number of votes they have may differ.

50. Taichi Sakaiya, "Issennichi no henkaku: 'Saiteki kōgyō shakai' Nihon no kōei to genkai" (One thousand days of change: The glory and limits of Japan, "the optimal industrial society"), *Voice* (Nov. 1986), pp. 126–48.

51. For example, at one time, even when criminal offenses were committed on campuses, many Japanese universities refused to let the police on campus, citing the university's "autonomy." Even today, university students do not recognize freedom of opinion as one of the fundamental principles governing the university. Thus, in recent years, on many Japanese university campuses, the majority of students have not hesitated to deny fellow students who belong to the Genri Undō (Fundamentalism Movement) group the right to participate in student government on the grounds that they are "undemocratic" or are spies working for a foreign country. In short, they take it for granted that if there are people who are hated by all of them, then it does not matter how much they discriminate against them, bully them, or treat them like outcasts. In this regard it is quite likely that outside observers, or insiders made the object of such bullying and discrimination, will conclude that the Japanese do not understand or respect human rights.

52. Such mediation may be another reason why Japanese organizations are considered "undemocratic," insofar as the interests and opinions of some groups, usually minorities, are thereby muffled and suppressed. One should not, however, overlook the fact that the unit veto for everyone is the main principle in most Japanese organizations, especially network organizations, and hence *wa* does not always prevail, or is not necessarily welcomed by everybody. Neither should one overlook the fact that, for the same reason, *wa* can often work in the oppposite way—namely, causing the majority to compromise with the minority.

53. Introduction to Karl Polanyi, *The Livelihood of Man*, ed. H. W. Pearson (New York: Academic Press, 1977), pp. xxxiii, xxxvi.

54. Ibid., p. xxxvi. Thus Polanyi uses the terms *market* and *exchange* in a narrower sense than I do. Polanyi's "exchange" is one special case of mine.

55. Ibid., p. xxxiii.

56. Ibid., p. xxxvi.

57. In their essay in this volume, Murakami and Rohlen adopt a different approach in dealing with this type of mutual act: they regard them as cases of "social exchange." The "administrative network" of Thomas Lifson (see his essay in this volume) thus belongs to, or includes, this type of network.

58. Paramarkets can include simultaneous two-way transactions in goods and services that on the surface resemble exchange, the crucial distinction being that the mutual act of reciprocation does not conclude there. For example, a transaction in which a buyer has made a payment and thus acquired goods may appear to be a typical exchange, but, if the buyer feels he has paid less than the market price (creating a debit to the seller) or, conversely, has paid more than the market price (creating a credit to the seller), and the seller agrees with this assessment, then that mutual act falls into the category of reciprocation rather than exchange.

59. Of course, there are many exceptions to this rule. In both hierarchical and network organizations, the possibility always exists that information wil circulate in a way at variance with the stipulated rules. In such cases, there may be information exchange (in a market sense) or reciprocation (in a paramarket sense).

60. This occurred at the Amagi Seminar organized by the Aspen Institute and Japan IBM held in October 1986, of which I served as a co-moderator. See also the works cited in note 29 above.

61. See Rothschild-Whitt, "Collectivist Organization." The author argues that in the first place, they came into existence as separate organizations outside the existing bureaucratic organizations, and that in the second place, American individualist culture does not seem to be a favorable environment for the survival, let alone flourishing, of such organizations.

62. Personal communication, such as ordinary conversation, exchange of letters, or telephone conversation, takes place among a restricted number of people, usually in a one-to-one fashion. Mass communication on the other hand, takes place on a massive scale between a few "senders" and an extremely large number of "receivers" in a one-sided, one-to-many fashion. In contrast, *group communication* takes place interactively among middle numbers (hundreds to thousands) of people in an *n*-to-*n* fashion. One interesting outcome of the spread of this last form of communication in recent years, mainly as computer-aided telecommunication, is that elements of "collectivist orientation" or preference for mutual understanding and cooperation through "consensus/inducement"-oriented mutual acts have been consciously introduced *into* existing bureaucratic organizations. See Hiltz and Turoff, *Network Nation*; Lipnack and Stamps, *Networking Book*; and Deward and Rheingold, *Electronic Citizenship*.

63. What is extremely important at this juncture is to assess, as accurately as possible, the implications of current changes in people's consciousness in the Western world, changes that may be called a paradigm shift away from individualism. It may be that Westerners are finally being liberated from the cultural constraints of individualism so that they can see, understand, and value the "contextual" and networking-oriented elements that have long been in existence in their own society. Similarly, the Japanese may on their part be discovering the existence and the value of "individual" and independence-oriented aspects of their own society. Be that as it may, I argue here that these different societies are similar to one another in an objective sense. What makes them subjectively different is culture, the peculiar cognitive and evaluative framework that members share and use, subconsciously most of the time.

64. See Rothschild-Whitt, "Collectivist Organization."

65. At the same time, however, it is also likely that one's mind is closed at least partly because of awareness of one's weakness and inferiority as an independent actor. A natural defense is then to insulate oneself informationally, under the guise of "autonomy," by obstinately rejecting disclosure of information about oneself and not lending an ear to advice or criticism from outside. Another way of coping is to welcome imposition of detailed regulations and rules on group members. Both of these seem to be occurring in schooling in today's Japan. See, e.g., Harry Wray, "Kokusai shugi o habamu Nihon no kyōiku" (Education in Japan is preventing internationalism), *Chūō Kōron*, Sept. 1989, pp. 160–75.

66. This inequality in credibility and depth of reciprocal relations in the paramarket is different in nature to the inequality of the distribution of wealth in the market. At least theoretically, the price of a commodity in a market will

not change according to the buyer. Anyone can buy a given commodity if willing to pay the seller's price, whether rich or poor, a newcomer to the market or an old-timer there. In this sense, the participants in a market are all equal, but this is not the case in a paramarket.

67. As far as I know, it was Isaiah Bendasan's *Nihonjin to Yudayajin* (The Japanese and the Jews) (Tokyo: Yamamoto Shoten, 1970) that first questioned the necessary validity of decisions made unanimously in Japan.

68. The two major political parties in Japan, the Liberal Democratic Party and the Japan Socialist Party, do not quite have the structure of modern bureaucratic organizations and often suffer from inability to reach decisions promptly and execute them effectively. One remedy for this, proposed repeatedly, particularly for the LDP, is to "modernize" by dissolving the various "factions" and reorganizing the party into a more centralized organization, both administratively and fiscally. Most LDP members, ashamed that their party is still at a "premodern" level, have accepted this as the only rational solution, at least theoretically, but there has never been any serious attempt to implement it, simply because it is so unrealistic. Whenever the factions have solemnly been declared to be dissolved, they turned out not to be or were soon revived. In recent years there have been voices, though still a minority, stressing the positive roles that factions play and offering a different scheme for reform while preserving the network nature of the organization. See, e.g., Ken'ichi Kōyama, "Jimintō no 'bunkatsu, min'eika' o" (A call for "divestiture and privatization" of the Liberal Democratic Party), *Sankei*, Aug. 8, 1989, which proposes reconstituting the LDP as a loose federation of former factions, reorganized into "political parties"—that is to say, more independent, policy-oriented, formal institutions.

69. See Eiichi Katō, *Toshi no fukushū* (Revenge of the city) (Tokyo: Taiyō Kikaku Shuppan, 1983), for a richly suggestive description and analysis of the "Mejiro machine." See also Shichihei Yamamoto, *Nihonjin to genshiryoku* (The Japanese and nuclear power) (Tokyo: KK World Press, 1976), p. 20, for the three circular steps reasoning about the ponderous decision-making process of today's Japan: (1) Japan will soon decline and perish if this impotence in decision making continues; (2) however, we have always been like this and yet somehow have been doing well, so we shall probably manage to do well in future too; (3) even though we have so far done alright, the world has changed greatly, so the familiar old ways of doing things do not hold any more.

Aoki: Decentralization–Centralization

1. James C. Abegglen, *The Japanese Factory: Aspects of Its Social Organization* (New York: Free Press, 1958), p. 129.

2. Ibid., p. 130.

3. Ronald Dore, *British Factory, Japanese Factory: The Origins of National Diversity in Industrial Relations* (Berkeley: University of California Press, 1973), p. 264.

4. Ibid., pp. 338–39.

5. Ibid., p. 340.

6. A conspicuous example of the universalist view may be found in the habitual thinking of neoclassical economists, who analyze the Japanese economy using the toolbox developed within the Anglo-American academic community. Japanese firms are assumed to be maximizing profits just as Western firms do, and Japanese households are assumed to maximize their utilities like Western households: their decentralized decisions are made mutually consistent through the workings of markets operating efficiently according to the law of supply and

demand. Neoclassical economists may recognize certain cultural and/or institutionally unique factors, such as the high savings propensity of Japanese households and slower adjustment of employment by firms in response to business cycles, but those phenomena may be dealt with only as differences in tastes exogenous to the model or by introducing "employment adjustment costs." In other words, the possible influence of cultural factors may be contained in a black box in the economists' model. The Japanese economic system is thus treated as basically homeomorphic to the Western system.

7. Koike's main work is *Shokuba no rōdō-kumiai to sanka* (The labor union and participation on the shop floor) (Tokyo: Keizai Shinposha, 1975). Major points of this book are succinctly summarized for English readers in "Skill Formation Systems in the U.S. and Japan: A Comparative Study," in Masahiko Aoiki, ed., *The Economic Analysis of the Japanese Firm* (Amsterdam: North-Holland, 1984). An English translation of a collection of Koike's various articles has been published as *Understanding the Industrial Relations in Japan* (London: Macmillan, 1988). See also "Skill Formation in Mass Production: Japan and Thai," *Journal of the Japanese and International Economies*, Vol. 1 (1987), pp. 408–40.

8. William G. Ouchi, *Theory Z: How American Business Can Meet the Japanese Challenge* (Reading, Mass.: Addison-Wesley, 1981); Ezra F. Vogel, *Japan as Number 1: Lessons for America* (Cambridge, Mass.: Harvard University Press, 1979).

9. *Igirisu no kōjō, Nihon no kōjō,* trans. Yasushi Yamanouchi and Koichi Nagai (Tokyo: Chikuma Shobo, 1986), p. xii.

10. Ibid.

11. Ronald Dore, *Taking Japan Seriously: A Confucian Perspective on Leading Economic Issues* (Stanford: Stanford University Press, 1987).

12. Hurwicz's works are highly mathematical. Nonmathematical readers are referred to Leonid Hurwicz, "The Design of Mechanisms for Resource Allocation," *American Economic Review*, Vol. 63 (1973), pp. 1–30 and "Mechanism and Institutions," in Takashi Shiraishi and Shigeto Tsuru, eds., *Economic Institutions in a Dynamic Society* (New York: Macmillan, 1989), a volume in the International Economic Roundtable Conference Series.

13. See Masahiko Aoki, "Horizontal v. Vertical Information Structure of the Firm," *American Economic Review*, Vol. 76 (1986), pp. 971–83; *Information, Incentives, and Bargaining in the Japanese Economy* (Cambridge: Cambridge University Press, 1988), chap. 2; "The Participatory Generation of Information Rents and the Theory of the Firm," in Masahiko Aoki, Bo Gustafsson, and Oliver E. Williamson, eds., *The Firm as a Nexus of Treaties* (London: Sage Publications, 1989). In the first two works, I use the adjective *horizontal* instead of *decentralized* to denote the same informational structure. But there should not be any confusion. It is to be noted, however, that the distinction here between the centralized and decentralized systems is different from the traditional one used by economists. In the traditional scheme, the centralized system is synonymous with the command system, whereas the decentralized system is often identified with the price mechanism.

14. Aoki, "Participatory Generation of Information Rents."

15. See W. Bentley McLeod and James M. Malcomson, "Reputation and Hierarchy in Dynamic Models of Employment," *Journal of Political Economy*, Vol. 96 (1988), pp. 832–54; Aoki, *Information, Incentives, and Bargaining*, chap. 3.

16. Paul Milgrom and John Roberts, "Bargaining Costs, Influence Cost, and the Organization of Economic Activity," in J. Alt and K. Shepsle, eds., *Rational Perspectives on Political Economy* (Cambridge, Eng.: Cambridge University Press, 1990), pp. 57–89.

17. Joseph Stiglitz, "Incentives, Risks, and Notes Toward a Theory of Hierarchy," *Bell Journal of Economics*, Vol. 6 (1975), p. 570.

18. Yasusuke Murakami, "*Ie* Society as a Pattern of Civilization," *Journal of Japanese Studies*, Vol. 10, No. 2 (1984), pp. 308–9.

19. Ibid., p. 357.

20. Ibid., p. 309.

21. Aoki, *Information, Incentives, and Bargaining*, chaps. 3 and 4.

22. See, e.g., Dore, *British Factory, Japanese Factory*, and Koike, *Shokuba no rōdō-kumiai*.

23. See Aoki, *Information, Incentives, and Bargaining*, chap. 2, on the *kanban* system.

24. D. Eleanor Westney and Kiyonori Sakakibara, "Comparative Study of the Training, Careers, and Organization of Engineers in the Computer Industry in Japan and the U.S." (MS, 1985).

25. Masahiko Aoki and Nathan Rosenberg, "The Japanese Firm as an Innovative Institution," in Shiraishi and Tsuru, eds., *Economic Institutions in a Dynamic Society*.

26. Aoki, *Information, Incentives, and Bargaining*, chap. 7.

27. Ibid.

28. This is only one aspect of ministries, however. Each ministry has another face as an autonomous delineator of public interest beyond specific jurisdictional interests. Otherwise, the ministry may fail to mobilize political resources in competition with other ministries. The dual characteristic of the ministry is a natural consequence of the bureaucratic motivation to enhance its political stock. See Aoki, *Information, Incentives, and Bargaining*, chap. 7.

29. Iwao Nakatani, "Seikinin kokka—Nihon—e no sentaku" (Choices open to the responsible state—Japan), *Asteion* (Fall 1987), pp. 38–40.

30. I would emphasize the need for "endogenous" overcoming of possible malfunctions in the Japanese bureaucracy caused by the failure of the duality principle. Some might expect "external" forces, such as national crises and foreign pressure, to solidify the diverse interests of ministries under such conditions, but the fact that rivalry between the Imperial Army and the Imperial Navy never ceased throughout World War II contradicts this expectation. Wartime experience also provides cases supporting the theoretical proposition that diffused sharing of knowledge is not effective in "drastically changing environments." For example, in order to boost morale in combat units before launching important tactical operations, Japanese soldiers were given a general picture of the strategy of which they were a part. As a result, when they were captured, both their interrogation and their diaries provided valuable information to the enemy (the U.S. Army prohibited soldiers from keeping diaries). See Ambassador Koichiro Asakai, "Watashi no rirekisho," *Nihon Keizai Shinbun*, March 6–7, 1988.

31. Chie Nakane, *Japanese Society* (Berkeley: University of California Press, 1970).

32. Ibid., p. 63. Emphasis added.

33. H. Itami, *Jinponshugi* (Peoplism) (Tokyo: Chikuma Shobo, 1987), chap. 2.

34. On the sharing aspect of the Japanese firm and its game-theory analysis, see Masahiko Aoki, *The Cooperative Game Theory of the Firm* (Oxford: Oxford University Press, 1984); "The Japanese Firm in Transition," in Kozo Yamamura and Yasukichi Yasuba, eds., *The Political Economy of Japan*, Vol. 1, *The Domestic Transformation* (Stanford: Stanford University Press, 1987), pp. 263–88; *Information, Incentives, and Bargaining*, chap. 5; and "Participatory Generation of Information Rents."

35. James Lincoln, Mitsuyo Hanada, and Kerry McBride, "Organizational Structures in Japanese and U.S. Manufacturing," *Administrative Science Quarterly*, Vol. 31 (1986), pp. 334–64.

36. Nakane here seems to imply by the *tate* principle only the CP aspect of the Japanese organizational mode, and denies the CI aspect, contrary to her assertion quoted in the previous section.

37. Nakane, *Japanese Society*, pp. 68–69.

38. For the work system of rice production and the importance of the irrigation system, see Thomas C. Smith, *The Agrarian Origin of Modern Japan* (Stanford: Stanford University Press, 1959).

39. Hajime Tamaki and Isao Hatade, *Fūdo* (Tokyo: Heibonsha, 1974).

40. Thomas P. Rohlen, "The Company Work Group," in Ezra Vogel, ed., *Modern Japanese Organization and Decision-Making* (Berkeley: University of California Press, 1975), pp. 208–9.

41. See Koike, "Skill Formation Systems," p. 63.

42. Ibid.

43. Murakami, "*Ie* Society," p. 356.

44. In this sense, it is interesting to note that a true hybrid, New United Motors Manufacturing, Inc., formed by the two giant Japanese and American firms, Toyota and GM, is experimenting with a Japanese-type work team composed of seven members, among whom jobs are rotated under the direction of the team leader, but implementing a much simpler structure of ranking. There are only two pay levels, skilled and unskilled, with annual bonuses. Team leaders made 50 cents more per hour in 1986, but there are no "pay-for-knowledge" differentials, which had failed in previous experiments with operating-team systems in other GM factories in the South. See Harry Katz, *Shifting Gears: Changing Labor Relations in the U.S. Auotomobile Industry* (Cambridge, Mass.: MIT Press, 1985), for a description of this experiment.

45. On the sharing of information rents, see Aoki, "Participatory Generation of Information Rents."

46. Fred Foulkes, *Personnel Policies in Large Nonunion Companies* (Englewood Cliffs, N.J.: Prentice-Hall, 1980).

47. Henry Rosovsky, *The University: An Owner's Manual* (New York: Norton, 1990), chap. 2.

48. Aoki and Rosenberg, "Japanese Firm."

Iwata: The Japanese Enterprise

1. For the content of such arguments and details of the controversy surrounding the topic, see Ryushi Iwata, "*Nihon-teki keiei*" *ronsō* (Polemics on "Japanese management") (Tokyo: Nihon Keizai Shimbunsha, 1984).

2. For representative arguments from this perspective, see the works of Nishiyama and Matsumoto, including Tadanori Nishiyama, *Gendai kigyō no shihai kōzō: Kabushiki gaisha no hōkai* (The control structure of contemporary enterprise: The collapse of joint-stock companies) (Tokyo: Yūhikaku, 1975); *Shihai kōzō ron: Nihon shihon shugi no hōkai* (On control structure: The collapse of Japanese capitalism) (Tokyo: Bunshindō, 1980); *Nihon wa shihon shugi de wa nai* (Japan is not a capitalist nation) (Tokyo: Mikasa Shobō, 1981); and *Datsu shihon shugi bunseki: Atarashii shakai no kaimaku* (Analysis of post-capitalism: The start of a new society) (Tokyo: Bunshindō, 1983); and Kōji Matsumoto, *Kigyō-shugi no kōryū: Nihon-teki pawā no shuyaku* (The rise of corporatism: The hero of Japanese power) (Tokyo: Nihon Seisansei Honbu, 1983), introduction.

3. See Nishiyama, *Gendai kigyō no shihai kozō*.

4. Nishiyama, *Nihon wa shihon shugi de wa nai*, p. 110.

5. Ibid., pp. 110–11.

6. Ibid., p. 98.

7. Matsumoto, *Kigyō shugi no kōryū*, Introduction.

8. Nishiyama and Matsumoto concentrate mainly on the strength of the Japanese managerial system, although they are aware of its weaknesses.

9. Dore has made similar observations about Hitachi. See Ronald Dore, *British Factory, Japanese Factory: The Origins of National Diversity in Industrial Relations* (Berkeley: University of California Press, 1973), p. 260.

10. Based on his observations at Hitachi, Dore reports that union leaders show strong interest in the company's performance, similar to that of managers. Ibid., p. 200.

11. Nishiyama, in comparison, does not ignore the cultural dimensions. However, he only points out its relevance to the argument of his framework and does not attempt systematically to analyze this factor.

12. Yasukazu Takenaka, *Nihon-teki keiei no genryū* (The origins of Japanese management) (Kyoto: Minerva Shobō, 1977), pp. 12–13.

13. Mitsui Bunko, *Mitsui jigyōshi shiryō* (The history of Mitsui business), Vol. 2 (Tokyo, 1977), pp. 356–57.

14. Mitsui Ginkō, *Mitsui ginkō hachijū-nen-shi* (The 80-year history of Mitsui Bank) (Tokyo, 1957), pp. 82–85; and see *Mitsui jigyōshi shiryō*, Vol. 3, pp. 5–16 for more information.

15. Tokushichi Nomura, who built his Nomura *zaibatsu* empire from a stockbrokerage, was well known for his ideal of "mutual support" and for his bold promotion of his employees. Fujimoto, too, based his business philosophy on the idea of "mutual support": coexistence and coprosperity with his employees and the general public.

16. See Ryushi Iwata, *Kyogyō no kenkyū* (The study of quasi[i.e., dishonest]-business) (Tokyo: Nihon Keizai Shimbunsha, 1987).

17. Such disputes, however, were seen mainly between workers and their supervisors. The relationship between white-collar employees and managers did not change as drastically. See Kazuyoshi Hosoi, *Jokō aishi* (The tragic history of female workers) and Shigemi Yamamoto, *Ah, Nomuge toge: Aru seishi jokō aishi* (Ah, Nomugi Pass: The tragic story of female silk-reelers), for eloquent descriptions of the consequences of the view of workers as dispensable.

18. The participants in this joint study were Yutaka Kasugai (who undertook the case of Mitsui), Shōichi Asajima (Mitsubishi and Sumitomo), Masaru Udagawa (Nissan), Takeshi Ōshio (Nichitsu), and Satoshi Saitō (Riken). Each of these individuals has contributed a great deal to the field. See Shōichi Asajima, ed., *Zaibatsu kinyū kōzō no hikaku kenkyū* (Comparative studies of the financial structure of zaibatsu) (Tokyo: Ochanomizu Shobō, 1987).

19. Ibid., p. 156.

20. Ibid., p. 213.

21. Ibid., p. 401.

22. Esyun Hamaguchi, *"Nihon rashisa" no saihakken* (The rediscovery of "Japaneseness") (Tokyo: Nihon Keizai Shinbunsha, 1977).

23. Ibid., pp. 77–79.

24. Richard T. Pascale and Anthony G. Athos, *The Art of Management* (New York: Simon & Schuster, 1981), p. 65.

25. Wada Toyoji Den-Hensanjo, *Wada Toyoji den* (The biography of Wada Toyoji) (Tokyo, 1926), pp. 184–85.

26. Mitsui Ginkō, ed., *Mitsui ryōgae-ten* (Mitsui exchange shop) (Tokyo, 1983), p. 137.

27. Mitsubishi Shashi Kankōkai, *Mitsubishi shashi* (Mitsubishi company documents) (Tokyo: University of Tokyo Press, 1976), Vol. 3, pp. 2–3.

28. Kamekichi Takahashi, *Kabushiki gaisha bōkoku ron* (On joint-stock companies ruinous to the state) (Tokyo: Manri-kaku Shobō, 1930).

29. I have often been asked by Americans whether *kigyō shugi* ("corporatism") could be adopted in the United States. In responding to such inquiries, I make it a rule to point out that the problem has two sides: business principles and employee attitudes. In my opinion, how the individual relates himself to the group is the most important factor in employee attitudes.

30. See, e.g., Ryushi Iwata, *Nihonteki keiei no hensei genri* (The organizational principles of Japanese management) (Tokyo: Bunshindō, 1977) and *Keieitai no seichō to kōzō henka: Seichō purosesu moderu no tankyū* (The growth of business organizations and their structural change: A search for process models) (Tokyo: Bunshindō, 1986).

31. Hamaguchi, *"Nihon rashisa" no saihakken.*

32. Today's youth seem to have begun to perceive their relations with their affiliated groups in a different way. See Ryushi Iwata, *Nihon no keiei soshiki* (Japanese managerial organizations) (Tokyo: Nihon Keizai Shimbunsha, 1985).

33. This observation was made by one of my colleagues at Musashi University, Professor Saturo Yoshida, who accompanied the tour.

34. Dore, *British Factory, Japanese Factory*, pp. 223–24.

35. On changes in the environment and measures for adjustment, see Ryushi Iwata, ed., *Nihon-gata keiei shisutemu no shōrai* (The future of Japanese-type managerial systems) (Tokyo: Ōkurasho Insatsukyoku, 1984).

Imai: Japan's Corporate Networks

1. See Ken-ichi Imai and Hiroyuki Itami, "Interpenetration of Organization and Market: Japan's Firm and Market in Comparison with the U.S.," *International Journal of Industrial Organization*, Vol. 2, No. 4 (Dec. 1984), pp. 285–310.

2. Peter M. Blau, *Social Exchange and Power in Social Life* (New York: Wiley, 1964).

3. Joseph A. Schumpeter, *Capitalism, Socialism, and Democracy*, 4th ed. (London: George Allen & Unwin, 1952), p. 83.

4. Phil Blackburn, Rod Coombs, and Kenneth Green, *Technology, Economic Growth and the Labour Process* (London: Macmillan, 1985), has much to offer for analyzing the world economy from this viewpoint.

5. Keiichirō Nakagawa, "Dai 2 ji taisen zen no Nihon ni okeru sangyō kozō to kigyōsha katsudō" (Industrial structure and entrepreneurial activities in Japan before World War II), *Mitsui bunko ronsō*, No. 3 (1969).

6. Nathaniel H. Leff, "Industrial Organization and Entrepreneurship in the Developing Countries: The Economic Groups," *Economic Development and Cultural Change*, Vol. 26, No. 4 (July 1978) and "Entrepreneurship and Economic Development: The Problem Revisited," *Journal of Economic Literature*, Vol. 17, No. 1 (Mar. 1979).

7. Joseph A. Schumpeter, *The Theory of Economic Development*, trans. Readers Opie (Cambridge, Mass.: Harvard University Press, 1951), pp. 65–74.

8. For a general description of Japanese economic development in relation to the Western economy, see Henry Rosovsky, *Capital Formation in Japan, 1868–1940* (Glencoe, Ill.: Free Press of Glencoe, 1961), chap. 4.

9. Michael Y. Yoshino and Thomas B. Lifson, *The Invisible Link: Japan's Sogo Shosha and the Organization of Trade* (Cambridge, Mass.: MIT Press, 1986), p. 23.

10. Readers are referred to the following publications: Shigeaki Yasuoka, ed., *Nihon no zaibatsu* (Japanese zaibatsu) (Tokyo: Nihon Keizai Shimbun-sha, 1976); Shigeaki Yasuoka, ed., *Zaibatsu keisei shi no kenkyū* (Study of the history of zaibatsu formation) (Tokyo: Minerva Shobō, 1970); John G. Roberts, *Mitsui: Nihon ni okeru keizai to seiji no 300 nen* (Mitsui: 300 years of economics and politics in Japan), trans. Yoshio Ando and Reiko Mitsui (Tokyo: Diamond, 1976); Yasuo Mishima, *Mitsubishi zaibatsu shi: Meiji hen* (History of the Mitsui zaibatsu: Meiji era) (Tokyo: Kyōiku-sha, 1979); Shōichi Asashima, *Sengo ki Sumitomo zaibatsu keieishi* (Postwar Sumitomo zaibatsu management history) (Tokyo: Tokyo Daigaku Shuppankai, 1983).

11. See John Scott, "Theoretical Framework and Research Design," in Frans N. Stokman, Rolf Ziegler, and John Scott, eds., *Networks of Corporate Power: A Comparative Analysis of Ten Countries* (Cambridge: Polity Press, 1985).

12. See Yasuoka, ed., *Nihon no zaibatsu*, pp. 30–31.

13. As a suggestive analysis, see Richard E. Caves and Masu Uekusa, *Industrial Organization in Japan* (Washington, D.C.: Brookings Institution, 1976).

14. Mitsubishi Economic Research Institute, *Mitsui—Mitsubishi—Sumitomo* (Tokyo, 1955).

15. George C. Allen, "Japanese Industry: Its Organization and Development to 1937," in Elizabeth B. Schumpeter, ed., *The Industrialization of Japan and Manchukuo, 1930–1940: Population, Raw Materials and Industry* (New York: Macmillan, 1940).

16. Eleanor M. Hadley, *Antitrust in Japan* (Princeton: Princeton University Press, 1970).

17. Schumpeter, *Capitalism, Socialism, and Democracy*, pp. 131–42.

18. Hadley, *Antitrust in Japan*, p. 10.

19. The basic literature is Mochikabu Kaisha Seiri Iin Kai (Shareholding Company Liquidation Committee), ed., *Nihon zaibatsu to sono kaitai* (Japanese zaibatsu and their dissolution) (1951), and *Shiryo hen* (Background material to *Nihon zaibatsu to sono kaitai*) (1950).

20. Yoshitarō Wakimura, "Sengo keiei shi no shuppatsu ten: Zaibatsu kaitai" (Starting point of postwar management history: Zaibatsu dissolution), *Business Review*, Hitotsubashi University, Vol. 31, No. 2 (Oct. 1983), pp. 88–98.

21. On the role of intercorporate shareholding, see Masahiko Aoki, "The Japanese Firm in Transition," in Kozo Yamamura and Yasukichi Yasuba, eds., *The Political Economy of Japan*, Vol. 1, *The Domestic Transformation* (Stanford: Stanford University Press, 1987), pp. 279–82.

22. See Ken-ichi Imai, "Japan's Industrial Organization," in Kazuo Sato, ed., *Industry and Business in Japan* (Armonk, N.Y.: M. E. Sharpe, 1980); also, George C. Eads and Kozo Yamamura, "The Future of Industrial Policy," in Yamamura and Yasuba, eds., *Political Economy of Japan*, Vol. 1.

23. A detailed discussion is given in Imai and Itami, "Interpenetration of Organization and Market."

24. See Ken-ichi Imai, "Japan's Changing Industrial Structure and United States–Japan Industrial Relations," in Kozo Yamamura, ed., *Policy and Trade Issues of the Japanese Economy: American and Japanese Perspectives* (Seattle: University of Washington Press, 1982).

25. For an example of investment decisions in the iron and steel industry, which formed the nucleus of postwar industrial develoment, see Seiichirō Yonekura, "Sengo Nihon tekkōgyō shiron—sono renzokusei to hi renzokusei" (A

preliminary essay on the postwar Japanese iron and steel industry: Its continuation and discontinuation), *Business Review*, Hitotsubashi University, Vol. 31, No. 2 (Oct. 1983), pp. 67–87.

26. As to the general explanation of the subcontracting system, see Masu Uekusa, "Industrial Organization: The 1970s to the Present," in Yamamura and Yasuba, eds., *Political Economy of Japan*, Vol. 1, pp. 499–506.

27. Benjamin Klein, Robert G. Crawford, and Arman A. Alchian, "Vertical Integration, Appropriable Rents, and the Competitive Contracting Process," *Journal of Law and Economics*, Vol. 21, No. 2 (Oct. 1978), pp. 297–326.

28. This is a controversial argument made in the seminal work of Ellsworth Huntington, *Civilization and Climate* (New Haven: Yale University Press, 1915). Too much emphasis on climate may, of course, be misleading, yet I believe there is some truth in the claim that climatic conditions caused Europe to industrialize. See also H. R. Trevor-Roper, *The Crisis of the Seventeenth Century: Religion, the Reformation, and Social Change* (New York: Harper and Row, 1968), chap. 2.

29. For further details, see Ken-ichi Imai, Ikujiro Nonaka, and Hirotaka Takeuchi, "Managing the New Product Development Process: How Japanese Companies Learn and Unlearn," in Kim B. Clark, Robert Hayes, and Christopher Lorenz, eds., *The Uneasy Alliance: Managing the Productivity-Technology Dilemma* (Cambridge, Mass.: Harvard Business School Press, 1985).

30. Michael J. Piore and Charles F. Sabel, *The Second Industrial Divide: Possibilities for Prosperity* (New York: Basic Books, 1964).

31. Friedrich A. Hayek, "The Use of Knowledge in Society," *American Economic Review*, Vol. 35, No. 4 (Sept. 1945), pp. 519–30.

32. William R. Ashby, "Principles of the Self-organizing Dynamic System," *Journal of General Psychology*, Vol. 37, No. 2 (Oct. 1947), pp. 125–28.

33. Suggestive discussion is given in Erich Jantsch, "Unifying Principle of Evolution," in Erich Jantsch, ed., *The Evolutionary Vision: Toward a Unifying Paradigm of Physical, Biological, and Sociological Evolution* (Boulder, Colo.: Westview Press, 1976).

34. For the basic concepts, I am indebted to Devendra Sahal, "Structure and Self-organization," *Behavioral Science*, Vol. 27, No. 3 (July 1982), pp. 249–58.

35. Israel M. Kirzner, *Competition and Entrepreneurship* (Chicago: University of Chicago Press, 1973).

36. Chie Nakane, "Network—Tōnan-Ajia teki ningen kankei" (Network: Human relationships in Southeast Asian countries), in Chie Nakane, *Shakai jinrui gaku* (Social anthropology) (Tokyo: Tokyo Daigaku Shuppankai, 1987).

Lifson: Managerial Integration in America

1. John Roberts, *Mitsui: Three Centuries of Japanese Business* (New York: Weatherhill, 1973), p. 97. On the early history of Mitsui, see also Johannes Hirschmeier and Tsunehiko Yui, *The Development of Japanese Business* (London: George Allen & Unwin, 1981), pp. 133–38, and Seiichiro Yonekura, "The Emergence of the Prototype of Enterprise Group Capitalism" (Institute of Business Research, Hitotsubashi University, Tokyo, 1985).

2. On Mitsui's role as a model for the development of the institution of the *sogo shosha*, see M. Y. Yoshino and Thomas B. Lifson, *The Invisible Link: Japan's Sogo Shosha and the Organization of Trade* (Cambridge, Mass.: MIT Press, 1986), chap. 2.

3. Mitsui bought 50 per cent of Alumax from AMAX, Inc. See Yoshi Tsurumi,

Multinational Management: Business Strategy and Government Policy (Cambridge, Mass.: Ballinger, 1984), pp. 416–34.

4. Michael Mandel, "Japan is the Biggest U.S. Investor—but Exactly How Big?" *Business Week*, May 1, 1989, p. 20, bases this assessment on the U.S. Bureau of Economic Assessment. Other data are drawn from the Japanese Ministry of Finance and Association for Foreign Direct Investment in America, *Periodic Review of Selected Statistics on Foreign Direct Investment in the United States, 1980–1988* (Washington, D.C., 1989).

5. Ryutaro Komiya, "Japan's Foreign Direct Investment: Facts and Theoretical Considerations," in Silvio Borner, ed., *International Finance and Trade in a Polycentric World* (Basel: International Economic Association, 1987), p. 245. Among the problems with statistics from the Ministry of Finance (upon which Figures 1–3 are based) are their basis in approvals of investments, rather than the actual investments implemented; their failure to include unrepatriated retained earnings; their inclusion of certain types of loans and bonds whose repayment is not deducted; and their failure to include loans or equity obtained overseas. There are thus elements that tend both to overstate and to understate the net level of foreign assets falling under Japanese control. There is no way at all to know where the balance lies.

In addition to statistics provided by the Ministry of Finance, the Ministry of International Trade and Industry (MITI) and the Bank of Japan also publish statistics on Japanese foreign direct investment. The three sets of statistics provided by the three agencies are gathered by different methodologies, which are mutually incompatible.

6. Quoted in Daniel Burstein, *Yen! Japan's New Financial Empire and its Threat to America* (New York: Simon & Schuster, 1988), p. 156.

7. From a radio broadcast on WMCA, New York City, quoted in *Manhattan, Inc.*, June 1989, p. 96.

8. Quoted in Burstein, *Yen!*, pp. 156, 159.

9. This definition is very similar to that of Komiya, "Japan's Foreign Direct Investment," p. 242.

10. See Yoshino and Lifson, *Invisible Link*, for an account of the *sogo shosha's* development and role in the Japanese economy and foreign trade and investment.

11. A definitive history of Japanese business in the United States has yet to be written. One source of data about the early years of the *sogo shosha* is Thomas B. Lifson, *Mitsubishi Corporation (B): Americanization at MIC* (Boston: HBS Case Services, 1981). For a more general history, see Komiya, "Japan's Foreign Direct Investment." For an account of Japanese multinational firms in the United Kingdom, see Malcolm Trevor, *Japan's Reluctant Multinationals: Japanese Management at Home and Abroad* (New York: St. Martin's Press, 1983).

12. Christopher Bartlett and Hideki Yoshihara, "New Challenge for Japanese Multinationals: Is Organization Adaptation Their Achilles' Heel?" *Human Resource Management*, Vol. 27, No. 1 (Spring 1988), pp. 26–27, cite a similar vicious circle in their study of contemporary Japanese multinationals.

13. Komiya, "Japan's Foreign Direct Investment," pp. 248–54.

14. See ibid., pp. 251–52, for an account of the conditions of overall FDI.

15. Norm Alster, "Unlevel Playing Field," *Forbes*, June 26, 1989, pp. 53–58.

16. M. Y. Yoshino, *Japan's Managerial System: Tradition and Innovation* (Cambridge, Mass.: MIT Press, 1968), chap. 6.

17. Two works published in 1981, for example, painted highly idealized versions of human-resource practices in Japanese firms: William Ouchi, *Theory*

Z: How American Business Can Meet the Japanese Challenge (Reading, Mass.: Addison-Wesley, 1981), and Richard Tanner Pascale and Anthony Athos, *The Art of Japanese Management* (New York: Simon & Schuster, 1981).

18. Kenneth B. Noble, "A Clash of Styles," *New York Times*, Jan. 25, 1988, p. D1.

19. Carolyn Skorneck, "Blacks, Women Win $6 Million from Honda," *Detroit Free Press*, Mar. 24, 1988, p. 10B.

20. Ibid.

21. Kathleen Pender, "Japanese Firm's Units Face Bias Counts," *San Francisco Chronicle*, May 31, 1989, pp. C1, 16.

22. Robert E. Cole and Donald R. Deskins, Jr., "Racial Factors in Site Location and Employment Patterns of Japanese Auto Firms in America," *California Management Review*, Vol. 31, No. 1 (Fall 1988), pp. 9–22.

23. Michael Speiess, Jack Hardy and Benjamin F. Rountree v. C. Itoh & Co. (America), 643 F 2d 353, was the first major such case. An analysis of this case is contained in S. Prakesh Sethi, Nobuaki Namiki, and Carl Swanson, *The False Promise of the Japanese Miracle* (Marshfield, Mass.: Pitman, 1984), pp. 55–85. Lisa M. Avagliano et al. v. Sumitomo Shoji America, 102 S. Ct. 2374 (1982), was the first major sex discrimination case against a Japanese firm based on failure to promote. Both cases have since been settled out of court, though other cases have been filed against the same defendants and other Japanese white-collar employers.

24. Power and influence are very complicated phenomena in organizations, involving both formal and informal aspects. For a sampling on the subject, see John Kotter, *Power in Management* (New York: AMACOM, 1979); Jeffrey Pfeffer, *Power in Organizations* (Marshfield, Mass.: Pitman, 1981); Samuel B. Bachrach and Edward J. Lawler, *Power and Politics in Organizations* (San Francisco: Jossey-Bass, 1980); and Edward J. Lawler III and John Grant Rhode, *Information and Control in Organizations* (Pacific Palisades, Calif.: Goodyear, 1976).

25. Kazuo Nomura, a Washington consultant, quoted in William Glasgall, Leah J. Nathans, and Ted Holden, "Tokyo Brokers Beat a Retreat from the Street," *Business Week*, Feb. 13, 1989, pp. 42–43.

26. Noble, "Clash of Styles."

27. Bartlett and Yoshihara, "New Challenge for Japanese Multinationals," pp. 25–26.

28. Thomas B. Lifson, "The Sogo Shosha: Strategy, Structure, and Culture" (Ph.D. diss., Harvard University, 1978), and Yoshino and Lifson, *Invisible Link*.

29. For a detailed empirical example of this type of network use, see Yoshino and Lifson, *Invisible Link*, chap. 5.

30. This analysis of exchange and reciprocity is indebted to the work of Peter Blau, *Exchange and Power in Social Life* (New York: Wiley, 1964). See also George Homans, *The Human Group* (New York: Harcourt, Brace & World, 1950); Peter Ekeh, *Social Exchange Theory: The Two Traditions* (Cambridge, Mass.: Harvard University Press, 1974); and Kenneth J. Gergen, Martin S. Greenberg, and Richard H. Willis, *Social Exchange: Advances in Theory and Research* (New York: Plenum, 1980).

31. Hiroshi Wagatsuma, "Internationalization of the Japanese: The Group Model Reconsidered," in Mannari Robert and Harumi Befu, eds., *The Challenge of Japan's Internationalization: Organization and Culture* (Tokyo: Kodansha, 1983), hypothesizes that when in a group of significant others, Japanese have a strong tendency to conform to group opinions.

32. In addition to core staff who have a career-long commitment to the firm, Japanese companies commonly employ other categories of labor, such as temporary workers of various sorts and subcontractor-supplied workers. For more on the concept of the core staff, see Yoshino and Lifson, *Invisible Link*, pp. 136–52.

33. On the same phenomenon in the United States, see Terrence E. Deal and Allan A. Kennedy, *Corporate Cultures: The Rites and Rituals of Corporate Life* (Reading, Mass.: Addison-Wesley, 1982).

34. See Ruth Benedict, *The Chrysanthemum and the Sword: Patterns of Japanese Culture* (1946; New York: New American Library, 1974); Takie Lebra, "Reciprocity and the Asymmetric Principle: An Analytic Reappraisal of the Japanese Concept of On," *Psychologia*, Vol. 12, No. 3–4 (1969), pp. 129–38.

35. Also known as the "Tale of the 47 Ronin," the most popular epic of the Japanese stage and screen centers on the years of hardship endured by a group of samurai who sacrifice everything to avenge their master's unjust death, thereby discharging their obligation to him.

36. T. Kawashima, "Dispute Resolution Among the Japanese," in A. von Mehren, ed., *Law in Japan* (Cambridge, Mass.: Harvard University Press, 1963); and H. Tanaka and M. Smith, *The Japanese Legal System* (Tokyo: University of Tokyo Press, 1976).

37. Merry White, *The Japanese Educational Challenge* (New York: Basic Books, 1987), p. 23.

38. Ouchi, *Theory Z*.

39. See Thomas P. Rohlen, *For Harmony and Strength: Japanese White-Collar Organization in Anthropological Perspective* (Berkeley: University of California Press, 1974), and Yoshino and Lifson, *Invisible Link*, on entry to the firm.

40. On game theory, see Thomas C. Schelling, *The Strategy of Conflict* (London: Oxford University Press, 1960).

41. Vladimir Pucik, "Promotions and Intraorganizational Status Differentiations Among Japanese Managers," *Proceedings of the Academy of Management* (Annual Meeting, San Diego, 1981), pp. 59–63.

42. Ralph E. Winter, "Okuma's Hendrick Aims to Make Unit Top Machine Builder in the U.S.," *Wall Street Journal*, May 23, 1989, p. B12; and Robert Guenther, "Matsushita, in a First, Names Kraft, an American, as President at U.S. Unit," ibid., Mar. 15, 1989, p. B10.

43. Bartlett and Yoshihara, "New Challenge for Japanese Multinationals," p. 36.

Shimada: Labor-Management Relations

I would like to express my sincere gratitude to Henry Rosovsky, Hugh Patrick, and other JPERC participants for their kind, constructive, and serious comments. Needless to say, however, I am solely responsible for any remaining errors. Thanks also to the Mitsubishi Seimeikai Foundation for generously providing a research grant in 1987, which partially supported research for this essay, and to the International House of Japan for its careful administrative assistance.

1. John T. Dunlop, in *Industrial Relations Systems* (New York: Holt, 1958), postulates the existence of a set of values shared by the main actors of an industrial-relations system at any point in time; these values are consistent with the broader contexts of such systems. Some of the features of what I here term *industrial culture* may be viewed as traits of what is generally called *deep culture*.

In this essay, I focus on the institutional and organizational nature of culture, which influences and molds behavioral patterns.

2. Chie Nakane, *Japanese Society* (Berkeley: University of California Press, 1970), argues that the roles of employees are often not well defined in Japanese organizations, and that employees' unlimited commitment to the organization is therefore likely to be expected to be just like the unlimited commitment of family members to the family. Kazuo Okochi, "Nihonteki rō-shi kankei no tokushitsu no hensen" (Special characteristics of Japanese industrial relations and their changes), *Nihon Rōdō Kyōkai zasshi* (Monthly journal of the Japan Institute of Labour), Vol. 1, No. 1 (1954), suggests that the "ethos (culture)" of agrarian families in Japanese agrarian village communities was transferred to industrial factories and came to characterize labor-management relations, which emphasized the master-client relationship in the early phase of Japanese industrial development. Hiroshi Hazama, *Nihon rōmukanri-shi kenkyū* (A study of the history of Japanese labor management: The formation and development of the family management system) (Tokyo: Diamond, 1964), traces the origin of Japanese-style management and industrial relations back to the commercial family system in the feudal era. Wakao Fujita, *Nihon rōdō kyōyaku ron* (Collective labor agreement in Japan) (Tokyo: Tokyo University Press, 1961), found an institutional origin of the organizational principles of Japanese-style management organized around the principle of the length-of-service reward system in the hierarchical structure of the feudal government system of preindustrial society.

3. Masumi Tsuda, "Nenkō-joretsu chingin to nenkō seido" (Length-of-service wages and the length-of-service reward system), in M. Shinohara and N. Funahashi, eds., *Nihon-gata chingin kōzō no kenkyū* (A study of the Japanese-style wage structure) (Tokyo: Rōdō Hōgaku, 1961), points out that this rapid introduction of Western technology resulted in poor development of the standardization of work and thus gave rise to a length-of-service reward system only ambiguously related to the skill level of workers.

4. Solomon B. Levine and Hisashi Kawada, *Human Resources in Japanese Industrial Development* (Princeton: Princeton University Press, 1980), provide a comprehensive survey of historical developments in the vocational training and education systems of both private corporations and public institutions during prewar Japanese industrial development. I have discussed the relationship between human-resource-development strategy and industrial relations in some depth by focusing on the early experience of the Yawata Steel Corporation in Haruo Shimada, "Nenkō-sei no shiteki keisei ni tsuite" (Historical formation of the lifetime commitment system: A case study of the Yawata Basic Steel Corporation, 1896–1934), *Mita Gakkai Zasshi* (Mita journal of economics), Vol. 61, No. 4 (1968).

5. Koji Taira, *Economic Development and the Labor Market in Japan* (New York: Columbia University Press, 1970), emphasizes the importance of a human-resource-development strategy as a critical cause of the long-term employment practice of Japanese corporations and rejects anthropological values of lifelong commitment as an explanatory factor.

6. The Trade Union Law, which endorses workers' rights to organize themselves, was enacted immediately after the war in December 1945. Under the perceived encouragement of SCAP, workers organized quickly and trade union organizations soon prevailed. The proportion of organized workers relative to paid employees increased from practically zero in 1945 to 46.4 per cent in 1956 and rose to a peak of 54.6 per cent in 1979. See Haruo Shimada, "Japanese Trade

Unionism: Postwar Evolution and Future Prospects," *Labour and Society* (ILO), Vol. 13, No. 2 (Apr. 1988).

7. For a comprehensive account of the critical features of Japanese enterprise unions, see Taishiro Shirai, "A Theory of Enterprise Unionism," in Shirai, ed., *Contemporary Industrial Relations in Japan* (Madison: University of Wisconsin Press, 1983).

8. A detailed study of the forerunners of enterprise unions in the metalworking industry in the prewar period is presented in Ryuji Komatsu, *Kigyōbetsu kumiai no keisei* (Development of enterprise unionism) (Tokyo: Ochanomizu Shobō, 1971).

9. Annual man-days lost per 10 employees were 4.6 for the latter half of the 1940s and 4.5 for the first half of the 1950s. These figures are roughly comparable to the American experience of the 1970s, when an average of 5.1 days were lost annually per 10 U.S. workers. The most notable examples of labor disputes in these turbulent years of Japanese labor history include the 56-day strike of Toshiba unions and strikes in the power industry in 1946; a well-known attempted general strike, led chiefly by workers in the public sector in 1947; a large-scale strike of postal workers in 1947; antidismissal disputes and strikes by the Hitachi union and by National Railways workers in the late 1940s; a 63-day strike of coal miners and a power industry strike in 1952; a 113-day strike of miners and a strike at Nissan in 1953; and strikes by steel workers in 1954. For detailed information about labor disputes, see Ministry of Labor, *Shiryō rōdō undōshi* (Documents of the labor movement), annual, and Haruo Shimada, "Japan's Postwar Industrial Growth and Labor-Management Relations," *Proceedings of the 35th Annual Meeting of the* [U.S.] *Industrial Relations Research Association*, Dec. 28–30, 1982.

10. A comprehensive analysis of the labor movement during the turbulent years right after World War II is given in Joe Moore, *Japanese Workers and the Struggle for Power, 1945–1947* (Madison: University of Wisconsin Press, 1983).

11. Sōhyō was organized in 1950 with the participation of three million workers representing 17 industrywide union federations, which united to counter communist-led union movements. However, with growing pressure against labor movements from both management and political circles, and in the increasingly severe international environment of cold war confrontation after the San Francisco Peace Treaty in 1951, Sōhyō rapidly grew critical of SCAP and U.S. policies. For a thorough summary of the labor movement during this period, see Hisashi Motoi, ed., *Nihon rōdō undōshi* (History of the Japanese labor movement), new ed. (Tokyo: Rōmu Gyōsei Kenkyūjo, 1983).

12. Andrew Gordon offers a brief review of developments in labor-management relations in this period, particularly from the viewpoint of management regaining control, in *The Evolution of Labor Relations in Japan: Heavy Industry, 1853–1955* (Cambridge, Mass.: Harvard University Press, 1985).

13. Nikkeiren issued a resolution at its ad hoc Extraordinary Convention in 1949 entitled "Resolution on New Labor Management," which was followed by the document "Nikkeiren's View on New Labor Management" in May 1950. The association's main objective was to restore and establish the right and initiative of management in labor-management matters. To this end, Nikkeiren tried to introduce and develop various labor-management programs, such as personnel evaluation schemes, a pay-by-job system, management training programs, and the Training Within Industries method. For further details, see Taishiro Shirai, *Gendai Nihon no rōmu kanri* (Labor management in contemporary Japan) (Tokyo: Tōyō Keizai, 1982). See also Gordon, *Evolution of Labor Relations*, for a description

456   Notes to Pages 272–73

of the attempts made by management to regain control in the workshop and developments in labor-management relations during this period.

14. Following an unsuccessful attempt at a general strike in February 1947, General Douglas MacArthur sent a letter to the Japanese government suggesting limits on the right of public workers to strike. In response, the government issued Ordinance No. 201 confirming the policy of limiting government employees' right to strike. It followed in the same vein with amendments and new legislation, including amendment of the National Public Employees Law (1948) and enactment of the Public Corporation Labor Relations Law (1949) and the Local Public Employees' Law (1950). In this general review and revision of the legal framework of labor-management relations toward stricter regulation, a major amendment of the Trade Union Law in 1949 aimed at giving formal assurance that trade unions would be genuinely independent organizations. The amendment limited union activities during work hours and prohibited automatic renewal of collective labor agreements and employers' paying for full-time union officers. The main thrust of the amendments was to limit the degree of freedom of the union movement. See Haruo Shimada, *Rōdō keizaigaku* (Labor economics) (Tokyo: Iwanami Shoten, 1986), esp. chap. 8.

15. A detailed review and analysis of some of the major labor disputes during the 1950s may be found in Wakao Fujita and Shobei Shiota, eds., *Sengo Nihon no rōdō sōgi* (Labor disputes in postwar Japan) (Tokyo: Ochanomizu Shobō, 1963; rev. ed., 1977). Systematic and comprehensive data are compiled in Ministry of Labor, *Shiryō rōdō undōshi*.

16. In a classical work, Fujita provides an insightful and detailed analysis of the background, critical factors for its formation, and consequences of the second union and its implications for the nature of Japanese unionism, based on a case study of the second-union problem of a coal mine. See Wakao Fujita, *Daini kumiai* (The second union: Toward the development of a unified union movement) (Tokyo: Nihon Hyōron Shinsha, 1955).

17. Keizo Fujibayashi, *Rō-shi kankei to rō-shi kyōgisei* (Labor-management relations and the joint-consultation system), Study Series No. 1, Institute of Labor and Management Studies, Keio University (Tokyo: Diamond, 1965), provides a good review of early experiences in the development of the joint-consultation system in Japan and its theoretical interpretation.

18. Minoru Takano, who had been a key advocate of local political struggles through worker-farmer alliances, lost his position as chairman of Sōhyō to Kaoru Ohta, who proposed an economically oriented union movement.

19. Toward the end of 1954, the Private Sector Joint Struggle Committee was organized by five industrywide federations of unions: synthetic chemical, coal mining, private railways, electric power, and paper and pulp. In January 1955, three more federations—metalworking, chemicals, and electric appliances—joined the committee. With the participation of these eight union federations, Shuntō was begun. The Shuntō movement has grown steadily since then by incorporating other major union federations, such as those of the steelworkers, public-sector workers, and shipbuilders. By the end of the 1960s, as many as five million workers had been organized.

20. The three basic principles of the productivity campaign of the Japan Productivity Center, which was established in 1955, were (1) to protect employment or prevent unemployment in the process of promoting productivity improvement; (2) to determine specific methods of improving productivity through labor-management joint consultation, taking into account the specific conditions in firms and industries; and (3) to make sure that fair distribution of the gains

from productivity improvement was made among management, labor, and the public (consumers) in accordance with prevailing conditions in the national economy. These principles were adopted partly to invite the labor camp, which had been skeptical, to participate in the productivity movement. For details, see Japan Productivity Center, *Seisan sei undō 30 nenshi* (30-year history of the productivity movement) (Tokyo, 1985).

21. Visits by the American quality-control statisticians Drs. William E. Deming and Joseph M. Juran had a significant impact on the quality-control campaigns in Japanese industrial circles. In the 1950s the Japanese Union of Scientists and Engineers launched organized efforts to promote quality-control movements throughout Japanese industry.

22. Many Japanese companies received technological transfers through inter-company relationships. The relationships between General Electric and Toshiba, Philips and Matsushita, and Austin and Nissan are well-known examples. See Yutaka Kosai, *Kōdo seichō no jidai* (The era of rapid economic growth) (Tokyo: Nihon Hyōronsha, 1981).

23. The Toyota method of production was originally developed by Tai-ichi Ohno. There is much available literature on this famous method of production, including the brief, yet comprehensive, explanation of its primary objectives, motivations, and features found in Tai-ichi Ohno, *Toyota seisan hōshiki* (The Toyota production system) (Tokyo: Diamond, 1978). A detailed analysis of the method is available in Yasuhiro Monden, *Toyota Production System: A Practical Approach to Production Management* (Atlanta: Industrial Engineering and Management Press, 1983). A good review of the historical development of this method is given in Michael A. Cusumano, *The Japanese Automobile Industry: Technology and Management at Nissan and Toyota* (Cambridge, Mass.: Harvard University Press, 1985).

24. The theoretical scheme and tips for application of the concept of total quality control developed by Ishikawa and others is provided in Kaoru Ishikawa, *What is Total Quality Control? The Japanese Way*, trans. David J. Lu (Englewood Cliffs, N.J.: Prentice-Hall, 1985).

25. In the process of the campaign to promote and disseminate the labor-management joint-consultation system, the Japan Productivity Center publicized a series of reports that reviews experiences with the joint-consultation system in the early 1960s and discusses its merits and problems. These reviews emphasize an important merit of the system: advance joint consultation was extremely useful for technological innovation because management and labor could share information beforehand and thereby adjust to new situations by minimizing conflict and friction. See Japan Productivity Center, *Seisan sei undō 35 nenshi*, esp. chap. 3.

26. By the mid 1970s, more than 70 per cent of enterprises with 100 or more employees were found to have a labor-management joint-consultation system. See *Survey on Japanese Labor-Management Relations* (Tokyo: Ministry of Labor, 1977).

27. In the case of NKK (Nippon Kokan Co.), the introduction of the *sangyō-cho* (foreman) position simplified the workshop management system by concentrating many of the functions that other management and staff members had performed in the foreman's position. See Shirai, *Gendai Nihon no rōmu kanri*.

28. In the case of the transfer of workers, for instance, the role of the foreman as a relayer of information becomes critical. It is largely because of the advice of a foreman that management is able to choose particular workers for transfer. Workers in turn often receive informal and preliminary consultation with the foreman before transfer plans are made.

29. Indeed, this is an important by-product of small-group activities such as quality-control circles (QCC). Taking advantage of this feature of small-group activities, management often utilizes the performance record of participants in such activities as critical data to evaluate their leadership capability and aptitude for teamwork; such data are often used to make recommendations for promotion. In many companies, during development of QCC activities, it was a more or less common trend that junior workers increasingly took on the role of a circle leader. This suggests the small-group activities are used more and more as an informal arena of personnel evaluation, as well as being sessions for quality improvement.

30. With the development of corporate organization, one might say that what Doeringer and Piore term a well-structured "internal labor market" has developed in many major Japanese corporations. See Peter B. Doeringer and Michael J. Piore, *Internal Labor-Markets and Manpower Analysis* (Lexington, Mass.: D. C. Heath, 1971).

31. For detailed discussion of the development of labor management during this period, see Shirai, *Gendai Nihon no rōmu kanri*, chap. 6.

32. An experienced executive manager of labor relations in a major steel company described the experience during this period as "one of building an equal partnership between management and unions based on mutual trust." However, a quick review of the kind of building blocks that form the basis for a company finally enjoying such a partnership shows the development of a highly complex and mutually determined system of labor-management relations. See Hyuga Orii, *Rōmu kanri 20 nen* (20 years of labor management experience) (Tokyo: Tōyō Keizai Shimpōsha, 1973).

33. Some unions in the private sector, such as Zenkin Dōmei (the Federation of Metalworkers) and Zensen (the Federation of Textile Workers), and some unions in the public sector have union leaders without employee status. However, union officials in most unions in the private sector maintain employee status and after retirement from a company are eligible for retirement fringe benefits.

34. Some economists have emphasized the difference in initial conditions between the two oil crises as a primary reason for the difference in subsequent economic performance. The views of a leading proponent of this argument are expressed in, e.g., Masaru Yoshitomi, *Nihon keizai: Sekai keizai no aratana kiki to Nihon* (The Japanese economy: A new crisis of the world economy and Japan) (Tokyo: Tōyō Keizai Shimpōsha, 1981). Others point to the influence of other factors, such as a learning effect between the two experiences. See, e.g., Takao Komine, *Sekiyu no Nihon keizai* (Oil and the Japanese economy) (Tokyo: Tōyō Keizai Shimpōsha, 1982). I have elaborated elsewhere on the importance of the information-sharing network developed during the late 1970s in the wake of the oil crisis. Comprised of the local and national levels of management, labor, and government, the network played a critical role during the second oil crisis in persuading labor to share the costs of economic adjustment in terms of wage moderation. See Haruo Shimada, "Wage Determination and Information Sharing: An Alternative Approach to Incomes Policy?" *Journal of Industrial Relations* (June 1983), pp. 177–200.

35. The annual increases in labor productivity were: 1976, 12.2 per cent; 1977, 5.2 per cent; 1978, 8.6 per cent; 1979, 11.0 per cent; and 1980, 6.3 per cent. See Ministry of International Trade and Industry, *Production Index of Mining and Manufacturing*, annual, for the years in question.

36. Real wages declined by 1.6 per cent, the first decrease since the annual wage offensive had begun 25 years earlier.

37. See Ohno, *Toyota seisan hōshiki*, and Monden, *Toyota Production System*.

38. See, for instance, Nihon Nōritsu Kyōkai, *Mazda no genba kakushin* (Mazda's innovations in the workshop) (Tokyo: Nihon Nōritsu Kyōkai, 1984).

39. Employment levels declined as follows in a few sample industries between 1977 and 1984: the textile and weaving industry, from 270,000 workers to 190,000; the ferro-alloy industry, from 11,000 to 5,000; the shipbuilding industry, from 250,000 to 120,000; the aluminum-refining industry, from 10,000 to 4,000; the petroleum and chemical industry, from 40,000 to 30,000; and the paper and pulp industry, from 78,000 to 64,000. See Haruo Shimada, "Employment Adjustment and Employment Policies: Japanese Experience" (Paper presented at the workshop on Trade Policy for Troubled Industries: Worker and Community Aspects of Adjustment, Institute for International Economics, Washington, D.C., Sept. 1988.).

40. See Haruo Shimada, "The Japanese Labor Market After the Oil Crisis: A Factual Report (I) and (II)," *Keio Economic Studies*, Vol. 14, Nos. 1 and 2 (1978). A shorter version is available in OECD, *Structural Determinant of Employment and Unemployment*, Vol. 2 (Paris, 1979), pp. 335–44.

41. Yoshiji Miyata, then chairman of the Japan Federation of Steelworkers' Unions, advocated this principle most vocally.

42. See Shimada, "Wage Determination and Information Sharing."

43. Adjustment costs to absorb the shock were shared by the three parties: by workers, in the form of moderate wage increases relative to growth and inflation of the economy; by employers, in the form of lost profits; and by the government, in the form of a running deficit.

44. Japan is the only nation to have a special "council" become an affiliate of the International Metalworkers' Foundation. Normally, each metalworkers' union in a country joins the IMF independently. However, having a special council may have helped member unions enjoy greater opportunities for exchanging and sharing relevant information on economic and industrial conditions.

45. The total value of privately owned land in the greater Tokyo region (including the neighboring prefectures of Saitama, Kanagawa, and Chiba) rose by 55 per cent in 1986 and reached 600 trillion yen according to an estimate prepared by the Economic Planning Agency based on the data from annual reports on stock values of National Economic Accounting (*Kokumin Keizai Keisan*).

46. Shinohara pointed out in 1986 that the "windfall" profit the Japanese economy gained by savings on the cost of imports owing to the increased value of the yen between 1985 and 1986 amounted to 11.8 trillion yen. Miyohei Shinohara, "Dai-genzei ni hittehi suru endaka genyuyasu" (Increased values of the yen and reduced oil payment well compare with a major tax reduction), *Ekonomisuto*, Apr. 6, 1986. The Economic Planning Agency later publicized its first estimate of such gains for the two-year period of 1965 to 1967 as nearly 30 trillion yen.

47. An estimate prepared by the Ministry of Labor for 1987 indicates that the wages of Japanese workers are now among the highest in the world. Based on the April 1987 exchange rate, and taking Japan's wage rate as 100, average hourly wage rates for male production workers were 110 for the United States, 130 for West Germany, 77 for the United Kingdom, and 89 for France. Average annual earnings for the same category of workers were 100 for Japan, 99 for the United States, 100 for West Germany, and 67 for both the United Kingdom and France. Since 1987, the yen has been revalued to as much as 120 yen to the dollar, making the nominal value of the wages of Japanese workers even higher relative to, for example, U.S. workers.

48. Using data for 1985, the OECD calculated that the purchasing power parity (PPP) of Japanese yen and U.S. dollars is 220 yen for one dollar. Since PPP does not fluctuate as rapidly as exchange rates in the international money market, the abrupt and drastic increase in the exchange rate of the yen after September 1985 rapidly increased the gap between PPP and the yen exchange rate. See OECD, *Purchasing Power Parities and Real Expenditures, 1985* (Paris, 1987). The Ministry of Labor's estimate of the PPP of the yen for consumption items for 1985 was 231 yen for one U.S. dollar.

49. According to the Ministry of Labor estimates mentioned above, using 1985 data and taking U.S. price levels as 100, Japanese price levels were 251 for foodstuffs, 191 for utilities, 166 for housing (rent and other expenses), 126 for clothing, 170 for education and recreation. Taking West German levels as 100, Japanese price levels for the same items were 129, 152, 168, 114, and 115 respectively.

50. One may say that very heavy "invisible taxes" are levied on Japanese workers for important daily consumption items. See, e.g., Kenichi Ohmae, "Get Angry Against Invisible Taxes!" *Bungei Shunjū,* Apr. 1987.

51. As of 1986, according to Ministry of Labor estimates, Japanese production workers in the manufacturing sector worked on average 2,150 hours a year, while comparable workers worked 1,924 hours in the United States; 1,938 hours in the United Kingdom; 1,955 hours in West Germany; and 1,643 hours in France.

52. Aggregate employment conditions improved remarkably following early 1987. The unemployment rate hit its postwar peak of 3.1 per cent in May 1987 but was reduced rapidly to 2.5 per cent by June 1988. The ratio of job openings to applicants compiled at the Public Employment Service Offices, a more sensitive measure of labor-market conditions, soared from 0.6 in spring 1987 to 1.1 in summer 1988.

53. In 1987, for example, the ratio of job openings to applicants was 1.9 for workers under 20, but 0.4 for ages 50 to 54, 0.2 for ages 55 to 59, and as low as 0.1 for ages 60 to 64. These age differentials are quite stable regardless of business conditions.

54. In spite of a short-run boom since 1987, major steel corporations are reducing their work forces by some 40,000 from a total of about 170,000 within say, three or four years to meet the objective of restructuring the industry to be more efficient and competitive. Shipbuilding is another industry in which the work force was reduced drastically in a major scaling-down of productive capacity. The industry employed about 250,000 workers in the early 1970s, but employment fell to about 70,000 by the early 1980s and underwent further adjustment in the late 1980s to reach the level of 40,000 workers.

55. Prices in greater Tokyo recorded drastic increases in 1986 and 1987. The prices of land in the business district rose on average by 23 per cent in 1986 and 76 per cent in 1987, and the price of residential land by 8 per cent in 1986 and 68 per cent in 1987. Average land prices in the greater Tokyo area also increased by 24 per cent in 1988. See Land Planning Agency, *Survey of Prefectural Land Prices: The Review of Standard Prices,* annual.

56. Takao Komine, *Kabuka, chika hendō to Nihon keizai* (Fluctuations of stock and land prices and the Japanese economy) (Tokyo: Tōyō Keizai Shimpōsha, 1989), presents a preliminary analysis of the effect of drastic increases in land prices on asset distribution. Those who already owned land benefited from increases in land prices, but those who wished to purchase real estate for the first time after the increases, absent other land to sell, suffered seriously.

57. For the past two decades, a relative increase in the tax burden of wage

and salary earners and a relative decrease in the share of the self-employed and corporations have been more or less secular trends. The percentage of revenues from income tax on earnings increased from 14.7 in 1970 to 20.0 in 1980 and to 21.8 in 1986. In contrast, the share of corporate income tax in total revenues declined from 33.0 per cent in 1970 to 31.5 in 1980 and to 30.6 in 1986. The share of tax reported by self-employed workers, such as farmers, small shop owners, and physicians, also declined, from 9.0 per cent in 1970 to 8.6 in 1986.

58. The major tax reform of 1988 introduced an across-the-board consumption tax of 3 per cent of sales value, which will have a complex impact on the redistribution of income, but the reform did not introduce effective measures to control the distribution of assets, despite the fact that a major public concern, and one hope for the tax reform, was to correct the widened asset differentials generated by the acute inflation of land prices and share values in the stock market.

59. Trade negotiations over agricultural products such as beef and citrus fruit in recent years between Japan and the United States symbolize governmental efforts to open the Japanese market to international competition. The fact that the proportion of manufactured goods in total Japanese imports rose from less than 30 per cent to more than 50 per cent between 1985 and 1988 clearly indicates that market forces are operating to introduce cheaper foreign products into the Japanese domestic market.

60. The primary objective of national confederations of trade unions, such as Rengo (the Japan Private Sector Trade Union Council) and Sōhyō, is the enrichment of the quality of workers' lives to the level enjoyed by their European and U.S. counterparts. Their basic recognition of the status quo is that despite high nominal income, the quality of life of Japanese workers is far behind their European and U.S. counterparts' in terms of both real standard of living and working hours. To increase real standard of living, high domestic prices must be reduced to levels comparable to those in Europe and the United States. The principal measure to achieve this goal is to open Japanese markets to international competition and introduce cheap foreign goods. On this general point, there is no disagreement among the different segments of the labor movement. See, e.g., the 1988 and 1989 issues of *Rengō hakusho: Seikatsu kaizen tōsō no tameno shiryo to bunseki* (White paper of the Japanese Private Sector Trade Union Confederation: Materials and analysis of trade union struggles for a better life), and Kokumin Shuntō Renrakukai (Association for People's Spring Struggle), *Kokumin Shuntō hakusho* (White paper for People's Spring Struggle for a better life).

61. For example, the Japan Socialist Party had only five seats in the House of Representatives in 1988.

62. The labor force fully involved in farming has been reduced to about 4 million in recent years, but if agriculture is to be rationalized to increase its labor productivity to a competitive international level, its labor force will have to be reduced considerably more. Yasuhiko Yuize, "Kome jiyūka ni dankai de" (Liberating the rice trade by a two-step procedure), *Japan Economic Newspaper*, Oct. 16, 1986, estimates, based on his simulation analysis, that the number of households engaged in rice production should be reduced from the current 250,000 families to 150,000–200,000 fully engaged farming families to double labor productivity. Similar arguments apply to such labor-intensive sectors as the distribution and service industries, employing 15 and 8 million workers respectively.

63. The Fourth National Plan for Comprehensive Development adopted in 1988 acknowledges this issue and addresses itself to developing core cities to

facilitate more effective distribution of economic resources throughout the Japanese archipelago.

64. The central government has a virtual monopoly on authority to grant permission and allocate funds to local public and private agencies to conduct projects in almost all spheres of public administration. This dominant central control exists not only for governmental organizations but often also for large private corporate organizations that have well-structured bureaucratic control systems. Under such circumstances, local branches have only limited discretion in mobilizing and allocating resources in the interest of local communities.

65. The idea of *"furusato* [homeland] creation" proposed by the Takeshita cabinet can be interpreted as an attempt to provide municipalities with an opportunity to reverse this unilateral flow of initiative from the central authority to local governments. The proposal encourages local communities to propose new policy ideas by granting 100 million yen to each of some 3,000 local municipalities and making the central government react to them.

66. The idea of reducing the tax on land sales and increasing the real estate tax for holding it has been suggested repeatedly by both policy planners and experts, but it has not been implemented, primarily because of its political unpopularity. Reducing taxes for those who sell land gives the impression to the public of enriching the rich; increasing the real estate tax for holding land is seen as punishing the large number of ordinary people who own houses on small pieces of land and who cannot be blamed for rising land prices. Indeed, in the face of the drastic increase in land prices in 1986 and 1987, local governments tried to moderate increases in real estate taxes, encouraging the owners to hold on to land so as to take advantage of future increases in land values and consequently reducing the amount of land for sale.

67. The Takeshita administration stipulated in 1987 that each ministry relocate at least one agency or office outside Tokyo in an attempt to counter the trend toward excessive concentration of resources in Tokyo, but it is doubtful how much substantial effect this kind of measure will have.

68. Many experts and organizations have proposed ideas for moving political and administrative functions out of Tokyo to a new capital city to be constructed. For a comprehensive account of both the background factors and policy proposals on this issue, see Kazuo Yawata, *Tōkyō shūchū ga Nihon o horobosu* (Excessive concentration in Tokyo will destroy Japan) (Tokyo: Kōdansha, 1987).

69. From the very beginning, there have been distinct differences between the two major camps of the labor movement, Rengō and Sōhyō, on the issue of tax reform. While recognizing the importance and merit of the introduction of an indirect tax for wage earners relative to other categories of taxpayers, Rengō exerted maximum pressure on the government by resisting early introduction of the new tax to force the government to adopt serious measures to correct inequitable features of the current tax system, particularly with respect to asset taxes. In contrast, Sōhyō more or less rejected a new consumption tax outright.

In the course of public debate and the political process in the Diet, this difference is reflected in the different attitudes of the Democratic Socialist Party, supported mainly by Rengō-affiliated unions, and the Japan Socialist Party (JSP), supported mostly by Sōhyō unions. The JSP, together with the Japan Communist Party (JCP), consistently refused to admit, or even participate in the process of examining, the bill, but the JSP and other opposition parties compromised with the Liberal Democratic Party (LDP) at the final stage of modifications to the bill. In this process, the difference of views grew increasingly apparent, even among Rengō-affiliated unions. For example, unions in the textile industry maintained a relatively negative stance, reflecting concerns about the potentially negative impact of the new tax on textile sales, but the auto workers' union favored the new tax because it would replace the previous heavy automobile tax and would consequently stimulate purchase of new cars.

Having obtained the conditional support of the DSP and other opposition parties in the final stages of the legislative debate, the LDP felt confident that it could pass the bill before the end of 1988, even in the face of strong opposition from the JSP and JCP. Although the package of bills finally passed was modified by political compromise in response to the demands of the JSP, Komeitō, and other "cooperative" opposing parties, it was far from what the opposition had originally wished for to correct inequities, particularly in the area of taxes on assets.

70. Unions tend to emphasize institutional and policy reforms increasingly strongly, recognizing that wage increases alone will not enrich workers' lives. Rengo, for instance, has made it a rule to compile demands in the areas of government policy and institutional reform systematically around June every year in an attempt to exert timely pressure and influence on the budgetary process.

71. A comprehensive analysis of the relationship between Japanese unions and political parties may be found in Taishiro Shirai, "Japanese Labor Unions in Politics," in Shirai, ed., *Contemporary Industrial Relations in Japan*. Dōmei was dissolved prior to the formation of Rengo in November 1987. However, Dōmei's regional organizations will remain as they have been.

72. See Yoshiro Kutani, "Japanese Trade Unions and Politics" (Paper presented at the Conference on Comparative Studies of Labor in Japan and the United States, East-West Center, Honolulu, Aug. 1985).

73. The Labor Union Congress for Policy Promotion, a forerunner of Rengō, made a special effort to strengthen unions' contact with the LDP and relevant government agencies.

74. Since the unification of labor organizations, the relationship between unions and political parties has grown somewhat fluid.

75. A survey of some 300 major enterprise unions in the private sector revealed that a member's contribution to the union, on average, amounts to 1.64 per cent of regular monthly pay in Japan. The data are from a survey conducted by Asia Shakai Mondai Kenkyūjo (the Research Institute of Asian Social Problems) for 1978. Public-sector unions collect considerably higher contributions, which may well amount to 2.5 per cent of monthly pay. In addition, some unions, particularly in the public sector, collect special contributions for strike funds. Overall, it is probably safe to say that Japanese unions on average collect contributions from members of as much as 2 per cent of their monthly pay. See, for further discussion, Norikuni Naito, "Trade Union Finance and Administration," in Shirai, ed., *Contemporary Industrial Relations in Japan* (Madison: University of Wisconsin Press, 1983).

76. See Shirai, "Theory of Enterprise Unionism," and Naitō, "Trade Union Finance and Administration," in Shirai, ed., ibid.

77. Many leaders who started in the tradition of the old Sōdōmei unions lack employee status (examples may be found in Zenkindōmei and Zensen), as do many leaders of public-sector unions (primarily because they were deprived of employee status for engaging in illegal disputes).

78. In contrast to the confrontational attitude of Nikkeiren led by Bunpei Otsuki up to 1986, the new administration led by Eiji Suzuki since 1987 seems

to emphasize a joint problem-solving approach, particularly in dealing with national structure and policy issues.

79. Nikkeiren began regular consultation with Rengo on various policy issues of mutual concern in spring 1988. In fall 1988, these two organizations jointly organized a public conference on the issues of land and housing. For implications of such joint activities, see Haruo Shimada, "Rōshi kyotō no ippo o fumidase" (Labor and management need to organize joint campaigns for structural reform), *Ekonomisuto*, Feb. 16, 1988.

Cole: Cultural and Social Bases of Japanese Innovation

I am indebted to the East Asia Program of the Woodrow Wilson International Center for Scholars for providing the congenial intellectual and physical environment that allowed me to pursue this research. The section of this essay entitled "Search, Discovery, and Transmission" appears in slightly different form in chapter 6 of my *Strategies for Learning: Small-Group Activities in American, Japanese, and Swedish Industry* (Berkeley: University of California Press, 1989). It is used here by permission of the University of California Press.

1. See Thorstein Veblen, *Imperial Germany and the Industrial Revolution* (1915; reprinted, Ann Arbor: University of Michigan Press, 1966); Henry Rosovsky, *Capital Formation in Japan, 1868–1940* (New York: Free Press, 1961); and Ronald Dore, *British Factory, Japanese Factory: The Origins of National Diversity in Industrial Relations* (Berkeley: University of California Press, 1973).

2. Kazushi Ohkawa and Henry Rosovsky, *Japanese Economic Growth* (Stanford: Stanford University Press, 1973).

3. Cole, *Strategies for Learning*.

4. See, e.g., M. Kohn, "Occupational Structure and Alienation," *American Journal of Sociology*, Vol. 82 (July 1976), pp. 111–30.

5. Kazuo Koike, *Shokuba no rōdō kumiai to sanka* (The labor union and participation on the shop floor) (Tokyo: Tōyō Keizai Shimpōsha, 1975).

6. Aoki goes on to argue convincingly that such benefits can be reaped only when strategic decision making is conducted on a centralized basis to ensure the maximization of firm-level interests, but that is not a matter that will be pursued in this essay.

7. Kiichi Fujino, "Company-wide Software Quality Control (SWQC)," in *Proceedings of the International Conference on Quality Control, 1987* (Tokyo: Japanese Union of Scientists and Engineers, 1988), pp. 459–64.

8. H. Peter Dachler and Bernhard Wilpert, "Conceptual Dimensions and Boundaries of Participation in Organizations: A Critical Evaluation," *Administrative Science Quarterly*, Vol. 23 (May 1978), pp. 1–39.

9. For most of the period under consideration, the major focus of the small-group activity movement in Sweden was the model set by the self-managing team. Only in the early and mid 1980s did a modest movement toward quality circles develop. The circles contained a set of problem-solving methodologies and a specific task orientation that was previously lacking in the operation of the self-managing teams.

10. Cf. Arne Kalleberg and James Lincoln, *Culture, Control, and Commitment* (New York: Cambridge University Press, 1990).

11. Kimiyoshi Hirota and Toshio Ueda, *Shōshūdan katsudō no riron to jissai* (Theory and practice of small-group activities) (Tokyo: Nihon Rōmu Kenkyūkai, 1975), p. 25.

12. Shoji Shiba, "Japan, Today and Yesterday: Its Secret for a Successful Development" (paper presented at the Manila Hilton Hotel, Nov. 25, 1983).

13. Hirota and Ueda, *Shōshūdan katsudō*, p. 40.

14. Ibid.

15. Cf. Haruo Shimada, *Hyūmanueā no keizaigaku* (The economics of human-ware) (Tokyo: Iwanami Shoten, 1988).

16. Kenji Okuda, "Nihon keiei kanrishi no ichi teiryū" (An undercurrent in the history of Japanese management: Recognition of work groups as an open system), *Nihon rōdō kyōkai zasshi*, Vol. 29 (May 1987), pp. 2–12. Some neo-Marxists would respond that the workers are participating in and concealing their own exploitation (see, e.g., Michael Burawoy, *The Politics of Production: Factory Regimes Under Capitalism and Socialism* [London: New Left Books, 1985]). This is not an issue that can be resolved by social science, however, but is rather a matter of ideology.

17. Rosabeth Kanter, *The Change Masters* (New York: Simon & Schuster, 1983), pp. 44–46.

18. New York Stock Exchange, *People and Productivity: A Challenge to Corporate America* (New York, 1982), p. 22.

19. Frederick Emery and Einar Thorsrud, *Form and Content in Industrial Democracy* (London: Tavistock Publications, 1969) (originally published in Norwegian as *Industriel Demokrati* (Oslo: Universitetsförlaget, 1964), p. 86.

20. Heinz Leymann, *Kan Arbetslivet Demokratiseras?* (Can work life be democratized?) (Stockholm: Management Media, 1982), p. 47.

21. See Swedish Employers' Confederation, *Samtal in Matfors* (Talks at Matfors) (Stockholm, 1971).

22. F. Emery and E. Trist, "Socio-Technical Systems" (1960), reprinted in F. Emery ed., *Systems Thinking* (London: Penguin Books, 1969).

23. George Homans, "The Study of Groups," in David Sills, ed., *International Encyclopedia of the Social Sciences*, Vol. 6 (New York: Macmillan/Free Press, 1968), p. 259.

24. See A. Cherns, *Using the Social Sciences* (London: Routledge & Kegan Paul, 1979).

25. E. Rhenman, *Företagsdemokrati och Företags Organisation* (Industrial democracy and industrial management) (Stockholm: Norstedt, 1964).

26. See, e.g., E. Thorsrud and F. Emery, *Medinflytande och engagemang i arbetet* (Participation and engagement in work; original title *Mot en ny bedriftsorganisasjon*) (Stockholm: Utvecklingsrådet för samarbetsfrågor, 1969), pp. 21–23.

27. Swedish Employers' Confederation, *Samtal in Matfors*; Pär Törner, *The Matfors Report* (Stockholm: SAF, 1976) (originally published in Swedish in 1971).

28. Stefan Agurén and Jan Edgren, *New Factories* (Stockholm: SAF, 1980).

29. Volvo Corporation, Workshop on Production Technology and Quality of Working Life, Gothenburg, Sweden, Nov. 14–15, 1984.

30. Anders Mellbourn, "MBL inte så Dålig som sitt Rykte," *Dagens Nyheter*, Apr. 29, 1984, p. 16.

31. Kurt Lewin may come about as close as we can to the intellectual godfather of industrial applications of small-group activities.

32. Juji Misumi, "Action Research on Group Decision Making and Organizational Development" (Paper presented at the 22d International Congress of Psychology, Leipzig, 1980).

33. James Halpin, *Zero Defects* (New York: McGraw-Hill, 1966).

34. Kenji Okuda, "Nihon nōritsu undōshi" (History of the Japanese efficiency movement), *IE Review*, Vol. 9, Nos. 5–6; Vol. 10, Nos. 1–3 (1968–71).

35. Okuda, "Nihon keiei kanrishi."

36. Riemon Uno, *Nōritsu zōshin no riron to jissai* (Theory and reality of efficiency improvement) (Osaka: Kōgyō Kyōikukai, 1921), pp. 35–45.

37. It is easy enough to find some prewar practice that conforms to contemporary small-group activity and to claim that it is therefore a traditional practice rooted in Japanese culture. One author for example claims to find the roots of quality circles in the *ikki* system of collective decision making that originated in the thirteenth century (Shichibei Yamamoto, "The Historic Roots of Japanese Corporate Culture," *Journal of Japanese Trade & Industry*, Vol. 1 [Jan.–Feb. 1985], pp. 62–65). Such efforts have a mystical element and function more as ideology than as social science; to make such claims without establishing the causal linkages between past practices and current behavior is unacceptable.

38. Armand Feigenbaum, *Total Quality Control*, 2d ed. (New York: McGraw-Hill, 1961).

39. Japanese Union of Scientists and Engineers, *QC sākuru katsudō un'ei no kihon* (Foundation of the operation of QC-circle activities) (Tokyo, 1971).

40. Kaoru Ishikawa, interview with Robert E. Cole, Tokyo, 1977.

41. Okuda, "Nihon keiei kanrishi."

42. Japanese Union of Scientists and Engineers, *Genba to QC* (The workplace and quality control), Vol. 1 (Tokyo, April 1962).

43. Taishiro Shirai, "A Theory of Enterprise Unionism," in Taishiro Shirai, ed., *Contemporary Industrial Relations in Japan* (Madison: University of Wisconsin Press, 1983), pp. 117–43.

44. R. E. Cole, *Work, Mobility, and Participation: A Comparative Study of American and Japanese Industry* (Berkeley: University of California Press, 1979), pp. 41, 171–73; Kazuo Koike, "Internal Labor Markets: Workers in Large Firms," in Shirai, ed., *Contemporary Industrial Relations*, pp. 29–61.

45. Charles Kepner and Benjamin Tregoe, *The Rational Manager* (New York: McGraw-Hill, 1965).

46. Peter Arnesen, personal communication, 1988.

47. R. Miller and D. Sawers, *The Technical Development of Modern Aviation* (New York: Praeger, 1970).

48. Jan Helling, director of Saab Scania, Trollhättan, Sweden, interview with Robert E. Cole, Nov. 1986.

49. Cf. Roger Rowand, "U.S. Lag in Global Technology Cited," *Automotive News*, Apr. 8, 1985.

50. Shin'ichi Takezawa, "The Quality of Working Life: Trends in Japan," *Labour and Society*, Vol. 1 (Jan. 1976), p. 31.

51. Edward Lawler III and Susan Mohrman, "Quality Circles After the Fad," *Harvard Business Review*, Vol. 63 (Jan.–Feb. 1985), pp. 65–71.

52. Elsewhere in this volume, Aoki also attacks the adequacy of purely culturally inherited small-group activity as a sufficient explanation for Japanese economic performance, but he does so from a different perspective than the one adopted here.

53. To be sure, in some cases there was an element of spontaneous support among workers for these developments, as well as opportunistic leadership on the part of opposition union leaders; otherwise management would not have succeeded.

Rohlen: Learning

For helpful comments on earlier drafts, I wish to thank Harry Rowan, Nate Rosenberg, Ed Steinmueller, and Steve Wheelwright. The many suggestions of other participants in the Japan Political Economy Research Committee conferences are also gratefully acknowledged.

1. For a very useful review of the subject of learning as studied by economists, see William Edward Steinmueller, "Microeconomics and Microelectronics: Economic Studies of Integrated Circuit Technology" (Ph.D. diss., Stanford University, 1987). The term *learning* has recently been appearing with increased frequency in studies of Japan, e.g., in Bill Ford, "A Learning Society: Japan Through Australian Eyes," in John Twining et al., eds., *World Yearbook of Education, 1987* (London: Kogan Page, 1987), and Richard T. Pascale, "Honda: The Learning Organization" (MS, June 1988).

2. The interested reader should consult three recent books that relate Japan's education system and socialization pattern to the nation's recent economic success: Thomas P. Rohlen, *Japan's High Schools* (Berkeley: University of California Press, 1983); Merry I. White, *Japan's Educational Challenge: A Commitment to Education* (New York: Free Press, 1987); and Benjamin Duke, *The Japanese School: Lessons for Industrial America* (New York: Praeger, 1987).

3. I wish to point out here that the topic of learning is rarely considered inclusively. Rather, it is studied piecemeal, as, for example, in the study of formal education or vocational training, or human-resource development, or on-the-job training, or corporate education, or media, or scientific innovation, or information networking, and so forth. For this reason, among others, the subject has not emerged clearly as a central concern in comparative political economy. Interdisciplinary barriers and the absence of a unifying sense of problem have both also contributed to this state of affairs.

4. See the very interesting general review of the subject of the rise and fall of national economic systems provided in Moses Abramovitz, "Catching Up, Forging Ahead, and Falling Behind," *Journal of Economic History*, Vol. 46, No. 2 (June 1986), pp. 385–406. While Japan is obviously this century's most interesting case of prolonged and rapid development, the topic of learning is but one angle from which to approach the overall issue.

5. See Thomas C. Smith, *Native Sources of Japanese Industrialization, 1750–1920* (Berkeley: University of California Press, 1988), for extended discussion of many of the considerations involved in relating premodern social patterns to the process of Japanese industrialization.

6. Ronald Toby, "Seek Knowledge Throughout the World: International Information and the Formation of Policy in Edo-Period Japan and K'ang-hsi Era China" (MS), pp. 47–58.

7. See Eleanor D. Westney, *Imitation and Innovation: The Transfer of Western Organizational Patterns to Meiji Japan* (Cambridge, Mass.: Harvard University Press, 1987), for a detailed account of institutional borrowing in a number of key areas of public life.

8. Hiroshi Irie, "Apprenticeship Training in Tokugawa Japan," *Acta Asiatica* (Tokyo: Toho Gakkai, 1988), p. 16.

9. The most interesting, broadest-gauged study of Japanese borrowing is George B. Sansom's *The Western World and Japan: A Study in the Interaction of European and Asiatic Cultures* (New York: Knopf, 1950).

10. Numerous scholars have pointed to an inclination in Japanese social-psychological make-up to contextual thinking and "other-orientedness," but the

case has never been made better than by Takie Sugiyama Lebra, *Japanese Patterns of Behavior* (Honolulu: University of Hawaii Press, 1976). Exaggerations in this sphere are virtually an occupational hazard for those who attempt to make generalizations about culture, yet the fact remains that this is an important point of differentiation from Western thinking and behavior in the sphere of international learning.

11. For a useful general account of this subject, see Ronald Dore, *Education in Tokugawa Japan* (Berkeley: University of California Press, 1965).

12. This is a point made at length by Roy Hofheinz and Kent Calder, *Eastasian Edge* (New York: Basic Books, 1982).

13. White, *Japanese Educational Challenge*, p. 57, discusses Ninomiya as a symbol in greater detail.

14. So pervasive is this general emphasis on improvement through learning that Robert J. Smith in his *Japanese Society: Tradition, Self and the Social Order* (Cambridge: Cambridge University Press, 1983), pp. 106–36, has termed Japan "the perfectible society." His key point is that the assumption of perfectibility is not limited to the economic sphere in the least, but rather is found in such public efforts as those aimed at reducing crime and traffic accidents, improving health, and managing a vast array of urban problems. Continuous improvement is also part of the individual life course as pointed out in my article "The Promise of Adulthood in Japanese Spiritualism," *Dædalus* (Spring 1976), pp. 125–43.

15. For overviews of the modern history of education, see esp. Tokiomi Kaigo, *Japanese Education: Its Past and Present* (Tokyo: Kokusai Bunka Shinkokai, 1968), and Rohlen, *Japan's High Schools*, chap. 2, pp. 45–76.

16. Quoted in Daikichi Irokawa, *The Culture of the Meiji Period* (Princeton: Princeton University Press, 1985), pp. 54–55.

17. See Solomon B. Levine and Hisashi Kawada, *Human Resources in Japanese Industrial Development* (Princeton: Princeton University Press, 1980), and Koji Taira and Solomon B. Levine, "Education and Labor Force Skills in Postwar Japan" (Final report prepared for the Japan Study, Education and Employment Section, National Institute of Education, 1986).

18. On this point much has been written. On Meiji Japan, see esp. Ivan Parker Hall, *Mori Arinori* (Cambridge, Mass.: Harvard University Press, 1973). For discussion of distinctively Japanese qualities in the postwar period, see Catherine Lewis, "Creativity and Japanese Education" (Unpublished study done for the Japan Project, U.S. Department of Education, 1987); Rohlen, *Japan's High Schools*; and White, *Japanese Educational Challenge*.

19. This should not be misunderstood to mean that numerically private education is a small part of the whole. At the high-school level, roughly a quarter of all students attend private schools, and at the level of higher education, 70 per cent of university and 80 per cent of junior college students are enrolled in private institutions. The dominance of the public side is predicated primarily on prestige, resources, and government control of standards.

20. Hall, *Mori Arinori*, offers a detailed portrait of policymaking in early Meiji educational development and its relationship to the general effort to strengthen the nation.

21. Masakazu Yano, "Personal Income Distribution and Its Influence on Education in Japan" (MS, Research Institute for Higher Education, Hiroshima University, 1986), is the most recent study of the relationship of education to income distribution in Japan.

22. Consider, for example, the fact that regional dialects made vernacular

conversation almost unintelligible between people of little education from different areas of the country at the end of the Tokugawa period.

23. On this and the following points regarding political compliance, see Rohlen, *Japan's High Schools*, pp. 210–40. The interested reader should also consult the symposium "Social Control and Early Socialization," *Journal of Japanese Studies*, Vol. 15, No. 1 (Winter 1989).

24. For a good introduction to this and a number of other topics, see U.S. Department of Education, *Japanese Education Today* (Washington, D.C.: Government Printing Office, 1987).

25. Rohlen, *Japan's High Schools*, pp. 77–110, contains a detailed account of the competition at the middle- and high-school levels.

26. The actual figure for 1985 is 47 per cent, up from 37 per cent in 1975. Figures for *juku* attendance by students in elementary schools doubled in the same decade according to Ministry of Education, *Gakushū juku chōsa* (Tokyo, 1986).

27. See also Thomas P. Rohlen, "The Juku Phenomenon: An Exploratory Essay," *Journal of Japanese Studies*, Vol. 6, No. 2 (Summer 1980), pp. 207–42.

28. According to a 1986 Ministry of Education survey reported in the Japan Foundation Newsletter (July 1986), Japanese families were on average paying ¥170,000 ($1,037 at $1 = ¥130) per child in elementary school, ¥210,000 ($1,615) per child in junior high school, ¥267,000 ($2,053) per child in public high school, and ¥551,000 ($4,238) per child in private high school in 1985. The ministry estimated that ¥335 billion ($2.57 billion) was spent by families on educational expenses unrelated to school for students up to the twelfth grade. The average costs of education (excluding living and travel expenses) for families with university students was ¥666,900 ($5,130). Although some of these expenses seem reasonable in comparison with the costs of private secondary and university educations in the United States, they come at the end of a process that costs more at earlier levels, and they represent generally mediocre quality compared to the elite public institutions.

29. See Thomas P. Rohlen, "Is Japanese Education Becoming Less Egalitarian: Notes on High School Stratification and Reform," *Journal of Japanese Studies*, Vol. 3, No. 1 (Winter 1977), pp. 37–70, for an early account of the phenomenon and its causes. If anything, recent prosperity has increased this tendency.

30. See Yano, "Personal Income Distribution." The Ministry of Labor's 1981 white paper *Rōdō hakusho* (p. 142) also contains a calculation of the rate of return to males employed in manufacturing of a university education for the period 1966 to 1980. The results show an overall decline from 8.2 per cent (annual) to 5.2 per cent, with an even steeper decline for those working in the largest firms (9 per cent to 5.1 per cent). Furthermore, while 8.2 per cent represented a better return than one-year time deposits in 1966, the situation was reversed by 1980, in part because rates of return on savings improved considerably.

31. Investment in education seems to me to be highly segmented and not made with any conscious sense of comparative return. One might still want to compare the rate of return on education with other investments. Savings account rates have also fallen and have generally been lower than for education. Land investments have paid handsomely until recently, but have required larger amounts of initial capital. Stocks have definitely provided a better return. The most interesting issue is the prospect of liberalization of the financial system and what it might do for rates of return for small investors comparing education to, say, savings.

32. This result is particularly well demonstrated in the cross-national tests of math and science conducted since the mid 1960s.

33. See Thomas P. Rohlen, "The Education of Koreans in Japan," in Changsoo Lee and George De Vos, eds., *Koreans in Japan* (Berkeley: University of California Press, 1981), for an extensive discussion of this issue.

34. Ministry of Education, *Waga kuni no bunkyō seisaku: Showa 63* (Tokyo, 1988), p. 268.

35. OECD, *Public Expenditure on Education*, OECD Studies in Resource Allocation, No. 2 (Paris, 1976).

36. The most useful discussion of this and other problems is contained in William J. Cummings, *Educational Policies in Crisis* (New York: Praeger, 1986).

37. Lawrence P. Greyson, "Japan's Intellectual Challenge," *Engineering Education*, published in three parts (Dec. 1983 and Jan. and Feb. 1984), provides the best available account of Japanese education for engineers. In 1984, 55 per cent of all doctoral degrees in engineering in the United States went to foreign nationals.

38. A number of recent comparative studies have found much higher ratios of engineers to production workers in Japanese manufacturing. See Andrew Weiss, "The Truth About Japanese Manufacturing," *Harvard Business Review* (July–Aug. 1984), pp. 119–25, and Ramchandran Jaikumar, "Postindustrial Manufacturing," *Harvard Business Review* (Nov.–Dec. 1986). Both emphasize this factor in their explanations of Japanese manufacturing leadership. Mark Fruin (lecture at Stanford University, 1987) has shown that the Japanese use of developmental factories with very high ratios of engineers is part of a product/manufacturing development sequence that is more complex than in the United States and more intensively "engineered" at the initial stage of manufacturing.

39. In this regard, see the chapter in this volume by Murakami and Rohlen.

40. Cross-national test results are provided in Torstein Husen, ed., *International Study of Achievement in Mathematics: A Comparison of Twelve Countries* (New York: Wiley, 1968); L. C. Comber and John P. Keeves, *Science Achievement in Nineteen Countries* (New York: Wiley, 1973); Harold W. Stevenson, *Making the Grade: School Achievement in Japan, Taiwan, and the United States* (Stanford: Center for Advanced Studies in the Behavioral Sciences, 1973); and James W. Stigler and Michelle Perry, "Cross-Cultural Studies of Mathematics Teaching and Learning: Recent Findings and New Directions" (MS, 1987).

41. For an account of these subjects as taught at the high-school level, see Rohlen, *Japan's High Schools*, pp. 241–70.

42. This assertion is based on the following considerations: (1) actual time in school to twelfth grade (Japanese children not only attend school 60 more days a year than Americans, for example, but also begin preschool earlier and in larger numbers and have much lower absenteeism rates), (2) the curriculum (in many subjects, the level of information and problem-solving skills of high-school seniors in Japan is equivalent to second- and third-year university levels in the United States), (3) international test results, and (4) weekly hours of homework (40 per cent of Japanese high-school seniors, for example, do at least 10 hours of homework a week, compared to 10 per cent for Americans).

43. It is worth noting here that school absences not owing to illness are also greater in the United States. Whereas over half of all Japanese high-school students surveyed had no such absences, only a quarter of the American sample did. See William Fetters et al., "Schooling Experiences in Japan and the United States: A Cross-National Comparison of High School Students" (U.S. Department of Education, National Center for Education Statistics, 1983).

44. Over 200,000 mostly male and academically strong students, known in Japan as *rōnin*, sit out for one or more years after high-school graduation studying to retake entrance exams to desirable universities.

45. See Rohlen, *Japan's High Schools*, pp. 294–301, for comparative figures on delinquency and school violence.

46. See, e.g., Fetters et al., "Schooling Experiences." Rohlen, *Japan's High Schools*, also contains extensive discussion of the differences in adolescent time allocation between Japan and the United States.

47. Fetters et al., "School Experiences."

48. Catherine Lewis, "Cooperation and Control in Japanese Nursery Schools," *Comparative Education Review*, Vol. 28, No. 1 (1984), pp. 69–84, and Lois Peak, "Learning to Go to School in Japan: The Transition from Home to Preschool Life" (Ph.D. diss., Harvard University, 1977).

49. Lewis, "Cooperation and Control," and Peak, "Learning to Go to School."

50. The essay by John Haley in this volume is particularly pertinent here. See also Thomas P. Rohlen, "Order in Japanese Society: Attachment, Authority, and Routine," *Journal of Japanese Studies*, Vol. 15, No. 1 (Winter 1989), pp. 5–40, for a general analysis of the relationship of socialization in Japanese early education to patterns of order and social control in general.

51. Fetters et al., "Schooling Experiences."

52. Harold W. Stevenson, "Classroom Behavior and Achievement of Japanese and Chinese and American Children," in Robert Glazer, ed., *Advances in Instructional Psychology* (Hillsdale, N.J.: Elbaum, 1985), and Stigler and Perry, "Cross-Cultural Studies."

53. See Duke, *Japanese School*, for an extensive argument regarding the relationship of schooling in Japan to work skills and habits.

54. The issue of equality is most thoroughly presented by William K. Cummings, *Education and Equality in Japan* (Princeton: Princeton University Press, 1980).

55. See, e.g., Tetsuya Kobayashi, "The Internationalization of Japanese Education," *Comparative Education*, Vol. 22, No. 1 (1986), pp. 65–72.

56. See John Zeugner, "Japan's Noneducation," *New York Times*, June 24, 1983.

57. Comparing themselves to patterns observed among the Western elite, Japanese often criticize their countrymen for not pursuing learning on their own once out of school. My own impressions do not support this criticism.

58. See, for example, James C. Abegglen and George Stalk, Jr., *Kaisha: The Japanese Corporation* (New York: Basic Books, 1985).

59. For very useful accounts of this development in the auto industry, see Yasuhiro Monden, *The Toyota Production System* (Atlanta: Industrial Engineering and Management Press, 1983), and Michael A. Cusumano, *The Japanese Automobile Industry: Technology and Management at Nissan and Toyota* (Cambridge, Mass.: Harvard University Press, 1985).

60. See Abegglen and Stalk, *Kaisha*, pp. 67–118, for discussions of this topic that are useful in illustrating Japan's comparative accomplishments, but that seriously understate the role of learning and organization.

61. Jaikumar, "Postindustrial Manufacturing," p. 70. The author also notes that whereas American CNC machines had a utilization rate of 52 per cent, the Japanese rate was 84 per cent.

62. See Kazuo Koike, "Human Resource Development and Labor-Management Relations," in Kozo Yamamura and Yasukichi Yasuba, eds., *The Political*

Economy of Japan, Vol. 1, *The Domestic Transformation* (Stanford: Stanford University Press, 1987).

63. William J. Abernathy et al., "The New Industrial Competition," *Harvard Business Review* (Sept.–Oct. 1981), pp. 68–113, and Steven Wheelwright, personal communication regarding his research on Japanese product development.

64. For a largely parallel analysis, but one that does not center on learning per se, see Haruo Shimada and John Paul MacDuffie, "Industrial Relations and 'Humanware'" (Working Paper No. 1855–88, Alfred P. Sloan School of Management, MIT, December 1986). For perhaps the most extensive and systematic presentation of the interrelationship of management, organization, and manufacturing technology as it has evolved toward continuous learning and continuous innovation, see Steven Wheelwright and Henry E. Riggs, "Advanced Manufacturing Processes and the Search for Competitive Advantage" (MS, 1987).

65. See Thomas P. Rohlen, *For Harmony and Strength: Japanese White-Collar Organization in Anthropological Perspective* (Berkeley: University of California Press, 1974), for a discussion of one such program. Avice Saint, *Continuous Learning Within Japanese Organizations* (San Francisco: Far West Laboratory for Education Research and Development, 1982), offers rather cursory information on this subject for 16 large Japanese firms.

66. Rohlen, *For Harmony and Strength*; Saint, *Continuous Learning*; Tadashi Amaya, *Human Resource Development in Industry* (Tokyo: Japan Institute of Labor, 1983); and Shimada and MacDuffie, "Industrial Relations and 'Humanware.'"

67. While ostensibly "voluntary," there is much management behind-the-scenes manipulation and even more social pressure to participate. The focus of quality-circle activity is operational problems, not issues of general management or worker satisfaction. Very little managerial prerogative is handed over when problem solving is delegated.

68. Based on several days of interviews with Jusco executives in March 1982.

69. Unpublished internal report, Westinghouse Corporation, 1981.

70. Amaya, *Human Resource Development*, reports that large Japanese firms have recently been taking a greater interest in executive training.

71. This is not to deny that the Japanese are very inclined to invest heavily in new equipment, but to underscore the fact that such investments are more integrated with human and organizational factors and tend to be made more incrementally.

72. The study is being conducted at Harvard Business School by Professors Kim Clark and Steven Wheelwright, and this is based on discussions with them about their work.

73. Many kinds of gains may show up simply as enhanced service (an unmeasured aspect of service as a "product") rather than as lower cost. Certainly, on a comparative basis, Japanese retailing provides greater customer service, but at a greater cost. Large-scale organizations in the service sector have simply not been studied adequately or compared cross-nationally in a manner that might provide insights into this very important matter. This does not detract from the suspicion that in the service sector, learning does not translate as directly into economic growth as in the manufacturing sector.

74. Thomas P. Rohlen, "Technological Borrowing and Innovation in a U.S.–Japan Joint Venture" (MS, 1976).

75. The soft technologies of learning can also be borrowed, but they must be institutionalized to be valid. Neither nations nor companies are inclined to hide or protect their learning technologies, nor are they likely to put monetary value on them. Yet borrowers interested in hard technology are frequently unable to

perceive the learning technology that surrounds its use. Furthermore, because of social and cultural differences, most learning technology can only be borrowed effectively if it is adapted carefully to the existing conditions of the new host nation. Once created, however, learning technology becomes part of the pool of intangible assets useful in the further evolution of a society's relationship with hard technology and with economic growth.

76. For a very pertinent discussion of this issue, see James Lardner, "The Terrible Truth About Japan: They Didn't Steal our VCR Technology—They Invented It," *Washington Post*, June 21, 1987.

77. Daniel I. Okimoto and Gary R. Saxonhouse, "Technology and the Future of the Economy," in Yamamura and Yasuba, eds., *Political Economy of Japan*, Vol. 1.

78. David McConnell, personal communication regarding his research on the JET program and internationalization.

Lebra: Gender and Culture

Earlier drafts of this essay were read and commented on by Hugh Patrick, Henry Rosovsky, Shumpei Kumon, and James Roberson, among many others. Their helpful suggestions, which convince me of the value of collaborative work, were partly incorporated into the final version, but needless to say, responsibility for any remaining errors rests with me. Fieldwork was conducted while I was a Japan Foundation research fellow, and I was the recipient of grants from the Social Science Research Council and the University of Hawaii Japan Studies Endowment Fund and of a Universitiy of Hawaii Fujio Matsuda Scholar award while I was writing the essay. I am grateful to all these individuals and institutions.

1. Stanley Cromie and John Hayes, "Toward a Typology of Female Entrepreneurs," *Sociological Review*, Vol. 36 (1988), p. 93.

2. James C. Abegglen, *The Japanese Factory: Aspects of Its Social Organization* (Glencoe, Ill.: Free Press, 1958), pp. 22–23.

3. For Robert E. Cole, the dual structure refers to the size of enterprise, and the duality of job security is inherent in the size duality. See Cole, *Japanese Blue Collar: The Changing Tradition* (Berkeley: University of California Press, 1971), pp. 37–40. To the two kinds of dualism, Hugh Patrick (in a personal comment) adds a third: "competitive sectors" versus "protected sectors."

4. Hugh T. Patrick and Thomas P. Rohlen, "Small-Scale Family Enterprises," in Kozo Yamamura and Yasukichi Yasuba, eds., *The Political Economy of Japan*, Vol. 1, *The Domestic Transformation* (Stanford: Stanford University Press, 1987), p. 354.

5. Rodney Clark, *The Japanese Company* (New Haven: Yale University Press, 1979), pp. 64–73.

6. Rōdōshō Fujinkyoku, ed., *Fujin rōdō no jitsujō* (Tokyo: Ōkurashō Insatsu-kyoku, 1987), table 20.

7. Kazuo Koike, "Workers in Small Firms and Women in Industry," in Taishiro Shirai, ed., *Contemporary Industrial Relations in Japan* (Madison: University of Wisconsin Press, 1983).

8. Sōrifu, *Fujin no genjō to shisaku: kokunai kōdo keikaku dai 4 kai hōkokusho* (Tokyo: Gyōsei, 1985), p. 80.

9. Rōdōsho Fujinkyoku, ed., *Fujin rōdō no jitsujō*, table 41.

10. When all working women are grouped into the categories of employed, self-employed, and family workers, the number of employed women turns out to have been steadily rising, and by 1983 they constituted up to 66 per cent of

all women workers. The reverse trend is observable among family workers, and the self-employed constitute the lowest proportion, with little change over time. See Sōrifu, *Fujin no genjō to shisaku*, pp. 70–71. But it should be noted that "the employed" include all sizes of enterprises as employers.

11. Patrick and Rohlen, "Small-Scale Family Enterprises," p. 340.

12. Women are more likely to become permanent employees in small family enterprises than in large corporations, but then, as Ito points out, their promotion has a ceiling below the managerial level because management tends to be monopolized by the owner family. See Barbara Darlington Ito, "Entrepreneurial Women in Urban Japan: The Role of Personal Networks" (Ph.D. diss., University of Iowa, 1983), p. 130.

13. Yōko Satō, "Hataraku josei wa dō kawattaka," in Hiroko Hara and Meiko Sugiyama, eds., *Hataraku onnatachi no jidai* (Tokyo: Nippon Hōsō Shuppan Kyōkai, 1985), pp. 26–27.

14. Frank K. Upham, *Law and Social Change in Postwar Japan* (Cambridge, Mass.: Harvard University Press, 1987), p. 129.

15. Ito, "Entrepreneurial Women in Urban Japan." We might add that, although a woman's own business is likely to be thus gender-bound, her participation in a family business her husband established or inherited is not hampered by her gender. As a part of her domestic role, she is able and expected to participate in, become a mainstay of, and exercise leadership in even a typically male business such as a lumber mill. See Takie Sugiyama Lebra, *Japanese Women: Constraint and Fulfillment* (Honolulu: University of Hawaii Press, 1984), pp. 222–23.

16. Sōrifu, *Fujin no genjō to shisaku*, p. 9.

17. See Naikaku Sōridaijin Kanbō Shingishitsu, *Fujin no seisaku kettei sanka o sokushin suru tokubetsu katsudō kankei shiryō* (Tokyo, 1985), p. 31, and Patricia G. Steinhoff and Kazuko Tanaka, "Women Managers in Japan," *International Studies of Management and Organization*, Vol. 16, No. 3–4 (1987), pp. 108–32. This extreme asymmetry in the distribution of managerial positions pervades the public sector, national and local, as well. A nurse employed by the municipal government of a provincial city complained to me that all the employees of the public health section were women in nursing or other health-care professions, except the section chief (*kachō*), whose sole contribution was "being male."

18. Clark, *Japanese Company*, p. 194.

19. Susan J. Pharr, "Status Conflict: The Rebellion of the Tea Pourers," in Ellis S. Krauss, Thomas P. Rohlen, and Patricia G. Steinhoff, eds., *Conflict in Japan* (Honolulu: University of Hawaii Press, 1984).

20. James McLendon, "The Office: Way Station or Blind Alley?" in David W. Plath, ed., *Work and Lifecourse in Japan* (Albany: State University of New York Press, 1983), p. 166.

21. Ibid., p. 168.

22. See Koike, "Workers in Small Firms and Women in Industry."

23. Yasuko Muramatsu, "Kibokan kakusa: danjo kan no chingin kakusa o umidasu haikei," in Hara and Sugiyama, eds., *Hataraku onnatachi no jidai*, p. 110.

24. Meiko Sugiyama, "Nippon ni okeru hataraku hahaoya no jittai," in Sumiko Iwao and Meiko Sugiyama, eds., *Hataraku hahaoya no jidai* (Tokyo: Nippon Hōsō Shuppan Kyōkai, 1984), p. 2.

25. Anne E. Imamura, *Urban Japanese Housewives: At Home and in the Community* (Honolulu: University of Hawaii Press, 1987), p. 19.

26. Ibid., pp. 125, 134.

27. Suzanne H. Vogel, "Professional Housewife: The Career of Urban Middle Class Japanese Women," *Japan Interpreter*, Vol. 12, No. 1 (1978), pp. 16–43.

28. Rōdōshō Fujinkyoku, ed., *Fujin rōdō no jitsujō*, p. 35.

29. Ito, "Entreprenuerial Women in Urban Japan," p. 129.

30. McLendon, "The Office," p. 164.

31. Fujin Mondai Kikaku Suishin Yūshikisha Kaigi, *Fujin mondai kikaku suishin yūshikisha kaigi iken* (Tokyo, 1987), pp. 76–77.

32. Ito, "Entrepreneurial Women in Urban Japan."

33. Hiroko Hara, "Danjo no betsu o koeta tayōsei o zentei ni," introduction to Hara and Sugiyama, eds., *Hataraku onnatachi no jidai*, p. 12.

34. Michiko Hasegawa, "'Danjo koyō byōdōhō' wa bunka no seitaikei o hakai suru," *Chūō Kōron*, May 1984, pp. 79–87.

35. Fujin Mondai Kikaku Suishin Yūshikisha Kaigi, *Fujin mondai kikaku suishin yūshikisha kaigi iken*, p. 75.

36. For a refutation of the M-curve stereotype, see Karen C. Holden, "Changing Employment Patterns of Women," in Plath, ed., *Work and Lifecourse in Japan*.

37. The housewife's stress, in connection with Confucian ideology, is discussed in Takie Sugiyama Lebra, "The Confucian Gender Role and Personal Fulfillment for Japanese Women," in Walter H. Slote, ed., *The Psycho-Cultural Dynamics of the Confucian Family: Past and Present* (Seoul: International Cultural Society of Korea, 1986).

38. *Hawaii Hochi* (daily), July 11, 1988.

39. Sōrifu, *Fujin no genjō to shisaku*, p. 13.

40. What comes to mind here is the rejection of Louis Dumont's contention (*Homo Hierarchicus: The Caste System and Its Implications*, rev. ed. [Chicago: University of Chicago Press, 1980]) that the Indian caste ideology centering on the pure-impure opposition is commonly shared across castes. Critics have attacked this as a Brahmanic view, contradicted by the Untouchables' bottom-up perspective. See Joan Mencher, "The Caste System Upside Down, or the Not-so-Mysterious East," *Current Anthropology*, Vol. 15 (1974), pp. 469–93; and Gerald D. Berreman, "The Brahmanical View of Caste," in his *Caste and Other Inequities: Essays on Inequality* (Meer, India: Folklore Institute, 1979).

41. Naikaku Sōridaijin Kanbō Shingishitsu, *Fujin no seisaku kettei sanka o sokushin suru tokubetsu katsudō kankei shiryō*, p. 5.

42. Rōdōshō Fujinkyoku, ed., *Fujin rōdō no jitsujō*.

43. Ryōko Akamatsu, *Danjo koyō kikai kintō-hō oyobi kaisei rōdō kijun-hō* (Tokyo: Nippon Rōdō Kyōkai, 1985).

44. Lebra, *Japanese Women*.

45. Shumpei Kumon, personal comment.

46. Nowadays, Japanese are learning how to enjoy leisure, necessitating an overhaul of workaholism. But whether Japanese are traditionally workaholic is questioned by Sepp Linhart, "From Industrial to Postindustrial Society: Changes in Japanese Leisure-Related Values and Behavior," *Journal of Japanese Studies*, Vol. 14, No. 2 (Summer 1988), pp. 271–307.

47. Takie Sugiyama Lebra, "Japanese Women in Male Dominant Careers: Cultural Barriers and Accommodations for Sex-Role Transcendence," *Ethnology*, Vol. 20 (1981), pp. 291–306.

48. Mary C. Brinton, "The Social-Institutional Bases of Gender Stratification: Japan as an Illustrative Case," *American Journal of Sociology*, Vol. 94 (1988), pp. 300–334.

49. McLendon, "The Office," p. 160.

50. Ibid.

51. See David W. Plath, *Long Engagements: Maturity in Modern Japan* (Stanford: Stanford University Press, 1980), and Brinton, "Social-Institutional Bases of Gender Stratification."

52. Chie Nakane, *Tate shakai no ningen kankei* (Tokyo: Kodansha, 1967).

53. Lebra, *Japanese Women*, pp. 243–44.

54. Brinton, "Social-Institutional Bases of Gender Stratification."

55. Ibid.

56. Takie Sugiyama Lebra, "The Dilemma and Strategies of Aging Among Contemporary Japanese Women," *Ethnology*, Vol. 18 (1979), pp. 337–53. The male counterpart of junior-senior exchange is the patron-benefactor being reciprocated by his protégé with loyalty. The latter, as he reaches his career prime, commands resources with which to patronize his patron, who has now passed his peak. The retired senior is likely to be helped by the junior to find a second job.

57. McLendon, "The Office," p. 169.

58. Lebra, *Japanese Women*.

59. Nancy Chodorow, "Family Structure and Feminine Personality," in M. Z. Rosaldo and L. Lamphere, eds., *Woman, Culture and Society* (Stanford: Stanford University Press, 1974), p. 57.

60. *Shūkan Daiamondo*, Feb. 19, 1983, Feb. 18, 1984, and Feb. 23, 1985.

61. Ito, "Entrepreneurial Women in Urban Japan."

62. For locating informants I owe thanks to Sadako Kuga, Fusako Baba, Michiko Kanda, Takako Hirano, and the staff of the Tokyo Chamber of Commerce and Industry. The views they shared with me of prominent businesswomen were also helpful.

63. In this sense, Mrs. A is not an entrepreneur in the strict sense, while all the other women are.

64. Eleanor Brantley Schwartz, "Entrepreneurship: A New Frontier," *Journal of Contemporary Business*, Vol. 5 (1976), pp. 47–76.

65. See Robert D. Hisrich and Candida G. Brush, "The Woman Entrepreneur: Management Skills and Business Problems," *Journal of Small Business Management*, Vol. 22 (1984), pp. 30–37; *The Woman Entrepreneur: Starting, Financing and Managing a Successful New Business* (Lexington, Mass.: D.C. Heath, 1985); and Sandra Winston, *The Entrepreneurial Woman* (New York: Newsweek Books, 1979).

66. Cromie and Hayes, "Toward a Typology of Female Entrepreneurs," p. 100.

67. See Lebra, *Japanese Women*, pp. 96–97, 230–32; and "Japanese Women in Male Dominant Careers."

68. This point echoes the comparative study of the attitudes of Japanese and American children toward schoolwork by Hiroshi Azuma and his colleagues, "Receptive Diligence and Teachability: A Cross-Cultural Discussion of Motivation in Education" (Paper presented at the International Congress of Psychology, Acapulco, 1984). It was found that to carry out a task, American children must be intrinsically interested in the task, whereas Japanese children can be diligent in performing the task without being interested in it.

69. The house register (*koseki*) is a family legal document filed at a local government office, based on the family's legal place of residence. Family members are identified by name, kinship status, and reason for entry into the register (e.g., birth, marriage, adoption). To have one's name on a koseki amounts to legitimization of one's existence as a Japanese citizen. Divorce means the removal of a spouse from the koseki. Under the prewar civil code, the koseki was a legal expression of the "house" (*ie*) that transcended and controlled its individual constituents. The postwar civil code, which does not recognize the ie as a legal

unit, has outmoded the concept of koseki, and yet the latter, still in existence in a simplified and contradictory version, continues to bind all Japanese.

70. *Katakana* is a Japanese syllabic writing system, distinguished from the more commonly used syllabary, *hiragana*, and from Chinese characters. The katakana syllabary is used to transcribe special categories of referents, foreign words being a major such category.

71. George P. Murdock and Caterina Provost, "Factors in the Division of Labor by Sex: A Cross-Cultural Analysis," *Ethnology*, Vol. 12 (1973), pp. 203–25.

72. Lebra, *Japanese Women*.

73. Liza Crihfield Dahlby, *Geisha* (Berkeley: University of California Press, 1983), describes how geisha and wives live in two disjointed role realms.

74. The Equal Employment Opportunity Law (Danjo koyō kikai kintō hō) was pased in May 1985, the culmination of many years of painstaking study and planning by leaders in and out of the government, and came into effect in April 1986. Estimates of the changes in employment practices likely to be brought about by this law inevitably vary, partly depending upon whether the estimator is an employer or employee. Revolutionary change is anticipated in some quarters (recall Hasegawa's argument), but many observers find a basically conservative feature in the law. What is pointed up, above all, is the wording in which the employer is supposed to "strive" to ensure equal oppportunity in recruiting, hiring, allocating, and promoting workers. It is argued that this terminology, phrased as "the duty to strive" (*doryoku gimu*), strips the equality stipulation of its coercive power. The choice of the term *kintō*, instead of *byōdō*, for the title of the law, also seems, in my view, to soften its egalitarian content, even though this may not have been intended by the formulators. See Akamatsu, *Danjo koyō kikai kintō-hō oyobi kaisei rōdō kijun-hō*, for the interpretation of a government representative who was deeply involved in the formulation of the law, and Masahiro Kuwabara, *Danjo koyō byōdō no un'yō kijun: Kanada, Amerika, to Nippon no kintō-hō ni terashite* (Tokyo: Sōgō Rōdō Kenkyūjo, 1980) for an outsider's view in comparison with the Canadian and U.S. laws.

75. Hayao Kawai, "Violence in the Home: Conflict Between Two Principles— Maternal and Paternal," in Takie S. Lebra and William P. Lebra, eds., *Japanese Culture and Behavior: Selected Readings*, rev. ed. (Honolulu: University of Hawaii Press, 1986).

76. This difficulty in delegating responsibility to subordinates has also been noted with respect to American women managers. See Margaret Hennig and Anne Jardim, *The Managerial Woman* (Garden City, N.Y.: Anchor/Doubleday, 1977).

77. Rohlen has also noted that the emotional vulnerability of women workers poses a problem for managers. See Thomas P. Rohlen, *For Harmony and Strength: Japanese White-Collar Organization in Anthropological Perspective* (Berkeley: University of California Press, 1974), p. 103.

78. Victor W. Turner, *The Ritual Process: Structure and Anti-Structure* (Chicago: Aldine, 1969).

79. Marriage tends to be postponed in proportion to the increasing number of women receiving higher education and being employed after graduation, which accounts for the decline in the marriage rate over the past decade. The proportion of single women decreases as age goes up: 78 per cent of women at age 20–24; 24 per cent at 25–29; 9 per cent at 30–34. The divorce rate has gone up from 1.07 per 1,000 of the population in 1975 to 1.51 in 1983. See Sōrifu, *Fujin no genjō to shisaku*, pp. 116–17. Nevertheless, marrying at 23 to 25 remains the norm for the majority of women.

80. Lebra, "Japanese Women in Male Dominant Careers."

81. Katherine S. Newman, "Symbolic Dialects and Generations of Women: Variation in the Meaning of Post-Divorce Downward Mobility," *American Ethnologist*, Vol. 13 (1986), p. 240.

82. Glenda Roberts, personal comment.

83. Takie Sugiyama Lebra, "Japanese Women and Marital Strain," *Ethos*, Vol. 6 (1978), pp. 22–41.

84. Ito, "Entrepreneurial Women in Urban Japan," p. 280.

85. Brian Moeran, "Individual, Group and *Seishin*: Japan's Internal Cultural Debate," in Lebra and Lebra, eds., *Japanese Culture and Behavior*.

Index of Names

In these indexes, "f" after a number indicates a separate reference on the next page, and "ff" indicates separate references on the next two pages. A continuous discussion over two or more pages is indicated by a span of numbers. *Passim* is used for a cluster of references in close but not consecutive sequence.

General Index

Abortion rates, 21–23
Activism, 17–18, 27–28, 60–61
Actors, in network model, 114–15,
437n.24
Adjudication, 45
Administrative Enforcement Law, 53
Administrative guidance, 32, 54, 91–
96 passim. See also Government
Administrative networks, 111, 235,
247–48; reciprocity in, 249–52, 259;
culture and, 253–58; selectivity of,
259; efficiencies of, 260–68
Affiliation, 255–58 passim
Affirmative action issues, 243–45
Age: discrimination, 243; learning
capacity and, 355; female
employment and, 366, 371, 376–81;
life expectancy, 373, 375; life
schedule, 376–78; social relations
and, 378–81
Agency for Personnel Administration,
158
Agricultural sector: culture and, 13–
14, 164–65; social exchange aspects
of, 97, 100; low productivity of, 281,
283; industrial culture and, 454n.2;
labor force reduction in, 461n.62
Altruism, 387–88
Aluminum industry, 238
Amakudari, 157f
Ambition, 257
American management: Japanese
practices in, 3–4; mutual learning
potential of, 147; ownership and

control patterns of, 173ff; Swedish
adoption of, 301; Japanese
adaptation of, 304–10; small-group
activities and, 310–14; international
developments and, 312–13;
insularity of, 312–13, 315;
participation concepts of, 318;
learning attitudes and, 347–48. See
also Japanese business in America;
Quality circles
American subsidiaries, see Japanese
business in America
Ancestors, authority of, 47–48
Antitrust activity, 215
Apprenticeship traditions, 325–26, 358
Asia's New Giant (Patrick and
Rosovsky), 1
Astrology, 21–23
Authority: in Japanese government,
32–34; defined, 34; of parents, 47–
48; external economic forces and,
91; American vs. Japanese concepts
of, 194; zaibatsu and, 207; education
and, 343; in women's businesses,
403–8
Autocratic system, 129
Automation, 356
Automotive industry, 162, 237ff, 353,
446n.44
Autonomous work groups, 301–4
Autonomy, self-organization and,
223f

Bank(s), 57, 212, 239–40, 451n.11

Library of Congress Cataloging-in-Publication Data

The Political economy of Japan.

"Under the general editorship of Yasusuke Murakami
and Hugh T. Patrick."
Includes bibliographies and indexes.
Contents: v. 1. The Domestic transformation / edited
by Kozo Yamamura and Yasukichi Yasuba—v. 2. The
changing international context / edited by Takashi
Inoguchi and Daniel I. Okimoto—v. 3. Cultural and
social dynamics / edited by Shumpei Kumon and Henry
Rosovsky.
    1. Japan—Economic conditions—1945–   .
2. Japan—Economic policy—1945–1989.
3. Japan—Foreign economic relations.   I. Murakami,
Yasusuke, 1931–   .   II. Patrick, Hugh T.
HC462.9.P57   1987   338.952   86-30037
ISBN 0-8047-1380-4 (v. 1 : alk. paper)
ISBN 0-8047-1381-2 (pbk. : v. 1 : alk. paper)
ISBN 0-8047-1448-7 (v. 2 : alk. paper)
ISBN 0-8047-1481-9 (pbk. : v. 2 : alk. paper)
ISBN 0-8047-1991-8 (v. 3 : alk. paper)
ISBN 0-8047-1992-6 (pbk. : v. 3 : alk. paper)

This book is printed on acid-free paper